THE OLD-HOUSE
JOURNAL
COMPENDIUM

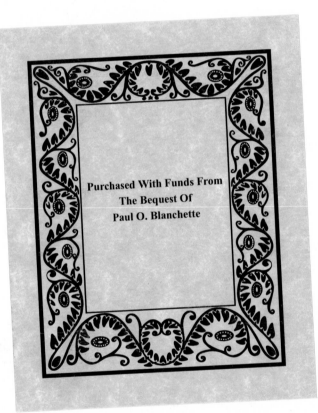

THE OLD-HOUSE
JOURNAL
COMPENDIUM

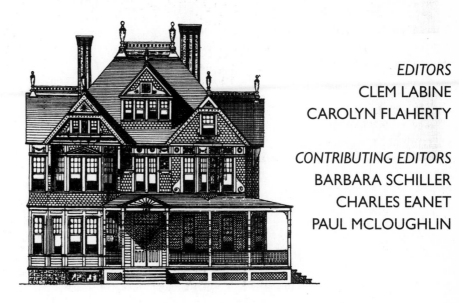

EDITORS
CLEM LABINE
CAROLYN FLAHERTY

CONTRIBUTING EDITORS
BARBARA SCHILLER
CHARLES EANET
PAUL MCLOUGHLIN

THE OVERLOOK PRESS
Woodstock • New York

This edition first published in the United States in 2008 by
The Overlook Press, Peter Mayer Publishers, Inc.
Woodstock & New York

Woodstock:
One Overlook Drive
Woodstock, NY 12498
www.overlookpress.com
[for individual orders, bulk and special sales, contact our Woodstock office]

New York:
141 Wooster Street
New York, NY 10012

Designed by Tony Meisel

Cataloging-in-Publication Data is available from the Library of Congress

Manufactured in the United States of America
ISBN-10 – 1-59020-016-0 / ISBN-13 – 978-1-59020-016-2
10 9 8 7 6 5 4 3 2 1

To
EVERETT ORTNER
—without whom this book and
The Old-House Journal
would not exist.

"Old buildings are not ours. They belong, partly to those who built them, and partly to the generations of mankind who are to follow us. The dead still have their right to them: That which they labored for . . . we have no right to obliterate.

"What we ourselves have built, we are at liberty to throw down. But what other men gave their strength, and wealth and life to accomplish, their right over it does not pass away with their death."

— JOHN RUSKIN

CONTENTS

PREFACE

THIS IS A HOME-MADE BOOK . . . literally. The inspiration for these pages sprang directly from my experience in restoring our home—an 1883 Victorian brownstone in the Park Slope section of Brooklyn. The building was a shabby rooming house when we acquired it . . . but there was enough of its original detailing intact to encourage my wife and me to believe that we could make it our home.

IT WAS DURING THE PROCESS of transforming the house from its rundown condition back to its original elegance that the idea for *The Old-House Journal* was born. So I left the major publishing house where I had worked for 15 years and plunged into publishing my own "how-to" newsletter. The brownstone not only provided much of the article inspiration for *The Old-House Journal*—it also housed its editorial offices for 5 years.

THE TOP THREE FLOORS sheltered our family: Three children, two cats, an iguana, innumerable gerbils, and a ubiquitous dog. On the ground floor we carved out space where we could create the first pages of what was to become *The Old-House Journal*. Thus at some points, the editors were going straight from the plaster tubs to the typewriters. It made for messy working conditions, but it was really first-hand information!

THE OLD-HOUSE JOURNAL is a monthly newsletter specializing in how-to information for restoring houses built before 1920. The publication was very much part of the urban revival that took place in the 1960s and 70s as the lure of old houses led people to buy and fix up homes in declining neighborhoods.

THE BULK OF THIS COMPENDIUM is made up of pages reprinted directly from *The Old-House Journal*. It covers material published between October 1973 and December 1977. Because *The Old-House Journal* is an ongoing communication process between readers and editors, you'll find in some instances different ways of doing things reported at various points in time. All the techniques work; you can select the one that best fits your needs and the materials at hand.

THERE WILL ALSO BE some stylistic inconsistencies in the text because these pages have appeared at various times over five years. It would have been impossible to go back and change all of these minor inconsistencies without remaking all the pages. So we are presenting the pages just as they were seen by the readers originally . . . . confident that the technical information is accurate and helpful.

THE COMPENDIUM is also a "work in progress" in that it does not present an answer for every conceivable old-house problem. New answers and new techniques are being discovered each day . . . and the editors present them in the pages of *The Old-House Journal* as they come along.

BUT IN THIS COMPENDIUM you'll find more solutions to the tricky problems that old houses pose than have been put together between two covers heretofore. Old houses are a way of life . . . an exciting and creative way of life. We hope these pages will help you to better understand and deal with your particular old house. Most important, we hope that this Compendium will stimulate you to want to learn more. Because there's always more to learn.

Clem Labine, Editor
The Old-House Journal

Buying Your Old House

BUYING YOUR OLD HOUSE

WHY AN OLD HOUSE?

WHY GO THROUGH IT ALL? Why put up with the uneven floors, antique plumbing, cracked plaster ... and the hundreds of other ills that an old house falls heir to? There are dozens of different reasons that draw people to old houses. But the end result is always the same: Once you're hooked on an old house, you can't live anywhere else.

SOME LOVE THE DESIGN, materials and workmanship in old houses: Real hardwoods, moulded plaster, marble mantels, fine joinery—and the unmistakable sense that somebody *cared* when the house was built. It is literally true that "they don't build them like that any more." Even if you could find the craftsmen, in many cases you can no longer get the materials—especially the fine woods—that went into many old houses.

OTHERS ARE ATTRACTED by the large, grand spaces that only an old house offers. There is a sense of well-being and uplifting of the spirit that you encounter only in these generously proportioned old rooms.

STILL OTHERS LOVE the sense that an old house is a living artifact from the past. The builder and previous owners may have passed on, but the house remains ... bearing witness to these previous lives in previous times. The house retains the imprint of all who have lived and loved within its walls.

THEN THERE'S THE ECONOMICS. For less money than it costs to buy a standardized new house, you can own a sturdily built old house with generous space, interesting room arrangements, and attractive architectural details inside and out. For the owner with sufficient time and energy, even a sadly rundown or abandoned house can become a charming—or even luxurious—home at an affordable price.

OTHERS ENJOY the idea that their house is one-of-a-kind. No matter if the house was built right out of a standard pattern book, each old house acquires a unique personality from the imprint of years of habitation. There's no other house quite like it.

AND IN RURAL AREAS, you'll find that the old houses often have pre-empted the best building sites—those offering the most attractive views and best drainage conditions.

ALL THESE ELEMENTS contribute to the romance of old houses. The style, the feeling of history, the exotic materials and finishes, the sense of quality ... all are part of the lure. And if the house is in need of help, the lure can be all the greater.

BUT WHATEVER THE INITIAL attraction, old-house lovers find that restoration is an enormously involving and creative process. It is the PROCESS that holds the key to the excitement. Every old house has its special story to tell. Discovering that story and remaining faithful to it is the key to a happy restoration.

THE GOAL is not to have the house completed by any specific date. Rather, the goal is to enrich yourself with the history, design, craftsmanship and social background that is relevant to your house. When you proceed in a thorough way, you will find that your old house becomes more than just a shelter; it is an experience. When you are through, you not only have a beautifully restored house; you will find yourself enriched in ways you never dreamed possible. And you'll also have a very tangible, inflation-beating real estate asset.

KEEPING UP AN OLD HOUSE is keeping faith with the past—and the future!

IS AN OLD HOUSE FOR YOU?

AN OLD HOUSE is not everyone's cup of tea. An old house is a way of life and a state of mind as much as it is a shelter from the storm. And, frankly, not everyone has the emotional makeup and patience that an old house demands. The spiritual rewards that the non-old-house types get from the house are not sufficient to make up for the headaches of falling plaster and leaking pipes.

AS MUCH AS ANYTHING, restoring an old house is an act of respect . . . respect for the architectural integrity of the structure, and respect for the people and historical forces that produced it.

AN OLD HOUSE ALSO REQUIRES patience . . . patience to go through the detailed learning and planning process set forth in the following pages. Because of the need for historical research and planning, an old house takes up more learning time than its newer cousins. In addition, you need the patience to put up with the many material infirmities that an old house succumbs to.

A GOOD SENSE OF HUMOR is also essential. How would you react if you were getting ready for your own party on Saturday night and the plaster ceiling in the front hall fell on the newly varnished floor? If you would laugh—because it hurts too much to cry—then you have the makings of an old-house person.

OLD-HOUSE PEOPLE are creative masochists. Creative, because restoration is an exciting process that develops your imagination and ingenuity. Masochistic because of the seemingly endless string of major and minor disasters that will overtake you before the house is done.

OLD HOUSES aren't for everyone. But if you have the right predisposition and adventurous temperament, you'll find restoration one of the most rewarding experiences of your life.

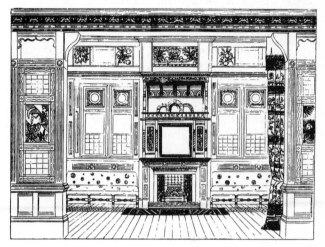

PICKING THE NEIGHBORHOOD

THERE'S AN AXIOM in the real estate business that declares: "The three most important factors in determining the value of a house are: (1) Location; (2) Location; and (3) Location." While that may be overstating the case a bit, it points out that no house exists in isolation from its environment.

OLD-HOUSE BUYERS are apt to get carried away by beautiful parquet floors, stained glass windows, carved oak wainscotting, etc., and blind themselves to the adjacent neighborhood. In older cities, especially, you are likely to find architectural gems in areas that are described sometimes as "colorful" and other times as "slums."

THERE IS (or should be) a trade-off between the price of the house and the desirability of the neighborhood. Many people have found great bargains buying an old house in a run-down area and banking on the restoration movement to improve the neighborhood. In cities all across the U.S., the restoration process has reversed the tide of urban decay. Georgetown in Washington, Park Slope in Brooklyn, Haight-Ashbury in San

Photo of 199 Berkeley Place. The brownstone that started it all.

Francisco . . . all are examples of once-deteriorating neighborhoods that have become fashionable (and expensive). People who bought old houses at the low point in a neighborhood's cycle have seen their investments double and double again.

OTHERS, HOWEVER, have purchased homes in run-down neighborhoods that never did turn around. When this happens, any resale is usually at a loss.

IN EVALUATING A NEIGHBORHOOD, you have to ask yourself honestly how much "pioneering" you are willing to do. If you have reservations about a particular area, you're best off seeing if you can find any kindred spirits who have already moved in. See how they like it. Scaffolds, trash haulers and other signs of renovation are always reassuring, as are the sounds of hammering, sawing and floor sanding. Walk the streets in both daylight and darkness to get a feel of the place. If you have children, the presence of other children on the block will be an asset. Likewise, you'll want to look into schools.

THIS IS NOT TO SAY that you should not be the first restorer into a neighborhood in the hopes of sparking a turnaround. Just realize that you'll have to work on two projects simultaneously: Improving your house and improving the neighborhood. Be prepared to help organize house tours and other such promotional activities designed to entice likeminded folks to buy houses. In every turn-around situation, *someone* has to be first. If that person is you, then just be sure the price you pay for the house is sufficiently low to compensate you for the investment of time and money you'll have to put into both house and neighborhood.

IF YOU DECIDE to buy an old house in a marginal neighborhood, be prepared for a chorus of "You're crazy" from friends and relatives. If you have carefully thought through your decision, then you can safely ignore them all! People can never imagine anyone selecting a lifestyle different from the one they have chosen for themselves. They'll see your decision as a threat to their own set of values.

BUT IN FACT, all of the negative comments can be very useful to you. They'll inspire an "I'll show them" attitude that can get the adrenalin going and provide a lot of energy to get on with the demanding tasks of restoration.

SELECTING THE HOUSE THAT'S RIGHT FOR YOU

WHILE IT'S TRUE that restoring an old house can be an exciting and creative process, it's also true that an old house can be a money-gobbling trap for the unwary. So it's important that you set out on the adventure with your eyes wide open.

ANY OLD HOUSE can be beautifully restored—no matter how decrepit its condition—given sufficient amounts of time, energy and money. So it is vital that you realistically evaluate how much of the three you have . . . measured against how much of the three a particular old house will require. The fun will quickly vanish from the experience if you get in over your head.

TO A LARGE EXTENT, there is a direct trade-off between time and money. The more time you can spend working on the house yourself, the less money you'll need. However, most novices tend to drastically underestimate how much time a restoration will require.

SO BEFORE YOU ALLOW YOURSELF to get carried away by a beautiful stained glass window or marble mantel, try to make a rational evaluation of how much time, money and energy the house will require. And compare these demands with your supply of same. At this point, the professional opinion of a house inspector will definitely be worthwhile. We'll say more about this later.

IF YOU HAVE A GUT FEELING that a particular house may be too much for you, then it probably is! In evaluating old houses, "The Rule of Two" usually holds true. "The Rule of Two" states: "An old house requires twice as much time and twice as much money as originally assumed." The classic mistake is to significantly underestimate the time and money that an old house will demand. Thus if you feel at the *outset* that a particular house is more than you can handle, then you are probably more correct than you even realize.

THESE CAUTIONARY WORDS are not designed to scare you out of buying an old house. Quite the contrary. The purpose is to help you make a realistic appraisal so that you'll find a house that you'll be happy with—and vice versa.

YOUR HOUSE'S STYLE

THE BEST WAY TO BEGIN the search for your special old house is to become familiar with the common old-house styles and their architectural details. The illustrations on the following pages will help you become familiar with the basic shapes and features. Few houses, however, represent a "pure" style. Architects and builders were continually experimenting with new combinations of traditional details. Too, houses are frequently altered over the years as tastes change. Today, a Colonial house may well have Victorian additions . . . and a Victorian house may have Colonial Revival additions. Careful study is required to determine what is original to a house and what may have been added.

AS AN INTRODUCTION, on the following pages you'll find sketches of the most common old-house styles–along with a brief description of the characteristics of each.

COLONIAL 1690–1760 >

CHARACTERISTIC DETAILS: Large central chimney; narrow clapboards; simple frames around doors and windows; few—if any—small windows (lights) around doors. Windows had numerous small panes—frequently 12 over 12. In South, similar designs were executed in brick. Few have survived without addition of wings, ells and lean-tos, and other changes in details.

< SALTBOX 1700–1770

CHARACTERISTIC DETAILS: The roof line defines the saltbox. It evolved from the practice of adding a lean-to on the back of a house in order to gain extra space. Sometimes a change in the angle of the back roof shows where the lean-to was added. The design became so popular that some houses were built with the long back roof as part of the original structure.

CAPE COD 1710–1830 >

CHARACTERISTIC DETAILS: Frame structure, one and one-half stories high; low pitched roof; large central chimney; no dormers. Light for attic comes from windows in gable ends. To increase attic headroom, builders sometimes used a bowed ("ship's bottom") roof. Originally covered on all sides and roof with wood shingles that weathered gray. Later houses used clapboards. Three basic designs: Half House—two windows to side of front door; Three-Quarters House—two windows to one side of door and one to the other; Full Cape—two windows to each side of door.

EARLY GEORGIAN 1720—1760 >

CHARACTERISTIC DETAILS: Symmetrical design based on Roman classicism. Set on high foundation, with emphasis on entrance bay in middle of house. Wide panelled door had row of rectangular lights in door, or transom light above. Columns or pilasters frequently framed door, with pediment above. Plain colonial eaves were replaced with cornice, often with classical features such as dentils. When dormers were used, they had triangular pediments and were spaced symmetrically. Usually had pitched roof; sometimes hipped. Executed in brick or wood.

< LATE GEORGIAN 1760—1780

CHARACTERISTIC DETAILS: Heavy use of classical details . . . doorways surrounded with pilasters or columns, surmounted by cornice and/or pediment; semi-circular fanlight over door. Palladian (triple) window on second floor in center. Cornice on window caps. More elaborate houses would have projecting entrance pavilion topped by a pedimented gable. Use of columns and pilasters became more lavish, as did use of classical details in the cornice. Corners on masonry houses usually had stone quoins; on wood houses the quoins were often simulated in wood.

FEDERAL 1780—1820 >

CHARACTERISTIC DETAILS: After the Revolution, house designers rejected much of the classical decoration of Late Georgian, but retained basic Roman symmetry. The result is often hard to distinguish from Early Georgian. Doorways retained pilasters and columns, usually topped with flat entablature. Elliptical fanlights over doors were popular. Simple frames around windows; corners unmarked by quoins or pilasters. Hipped roofs became more common, sometimes rimmed by a balustrade. Flat boarding sometimes used on exterior for a more classical effect.

< GREEK REVIVAL 1815—1840

CHARACTERISTIC DETAILS: Emphasis on columns (or pilasters), capitals and low triangular gabled pediment—all to create the effect of a Greek temple. Focus shifted from the long side of the house to the gabled end. Pedimented gable appears to rest on classical entablature, which is in turn supported by columns. More elaborate homes had a columned entrance portico—especially popular in the South. Windows are strongly vertical, with 6-over-6 panes. Lines are simpler and cleaner than Roman-influenced Georgian.

GOTHIC REVIVAL 1835—1880 >

CHARACTERISTIC DETAILS: Objective was to recapture the romance of medieval buildings. Emphasis was on vertical effect, achieved through multiple sharply pointed gables with slender finials at the peaks. Windows were tall and slender, sometimes topped with a lancet arch. Casement windows with leaded diamond-shaped panes were also popular. Wooden verge boards under eaves—and other decorative woodwork—was cut with medieval motifs such as trefoils, quatrefoils, gothic crosses and other pointed symbols.

< CARPENTER GOTHIC 1870—1910

CHARACTERISTIC DETAILS: Sawn wood ornament at peaks of gables, in verge boards under gables, and on porches. Even porch railings and aprons sometimes have sawn patterns. Designs may be holes and slots cut out of wood—or pieces applied to other boards. Sawn brackets appear on porch posts and on cornice. Ornament depends more on whim of the carpenter/builder than on any architectural style. This type of ornament also called "gingerbread."

< QUEEN ANNE 1875—1900

CHARACTERISTIC DETAILS: A picturesque massing of variety of shapes and textures in a non-symmetrical composition. Gables, dormers, chimneys, round turrets and oriel windows used freely. Porches feature delicately turned spindlework; horizontal decorative bands. Brick chimneys usually fluted, with large caps. In brick, terra cotta used for decoration. In wood, smooth boards are mixed with clapboards and shingles for variety.

MANSARD 1860—1885 >

CHARACTERISTIC DETAILS: Easily recognized by highly distinctive roof line. Extra living space on top floor is gained by bending out the slope of the roof. The Mansard roof is pierced by a dazzling variety of dormer windows: Rectangular, pointed, gabled, round—even double rows of dormers. Dormers often ornamented with pediments and console buttresses. Slate often used on steep slope of roof. Also called Second Empire style.

< ITALIANATE MANSION 1845—1885

CHARACTERISTIC DETAILS: This style is loosely based on Italian Renaissance models. It is highly symmetrical, often constructed in stone . . . or wood painted to look like stone. Roof is often flat, with belvedere or cupola on top. Roof overhang is large, and accented by a deep, highly decorated cornice featuring massive brackets. Tall windows with ornamental hoods dominate side walls; windows and door openings often have round or arched tops. Various other Renaissance features such as corner quoins and balustrades are sometimes found.

ITALIAN VILLA 1835—1885 >

CHARACTERISTIC DETAILS: Designed to resemble Italian country villas. Asymmetrical arrangement of squared shapes and lines. Flat or low-pitched roofs; extended eaves that emphasize deep and heavy cornices set with ornate brackets. Plain horizontal decorative bands. Tall, slender windows, some with rounded heads. Square-pillared porches; semi-circular arches; tall square tower or cupola; balconies set on stout, ornate brackets.

< VERNACULAR ITALIANATE 1865—1885

CHARACTERISTIC DETAILS: Many thousands of houses were constructed by carpenter/builders based on loose adaptations of the "pure" Italianate models. These adapted versions often have projecting bay windows of one or two storeys. There's often a broad columned porch with decorative brackets. The roof is accented with a massive cornice with large brackets. Tall windows placed in bays dominate; window frames are usually ornate. Tops of windows and doorways are often rounded. Siding in panelled wood or clapboard.

STICK STYLE 1875—1900 >

CHARACTERISTIC DETAILS: A uniquely American style in which exterior decorative boards are used to give an exaggerated sense of structural support. An outgrowth of the Queen Anne and other picturesque styles, the house features an asymmetrical massing of shapes and variegated surface textures. Siding may be horizontal or vertical boards—or shingles—but the siding is always broken up into panels with flat wooden trim boards. There can be additional trim boards in "X" patterns to suggest structural bracing. Eaves are often decorated with brackets or braces.

SHINGLE STYLE 1885—1900 >

CHARACTERISTIC DETAILS: Wooden shingles are the usual covering for both roof and walls, sometimes with fieldstone foundation or ground floor. An outgrowth of the Queen Anne movement and Colonial Revival, houses are usually 2 or 2-1/2 storeys high with 45° gables or gambrel roofs. Often has large porches, but roof overhangs are small. Roof often has dormer or "eyebrow" windows. Exterior is more controlled with fewer projections than many other late Victorian styles. Sometimes butts of shingles are cut in decorative patterns, but more often are left square.

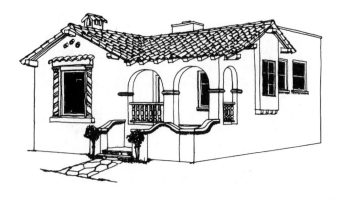

< BUNGALOW 1900—1930

CHARACTERISTIC DETAILS: Simple wood frame construction with clapboard, shingle or stucco sheathing. Main roof usually extends forward to cover front porch. Square "elephantine" porch posts; broad roof overhang with exposed rafter ends and sometimes knee brackets. Chimney and porch foundation often made from fieldstone. Has a plain block-like appearance with simple, informal open floor plan. Generally one full storey with a second storey under the roof. Projecting beams and trellises are common; roofs generally covered with wood or composition shingles.

MISSION REVIVAL 1895—1940 >

CHARACTERISTIC DETAILS: Originating in California, this style spread to other parts of the Southwest and Florida. Major features are rough-textured stucco or concrete walls, sloping roofs covered with half-cylinders of red tile, and openings with round-headed arches. General shape is squarish and blocky. Arcades are common feature around porches. Decoration is quite spare, usually limited to a simple treatment of eaves, large moulded balusters on railings, and coping or string courses to delineate floor lines. Interiors often have heavily beamed ceilings.

< CLASSIC AMERICAN FARMHOUSE 1800—1920

CHARACTERISTIC DETAILS: This vernacular structure is a direct descendant of the Colonial house. They have been built in rural areas from the 1700s up to the 1900s. It has a large boxy shape, usually 2 or 2½ storeys high; small roof overhang; simple treatment of the cornice. Windows are placed symmetrically in bays. Wings and ells often show where additions have been made. Horizontal clapboard siding predominates, with narrow corner boards; trim around doors and windows is often simple, flat boards. Broad porches were often added in late 19th century.

COLONIAL REVIVAL 1885—PRESENT >

CHARACTERISTIC DETAILS: This style represents an attempt to go back to the U.S.'s architectural roots by re-using details from the Colonial Georgian and Federal styles. But they are grafted onto the larger houses of the late Victorian era, so the end result is heavier and more boxy than the originals. Typical features are symmetrical layout of facades, hipped or gabled roof, dormers, plus classical details such as columned porches, Palladian-style triple windows, dentilled cornices, roof balustrades. Doorways frequently have fan-lights and slender sidelights.

< TUDOR REVIVAL 1885—PRESENT

CHARACTERISTIC DETAILS: This is a revival style designed to capture the rustic charm of "Merrie Olde England" by imitating the half-timbered houses of Elizabethan structural framing. Area between the timbers is sometimes filled with stucco like the original; more often with wood painted light colors. Verge boards sometimes decorated eaves under the gables, and there may be finials and pendants at the peaks. Roofs can be slate; windows have small panes.

PRAIRIE STYLE 1895–PRESENT >

CHARACTERISTIC DETAILS: This style originated in Chicago with the so-called Prairie School of architects, with primary inspiration coming from Louis Sullivan and Frank Lloyd Wright. Primary characteristic is the low, spread-out appearance, with heavy emphasis on horizontal lines. Much of the earlier 19th-century architecture emphasized vertical lines. This style features broad, low overhanging roofs and bold juxtaposition of masses. Windows occur in horizontal bands. Exterior is basically undecorated. Side walls can be stucco, Roman brick, random ashlar stone or stained wood.

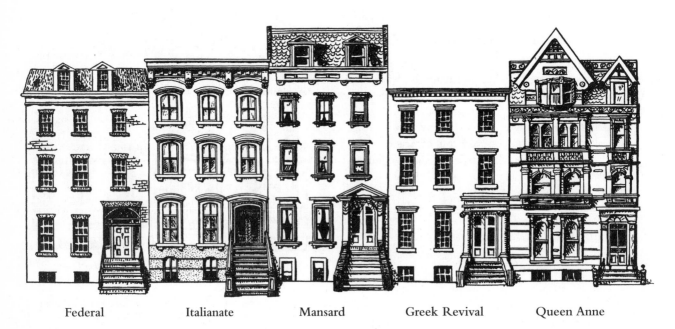

| Federal | Italianate | Mansard | Greek Revival | Queen Anne |

CITY ROW HOUSES: Although they had only the front surface to work with, designers captured the essence of various styles in row houses ... Doorways with fanlights and sidelights in Federal; arched windows and heavy brackets on Italianate; using the Mansard roof with countless dormer variations; dentilled cornice with classical columns and architrave on Greek Revival doorway; dazzling variety of gables, bays, textures and horizontal banding on Queen Anne.

APPRAISING THE STRUCTURE

THE GUIDE to old-house styles tells you what *kind* of house you are looking at. But it takes a different type of appraisal to judge what physical shape the structure is in. You want to avoid taking on a house that will consume more time and money than you have available. The art lies in predicting *in advance* approximately what will be required to put the house back into the shape you'd like.

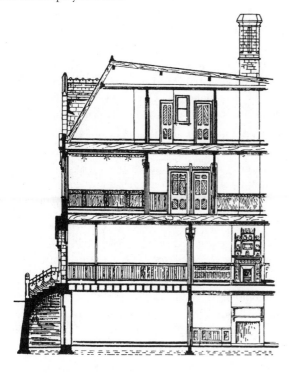

THE FOLLOWING checklist gives a rundown of 73 of the most common defects. This will help you eliminate those houses that are too rundown for you to consider.

COME PREPARED

WHEN SETTING OUT on an old-house inspection, you should have with you: Flashlight, small magnet, plumbline (string with small weight will do), penknife, a marble, pair of binoculars, pad and pencil, and an inspection checklist. Wear old clothes so you can closely inspect important places like the cellar and underneath porches.

THE ROOF

A sound, tight roof is the first line of defense against the #1 enemy of an old house: Water. If the roof is in bad shape, you should plan on repairing—or replacing—it right away.

1. Type of roof on house (arranged in approximate order of longevity):

Slate (1)	Wood Shakes (6)
Copper (2)	Wood Shingles (7)
Ceramic Tile (3)	Galvanized Steel (8)
Tar & Gravel (4)	Asphalt Shingles (9)
Asbestos Tile (5)	Roll Roofing (10)

2. Pitched Roof: Any sign of missing, broken or warped shingles or tiles? (This could mean roof will have to be replaced soon. It can also mean that there is water damage inside.)

NOTE: Binoculars can give you a good close-up view if it is impossible to actually get up on the roof.

3. Asphalt shingles: Are the mineral granules getting thin and do edges of shingles look worn?

4. Asphalt shingles: Does roof look new but lumpy? (New roof may have been applied directly over old shingles. No way to tell what sins may have been covered over.)

5. Flat roof: Any sign of bubbles, separation or cracking in the asphalt or roofing felt? (Roofing should be flat and tight to roof; it shouldn't feel squishy under foot.)

6. Flashing around chimneys & valleys: Any sign of rusty, loose or missing flashing? (Flashing is the weakest part of any roof. Copper is the best flashing and will show a green patina.)

7. Chimneys: Is the masonry cracked or crumbling?

8. Do the old chimney flues have a tile lining? (If not, they could be a fire hazard in conjunction with wood-burning fireplaces.)

9. Gutters: Are there any loose, rotted or missing gutters?

10. Does the ridge of the roof sag? (This could be normal settling that comes with age—or it could be caused by rotted rafters. Check further!)

11. Cornice: Is there badly peeling paint on the cornice—

especially the underside? (This can be sign of a roof leak that is spilling water into the cornice.)

EXTERIOR WALLS

1. Do exterior walls seem plumb? (You can check with a plumb line; a weighted string will do. Out-of-plumb walls can be a sign of serious foundation problems.)

2. Sight along exterior walls. Any sign of major bulges? (This could signal major structural flaws.)

3. Do doors line up squarely in their frames? (Out-of-square doors can be another sign of possible foundation trouble.)

NOTE: Almost all old houses settle in a haphazard manner. So signs of sag are not necessarily a major drawback. But it does mean a thorough investigation should be made to find the root causes. Some sags require no remedy; others can be cured with a few extra support posts. Still others may require major foundation surgery.

4. Is decorative woodwork firmly attached to house and tightly caulked to prevent water penetration?

5. Is exterior paint fresh and in good condition?

6. If paint is not new, is it powdering and chalking to a dull powdery surface? (This is the way old paint should look.)

7. Is paint peeling, curling and blistering? (This could mean a serious water problem—either a leak or lack of sufficient vapor barrier in wall.)

8. Are there open joints around door frames, window frames and trim? (These will have to be caulked.)

9. Are joints between dissimilar materials (e.g., wood and masonry) well protected with flashing or caulk?

10. Is putty around window glass sound and well painted?

11. Masonry Walls: Any signs of cracks? (Horizontal cracks and hairline cracks in bricks are not a major problem; cracks that run vertically through bricks and mortar are more serious.)

12. Is mortar soft and crumbling; are bricks missing or loose? (Loose masonry is vulnerable to attack by water … and having a masonry wall repointed with fresh mortar is expensive.)

13. Has masonry been painted? (It will have to be re-painted about every 5 years, or else stripped—a major task.)

14. Stonework (especially sandstone): Any sign of spalling, cracking or crumbling of the stone? (This can be expensive to repair.)

15. Clapboards: Are many loose, cracked or missing? (This is an open invitation to water—and rot.)

16. Shingles: Are they thick and well nailed? (Thin, badly weathered shingles may have to be replaced.)

17. Do shingles have a natural finish? (Natural finishes are easier to re-apply to shingles than is paint.)

TERMITES & ROT

1. Termites: Any sign of veins of dirt on interior or exterior walls? (These are termite mud tunnels. Look for them on foundation, under porches, steps and on cellar walls.)

2. Does wood near the ground (both outside and inside) pass the "pen knife test"? (Wood should be probed with penknife to test for soundness. Check areas such as cellar window frames, sills, floor beams and posts, porches and steps.)

NOTE: Unsound wood can be caused by either termites or rot. Rot can be arrested by shutting off the source of moisture. Termites call for chemical warfare. If at all unsure about the cause of bad wood, call in the experts.

3. Is all exterior wood at least 6–8 in. above the ground? (If not, this is an inviting target for termites and/or rot.)

4. Is there any vegetation close to the house? (Vegetation holds moisture in wood; be sure to check behind it for rot.)

5. Any signs of rot in cornice or attic beams? (Leaking roofs and gutters often spill water into top of house where it goes undetected for long periods.)

THE ATTIC

1. Any sign of leaks (such as dark water stains) on the underside of roof, especially around chimneys, valleys and eaves?

2. Is attic adequately vented? (Check especially for signs of mildew on underside of roof boards.)

INSULATION

NOTE: Most houses before 1940 had no built-in insulation. However, some old houses will have had insulation added.

Houses with brick or stone walls rarely have any wall insulation. With cost of fuel soaring, a well-insulated house is a big asset.

1. Attic: Any loose fill insulation visible between attic floor joists? (This is best place for attic insulation.)

2. Has insulation been blown into side walls? (You may have to take owner's word for this. In cold weather you can tell how good wall insulation is by feeling the inside of an exterior wall and comparing with temperature of an interior partition. They should feel about the same.)

INTERIOR SPACES

1. Are there any signs of damp plaster? (This means leaks coming either from roof or internal pipes. Check especially top-floor ceilings, the inside of exterior walls, and ceilings and partitions under bathrooms.)

2. Is there any loose plaster in walls or ceilings? (Cracks in plaster are par for the course—but plaster that is spongy when you push on it will have to be repaired or replaced.)

3. Is there a noticeable bounce to the staircase when you jump on it? Are there any noticeable gaps between treads, risers and side stringers? (Substantial vibration may mean structural problems that will be quite costly to correct.)

4. Is flooring original and in good repair? (Floors covered with carpet or linoleum can harbor many problems—especially if you want to restore the original flooring.)

5. Do floors have a pronounced sag or tilt? (Simple test: Place a marble on the floor and see if it rolls away. This could just be normal settling or serious structural flaws. Check for cause.)

6. Do floors vibrate and windows rattle when you jump on floors? (This is symptom of inadequate support. Among possible causes: Undersized beams, inadequate bridging, cracked joists, rotted support posts. Often this can be cured fairly simply with a few new support posts.)

7. Windows: Do sashes move up and down smoothly?

8. Do window frames show signs of substantial water leakage? (Look for chipped and curling paint at bottom of sash and sills. Although quite unsightly, this can be cured with caulk, putty and paint.)

9. Are fireplaces operational? (Evidence of recent fires in the fireplace is a reassuring sign. Peek up the chimney; if you can see daylight you at least know the flue is clear.)

10. Are there smoke stains on front of mantel? (This is a sign of a smoky fireplace. It can be cured—but it is a bother.)

FOUNDATION

1. Is there a dug cellar with wood sills resting solidly on a masonry foundation well above ground level? (Some old structures have "mud sills"—heavy beams resting directly on the ground. These eventually have to be replaced, which is a major undertaking.)

2. Is mortar in foundation soft and crumbling? (This is not necessarily serious as long as there's no sign of sag in the structure; ditto for foundation walls laid dry—without mortar.)

3. Are there any vertical cracks in the foundation wall? (This could be serious, or it could be from settling that stopped years ago. Have an engineer check it.)

4. Does ground slope away from foundation so that rain water drains off?

5. Do downspouts have splash blocks to divert water away from house? (If downspout goes into ground, be sure it isn't pouring water into the earth next to the foundation—a flooded basement is the likely result.)

THE CELLAR

1. Do sills (the wood beams at the top of the foundation walls) show signs of rot or termites? (Probe with penknife.)

2. Any sign of dampness on the underside of floors around pipes? (If leaks have gone undetected for some time, there could be substantial wood rot.)

3. Does basement show signs of periodic flooding? (It's a good sign if current owner stores important tools and papers on cellar floor. Bad signs: Rust spots, efflorescence or mildew on walls, material stored on top of bricks to raise it above floor level.)

4. Any sign of sagging floors, rotted support posts or jury-rigged props to shore up weak flooring?

5. Are the water pipes and large waste pipes in good condition? (The cellar is the best place to evaluate the over-all condition of the plumbing. For example, look for patches on the waste pipes; it's an indicator of advanced age. Replacement is expensive.)

ELECTRICAL SYSTEM

1. Does wiring in cellar appear to be a rat's nest of old frayed wires?

2. Does main power box in cellar have at least 100 amp. capacity? (An up-to-date installation will have capacity marked on it. An old fuse box with only 3–4 fuses in it means there may only be 30–40 amp.—far too little. A re-wiring job will be needed.)

3. Do all ceiling light fixtures have wall switches?

4. Is there at least one electrical outlet on each wall in every room?

5. Is there any sign of surface-mounted lampcord extension wiring? Multiple cords plugged into a single outlet? (This is a tell-tale of underwiring. Expect to hire some electricians.)

PLUMBING

1. Are water pipes copper or brass? (If they are, magnet won't stick to them. Copper or brass is longer-lasting than galvanized iron. Magnet won't stick to lead piping either. Lead will be soft and silvery when scratched with penknife. Lead piping will probably have to be replaced shortly.)

2. Is water pressure adequate? (Test by turning on top floor sink faucets; then turn on bathtub and flush toilet. If water slows to a trickle, piping may be inadequate or badly clogged with scale.)

3. Is plumbing connected to a city sewer system?

4. If there is a septic tank, was it cleaned in the last 3—4 years? (Overloaded septic tanks are common source of trouble. It's best to call serviceman who did last cleaning and get his opinion of the system. Repairs can easily run over $1,000.)

5. Is water supply from:

     City main?   Drilled well?   Shallow well?

NOTES ON WATER SUPPLY: City main is the most dependable source; shallow (dug) well is the least desirable. If water is from a well it is best to get it analyzed by the County Agent for fitness. If water is from a spring, beware of claims that "spring never runs dry" unless you can verify it. You may end up paying to drill a well during a long dry summer.

HEATING SYSTEM

1. Was heating plant originally designed to burn coal? (If so, it is probably more than 25 years old and may be a candidate for replacement.)

2. Does heating system operate satisfactorily? (You can test system even on a summer day: Move thermostat setting above room temperature. Heat from a hot-air furnace should appear at registers within a few minutes; in a steam or hot-water system radiators should heat up in 15—20 min.)

3. Will fuel bills present you with any unpleasant surprises? (Copies of fuel bills from the last heating season are the best measure of the heating system's efficiency.)

4. Is capacity of hot water heater at least 40 gal.? (This is minimum required by a family of 4 with an automatic clothes washer.)

5. Any sign of leaks or rust spots on the hot-water heating tank? (Check by peeking through small door that gives access to the pilot light.)

6. On steam heating systems, do floorboards around radiators show signs of black stains and rot? (This comes from leaks and indicates system hasn't been well maintained.)

⚜

ONCE YOU'VE FOUND A HOUSE that seems both appealing and practical, it's time to engage a professional house inspector. His fee—usually in the $100—150 range—is a small price to pay for decreasing the risk in an investment of many thousands of dollars. Your house inspector should provide a written report listing all the physical defects he could find. He should also be able to give you ballpark figures on what it would cost to remedy each of the defects he finds.

IF YOU'VE NEVER READ a report from a house inspector, beware: They can be pretty scary documents. If you are the nervous type, you could wind up never buying a house, because these reports are invariably negative. You have to realize that you are paying the inspector to find everything *wrong* that he can possibly find. He doesn't want his clients coming back in anger later to accuse him: "You didn't tell me about so-and-so." Thus he's going to list every little thing he finds. You can be sure if a house inspector went through the White House, he could come up with plenty of negative facts to put in his report.

THE ART OF reading a house inspector's report is in separating the immediate and consequential from the trivial and long-range. If he comes up with expensive corrections that have to be done immediately, then you have to add those costs to the price of the house. Other defects will be minor things that you can correct yourself. Still others will be long-range problems that it would be nice to correct . . . but they can wait until time and budget allow.

BEAR IN MIND ALSO that the house inspector won't recommend that you buy or not buy any particular house. His job is merely to underscore all of the negative (and positive) elements of the structure. After you have the facts, the decision to buy or not buy is yours alone.

IN SELECTING A HOUSE INSPECTOR, he or she need not be a professional engineer (although it is always reassuring to see the initials "P.E." after a house inspector's name). He should definitely not have any ties to the real estate broker who is showing the house, nor any connections with any contractor you may be thinking of using. Word-of-mouth from recent home buyers in your neighborhood is the best way to find a reliable inspector. Lawyers who specialize in real estate in your area are also a good source of recommendations.

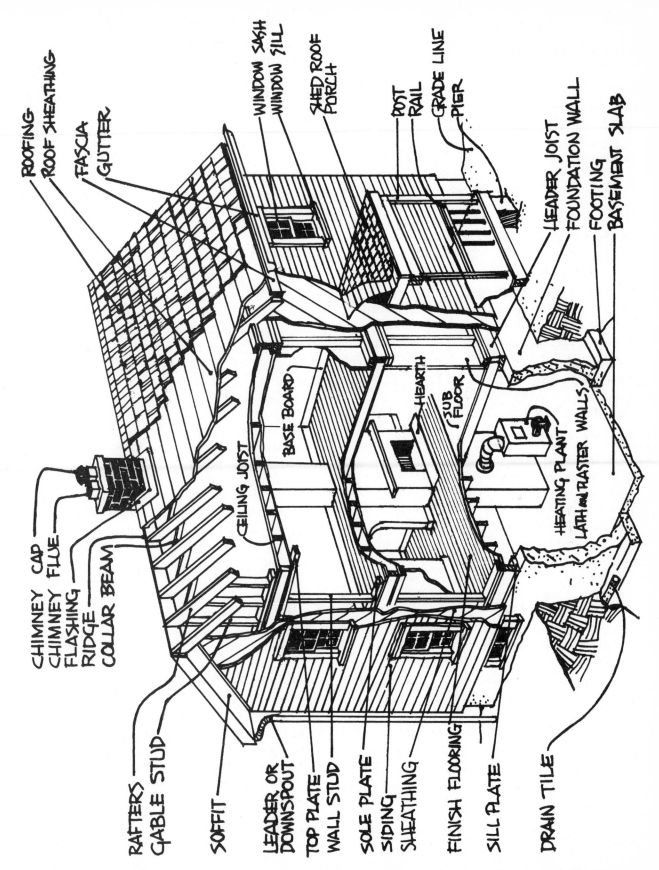

ROOFING
ROOF SHEATHING
FASCIA
GUTTER

WINDOW SASH
WINDOW SILL
SHED ROOF PORCH

POST
RAIL
GRADE LINE
PIER

LEADER JOIST
FOUNDATION WALL
FOOTING
BASEMENT SLAB

BASE BOARD

CEILING JOIST

HEARTH

SUB FLOOR

HEATING PLANT
LATH and PLASTER WALLS

CHIMNEY CAP
CHIMNEY FLUE
FLASHING
RIDGE
COLLAR BEAM

RAFTERS
GABLE STUD

SOFFIT

LEADER OR DOWNSPOUT
TOP PLATE
WALL STUD
SOLE PLATE
SIDING
SHEATHING
FINISH FLOORING
SILL PLATE
DRAIN TILE

If there is a neighborhood preservation group, you can probably get a couple of names from them.

THE PURCHASE

THE ACTUAL PURCHASE and closing on the building is pretty straightforward—once you have your mortgage squared away. Since the mortgage market varies so much from month to month and from area to area, it's impossible to say anything specific here—except to note that it is getting a *little* easier to get a mortgage on an old house. Banks and insurance companies have been refusing to lend money or write insurance in many areas where old houses are found (a practice called "redlining"). In redlined areas it has been extremely difficult to get a mortgage—no matter how sound the building and how reputable the buyer.

THE UNFAIRNESS of redlining and the disastrous impact it has had—especially in the older cities—has become apparent and this pernicious practice is somewhat less common that it was a couple of years ago. In a few cases, companies have changed their policies voluntarily. In other cases, the threat of corrective legislation from state legislatures has helped redlining banks and insurance companies to see the error of their ways.

YOUR REAL ESTATE ATTORNEY will handle all the details of the closing for you. Having a good attorney—familiar with the real estate in your neighborhood—is an enormous help in reducing the inevitable anxiety that comes with buying *any* house, new or old. Again, the best way to find a good attorney is by word-of-mouth referrals from people who have already purchased old houses in your neighborhood.

A WORD ABOUT WORRY: Buying an old house is, for most of us, a great emotional trauma. You'll wake up in the middle of the night in a cold sweat absolutely sure that you've made a horrible mistake. But if you've done your homework carefully by the light of day, you can safely ignore these dark nights of the soul. Take comfort, because just about every old-house buyer has gone through these second thoughts and has gone on to conquer both the fears and the house.

⚜

AFTER THE PURCHASE

ONCE YOU (AND THE BANK) own the house, there is a great urge to rush all about and start doing everything that needs doing—all at one time. RESIST THAT URGE! In the process of making quick "improvements," it's easy to destroy the antique character of the house ... obliterating the reasons for which you bought the house in the first place. All too often, after people have been in a house for a few years, they regret some of the early work that they did.

THE ONLY THING that's important to get done right away is to make the house weathertight. Water is the bitter enemy of an old house. And whether the water is coming from a leaking roof, holes in the cornice or siding, a rotten gutter or leaking pipes, stopping the water is your first priority. Water will rot wood, attract insects, spoil plaster, infiltrate masonry, and try in every possible way to reduce your home to a pile of dust.

YOUR HOUSE INSPECTOR should have spotted many of the water problems for you, and they should be listed in your report. Specific tips on combatting water penetration will be found in the section on rot further on in this Compendium.

ONCE YOUR HOUSE IS DRY and protected, you are ready to start the exciting part: the restoration. Realize at the outset that, if this is your first old house, it's impossible for you to know everything you should know before tackling the house. It's the homeowner's version of Catch-22: "Before restoring an old house, you should have plenty of experience. But the only way you get experience is by restoring an old house."

EVEN IF YOU MEMORIZE every word in this book, there will be (or should be) lots of questions remaining. Inevitably, there will be much that you learn as you go along. Bear in mind what was said earlier: The most important aspect of restoration for you should be the PROCESS of doing it. By learning as much as you can *before* you start the hands-on work, you can accomplish two things: (1) You minimize the chances of making really dumb mistakes; (2) It makes the process more fun and personally rewarding for you.

IT'S CRUCIAL at the outset to have the right attitude about your house . . . a combination of respect plus a sense of perspective about time. Your house has been standing for many decades. And it will last for several more *centuries* if properly cared for. Getting things done by "next week" is not important. What *is* important is avoiding irreversible mistakes that will disfigure the house for all the years to come.

THE THREE VITAL INGREDIENTS

THERE ARE THREE VITAL INGREDIENTS in the revival of an old house: The plan, the materials, and the workmanship. And of the three, far and away the most important is *The Plan*. Alas, planning seems so boring when you could be doing highly visible things like stripping paint or knocking down sheetrock walls. But most of the amateur's mistakes are made during this early pell-mell rush to "make progress." A well-intentioned but uninformed restorer can cause more damage to an old house in a few weeks than decades of neglect.

REMUDDLING

Merely by changing small architectural details—like windows—you can destroy much of the character of an old house.

Original: Greek Revival

Original: Gothic Revival

"REMUDDLED"

"REMUDDLED"

THE CORRECT APPROACH is to work out a master plan for the entire house before ever lifting a hammer. Then make sure that each activity conforms to the plan.

THE MASTER PLAN

THERE ARE SEVEN GUIDELINES to making a successful master plan . . . one that will do credit to you and your house:

(1) LIVE IN THE HOUSE, if possible, before doing any work on it. Get the feel of the place. The only real way to figure out how a house works . . . and how you use it . . . is to live in it a while. Often, the original designer had some clever ideas built in that don't become apparent until you've spent some time in the house.

(2) BE GENTLE. Most people are far too aggressive in approaching an old house. The less one knows, the more apt one is to rip out, change and remodel. Thoughtless "remuddling" not only costs a lot of money, but it can also lower the long-term market value of your home by destroying the original architectural character. In developing your plan, see how *little* you can do to the original material in the house and still have it be comfortable.

(3) READ, RESEARCH . . . and read some more. The more you learn about the style of your house, the previous owners, and the influences that went into its design, the more likely you are to change your mind about what you want to do to the house. Usually, the more you learn, the stronger your desire to restore (or preserve) the original character.

(4) DON'T DO ANYTHING that can't be undone In setting your plan, try to avoid "irreversible changes"—those that permanently alter the character and appearance of the house. An old house is really a cultural trust. We have no right to destroy good work that was done by previous generations. Rather, we have a *responsibility* to preserve that good work for the generations that come after us.

FOR EXAMPLE, putting up aluminum siding is not an irreversible change per se (even though it is usually inadvisable) because the original wooden siding remains underneath. But if the siding contractor in applying the aluminum rips off some woodwork trim in the process, then this represents a permanent and irreversible loss to the house.

CHANGING A PAINT COLOR or wallpaper are examples of reversible changes, because someone at a later date can always change the paint color or hang a different wallpaper.

(5) REPAIR RATHER THAN REPLACE. Try to salvage and repair the original material in the house. You can accomplish minor miracles with plaster, putty, linseed oil and paint . . . as you'll see later in this book. The operative phrase for old

buildings is: "Daily care and conservative repair."

FOR EXAMPLE, the plaster in a ceiling may be badly damaged and require replacement. A contractor will usually want to rip everything out and start anew. But usually it's possible to break out and replace the flat ceiling plaster without destroying the cornice mouldings or the center ceiling medallion. It will take a bit more time to salvage the original material in this way . . . and so the contractor will never do it unless the owner insists upon it. (The phrase "It can't be done!" is the first thing taught in contractors' school.)

IF YOU HAVE TO REPLACE original elements, make sure the replacements are as close to the original as possible. For example, if you find you have to replace original one-over-one windows, don't install small-paned Colonial style sash in their stead.

(6) TO THINE OWN STYLE BE TRUE. Don't try to make an old house over into something it's not. The most common mistake is to try to "Colonialize" late 19th century houses to suggest that they are older than they really are. It never works! Each style has its own proportions and details. To try to make a Victorian house look Colonial just creates a hybrid that looks silly. No matter how many porches are ripped off, Federal eagles and neo-Georgian doorways installed, or how many fake vinyl shutters tacked on, the house will never look Colonial.

EVERY OLD HOUSE had an *original design concept*. This is true whether it was designed by a famous architect or erected by an anonymous carpenter/builder. Discovering that basic design concept—and remaining true to it in your restoration—is the key to most successful old-house revivals. By preserving and enhancing the original design you get a clarity and coherence of vision . . . a unified effect that otherwise gets lost if you start muddling in new design elements that don't fit with the old architecture.

NEVER FEEL APOLOGETIC that your house isn't "old enough" just because it wasn't built before the American Revolution. Each house, whether built in 1720 or 1920, is an

To Thine Own Style Be True: A late 18th-century Virginia room.

To Thine Own Style Be True: A circa 1870 Queen Anne Hall.

example of a particular architectural style. The most satisfying course—for you, the house, and succeeding generations—is to preserve or restore the house according to its original design.

THE ECONOMIC CLINCHER: It's almost always cheaper to restore along the original lines of the house than it is to try to "remuddle" it to a different look.

(7) GET HELP—free and otherwise. Lots of organizations, books and publications are available to help you analyze your house and plan out the best course of action.

THERE ARE NUMEROUS BOOKS on the old architecture of specific cities and towns. Your local library or historical society should have a collection of these. Your local historical society will often have photographs of old houses in your community. If they don't have a photo of your particular house, they'll often have pictures of ones similar to it.

BEYOND THE FREE HELP, you may want to call in an architect or other restoration professional. We'll discuss working with architects in a following section.

SPECIFICS OF YOUR MASTER PLAN

YOUR MASTER PLAN has to take two sets of needs into account: (1) The living needs of you and your family; (2) The need to protect the historical character and integrity of the house. Sometimes these two sets of needs overlap and conflict. All you can do in these circumstances is work out the best possible compromise . . . keeping in mind that the house will probably be around a lot longer than you.

TO START COMBINING all of your historical research with the physical needs of the house, you need a way to organize your information. Some people like file folders. Most find that 3-ring binders are most convenient. The method you

use is not important—just so long as you have some definite system. If you rely on random sheets of paper piled atop your desk, sooner or later you're going to lose some vital notes.

MOST PEOPLE BUILD THEIR RECORDS according to specific areas of the house; e.g., North Facade, Front Parlor, Back Bathroom, etc. Start your file by including all the historical information you've uncovered: Original paint colors and finishes, original architectural details that may be missing or that need repair, original uses and appearances of various rooms, and—if you are lucky—any old photographs of the house that you've been able to locate. Then, through photos, notes and drawings, you will want to list as much as you can about conditions as you found them.

A WORD ABOUT PHOTOGRAPHS: Many newcomers to old-house restoration underestimate the importance of "before" photographs. They are essential if you are working on a house with any historical significance, and a great convenience for "ordinary" houses. At the time, photos may seem like a bother, because you are *sure* that everyone will remember exactly how dismal conditions were. Not so. Once restoration begins, it is amazing how quickly you forget important details.

FOR HISTORIC HOUSES, photos are vital because they provide an ongoing, permanent record of what has happened to the house. And for "ordinary" houses, photos can be a big help in talking with architects and contractors. Also, your "before," "during," and "after" pictures become a life-long joy to you and your family when the restoration is finally finished.

FOR YOUR OWN ENTERTAINMENT, you may want some of your pictures in color. But for the permanent record, you should have black & white photos. After a few years, some color prints begin to fade. So if you want pictures that your grandchildren will cherish, you are best off with black & white.

AFTER YOU HAVE DOCUMENTED existing conditions, start adding notes and sketches of changes that may be needed. Within the need to preserve the architectural character of your house, you also have to allow for such things as:

• Adequate and well-located storage space

• Privacy for family members

• Space for hobbies and projects

• Play space for children

• Ease of maintenance

• Flexibility (the toddler on the tricycle becomes the teenager with the stereo)

DOORS DESERVE A SPECIAL MENTION. Most old houses were fitted with doors at each room entrance. If these doors survive, today's homeowners—influenced by modern

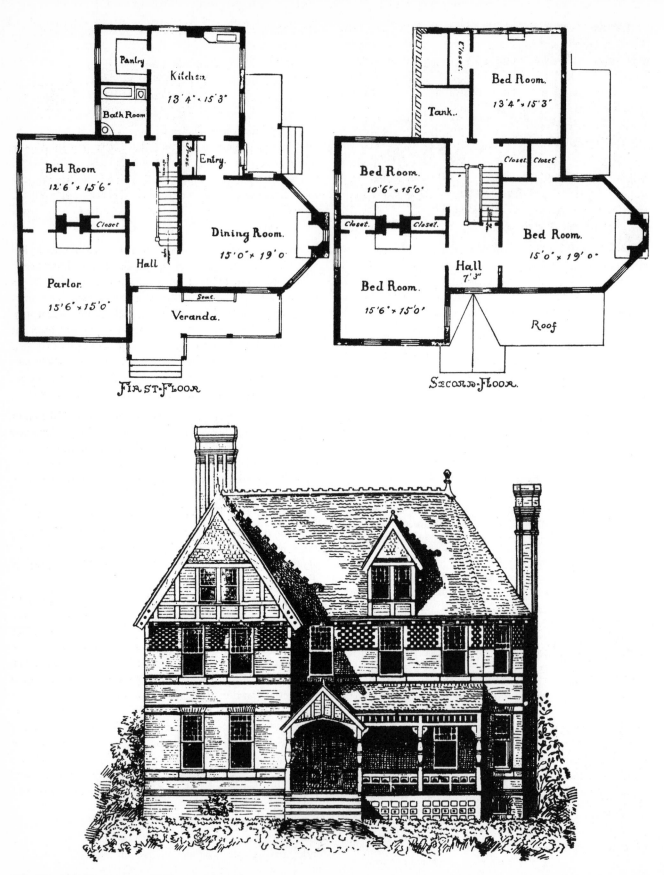

Pantry.

Kitchen.
13'4" x 15'3"

Bath Room

Entry.

Bed Room
12'6" x 15'6"

Closet

Dining Room.
15'0" x 19'0"

Hall

Parlor.
15'6" x 15'0"

Seat.

Veranda.

FIRST·FLOOR

Closet

Tank.

Bed Room.
13'4" x 15'3"

Closet Closet

Bed Room
10'6" x 15'0"

Closet. Closet.

Bed Room.
15'0" x 19'0"

Hall
7'3"

Bed Room.
15'6" x 15'0"

Roof

SECOND·FLOOR

"open plan" design—are often tempted to remove them. These partions and doors, however, had one practical use that is becoming relevant again today. They served to close off unused rooms so that you didn't have to heat unoccupied spaces. With soaring heating and air conditioning bills the ability to close off unused portions of the house is a highly desirable feature.

HAVING ZEROED IN on your practical needs, expand your vision outward. Look at historic houses of comparable vintage in your surrounding area. Go on house tours in restoration neighborhoods. And consult reference works and periodicals on historic architecture and design. (See bibliography.) Add pertinent ideas to your file.

NOTE NEXT IN YOUR PLANNING BOOK all changes that must be made in the mechanical systems: Heating, plumbing, wiring and air conditioning. Any changes in these systems involve messy work, frequently tearing open walls and the like. All of this work has to be done before any of the closing, finishing and decorative work can take place. You have to think through very carefully at this stage exactly where you want to locate toilets, sinks, all electrical outlets, ceiling fixtures, control switches, etc.

A COMMON MISTAKE, for example, is not to anticipate all of the electrical outlets and boxes for lighting fixtures that will be needed. It's easy enough to put them in while the electrical contractor is working on the place. But it's a major headache to add an outlet or a wall switch after all the surfaces are plastered, painted and papered. If you have planned each room down to the minute details, then the need for outlets will the apparent. And if there's any doubt, have the extra outlets put in. There's no sense spoiling your restoration with a rat's nest of extension cords because of a failure to plan properly.

CENTRAL AIR CONDITIONING presents special problems for old-house restorations. The need for ductwork in-

The kas was the early Dutch colonists' answer to storage problems.

volves cutting and encasing that can mar some of the original architectural details. Keep in mind that houses built before 1930 were designed as natural cooling machines. With proper use of shutters, awnings, shades, vents—and perhaps old fashioned ceiling fans—you can take advantage of natural ventilation that, in many sections of the country, will keep the house sufficiently comfortable on all but the hottest days. (See the section on "The Energy-Efficient Old House.") When air conditioning is needed, room window units can give the required cooling without permanent damage to the house.

STORAGE presents another special problem in old houses. People 150 years ago didn't have as many things cluttering their lives. So they didn't need as much storage capacity. Before you assume that you have to have built-in storage for everything, consider the solution that was often used in the 19th century: Free-standing armoires and storage chests. These can be picked up fairly inexpensively at flea markets, antique auctions and such places. This solution not only eliminates the mess and expense of building closets, but also adds to the period look of the home and avoids permanent changes to the structure.

ONCE YOU'VE DEVELOPED rough ideas about what you'll require for kitchen, bath, laundry and storage areas, you must determine whether you have enough floor space for everything you'd like to do. This calls for measured-scale drawings. If you are working with an architect, this is the first thing he'll do. If you're acting as your own designer, then taking the time to make your own set of measured drawings is worthwhile, if changes of any magnitude are planned. By working to scale on paper, you quickly discover whether there's enough space to turn that pantry into a bathroom, or if that maid's room has the potential to become a breakfast room. Too, discussions with workmen are very simple when you have a precise drawing of what the final result is supposed to look like.

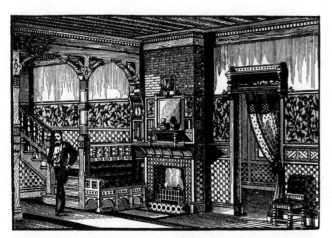

Heavy curtains, called portieres, were often hung in doorways to keep out drafts.

Rehabilitating old fireplaces is one of the complex tasks that often occur during a restoration.

IF YOU ARE LUCKY, sometimes you can find a set of measured drawings on file at your building department. You should be allowed to make a copy. On rare occasions, the previous owners can provide plans for the house. If you do start with someone else's plans, be sure to spot-check the accuracy of the scaling and make sure that the plans fully reflect the house as it looks today.

HIRING AN ARCHITECT

IF THERE IS a lot of basic work that has to be done in the house, such as installing a new heating plant, new plumbing and wiring, removing extraneous partitions, etc., you may want to hire an architect. However, this is not quite as simple as it sounds. (Nothing in an old house ever is!) Some architects are the best friends old houses ever had. Other architects are their worst enemies. When you are hiring one, you have to be able to tell one from the other.

THE ARCHITECTS TO AVOID are those who view an old house merely as a blank canvas upon which they can show off

their own creativity. This type of architect is unable to subordinate his or her ego to the original design concept of the house. They can't wait to start tearing things out in order to make their "improvements."

AT THE OTHER END OF THE SPECTRUM there are architects who understand and respect old buildings, and who derive immense satisfaction from restoring the original charm and character. This type of architect knows more about old houses than you'll ever be able to learn . . . and will earn his or her fee many times over.

PROS & CONS OF USING A RESTORATION ARCHITECT

Some Advantages

• Has intimate knowledge of the problems old houses present

• Can save time and money by avoiding costly mistakes

• By asking pertinent questions, he helps you clarify your needs

• Knows qualified contractors and craftsmen

• Will write tightly defined bid specifications

• Can supervise workmen to ensure top-quality results

Some Disadvantages

• An architect-managed job is usually accomplished in one big spurt

• Rapid pace of work means big cash outflow at one time

• Rapid pace of work makes it difficult and/or expensive to change your mind

• A persuasive architect can sometimes talk you into things you regret later—especially if you haven't fully worked out your own master plan

---

IT'S NOT EASY for the novice to tell which type of architect he's dealing with. The safest course is to ask around for recommendations from people who have had work done . . . or get recommendations from the local historical society or preservation organization. You can also call the local chapter of the American Institute of Architects or nearby schools of architecture to get names of architects who specialize in domestic restorations.

ANY ARCHITECT you approach should be happy to show you examples of his or her work and refer you to previous clients. Be sure to check with these former clients and see

This mid-1890 Queen Anne house in Vallejo, California, has suffered a typical remodelling–the removal of its architectural features.

Now restored (fortunately there was a photographic record of its original state) and painted in a Victorian manner, the house has regained its former charm.

their houses. Old-house people who have had a happy experience with an architect will usually be willing to show you their homes. An on-site inspection will give you an idea of the design approach of the architect and the level of excellence in the finished details.

DON'T HIRE AN ARCHITECT with whom you don't feel personally comfortable, no matter how gifted he or she may be. Restoring your home is a highly individual experience, and you should enjoy working with the architect whom you select.

HAVING CHOSEN YOUR ARCHITECT, go meet him or her armed with the information you have gathered and the preliminary plans you have made. And be very explicit about your budget. Many complaints about architects' disregard for the client's purse arise from the client's reluctance or inability to provide realistic budget figures.

AFTER YOUR INITIAL MEETING, the architect will draw up a letter of agreement stating his charges per hour for the various skills involved, a schedule of payments, and a projected figure for the total architectural work that cannot be exceeded without your approval. Don't hesitate to request changes in some of the terms. The scope of an architect's work is negotiable, and so fees can vary accordingly. Request weekly or monthly billing that will enable you to keep track of hours spent and how fast the dollars are being used up.

FEES FOR AN EXPERIENCED ARCHITECT will usually range from 10% to 20% of the total cost of the project when he or she is working on a percentage basis. His basic services can include any or all of the following:

1. Design and Development: Measuring and making an accurate plan of existing conditions; developing a list of the client's needs; designing and drawing new plans, layouts and elevations.

2. Construction documents: Providing working drawings; accurate and fully scaled detail drawings; and bid specifications:; written descriptions of the work, materials to be used, and methods for execution.

3. Supervision of contractors: Organizing (with the advice and consent of the owner) the bidding for the job; evaluating bids and selecting contractors; drawing up the construction contract; acting as owner's agent in making payments and ordering changes; on-site inspection of work in progress; quality control.

IF YOUR HOUSE requires extensive changes and complicated preservation work, you may need all these services from an architect. But most restoration jobs don't require them all—and many architects are quite happy for you to select from their full range of services on an à la carte basis. In such cases, you'd pay for the services on an hourly rate. (Some architects will work only on an hourly rate on domestic restoration jobs

SAMPLE SPECIFICATIONS

Modify or make more specific as conditions warrant. Be sure that every detail not spelled out on the plans is covered by a written specification. Specifications should tell not only what is to be done, but also who is to do it.

Bathroom

Floor will be 1-in. hexagonal white unglazed ceramic tile set in concrete. Kohler fixtures (client to specify; contractor to supply). There will be a wainscot of white glazed ceramic tile 2" × 4" laid horizontally to a height of 50 in. with glazed trim at all edges and corners. Wainscot to be set in concrete bed. Walls and ceiling above wainscot to be 5/8-in. waterproof sheetrock. Ceiling light, medicine cabinet and two small sconces client to supply; contractor to install. Wall and ceiling to receive prime coat and finish coat of PPG semigloss enamel; client to specify colors.

Ceilings

All loose plaster to be reinforced by 3-in. screws and washers attached to joists. Washers to be covered by joint compound feathered to 18 in. on all sides. All cracks to be mended with cloth tape and joint compound. Sections of missing plaster to be filled with 3/8-in. sheetrock shimmed to level of old plaster. Joints between sheetrock and old plaster to be sealed with cloth tape and joint compound.

Walls

Remove all wallpaper down to bare plaster. Cracks in corners and other cracks designated as Structural Cracks to be patched with Krack-Kote. Other cracks to be patched with cloth tape and joint compound. Feather and sand for smooth finish. Use PPG paints for one prime coat and one finish coat. All joints between plaster and woodwork to be filled with acrylic caulk.

Floors

Strip oak floors to be sanded; make three (3) passes with fine sandpaper. All corners to be hand-scraped. Client to inspect floor for sanding marks before finish is applied. Finish with one thin coat of gym seal varnish followed by two (2) coats of high-gloss gym-coat varnish. Allow at least 24 hr. drying time between coats.

Parquet floors shall be sanded starting with medium-grade paper. DO NOT use coarse paper on parquet. Otherwise, finish as above.

Finish Carpentry

All finish carpentry to be as specified on plans. Repair five (5) cornices at top of window and door casings on first floor. Missing pieces to be fabricated as required from top grade American Black Walnut. Finish to match existing woodwork with three (3) coats of hand-rubbed shellac. All nail holes to be filled with linseed-oil putty colored to match wood. Carpenter to install all hardware (client to furnish).

Similar specifications may also be needed to cover such things as:

Roofing	Plumbing
Exterior Woodwork	Electrical & Mechanical
Exterior Masonry	Hardware & Fittings
Tile Work	Heating & Air Conditioning
Demolition & Removal	Security System
Ironwork	

since the construction contracts often aren't large enough to allow them to fully recover their fees on a straight percentage basis.)

HOURLY FEES FOR ARCHITECTS are usually in the $30—50/hr. range. When you work with an architect on an hourly basis, he or she is essentially acting as a consultant on your job. You can use the architect on the most creative tasks . . . while you may opt to pick up some of the chores like supervising of the contractors and workmen.

IF YOU HAVE more time and energy than cash, a good method is to have the architect design a master plan that will enable you to do the work in stages . . . one project leading smoothly to the next. In this way, you can have the work proceed at the rate your personal finances permit—but you have the security of knowing that the scope of the entire project has been carefully thought through and that the sequence of work is logical.

THE GENERAL CONTRACTOR

ALSO KNOWN AS THE "GC," the general contractor is a person who claims to be able to handle a restoration or renovation job from start to finish. He will supply, schedule and supervise all of the trades involved: Carpenters, electricians, masons, etc. He will help select materials and equipment and will procure them. He'll pay the bills and do the bookkeeping. And he'll get whatever permits are required by local building regulations.

FOR THIS WORK, and for his knowledge and experience, the GC plans on making a gross profit of about 33% of the total cost of the job. To achieve this profit goal, he charges you a fee that represents about a 50% markup over his direct costs for labor and materials.

YOU DON'T HAVE TO HIRE a GC for all the work. You can subcontract with one or more of the trades directly and have each subcontractor—mason, carpenter, painter—be responsible for insurance for his workers and for the filing of any necessary papers and permits. (Making sure that workmen on your property are covered by Workmen's Compensation Insurance is your responsibility. If there should be an accident—and they aren't covered by insurance—you as the homeowner may be liable.)

WHEN YOU PARCEL OUT WORK to subcontractors, you are essentially acting as your own general contractor. This will inevitably mean more time—and perhaps more grief—on your part. You will be responsible for making sure that the subcontractor shows up on time, that his efforts are coordinated with other subcontractors, that he properly understands your instructions, etc. In return for this additional aggravation, you do get the advantage of tighter control over the job—providing you know clearly what you want done.

ANOTHER ADVANTAGE to acting as your own general contractor is that you have greater control over the pace of the work. And you won't have to make as many snap decisions. For example, the General Contractor might come rushing up to you and say that the carpenter needs to know the height of the chair rail immediately because the plasterers are waiting to start work as soon as the carpenter finishes.

FINDING A RELIABLE GENERAL CONTRACTOR or subcontractor who understands the special problems of old houses is not easy. Just thumbing through the Yellow Pages is a chancy business. And you can't really depend on lawsuits for redress if you end up with a result that makes you unhappy. Since litigation is so expensive and time-consuming, basically your construction contract is only as good as the person who signed it. That is why the selection of the right person is far more important than your legal position as defined on the contract.

TO GET NAMES OF CONTRACTORS, consult friends and neighbors, architects, building supply companies, real estate lawyers—and perhaps even the bank that holds your mortgage. After you have about five likely sounding prospects, check out jobs they have worked on recently—and talk to the property owners. Bear in mind when talking to people who you don't know that few will admit to flaws by careless workmen that might diminish the value of their property. So be prepared to read between the lines . . . and if the recommendation seems lukewarm listen intently for what they *don't* say.

NARROW YOUR CHOICE down to two or three and then get bids for your job. Keep in mind that in order to get a carefully figured price, the contractor must know *exactly* what he is bidding on. If there are elements to the job that aren't clear, the contractor must add dollars to his bid to protect himself against surprises. Supply the contractor with copies of plans, working drawings and specifications. Remember that it is almost impossible for specifications to be too detailed. Far more difficulty is caused by vague (or nonexistent) specifications than by overly detailed ones. Be sure that every detail that is not spelled out on the plans is covered by the accompanying written specifications.

CHOOSING A CONTRACTOR

ONCE YOU HAVE THE BIDS, don't automatically grab the lowest one. Also *listen* to the way various bidders talk about the job. Some contractors are more willing than others to take the special pains that old-house work requires. This special care takes time. So it is possible that the contractor who is right for your house will not have the lowest bid. On the other hand, by having several bids in hand, you can tell if any single contractor is trying to take you to the cleaners.

THE AGREEMENT you sign with a contractor should be regarded more as a helpful working document than as a paper setting forth each party's legal rights. Like the specifications, the contract should be very detailed, because it spells out what you expect of the contractor and vice versa. Most disputes arise not from skullduggery on the contractor's part, but rather from genuine misunderstandings. The best way to avoid misunderstandings is to PUT IT IN WRITING.

THE CONTRACT you sign should cover all of these points:

• The full price of the job.

• The specific work the contractor agrees to. Be sure that the plans and written specifications that were part of the bidding process become a legal part of the contract. Type and quality of materials to be used should be spelled out.

• The date work is to begin—and a time schedule of how the project should proceed, step by step.

• A schedule of payments. A common arrangement is one payment (often one-third) when work begins, another payment at the halfway point, and the balance upon completion.

• Who supplies what. The contract or your written specifications should spell out any appliances or fixtures that you expect the contractor to buy and furnish as part of his contract. If you have a specific brand and model in mind, spell it out. (Leaving fixture selection to contractors sometimes results in unpleasant surprises. He may install a bathtub that he thinks is a great bargain but which you think is hideous.)

• Patching and cleanup. Details like who is responsible for removal of debris and cleanup should be spelled out. If you expect an electrician or plumber to patch all the holes he has made, specify this and also the kind of finish on the patch that you expect. Most plumbers and electricians base their prices on the assumption that you'll patch any holes they make and that you will dispose of their debris. If you want your house "broom clean" at the end of each day's work, spell this out.

FIRST THINGS FIRST

IF YOUR RESTORATION is being supervised by an architect or general contractor, then he or she will schedule events and see that work occurs in the proper sequence. But if yours is a do-it-yourself job—or you are acting as your own general contractor—then it's your responsibility to schedule the work.

ALTHOUGH NO TWO RESTORATIONS ARE ever the same, this is the order in which activities usually occur:

1. Research and Planning: The importance of thorough investigation and planning has been emphasized previously.

2. Weatherproofing: The house must be protected from the elements, especially water penetration. If there are roofing problems, leaking gutters, missing siding, etc., make these repairs first.

3. Demolition: If the restoration plan calls for removal of extraneous sinks and cabinets (frequently a legacy of roominghouse conversions), now is the time to do it. Old electrical wiring, plumbing and extraneous partitions should also be removed. Homeowners often prefer to do demolition themselves because it doesn't require special skills and they can save money. Demolition, however, does require careful planning to make sure that you don't inadvertently destroy valuable architectural details and original house fabric.

4. Removal of Debris: It's often convenient to rent a bulk trash container that can be parked outside your house. If you are having workmen carry debris for you, try to be on hand to double-check what they are throwing out. Sometimes, precious pieces of architectural ornament that you had carefully set aside will look like junk to the workmen and they will cheerfully toss it in the trash hauler. Also, scavenge the debris for any seasoned lumber, mouldings, etc., that you can recycle.

5. Framing, Flooring and Structural Work: Install new beams where required, repair or replace any exterior windows and doors, frame out new partitions, install flooring, and framing for closets.

6. Rough Plumbing: Plumbing is messy work. Holes may have to be punched through floors, walls and ceilings. Be sure to discuss with the plumber any holes he plans to make. Plumbers tend to think solely of making it easy to run their pipes ... not of preserving the architectural beauty of your house. Plumbers are notorious for cutting through any beams that happen to be in their way, even though the cuts may weaken the structure. By careful planning, it is usually possible to run all necessary pipes without damaging decorative plaster or other important architectural details. But the plumber won't take these extra pains unless you discuss them with him *in advance* and he understands your concerns.

SUPPLY PIPES, waste pipes, vents and heating lines should all be thoroughly tested before partitions are sealed up.

7. Electrical Wiring: Running wires through plastered walls and ceilings usually requires punching holes. But this can almost always be done without damaging decorative plaster

detail. As with plumbers, be sure to discuss with electricians the routes they plan for their wires and let them know your concern about cornices, ceiling medallions, etc.

BE SURE THAT you have checked the wiring plan very thoroughly to make sure that you have anticipated future needs. All wiring, lights and outlets should be tested before any partitions are sealed up.

8. Bathroom and Kitchen Fixtures: Tubs, toilets, sinks and tile work can be put in at this point.

9. Inspection: Before any partition closing is done, make a thorough inspection of all work and compare it against your plans and specifications, making a list of any corrections that have to be made. Perhaps the electrician forgot an outlet, or the plumber installed a basin crooked.

10. Walls and Ceilings: Install plaster and/or sheetrock as required. (Plaster is the preferred material for old houses.) Tape and patch cracks. Any new plaster should cure for at least two weeks before painting.

11. Finish Carpentry: Install mouldings, hang doors, add door and window trim, etc. Hardware should be mounted at this point, although some items like escutcheons for door knobs may have to be removed during final painting.

12. Install Electrical Fixtures: Chandeliers, sconces and the like should be installed before painting, as there may be some minor plaster damage that will require patching.

13. Painting: This is the moment that brings about a magical change. Just be sure that electrical fixtures and the like are carefully masked. Some hardware, such as door knob escutcheons, window latches, etc., should be removed and remounted after the paint has dried.

14. Finishing of Floors: Sand and finish new flooring. If you have antique wide-board flooring, you'll want to scrape or sand these by hand. The big electric floor sanders grind all the distinctive wear marks out of the old wide boards and reduce them to a flat sameness. In applying floor finish, allow sufficient drying time between coats (consult label) and remember that two thin coats are better than one thick coat.

BETTER TO PRESERVE THAN RESTORE; BETTER TO RESTORE THAN REMODEL.

THERE ARE SIX WORDS starting with "R" that are used in connection with work on old houses: (1) Restoration; (2) Renovation; (3) Rehabilitation. (4) Remodeling; (5) Recycling; and (6) Reconstruction. And for good measure, there is one "P" word: Preservation. These words are not interchangeable; they define a particular attitude and way of approaching an old building. The word that you select to describe your own activities is important, because it defines the relationship between you and the house.

IN GENERAL, it is always best to preserve . . . and better to restore than remodel. When in doubt, take the most conservative course. That means the method that is the least intrusive . . . the one that disturbs the original material the least.

THE IDEAL COURSE OF TREATMENT for an old building is a program of daily maintenance that keeps it from getting into a run-down condition. When a part reaches a state where it can't be maintained (preserved) any longer, the repair should be done in a way that retains as much of the original as practical. The new patch should duplicate the original in appearance, shape and texture.

IN THIS BOOK, you'll find that the emphasis is on preservation and restoration. Old houses have a richness of styling, ornamentation and finish that make them a great environmental resource. They simply can't be duplicated by today's building methods. Too many of these fine old houses have already vanished. To allow the remaining old buildings to decay, to be defaced or demolished is a cultural crime.

IT IS IMPERATIVE that more people start taking an active role in preserving our architectural heritage . . . for the enrichment of our own built environment, and for the enjoyment of generations yet to come.

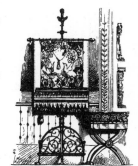

PRESERVATION—Keeping an existing building in its current state by a careful program of maintenance and repair.

RESTORATION—Returning a building to the appearance it had at some previous point in

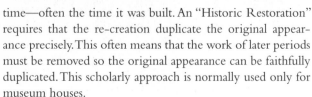

Dining room (left) and Library (right) as illustrated in an 1863 book on home decoration.

time—often the time it was built. An "Historic Restoration" requires that the re-creation duplicate the original appearance precisely. This often means that the work of later periods must be removed so the original appearance can be faithfully duplicated. This scholarly approach is normally used only for museum houses.

FOR OLD HOUSES that function as homes, the approach normally taken is an "Interpretive Restoration" or an "Adaptive Restoration." In an Interpretive Restoration, the house is restored in keeping with the original architectural style of the house. The decoration and furnishings are of a period appropriate to the house—without attempting to precisely duplicate the original appearance of the exterior and interior down to the last detail.

IN AN ADAPTIVE RESTORATION, the basic architectural features of the house are retained, but the decoration and furnishings may be handled in an eclectic or contemporary fashion.

RENOVATION—Making a structure sound and reusable, without any special regard to the period architectural appearance.

REHABILITATION—Same as Renovation.

RECYCLING—The process of repairing or rehabilitating old buildings so they can be used again. Recycling done with an historical perspective may be termed "restoration." Recycling without any historical sensitivity is "renovation" or "rehabilitation."

REMODELLING—Changing the appearance of a structure, inside or out, by removing or covering over original details and substituting new materials and forms.

RECONSTRUCTION—Re-creating an historic building that has been destroyed by erecting a new structure that duplicates the original as closely as possible. A reconstruction may be built with new materials, or old recycled building materials.

THE INTERPRETIVE RESTORATION

By Clem Labine

A dining room wall that exemplifies the finest decoration in the American style at the end of the 18th century with fine woodwork details by Samuel McIntyre.

A SUBTITLE for this section could be: "Don't Feel Imprisoned By Mediocre Taste." Old-house owners who feel a responsibility about the historical character of their homes often worry greatly about whether what they are doing with their houses is a true reflection of the "original." They feel guilty if what they are doing is not an historically accurate duplication of what the original owners did. These homeowners worry a great deal about whether or not their work is "authentic."

THIS SECTION IS DESIGNED to eliminate *needless* guilt and anxiety. Granted, an old house entails special obligations: Everything you do to the house should be in keeping with the spirit and tradition of that particular style. To thine own house be true. But the search for historical authenticity can be carried to extremes that make the house a burden rather than a joy.

SOME PEOPLE will make changes from the original—and then feel guilty about it. Others will slavishly reproduce some of the original decorative treatments—even though they personally don't like it. The objective of this article is to help you distinguish between important and unimportant changes. Worry about the important ones—and have fun in the areas that allow you some creative freedom.

I AM ASSUMING in this discussion that your old house is like mine; i.e., it is not an historically important home. It wasn't designed by a famous architect; nobody famous ever lived there; nothing important ever happened there; and it is not a particularly exquisite example of any particular architectural style. In other words, it is an "ordinary" old house.

IN SOME WAYS, it is harder to restore the "ordinary" house than the historically important one. With the historical house, your course is clear: You want to make it as close to the historical original as possible. But with the "ordinary" old house there is less precedent to guide you.

THE FIRST STEP in restoring an "ordinary" old house is to make a distinction between reversible and irreversible changes.

REVERSIBLE WORK

WE START WITH the premise that an old house is a cultural trust. Any house that has survived for 60 years or more in our throw-away culture has a special claim on our sympathy and attention.

FURTHER, we have no moral right to destroy good craftsmanship of past generations. Creations of the past belong as much to the dead and to the generations yet to come as they do to us. We can tear down and meddle all we want with our own constructions. But good work on which previous generations have lavished their time and treasure we have no right to destroy. We have a responsibility to future generations to pass along today's old houses intact.

IN DEFINING "intact," however, we must make a distinction between the decorative *appearance* of a house and the *fabric* of a house. We should always be very hesitant to destroy or change the original fabric of a house. But there are many ways that we can alter the appearance of the house—in ways that suit our own tastes—that still remain faithful to the spirit and character of the structure.

THIS DISTINCTION is based on what may be *reversible* at a later date. Should someone come along after you (or if you should change your mind at a later date) and wish to restore the exact original appearance of the house, the work you have done should be easily *undone*; i.e., be easily reversible.

A SIMPLE EXAMPLE of reversible work is paint and wallpaper. Changing a paint color is easily reversible by merely adding another color on top. And wallpaper can be easily stripped off when a different wall treatment is desired.

THE ONLY TIME a painting operation becomes partially irreversible is when all paint layers are stripped off, thereby eliminating the historic record of the changes in finishes that were laid down since the house was built. When it is necessary to strip paint in a museum house, they avoid this obliteration problem by always leaving small sections unstripped in unobtrusive places. Thus a complete record is intact, should it ever be necessary to trace the entire paint history.

EVEN SOMETHING AS DRASTIC as adding aluminum siding over old clapboards can be considered reversible (even

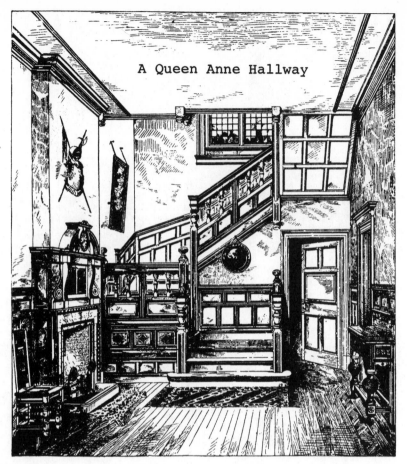

A Queen Anne Hallway

though we don't recommend it). The original material of the house still exists under the new siding. The thousands of people around the country who are ripping off 1940s asbestos and asphalt siding from old houses testify to the reversibility.

HOWEVER, if the contractor (as they often do) removes some of the wooden trim from the exterior then the job becomes less reversible. The only way to re-create the original appearance of the exterior would be to find a pattern and duplicate the original trim—often an impossible task. Once the ornamental woodwork is gone, it's doubtful that the house will ever again regain that architectural feature.

LIKEWISE, putting in a sheetrock partition is usually reversible—if it is carefully done so that not much of the original fabric is destroyed. But tearing down an ornamental plaster ceiling to replace it with sheetrock is *irreversible*.

THE INTERPRETIVE RESTORATION

THE DISTINCTION between reversible and irreversible work makes it easier to see where we can express our individual tastes in restoring our particular old house. Many aspects of the decoration—both interior and exterior—involve

Mid-19th-century drawing room in the Gothic style.

reversible work. And it is in this area that we can express our own taste without the slightest twinge of guilt. As long as you aren't damaging the fabric of the house, indulge yourself.

A CONCEPT that you may find useful is the "interpretive restoration." An interpretive restoration is one that is in the style of the period, without necessarily being a faithful duplication of what may have been in the house originally.

EVEN IN HOUSE MUSEUMS where the original structure is intact, a curator may have to resort to an interpretive restoration for one or more of the rooms. If there isn't enough documentation of the original decoration and furnishings, then the curator has to start making educated guesses based on whatever fragmentary evidence is available combined with knowledge of the styles of the period.

OBVIOUSLY, if your house had some exquisite decorative feature, such as painted stencil-work or scenic wall or ceiling paintings, it is very desirable to preserve or restore these details to the fullest possible extent. But many old houses never had such fine finishes inside. And that's where the interpretive restoration comes in.

FOR YOUR HOUSE

HERE ARE SOME OF THE CASES in which an interpretive approach may be most practical:

• You have no idea what the original interior looked like, but you would like to decorate in the style of the period. The house itself provides little physical evidence, and there are no photos or written evidence that you can locate.

• You have some idea of what the interior looked like (from physical or photographic evidence) but you find that your personal taste is at considerable variance from what a faithful

historical restoration would dictate. In effect, you would be spending a lot of time and money to recreate an interior that you didn't like.

• You have some evidence of what the interior should look like, but you simply don't have the budget to recreate all that would be required. This is not uncommon when people buy large, run-down 19th century houses that had been mansions when originally built. In this case, you might choose to do a low-budget interpretive restoration . . . keeping your options open in case you come into more money at a later date.

THE BASIC APPROACH to the interpretive restoration is to steep yourself in the social and decorative arts history of the period that relates to your house. Visit house museums of a similar period. Read every book you can get your hands on. Talk to people at your local historical society. And, of course, keep reading *The Old-House Journal*. Read, research . . . and read some more.

KEEP A FOCUS

THE TIME FRAME you select for your interpretive restoration might have a latitude of 10—20 years. The most important factor is not which time frame you pick, but rather that you stay faithful to the spirit of whichever time frame you select. This gives the end result a unity and clarity of concept that makes it look "designed" rather than just thrown together. Old is not enough; the idea is to put the house together with a coherent theme.

ALSO, BY SELECTING a time frame that is within 10–20 years of the house's construction, you'll have decorative details that accent and harmonize with the architectural elements of the house, rather than clashing with them.

SELECTING A TIME FRAME of 10–20 years gives you plenty of latitude to find decorative schemes that please you. Within every period there were movements and countermovements . . . the elaborate and the simple . . . so that you can find models to suit your taste. For instance, Art Nouveau is a style that reached its zenith between 1890–1905, but could fit right in with a Queen Anne/Eastlake house built in 1880 because the Art Noveau designs were just an extension of the Aesthetic Movement designs that were used initially in Queen Anne homes.

FOCUSING ON A SINGLE ERA actually makes decorating less confusing, because it automatically enables you to eliminate many choices from consideration. If you have a Colonial Revival house with Georgian details, you know that you want Williamsburg-type English reproductions and antiques. So if you see a Tiffany-style lamp shade for sale, no matter how lovely, you can pass it by without a qualm because you know

THE FACE OF THE ENEMY

Building supply dealers and manufacturers will urge you to deface your old house by encasing it in this year's fad product. (Name deleted from this actual ad to protect the guilty!)

it isn't relevant for what you are doing.

IF THERE IS A SUBSTANTIAL budget for the project, it could be worthwhile to engage a restoration architect or interior designer who has knowledge of the period of interest to you. A competent professional will have more knowledge than you can ever hope to acquire in spare-time study. Even if you use a professional, however, you still want to learn as much as you can yourself before ever talking to the pro.

THE MORE YOU AS CLIENT KNOW, the better able you are to talk intelligently with the professional and get the most out of him or her. Besides, the process of self-education in the design idiom of past periods is one of the most enjoyable parts of restoring your old house.

INTERPRETIVE TRADE-OFFS

BUDGETS OR PRACTICAL considerations often dictate that not every detail from a particular decorative style can be duplicated. For example, many moderately furnished parlors had elaborate draperies that gave a rich feel to the room. Because of the cost of these heavy fabrics today—and the extraordinary upkeep required—a homeowner may wish to keep the window treatments simple or non-existent. But elaboration that is lost at the windows can be added elsewhere. For example, a rich wallpaper pattern or stencilled treatment of the ceiling can be used, which would keep the luxurious feeling.

OFTEN BUILDERS would erect houses with wood-work and plasterwork in the most "modern" designs because the latest pattern books had made their way into the hands of the architect or contractor. However, especially in the Western parts of the U.S., the interior decorating ideas lagged behind the construction styles. Thus in 1885 you might see a homeowner decorating an Eastlake-style house with mid-Victorian cabbage roses. Today, the owner of that house could choose to make interpretive stylistic corrections and decorate with William Morris papers.

EARLY AMERICAN WALLPAPERS, readily available today, are another interesting example of interpretive restora-

tion. These papers are sold as "documentary" papers, but often the original document is *not* a wallpaper. Rather the patterns are frequently taken from fabrics, book endpapers, china, etc. But this is no reason for the owner of an 1830 Greek Revival house not to use an appropriate paper—even though the house in 1830 probably only had painted walls. Before 1840, the only wallpapers available in the U.S. were expensive materials imported from England, France and elsewhere. Therefore, all but the most luxurious houses went without paper. However, one of the "interpretive" papers can be an appropriate, practical and inexpensive way to capture the flavor of the era.

ANOTHER CONSIDERATION: Many late 19th century homes (except those of the very wealthy) were not decorated with the latest fashions . . . simply because the owners did not have access to the fancy stores of New York and Philadelphia. Rather, these homes were often furnished out of the catalogs of the day. But there's no reason why today's owner of a Colorado Queen Anne house can't play "what if . . ." and proceed as though the original owners had access to the best stores and taste of the era.

SOME CRITICS of interpretive restorations say that it is "gilding the lily" to put in period effects that were not present in the original. And of course it can be overdone. One would not want to install an elegant Georgian interior in a simple Colonial farmhouse, nor a Rococo Renaissance Revival interior in a 19th-century workman's cottage. But that's where the "What if . . ." part of the exercise comes in. If the best design minds of the period had been used on your house, they wouldn't have overdone it either. They might have developed a richer-looking interior than your house originally had . . . but it would have been very much in keeping with the style and proportions of the house.

A Case History . . .

THE INTERPRETIVE RESTORATION

By Clem Labine

IN THE PREVIOUS SECTION, I set out some of the basic principles for an interpretive restoration . . . one that is faithful to the original period and style of the house, without necessarily being an exact duplication of what was originally in the structure. Now let me illustrate how I applied these principles in the restoration of the dining room in my 1883 brownstone.

THE HOUSE, located in the Park Slope section of Brooklyn, had been a rooming house when my wife and I purchased it. The house had been cut up into numerous apartments, with sheetrock partitions dividing up the original grand spaces, and sinks and stoves seemingly in every corner. Very little evidence of the original appearance remained, except for the walnut woodwork—most of which was still intact under countless layers of paint.

THROUGH DOCUMENTARY RESEARCH, we learned that the house had been built in 1883 by a speculative builder, and had been rented out for two years before a purchaser finally came along. Given the speculative nature of the house's start in life, it seemed unlikely to us that the house ever had a very elaborate interior-decorating scheme.

WE ALSO LEARNED that the man who purchased the house in 1885 had worked in a brokerage firm on Wall Street. From the little fragments we found, Mr. Blackwell seemed to be a solid citizen—but not a man of unusual wealth. Therefore, it seemed unlikely to us that the new owners would have dramatically upgraded the decoration in their new home.

EVIDENCE FROM THE HOUSE

PAINT SCRAPINGS and other archeological evidence tended to support this hypothesis. The original finishes that we could find seemed rather mediocre . . . not at all indicative of the best taste of the 1880's.

WE UNCOVERED, for example, fragments of three wallpapers that, if not original, were from an early decorating scheme. One of them was a very attractive Art Nouveau pattern. But the others were quite pedestrian. We wouldn't have wanted to reproduce them—even if the budget would have allowed it.

WHEN WE STEAMED the calcimine paint off the dining room ceiling, we found what seemed to be the original paint finish: A brownish purple that could best be described as the color of liver. It was definitely a color that could be called "interesting," but was not one that my wife and I felt we could live with.

DURING THE WORK on the ceiling, we also uncovered evidence of a turn-of-century remodelling that involved (among other things) removal of an ornate plaster medallion and its replacement by a much smaller, simpler circular medallion. This presented an immediate question: Should we attempt to recreate a medallion like the original, or work with what we had?

IT WAS AS WE PONDERED all these factors that we opted for an Interpretive Restoration.

'WHAT IF . . .'

FOR OUR INTERPRETIVE restoration, we started by going back to the original design idea of the house . . . to see what the structure itself would suggest. The dominant decorative feature, inside or outside the hous, is the walnut woodwork with the large carved crowns. Research into the style books of the day showed that these linear, geometric ornaments were basically inspired by Charles Locke Eastlake and the English Aesthetic or Art Movement. This discovery gave us the starting point we needed.

WE THEN POSED the "what if" question: What if one of the leading aesthetic designers of the time had been retained to decorate the house? What might the house have looked like? For our "leading designer," we chose Christopher Dresser—an English design genius of the late 19th century. We selected Dresser because of the power and originality of his designs—and because he had published a great deal. So there was a large body of printed work available for review.

FORTUNATELY, several of Dresser's works are available in inexpensive reprint editions. And through a friend who is a book collector, I also had access to one of Dresser's original volumes. The color plates were immensely helpful in color selection.

NEXT, we made the decision to emphasize painted decoration. Part of the reason was that Dresser had a preference for flat, sylized decoration, such as stencilled ornament. Equally, very little is available today in Aesthetic Movement papers and fabrics. But you can still buy paint and reproduce any painted decoration that you see in a book or in a museum.

THE DECISION to use painted decoration also solved the problem about what to do about the small replacement ceiling medallion. Dresser didn't like the large cast ceiling medallions; he preferred a flat painted ceiling ornament. So we decided to keep the existing small plaster circle and add a painted ornament around it.

NEXT STEP WAS to select the patterns to reproduce. The pattern for the ceiling and center ornaments came from Dresser's "Modern Ornamentation." Similarly, dado and frieze paper were adapted from other Aesthetic Movement sources.

DURING (above): A rooming-house bathroom had been built into the dining room alcove. Photo shows midway point in the restoration. Partitions and bathroom fixtures have been removed, the floor replaced, and the cut for the bathroom door is ready to be re-sealed. Behind bathroom partition was found a turn-of-century wall treatment in very damaged condition.

AFTER (below): Dining room restored in the Aesthetic fashion of the 1880's. Photos by Jim Kalett

CANVAS FIRST

OF COURSE, before any of the decorative work could be done, there was an enormous amount of repair work to be executed—on woodwork, ceiling, walls and floor. But since this was relatively straightforward (albeit endless) work, I'm not going into details here. The "During" photo on this page hints at the amount of work done.

ONE UNUSUAL FACET of the preparation work was the application of canvas to the ceiling and walls before any paint was laid down. Since so much time and effort was being put into the painted decoration, it seemed worth this extra step to ensure that the painted ornament wouldn't be damaged by minor plaster cracks. The "canvas" is actually a white vinylized fabric—applied just like wallpaper—and is available through large wallpaper and decorating outlets.

AFTER THE PREPARATION work was completed and the patterns selected, it was just a matter of layout and execution. Most of the decoration was stencilled. There were about 200 man-hours that went into the decoration. Howard Zucker and Helmuth Buecherl made invaluable contributions in the layout and application of the painted ornament.

THE RESULTING ROOM in the Aesthetic manner is not an attempt to duplicate what was originally in the house. But it is very much in keeping with the spirit of the times when the house was built. And, most important to me, the room is fun to be in. I understand all of the social history behind the decoration—and was part of the process that created it.

Left: Painted ornament—based on Christopher Dresser designs—was added around the small plaster medallion that had been installed in a 1900 remodelling. Dresser preferred flat painted ornament rather than three-dimensional plaster.

Below: Large crowns on woodwork established the stylistic theme for the rest of the decoration: Sunflowers in the Aesthetic manner. Ceiling and cove are stencilled. The frieze paper was silk screened by a friend, Charles Eanet.

Above: The dado was created by stencilling the stylized sunflowers over a glazed background; lines were produced with a striping brush and straightedge after stencils dried. Dust band above dado is a three-color stencil.

Getting to Know Your Old House

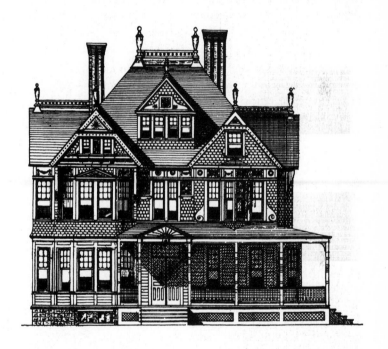

GUIDLINES FOR REHABILITATING OLD BUILDINGS

RESTORING AND REHABILITATING old buildings is becoming so popular that almost as many crimes are being committed by misguided remodelers as were committed in the 1960s by the "clear and destroy" bulldozers of the urban renewal forces.

PEOPLE HAVE FOUND that it is the older buildings and neighborhoods that give cities and towns their own special character. Often badly neglected for decades, these old buildings—both residential and commercial—are increasingly being recognized as an under-valued asset.

FURTHER, it has become clear that it does little good to restore a single structure if the neighborhood around it continues to decay. Thus the accent today—for both homeowners and government officials—is on neighborhood preservation. Many old buildings that lack outstanding architectural merit nonetheless become important when viewed in the context of the street or neighborhood.

BUT THIS KNOWLEDGE ALONE does not arm the individual homeowner or local official with the proper know-how to handle the rehabilitation of an old building. Often the overzealous remodeler will destroy the essential character of the structure he set out to save—through a series of seemingly small but critical mistakes.

THE UNDERLYING PRINCIPLE is that when bringing an old house or commercial structure up to modern functional standards, it is essential that its architectural character not be destroyed in the process. What follows is a set of 9 principles that should guide the rehabilitation of any old building . . . be it an 1855 Italianate house or a 1910 office building. Specific applications of the principles are shown in the "do's and don't's" on the following three pages.

THE 9 BASIC PRINCIPLES

• Every reasonable effort should be made to provide a compatible use for buildings that will require minimum alteration to the building and its environment.

• Rehabilitation work should not destroy the distinguishing qualities or character of the property. Removal or alteration of historic material or architectural features should be held to a minimum.

• Deteriorated architectural features should be repaired rather than replaced whenever possible. When replacement is necessary, new material should match material being replaced in composition, design, color, texture and other visual qualities.

• Replacement of missing architectural features should be based on accurate duplication of original features insofar as possible.

• Distinctive stylistic features and examples of skilled craftsmanship—which are scarce today—should be treated with sensitivity.

• Many changes to buildings and environments that have been made over the years are evidence of the history of the building and the neighborhood. These alterations may have developed significance in their own right and this significance should be respected.

• All buildings should be recognized as products of their own time. Alterations to create earlier appearances should be discouraged.

• Contemporary design for new buildings in old neighborhoods and additions to existing buildings or landscaping should not be discouraged if the design is compatible with the size, scale, color, material, and character of the neighborhood.

• Whenever possible, additions or alterations to buildings should be done so that if they were to be removed in the future, the essential form and integrity of the original building would be unimpaired.

THE ENVIRONMENT

TRY TO:	AVOID:
Retain distinctive features such as the size, scale, mass, color, and materials of buildings, including roofs, porches, and stairways that give a neighborhood its distinguishing character.	Introducing new construction into neighborhoods that is incompatible with the character of the district because of size, scale, color and materials.
Use new plant materials, fencing, walkways, and street furniture that are compatible with the character of the neighborhood in size, scale, material, and color.	Introducing signs, street lighting, street furniture, new plant materials, fencing, walkways and paving materials that are out of scale or inappropriate to the neighborhood.
Retain landscape features such as parks, gardens, street furniture, walkways, streets, alleys, and building set-backs which have traditionally linked buildings to their environment.	Destroying the relationship of buildings and their environments by widening existing streets, changing paving material, or by introducing poorly designed and poorly located new streets and parking lots or introducing new construction incompatible with the character of the neighborhood.

BUILDING: LOT

TRY TO:	AVOID:
Retain plants, trees, fencing, walkways, and street furniture that reflect the property's history and development.	Making hasty changes to the appearance of the site by removing old plants, trees, etc., before evaluating their importance in the property's history and development.
Base all decisions for new work on actual knowledge of the past appearance of the property found in photographs, drawings, newspapers, and tax records. If changes are made they should be carefully evaluated in light of the past appearance of the site.	Over-restoring the site to an appearance it never had.

BUILDING: EXTERIOR FEATURES

Masonry Buildings

TRY TO:	AVOID:
Retain original masonry and mortar, whenever possible, without the application of any surface treatment.	Applying waterproof or water repellent coatings or other treatments unless required to solve a specific technical problem that has been studied and identified. Coatings are frequently unnecessary, expensive, and can accelerate deterioration of the masonry.
Dupliate old mortar in composition, color and textures.	
Duplicate old mortar in joint size, method of application, and joint profile.	Repointing with mortar of high Portland cement content can create a bond that is often stronger than the building material. This can cause deterioration as a result of the differing coefficient of expansion and the differing porosity of the material and the mortar.
Repair stucco with a stucco mixture duplicating the original as closely as possible in appearance and texture.	
Clean masonry only when possible to halt deterioration and always with the gentlest method possible, such as low pressure water and soft natural bristle brushes.	Repointing with mortar joints of a differing size or joint profile, texture or color.
	Sandblasting brick or stone surfaces; this method of cleaning erodes the surface of the material and accelerates deterioration.
Repair or replace where necessary, deteriorated material with new material that duplicates the old as closely as possible.	Using chemical cleaning products which could have an adverse chemical reaction with the masonry materials, i.e., acid on limestone or marble.
Replace missing architectural features, such as cornices, brackets, railings and shutters.	Applying new material which is inappropriate or was unavailable when the building was constructed, such as artificial brick siding, artificial cast stone or brick veneer.
Retain the original or early color and texture of masonry surfaces, wherever possible. Brick or stone surfaces may have been painted or whitewashed for practical and aesthetic reasons.	Removing architectural features, such as cornices, brackets, railings, shutters, window architraves, and doorway pediments. These are usually an essential part of a building's character and appearance, illustrating the continuity of growth and change.
	Indiscriminate removing of paint from masonry surfaces. This may be historically incorrect and may also subject the building to harmful damage.

BUILDING: EXTERIOR FEATURES

Frame Buildings

TRY TO:

Retain original material, whenever possible.

Repair or replace where necessary deteriorated materials with new material that duplicates the old as closely as possible.

AVOID:

Removing architectural features such as siding, cornices, brackets, window architraves and doorway pediments. These are in most cases an essential part of a building's character and appearance, illustrating the continuity of growth and change.

Resurfacing frame building with new material which is inappropriate or was unavailable when the building was constructed such as artificial stone, brick veneer, asbestos or asphalt shingles, plastic or aluminum siding. Such material also can contribute to the deterioration of the structure from moisture and insect attack.

Changing the original roof shape or adding features inappropriate to the essential character of the roof such as oversized dormer windows or picture windows.

Roofs

TRY TO:

Preserve the original roof shape.

Retain the original roofing material, whenever possible.

Replace deteriorated roof coverings with new material that matches the old in composition, size, shape, color, and texture .

Preserve or replace, where necessary, all architectural features that give the roof its essential character, such as dormer windows, cupolas, cornices, brackets, chimneys, cresting, and weather vanes.

Place television antennae and mechanical equipment, such as air conditioners, in an inconspicuous location.

AVOID:

Applying new roofing material that is inappropriate to the style and period of the building and neighborhood.

Replacing deteriorated roof coverings with new materials that differ to such an extent from the old that the appearance of the building is altered.

Stripping the roof of architectural features important to its character.

Placing television antennae and mechanical equipment, such as air conditioners, where they can be seen from the street.

Windows and Doors

TRY TO:

Retain existing window and door openings including window sash, glass, lintels, sills, architraves, shutters and doors, pediments, hoods, architraves, steps, and all hardware.

Respect the stylistic period or periods a building represents. If replacement of window sash or doors is necessary, the replacement should duplicate the material, design, and the hardware of the older window sash or door.

AVOID:

Introducing new window and door openings into the principal elevations, or enlarging or reducing window or door openings to fit new stock window sash or new stock door sizes.

Altering the size of window panes or sash. Such changes destroy the scale and proportion of the building.

Discarding original doors and door hardware when they can be repaired and reused in place.

Inappropriate new window or door features such as aluminum storm and screen window combinations that require the removal of original windows and doors or the installation of plastic or metal strip awnings or fake shutters that disturb the character and appearance of the building.

Porches and Steps

TRY TO:

Retain porches and steps that are appropriate to the building and its development. Porches or additions reflecting later architectural styles are often important to the building's historical integrity.

Repair or replace, where necessary, deteriorated architectural features of wood, iron, cast iron, terra-cotta, tile, and brick.

Repair or replace deteriorated material with new material that duplicates the old as closely as possible.

AVOID:

Removing or altering porches or steps.

Stripping porches and steps of original material such as hand rails, balusters, columns, brackets, and roof decoration of wood, iron, cast iron, terra-cotta, tile and brick.

Applying new material that is inappropriate or was unavailable when the building was constructed, such as artifical cast stone, brick veneer, asbestos or asphalt shingles, or plastic or aluminum siding.

Enclosing porches and steps in a manner that destroys their intended appearance.

BUILDING: EXTERIOR FINISHES

TRY TO:

Discover and retain original paint colors, or repaint with colors based on the original to illustrate the distinctive character of the property.

AVOID:

Repainting with colors that cannot be documented through research and investigation to be appropriate to the building and neighborhood.

BUILDING: INTERIOR FEATURES

TRY TO:

Retain original material, architectural features, and hardware, whenever possible, such as stairs, handrails, balusters, mantel-pieces, cornices, chair rails, baseboards, paneling, doors and doodrways, wallpaper, lighting fixtures, locks, and door knobs.

Repair or replace where necessary, deteriorated material with new material that duplicates the old as closely as possible.

Retain original plaster, whenever possible.

Discover and retain original paint colors, wallpapers and other decorative motifs or, where necessary, replacing them with colors, wall-papers or decorative motifs based on the original.

AVOID:

Removing original material, architectural features, and hardware, except where essential for safety or efficiency.

Installing new decorative material that is inappropriate or was unavailable when the building was constructed, such as vinyl plastic or imitation wood wall and floor coverings, except in utility areas such as kitchens and bathrooms.

Destroying original plaster except where necessary for safety and efficiency.

PLANNING AND FUNCTION

TRY TO:

Use a building for its intended purposes.

Find an adaptive use, when necessary, which is compatible with the plan, structure, and appearance of the building.

Retain the basic plan of a building, whenver possible.

AVOID:

Altering a building to accommodate an incompatible use requiring requiring extensive alterations to the plan, materials, and appearance of the building.

Altering the basic plan of a building by demolishing principal walls, partitions, and stairways.

NEW ADDITIONS

TRY TO:

Keep new additions to a minimum and make them compatible in scale, building materials, and texture.

Design new additions to be compatible in materials, size, scale, color, and texture with the earlier building and the neighborhood.

Use contemporary designs compatible with the character and mood of the building or the neighborhood.

AVOID:

Making unnecessary new additions.

Designing new additions which are incompatible with the earlier building and the neighborhood in materials, size, scale, and texture.

MECHANICAL SERVICES: HEATING, ELECTRICAL, AND PLUMBING

TRY TO:

Install necessary building services in areas and spaces that will require the least possible alteration to the plan, materials, and appearance of the building.

Install the vertical runs of ducts, pipes, and cables in closets, service rooms, and wall cavities.

Select mechanical systems that best suit the building.

Rewire early lighting fixtures.

Have exterior electrical and telephone cables installed underground.

AVOID:

Causing unncecessary damage to the plan, materials, and appearance of the building when installing mechanical services.

Cutting holes in important architectural features, such as cornices, decorative ceilings, and paneling.

Installing "dropped" acoustical ceilings to hide inappropriate mechanical systems. This destroys that proportions and character of the rooms.

Having exterior electrical and telephone cables attached to the principal elevations of the builidng.

SAFETY AND CODE REQUIREMENTS

Investigate variances for historic properties afforded under some local codes.

Install adequate fire prevention equipment in a manner that does minimal damage to the appearance or fabric of a property.

Provide access for the handicapped without damaging the essential character of a property.

HOW TO RESEARCH AND DATE YOUR OLD HOUSE

RESEARCHING AN OLD HOUSE is something that most owners put off "until the more important things are done." Unfortunately, this common attitude is exactly the WRONG way to approach a vintage house. It's like setting out to build a house without constructing a foundation.

SURE, you have to make sure that the roof doesn't leak and that the termites aren't about to run off with the place. But once the structure is stabilized, the research work should be high on the list of priorities.

WHEN RESTORING AN OLD HOUSE, the goal is to do work that is in keeping with the style and tradition of the structure. Among other things, the in-character restoration is the best way to preserve the long-term market value of the property. But to do high-quality restoration work, you have to know what the house was like originally. And that means research . . . at the outset.

INVARIABLY, when someone does rehabilitation and decorating work before finding out everything possible about the house, he or she regrets doing certain things. But then it is too late; the work is done and the money is spent.

IN RESEARCHING a house, you are looking for answers to questions such as the following:

• Who built the house and when?

• What style is it?

• What did the house originally look like—inside and out?

• Who owned and lived in it?

• What were the cultural forces at work when the house was built?

ONCE YOU'VE IMMERSED YOURSELF in the history of the house, you begin to feel differently about the building. It acquires a new personality—and makes you change your ideas about what you want to do to the structure. Usually, the desire to make changes decreases and the desire to restore in a period fashion increases. You become less eager to tamper with a house that has meant so much to so many.

THERE ARE FOUR basic sources for historical information about your house: (1) Oral history; (2) Documentary sources; (3) Inferred data; (4) Physical evidence.

ORAL HISTORY is just a fancy name for talking to every-one who might know anything about the house in its earlier days. Obviously, this technique will be more fruitful for houses built after 1890 than it will be for older dwellings.

THE HUMAN LINKS

BY STARTING with the most recent occupants, you may be able to trace the chain of owners. If you're lucky, the house will have been lived in by fewer than five families. Luckier still, you may find relatives of these families still in the area. In addition, you can probably gather names of other people associated with the house (former neighbors, friends of the family, housekeepers, etc.). These people can often add helpful details—especially when members of the owners' families can't be found.

CONSULTING LOCAL TELEPHONE DIRECTORIES should tell whether any of these people—or their relatives—are still in the area. Phone calls or letters/questionnaires can quickly determine whether these folks have any helpful data.

SOME OF THE INFORMATION you'd hope to get: Colors inside and out, type and placement of furniture, uses of various rooms, what was done to cool house in summer and heat it in winter, how holidays were celebrated, decoration of the house, etc.

AND ALWAYS . . . you are looking for old photos of the house that people will let you borrow to have duplicates made.

IN PERSONAL INTERVIEWS, it's a good idea to have a written checklist to guide you. When dealing with people's recollections, it is very easy to get sidetracked by interesting—but irrelevant—stories. One word of caution: Memory is a fragile thing. People may tell you some charming details. But before you accept anyone's recollection as gospel, try to get verification from another source.

DOCUMENTARY EVIDENCE

USUALLY THERE ARE one or more public offices where you can find records relating to your property. The later the house was built, the greater the likelihood of finding specific information. Records and deeds from before 1850 tend to be

| Colonial 1690–1760 | Saltbox 1700–1770 | Cape Cod 1710–1830 | Early Georgian 1720–1760 |

rather vague and relate more to the land than to dwellings. Also possible: None of the old records exist anymore due to loss by fire.

PROCEDURES FOR FILING public documents vary from town to town. So you'll have to discover any local idiosyncrasies for yourself.

THE BUILDING DEPT. is the best source of information about your house—if they were issuing building permits at the time your home was built. Among the information you may be able to glean from these records:

• Date building permit was issued

• Name of owner

• Name of architect and builder

• Cost

• Type of heating plant, roof and basic materials used

• Floor plans that show placement of major fixtures

• Dates and types of major alterations

TO LOCATE BUILDING DEPT. DATA, normally you need to know your block number and lot number. This can be obtained from your deed, from maps in the Building Dept., or from plat books (more on these later).

OFTEN, ONLY SUMMARY INFORMATION (such as a permit number) will be recorded on an index card that is used as the primary working reference for your property. Getting the detailed information requires digging out the original permit from the archives. This can be a time-consuming chore—and may require special permission. So don't expect Building Dept. personnel to welcome your inquiries with a big smile. But polite persistence will usually get you the assistance you need.

DELVING IN THE DEEDS

SECOND SOURCE of information is the office that registers real estate transactions. This source will give you names and dates of owners of the property—and sometimes sketchy information about the dwelling on the property.

ONE CAUTION about deed information: When the deed goes back to the 1700s or early 1800s, you can't automatically assume that the structure you own is the same one referred to in the earliest deed. Fire may have destroyed the original house and you may be living in a replacement built at a later date.

ALSO, HOUSES WERE MOVED with surprising frequency in the old days. It is possible that your house was built at another site and then moved onto your land at a later date.

THE PLAT BOOKS

PLAT BOOKS (large scale maps showing lots and buildings on each block) are available for most large communities going back into the 19th century. These maps, originally drawn up for insurance purposes, can be an invaluable research tool. For example, if you can't locate a building permit for your house, you can go back through the plat books (which were issued annually) to see the first year when a house was indicated for your lot.

BY COMPARING PLAT BOOKS from year to year, you can also see how a neighborhood developed, when water and sewer lines appeared, etc. Plat books should be available through your historical society or public library.

DIGGING IN DIRECTORIES

DURING THE LATE 1800s and early 1900s many cities had directories that listed people at their home addresses. These were precursors of the telephone book. Often, these directories also included occupational information. These directories can be especially helpful if other official records have been lost or destroyed.

SOME OF THESE DIRECTORIES were organized by address. In this case, you can look back and see the oldest entry you can find for someone living at your address. Other directories were arranged alphabetically by last name. In these cases, you have to have names from the deed records in order to know who to look up. When occupations and titles are given, often you can watch the rise (or fall) of an individual's

Late Georgian 1760–1780

Federal 1780–1820

Greek Revival 1815–1840

Gothic Revival 1835–1880

fortunes by looking him up in successive directories.

THESE DIRECTORIES—if compiled for your community—should be available through your public library or historical society.

IF ANY OF THE HOUSE'S OWNERS were prominent citizens, you may be able to locate a detailed obituary for them through your library.

FEDERAL CENSUS INFORMATION—although confidential for this century—is available before 1880. In your area Federal Archive and Record Center you may be able to locate census questionnaires filled out by the families living in your house.

YOUR LOCAL HISTORICAL SOCIETY can also be a goldmine of pictorial information. It may have photographs of your particular house. At the very least, you can usually find old photos of your neighborhood and of houses similar to yours.

THE EDUCATED GUESS

WHEN NO WRITTEN RECORDS can be found, you have to fall back on information you can infer from the house itself. In other words, an educated guess. Houses built before 1830 provide many clues from the material in the house itself. Up to that time, most construction materials were handmade—and there are enough variations in materials and methods to provide dating clues. More on this later.

AFTER 1830, machine technology began to spread rapidly. Materials and methods became more uniform during successive decades of the 19th century. So it is very difficult to date late 19th century houses from the material alone. Rather, you have to look at the architectural details of the house . . . inside and out. A good first approximation of age can be gleaned from a knowledgeable reading of the style and decorative features.

INFERENCES FROM THE ARCHITECTURAL style are based on knowing that tastes in domestic architecture have gone through well-defined phases. But two precautions must be observed in drawing conclusions: (1) Styles were in fashion at different times in different parts of the country; (2) You must learn about the false clues that a house can give off (more below).

IN INTERPRETING the style of your house, it's imperative that you become familiar with the architectural peculiarities of your area—in addition to knowing what the standard style books say. For example, new styles tended to appear first in the cities of the East. It could take 20–30 years for a style to show up in remote rural areas or far in the West. One of the references listed on the previous page gives some helpful guidance on when various styles appeared in major sections of the U.S.

BEWARE MISLEADING CLUES

A COMMON ERROR made in looking for age clues in the style of a house is to try to make a determination based on the

Italiante 1845–1885

Mansard 1855–1885

Queen Anne 1875–1900

Carpenter Gothic 1870–1910

Door ca. 1879

entire physical mass. This approach overlooks the fact that very few old houses stand exactly the way they were built. Over the years, various "improvements" are made. Material is added—or taken off.

FOR EXAMPLE, a simple colonial-style farmhouse built in 1800 might have undergone extensive renovation in 1860. A typical remodelling would have called for raising the roof, adding a fancy bracketed cornice, plus new chimneys and porches. To the casual observer, it would look like a typical mid-Victorian Italiante home. Only closer examination would reveal the building's earlier origins.

ALSO CONFUSING to the beginner is the tendency of many carpenter/builders (and architects, too) to combine in a single dwelling the elements from several different styles that pleased them. Any attempt to hang a single style label on such a building is doomed to failure.

THE KEY LIES IN STUDYING each detail in the house: Windows, doors, cornice, porches, chimneys, roofline, siding, ornament, interior woodwork, mantels, etc. The styling and combinations of many of these elements can give age clues to within 10 years. If all pieces seem to match up in age, then you have a pretty good idea of what you are dealing with. If there seems to be a big disparity in the age of the parts so that you're utterly confused, then it may be time to call in the experts.

OBVIOUSLY, this process of stylistic analysis will go a lot faster with the guidance of a professional architectural historian. But the homeowner who puts his or her mind to it can usually usually learn enough about local architecture to pinpoint the age of the house to within 10–15 years.

PHYSICAL EVIDENCE

PHYSICAL EVIDENCE is mainly of value for houses built before 1840. After that date, there aren't enough variations in materials and methods to be very helpful. Dating from physical evidence is tricky for the experts—so obviously most homeowners can't expect to come up with accurate results without a lot of study. What follows is a brief review of the kinds of

things a trained antiquarian would look for.

FIRST, you don't draw any conclusions from a single piece of evidence. Rather, you try to date as many pieces of material as you can—and then see what patterns develop. For example, it's easy to be led astray by the propensity of old-time builders to re-use building materials. (Recycling was not invented by the current generation!) You could very well find hand-wrought nails and hardware made in 1790 being used in a house built in 1830.

AMONG THE ELEMENTS that can yield up dating clues: Nails; latches & hinges; timber framing; sash & window glass; plaster lath; woodscrews; doors; fireplaces & chimneys; paneling. Here is a brief sampling of the dating characteristics of some of these elements:

NAILS: All nails were hand-wrought up until the 1790s. Then a series of technical developments made possible machine-made nails. Nail manufacture changed several times up until the wire nail took over after 1850. So a good sampling of nails can help you date a house as before 1790; or a date somewhere between the 1790's and 1840–50; or after 1850.

SCREWS WITHOUT POINTS were in wide use up until 1846. New machinery at that date made it possible to make screws with points—which won rapid acceptance. So the existence of screws without points in old hinges, etc., indicates a house was probably built before 1846.

MOULDINGS ON ORIGINAL DOORS give clues (see diagram anext page). Until about 1835, all mouldings were cut as an integral part of the door with hand moulding planes. When cheap machine-cut strip mouldings started to become available, many builders quickly adopted them. Any door with these separate moulding strips was made sometime after 1835. However, doors with integral mouldings were still being made after 1835 in some areas where strip moulding wasn't

Old Nails Yield Dating Clues

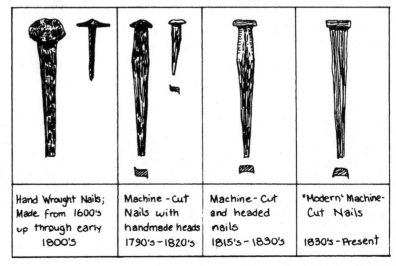

Hand Wrought Nails; Made from 1600's up through early 1800's	Machine-Cut Nails with handmade heads 1790's – 1820's	Machine-Cut and headed nails 1815's – 1830's	"Modern" Machine-Cut Nails 1830's – Present

available—or by old-time carpenters who wouldn't abandon the old ways.

LATCHES AND HINGES can also yield dating clues. Unfortunately, in many cases the original latches may have been replaced. The best place to look for original hardware is in the minor rooms on upper floors, attic doors, etc. In some cases these less important spaces were ignored when other areas were "modernized." Two common hand-wrought latch types and approximate dates are shown at the left. Detailed information on dating old hardware is given in the booklet described at the bottom of this column.

A HOUSE FRAME made up of large 6"×6" (or larger) timbers held together with wooden pegs indicates the house was built before 1840. Balloon framing—based on 2×4's—came into use in the 1840s. You can usually see the framing members in the attic. The attic is also a good place to look for other original materials, nails, etc., and for signs of alterations.

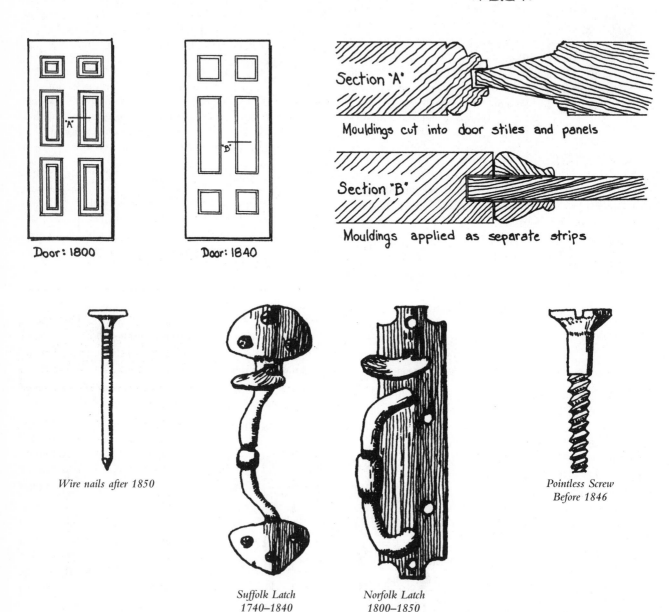

Door: 1800

Door: 1840

Section "A"

Mouldings cut into door stiles and panels

Section "B"

Mouldings applied as separate strips

Wire nails after 1850

Suffolk Latch
1740–1840

Norfolk Latch
1800–1850

Pointless Screw
Before 1846

CATALOGUE YOUR HOUSE'S SECRET PASSAGES

IT'S THE ONLY WAY THERE IS TO DO IT! These are the emphatic words of the plumber when he's explaining why he plans to run his pipe right through a highly conspicuous corner of your parlor, ruining some ornamental plasterwork in the process.

WHEN A PLUMBER OR ELECTRICIAN has to run a line, he naturally picks the path of least resistance. And that usually means straight through floors and ceilings. Exposed piping or electrical conduit obviously is visually objectionable to the homeowner. But what do you do when the workman stoutly maintains that there is no other way to run the line?

ANSWER: BEFORE THE WORKMAN ARRIVES, make an inventory of your house's secret passages—those hidden voids and tunnels inside the walls that extend through the floors, which greatly simplify stringing of wire and pipe. Some workmen will not take the trouble to hunt for these themselves, so you're best off having done your homework before the fellow arrives.

WHETHER YOU'RE RUNNING WIRE FOR NEW CIRCUITS and convenience outlets, or for a stereo, inter-com or alarm system—or pipes for a new kitchen—you'll find that one of the most precious architectural gifts the original builder could have bequeathed to you is a set of cellar-to-roof passages.

NOW, IT IS POSSIBLE to hide any conduit in just about any wall—if you are willing to pay for all of the hacking and patching that is required. But by knowing in advance what secret passages are available, it is likely you can achieve total concealment at no greater expense than what you'd be charged for exposed pipe or conduit.

THERE ARE THREE TYPES OF SECRET PASSAGES that are likely to offer ideal spaces for top-to-bottom or inter-floor runs. They are:

1. old hot-air ducts;

2. pipe chases;

3. voids next to chimneys.

IN HOUSES THAT WERE formerly heated by hot air there be unused air ducts in the walls. In city row houses, these ducts were usually built into the brick common walls. Finding these ducts will be a job of varying complexity—depending on how thoroughly the house has been renovated. Mapping out these old air ducts is extremely valuable, however, because they can make the bringing up of both wire and pipe from the basement a relatively simple matter.

IF YOU'RE LUCKY, the previous occupants will have left the old hot-air registers in the rooms. That shows exactly where the old ducts ended. There are two types of ducts to contend with: The Branch Duct and the Mainline Duct. The mainline is most valuable because it rises from the cellar in a straight line.

YOU CAN DETERMINE WHICH TYPE of duct you've located by using a piece of string or fishline and a small weight (such as a bunch of washers). Simply drop the line through the register and note how far it goes down before hitting bottom.

IF YOU HAVE A BRANCH DUCT, it can still be used to run wire, since the bends can be negotiated with electrician's snakes. But a branch duct is virtually useless for plumbers; they'd have to break open the wall at the bends.

NEXT PROBLEM is to find where the ducts start in the cellar. It's likely that the openings for the air ducts in the cellar have been bricked over. But you shouldn't have much difficulty locating the patch(es) at the top of the cellar wall. A brick-and-mortar patch can be removed with a hammer and cold chisel.

IF NO REGISTERS have been left in the wall, a little more detective work will be required to locate abandoned ducts. From the cellar, you can find where the ducts start up the wall. Tapping on walls in rooms above the spot where the duct starts can locate covered-over registers on the main-line duct.

BRANCH DUCTS WILL HAVE to be located by the wall-tapping ritual and an exploratory nail here and there where you suspect there's a covered-over register. (Any holes made in this exploratory process can be easily patched with spackle.)

PIPE CHASES ARE THE NEXT BEST SOURCE of secret passages. A chase is a vertical channel in a wall through which pipes pass from floor to floor. Most pipe chases that include waste lines will go from the cellar to the top of the house, since waste lines have to be vented to the roof.

IN HOUSES WITH SLIDING PARLOR DOORS, the ends of the door pockets frequently contain passages for gas pipes.

IN OLD WOODEN FRAME HOUSES, another place to look for voids is next to chimneys. Since interior chimneys constituted a wide bulge in a room anyway, old-time builders seemed to leave a little space between framing beams and the chimneys just for the heck of it.

IF YOU HAVE AN ATTIC, you may be able to determine by inspection and exploration with a weighted line whether there's such a void next to your chimney. Inspecting the framing in the cellar may also give clues as to how closely the framing beams have been brought up to the chimney. Otherwise, you'll have to resort to artful tapping to see if there are usable voids next to the chimney.

Void In Framing Next To Chimney

IN SHORT, there's no precise formula that will absolutely locate the secret passages in your particular house. But armed with these guidelines, you can be your own house detective and map out the tunnels hidden within your own walls. With this knowledge, you'll know whether that next line-stringing job really is "impossible."

Replace Register With An Outlet

Electricians may tell you not to consider installing electrical outlets on brick walls because of the difficulty in running wire. But most common walls in city row houses contain an old hot-air duct—which makes it relatively easy to install an outlet where the register used to be. While you're at it, you may want to convert every old register on that duct to a convenience outlet.

Here are the steps that you or the electrician would follow:

1. Rip off the register grill. If screws are rusted tight, gentle persuasion with a pry bar will have to be used.

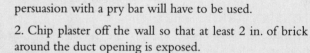

2. Chip plaster off the wall so that at least 2 in. of brick around the duct opening is exposed.

3. Drop a weighted string down through the duct and pull wire up from the cellar. Standard circuit connections are made at the cellar box.

4. Cut a piece of 1/2 in. sheetrock or rock lath so that it covers the exposed brick area.

5. Cut hole in the sheetrock to hold an electrical box. Secure box to sheetrock with clips. Connect wire to box.

6. Secure sheetrock to wall with masonry nails driven into mortar.

ROOFS AND WINDOWS

REPAIRING SLATE ROOFS

SLATE IS AN ATTRACTIVE AND EXTREMELY durable roofing material. Therefore, if your old house has a slate roof—either showing or else covered by a more "modern" roofing material—every attempt should be made to repair and restore the existing slate. This will probably mean fighting off hordes of roofing contractors who will tell you that it is "impossible" to repair slate and who instead want to sing the praises of the line of asphalt shingles they are pushing this month.

WHILE THE INITIAL COST of repairing a slate roof will often be higher than an overlayment of modern materials, the longer service life of slate usually makes up for this higher cost. And none of the contemporary materials can match the beauty of a well-laid slate roof.

MR. AVERAGE ROOFING CONTRACTOR is probably right on one count: If he insists that it can't be done, then it does mean that he can't do it! Slate is, in fact, a tricky material for roofers who are not experienced in its installation and repair. Many problems that you see today in old slate roofs are not the fault of the material itself, but rather are caused by faulty installation.

LEAKS IN SLATE ROOFS are normally caused by one of two conditions: (1) Deteriorated flashings; (2) Missing slates. If visual inspection doesn't reveal any missing slates, then the flashings are the likely culprit. More about this later.

SLATES COME LOOSE usually for one of two reasons: The slate itself has cracked, or the nails holding it have rusted through. Slates are subject to frost damage—especially in the upper half, which is kept damp by the overlapping slate above. Because slate is a natural product—cut from a sedimentary rock—there are liable to be a few slates in a roof that are more porous than the others and thus subject to cracking by absorbing water. Should a frost follow, the water will freeze and expand, subjecting the slate to mechanical stress.

MORE SERIOUS is the slate that let go because its holding nails rusted through. If it happened to one set of nails, there is the likelihood that it will be happening soon to other slates. This is definitely caused by faulty installation. If the condition becomes serious, it may require lifting all of the old slates and relaying them—this time using copper nails.

MOST OFTEN, however, the problem is just one of replac-ing a few broken slates. While this is not often thought of as a do-it-yourself job, it can be done by a competent handyperson—who is not afraid of heights! If there are any doubts in your mind, however, you are probably best off seeking out a roofer with experience in handling slate.

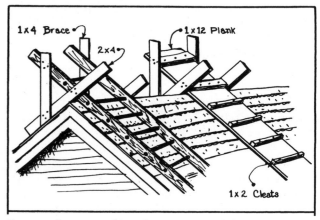

Two types of supports used in roofing repair to provide footing and distribute weight evenly over large area.

SLATE IS A BRITTLE MATERIAL; roofers (or you) should never step directly on the slates—they may break. Experienced roofers use various types of supports to distribute their weight while they are working on the slates.

TO REPLACE A BROKEN SLATE, first step is to remove the remainder of the broken slate and/or the nails that originally held it. This is accomplished with a roofer's tool called (appropriately) a slate nail cutter. If you don't happen to have one of these laying around your toolbox—and you can't buy one at your friendly neighborhood hardware store—a workable version can be fabricated at a local metalworking shop.

SLIDE THE NAIL CUTTER up under the broken slate and hook it around the nail. Strike the cutter with a hammer, moving the cutter sharply downward. This will cut the nails and free the end of the damaged slate.

IF THERE'S ONLY A SHORT STUB of slate left, you may also be able to cut the nails by sliding a hacksaw blade up under the old slate and cutting the nails by sawing.

AFTER THE BROKEN SLATE and nails have been removed, a copper holding tab is nailed in the seam between the slates, as shown in the diagram. The copper strip should be at least two inches wide and long enough to extend up under the slates as shown. Be sure to use copper nails. The replacement slate is then slipped into position and the copper tab is bent up to hold the slate in place. Any excess copper strip beyond that needed to form a mechanically secure hook is cut off with tinsnips.

Copper Holding Tab Nailed In Place

Slate Inserted And Tab Bent Up

Strike With Hammer

Nail Slots

Slate Nail Cutter

Nails To Be Cut

Broken Slate

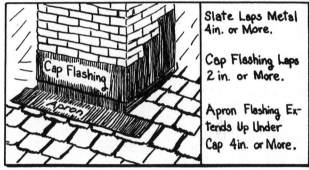

Cap Flashing

Apron

Slate Laps Metal 4 in. or More.

Cap Flashing Laps 2 in. or More.

Apron Flashing Extends Up Under Cap 4 in. or More.

FLASHING

LEAKS IN FLASHING often show up as wet spots on walls and ceilings. Inspect the flashings at those points—and above—in valleys, and around chimneys, dormers, etc. Around chimneys the flashing may come loose at the top where it is set into the mortar. Where mortar has loosened and fallen out, it should be repointed. Liberal use of roofing compound or flashing cement will seal small holes and cracks.

IF EXPOSED METAL FLASHING shows signs of rusting, it can be wire-brushed and painted with a good-quality metal primer. The paint coat should be renewed as required to prevent further rusting. If the flashing in the valley is rusted through or too narrow, some slates will have to be taken up and the flashing replaced. This isn't too difficult in an open valley (where you can see the flashing) but is quite a production with a closed valley (where the slates have been laid over the flashing).

VERY OLD SLATE ROOFS sometimes fail because the holding nails have rusted away. In these cases, the slates may have to be removed and the entire roof re-laid, including the underlay materials. If the decision is made to remove all the slates, you should take advantage of this opportunity to give the roof timbers a thorough inspection. All loose boards should be renailed, and any decayed boards replaced. Before laying down the new roofing felt, the sheathing boards should be swept clean, and protruding nails set in.

ALL SLATES THAT ARE STILL in good condition can be re-used. Use corrosion-resistant large-headed slating nails. Nails should not be driven too tightly—they should barely touch the slate. This is exactly opposite from the technique used in laying wood shingles, where you want the nails driven tight.

ROOFING WITH WOOD SHINGLES

By C. R. Meyer

WOOD SHINGLES WERE the standard roofing material in America throughout colonial days, and continue today as the roofing treatment of choice in many locations across the country.

COLONISTS ON THE ATLANTIC coast split shingles from native white pine and other timber species. During the 1700s most of the nation's shingles came from New Jersey cedar swamps. The popularity of that material was so great that by the 1800s the natural stands had all been depleted. It was then discovered that the swamps had as many logs under them as they had had over them.

THE SWAMP BOTTOMS were covered with layers of old cedar, some of the logs having lain there for hundreds of years. The supply, cut off as it was from oxygen, was perfectly preserved and served as a major source of shingle wood from that time up to the Civil War. Cedar continues today as the nation's most popular shingle wood, although the supplies now come not from New Jersey swamps, but primarily from the red cedar forests of the Pacific Northwest.

THE STORY of the New Jersey swamp bottoms is not just an interesting tale but an instructive one as well. It points at the fact that wood will not rot if deprived of oxygen, nor will it decay in the absence of light or moisture. Those oxygen-free New Jersey cedars had been preserved by continued submersion. It is the variations of moisture and temperature that are the principal decay-causing factors in wood deterioration. Thus, wood exposed to conditions that favor decay deteriorates more rapidly in warm, humid areas than in cool, dry ones. High altitude locations generally are less conducive to deterioration than low ones since the warm growing season for decay-causing fungi is shorter.

CONTROL OF NATURAL FORCES involved in wood deterioration is not practical, but the use of wood species such as cedar, with a high natural decay resistance, combined with proper application can help prolong the life expectancy of a wood roof. In addition, in certain instances the application of commercially marketed solutions of fungicides such as pentachlorophenol to the roof will kill moss and fungus and prevent their growth for some time. These solutions can be quite toxic to both plants and animals, however, if not used correctly. Follow directions carefully.

LEAKAGE PROBLEMS associated with wood shingle roofs often occur because the roof has deteriorated over the years due to lack of proper maintenance. Moss will build up on shaded portions of a roof and in time will force the shingles apart, allowing moisture to enter. Dirt and debris can accumulate on a poorly maintained roof surface, slowing the run-off of water and allowing the shingles to absorb moisture, inviting fungus attack. Even the most decay-resistant woods will show signs of rot if they are allowed to stay damp over extended periods of time.

WHEN SHINGLES become pulpy and soft from rot, weather extremes to which they were immune when sound will help accelerate deterioration. The roof will become especially susceptible to driven rain and wind.

REROOFING

WHEN THE DECISION is made to reroof a house with wood, the choice of whether or not to roof over the existing surface must be faced. Many roofers seem to be of the opinion that there really is no choice, that the old roof *must* come off–it isn't so!

SUCCESSFUL OVERROOFINGS HAVE BEEN going on for years. The prejudice against the maneuver seems to lie in the fact that the result tends to look lumpy at times. Rather than taking the time to explain why the rocky roof job wasn't his fault, most roofers would rather avoid them altogether. There are numerous advantages to leaving the old roof intact.

OVERROOFING provides a double roof with extra insulation value and storm protection. The interior is safe from the weather during the application period. Eliminated is the mess in the yard along with the corresponding clean-up; and one is saved the misery of stripping the old roof off.

THERE ARE DISADVANTAGES AS WELL. It may be very difficult to find a sound surface in which to nail. As mentioned previously, overroofing onto a badly disintegrated roof may cause the finished surface to appear very irregular. Any roof sheathing that proves to be rotten must be replaced; this procedure isn't possible without removing the roof over it, so any roof with a preponderance of bad sheathing might as well be stripped completely. One last remark on stripping off old roofs: Many areas of the country have building codes that limit the total number of roofs on a structure; three is common.

OVERROOFING

WHERE OLD ROOFING is to remain, a six-in.-wide strip of the existing shingles must be removed from all eaves and gable edges around the perimeter of the roof. Onto this stripped-back area new boards of 1-in. thickness (1x6) should be applied.

THESE BOARDS PROVIDE a sturdy base at the edges of the roof and conceal the old roof from view, eliminating the "Dagwood sandwich" look one so often sees at the eaves of an overroofed house.

NEXT, THE EXISTING RIDGE covering must be taken off and replaced with a strip of bevel siding on either side, with the butt edges overlapping at the peak. This step precludes the formation of a mound of roofing material at the ridge where roofing is applied in extra layers. (See figure 1)

NAILING OF THE SHINGLES is extremely important. Use nails that are able to penetrate at least one-half in. into the roof sheathing underneath the old roof. In most cases this would be either 5 penny (1¾ in. long), or 6 penny (2 in. long) nails. Be sure to use rust-resistant nails. Aluminum nails will do, but there is nothing like a hot-dipped zinc-coated nail for holding power. Ordinary galvanized nails, like aluminum ones, are rust resistant but smooth.

TRY TO ASSURE THAT any flashing used is of the same material as the nails. Don't mix aluminum flashing with galvanized or vice-versa. The dissimilar metals will react with each other. Don't use bright or blued steel nails as they are not rust resistant.

TO BEGIN THE SHINGLE COURSING, first determine the exposure required on the roof. The exposure is the amount of each shingle exposed to the weather. Red cedar shingles come in three lengths: 16, 18, and 24 inches. To determine the exposure, see the accompanying chart. Shingles are not recommended for a rise of under 3 in. in 12 in. of "run." (See chart ar right.)

NEXT, BEGIN with a double thickness of shingles at the bottom edge (eave) of the roof, applied over the new 1x6 strip board. In very cold climates it is recommended that a strip of smooth-surface 45-lb. roll roofing be laid under the shingles at the eaves to act as a waterstop for any moisture backed up by ice dams formed during cold spells. Ice dams often build up on the

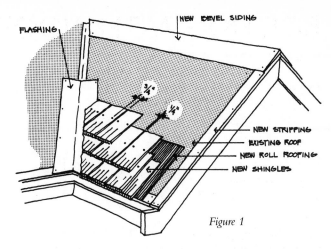

Figure 1

overhang of roofs and in gutters causing melting snow water to back up under shingles. Damage to ceilings inside and to paint outside results. Lay the roofing over the eaves, extending it upward well above the inside line of the wall.

LET THE SHINGLES PROTRUDE over the eave edge to assure the proper drip into the gutter. About 2 in. would normally be sufficient. After the first course is laid at the eave, tack a long, straight board onto the shingles 5 in. or more up from the edge, depending upon the exposure desired. The

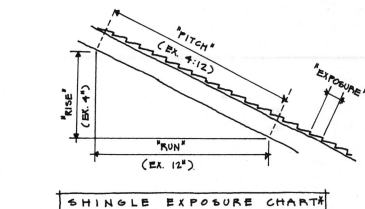

	SHINGLE LENGTH		
ROOF PITCH	16"	18"	24"
EQUAL TO of MORE THAN 4:12	5"	5½"	7½"
LESS THAN 4:12	3¾"	4¼"	5¾"
LESS THAN 3:12	SHINGLES NOT RECOMMENDED		

SHINGLE EXPOSURE CHART

*as recommended by the Red Cedar Shingle and Handsplit Shake Bureau.

board will act as a straight edge to line up the next rows of shingles. Start the next row against this guide and nail each shingle down using the proper length and type of nail, two to a shingle only. Now matter how wide the shingle, use only two nails.

PLACE THE NAILS NO FURTHER than 3/4 in. from the side of the shingle and make sure that the next row above will cover the nails by about one in. Drive the nails until the heads meet the shingle surface, but not further, as nails have less holding power when driven with the heads into the shingle surface. (Especially if they cause the shingles to split.)

SPACE SHINGLES 1/4 in. apart, allowing the individual shingles to expand and prevent possible warping. Joints between the shingles should be offset at least 1-1/2 in. from the joints between shingles in the course below. Joints in succeeding courses should be spaced so that they do not directly line up with joints in the second course below.

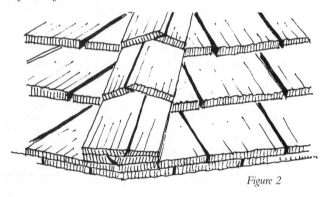

Figure 2

WHEN THE RIDGE is reached at last, choose shingles of uniform width, 3 to 5 in. Cut back the edges on a bevel and alternate overlap. A great deal of time and effort can be saved here if factory assembled hip and ridge units are available. (See figure 2)

VALLEYS CAN BE ESPECIALLY troublesome. Most roof leaks occur at points where water joins to run off the roof, or where the roof abuts a vertical surface. In these potential problem areas use metal valleys and flashings to maintain a watertight roof. Extend valley flashings beneath shingles at least ten in. on either side of the valley center if the roof pitch is less than 12 in.

FOR STEEPER ROOFS, the valley sheets should extend at least seven in. up either side. As the roof shingles are laid, those which adjoin valleys should be trimmed parallel with the valleys to form a six in. wide gutter. Be sure that the grain of the shingles is the same as it is in the main body of the roof to maintain a pleasing appearance. Keep nails as far from the valley center as possible. If you pre-cut shingles to be used in the

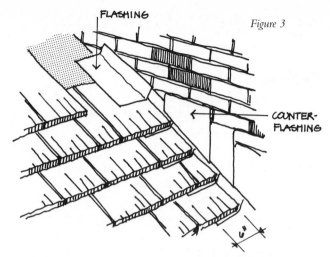

Figure 3

valleys from wide shingles found in the bundles, you will have a good supply of the proper size. Furthermore, the sections cut off can often be used on the other side of the roof hips.

ANYTHING WHICH PROTRUDES through the roof or abuts it should be flashed and counter-flashed to prevent water leakage. Flashing should extend at least 6 in. under the shingles and should be covered by counter-flashing. (See figure 3)

VENT PIPE FLASHING can cause problems if not applied in the proper manner. Allow the flashing to show on the down-slope side of the vent. The inexperienced person trying for a neat appearance will often try to cut the shingles out all around the vent. This will have the effect of forming a dam on the downhill side, creating a place for debris to collect and subsequently backing up runoff water. By leaving the down-slope side of the flashing showing, debris will wash away. One should also allow about one in. clearance around the vent pipe on the other three sides to assure that no debris will hang up a these points.

A COUPLE OF MORE POINTS. To avoid leaks, wood shingle roofs should not be subjected to unusual strains. If it is essential to walk over a roof for any reason, wear soft soled shoes and tread lightly. When applying the roof, the same rule pertains; never wear spiked footwear. And finally, when the roof is completed, keep it clean. Assure that no leaves and twigs are lodging behind the chimney or vent pipes. With proper care, the wood shingle roof you have applied should give years of durable service.

FLAT ROOF REPAIRS

WHILE MUCH IS PRINTED in magazines about fixing shingle roofs, little is said about repair of flat roofs—the type found on many old row houses.

A FLAT ROOF is usually constructed of one of two types of materials:

      a. Tar-and-Gravel

      b. Roll Roofing

ROLL ROOFING is most frequently found today; tar and gravel is an older type of construction. Since roll roofing is more common, we'll look first at fixing this type of roof.

ROLL ROOFING—which basically is felt impregnated with tar—is subject to cracking and blistering due to action of the sun and wind. By checking your roof a couple of times a year you can locate potential trouble spots before they become actual leaks.

FLAT-ROOF REPAIRS are based on generous use of roofing asphalt (compound). There are two basic grades:

• Trowelable Asphalt: This is the thickest type. It contains asbestos fibers to give the coating more body. As the name implies, it's applied with a trowel. It's the type used in most roof repairs.

• Brushable Asphalt: Thinner in consistency, this is plied with a long-handled brush. It's used mainly in preventive maintenance coatings.

THE MOST serious problem with roll roofing is cracking and blistering.

IN BLISTERED areas, the roofing felt has separated from the lower layers and is more vulnerable to cracking and leaks. Blisters can be repaired as shown at the right.

IF THE PATCH is large (over 8"), it's advisable to cover the patch with a new piece of roofing felt, which is nailed in place and covered with asphalt.

IF THE AREA is too badly worn or frayed for the slit-and-patch technique, then part of the roofing must be replaced. Carve out a square-shaped section as shown—lifting out only as many layers as are damaged.

SHAPE MATCHING patches from new roofing felt, cutting out as many as there

PATCHING BLISTERS

Slit blister down the middle.

Force asphalt under slit.

Nail on both sides of cut.

Cover nails with asphalt.

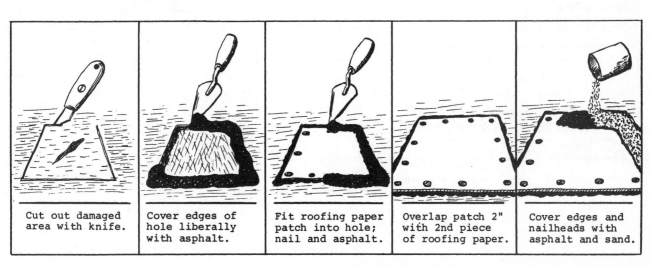

| Cut out damaged area with knife. | Cover edges of hole liberally with asphalt. | Fit roofing paper patch into hole; nail and asphalt. | Overlap patch 2" with 2nd piece of roofing paper. | Cover edges and nailheads with asphalt and sand. |

were layers removed. Each patch should be firmly embedded in asphalt; stamp on them with your feet to ensure firm anchoring.

CUT A FINAL PATCH that is 2" larger than the opening cut in the roof. Spread asphalt under all the edges, then nail in nailheads and patch seams with roofing asphalt.

DURING YOUR ROOF INSPECTION, you should also check the edge for any signs of curling that would allow wind-blown rain to be forced under the roof. If edge is curling, nail down and cover nailheads with asphalt.

ALSO PAY PARTICULAR ATTENTION to the flashing areas where skylights, chimneys, hatches and vent pipes meet the roof. If you detect any signs of cracking, daub liberally with roofing asphalt.

WHEN APPLYING ROOFING asphalt, brush well with a whisk broom to remove all dirt and dust in order to ensure good adhesion. If after brushing the surface still seems exceptionally dry and dusty, you can brush on a thin coat of benzine paint thinner or turpentine to increase adhesion of the asphalt.

THE ROOFING ASPHALT you use for patches is also subject to drying and cracking from the sun. To retard drying, you should cover the final layer of roofing compound with sand or gravel. This material helps reflect the sun's rays. Alternately, you can paint the patch with brushable roofing coating every year or so. This helps restore the oil to the asphalt.

NAILS USED in roofing work, of course, are the broad-headed galvanized roofing nails. The broad heads provide maximum holding surface for the roofing felt, and the shanks have serrations that make them more resistant to working loose. These nails are driven down flush with the top of the roofing felt, but never so deeply that they cut into the roofing material.

IF YOU HAVE A TAR-AND-GRAVEL ROOF, it's probably many years old and should be treated gingerly. If you call in a roofer to repair it, he will probably want to replace it with roll

Areas Subject To Curling & Cracking

roofing. This will be doubly expensive because they first have to cart away all the gravel.

HOWEVER, a tar-and-gravel roof—properly maintained—can last indefinitely. This type of roof is composed of several layers, as shown in the diagram. The gravel's function is to reflect the sun's rays and retard the drying and cracking of the tar layers. It's the tar that actually provides the waterproof seal.

TAR-AND-GRAVEL roofs usually give trouble at the edges, and in areas where the gravel has been washed away. They are especially subject to cracking at the edges where the roof curls upward at a parapet.

IF YOU FIND CRACKS at an upward-curling edge, repair as shown in the diagram. To provide structural integrity to the patch, use either roofing membrane (available at building supply stores), or ordinary felt thoroughly soaked with asphalt. (Regular roofing felt is too stiff to adhere tightly to the curve.)

IF THERE ARE any places where the gravel has washed away, that area should be coated with brushable roofing coating, then covered with loose gravel scavenged from another section of the roof. If there's no loose gravel you can find, then sprinkle the area with sand.

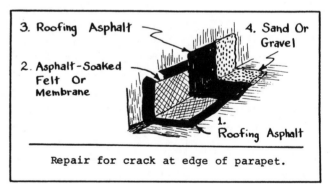

3. Roofing Asphalt
4. Sand Or Gravel
2. Asphalt-Soaked Felt Or Membrane
1. Roofing Asphalt

Repair for crack at edge of parapet.

NO MATTER HOW CAREFUL you are during these roof repairs, you and your tools are going to come down covered with asphalt roofing compound. Both you and your tools are readily cleaned up with benzine paint thinner, however.

GRAVEL
Tar
Roofing Paper
ROOF BOARDS

CHIMNEY CHECK-UP

WHILE YOU'RE inspecting the roof, check on the condition of your chimneys. Are flashings watertight? If not, coat liberally with asphalt roofing compound.

ALSO CHECK CONDITION of the mortar joints. Any soft or loose mortar will admit water during the winter, and when it freezes more loosening will result. Chip out all loose mortar with an old screwdriver or a small cold chisel.

REPACK JOINTS with fresh mortar, employing a small pointing trowel. Wet bricks thoroughly before laying in the mortar. If you're not using a pre-packaged mortar mix, make a mortar of 3 parts sand, 1 part portland cement and ½ part hydrated lime. (The lime makes the mortar adhere better to the bricks.) After packing in fresh mortar, smooth the joint with a pointing tool ("slicker") or a wooden dowel.

ONCE ALL THE mortar joints are dry, coat the chimney with a colorless masonry sealer to prevent further water penetration. Alternately, if the chimney is in an area where appearance is not important, you could coat the chimney with asphalt.

A RESTORATIONIST VIEW OF WINDOWS

FENESTRATION—the art of placing window openings in a building wall—is one of the most important and least understood elements controlling the exterior appearance of a house. Just as eyes give character to the human face, so windows give character to a house. In fact, our word "window" comes from an old Norse word meaning "wind's eye"—having originated in a time when windows were merely holes in the walls.

AND JUST AS THERE'S MORE to the eye's appearance than the eyeball, so there's more to a window than glass. An eye gets much of its character from the brows, lashes and shadows beneath the eye. A window gets its character from the detailing that surrounds the glass. Among the factors affecting the appearance of windows are:

• Size, shape and spacing of the window openings;

• Type of sash;

• Number of lights in the sash;

• Ornamentation surrounding the sash.

ASSUMING THAT THE ORIGINAL architect or housewright did a competent job in design and construction of the house, the owner will make changes in windows only at great peril to the integrity of the house. Or, if previous owners have made a botched attempt to "modernize" windows, today's owner should seriously consider what could be done to restore the original treatment.

ONE VERY BASIC design element is the size of the light, or pane. In early America, all glass was hand-blown, so it was impossible to make large panes of glass. This required use of many lights in a window, held in a frame of wood muntins. The result was the familiar 12 over 12 windows that are so characteristic of early American homes. Homeowners were always clamoring, however, for windows with bigger and bigger panes—because they gave more light and because windows were taxed on a per-pane basis. When glassmaking improved in the 1800s, 2 over 2 and 1 over 1 windows became the order of the day. And houses were designed with the effect of large panes of glass in mind.

IN THE EARLY 20th century, two separate trends in architectural fashion conspired to raise havoc with the fenestration of some fine old houses. First came the colonial revival—sparked by a legitimate interest in early architecture in the American colonies. But this movement led to gross abuses. Everyone with a house built after 1830 apparently felt guilty about not having a real colonial home . . . so many homeowners compensated by installing pseudo-colonial multi-paned sash in Victorian houses meant to have large 1 over 1 windows. The result often looks downright silly.

Old-House Sash Arrangements

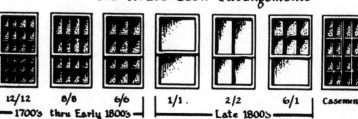

| 12/12 | 8/8 | 6/6 | 1/1 | 2/2 | 6/1 | Casement |
| 1700's thru Early 1800's | | | Late 1800's | | | |

Inappropriate Modern Sash

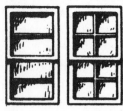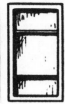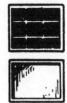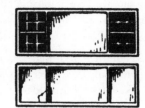

SOME HOUSES BUILT IN THE LATE 19th and early 20th century attempted to come to terms with the colonial revival through compromise: The 6 over 1 window. The top sash with its 6 lights was a bow to the colonial heritage with its quaint small-paned sash. The single bottom pane was acknowledgement of glass-making technology that permitted manufacture of large light-admitting windows. Although it smacks of "committee design," the 6 over 1 window has the virtue of being part of the building's original fabric—and part of an over-all design that was predicated on the appearance of these compromise windows.

A SECOND CRISIS for old houses occurred in the 20th century with the advent of modern architecture and its rejection of everything Victorian. In their search for a simplified architecture, designers rejected everything traditional, including window sash. Thus there was a period when new construction emphasized horizontal rather than vertical lights. Some owners of old houses, not wanting to seem old-fashioned, were sure they could make their homes look "modern" if they installed modern window sash. The results were usually disastrous.

LOOK AT ANY HOUSE built prior to 1920. Almost without exception, you'll find that the panes of glass are rectangles, with the long side pointing up. Installing horizontal window panes in a house designed for a vertical effect yields a very disconcerting result.

THE ULTIMATE PROBLEM presented by the horizontal look is the picture window. Many people like the vistas presented by a large expanse of horizontal glass in the wall. But a picture window in the side of a house that otherwise retains its old sash totally unbalances the original architectural composition. Mixing of window styles is rarely carried off successfully.

ABOUT THE ONLY WAY a picture window can be incorporated successfully into an old house is if a new wing or ell is being added. In this case, the addition can be designed for new fenestration, and the whole design made harmonious with the older section of the house.

Rather Silly!

OTHER STRANGE THINGS are done with shutters and blinds. On many houses, blinds have the same function as wings on a chicken—they are merely vestigial reminders of some long-forgotten purpose. Because shutters and blinds have become purely decorative, one frequently sees some ludicrous arrangements: Tiny shutters tacked on the ends of huge picture windows . . . one shutter perching between two windows . . . vinyl substitutes that clearly won't close. The list of absurdities could go on and on. The reasoning seems to be that any house that carries the merest suggestion of shutters somehow instantly acquires the romance of an old house.

THERE'S ONE SPECIAL CASE where shutters and blinds can be a drawback—even on houses that had them originally. That's when there is unusually fine detailing on the side of the window casing. Shutters will completely obscure this ornamentation. So either the shutters or the window detailing have to be sacrificed.

Original Window Opening
In Brick Rowhouse Wall

THE ULTIMATE butchering that can be done to an old house is the reduction of window openings so that smaller, modern sash can be used to replace deteriorated, old sash. This is such obvious folly that it wouldn't seem worth mentioning—except that countless old houses bear the scars of such "improvements," which are usually done in the name of saving money. The reasoning is that using standard sash will cost less. Yet the money that is saved by using standard sash is burned up with the additional expense of changing the opening; by the time the carpenters and masons are paid, the owner could have had sash custom-made. And the building wouldn't be permanently marred.

BAD: Brick Infill Used
To Reduce Opening For
Modern Sash

WITH WINDOWS, the conservator's slogan of "Daily Care and Conservative Repair" is especially apt. The restorer's approach to windows can be summarized:

• Don't change original sash. Wooden sash can be preserved indefinitely with caulk, wood preservative, putty and paint.

• If previous owners have allowed window sash to totally rot away, replace with sash that is consistent with original design of the house.

• Never remove ornamentation surrounding a window.

• If ornamentation is missing or beyond repair, replace or duplicate as closely as possible. If it is impossible to totally duplicate original detailing, at least replace with a unit that duplicates the mass of the original. Thus to the eye, the rhythm and line of the structure will remain unchanged.

A WINDOW REVIEW

ONE OF THE MOST distinctive window styles is a triple window known as a Palladian. The center window has an arched head and the side windows are narrower with arched or square heads. It was originally called a Venetian window from 16th century Venetian architecture. When introduced in England in 1615, it took on the name of its creator, Andrea Palladio. This elegant form has been popular in both Southern and New England homes since 1750 with many variations in the tracery of the elliptical heads and the

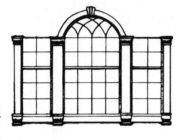

pilasters between the windows. The Palladian motif is often repeated in the entranceway with a similar fanlight over the door. A Palladian motif is always a prominent architectural feature of a house.

THE TRIPLE WINDOW differs from the Palladian in its lack of an arched head in the center window. Any tripartite group of windows with square heads is simply called a "triple window." There are endless variations, often featuring small or diamond-shaped lights in narrow side windows.

A POPULAR FEATURE OF many houses of varying styles and age is the bay window. An architectural projection with a group of windows in it, a bay begins at ground level but may rise several storeys. A pleasing way to let more light in, many houses feature more than one bay window in their design.

AN ORIEL WINDOW is similar in form to a bay window with as many variations. The difference is that the oriel window begins on an upper storey of the house. An oriel may extend upward two or more storeys. It remains an oriel as long as there is not a bay at the ground level. Often very decorative, added detail is found in the corbels which support the structure. An oriel window is sometimes referred to as a "bow" window.

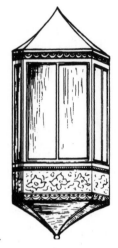

THE LATTICE WINDOW HAS diamond-shaped leaded lights. Also called a lozenge window because of the diamond shapes. A lancet window is a tall, narrow window with an arched top, very often with diamond-shaped lights. The double-lancet window illustrated at the right is a typical combination of the lancet shape and lattice lights found in many gothic revival houses of the Victorian period.

ROSE WINDOW IS A lovely, old-fashioned name for a round window with radiating tracery. It is more often called a wheel window.

A DIOCLETIAN WINDOW is a semicircular window divided by wide uprights (mullions). The center portion is larger than the two sides. It is

neo-Palladian motif, derived from the Baths of Diocletian, and sometimes called a therm.

EYEBROW WINDOWS are low, inward-opening windows with bottom-hinged sash. They are attic windows built into the architrave of a house. They are sometimes called "lie-on-your-stomach" windows.

GABLED DORMERS are dormers with pointed roofs. They are found in many architectural styles and have been very popular for centuries. Victorians were particularly fond of the gabled dormer, often projected from a mansard roof. Many versions featured a hood, which extended out and over the structure, as the illustration below shows. The hoods gave the Victorian another place to add decorative woodwork in the current fashion.

Among the many ways that have been devised to bring more light into an attic floor are windows that project from the roof. They add more space to the interior and are known as dormers. If the roof slopes downward from the house they are known as shed dormers. Flat-roof projections are commonly called doghouse dormers.

WINDOWS AND PARTS

CASEMENT WINDOWS

A casement window is a single or double sash window that is made to open outwards by turning on hinges attached to its vertical edge. One of the oldest types of windows, it was in general use until the introduction of the moveable sash window in the 17th century. Casement windows have been a popular modern style of window, operated by a more sophisticated lever or worm gear.

DOUBLE-HUNG WINDOWS

A window is called double-hung when it has an outside sash that slides down and an inside one that goes up. The movement of the sash is controlled by chains or cords on pulleys with a sash weight.

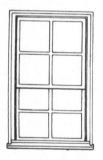

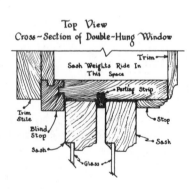

Top View
Cross~Section of Double-Hung Window

SASH

The framework in which the panes or lights are set.

LIGHTS

Referring to the panes of glass in a window, as in an eight "light" or twelve "light" window.

MUNTINS

The wood strips that separate the panes of glass in a window sash. There is a lot of confusion with the terms "muntin" and "mullion." However, "muntin" has become the term most often associated with old houses.

Muntins Became
Slimmer Over The Years

1750   1870

SILL

The lowest member beneath a door or window opening; the bottom cross-piece of a window frame.

STILE

The vertical strip at the sides of a window frame.

LINTEL

A piece of wood, stone, or steel placed horizontally across the top of door and window openings to support the walls immediately above the openings. Sometimes visible in masonry construction, the lintel is usually covered by framing and trim.

CAP

The cap is a decoracornice covering the lintel.

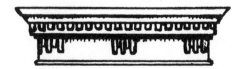

HEAD

The small window or top segment of a window above a major window. They are usually semicircular or rectangular and have small lights or tracery.

TRACERY

The branching of muntins to form a pattern on a window head. When a tracery window head is placed above a door it is called a fanlight.

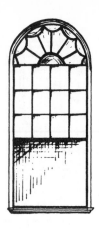

SHUTTERS AND BLINDS

The terms "blinds" and "shutter" are often used incorrectly. Both are constructed with top and bottom rails and side stiles. If the space inside is filled with slats, it is called a blind. If, instead of slats, the panel is solid it is a shutter.

THE FUNCTION OF blinds is primarily ventilation not decoration. If the blinds are shut in the early, cooler part of the day they will keep the cool air in while admitting some shady light through the slats. They can also be closed over an open window in the rain in order to let cool air in through the slats while protecting the open window.

Shutters were originally used to actually "shut up" the house in the owners absence. They offer an added protection against a break-in.

LATE 17th- and early 18th-century houses had casement or fixed windows. The panes were small (the older the house the tinier the panes.) These panes or lights were set in lead and the lattice window was common. Most of these early leaded windows were used to make bullets during the Revolutionary War and so very few can be found today.

GLASS FROM THIS PERIOD has an opalescent tinge and a wiggly surface testifying to its hand-made origins. The first double-sash windows had only one moveable sash with no counterweights. To hold these windows open a peg (usually kept handy on a chain) was inserted through a hole in the moveable sash and into a corresponding hole in the frame.

For good reason, this type of window was given the name "guillotine."

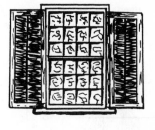

EVEN BEFORE THE REVOLUTIONARY WAR it had become fashionable to paint the putty dark colors to make the muntins seem more slender and the panes appear larger. By the end of the 18th century glass was being manufactured in this country and larger panes at lower cost became available. By this time, 6-over-6 windows were popular, a technological advance over the 12-over-12.

BY THE MIDDLE OF THE 18TH CENTURY, colonial manufacturing had become sophisticated enough to accommodate the burgeoning taste for classic architecture. The Palladian window, and variations of the triple and double window became popular. Georgian, Federal and New England houses featured decorative windows with semicircular and round shapes as well as head lights with delicate tracery.

VICTORIAN BUILDERS RECREATED windows in

every mode in their eclecticism. The lattice window and lancet window appeared during the Gothic Revival. Elaborate carvings topped windows, echoing gothic motifs. The Eastlake influence brought decorative trefoils and quatrefoils to window decorations. The oculus, or round window, was a favorite, often combined with lancets in gabled dormers.

THE POPULARITY OF dormers in gable, doghouse and shed form gave an added opportunity to combine window shapes and types.

AS THE VICTORIAN ERA raced through every previous cultural period in history in its use of design motif, the use of stained glass, many small lights for decorative heads or additional small decorative windows came into play.

CITY HOMES OF the Victorian period feature windows in endless variety. Since the 1-over-1 was commonly used for the sash itself, the decorative motif is usually found in caps, hoods, pediments, and other architectural features surrounding the window. In fact, one of the ways builders gave variety to the row house was to use a different decorative motif above and around the windows on each storey of the same house. Bay and oriel windows abounded, giving a pleasant irregularity to the city block.

THE GREEK REVIVAL STYLE borrowed from Roman and Egyptian architecture as well as Grecian, flourished around mid-19th century, giving the cityscape triangular pediments above large windows, in keeping with the large classic proportions.

THE GOTHIC REVIVAL added medieval tracery, Tudor arches, and many pointed windows.

THE HEAVY ROMANESQUE REVIVAL STYLE featured round-headed windows. Versions of the Diocletian window were common, often in large scale. Fluted columns were popular accompaniments to rectangular windows.

ITALIANATE, THE AUSTERE STYLE aping the Italian house of contemporary Italy, had simple windows that depended on the decorative motifs of the surrounding stonework for their interest. The related Renaissance Revival style added more decoration in the ornamental cornices popular for adorning windows.

THE MOST ECLECTIC QUEEN Anne style added many more bay and oriel windows, along with turrets and dormers. Carvel foliage decorated many lintels, and caps were ornately carved and had tall, graceful shapes. The Queen Anne style mixed rectangular, arched and elliptical shapes to a greater degree than previous styles.

A WALK THROUGH ANY neighborhood where old houses remain will reveal to a window-watcher a wealth of decorative detail that proves that a window is certainly as worthy to look at as to look through.

SEALING LEAKY WINDOWS

DOUBLE-HUNG WINDOWS found in many old houses are especially vulnerable to the winter elements. Through settling, warping and sagging, many gaps are created that provide entry points for both cold air and water.

SEEPING WATER will initiate an irreversible process of rot. And cold air leaking in can increase your winter fuel bill by as much as 20%.

KEEPING OUT water and cold air require two separate maintenance procedures. Let's start first with the water problem.

START by examining the joint where the window frame meets the building wall. There should be no gaps. If the old caulk has cracked or has fallen away, recaulking is a must. Here is the sequence of steps:

1. Renail any loose boards in the window frame.

2. With wire brush and putty knife, remove any loose caulk and accumulated dust and dirt.

3. Run a generous bead of caulk (about 3/8 in. across) into the joint. The caulk gun is a relatively simple tool to use; with a little practice you can run a smooth even bead anywhere.

IF AT ANY POINT the gap is so wide that it won't support the caulk, stuff the hole first with oakum. (Oakum—used by plumbers—is a tar-impregnated fibrous material that is available at hardware or plumbing supply stores.)

IF YOU ARE USING an oil-based caulk (the least expensive type) it should be painted to extend its life. Let the caulk dry for a couple of days to let a skin form; then paint.

NEXT EXAMINE the condition of the window frames and sills. Are there any open holes or cracks in the wood? These should be brushed with linseed oil, then filled with putty. If the paint has started to crack and peel, all loose paint should be scraped off with a putty knife

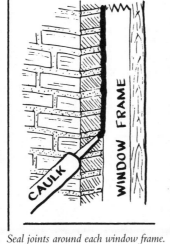
Seal joints around each window frame.

and wire brush. If the problem area is small, simple patch painting will do. If the entire paint film is in bad shape, you'd better repaint the whole window frame.

IF THE PAINT has peeled to the extent that lots of bare wood is showing, you should consider waterproofing the frame before repainting. Use a wood preservative containing pentachlorophenol (sold under brand names such as "Wood Good"). Apply a generous coating of this material—flowing on as much as the wood will absorb. This preservative not only acts to prevent rot, it also serves as a water repellant. It also seals the wood and provides better adhesion of the subsequent paint coat.

AFTER ALLOWING THE wood preservative to dry for 24 hours, paint in the usual manner. The preservative acts as a primer. However, two thin finish coats are better than one thick one.

NEXT CHECK THE PUTTY around the window glass. The putty's function is not to hold the glass in (the glazier's points do that). Rather, the putty's job is to keep water from seeping into the wooden frame. To do this, there must be a perfectly tight seal between putty and glass.

IF ANY PUTTY is loose or cracked, chip the loose material out with a putty knife. Then, using a wire brush, remove any dust and dirt from the putty channel. Next, paint the exposed area with linseed oil. (The oil in the frame will retard the drying and cracking of the new putty.)

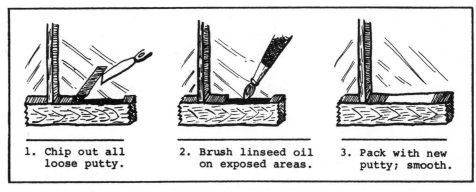

1. Chip out all loose putty.

2. Brush linseed oil on exposed areas.

3. Pack with new putty; smooth.

Then lay in a bed of fresh putty and strike off cleanly with a putty knife.

SILLS REQUIRE SPECIAL ATTENTION because they get the heaviest beating from water. If sills are completely bare of paint, start with the waterproofing treatment described above. If there are any cracks or holes, prime them with linseed oil and fill with putty. If there are areas that will need repainting, you can also use linseed oil to prime the wood. Allow linseed oil to dry for at least 24 hours before painting.

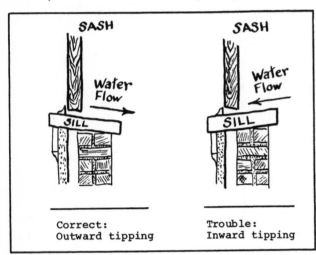

Correct:
Outward tipping

Trouble:
Inward tipping

WHILE WORKING on the sills, check their pitch with a level or a little water. Sills should pitch downward away from the window so that water flows away from the house. Sometimes settling and sagging results in sills that tip inward—and that means trouble. For temporary repairs, you can waterproof the sill with wood preservative and linseed oil—and seal cracks with putty and caulk to minimize leakage of water into the frame. But this condition will eventually require replacement of the sill—and possibly the entire frame.

ONE MORE WORD on sills. If you have a wooden sill meeting a stone or brick sill underneath, be sure the crack between the two is well sealed with caulk.

KEEPING COLD AIR OUT

UNFORTUNATELY, PINPOINTING AIR LEAKS is most easily done in the winter when the air is cold. Merely passing your hand around the window frame will tell you where air is coming in. However, winter is an uncomfortable time to do anything about the leaks.

WHILE THE WEATHER is still warm, you can spot potential leaks by looking for places where the sash doesn't seal tightly:

1. Do sashes fit snugly in the side frames?

2. Does bottom of upper sash mate tightly against top of lower sash?

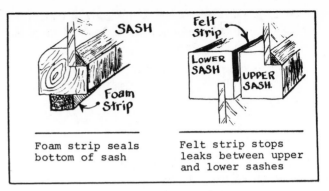

Foam strip seals
bottom of sash

Felt strip stops
leaks between upper
and lower sashes

3. Does upper sash close tightly against top of frame?

4. Does bottom of lower sash shut tightly against the sill?

ANY PLACE where the windows do not fit snugly is going to be a place where you will have a cold air leak.

IF IT'S A window that you will not have to open during the winter, the simplest way to cope with gaps is to use rolled caulking that is available at most hardware stores. Simply press this material into all the crevices around the inside of the window and forget it until spring.

IF YOU HAVE to operate the window, however, other procedures will be necessary. Fabric weatherstripping can be tacked to the inside of the window frame—but the result is really ugly.

FOR "INVISIBLE" weatherstripping, try the following:

1. Gaps at top and bottom of the window can be sealed by attaching adhesive-backed foam to the top of the upper sash and bottom of the lower sash. If you have trouble sticking on the foam strips because of dirt on the sashes, try putting a coat of contact cement on the sashes before pressing the foam in place.

2. Gaps between upper and lower sashes can be sealed by tacking a strip of felt or spring bronze to the top of the lower sash.

3. Windows that have too much play at the sides can have weatherstripping

Weatherstripping can be
tacked in place without
removing sash from frame

tacked in the side channels—without having to remove the window from the frame. You can use felt strips, zinc fringed with felt, or spring bronze for this purpose.

IN ADDITION to these gaps in the window frame, a surprising amount of cold air can leak in from the inside moldings around the window casing. Often these leaks leave tell-tale dirt marks on the wall. These can be filled with spackle as they are located.

STRIPPING HINT: Steel wool used to scrape off paint remover during the stripping process frequently leaves fine slivers of steel that must be removed before applying the finish. Passing a strong bar magnet over the surface will usually pick up slivers that have escaped the dust rag.

RESTORING ROTTED WINDOW SILLS

MANY TIMES A QUICK INSPECTION of window frames on an old house yields the verdict: "Window frames need to be replaced." Replacing window frames can be an expensive and/or time-consuming process. But in 4 cases out of 5, the verdict for total replacement is based on the condition of the sills—not the rest of the frames.

WHERE THE SILLS ARE IN SAD SHAPE, it often is possible to make restorative repairs that will extend the life of the wood for many years. It also helps avoid the search for woodwork that will match the original.

THERE ARE AT LEAST THREE techniques that can can be used to restore a rotted sill. All are acceptable—the choice depends upon availability of materials and which media you feel most comfortable working with. Basic principle is the same with all three techniques: You have to create a surface

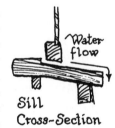

Sill Cross-Section

that will shed—not absorb—water. Therefore, all cracks and holes must be filled, and a smooth continuous surface created that tips away from the house.

ONE RESTORATIVE technique is based upon using a couple of marine products that are normally employed in boat repairs. An epoxy material—"Git-Rot"—can be used to saturate a partially rotted sill and arrest rot by encapsulating the fibers in resin. The surface can then be filled with another epoxy boat-repair product—Marine-Tex—which can be used to impart the proper water-shedding pitch. After the material dries, it can be painted in the normal manner. The

main drawback of this procedure is the difficulty in locating the materials. A boatyard or marine supply store is your best bet.

THE SECOND PROCESS relies on the carpenter's old standbys: Linseed oil and putty. The procedure can be used where the major problem is cracks and holes, and where the surface itself is basically intact. Scrape away all loose material with a putty knife and wire brush. Thoroughly soak the sill with pentacholorphenol wood preservative (such as "Wood Good") to kill any rot-causing organisms. After waiting a day, saturate the sill with boiled linseed oil. Wait another day, then saturate again with the linseed oil. After another day's wait, fill all cracks and holes with putty. Wait a couple of more days for a skin to form on the surface of the putty, then prime and paint.

THE THIRD PROCESS is used where the sill is badly deteriorated and the surface needs to be built up. You can use Plastic Wood—or make your own wood filler by mixing a paste of fine sawdust and a waterproof glue (such as Sears resorcinol glue). If more than ¼ inch must be built up, apply in two or more coats and allow to dry thoroughly between applications. After final coat has dried, sand, prime and paint.

TO PROTECT THE INTERIOR of the frame from water damage in the future, be sure the joint between the sill and the vertical side members is carefully caulked. Painting

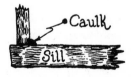

Caulk

Sill

the caulk after it has dried for a week—especially if it is the older oil-based type—will greatly extend its life.

CURING PROBLEMS IN DOUBLE-HUNG WINDOWS

DOUBLE-HUNG WINDOWS have been used since the middle of the 18th century. (The term "double-hung" stems from having two sashes able to move up and down independently within the window frame.) The double-hung design has proved very practical and adaptable . . . capable of surviving many changes in architectural fashions over the years.

EARLY VERSIONS of the double-hung window did not have counterweights to ease operation; they were held in an open position by spring plungers or pins. The addition of the counterweight in the 19th century allowed the sash to balance in any position without requiring any mechanical stops. Some modern replacement windows use spring ballasts instead of weights, but many of these have not proved as reliable and long-lasting as the old counterweight design.

EVEN IF YOU HAVE the old reliable double-hung windows with counterweights, you are sure to encounter problems from time to time. If you have never disassembled a window, the task might seem awesome at first. But once you understand the anatomy, it's not much of a trick.

STICKING SASH

SASHES MAY STICK in their frames because they have been painted shut—or because the wood has swelled during damp weather. In most cases, sashes that stick due to swelling will correct themselves as soon as the weather turns drier. If they continue to stick, more drastic measures will be needed, as described below.

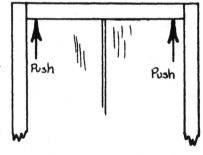

IF PAINT is the cause of sticking, try running the point of a sharp knife between the edge of the sash and the frame. This will break any bridged-over paint film. Then apply steady pressure to the sash near the side rails to work it free. (Pressure at the center may break the sash if it's really stuck.) HINT: To prevent sash from sticking after painting, run the sash up and down for several days until the paint film has thoroughly dried.

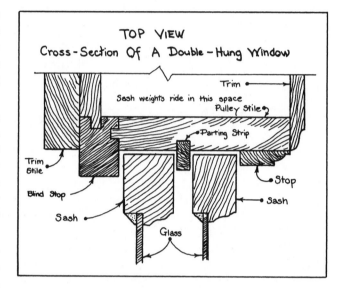

IF FURTHER PRYING is necessary to free up the sash, use a wide-bladed chisel or stiff putty knife. Don't use a screwdriver—it will mar the woodwork. After the sash is freed, if it still is binding use a chisel to scrape excess paint from the parting strip and both stops. With coarse paper, sand edges of the stops and parting strip that have been scraped.

IF THE SASH IS BINDING against the sides of the frame, try pounding the sides of the sash channel with a hammer and block of wood. This frequently will expand the channel a fraction of an inch—sufficient to free up the sash. As a final touch, lubricate the channel by rubbing with a bar of hard soap. Or use a commercial silicone lubricant.

IF NONE OF THE ABOVE succeeds in freeing the sash, you'll have to remove it (see below) and plane a little off one edge. Before reinstalling the sash, coat the planed edge with boiled linseed oil to retard moisture absorption (and resultant swelling).

REMOVING THE SASH

SEVERAL REPAIR OPERATIONS require removing the lower sash and, sometimes, the upper sash. First step is to remove the interior stop moulding that bears against the lower sash. Usually, it is necessary to remove only one of the stops.

BEGIN by running a razor blade or sharp knife down the crevice between the stop and the inside frame. This breaks the paint film and helps prevent chipping. Loosen the stop by prying with a stiff putty knife or chisel. (If the stop won't budge, it may be held with screws rather than nails. You'll have to locate the screw heads under the paint.)

TO REMOVE THE STOP, you have to bow the moulding sufficiently so that it will clear the mitered corners at top and bottom. This has to be done carefully to avoid breaking the stop moulding. (You may find that the stop is already broken into two pieces because one of your predecessors wasn't sufficiently gentle.) The job is made more difficult if the stop has been nailed with long finishing nails near top and bottom. You may not be able to bend the moulding enough to clear the nails from their holes in the frame. If this occurs, you'll have to remove the nails before the stop will come loose.

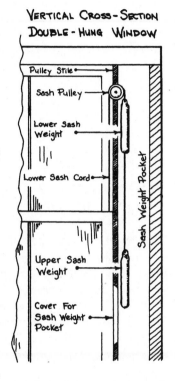

VERTICAL CROSS-SECTION DOUBLE-HUNG WINDOW

Pulley Stile
Sash Pulley
Lower Sash Weight
Lower Sash Cord
Sash Weight Pocket
Upper Sash Weight
Cover For Sash Weight Pocket

ONCE THE STOP is out, the bottom sash will swing free. If the weights are supported by a sash chain, you can make working with the lower sash easier by immobilizing the sash weight. Pull the weight to the top of the pocket by drawing down on the chain. Then slip a 2" common nail through the topmost link. This also prevents the weight from crashing to the bottom of the pocket when the chain is released from the sash.

ZINC WEATHERSTRIPPING complicates sash removal, since the metal strip will hold the sash in place. The zinc strip is held with small nails, which must be located and removed with screwdriver and pliers. Then sash will swing out as above.

THE SASHES are attached to their counterweights with either chain or sash cord. Cord is usually anchored in place by a knot in a hole bored in the top of the sash. (Sometimes cord is held with nails or wedges.) Chain may be held by nails or screws (screws are preferable) or by a spring twisted through the end of the chain and anchored in the hole in the top of the sash.

TO DETACH THE CORD from the sash, untie the knot—if you want to re-use the cord. However, if there is any sign of wear you might as well replace the cord while you have the window apart. In this instance, just cut the old cord off. (Hold onto the cord while cutting so that the sash weight doesn't smash into the bottom of the pocket.) Chain can be detached by removing the nails, screws or spring that holds it.

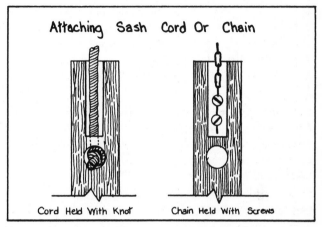

Attaching Sash Cord Or Chain

Cord Held With Knot   Chain Held With Screws

TO REMOVE THE UPPER SASH, take out the parting strip that separates upper and lower sash. Normally, this is just wedged into a groove in the pulley stile and held by friction. But odds are that it is also firmly held by several layers of paint. Cut the paint film by slicing the junction with a razor blade. Pry strip out with a putty knife. If the parting strip should accidentally break, you should be able to get a replacement at the lumber yard.

AFTER THE PARTING STRIP IS OUT, take the upper sash all the way down—and immobilize the sash weight with a nail through the sash chain. The upper sash will now swing free and can be detached as described above.

REPLACING SASH CHAIN & CORD

WHEN A SASH CHAIN or cord is broken the sash will fall when raised because there isn't sufficient counterweight to hold it against gravity. The window has to be taken apart to replace the broken linkage. Chain lasts longer than cord, so it is worthwhile to replace with chain even if the window is currently rigged with cord.

TO REPLACE A BROKEN CHAIN on the lower sash, only the lower sash need be removed. To replace a chain on the upper sash, you have to take out both the lower and upper sashes as described above.

WITH THE REQUIRED sashes removed, you next have to recover the detached sash weight—which is lying passive

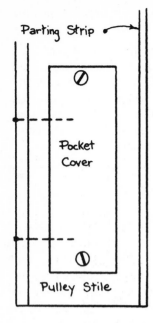

Parting Strip

Pocket Cover

Pulley Stile

and useless at the bottom of its pocket. To do this, you have to locate and open the pocket cover (see diagram at left). Sounds easy, but sometimes the cover is completely hidden by layers of paint. You may have to do a little creative scratching around. In theory, the cover is held in place by one or two screws. But on some old windows, the screw holes have gotten so chewed up that the screws no longer hold. As a result, frustrated householders in years past may have secured the cover with finish nails driven in from the side. If the nails have been countersunk, it may be impossible to pull them without digging up the woodwork. Instead, cut them by inserting a hacksaw blade in the crack between the pocket cover and the pulley stile.

ONCE THE COVER IS OFF, you can fish out the weight and remove the old chain or cord. Simplest way to thread the new chain or cord into place is to use a little helper nicknamed a "mouse." Tie a small nail or screw onto the end of some nylon fishline or similarly strong line. Tie the other end of the line onto the replacement chain. Push the weight over the pulley and feed line into the pocket. When your "mouse" shows up at the pocket cover opening, you can grab the line and pull the chain or cord through.

"Mouse"

PASS THE CHAIN THROUGH the hole in the sash weight and hook it with the metal C clip from the old chain (or buy some when you pick up your new sash chain). If you don't have any C clips, wrap the chain securely with copper wire.

(Ideal wire for this job can be scavenged from some old pieces of ≠14 BX cable.) While the weight pocket is open, check it for accumulated debris, protruding nails, etc., that could impede free movement of the weights.

GETTING THE CHAIN the right length is critically important. If too short, the sash won't come all the way down; if too long, you won't be able to raise the sash all the way because the weight will thunk into the bottom of the pocket.

BEST WAY TO GET THE RIGHT LENGTH is to measure the old piece. If for any reason this isn't possible, do the following: Draw the weight all the way to the top of the pocket until it bumps into the pulley. Fix the weight in position with a nail through the chain. Then with the sash in the lowermost position, measure off enough chain so that it can be secured in the sash slot with screws or the old coil spring. Allow yourself about an extra inch.

BEFORE REPLACING the pocket cover and stops, test the sash by moving it up and down to make sure that everything is working smoothly.

WHEN PUTTING BACK THE STOP MOULDING, it is best to pull all the old nails and set new ones in order to give yourself maximum flexibility in getting the proper fit against the lower sash. You want the moulding to be tight enough so that the sash doesn't rattle when the wind blows—yet loose enough to permit smooth movement up and down.

THROUGH TRIAL-AND-ERROR with the sash in both the raised and lowered positions, find the best place for the stop. Then—and only then—secure it in place with 4 or 5 1½" finish nails. It is advisable to re-check for smoothness of operation after each nail is driven. Sometimes the process of pounding the nails home moves the stop just enough to make the sash bind. And don't place nails within 12 in. of the top or bottom of the stop moulding. Or else, as described above, it will make things more difficult for you next time you have to disassemble the window. Perish the thought!!

CARE & REPAIR OF WINDOW SASH

WINDOW SASH IS ESPECIALLY VULNERABLE to water damage. On the outside, the interface between wood and glass—normally protected by putty—is often a source of moisture leakage into the wood. On the inside, during cold weather, windows are subject to condensation that runs down the glass and into the wood. Result: Peeling paint and the possibility of rot.

BECAUSE OF THE IMPORTANCE OF the right type and shape of window sash to the appearance of a house, every effort should be made to save the originals. Even sash that seems beyond salvage can be brought back to useful life. A little tender loving care can work miracles.

FIRST ITEM to check is whether joints in the sash frame are loosening—especially the lower rail. Open joints admit water, hastening the process of deterioration. Repair calls for removing the sash from the window frame. From the inside, carefully pry off the strip of wood that holds the lower sash in place. If the upper sash must be removed, the parting strip in the frame (between upper and lower sash) must also be pried out.

Reinforcing Angle

TO REINFORCE THE LOOSE CORNERS, the first job is to close up the gaps by forcing the rails back together. Sometimes they will just slide back; other times a strap or pipe clamp will be required. Then screw flat metal reinforcing angles in place. (Be sure to leave enough clearance so that the angle doesn't hit the frame or parting strip.) Drilling pilot holes for the screws, of course, makes the job much easier.

IF THE CONDITION OF THE FRAME permits, you can also reinforce the corners by drilling holes and tapping in glue-soaked dowels. Just be sure to use a waterproof exterior-grade glue. Or if the joints are really open and clean, you can just re-glue and clamp.

ANY LOOSE OR CRACKED PUTTY should be replaced following the procedure outlined in "Sealing Leaky Windows." Next comes the condition of the paint. If the sash has gone unpainted for many years, not only may the paint be cracked and peeling, but the wood itself may be bare, dried and fissured.

IF MUCH BARE WOOD has been exposed to the weather, follow this procedure: Scrape off any loose paint with putty knife and wire brush. Then thoroughly saturate the bare wood with a 50/50 mixture of boiled linseed oil and turpentine. Let dry a day and repeat the soaking. After the linseed oil has dried thoroughly (1–2 days) the sash can be primed and painted as usual with any high-quality oil-based exterior paint. Any holes and cracks should be plugged with linseed oil putty prior to painting.

SOAKING THE SASH WITH LINSEED OIL prior to painting lessens the likelihood of paint failure later on. The dry, fissured wood acts like a sponge for water. If any water gets into the sash, the wood would soak it up, tending to loosen the paint film above it. Filling the pores of the wood with linseed oil makes the mass of the wood more repellent to water entry.

ALSO CRITICAL IS THE WAY that the glass is installed in the sash. Obviously, in an old house you're going to live with what was done previously. But if you have to replace any panes, at least you can make sure that the new glass is installed properly.

HARDEST PART of replacing a pane of glass is getting rid of all the old putty. The rabbeted grooves should be cleaned down to the bare wood, taking care not to gouge the sash. Inevitably, some of the old putty will seem welded to the wood. If hammer and chisel have little effect, there are a couple of things you can do. Heat softens putty; you can use a propane torch or a soldering iron with the tip wrapped in aluminum foil (to keep tip from fouling). Chemicals can also soften putty. Among those that will work: Paint remover, lacquer thinner or muriatic acid.

NEW GLASS SHOULD BE CUT ⅛-in. smaller than the opening to allow for irregularities in the wood and for expansion and contraction.

EITHER LINSEED OIL PUTTY or latex putty—more commonly known as glazing compound—will be used to set the glass. The choice rests with personal preference. Glazing compound, the newer material, is claimed to be easier to work and longer lasting. Traditionalists prefer the linseed oil putty; properly protected with paint it will last quite satisfactorily.

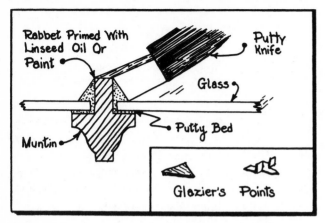

IF GLAZING COMPOUND IS BEING USED, the rabbeted groove should be primed with paint and allowed to dry. If linseed oil putty has been selected, the rabbets should be brushed with boiled linseed oil. This prevents the wood from sucking the oil out of the putty, which would cause premature cracking.

WHEN GLASS IS SET INTO THE SASH, it should not touch the wood anywhere. It should float in a bed of putty on all sides. This makes the best seal against moisture and helps prevent rattling window glass. To make the bed, spread a 1/16-in. layer of putty on the bottom and side of the rabbeted groove. Press glass gently to embed it in the putty. Putty should distribute evenly so there are no gaps visible between glass and putty anywhere.

NEXT, SET IN THE GLAZIER'S POINTS. You can also use the newer push-points (slightly easier to set) or just plain brads. These metal fasteners are what actually hold the glass in place—not the putty. On small panes, use two points to a side. On larger pieces, set points every 8–10 in.

AFTER POINTS ARE SET, make rolls of putty with your hand and press them around the edge of the pane. Form a smooth bevel by pressing down firmly with a stiff putty knife and drawing it slowly along the sash. A clean putty knife is essential to making a smooth bevel. To clean knife, keep a pad of steel wool handy that you've moistened with linseed oil. Clean putty knife on the steel wool when it starts to stick.

IF YOU HAVE TROUBLE getting the bevel smooth with the knife, give it a wipe with your thumb when no one is looking. Also: Be sure you don't make the bevel so wide that you can see it on the inside of the window.

PAINT IS ESSENTIAL for long putty life. The putty should be painted after a skin has started to form—usually after 3–4 days. Paint should extend slightly over putty onto the glass to make a watertight seal. Masking tape will help if you don't trust your hand.

PEELING PAINT ON THE INSIDE OF THE SASH is especially common. It's caused by moisture—either coming in from the outside as described above—or from condensation that forms during cold weather.

THERE'S NOT MUCH you can do about condensation short of installing storm windows. But the problem can be alleviated by treating the wood so that it won't absorb water. Scrape and wire-brush to remove as much loose flaking paint as possible. Then flow on a liberal coating of a 50/50 mixture of turpentine and linseed oil. (Do this only after the wood has thoroughly dried out.)

REPEAT APPLICATIONS every 2–3 days until the wood has absorbed as much linseed oil as it will take. Any cracks and holes then can be filled with linseed oil putty. Allow putty to dry firm on top for a week or so. Then prime and paint with any high-quality oil base paint.

OLD PEELING SASH rejuvenated in this manner and kept well-protected with paint at periodic intervals can have its service life extended almost indefinitely.

DETECTING & DEFEATING ROT

IN THE 19TH CENTURY, the Victorians developed a fondness for romantic ruins. "Pleasing decay" they called it. The decay is not so pleasing, however, when it is your house that is becoming the ruin.

FUNGI THAT CAUSE DECAY in wood are nature's scavengers. Their job in the life cycle is to break down dead wood and return it to the earth. Just because some of this dead wood may be part of your house is of no concern to these rot-causing creatures.

THUS IN PREVENTING ROT in wooden house timbers you are battling one of the basic forces of nature. The spores of the decay fungi are being continually produced by the billion and carried aloft on the wind. The air inside and outside your house, therefore, constantly carries the seeds of decay. The homeowner's only hope is to prevent the timbers from becoming an inviting home for these eager eaters.

WOOD CAN BE A LONG-LASTING building material. We have wooden structures in the U.S. that date from the 1700s—and there are timber structures in Europe that are many centuries older. There is, however, no such thing as total victory in the battle against rot—only temporary successes. Recognize, for example, that all wood that is continually exposed to the weather is going to have to be replaced sooner or later.

BUT AS LONG AS THE OLD-HOUSE OWNER is vigilant and conducts periodic inspections for decay-breeding conditions, the forces of decay can be kept at bay. All interior timberwork can be made to last indefinitely if the proper preventive maintenance procedures are followed.

KNOW THE ENEMY

ALMOST ALL HOUSE ROT is caused by fungi—plant-like organisms that grow without chlorophyll, true roots, stems or leaves. There are six categories of decay you might encounter around your house, ranging from mildly annoying to downright alarming.

• BLUESTAIN—A dark color caused by a fungus invading sapwood. The color can penetrate deep into the wood. The stain by itself does not seriously weaken the timber. But the presence of bluestain is an indicator of moisture conditions that could generate more dangerous forms of rot. Bluestain is often found around sources of moisture such as window sash, water pipes and bathroom fixtures. Stained wood is more vulnerable to water penetration—and thus prone to further decay. Color of this type of sapwood stain can range from brown through blue, steel-gray and black.

• MOLD—Also called mildew. Mold fungi form a powdery, loose mass on the surface of wood. Color of mold on softwood can range from orange and pink through green and black. Mold on hardwood usually shows up as dark spots. Although mold won't seriously undermine the strength of wood, like sapwood stain it can make the wood more susceptible to attack by more aggressive fungi.

• BROWN ROT—Caused by fungi that consume cellulose, brown rot imparts a brownish color to infected wood, plus a tendency to crack across the grain, then to shrink and collapse. The wood becomes very water absorbent and loses strength rapidly.

• WHITE ROT—Caused by fungi that consume both lignin and cellulose, white rot causes wood to lose color and appear whitish, leaving the affected member in a fibrous and stringy condition. The wood doesn't crack across the grain as with brown rot, and doesn't shrink or collapse until the rot is very advanced.

• SOFT ROT—Not as serious as other rots, soft rot is normally confined to the surface of wood. Exterior surfaces afflicted by soft rot tend to be severely cracked and fissured, both with and across the grain. But when the surface is scraped with a knife, you soon strike sound wood. Soft rot tends to occur on exterior surfaces that are frequently wet, such as shingles, window sash and shutters.

• WATER-CONDUCTING ROT—This most insidious type of rot fortunately is not too common in the U.S. Unlike other forms of rot that require water to be supplied externally, this fungus can carry its own water over considerable distances through its web-like structure. These tentacles deposit water in the sound wood, raising the moisture content and making it suitable ground for the fungus to grow and spread further. Because this fungus can carry its own water, it is sometimes called "dry rot," which is somewhat misleading since it does have to get water from somewhere in order to carry out its cycle of decay-and-spread.

One variety of water-conducting fungus—merulius lacrymans—is common in England and Europe and is known familiarly as "house rot." Another variety—poria incrassata—is found in the southern U.S. This type of decay can spread undetected inside partitions, revealing itself only after serious structural damage has been inflicted.

CONDITIONS THAT BREED ROT

ROT-CAUSING FUNGI need four basic elements in order to thrive: Oxygen, moisture, food and moderate temperature. By eliminating any one of these conditions you can control or eliminate rot.

KEEPING WATER OUT OF HOUSES

IN A HOUSE, the two most practical variables to control are the food supply and moisture. Excluding oxygen isn't possible—although some old-timers used this principle to store logs free from rot. They would simply submerge the logs in a fresh-water pond.

ROT FUNGI CAN ONLY START FEEDING in earnest on wood that contains moisture above the fiber saturation point (approximately 30% water, compared on an oven-dry basis). By comparison, the wood in a normal dry building contains about 12–14% moisture. Trouble only starts when this level of water is raised by moisture from an external source—such as from precipitation or from the soil. By locking out this excess moisture, you deny the fungi one of the four requirements for life.

YOU CAN ALSO MAKE THE FOOD SUPPLY—the wooden timbers—less appetizing by using preservatives that act as poisons. More about this later.

MOISTURE THAT CAUSES ROT usually comes from one or more of 4 sources: (1) Ground Moisture; (2) Rain & Snow; (3) Plumbing Leaks; (4) Condensation.

GROUND WATER will migrate from soil to the house through several avenues:

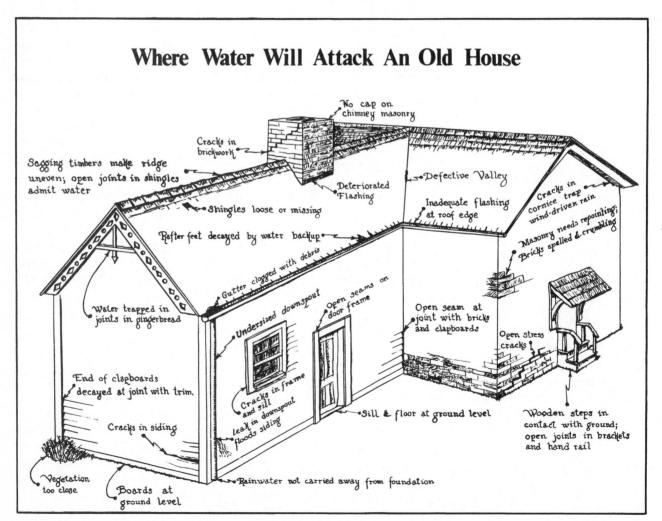

Where Water Will Attack An Old House

No cap on chimney masonry

Cracks in brickwork

Sagging timbers make ridge uneven; open joints in shingles admit water

Deteriorated Flashing

Defective Valley

Inadequate flashing at roof edge

Cracks in cornice trap wind-driven rain

Masonry needs repointing; Bricks spalled & crumbling

Shingles loose or missing

Rafter feet decayed by water backup

Gutter clogged with debris

Open seams on door frame

Open seam at joint with bricks and clapboards

Open stress cracks

Water trapped in joints in gingerbread

Undersized downspout

End of clapboards decayed at joint with trim.

Cracks in siding

Cracks in frame and sill

leak in downspout floods siding

Sill & floor at ground level

Wooden steps in contact with ground; open joints in brackets and hand rail

Vegetation too close

Boards at ground level

Rainwater not carried away from foundation

- Direct contact of wood with the soil. Sometimes the level of the earth around a house gradually rises over the years until the exterior woodwork is touching the soil. Porches and steps in particular are likely to have wood in contact with the earth. There should be at least 8-in. clearance between sills and the ground level.

- Condensation of water vapor in crawl spaces under the house.

- Strands of water-conducting rot will transmit ground water far into a wooden structure as described earlier.

- Capillary action in the foundation walls can carry water up several inches to wet the sills. Also, some old structures may have floor joists set into the foundation below the current ground level. The water that leaks into the masonry will cause rot in the ends of the beams.

RAIN AND SNOW

WATER FROM RAIN AND SNOW can find amazingly devious routes into a house. Water can be drawn into very thin cracks in wood joints—and will remain in such confined spaces for long periods.

ANY EXTERIOR SURFACE that has an open joint or seam that is unprotected by caulk or a paint film is subject to water penetration. The end grain of siding—especially where it meets vertical trim—is vulnerable. So are porch railings, door and window frames, shutters and decorative trim such as Victorian gingerbread. Lateral cracks in clapboards present an open invitation to rainwater. Until such boards are replaced, the cracks should be plugged with putty and painted.

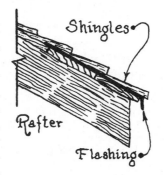

EDGES OF ROOFS are especially vulnerable. Gutters can become clogged with leaves, or, in the winter, by ice. Gutter blockage can cause water to back up under the roofing. This can result in water flooding down into the cornice and interior partitions. The proper eave flashing under the shingles will prevent such flooding—but an old house might not have adequate (or any) such flashing. The same type of flooding can occur during heavy downpours if the downspout isn't big enough to handle the run-off.

A WARNING SIGN of a water problem at the roof edge is peeling or blistering paint on the underside of the soffit. One way to deal with ice blockages in the winter is to place electric heating cables in the gutters. Another way to cope with troublesome gutters is to remove them altogether!

CRACKS IN STUCCO or other masonry walls can also admit enough water to generate rot in the wooden sheathing underneath.

RAINWATER SPLASHING against a hard surface on the ground level can also rebound high enough to

keep the siding unduly wet. Vegetation that is growing too close to the house can also raise moisture levels in the siding to a point where it will be hospitable for rot fungi.

LEAKY PLUMBING

MOST PLUMBING LEAKS are discovered before they can do too much damage as far as rot is concerned. The major exception is the bathroom, where it is possible for fixtures to develop slow leaks that will gradually soak partitions without attracting much attention until considerable damage has been done.

CRACKS IN TILE GROUT in floors and tub enclosures can admit enough moisture to rot timbers—and the process will probably be slow enough so that it won't be discovered until structural damage has been done. Gaps in tiling around bathroom fixtures should be kept closed with silicone caulk. Loose grout should be removed and re-grouted, then water-proofed with silicone. The homeowner should also be on the lookout for loose and lifting tiles. Not only will they admit water—they may also signify that water has been penetrating for some time and that wood is rotting.

IF YOU HAVE A PANEL (usually located in a closet) that gives access to the back of tub and shower fixtures, you should open it occasionally to check for signs of leaks. If you don't have such a panel and are doing some restoration work around the bathroom that is creating a mess anyway, you should consider the practicality of installing a plumbing access panel where it won't be noticed.

CONDENSATION

CONDENSATION is the most insidious source of moisture, since the water comes from vapor in the air and not from an obvious source like rain or a leaky pipe.

CONDENSATION OCCURS WHEN warm, moisture-laden air contacts a cold surface. Warm air can hold more water vapor than cold air. So if the cold surface lowers the temperature of the air below its dew point, the excess water has to go someplace. It shows up as droplets of water on the cold surface.

THE EARTH IN A CRAWL SPACE beneath a house can be a source of moisture that will condense on sills and joists—especially if the house is air-conditioned in the summer. Corners are especially susceptible to condensation—and rot—because they get the least air circulation. Best way to combat condensation in a crawl space is to cover the ground with polyethylene sheets or strips of asphalt roofing paper.

WATER MAY ALSO CONDENSE on cold water pipes in humid weather. If this causes water to drip on structural wood, the offending pipe should be wrapped with the special insulation that is sold for this purpose.

CONDENSATION MAY ALSO OCCUR inside wall partitions on cold winter days when warm moist air from the interior contacts cold exterior walls. This is especially likely if a vapor-resistant barrier was installed under the siding. This problem should not occur if insulation has been installed with a vapor barrier on the inside wall. Water will also condense on window panes in winter, eventually causing soft rot and staining in the sash. Where this occurs, treat the sash with a pentachlorophenol preservative.

PREVENTING ROT IN OLD HOUSES

IN THIS CHAPTER, we'll look at specific measures to keep water from fostering rot fungi, and how to deal with rot once it has gained a foothold.

THE ROOF is the home's first line of defense against water—and it is a line that is frequently breached. The top floor and attic should be checked at regular intervals for the tell-tale stains that disclose that water is becoming an unwelcome visitor.

FINDING THE SOURCE of a roof leak is another matter, however. Water may travel for many feet under the roofing or along a rafter before emerging as a visible leak. If you are really lucky, the leak may be readily apparent from the underside—such as being able to see sunlight peeping through your roof. In this event, mark the spot by driving a nail upward through the roof. That will enable you to locate the exact spot when you go topside to patch.

MORE LIKELY, you won't be able to spot the exact source of the leak from below—so you'll have to make a visual inspection from the top of the roof. Start by locating the point on the top side that corresponds to the stain on the underside. This is accomplished by careful measurements from a reference

point, such as a chimney. Now you know that the source of the leak is at—or above—the point you've marked. The checklist on the next page is a guide to the common sources of roof leaks.

MOST MINOR ROOF LEAKS can be repaired with a daub of asphalt roofing compound. Additional life for the patch can be achieved by painting it with liquid roof coating.

EVERY ROOFING MATERIAL has a finite life-span, however, and when it starts to leak because of general material failure, it is time to completely re-roof. For example, wooden shingles have a life expectancy of 15–25 years. The surface of wood shingles gradually weathers away, making the shingles thinner and thinner. As the shingles slim down, they lose strength and tend to snap off in high winds. Wood shingles should be replaced when they have lost half their original thickness.

In northern climates, ice dams can form in gutters and valleys, causing water back-up during freeze-and-thaw cycles. Water backup under shingles will

Moss on shingle roof can form mini-dams that will cause leaks.

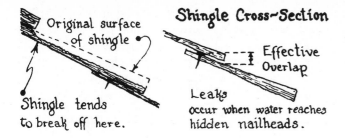

Original surface of shingle

Shingle tends to break off here.

Shingle Cross~Section

Effective Overlap

Leaks occur when water reaches hidden nailheads.

cause leaks in an otherwise water-tight roof. You can prevent ice dams from forming by placing electric heating cables in the affected gutters and valleys.

COMMON SOURCES OF ROOF LEAKS

• Cracks in chimney masonry

• Loose flashing around chimneys & valleys

• Loose or missing shingles

• Cracks caused by settling rafters

• Water backup from plugged gutters, or other debris, moss, etc.

• Protruding nailheads

• On flat roofs: bubbles & blisters; cracks where roofing abuts vertical surfaces

SIDING, DOORS & WINDOWS

EXTERIORS OF WOODEN BUILDINGS are normally protected by paint. Paint by itself is not a rot-preventer. Paint's function is to form a continuous film that will shed water . . . thereby depriving rot fungi of needed moisture. Once a paint film is broken, water can seep into the wood behind. The presence of moisture in the wood tends to blister and peel more paint . . . admitting more water . . . and the cycle accelerates.

CAULK AND PUTTY are used to plug holes and cracks in siding, to prevent the paint peeling process from ever getting started. Putty is used to plug nail holes and similar holes in a single piece. Caulk, which is more elastic, is used to

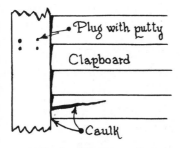

Plug with putty

Clapboard

Caulk

seal long cracks and joints—especially those between dissimilar materials (like brick and wood) where there will be differences in rates of expansion and contraction.

CRACKS THAT ARE TOO WIDE to be sealed with caulk by itself can first be stuffed with oakum—a specially treated rope-like material that is available at plumbing supply stores and major hardware outlets. The crack can then be spanned with one or more beads of caulk.

JOINTS AROUND door and window frames are quite vulnerable to water seepage—especially at the top. These joints should be thoroughly caulked. In addition, if any rebuilding of door or window casings is required, flashing should be installed over the drip cap as shown in the diagram. The flashing can be of non-corrosive metal—aluminum or copper—or waterproof felt. Flashing should also be used over the drip cap where the bottom clapboard meets the horizontal trim board at the sill.

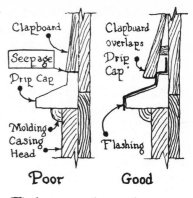

Clapboard

Seepage

Drip Cap

Molding Casing Head

Poor

Clapboard overlaps Drip Cap

Flashing

Good

Flashing over doors and window casings prevents seepage.

SIDING AND TRIM also benefit from liberal treatment with a high-quality wood preservative—as outlined below.

THE PREVENTER: PENTACHLOROPHENOL

PENTACHLOROPHENOL (sometimes affectionately referred to as "penta") is a great boon to the homeowner in the continuing battle against rot. Creosote—which for many years was the standard wood preservative—has the disadvantages of a persistent odor, plus rendering treated wood unsuitable for gluing or painting.

A GOOD PENTA-CONTAINING preservative (such as "Wood Good" or "Wood Life") not only has no lingering odor, but also performs two vital functions:

• The active ingredient—pentachlorophenol—is an effective poison for the various fungi that cause rot;

• The preservative also contains water repellents that keep moisture from penetrating the wood.

READY-TO-USE PRESERVATIVES normally contain 5% penta. Special concentrates containing 10% or 20% penta can be obtained when a higher concentration is desired to compensate for shallow penetration of preservative into the wood. Penta—unlike creosote—can be painted; in fact, it can act as a very effective primer. Because of the water repellents, moisture absorption into the wood is greatly retarded, which means that the paint is less likely to peel and blister over the years.

EXTERIOR WOOD SHOULD ALWAYS BE TREATED with preservative before installation. It's best to use wood that has been pressure-treated with preservative, since this process forces the preservative deeply into the wood. When using wood that hasn't been pre-treated, apply preservative by soaking or painting. The best on-site treatment is to submerge the wood in a tub of preservative for 15 min. Bricks can be used to hold the lumber submerged. Allow an additional 30 min. for the lumber to air-dry before installing. All cutting and drilling should be done before soaking so that preservative will penetrate all exposed surfaces.

IF SOAKING IS IMPOSSIBLE, the next-best thing is to apply preservative with a brush. Pay special attention to the end-grain, which is highly absorptive. End-grain will absorb a lot of preservative—just as it will absorb a lot of water if not properly treated. Even if you don't have a tub big enough to soak entire pieces of lumber, it frequently is possible to dunk the ends in a bucket of preservative for a few minutes. Brushing will be adequate for the middle sections. If dunking the ends is impossible, make sure that the end-grain gets a double application of preservative put on with a brush.

CAUTION: Pentachlorophenol is a poison—for people as well as fungi. Any skin that contacts preservative should be washed immediately with soap and water. In addition, some people may exhibit a special skin sensitivity to penta and should avoid working with the material altogether.

ON PROJECTS WHERE THE ENTIRE EXTERIOR has been replaced with new wood, you might want to consider finishing with an exterior stain (such as Cuprinol) rather than paint. These stains are a mixture of preservative plus pigment. Since they penetrate the wood rather than forming a film, you never have the peeling and blistering problems you can have with paint. Renewing a stain finish is a lot easier than repainting, too.

DEALING WITH ESTABLISHED DECAY

CONDUCTING AN INSPECTION FOR rot infestations once a year will enable the homeowner to isolate and correct rot conditions before they do any great harm—and while the remedies are relatively inexpensive.

ADVANCED ROT CONDITIONS are easy to recognize; it is less easy to recognize rot in its early stages. Decay usually causes wood to change color. Most often, the infected wood becomes darker. Some fungi, however, cause wood to lose color until the surface appears whitish.

WHERE DECAY IS SUSPECTED, you can use the "pick test" to make a definite determination. This test is based on the fact that decay causes the wood fibers to lose toughness. Jab an awl or ice pick at an angle into the piece of wood—preferably when wet. Pry up sample of the wood. Healthy

wood will produce long splinters. Rot-infected wood tends to lift in short sections, breaking across the grain, without creating splinters.

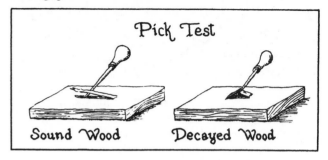

WHEN DECAY IS DISCOVERED, there are three steps—in ascending degrees of complexity—that can be taken, depending on the seriousness of the condition:

1. Eliminate the source of moisture so that the wood dries out completely. If there is evidence of only superficial rot, drying the wood is all that will be required to arrest the growth of rot fungi and to kill those that have gotten started.

2. If there is any doubt about the source of moisture being completely eliminated, the wood should also be treated with preservative. All joints and cracks must be flooded with penta solution. The goal is to get the penta as deep into the wood as water ever has penetrated. Several repeated applications will be more effective than one.

Exterior wood, such as porch posts, wooden steps, etc., that exhibit any sign of rot should be treated at regular intervals—at least every two years. The slightest infection by rot fungi increases the water absorptivity of the wood—and therefore increases the likelihood of accelerated fungi growth. Thus it is imperative to keep the wood fibers saturated with the water repellents in the preservative.

3. If the rot has materially weakened the wood, the affected members will have to be replaced. Preservative will arrest the growth of rot fungi—but it can't restore strength to wood that has been attacked. All infected wood should be cut back to healthy, non-decayed timber. Contrary to popular belief, infected wood will not contaminate adjacent healthy members—as long as moisture is not present. But if you leave some fungi-infected pieces in place and moisture should be re-introduced to the area, the spread of decay will be very rapid.

OBVIOUSLY, ANY REPLACEMENT LUMBER should BE thoroughly soaked with preservative before installing. For good measure, you should also brush and spray (an ordinary garden sprayer will do) preservative on all timber adjacent to the patch.

IN CASES INVOLVING NON-LOAD-bearing wood, it is possible to restore rotted sections by using some of the new epoxy materials.

Masonry and Energy Efficiency

RESTORING OLD BRICKWORK

By Frederick Herman, AIA

RESTORERS OF OLD HOUSES often fall victim to one particularly subtle error: Selecting the wrong materials. This is especially true when working on exterior brickwork and other types of masonry. The consequences of error can be quite serious . . . and the full impact won't be noticed for several years in some cases. Few newcomers to old houses seem to realize that what might appear to be a fine job of brickwork repair can do more damage over the long run than the repairs supposedly accomplished. This is especially true for structures and masonry dating from before the 1870s.

MASONRY IS NOT PERMANENT. It slowly ages and deteriorates. When you introduce new materials into a masonry wall you are changing the way that particular section will age and move in response to changes in the weather and temperature. These differences in rates of expansion and contraction can set up stresses that will wreak havoc over the years. Selecting the wrong material today will assuredly bring its day of reckoning tomorrow.

TODAY'S MASONRY MATERIALS are quite different from those used in the past . . . especially the mortars. Mortars used in early construction, disregarding clays, were basically "soft" lime mortar, i.e., a mixture of lime and sand. Such mortars often contained substantial impurities, were poorly mixed, and proportions of ingredients varied substantially. The result was a weak mortar.

WORKMANSHIP in old masonry walls often is poor. In the interior of walls, party walls, and other areas that did not show, the early masons often threw the materials together . . . with the bonding of brick and mortar being strictly problematical. In addition, the bricks themselves were often very soft—approaching the quality of unburnt clay. Adding further to the softness of old brickwork is the fact that over the decades the lime will slowly leach out of the mortar. To compensate for lack of quality, the early masons substituted quantity—in the form of thick walls.

THE END RESULT was a brickwork mass that was fairly plastic. Stresses caused by shifting foundations, changing loads, etc., could relieve themselves by movements within the wall itself. It is not unusual today for one to simply pull bricks out of an old wall by hand and find that the mortar has disintegrated—the lime having leached out, leaving the bricks resting on sand. The bricks themselves will often have returned to a sort of clay-like consistency . . . or have crumbled into pieces. If one is not familiar with old masonry, confronting such a situation can generate a real panic . . . the sickening fear that the whole structure is about to come tumbling down.

THE PERIL IN PORTLAND CEMENT

AT THIS POINT, RESIST AT ALL COSTS the temptation to run out to buy some modern mortar (premixed or otherwise) and some new bricks to quickly patch things up. If you do, you have just bought yourself some trouble for the future. No immediate action is required. What is needed far more is a thorough analysis of your particular problem. That old wall has been standing for a good many years . . . and it is highly unlikely that it is going to pick this moment to collapse. If your nerves are rattled, some judicious shoring will win additional time and give you peace of mind. Use this time to get expert advice.

THE TEMPTATION TO USE CONTEMPORARY materials such as portland cement mortar and modern hard burnt bricks will invariably lead to further trouble. Portland cement is a dense, unyielding material. When combined with modern bricks (for which it is well suited) it results in a rigid, inflexible wall. While this is fine if the wall is composed entirely of these materials, it is disastrous of these hard materials are mixed in with the old soft mortar and bricks.

THE NEW MATERIALS, due to their much greater strength, will not yield and give way to adjust to changing stresses like the old. New stress patterns will be created within the masonry and these will act most violently at the weakest point in the wall—which will be in the old brickwork. You will have patched one crack only to find that you have gotten two new ones.

ON EXTERIOR SURFACES exposed to the weather, the new hard materials will weather at a much slower rate than the old. In extreme cases, there are records of old masonry being eaten away as much as 1/8 in. per year in areas of high pollution and rapid changes in temperature and atmospheric conditions. In such situations, the hard new bricks and mortar will not budge. The repaired masonry may end up as a wall decorated with a network of projecting mortar joints.

SIMILARLY, great caution has to be exercised in trying to repair old stucco or in trying to build up the surface of spalled stonework. The new portland cement coating will be a rigid surface, with an entirely different rate of expansion and contraction than the area to which it is applied. This new surface, thick enough to have strength of its own (and this can be as little as 1/4 in. or less) can literally rip off the face of the old work to which it has been applied.

TIPS ON POINTING

IN REPLACING DETERIORATED MORTAR, here are a couple of other tips: (1) Remove old mortar to depth of 1 in. with hammer and cold chisel. Carbide wheels will damage the old bricks; (2) Flush particles from joints with garden hose; (3) Experiment with trowel and jointing tool to see which gives best physical match with shape of old joint. A tooled joint is the most watertight and gives best bonding. Remove excess mortar from bricks with stiff scrub brush.

Weathered

Tooled

THE BOND BETWEEN NEW CEMENT STUCCO and the old work will be subject to great stress due to differences in rates of expansion and contraction. Result: The older, weaker surface will give way. Examination of pieces that have broken off will usually reveal fragments of of brick, mortar and stone that the new stucco pulled off the old wall. Aside from temporary cosmetics, the new stucco has set up a situation that aggravated the very problem that was to have been corrected.

BEWARE OF ANOTHER TRAP: Color. There is a natural inclination to try to match the color and appearance of the new work to the old. For all intents and purposes this is impossible. Duplication of the effects on surfaces and color wrought by 100 years or more exposure to weather, soot and plain old age just can't be achieved outside laboratory conditions.

EVEN IF THE OLD MORTAR IS MATCHED EXACTLY in composition, the new mortar would look radically different if only because it's clean. Here the only answer is patience . . . letting the toll of time and nature blend the old and new. Or else resort to some temporary form of surface tinting. At all costs avoid using color within the mortar itself. A colored mortar will provide a match—but only for the moment. The aging process will soon emphasize the inherent color differences that exist between the old and new. Instead of matching colors, you have actually placed side by side two substances of inherently different color characteristics, which age will only emphasize.

EVEN WORSE is the desire "to make it all look like it was originally." This usually means that everything will be made nice, clean—and ruined—by sandblasting. Sandblasting is the best method invented to ruin old brickwork and shorten its life. Did you ever see a glazed header after sandblasting? No glaze left! Sandblasting will cut right through the outer face of brick and mortar to expose the soft underbody.

REMOVING THE OUTER SKIN of old bricks makes them more vulnerable to atmospheric attack. Too, porosity is increased and the bricks absorb more water. Damp walls might be an unwelcome after-effect. Sandblasting will also change the color of a wall. The interior body of a brick is almost invariably a different color than the outer skin that was exposed to the heat of the firing process. Claims that problems resulting after sandblasting can be solved with coats of sealants have to be taken with skepticism. Sealants are at best of a temporary nature and are of unproven durability over the long term.

WHEN YOU ARE ON YOUR OWN

OF COURSE, the real question is what do you DO when confronted with a masonry wall that needs repair. The preceding discussion has convinced you, hopefully, that the best thing is to consult an expert with experience in old masonry and the materials used. Even experts will disagree about certain details, however, because every old wall presents its own unique set of problems.

IF THERE ARE NO EXPERTS AT HAND, a careful examination of the old masonry may yield enough data for you to proceed on your own. First problem is to determine the type of mortar already in the wall. Lime mortar is soft and will crumble in your hand with a little pressure. It will disintegrate in water, with the lime leaching out. Portland cement mortar by contrast is hard and will not crumble; rather it cracks under stress. It will not dissolve in water.

LIME MORTAR derives its color from the sand that was used. You can tell a great deal about the sand by inspecting the particles that settle out after dissolving a sample in water. Portland cement mortars, on the other hand, are varying shades of gray (white portland cement is a comparatively recent innovation). Close inspection will also tell you a great deal about the color, hardness and porosity of the bricks in the wall.

MIXING AND MATCHING MORTAR

NEXT STEP IS TO GET A GOOD MASON and tell him what you found and instruct him to match things as closely as possible. If you have a mason who is inexperienced in working with old masonry—or if you have to proceed on your own—the safest course is to select materials that are as close as possible to that which is being repaired. In the case of bricks, this means reusing as much of the old brick as possible. Where you have to replace deteriorated bricks, and can't scavenge enough from the old wall, try to find other old brick from the same period of suitable color and size. In a pinch—and with some difficulty—contemporary handmade brick can be obtained that approach the old both as to color and consistency. This is a costly alternative.

TO DUPLICATE old lime mortars, the following is a frequently used formula that will yield a soft mortar . . . but is easier to work with than the original pure lime mortar. Mix one part portland cement by volume with 3 parts hydrated lime by volume. Add 3–5 parts by volume of sand to one part of the cement-lime mixture.

A SKILLED MASON is definitely the best person to mix the mortar and lay the brick. He knows how to handle such matters as width and shape of mortar joints, racking of the courses, and related problems. He will also make sure the whole thing doesn't collapse while he is working on it.

STUCCO REPAIRS are definitely not a do-it-yourself project. Minor stucco patching can be done by using a stucco formula similar to the lime mortar mixture outlined above. Old stucco, however, gets its color and texture from the coarseness of the sand. Various additives such as horse hair were not uncommon. These are hard to match. In addition, stucco work often involves large areas that require cleaning, scaffolding, etc. This is beyond most homeowner's capabilities.

HOPEFULLY THE POINTS DISCUSSED HERE have convinced you that masonry repairs require long-term solutions. It's a lot more complicated than putting on a new coat of paint.

CHEMICALLY STRIPPING PAINT FROM EXTERIOR MASONRY

By James G. Diedrich

PEOPLE WHO OWN PAINTED BRICK structures can derive four basic benefits from stripping off the paint layers and getting down to bare brick: (1) Long-term maintenance is simplified; (2) The architectural integrity of the building is enhanced; (3) The texture and color of the brick and mortar almost always have more visual appeal than the color that comes from a paint can; (4) Restoration of the original brickwork invariably increases public admiration and appreciation of the structure.

REMOVING PAINT FROM BRICKWORK is not a project to be undertaken lightly, however. There are two basic approaches: Mechanical removal (sandblasting) and chemical stripping. Although every project has its special problems, in most instances chemical stripping is the best approach. There are 5 ingredients to a successful paint stripping job:

• Time

• Some allowance of money

• A contractor's professional stripping formula (not a paint store product)

• Some training in use of the stripper

• A love for and appreciation of the original brick structure

OF COURSE, it is always possible to simply scrape and repaint a structure that is already painted. But in the long run I feel this is not desirable. First, and most important, the brick and stone in most old structures—especially those of the 19th century—was intended to be seen. It is true that the old European technique of painting the brick and pencilling the joints in white was used on some structures in America. But it was not widespread. More important, maintaining and re-painting this kind of detailed color scheme gets prohibitively expensive—especially as paint layers build up and cracking and peeling get to be more of a problem. And many people—me included—find this kind of painted brickwork aesthetically unappealing.

BECAUSE OF THE HIGH COST of painting the mortar joints, today paint is almost invariably applied over both the bricks and the mortar—thus eliminating the decorative relationship between the two. To me, this is an insult to the integrity of the building.

WHEN A BRICK STRUCTURE needs waterproofing, painting may be the least expensive solution—for the short term. But painting isn't even the simplest answer. Many of the commercial sealers are easier to apply than paint. You can do it yourself with an ordinary 2-3-gal. garden sprayer. And a good recommended sealer can have double the lifespan of most paint films. It's not uncommon for paint to start flaking and peeling within 2–4 years on brick.

ALTHOUGH IT HAS A LONG HISTORY as an exterior sealer, paint is less than a totally satisfactory material. As a sur-

Ten coats of paint were removed from this patch of Milwaukee Cream City brick with one application of ABR stripper—followed by washing and neutralizing.

Sandblasting to remove paint can have disastrous results—as in this particularly horrible example from an 1890 brick church in Milwaukee.

face film it will also lock water in the brick, and we have seen cases of serious deterioration of brick that occurred beneath the painted surface. Masonry must be allowed to breathe.

ONCE PAINT STARTS TO PEEL—as it will on older, soft common brick—it requires constant maintenance to keep the paint film intact. So you get into a constant cycle of scraping, wire-brushing and repainting. Patch-painting isn't very satisfactory, because the sun fades paint and the touched-up areas stand out like freckles. And if the whole surface is re-coated, after this sequence is repeated a number of times you end up with layer piled upon layer—which then begins to crack and look like a dried lake bed. Successive paint coatings then get thicker and thicker in hopes of filling in the cracks. The end result of this relentless process is a painted surface that looks like alligator skin. So even a confirmed enthusiast for painting eventually has to confront the necessity of removing old paint from a building—even if he just wants to paint it again.

IF A BRICK STRUCTURE is only dirty, please just clean it; don't start the paint covering process! Chemical cleaning of brick is a simple and inexpensive process . . . and can be handled as a do-it yourself project.

HOMEMADE FORMULAS for stripping paint from brick are not recommended. The article in the February 1975 Journal discussed the dangers in uncontrolled use of lye. Exterior paint stripping can be handled as a do-it-yourself job, however, if you have professionally formulated chemicals and take

Prior to repainting (right), 25 layers of peeling, cracked paint were removed from the cast iron columns and surrounding wood and sheet metal on this commercial building. Two applications of chemical stripper were required.

the time to learn how to use them properly. The ABR strippers are formulations of caustic mixed with emuslifiers, neutralizers plus a compound to make it thicker or thinner. The material is quite safe to use. I personally have been splashed in the face and hands with the stuff in my enthusiasm to get on with a job, and it washes right off with no ill effects.

APPLYING THE STRIPPER

EVERY JOB HAS ITS OWN PECULIARITIES, but in general here are the steps we go through in attacking a masonry stripping job:

1. By scraping out a paint chip, we get an idea of the number of layers of paint on the structure. This gives us an indication of how tough the job is going to be and whether it's likely that two coats of stripper will be required.

2. Based on the finding in (1), we mix up a test batch of stripper, increasing the viscosity (using methyl cellulose to make it thicker) in proportion to the number of paint layers to be removed. With higher viscosity, a thicker layer of the stripper will stick to the side of the structure.

Sometimes paint isn't the problem . . . just years of accumulated dirt and grime. This test patch shows how a chemical cleaner will quickly restore the original look.

3. We next try out a sample of the stripper on a test patch to see how long it takes to soak through all the layers. This can be as little as 1 hr. or as much as 24 hr. We find that 60% of the jobs we tackle can be handled with one application of stripper. Where more than one coat is required, we thoroughly

wash off the first coating and all the softened paint residue, then apply the second coat.

4. With the test results in hand, you're ready to apply the stripper to the building. This can be done with a large soft-bristle brush like a whitewash brush. For faster application, you can use a paint sprayer with the nozzle taken off so that the material flows onto the wall.

IF THE STRIPPER HAS TO STAY ON THE WALL for a number of hours, the surface may dry out—especially if it is exposed to direct sun. The surface of the stripper should be re-wet by lightly fogging with a fine water spray from a hose.

5. When the paint is totally softened, the stripper plus dissolved paint is hosed off the wall. You can use an ordinary garden hose with normal pressure. But it goes a lot faster if you use a high-pressure hose with 300–500 psi. water. This kind of equipment can be rented. If a second coat of stripper is needed, this is the time to put it on.

6. As soon as possible after hosing off the paint and stripper, the neutralizing acid is applied. A non-controlled acid, such as muriatic, will etch the mortar joints and possibly burn the bricks. We use our ABR 101 brick cleaner—which contains mild acids plus controlling agents—as the neutralizer. This can be put on with a large brush, or can be flowed on with a pressure sprayer.

THE NEUTRALIZER can be washed off within minutes of being applied. A high-pressure hose (300–500 psi.) definitely should be used for this operation. Reason: The neutralizing solution will also clean the dirt off the masonry, but the dirt particles can only be dislodged by high-pressure water.

BECAUSE THE STRIPPER DISSOLVES THE PAINT, clean-up is not a problem. If the residue is flowing onto a sidewalk, just wet the pavement beforehand and flush the material to a drain. There will be no stain. If the residue is falling onto earth, just thoroughly soak the ground in advance. The material will disperse into the ground quite neatly. Although plants and shrubs should be protected with plastic sheeting, the neutralizing agents in the stripper keep it from harming the soil—unlike lye stripping agents.

Acidic brick cleaner (which also serves as neutralizer for the caustic paint stripper) can be applied with a brush or ordinary garden sprayer.

Thorough flusing of the brick cleaner requires a high-pressue (300–500 psi.) hose to remove all surface dirt. This equipment can be rented.

A CAUSTIC APPROACH TO EXTERIOR PAINT REMOVAL

By Laurence J. Reilly

A KEY ELEMENT IN RESTORING any masonry structure is the removal of paint from originally unpainted surfaces. Paint was usually applied later to hide dirt (especially in urban areas) and deteriorated mortared joints. Proper architectural paint-vents are needed. Of the three, only the third presents a treatment that will leave the original surface intact, and is relatively easy. This article will deal with this third method, limited to masonry buildings covered with an oil base paint.

SINCE OIL BASE PAINT is acidic in nature, it will be chemically broken down by an oxidizer, or caustic base. The base used in this instance is caustic soda (lye), purchased at a chemical supply house in 100 pound kegs. Flakeing can make a building attractive but presents two major drawbacks. First,

it is not original (in most cases), and secondly, it leads to endless repainting as the surface again deteriorates and become dirty.

THERE ARE THREE OPTIONS OPEN to the owner who wishes to remove exterior paint: (1) sandblasting; (2) hand-scraping; (3) chemical solform at about 20¢ per pound. For smaller applications, household lye sold in supermarkets works just as well. It is a good idea before buying the larger quantity of lye to test the surface with a small batch of remover made up with household lye. The test sample is prepared in the same manner as the larger quantity.

REMEMBER THAT WORKING with any caustic requires a great deal of care. Rubber gloves with long wrists, hat, plastic face shield, long-sleeve shirt, etc., are musts. A rubberized, hooded slicker is ideal. If the solution gets on the skin, it should be washed immediately with plenty of water. It can also be neutralized with vinegar.

THE IDEA BEHIND THIS ENTIRE procedure is to stick the caustic to the painted surfaces, because a plain solution of caustic and water will not adhere to a vertical wall. A thickener is needed. This can be a number of products including Cab-O-Sil (fumed silica), fluffed calcium stearate or plain cornstarch. I used cornstarch and found it quite satisfactory—as well as inexpensive.

TO BEGIN, two non-metallic containers are needed. I prefer 5-gallon, plastic, joint-compound buckets. In one, put a quantity of the caustic and slowly add water, stirring gently until the caustic is dissolved. In the other bucket, put cold water and add the thickener. When using cornstarch, add until the water turns a milky white in color and stir until all lumps are dissolved. Then add the thickened solution to the caustic which should immediately become thick and syrupy. The strength of the remover varies directly with the amount of caustic used. I usually make about a gallon of each

This pre-Civil War brick townhouse in Trenton's Mill Hill Historic District is an example of the excellent exterior restorations of brick and frame houses being done in this area.

Low estate that had befallen the Thompson Triangle buildings is shown by this photo of the Round Corner House in 1968.

Now restored, the Round Corner House and adjacent Armstrong House provide pleasant apartments and offices (including Adams').

solution using perhaps a pound of caustic soda. The coverage will depend upon the painted surface to be stripped. Since there are so many variables, much individual experimentation is required.

A NYLON-BRISTLED PAINT BRUSH will not be affected by the caustic. Whenever possible, I use stiff, discarded brushes, because the remover will clean them like new, thus yielding a highly desirable bonus!

USUALLY, immediately upon application, the paint will start to break down. When there are many layers, only the top-most layers will come off at first. But remember, as in all types of paint removing, patience is the watchword. The longer the remover is on, the more paint it will remove.

ONCE THE SURFACE IS COATED, it should be kept moist. Moisten by gently sprinkling with just enough water to keep the remover intact without causing it to run. After about an hour, test the surface with a hard jet stream from a garden hose.

IF THE PAINT WASHES OFF down to the original surface, it is ready. If not, wait longer before testing again. In situations where there are many coats of paint, it is possible that the remover will not cut all the way through. In this case, the remover must be washed off and the entire process repeated. I once let a coat of remover remain for a week, and the paint was not completely removed.

HERE, HOWEVER, IS WHERE THE experimentation comes in, varying the strength of the solution. A handy tool is a pump that will increase the water pressure used in connection with a wand at the end of the hose, a knife-like jet of water can be produced that will lift the softened paint much more readily than a garden hose. These pumps and hose attachments are used in building-cleaning and probably can be rented.

ONCE THE PAINT IS REMOVED, the surface should be washed down with acid to neutralize any remaining caustic. Hydrochloric will remove dirt. Extreme care must be exercised whenever working with any of these acids as they will harm human tissue, plants, trees, parked cars, etc., as will the paint remover. These acids must also be thoroughly rinsed off with water.

WHEN WORKING ON THE EXTERIOR of a building, extreme care must be taken to properly protect adjoining properties. Check first with abutting owners and mask off any surfaces that might be contacted by any of the chemicals or the water used in their removal. Sheet-plastic works well as a protective covering, and is readily available.

THERE IS ALSO A POSSIBILITY that a permit may be required from the local building inspector, especially if the work is to be done on the front of a house.

THE REMOVED PAINT USUALLY GATHERS at the base of the building and after the water runs off, it can be shoveled into a waste container. Since the paint does not dissolve in water, I do not think there is any environmental damage from the water that runs off into storm drains.

ONCE A BRICK BUILDING HAS BEEN CLEANED, there is usually a tendency for the bricks to effloresce. This can be removed with muriatic acid and will sometimes disappear when a sealer is applied. The sealing should be done a week or two after the cleaning when the bricks are thoroughly dry. In older buildings, the water jets may rake loose mortar from the joints and make pointing necessary. Pointing is probably advisable in any case and a clean surface improves the adhesion of the pointing mortar.

MY OWN HOME was cleaned and treated in the way I have described with highly satisfactory results. I know of no commercially available process or material that removes paint from exterior masonry economically. With the current trend in architectural preservation and restoration, perhaps a better method will be available soon. Until then, the caustic and water approach will have to do.

REMOVING STAINS FROM MASONRY

By Theodore Prudon

STANDARD MASONRY CLEANERS generally remove only surface dirt and not stains. Most stain removal is done with the aid of a poultice. Poultices are also used when large amounts of water are undesirable as in interiors. A poultice is made by adding a solvent or chemical cleaning agent (or both) to water, into which an inert filler is stirred until the consistency of thick paste is achieved. The paste is then applied to the area to be cleaned.

THE INERT FILLER as an absorbent powder controls the rate of evaporation or reaction thereby giving the solvent or chemical cleaning agent the time to dissolve the stain. Upon evaporation or completion the solvent or cleaning agent is drawn out of the masonry into the absorbent powder together with the material that caused the stain. When the poultice is completely dried out, the powder with the stain material can be brushed off.

THE SELECTION OF THE cleaning agent or solvent depends upon the type of stain to be removed. A variety of chemically inert fillers can be used as filler materials for the poultices. Essential is that they are finely divided, have a high absorbency value and do not react with the chemical cleaning agent selected. Used are, for instance, talc, whiting, Fuller's Earth, bentonite, powdered silica, etc.

PRIOR TO APPLICATION, excess staining material, such as tar, should be scraped off. Sometimes stains are pre-wetted with water to prevent too deep a penetration of the chemical cleaning agent. Apply the paste in layers not much thicker than ¼ inch. To prevent too quick an evaporation, the poultice can be covered with sheets of polyvinyl, taped against the wall. Poultice can be re-wetted. Once dried out, the powder or dry paste can be scraped or brushed off with bristle brushes and wooden paddles or other non-metallic implements. If not effective, the application can be repeated. The area cleaned should be rinsed thoroughly with clean water to remove any chemical residue.

THE PROBLEM WITH removing stains from masonry is similar to that of fabric. The area cleaned with a poultice will appear as a "clean spot" because not only the stain but also all other dirt will be removed, while the remaining area is still soiled. Exposure over a period of time reduces this quite quickly but the best solution is to remove the stains at the same time that the remainder of the masonry is to be cleaned.

IRON AND CORROSION

MASONRY IS FREQUENTLY stained by the run-off of corrosion or rust from adjacent or embedded iron or steel. The removal of these stains is generally quite easy if the stain is not too deeply embedded. For light staining a solution of oxalic acid and water can be brushed or sprayed on. Solution is 1 lb. oxalic acid in one gallon of water or 1 to 10 parts by weight. A small amount of ammomium bifluoride is added to increase the effectiveness and speed of the removal. However, great care is necessary because the ammonium fluoride

gives hydrofluoric acid, which etches acid-sensitive materials including brick or glazed terra cotta. A second application might be necessary if the stain is too deeply embedded. Upon completion the area is to be rinsed carefully with clean water to remove all chemical residue.

A second method, used for deeply embedded stains, involves the use of a poultice. Sodium or ammonium citrate, glycerine and warm water are mixed in the proportions 1:7:6. An inert filler such as whiting or kieselguhr (which is not easily available) is added to form a thick paste. The mixture is applied to the stained area and left to dry for several days till the poultice can be brushed or scraped off.

LICHENS AND MOSSES

LICHENS AND MOSSES do grow on damp masonry, usually in shady locations or areas that are only sunlit for very short periods. Dampness of masonry can indicate problems in the masonry wall itself, although lack of moisture evaporation because of location is hard to remedy. Nevertheless these areas need watching. Lichens and mosses can be killed with a solution of zinc or magnesium silico fluoride (by weight, 1 part to 40 parts of water.) A commercial weed killer can also be used with care. Household detergents or bleaches might also prove successful. If growth is a result of location and exposure, the problem is likely to recur. Green stains that do not respond are probably vanadium stains.

COPPER AND IRON STAINS

STAINS FROM BRONZE AND COPPER are generally found as a result of the run-off from flashing, gutters, statuary and fasteners. Its removal is not too complicated. A mixture of 1 part ammonium chloride (sal ammoniac) and some 4 parts of talc or diatomite plus ammonium hydroxide or household ammonia is prepared till a thick paste is obtained. Placed upon the stain, this poultice is left to dry. The dried poultice can be scraped or brushed off with wooden or non-metallic tools. More than one application might be necessary before stain is removed. Upon completion the area is to be washed thoroughly with clean water.

OIL STAINS

THE REMOVAL OF PETROLEUM and lubricating oil stains is not unlike the removal of asphalt stains. After the excess on the surface is removed by scrubbing with soap, scouring powder and trisodium phosphate, a poultice with a solvent can be used. Solvents generally recommended are carbon tetrachloride, trichlorethylene, benzol and others. Care is necessary and good ventilation is required indoors because solvents are highly volatile. A poultice with 5% sodium hydroxide (caustic soda) followed by scrubbing is also effective. However, use of these alkaline solutions can cause efflorescence after completion.

ASPHALT AND TAR

TAR AND ASPHALT stains, usually caused by sloppy or temporary roof repairs, are more difficult to remove and cannot always be totally cleaned. After the excess material is scraped off (taking care that the surface is not damaged) a poultice made of inert filler and solvent can be used. Solvents are one of the following hydrocarbons: Xylene, toluene, trichloroethylene or mineral spirits. The solvent strength varies as does the evaporation rate; when solvent strength is high so is the rate of evaporation. A too rapid evaporation might reduce the effectiveness. Trichloroethylene has high solvency, while mineral spirits have less dissolving power and slow evaporation rate but are quite readily available. Benzene has similar characteristics but extremely toxic requiring special precautions. Because most of these solvents are highly volatile, flammable and sometimes toxic, extreme care is necessary, especially when used inside. If an emulsified asphalt stain is encountered, repeated treatments with a poultice of diatomaceous earth and toluene or benzol might be necessary.

ASPHALT STAINS might not be able to be removed completely. The success will not only depend upon the depth to which it is pentrated, but also upon the surface texture. If the surface is textured, rough or has many small crevices, residual fragments do occur. However, the visual impact of the stain will be substantially less. Washing and scrubbing after the poultice application with a detergent or scouring powder is desirable.

MANGANESE AND VANADIUM

SOMETIMES BRICK CAN STAIN in a particular manner as a result of its composition. Manganese gray or brown brick sometimes stains as a result of the manganese used to color the brick. Generally it will occur on the mortar joints but also sometimes on the brick itself as brownish stains. It is difficult to remove and not soluble in hydrochloric acid, while sulfuric acid is much too strong. After the wall is wetted, a solution of acetic hydrogen peroxide solution can be brushed or sprayed on. The solution is composed of one part acetic acid (by volume of 80% or stronger), one part hydrogen peroxide (30–35%) and 6 parts of water. When all the stains have been removed, they can possibly recur after a few days. Again they can be removed in the same manner.

VANADIUM STAINS on brick work are green, brownish-green or brown. They are frequently mistaken for organic growth of some sort. The origins are not quite clear, but areusually attributed to impurities within the masonry itself or as a result of metal anchoring or support systems, which can contain vanadium alloys. The stains might sometimes occur after chemical cleaning. Washing with hydrochloric acid (muriatic acid) is detrimental because it fixes the stains rather than removing them and turns them brown. These stains can be removed with strong caustic soda solution, which has to be left on the surface for some two or three days. It can be harmful to the brick masonry. Another possibility for removal is washing down with a solution of ethylene diamine tetra acid (EDTA) in one part to ten parts of water.

RESTORATION OF SANDSTONE

SANDSTONE (also called "brownstone") was a popular building material in the 19th century. Quarried in the Connecticut River Valley and in New Jersey, sandstone was easy to cut and carve when fresh from the quarry. Upon exposure to the air, the surface crystallized, making it much harder.

SANDSTONE is a durable building material—when properly cut and laid. Because it is a sedimentary rock, sandstone has a grain that corresponds to the layers of sediment that were laid down over the millenia before the material was converted to rock by geological processes. Sandstone ages well if its end-grain faces the weather. However, in many 19th-century applications, the grain was placed parallel to the weather side.

USE OF SANDSTONE IN THIS INCORRECT fashion leads to spalling and flaking of the stone—the the bane of many of today's owners of sandstone buildings. The villain of the piece is water. Sandstone is porous, and water will penetrate the stone. In winter, alternate thaw-and-freeze cycles allow water to get into the stone and then freeze and expand—splitting off some of the top layer.

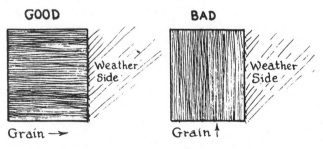

RESTORATION OF SANDSTONE falls into two major categories: (1) Repair and resurfacing of damaged stone; (2) Preventive maintenance to keep spalling from getting a start.

UNFORTUNATELY, repair and resurfacing of sandstone involves great amounts of tedious hand labor. As a result, it can be an expensive process to have done professionally.

IN THEORY, the resurfacing process is simple: (1) all loose stone is chipped out with hammer and cold chisel to get down to sound material; (2) a "scratch coat" of portland cement mortar is applied, building up to within 3/16 in. of the surface; (3) a final coat of brownstone stucco is troweled on. Brownstone stucco is simply a conventional portland cement mortar mix to which reddish pigments have been added.

THE PROCESS IS FAIRLY SIMPLE on flat surfaces, and small repairs are definitely within the capabilities of the home craftsman who enjoys working with mortar. The only tricks are to undercut the stone when chipping so that the patch will lock firmly, and to be sure the patch is level with the rest of the stone. This is readily done by working a straightedge back and forth across the width of the patch to strike it off flush. Careful work with trowel and wooden float will assure a level surface.

THE PROCESS GETS TRICKY when you have to restore carvings, moldings and curved surfaces on a sandstone building. Professionally, this work is almost invariably done by masons who were trained in Italy or Germany. And there aren't many such masons around anymore. The restoration process is the same as for flat surfaces: Deteriorated surfaces are built up with portland cement and finished off with brownstone stucco.

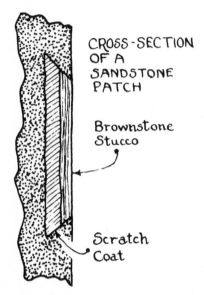

CROSS-SECTION OF A SANDSTONE PATCH

Brownstone Stucco

Scratch Coat

BUT RESTORING an elaborately carved lintel requires craftsmanship of a high order. Among other things, it may require constructing temporary forms on the building to allow cement to be cast in place. Special curved tools will also be used in re-creating moldings.

ANYONE WHO ENJOYS sculpture could probably develop the skills required to tackle this work. Among other things, you'd have to be adept at fashioning special tools that would be needed to duplicate ornate curves.

BECAUSE OF THE COMPLEXITY of building up shapes in masonry, some restorers have recreated lintels and other decoration out of wood. When treated with pentachlorophenol preservative (sold under such trade names as "Wood Good") and painted the color of sandstone, the end result is almost indistinguishable from the original. And as long as the wooden replica is painted regularly, it will last as long—or longer—than the sandstone on the rest of the building.

SINCE THE RESURFACING of sandstone is such a tedious and expensive process, it behooves the owner of a brownstone structure to take good care of the stone that hasn't started to deteriorate. This means waterproofing.

SIMPLEST waterproofing method is painting. One drawback of paint is that it will need to be renewed every three to five years—and it can get unsightly if it starts to peel. Particular care should be exercised in painting over fresh cement patches. If the patch isn't properly primed, the alkalies in the cement stucco will cause the paint to peel in a few months. Depending on the paint you've selected, etching the patch with muriatic acid or washing with a zinc sulfate neutralizing solution might be required.

IDEALLY, CEMENT STUCCO PATCHES should cure at least 8–10 weeks before painting. This can be impractical, however, if your contractor has rigged scaffolding and so has to complete the job all at once.

THE EXPERTS DISAGREE as to the best type of paint to use on exterior stonework—especially where there's been cement patching. So be forewarned that this is a problem area and don't automatically accept a contractor's word that his particular solution will "work fine." Your best defense is to ask your contractor for references on jobs he did a year or more ago—and then contact the owners to see how the paint job has weathered.

ANOTHER WATERPROOFING METHOD is to use clear sealers. Solutions of 5% silicone have been used for some time, but experience has shown that these coatings retain their water repellency only 1–2 years. Another type of sealer that has been gaining in popularity is based on mixed stearates (see box opposite). Stearates will retain water repellency for up to 10 years. Before any sealer can be applied, however, the stone should be thoroughly cleaned.

CLEANING AND SEALING STONE

MANY PRODUCTS are available for restoring sandstone, terra-cotta, limestone and other masonry surfaces.

Solvent cleaners (that wash off dirt) are said to be 50% less costly than older steam cleaning and sandblasting methods. To apply PSC's restoration cleaner, the product is diluted with 2 to 4 parts of water and applied liberally with a large brush to a surface that has been pre-wet. After 5 min., second application is put on if needed, then surface is thoroughly rinsed with fresh water.

Once surface is cleaned, a sealer can be applied. A sealer prevents water penetration into porous stone (thus retarding deterioration) and also helps prevent accumulation of dirt and grime. Both penetrating stearate-type sealers and acrylic surface-coating sealers are available.

THE ENERGYLEFFICIENT OLD HOUSE

By Clem Labine

WHILE IT IS IMPORTANT for old-house owners to pay attention to energy conservation, it's equally important that we not rush in thoughtlessly and tack on every gimmick that's being hustled by fast-buck salesmen. Much of energy conservation is common sense. Significant savings can be made by changing habits—without ever touching the house.

AS AN EXAMPLE OF the pitfalls that await the unwary, we recently saw an 1815 Greek Revival farmhouse that had an 1895 addition. The 1815 section had been insulated two years ago with loose fill blown into the side walls. Today, all the paint is peeling from the clapboards on the insulated walls. The 1895 section, which wasn't insulated, has its paint still intact.

OWNERS OF HISTORIC HOUSES, especially, should beware of taking steps in the name of energy conservation that will either alter the architectural character of the house or else harm the fabric of the structure. There are often less drastic methods that can achieve comparable results. For instance, re-examine the way you operate the house. These pointers seem self-evident, yet most of us have developed profligate habits that are a carryover from the era of cheap energy.

Changing Habits

HERE ARE JUST a few checkpoints against which you can measure your own energy-consciousness:

1. In winter, set thermostats at lowest possible settings. Insulate yourself with sweaters (that's easier and cheaper than insulating the house).

2. In summer, utilize natural cooling as much as possible before turning on the air conditioner (more on this later).

3. Don't heat (or cool) rooms that aren't in use. Close off areas of the house that aren't being occupied.

4. Reduce levels of illumination. (Contemporary interiors are over-lit by historical standards, anyway.) Besides the power consumed by lighting, heat from the lights adds to the cooling load in summer. If you are using an air conditioner, it puts you in the position of using electricity to make heat (in the lights) and electricity (in the air conditioner) to remove the very same heat.

5. Heating plant should be cleaned regularly for maximum fuel efficiency. If you can't do this yourself, have a service man to do it. The hot water tank should be flushed once a month to get rid of the sediment that accumulates at the bottom and which reduces heat transfer. If the furnace is an old coal boiler adapted to oil, consider replacing it with a new unit with higher fuel efficiency.

OPERATING THE HOUSE EFFICIENTLY

IN ADDITION to the above, there are a series of "soft technology" operational steps that were common in the old days, but which fell into disuse in the era of cheap energy. These steps help you control the environment within the house without heavy capital expense or consumption of energy.

A LONG-TERM STEP is the planting of deciduous (leaf-shedding) trees on the south and west sides of the house. The leaves shield the house from the sun in summer—and provide additional cooling vapors trough transpiration. Evergreen trees planted on the side of the house facing prevailing winter winds can also act as a windbreak.

Planting deciduous trees on south and west sides of a house is a traditional way to provide natural cooling.

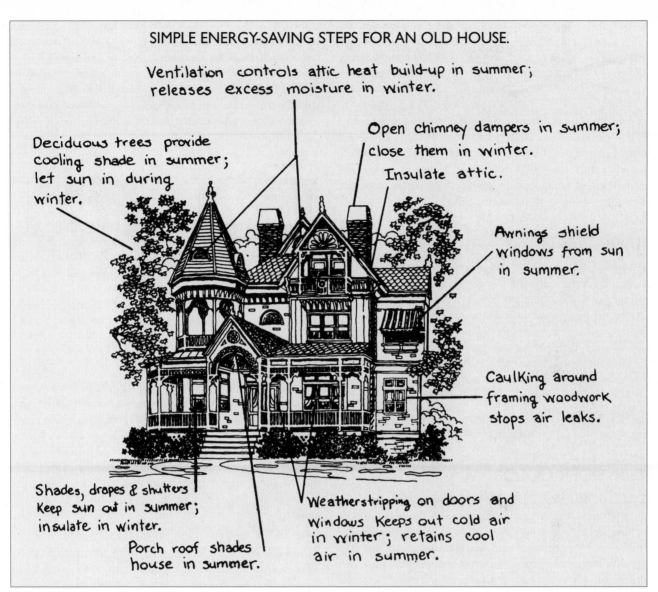

SIMPLE ENERGY-SAVING STEPS FOR AN OLD HOUSE.

Ventilation controls attic heat build-up in summer; releases excess moisture in winter.

Open chimney dampers in summer; close them in winter. Insulate attic.

Deciduous trees provide cooling shade in summer; let sun in during winter.

Awnings shield windows from sun in summer.

Caulking around framing woodwork stops air leaks.

Shades, drapes & shutters keep sun out in summer; insulate in winter.

Porch roof shades house in summer.

Weatherstripping on doors and windows keeps out cold air in winter; retains cool air in summer.

BEFORE PLANTING ANY TREES, however, consult an experienced nurseryman about proper placement of the young trees. Most people underestimate the size of adult trees—with the result that the house eventually has trouble with branches, fallen leaves in the gutters, etc. On the other hand, if trees are placed too far from the house, benefits are dissipated.

SHUTTERS, window shades, drapes and window awnings are old-fashioned—but effective—devices to control interior house climate. These devices are used to counter the fact that single-thickness window glass can allow an enormous amount of heat to enter—or escape from—a house.

IN THE SUMMER, the old-time householder would open up the house in the morning to let it fill with cool night air. Then as the sun began to heat things up, shutters and window shades would be drawn on the sunny side—and perhaps awnings let down also.

CONVERSELY, in winter, shutters and heavy drapes can be closed to prevent radiant heat losses to the cold side of the house. But on the sunny side, everything is pulled back from the windows to let the sun's warming rays stream in.

FIREPLACE DAMPERS are also an operational control. On warm days, the dampers can be opened to allow warm air to rise up the chimney, which promotes air circulation. On cold days, of course, the dampers should be closed to prevent heat from escaping.

FOR LATE 19TH-CENTURY and turn-of-century houses, portieres are an appropriate and attractive way to cut down on drafts within a house.

OLD-FASHIONED CEILING FANS have suddenly taken on a very practical—as well as nostalgic—look. They consume only as much power as a large light bulb . . . and far less than

an air conditioner. On all but the hottest days, the cooling provided by a ceiling fan is adequate. And there's another energy-saving aspect to ceiling fans: During the winter, a ceiling fan can help warm a high-ceilinged room. That's because hot air tends to rise and collect in a stratified layer at the top of a tall room. Running a ceiling fan at low speed recirculates the hot air back to the floor level—evening out the temperature in the room and lowering the fuel demand on the furnace.

RADIATORS

RADIATORS should get special attention; efficient transfer of heat from the radiator to surrounding air is critical to fuel conservation. Dust or clean radiators at least once a month during the heating season. Avoid painting radiators if possible; use radiator covers instead. If it is necessary to paint, use the special paint designed for this purpose. If an old radiator is crusted with paint, it would be a good idea to strip it. If you have a strong friend, the easiest way to strip a radiator is to remove it and take it to a shop that has a sandblasting rig.

YOU CAN INCREASE heat output from a radiator by placing a small fan on the floor and aiming it at the radiator.

CONSIDER COLOR

EXTERIOR PAINT COLOR has an impact on energy efficiency. In southern areas where cooling is the primary consideration, light colors reflect more of the sun's heat, keeping the walls cooler. In northern areas, where heating is the primary consideration, darker colors will absorb more of the sun's heat during the winter. Of course, paint color selection has to take into account aesthetics and historical precedent. But there are certain combinations that are both aesthetic and ecological disasters—such as a Victorian house in Buffalo, N.Y., that is painted white!

INSULATION

BECAUSE HEATED AIR rises, much of the heat loss from a house is through the roof. Every old house will benefit from attic insulation. Technical problems are few because it usually is possible to get the proper vapor barriers installed. It is essential that any insulated attic have proper ventilation to prevent condensation of moisture. Best way to insulate an attic is to put insulation between the attic floor joists with vapor barrier facing down. Worst place to install insulation is between the rafters directly against the roof boards. This doesn't allow for adequate ventilation under the roof.

INSULATION IN THE SIDE WALLS of an old house should be the LAST energy-saving step tried. Because of the difficulty of installing adequate vapor barriers, side wall insulation can cause serious paint peeling and rot problems. (The Sept. 1976 article discusses side wall insulation in greater detail.) Consider side wall insulation only after every other step in this article has been tried and the resulting energy savings evaluated.

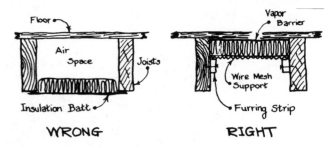

UNHEATED CRAWL SPACES under a house can benefit from insulation. See diagram for proper installation.

STORM WINDOWS

SINGLE-THICKNESS WINDOW GLASS plus gaps around old sash account for large heat losses. So storm windows are a logical energy-saving step. The only problem is finding windows that don't detract from the house's appearance. It is almost impossible to find wooden storm windows these days, so most of us have to come to terms with aluminum. Just avoid the raw aluminum look. Aluminum windows now come in a variety of pre-baked finishes. If you can't find a color that is compatible with your trim paint, buy white or the color that is closest to your desired color, and then paint them yourself.

CONDENSATION is frequently a problem with storm windows on old houses. If the storm windows leak cold air, you may find condensation on the inside windows. Usual solution: Caulking thoroughly between the storm window and the exterior window frame.

IF CONDENSATION OCCURS on the inside of the storm windows, it means that loose-fitting inside sash is leaking moisture-laden air into the space between the two windows. Usual solution: Using rope-type caulk to seal around the inside sash.

AIR INFILTRATION

AIR LEAKING THROUGH small cracks and holes in a building's exterior is a major source of heat loss (as well as heat gain in summer). If you add together all the small apertures on the typical old house (including cracks around doors and windows) you'd have a hole 5 ft. x 5 ft. or more. When you imagine all the heat that would escape on a cold winter

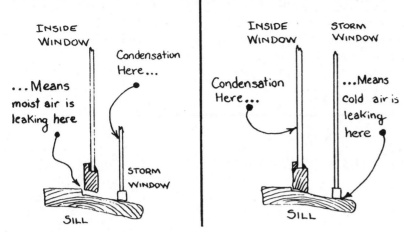

Two sources of storm window condensation.

day through an open 5 by 5 window, you see what a major problem air infiltration can be.

BECAUSE THE OPENINGS ARE SMALL, stopping them all up isn't as easy closing a single 5 by 5 opening. Reducing air infiltration involves a methodical series of steps:

• On wood structures, make sure that the exterior paint film is in good condition.

• On masonry structures, make sure that the mortar is sound. Repoint if necessary. Avoid, however, application of masonry sealers—except in highly unusual circumstances. Sealers can trap moisture in masonry walls and cause accelerated deterioration.

• Caulk all construction joints with a high-quality acrylic or butyl caulk. Fill all holes in exterior wood with putty or glazing compound.

• Caulk gaps in interior woodwork—especially where it butts plaster surfaces—and around electrical outlet boxes where necessary. You can tell which interior gaps need filling by passing your hand along the woodwork on a cold winter day. Chances are you'll be amazed by the amount of cold air you feel squirting into the room.

• Insert strips of felt between wide gaps in floorboards that allow cold drafts. Felt is better than any solid filler because it can expand and contract with the boards.

• Weatherstrip around doors and windows. This is especially important where there are no storm windows to cut down on drafts.

• On very old houses, check for gaps where the roof rafters meet the side walls. They may be big enough that you'll have to stop them up with fitted blocks of wood.

DON'T WORRY if you don't stop 100% of the air infiltration—a house has to take in some fresh air to replace oxygen used by respiration and combustion.

THE ALTERNATE FUEL FALLACY

SOME PEOPLE SEEM TO FEEL that all they have to do to solve the energy crisis is to switch to burning wood in a fireplace or stove. Besides the fact that a fireplace is the least efficient of all home heating systems, there is an additional fallacy in the switch-to-wood syndrome.

YOU CAN ONLY FEEL energy-vrtuous if: (1) You are burning only fallen wood; or (2) You are managing your own woodlot and are growing as much wood as you are burning.

TREES, although renewable, are not an infinite resource. There are many countries—including China—that have been stripped virtually bare of trees by wood-burning householders.

REGARDLESS OF THE SOURCE of the energy, the old-house owner's first priority should be to make your house consume LESS. If no one has ever fitted up your home for maximum energy savings, you should be able to save at least 25–40% of your annual energy consumption by following the steps outlined in this article.

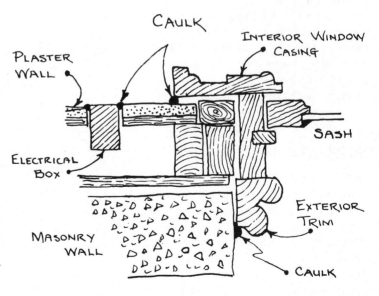

Caulk Helps Stop Air Infiltration

TOP VIEW – CROSS-SECTION — WINDOW FRAME

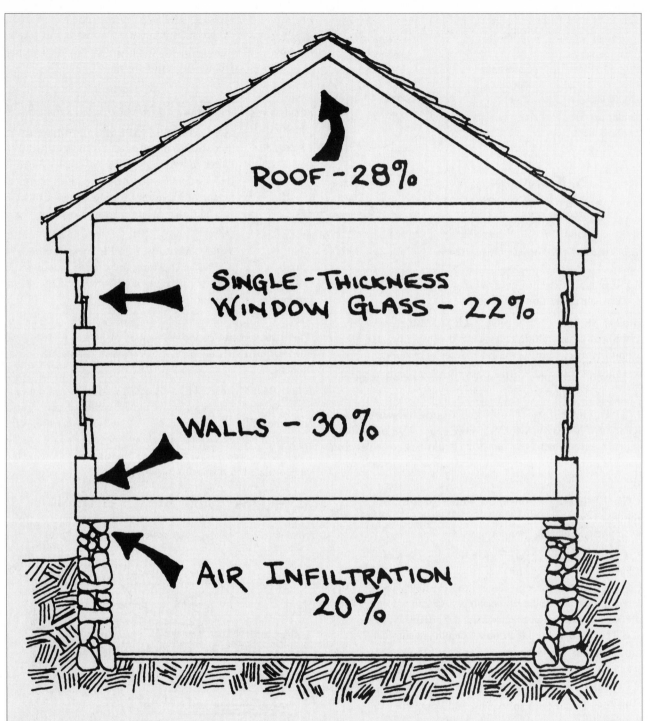

ROOF - 28%

SINGLE - THICKNESS
WINDOW GLASS - 22%

WALLS - 30%

AIR INFILTRATION
20%

Relative importance of sources of heat loss in the typical old house without insulation or storm windows. Heating, air conditioning and water heaters account for the bulk of energy consumed in the average household. This is where the greatest savings can be made.

INSULATION AND THE OLD HOUSE

By William N. Papian, P.E.

INSULATION'S JOB is to impede the flow of heat. In cold weather, you want to keep the heat inside; in hot weather you want to keep the heat out. Heat travels in three ways: By conduction, by radiation, and by convection. An effective insulation job takes account of all three.

CONDUCTION—Most heavy, dense materials are good heat conductors, e.g., metal, masonry, etc. Less dense materials, such as wood, are intermediate. Lightweight materials, such as fabrics, foamed plastics, spun fiberglass, etc., are poor conductors.

RADIATION—Heat travels through space, just as light does, by radiation. To block heat radiation, you need only insert an opaque material in the path of the rays. Most building materials—except glass—are opaque to heat radiation.

CONVECTION—Heated fluids, whether gases or liquids, rise and promote general mixing within the fluid. Thus, air convection helps to heat an entire room from a single wall "radiator" or baseboard convector. Convection is reduced by compartmenting and mechanically blocking fluid movement.

INSULATION VALUES

EFFECTIVE HOUSE insulation has to do all three things: Conduct poorly, block radiation and reduce convection. For example, fiberglass batting is a good insulation, even though glass is an intermediate conductor. The reason: The air that makes up the greatest volume of the material is about the poorest heat conductor we know. In addition, the several-inch-thick mat is opaque to light and heat radiation. And the great amount of air in the mat is largely blocked and compartmented into tiny volumes so that both internal and pass-through convection is kept very low.

THE FOLLOWING TABLE gives a rough indication of the relative insulation value of some ordinary building materials. You'll see that the best insulator in the table (expanded urethane) has almost 60 times the insulating value of the poorest material in the table (concrete).

	Resistance, R, per inch of thicknes
Concrete	0.1
Gypsum Plaster	0.2
Brick	0.2
Wood	1.3
Impregnated Sheathing	2.6
Fiberglass Blanket	3.4
Expanded Urethane	5.9

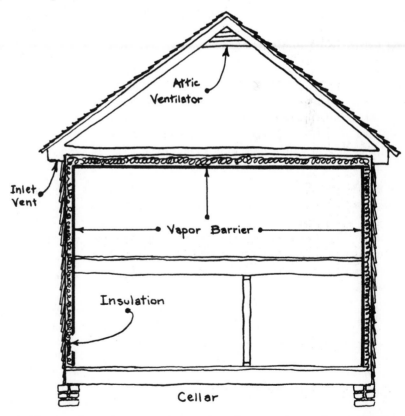

Ideal location of vapor barriers, insulation and ventilation in a 2-storey house with full basement.

WITH THESE PRINCIPLES in mind, let's look at some of the commercial materials and methods.

FOAMED PLASTICS

FOAMED PLASTICS are available primarily as boards (Styrofoam, for example). They have the highest insulation values—and are also the most expensive. Because the boards can be neither bent nor stuffed to fill a space tightly, this form is useful primarily in new construction or for fastening to basement walls. The foamed plastics are generally good vapor barriers.

PLASTICS CAN ALSO BE FOAMED in place, a technique advertised for side-wall work in old houses. Polystyrene, polyurethane and ureaformaldehyde resins are all being foamed in place by specialized contractors. Results have been mixed. At one extreme, the foams—applied through holes in the exterior siding or the interior plaster—may leave unfilled cavities. At the other extreme, the foams may burst some walls through loss of control or through swelling. Also, the odor of the ureaformaldehyde resin may persist for some time.

AN ADDITIONAL CAUTIONARY NOTE: Some foamed plastics emit toxic fumes when burning under certain conditions. Before installing any plastic foam insulation, your local fire marshal's opinion should be solicited.

ALUMINUM FOIL

ALUMINUM FOILS function primarily by reflecting radiation. In its simplest form it consists of a single sheet of foil so placed that it drastically reduces incoming or outgoing radiation. Aluminum is, of course, a good conductor, so that if both faces of a sheet touch adjacent surfaces it is no insulator at all. And if its reflective surface gets dirty, its insulating quality is reduced.

MOST COMMON FORM of foil insulation consists of several sheets of aluminum-faced paper separated from each other by short, angled strips of paper, also aluminized. The material comes flattened and rolled. A proper pull across the width of the material causes it to snap open and hold its shape, separating the shiny inside faces. Edge flanges allow for stapling to the studs of exterior walls during construction. A two-space type may yield an insulating value up to R–5. It is also a good vapor barrier when properly installed, is relatively fireproof, and impervious to damage from moisture or vermin. It is limited pretty much to new construction, however.

FIBERGLASS BLANKETS

FIBERGLASS BLANKETS are available in rolls or batts (4-ft. sections), in two widths (15 or 23 in.) in thicknesses up to 6½ in. There are a variety of facings: Single, double, paper, aluminum foil or unfaced. R values run approximately 3 to 3½ per inch, and the facings provide good vapor barriers. The material can be hung by its flanges between studs, laid or stuffed in place, or wrapped around objects like ducts.

FIBERGLASS rolls or batts are excellent for accessible areas: Attics, crawlspaces, half open walls, etc. Vapor-barrier problems must be kept in mind (see below). And it is wise to staple additional support under the material if it is placed in the ceilings of crawl spaces or between rafters from below.

ONE SPECIAL PRECAUTION should be taken with the blanket form of insulation. It should be installed so that gross air movements resulting from infiltrating wind or natural convection are effectively blocked. One example occurs when batts are stapled to the bottoms of the joists over a crawl space. This makes a neat-looking installation, but the air space between the batt and the subfloor is bound to cause trouble. There are bound to be leaks around the batting. These leaks will set up convection currents in the air space that will greatly reduce the insulation value.

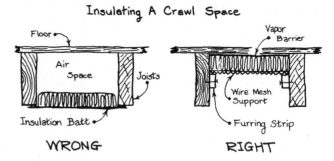

Insulating A Crawl Space

WRONG — RIGHT

SIMILAR PRECAUTIONS should be observed in insulating walls and floors. Careful stuffing and fitting is the only answer. For attic floors, additional protection against leaks and convection currents can be provided by adding some poured insulation on top of the fiberglass rolls or batts.

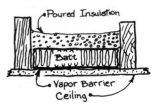

POURED AND BLOWN

AMONG THE INSULATIONS that pour or blow well are expanded mica, spun fiberglass (commonly called blowing wool) and cellulosic fibers. Expanded mica (Vermiculite is one trade name) is not used much for home insulation. Although it handles well, its granularity causes it to dribble out of small holes. It also packs down to a higher density than desired. It is costlier, for a given insulation value, than other types. R values run between 2.5 and 3 per inch.

FIBERGLASS WOOL (and it predecessor, rock or mineral wool) is the most frequently encountered in this class. It is not particularly suited for do-it-yourself application because it comes in a compacted form requiring a truck-mounted machine to shred and blow the stuff. It is fine for attic applications, with the following reservations: It is easily blown around by any wind or drafts in the attic, frequently being found piled back from eaves having soffit ventilation. It clings to shoes and clothing. Finally, some people have skin and mucous-membrane sensitivities to fiberglass and its dust.

FIBERGLASS WOOL would be a good candidate for blowing into the sidewalls of an old house except for its propensity to catch on nail ends, splinters, etc., leaving serious voids. Blowing wool R values are about 2.25 per inch, a bit lower than batts (although under the right conditions wool will pack more uniformly to give better overall results).

CELLULOSIC INSULATION

OF SPECIAL INTEREST to old-house owners is cellulosic insulation. This consists of short fibers of cellulose (often reclaimed paper) chemically treated to yield a reasonably fire-retardant material that pours or blows very well. Its R value is about 3.7 per inch, and it doesn't hang up unduly on small projections within walls. Although cost is slightly higher than its fiberglass counterpart, in my opinion this is the best material for side wall application in old houses.

CELLULOSIC INSULATION can be blown into side walls by a contractor with blowing equipment. In a typical house, holes 1 in. in dia. are made every 16 in. (to provide access to each between-stud cavity). This has to be repeated for each storey. In addition, fire-stops and between-storey framing may require additional holes. Holes can be made through the interior plaster or exterior siding. If large openings are available due to restoration activities, insulation may be poured in. Of course, it will trickle out if any holes or significant crevices exist below the pouring or blowing levels.

HOLES MADE FOR THE BLOWING NOZZLE are then closed with circular wooden plugs and finished over. It is possible for the adventurous do-it-yourselfer to rent equipment for blowing cellulosic insulation through 1 in. holes.

OF COURSE, pouring (or blowing) cellulosic insulation into between-joist spaces on attic floors is quite simple. It bothers sensitive skins and throats less than fiberglass, and is a bit more likely to stay in place.

MOST OF THE CELLULOSIC INSULATION used in the greater Washington, D.C., area is made by Cellin Manufacturing, P.O. Box 224, Lorton, Va. 22079. The root tradename for their product is "Cellin," followed by a suffix that indicates whether the product is for pouring (Cellin Craft), blowing (Cellin Pac), or spraying (Cellin Spray). Cost to have a contractor blow cellulose insulation into side walls varies from 35–75¢ per sq. ft. (depending on complexity of the job) including finishing over of the holes.

HOW MUCH?

BASED ON RECENT STUDIES—taking into account expected future prices—attics can profitably use insulation with total R values in the 20s or 30s. That corresponds to 6–8 in. of cellulosic fiber insulation. Side walls and crawl spaces can use half that amount. Pay-back periods (at present interest rates) are only a few years for installing that much insulation in uninsulated areas. Payout is closer to 10 years when doubling existing 1- or 2-in. amounts.

THE CONDENSATION PROBLEM

MOST PROBLEMS caused by improperly installed insulation result from an inadequate understanding of condensation mechanics. Peeling paint and serious rot conditions inside the walls may be the consequence . . . even though the house was perfectly sound before the insulation was put in. A detailed analysis of condensation causes and cures will appear in Part II of this article.

FOR AN UNUSED and unfloored portion of an attic that already has some insulation, it is usually worth it to add additional insulation if an additional inch or so will provide some modest cover over the floor joists. Wood is an intermediate conductor, and the joists usually account for about 10% of the floor area.

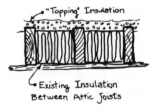

ELECTRICALLY HEATED HOMES can use half again as much inslation as the above figures indicate.

OTHER FACTORS

INSULATION may actually be a secondary consideration in an old house that has loose fitting old doors and windows. The amount of heat loss through these apertures is enormous. In these cases, caulking, weather stripping and storm windows and doors may well have the first priority. A dollar invested in these first-line measures usually has a better payout than an insulation job.

ALTHOUGH THIS ARTICLE was written primarily with winter heating in mind, the insulating measures described will also help considerably with summer cooling.

INSULATION AND THE OLD HOUSE

By William N. Papian, P.E.

MOST PROBLEMS CAUSED by improperly installed insulation stem from a poor understanding of the condensation factor. Moisture-laden air tends to travel to the outside through walls and ceilings. Kitchens, bathrooms and laundries throw off an amazing amount of water vapor—all of which has to go someplace. In a drafty old house, there are plenty of cracks and crevices that allow the water to escape harmlessly. If you suddenly turn around and tightly seal and insulate every crack, you may generate serious rot and paint peeling problems that you never had before. The solution is to make sure that all water-generating centers have adequate ventilation—and that you understand the principles of vapor barriers.

CONDENSATION PROBLEMS occur in cold weather. As moisture-laden warm air travels through walls, it will soon drop below the dew point and some of the moisture will start condensing out—almost always on the first hard surface it meets. The resulting dampness inside the wall can reduce insulation values and promote rot.

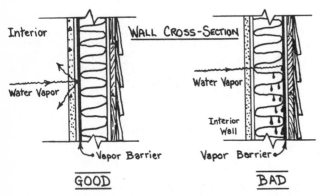

VAPOR BARRIERS are used to prevent moisture from getting inside the partitions in the first place. Vapor barriers should always be placed on the warm side of the insulation—NEVER on the cold side. For example, if you are pouring insulation in the attic floor, lay down a vapor barrier first. (Thin plastic sheeting is adequate.) With blanket insulations, be certain to place the kraft paper or aluminum-foil side toward the inside of the house.

IN SOME CASES—such as blowing insulation into a side wall—it is impossible to install a vapor barrier. In this case, you had better be sure the exterior wall is reasonably porous to air. Most clapboard exteriors are sufficiently porous. If events show that additional ventilation is needed, small wooden wedges can be inserted under the clapboards. In severe cases, metal vents can be used to provide the additional air flow needed to carry the water vapor away harmlessly.

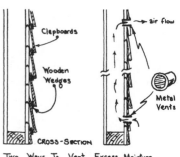

WHEN LOOSE FILL insulation has been used in side walls, it is also a good idea to make sure that the interior surfaces of the walls are as vapor-resistant as possible. This means spackling all cracks—especially those around window frames, baseboards, etc. Any electrical boxes in the outer walls should be carefully caulked to seal the space between the metal and the plaster. This type of sealing might seem unnecessary, but tests have shown that there is enough moisture loss through

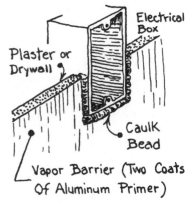

the perimeter of an outlet box to form a large ball of frost on the back face during extended cold periods. When this frost melts as the weather warms up, the water released can damage exterior paint films and promote rot inside the wall. In cold climates, sealing of the outlet boxes in insulated walls is especially important in rooms that generate a lot of water vapor, such as the bath and kitchen.

THE SAME PRINCIPLES used in sealing outlet boxes should be applied to all openings in an insulated outside wall. Such openings include exhaust fans in bath or kitchen, air registers and plumbing openings. (Even if your side walls aren't insulated, you should consider sealing these apertures just to cut down on heat loss.)

ADDITIONAL MOISTURE RESISTANCE can be added to side walls with blown-in insulation by coating with two coats of aluminum paint. The decorative paint can then be added on top of the aluminum. This does not offer as much vapor resistance as a continuous membrane—but it helps.

ATTIC PROBLEMS

MOISTURE ESCAPING from the house into the attic tends to collect in the coldest part of the attic. Condensation or frost on protruding nails, on the surfaces of roof boards, etc., indicates the escape of excessive amounts of water vapor from the heated rooms below. If a vapor barrier is not already present, place one between the joists UNDER the insulation. If the insulation is of the loose fill type, the best procedure is to scoop it all up and lay down thin plastic sheeting as described above. Sheeting should lap against the joists for best seal. Less effective—but better than nothing—is the painting of ceilings below the attic with two coats of aluminum paint.

MAKE SURE the vapor barrier fits tightly around ceiling lights and exhaust fans. Caulk if necessary. In addition, the attic should have both inlet and outlet ventilators. Recom-mended number and sizes of vents for various sizes of attics are given in government publications.

SOLID MASONRY WALLS

THE FULL MASONRY WALL, plastered on the inside, is difficult to insulate because there are no void spaces to fill with insulation. If you are willing to give up some interior space, then insulation can be added to the wall. One tech-nique is to cement insulating foam board directly to the wall. (This can be done with or without removing the old plaster.) The insulating board can be plastered, left exposed, or covered with any desired finish material.

ANOTHER ALTERNATIVE is to attach 2 x 2 furring strips to the wall on 16-in. centers. Then 1-in. blanket insulation can be stapled between the strips. Thicker insulation can be used if you use bigger furring strips. This same procedure can be used to insulate cold basement walls.

THE ABOVE TECHNIQUES have great drawbacks, obvi-ously, for historic houses or houses with rich interior detail. Not only do you lose the original plaster surface, but the trim around doors and windows has to be changed (or moved out) to accommodate the added wall thickness.

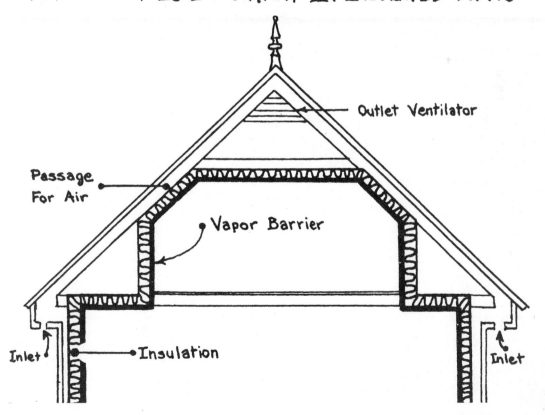

VENTILATION IS IMPORTANT IN INSULATED ATTIC

Outlet Ventilator

Passage For Air

Vapor Barrier

Inlet

Insulation

Inlet

A TYPICAL DILEMMA

TYPICAL of the questions that arise about insulation are contained in this letter from a *Journal* reader: "Two years ago we purchased an 1834 Greek Revival house—uninsulated. Some contractors have told us that blown insulation is best. Others tell us that this cuts off air circulation and causes condensation and wood rot. Also, wind enters under the house in one section where there is only a crawl space. Is there any reason why this space cannot be sealed?"

ANSWER: Blown cellulosic insulation should be satisfactory for the side walls. Its moisture handling ability is reported to be superior to fiberglass. Any small amount of moisture that enters the cellulose is absorbed, spread over a considerable volume, then is given up when the atmosphere is drier.

THE INTERIOR WALLS should be made as vapor-tight as possible, sealing all crevices as discussed earlier, and two coats of aluminum paint applied.

THE CRAWL SPACE can be fixed by fastening blanket insulation between the floor joists as detailed in Part I. The crawl space itself should not be sealed off. Enough ventilation should be allowed so that water vapor from the ground can be vented. Ventilation requirements are greatly reduced when plastic sheeting is used as a soil cover to retard evaporation of moisture from the earth.

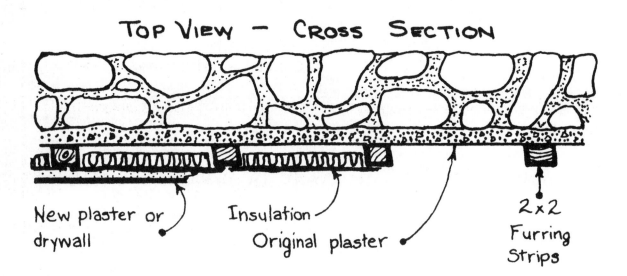

TOP VIEW — CROSS SECTION

New plaster or drywall

Insulation

Original plaster

2 x 2 Furring Strips

One Way To Insulate A Solid Masonry Wall

Wiring, Plumbing, Plastering

HOW TO MAKE AN ELECTRICAL SURVEY

OLD-HOUSE OWNERS frequently inherit a raggle-taggle electrical system. The first step in updating or expanding the system is to determine exactly how the circuits are divided and the amount of load on each.

HAVING A ROAD-MAP to your electrical system is especially valuable when you want to add outlets or lights; you can see which circuits are lightly loaded and which are filled to capacity. A complete index to your electrical system is also helpful when you want to kill power to a particular fixture; you can flip the correct circuit breaker right away without darkening the whole house with trial-and-error fumblings.

TO MAKE YOUR OWN ELECTRICAL SURVEY doesn't require any special tools—just several hours of time. You'll want to record the information in a good-quality bound notebook . . . the kind that will withstand years of use. It's also highly desirable to have a helper who can do a lot of the plugging and unplugging while you work at the fusebox.

THE BASIC PRINCIPLE of an electrical survey is simplicity itself: You start in one room and determine by trial and error which fuse or circuit breaker controls each electrical fixture. If you have an old fuse box, you may have to assign your own numbers to each fuse. You will need an on/off indicator for the outlets. You can use any small portable electrical appliance such as a radio or table lamp. Or you can make

you own indicator out of a pigtail socket (available at lighting stores) to which you attach a plug. If you have to work alone, you can save some back-and-forth by using a loud portable radio to indicate when power has been cut to an outlet But overhead lights require visual inspection . . . which may mean a lot of trips up and down the cellar stairs.

START BY MAKING A MAP of each room in the house, indicating each electrical fixture. Then note beside each fixture the number of the fuse or circuit breaker that controls it. When this is done, set up a second section in your notebook, listing—on separate pages—each circuit in numerical sequence. Then list under each circuit all the fixtures it controls, picking up the information from your room maps.

THIS CIRCUIT-BY-CIRCUIT LISTING usually reveals some surprising things. For example, one homeowner, who had just spent $1,600 on extensive rewiring, found that the electricians had put the refrigerator and dishwasher on the same circuit (major appliances should have their own circuits) while the solitary load on a nearby circuit was the fluorescent light on the kitchen stove!

ELECTRICAL SYSTEM IS CROSS-INDEXED BY CIRCUIT AND BY ROOM

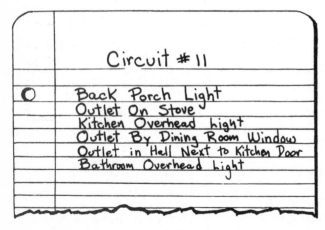

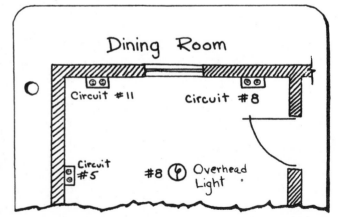

RUNNING ELECTRICAL WIRE 1

By James R. McGrath

OLD HOUSES were not designed for the miracles of all-electric living. While that may be a blessing in some ways, there *are* certain minimum standards of convenience and electrical safety you want your house to meet. A renovation of an old electrical system can be an expensive—and harrowing—process.

IN THIS ARTICLE we'll review one of the most vexing aspects of an electrical renovation—running wires through an old house. Whether you are doing the work yourself or having it done for you, these tips can be valuable. Electricians who are unfamiliar with old houses will often insist that wire can't be run between certain points . . . or that some ornate plasterwork will have to be hacked away . . . or that running exposed surface wiring is the only way a job can be accomplished.

BY STUDYING THE ANATOMY of your house—and planning exactly where the wire is to run—you'll be prepared for the "it can't be done" arguments. The easiest (and cheapest) way to run wire is through the "secret passages" built into your house—the pipe chases, vents, crawl spaces, etc. A guide to finding these hidden passages was contained in an article in the January 1974 issue of *The Journal*.

MANY ELECTRICIANS hate to work on old houses because the bulk of the work isn't electrical; it's more like carpentry. To run wire through partitions, under floors, behind walls and over ceilings requires an intimate knowledge of the innards of a house. That's why the two most important tools in running wire in an old house are not pliers and wire cutters, but rather plaster chisel and fish wire.

THE FOLLOWING GUIDELINES are based on the assumption that you're doing electrical work yourself (local codes permitting). But even if you're not familiar enough with electricity to handle 110-volt and 220-volt wiring, the same wire-running techniques also apply to such low-voltage applications such as doorbells, intercoms and hi-fi systems where there is no safety hazard involved.

THE FIRST RULE OF RUNNING WIRE IS: Always have a helper. My own experience has taught that having 4 hands on the job rather than 2 doesn't just make a job twice as easy. There are some wire snaking operations that are simply impossible to do by yourself. So before attempting any complicated wire running, be sure you have lined up a spouse or friend for help.

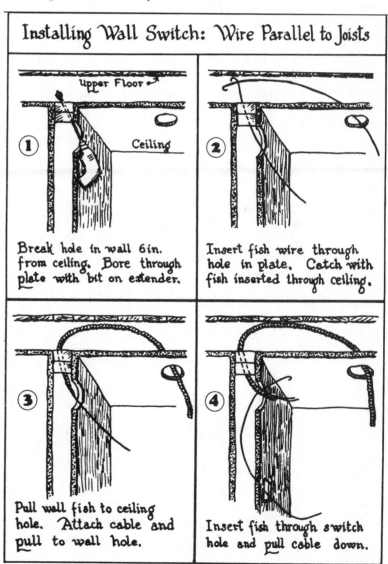

Installing Wall Switch: Wire Parallel to Joists

① Break hole in wall 6in. from ceiling. Bore through plate with bit on extender.

② Insert fish wire through hole in plate. Catch with fish inserted through ceiling.

③ Pull wall fish to ceiling hole. Attach cable and pull to wall hole.

④ Insert fish through switch hole and pull cable down.

GOING FISHING

KEY TO RUNNING ELECTRICAL CABLE in an old house is learning how to use fish wire (sometimes also called a "snake"). Electricians' fish wire is steel tape about 3/16 in. wide and 1/16 in. thick. It is flexible enough to go around corners, yet stiff enough not to buckle when being pushed through partitions. Fish wire is inexpensive, so you should have at least two long ones (about 30 ft.) and a couple of short ones (10 ft.)—plus a 4-ft. "hooker"—on hand if you are getting involved with any extensive projects.

THE THEORY OF USING FISH WIRE is simple enough. If you want to run BX electrical cable between points A and B in a partition, you simply break open small holes at A and B. Fish wire is pushed in at A and shoved into the partition until you (or your helper) can see it through the Point B hole. BX cable is then attached to the end of the fish wire at B and the fish is pulled back at A. The cable is threaded through the partition as the fish is withdrawn. Simple!

OF COURSE, reality is seldom as simple as theory. There are dozens of different obstacles lurking inside ceilings, floors and walls just waiting to snag your fish wire. A fish wire can hang up on a piece of lath, a chunk of old plaster, bridging, firestops, existing electrical wire—and even abandoned fish wire! (During a recent ceiling restoration, I found a highly serviceable 50-ft. fish between the joists that some long-departed electrician had abandoned after getting it impossibly snagged in some bridging. You could almost hear his cuss words as he tried to work it loose!)

BEYOND A FEW HINTS THAT I'LL PASS ALONG, about the only other counsel one can offer on using fish wire are the restorer's two stand-bys: Patience and Persistence.

BEFORE SENDING A FISH WIRE INTO A PARTITION, make sure you've made a neatly rounded hook on the end (this is a two-plier operation). By putting a good reverse bend on the end you'll help avoid snags when pulling back on the fish.

Reverse Bend

FISH HAVE A PRONOUNCED CURL in them because they are stored rolled up. This curl can be made to work for you. Orienting the curl in one direction tends to put the hook along one specific surface in a passage.

Curl carries fish into blockage. Try again!

Turning fish over puts hook against opposite surface. Push on!

If you hit a blockage, withdraw the fish and turn it over so the curl is facing in the opposite direction. This maneuver will force the hook to the opposite surface and will often take your fish by the obstacle.

THE OTHER TRICK TO USING FISH is developing the art of the wiggle. Often a fish can't be pushed by an obstacle with brute force. But by wiggling and shaking it—along with steady pressure—you can make the hook on the end jump around the obstruction.

WHEN THE RUN INVOLVES LINKING UP TWO FISH (as in the drawing above), even more patience is required. You have to depend on a combination of sound and touch to determine when the two fish are in contact, and then carefully withdraw one so that the two hooks link together.

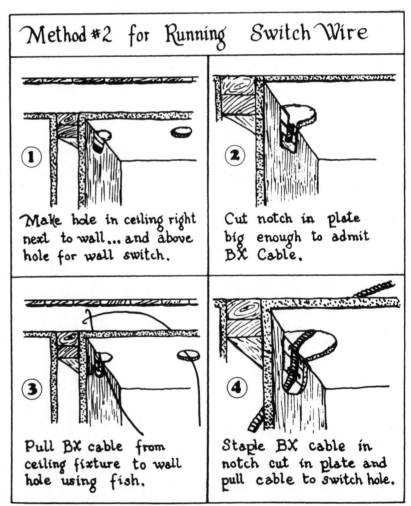

Method #2 for Running Switch Wire

① Make hole in ceiling right next to wall... and above hole for wall switch.

② Cut notch in plate big enough to admit BX Cable.

③ Pull BX cable from ceiling fixture to wall hole using fish.

④ Staple BX cable in notch cut in plate and pull cable to switch hole.

AS A LAST RESORT, if you find you can't get a fish beyond a certain point no matter what you try, you can always open the partition at that point. It's not an elegant solution, but you get at the problem quickly. And it is often better to spend 1 hour patching a hole—after having solved the problem—than to spend an hour in utter frustration trying to force a fish by an obstacle that just won't yield.

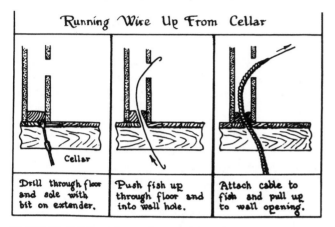

Running Wire Up From Cellar

Drill through floor and sole with bit on extender.

Push fish up through floor and into wall hole.

Attach cable to fish and pull up to wall opening.

BESIDES FISH WIRE, other tools you'll need for running electrical cable are a hammer, a cold chisel (for hacking plaster), a keyhole saw (for cutting lath), and a power drill with carbide-tipped bits (for drilling in plaster), spade bits (for boring beams) and a bit extender. And of course you'll need your standard kit of plaster patching tools.

PLANNING THE RUN

BEFORE SETTING hammer to plaster, consider all possible ways to get cable between the starting point and end point. For example, take the problem shown at the top right—a common one for old-house owners. To add a wall switch to a ceiling fixture, you have to run wire from ceiling to wall. First task is to note in which direction the ceiling joists run. It's much simpler to run wire in the void parallel to the joists than to cross the ceiling perpendicular to the beams—which requires a lot of cutting and notching.

IF YOU DON'T KNOW in which direction the joists run, you may be able to find out by probing with a wire through the hole at the ceiling fixture. Otherwise, you will have to do some probing with a nail or drill (holes can be readily patched with spackle).

IF YOU HAVE any leeway in locating the wall switch, obviously it will be easiest to place it on the wall directly under one of the between-the-joists voids.

BUT IF YOU HAVE NO choice about switch location and the wire has to run perpendicular to the

joists, you still have two choices. Instead of running across the joists, you could select Path #1 shown in the diagram above. The wire comes to the wall in a void parallel to the joists, then crosses the wall studs to the switch location. The choice depends upon the construction of the house. The across-the-wall method, although the longer path, does have the advantage of eliminating a lot of ceiling work that would have to be done on a ladder.

Problem: Run switch wire from ceiling light to Point A on wall.

THE ACROSS-THE-WALL METHOD is especially attractive if there is thick lath and plaster, plus a baseboard that is readily removed. In this event, you can gouge a channel for the cable in the plaster behind the baseboard and not have to worry about a lot of patching because the baseboard will conceal the cable. Crossing the ceiling joists is also simplified if you are working on the top floor. In this case, you can usually take the cable up and over through the attic or crawl space.

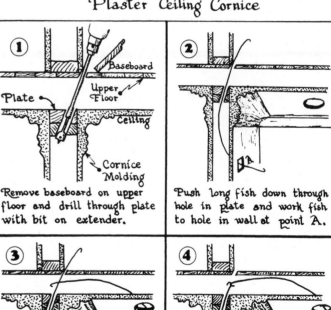

How To Run Cable Around Ornate Plaster Ceiling Cornice

① Remove baseboard on upper floor and drill through plate with bit on extender.

② Push long fish down through hole in plate and work fish to hole in wall at point A.

③ Insert fish through ceiling hole and wiggle it until it snags the first fish.

④ Pull first fish until it hooks ceiling fish. Attach cable and pull through to wall hole.

Top View: Ceiling Joists

A   Wall

Fixture O   B

To install wall switch for
ceiling fixture, it's simpler to
run wire to B ~ parallel
to joists ~ than to Point A
which requires crossing joists.

Top View: Ceiling Joists

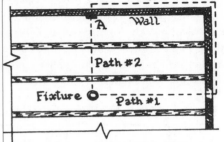

A   Wall

Path #2

Fixture O - - - Path #1

Path #1 to Point A allows
wire to be run parallel
to joists, then across wall.

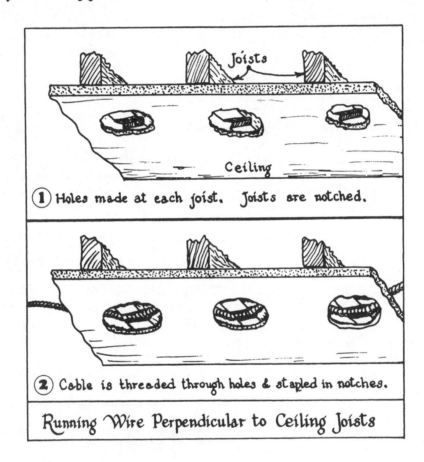

Joists

Ceiling

① Holes made at each joist.   Joists are notched.

② Cable is threaded through holes & stapled in notches.

Running Wire Perpendicular to Ceiling Joists

RUNNING ELECTRICAL WIRE 2

By James R. McGrath

MOST IN-WALL WIRE RUNS are related to the installation of wall switches or convenience outlets. Vertical runs of cable in walls between studs normally is quite simple. The one exception is when you encounter a firestop or horizontal bridging between the studs. (A firestop inhibits drafts inside walls and retards the spread of flames in the event of fire.) You will know that you've hit a horizontal brace if your fish wire won't pass, no matter how much you wiggle or twist it. Such a horizontal obstruction is passed by breaking open the plaster and notching the member. Exact location of the cross-member can be determined by noting how far the fish wire will penetrate the partition, or by dropping a weighted string into the wall.

Firestop inside wall may impede vertical runs of cable.

Studs

Firestop

Sole

FASTEST WAY to make the notch is to chip out the plaster with a cold chisel or an old screwdriver, then chew a channel through the lath and cross-member with a 1-in. spade

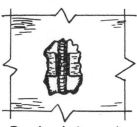

Break plaster and notch firestop to let cable pass through.

bit in your electric drill. Finish the notching with a hammer and chisel. If the notch has to be made in a wall that is papered, you can cut the paper in 3 places with a razor blade, making a flap that can be lifted and held out of the way with masking tape while you work. If the wallpaper is tightly stuck to the wall, you

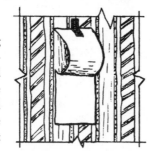

can loosen the paste by soaking the paper with warm water. After the cable has been run and the plaster carefully patched, the wallpaper can be pasted back in position and the incision will be practically invisible. (If you don't

have a small quantity of wallpaper paste on hand, you can use some white library paste—which is also water soluble—thinned with some additional water.)

HIDING BEHIND THE BASEBOARD

RUNNING WIRE perpendicular to the studs in a wall is a messy business at best because there is an obstacle—a stud—to be crossed every 16 in. Above the baseboard, the procedure is to break open the plaster at each stud and notch the lath and stud. Notch is made deep enough so that cable can be threaded through and stapled to the stud without making a bulge when the patching plaster is filled in. Because this process is so messy, it's obvious that you should try to get all of this type of wiring out of the way before doing any of the final decorating. When making notches in the studs, you should try to avoid breaking any lath, as this will weaken the plaster between

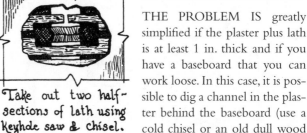

Holes are made at each stud. Studs are notched.

Cable is threaded through holes & stapled to studs.

the studs. Careful work with a keyhole saw and chisel will allow you to take out two half-sections of lath—giving plenty of room to pass the cable and yet maintaining the integrity of the continuous lath framework.

Take out two half-sections of lath using keyhole saw & chisel.

THE PROBLEM IS greatly simplified if the plaster plus lath is at least 1 in. thick and if you have a baseboard that you can work loose. In this case, it is possible to dig a channel in the plaster behind the baseboard (use a cold chisel or an old dull wood chisel). Run cable in the channel and fasten it to the studs with BX staples, then replace the baseboard. With this procedure, you don't have to worry about breaking up a decorated wall and you don't have to patch the plaster afterwards. This technique can be especially

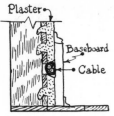

Plaster

Baseboard

Cable

Notch in plaster
between lath lets
cable run concealed
behind baseboard.

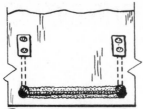

Points on same wall
can be connected by
removing baseboard and
making channel in plaster.

useful in adding a convenience outlet on a wall when you can use an existing outlet as the power source.

THE BASEBOARD usually can be pried loose by slipping a stiff putty knife behind it; it is usually just secured to the studs with finishing nails. Don't use a screwdriver for prying—it will mar the wood.

THE PLASTER AND LATH MAY NOT BE THICK ENOUGH to allow you to make a channel sufficiently deep to bury the entire cable. In this case, you'll have to notch each stud as described on the previous page and thread the cable behind the plaster. But by working behind the baseboard at least you don't have to worry about patching the holes.

THE BASEBOARD CAN BE REPLACED with a few finishing nails, with the heads countersunk and the holes filled with putty or spackle. Any unsightly gaps between the top of the baseboard and the wall can be filled with spackle before doing any touch-up painting.

LOOK FOR THE CLOSETS

TO RUN WIRE IN A ROOM in which you are reluctant to disturb the wall plaster, you may be able to take the wire across adjacent surfaces in adjoining rooms.

CLOSETS ARE PRIME CANDIDATES. Wherever possible, the cutting and notching required for cross-wall runs should be done on the inside of closet walls. This avoids damage to finished walls—and you don't have to be so fussy in patching closet interiors.

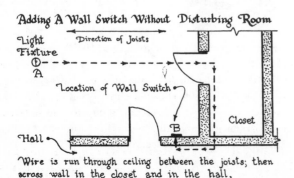

Adding A Wall Switch Without Disturbing Room

Direction of Joists

Light Fixture

Location of Wall Switch

Closet

Hall

Wire is run through ceiling between the joists; then across wall in the closet and in the hall.

IN THE EXAMPLE SHOWN BELOW, it is possible to get wire from the light fixture at Point A to the switch at Point B without ever disturbing the wall plaster in the room. The procedure is as follows: (1) Wire is run between the joists across the ceiling to the interior of the closet; (2) Inside the closet, holes are punched in the ceiling plaster and a couple of joists are notched to bring wire around the door opening; (3) Wire is brought down between studs in the closet to approximate height of switch; (4) Studs inside closet are notched and cable is threaded through wall. (Bringing cable across wall rather than ceiling avoids a lot of awkward overhead work); (5) Hole is punched through closet wall and cable is brought out to hall. Depending on condition of wall plaster, wire can be brought directly across the wall by notching the studs, or cable can be taken from the closet down between the studs and down the hall wall behind the baseboard; (6) Wire is brought up between the studs to the hole made for the new wall switch.

AROUND THE DOORS

SOMETIMES WHEN RUNNING CABLE BEHIND a baseboard to avoid damage to the wall you'll run smack into a doorway. It's possible, of course, to take cable around a door by notching studs—using the technique outlined previously. This is not a suitable procedure for a decorated wall, however.

USUALLY THERE IS a space of 1 inch or more between the door jamb and the framing studs. Wire can be run in this space—after you remove the casing on the doorway. The casing normally is held with finishing nails, and can be worked loose using a stiff putty knife. There may be some spacer blocks between the jamb and the frame that will have to be notched in order to recess the cable. After securing the cable in place using BX staples, the casing can be re-nailed, and the heads countersunk and filled with spackle or putty.

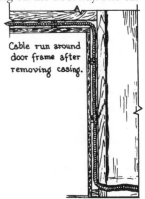

Cable run around door frame after removing casing.

NO TWO HOUSES ARE BUILT ALIKE and obstructions may show up in the most unlikely places. There's no substitute for common sense in working out some of these puzzlers. In many cases, the easiest route is not the most direct route; you're better off using a few extra feet of cable to save yourself aggravation. As a result, cable runs in old houses are generally longer than what would be required to do the same job in new wiring. I always specify ≠12 wire on all my old-house jobs to minimize voltage drops in these longer runs.

COPING WITH FRAYED ELECTRICAL WIRING

Many old houses have frayed electrical wires that can cause short circuits . . . . and possibly fires. Here are the danger signs to watch out for and what you can do to avoid rewiring the entire house.

MOST HOMEOWNERS have had this experience: You set out to install a new outlet, switch or ceiling fixture . . . and the insulation on the wire in the electrical box crumbles in your hand. Frustrating, yes. But it also signals bigger troubles ahead.

THE NATURAL TEMPTATION in such a situation is to wrap the offending wire with electrical tape, utter a fervent prayer and stuff the wire back into the box. However, crumbling insulation is symptomatic of advancing age in your electrical system—and should be given more thorough-going treatment.

THE BEST that comes out of such a condition is an eventual short-circuit that will blow a fuse or circuit breaker. The WORST would be current leakages and sparking that isn't large enough to blow a fuse—but is sufficient to cause a fire.

FRAYED WIRES ARE going to be common in houses that were wired in the 1920's or earlier. Now at age 80 or more, this wiring can be expected to show signs of senility.

WIRING IN MOST OLD HOUSES will be of the BX variety. This consists of a spiral metal armor (that also acts as a safety ground) and two or more rubber-insulated wires. Problems arise as the rubber becomes embrittled after prolonged exposure to air. The oxidized rubber may crumble away, allowing the two wires to contact each other (short circuit!), or allowing the hot wire to short out to the metal armor.

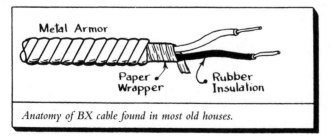

Anatomy of BX cable found in most old houses.

IN ADDITION to crumbling insulation, there is another warning sign that your wiring may be in a dangerously deteriorated condition: Current leakage from the hot (black) wire to the ground (white) wire.

Leakage can be detected with a neon-bulb circuit tester as indicated in the diagram. The ultimate symptom, of course, is a

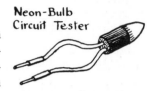

short circuit that blows a fuse or trips a circuit breaker. This is far preferable to the sparking that leakage can cause, however. Sparking leads to fires. When the fuse blows cleanly, the power is cut off and danger of fire is eliminated. And a blown fuse prompts immediate action to trace and cure the problem because otherwise the entire circuit is inoperable.

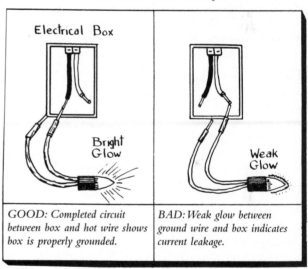

GOOD: Completed circuit between box and hot wire shows box is properly grounded.

BAD: Weak glow between ground wire and box indicates current leakage.

SOMETIMES CRUMBLING INSULATION can be dealt with merely by wrapping with electrical tape. There is the danger, however, that the crumbling insulation continues back into the box connector where it's not readily visible. If such is the case, it's a ready-made condition for a short circuit or fire.

AN ELECTRICIAN MIGHT TELL YOU that the only cure is to rip out all the old wiring and totally replace it. While such a step is doubtless the best solution, it is quite expensive—and messy. There is an in-between solution that is much less expensive and can extend the life of your old wiring by many years.

THIS IN-BETWEEN SOLUTION is possible because the insulation inside the armored section of the cable is almost always in far better condition than the insulation that has been directly exposed to the air for many years. So to get wire that has sound insulation, all you have to do is cut back a foot or so of the old BX armor and expose the wire that has been protected from air oxidation.

YOU MIGHT WISH to leave this task to an electrician. But if you live in an area where do-it-yourself wiring is permitted, here is what is involved.

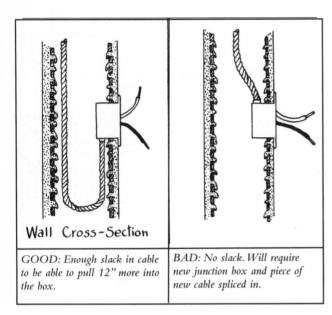

Wall Cross-Section

| GOOD: Enough slack in cable to be able to pull 12" more into the box. | BAD: No slack. Will require new junction box and piece of new cable spliced in. |

IF THE ELECTRICIANS who originally installed your wiring did a proper job, they left some slack in the BX cable into the box. You can then cut back the armor and get some fresh wire to work with. Here are the steps that you would follow:

1. BE SURE POWER IS TURNED OFF.

2. Chip away plaster around the box and unscrew box from the lath or stud.

3. Remove cable from box by loosening screws on cable clamp.

4. Pull slack cable out of wall and cut 12" off the BX armor. Be careful not to cut into insulation of the wires inside the armor. Insert plastic anti-short collar between end of armor and wires in the armor.

5. Cut off deteriorated section of wire and use the freshly exposed wire to reinsert into the box.

6. Re-clamp cable to box; re-mount box in wall; patch plaster.

Note: Detailed instructions on cutting of wire and mounting of electrical boxes is contained in the booklet cited below— or in any standard wiring text.

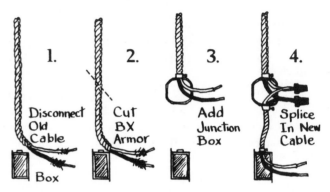

1. Disconnect Old Cable — Box
2. Cut BX Armor
3. Add Junction Box
4. Splice In New Cable

IF THERE ISN'T ENOUGH SLACK WIRE, the remedy is a little more complicated. What's involved is adding a junction box and splicing in a new piece of BX cable.

WHILE A MESSY JOB—because a bigger hole in the wall is involved—it's usually a lot less expensive (and less messy) than ripping out and totally replacing the old wiring.

JUNCTION BOXES and spliced wiring can be installed either in walls or ceilings. The hole that is left in the plaster is a relatively simple matter for you—or a plasterer—to patch.

WHEN THERE ISN'T enough old cable to cut back, new BX cable must be spliced in.

SANDING HINT

One frequently encounters complex curves that must be sanded. Next time, try making a sanding block out of an old deck of cards. The cards will adjust themselves to the curves and provide even sanding pressure.

CO-EXISTING WITH OLD PIPING

By Clem Labine

PLUMBING is something that most old-house owners would rather not think about. Piping can hardly be considered the most glamorous part of restoration. Yet you ignore plumbing at your peril. If water from leaking pipes doesn't ruin your walls and ceilings, then the plumber will when he is making the repairs.

OBVIOUSLY, the ideal situation when taking on an old house is to replace all old piping—especially if you are doing a top-to-bottom restoration and have the place torn up anyway. We'll deal in greater detail with the fine points of laying out a whole new system in later installments of The Plumbing Clinic.

FOR NOW, we are going to assume that for reasons of economy or convenience you've decided to do the minimum amount of plumbing work. So we'll review some of the characteristics of old plumbing systems and ways that you can get the most mileage out of antique pipes. But one final warning: Plumbing work is just about the messiest job there is—second only to plastering. So before spending many hours and dollars decorating a ceiling or wall, be sure you won't have to tear it all apart a few months later to get at a rotten pipe buried in the partition.

INSTALLATION OF MAIN PIPING is beyond most homeowners. In many areas building codes require such work to be done by licensed plumbers. Besides, most of us don't have the special tools and skills to cut, fit and join big hunks of metal pipe. The advent of plastic pipe—where permitted by the codes—has simplified installation, but most of us are content to let the pros handle the big jobs. The vast majority of plumbers will do a competent job—as long as you know precisely what you want done and insist on it.

WHAT THE OLD-HOUSE OWNER *can* do is learn how to make simple hook-ups (like attaching a sink to roughed-in pipes), make repairs and to supervise a plumber in his placement of new lines.

THE ABILITY TO MAKE REPAIRS in old piping—no matter how crude—will save you many dollars and much grief. With many plumbers today, you seem to have to work out an appointment weeks in advance. It's harder to see a plumber than a doctor. Heaven help you if you have a plumbing emergency on a Saturday evening of a holiday weekend. By being able to jury-rig repairs yourself you can at least keep the piping in service until you can arrange an audience with the plumber—and avoid extra charges for rush service.

YOUR ABILITY TO MAKE REPAIRS depends on two things: (1) Analyzing the plumbing system in advance of any difficulty so that you know what pipes go where and what each does; (2) Having on hand the tools and materials that you will need to make emergency repairs. Your plumbing tool box should pass the "Sunday Afternoon Test": That is, could you make repairs with tools and materials on hand when all the hardware stores are closed?

TEST THE SHUT-OFF VALVE

ALL THE BOOKS TELL YOU that the first thing to do when checking out your plumbing is to locate the main water shut-off valve. The main shut-off valve is your final line of defense in event of emergency. If a leak occurs—and you can't isolate the problem line quickly—then you have to be able to shut off the flow of water to the entire house.

WHAT THE BOOKS OFTEN DON'T TELL the old-house owner is to be sure to *TEST* the main shut-off valve to be sure it works. Sometimes, an old valve that has remained undisturbed for years will be rusted tight in the open position. No amount of twisting on the handle will budge some of these "frozen" valves. In fact, excessive twisting with a wrench may succeed only in breaking the handle. You don't want to discover that you have a frozen valve just when your basement is starting to fill up with water!

ABOUT THE ONLY WAY TO DEAL with a stuck valve is to liberally soak the valve with a penetrating lubricant like "Liquid Wrench." Give the valve a few raps with a hammer to help the Liquid Wrench penetrate—then leave the valve alone for a day. If this doesn't loosen the valve, repeat the dousing and rapping. After doing this two or three times, if the valve stem is still stuck—so are you! It means you'll probably have to replace the whole valve. In the case of houses connected to a water main, this means cutting off the water out at the street. This is definitely licensed plumber time!

The fellow next door to me once changed his own shut-off valve without having the water turned off at the street. He packed the main water pipe on the street side of the valve in dry ice. The water in the pipe quickly froze, forming an ice plug that kept the water back while he put on a new shut-off valve. It worked fine for Fred—he was an eternal optimist!—but is a very chancy procedure and definitely not recommended.

AFTER MAKING SURE that the main shut-off valve works, you ought to label this all-important valve with a big tag so that someone who is not familiar with the system could shut it off in your absence.

ONCE YOU'RE SURE you can cut off the flow of water to the house, you are ready to turn your attention to the rest of the system.

KNOW YOUR PIPING

EVERY HOUSE HAS TWO SEPARATE PARTS to its plumbing system: (1) The supply pipes; (2) The DWV (Drain-Waste-Vent) piping. The supply side is easy to understand. You obviously need a pipe for hot water and a pipe for cold water running to each fixture. About the only thing to watch out for on the supply side—other than leaks—are the materials of which the piping is made.

MOST MODERN INSTALLATIONS use soldered copper or plastic pipe. In older installations, you may find brass, galvanized iron—or even lead. Sometimes you'll even find creative combinations of these metals. (A sure invitation for trouble; joints between dissimilar metals corrode from galvanic action.)

GALVANIZED IRON AND LEAD are also trouble. Galvanized iron has a shorter life than other materials—and is prone to scale build-up. If you have low water pressure in your house—and you have galvanized iron supply pipes—it's likely that you are getting pressure drop from scaled-up pipes. It only takes one plugged up section at a key spot to lower pressure throughout the entire house. The only way to tell for sure if scaling is the culprit is to remove a section and take a look. If you find significant scaling, you had best be prepared to replace all the galvanized pipe.

FUNCTIONING OF THE DRAIN-WASTE-VENT is less well understood by many people—especially the venting system. Water flows to the sewer (or septic tank) through the drain lines. The problem is that sewer gas can also flow back through these same pipes into the house.

THAT'S WHY EACH PLUMBING FIXTURE should be fitted with a trap. Traps form a water seal that prevents sewer gas from leaking out through the fixture. (Contrary to popu-

lar myth, the primary function is *not* to catch rings and hair pins that fall into the drain!)

BUT A TRAP ALONE is not enough. Sewer gas can accumulate behind the trap and leak into the house through any joint that isn't gastight. So main waste stack (also called "soil stack") is carried up through the roof—and left open to the atmosphere. Any accumulated sewer gas is then vented harmlessly to the atmosphere and dispersed by the wind.

PIPE TYPE TEST

IF THERE IS ANY DOUBT about the material of which your piping is made, a magnet and small knife will tell you quickly:

• COPPER—Magnet won't stick. When scratched with knife, color showing is orange-gold.

• BRASS—Magnet won't stick. When scratched, color is yellowish gold.

• LEAD—Magnet won't stick. Soft when scratched with knife; color is silvery gray.

• GALVANIZED & CAST IRON—Magnet sticks.

Vent lines prevent vacuums in the main soil stack from siphoning water out of the traps. All vents must connect to highest point in the system.

IN ADDITION TO THE VENT on the main soil stack, there should be a vent line between every fixture trap and the main soil stack . . . a vent line that carries up above the highest plumbing fixture in the house. Reason: Water falling down the main soil stack (especially from a flushing toilet) can create a vacuum via the aspirator effect in all the horizontal waste lines connected to the stack. Thus, water in the fixture traps could be pulled into the main stack by the vacuum—breaking the protective water seal in the trap.

Falling Water

Vacuum

Drain Line

Main Soil Stack

THE TRAP IS PROTECTED by the vent pipe inserted between the trap and the main soil stack. This vent line—open to the atmosphere at the roof—equalizes pressure on both sides of the trap . . . so no water-siphoning vacuums can form.

WITH OLD PLUMBING, alas, you may find that some fixtures are not properly vented. In these cases, you can probably continue to live with them. Codes usually make allowances for leaving old piping in place as long as it is in working order.

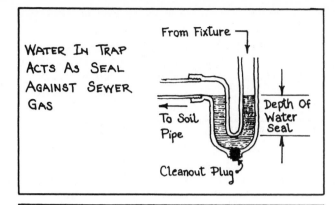

WATER IN TRAP ACTS AS SEAL AGAINST SEWER GAS

From Fixture

To Soil Pipe

Depth Of Water Seal

Cleanout Plug

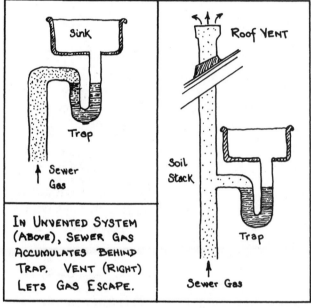

Sink

Trap

Sewer Gas

Roof Vent

Soil Stack

Trap

Sewer Gas

IN UNVENTED SYSTEM (ABOVE), SEWER GAS ACCUMULATES BEHIND TRAP. VENT (RIGHT) LETS GAS ESCAPE.

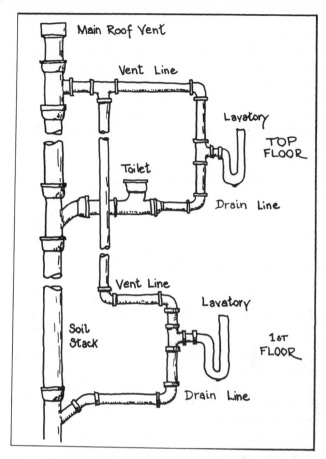

Main Roof Vent

Vent Line

Lavatory

TOP FLOOR

Toilet

Drain Line

Vent Line

Lavatory

Soil Stack

1st FLOOR

Drain Line

As for safety, as long as no one has been killed by sewer gas in the house in the last 100 years you can figure that there is no imminent peril. Many Brooklyn brownstoners have been peacefully co-existing with old lavatories that are not vented in accordance with the new codes.

IN ANY NEW PLUMBING WORK, however, all fixtures should be vented properly. (If common sense doesn't demand it, the plumbing inspector will!) The requirement for a vent doesn't present much of a problem when the work is being done on the top floor. On the ground floor, however, the requirement to run a vent line up to the top of the house can pose the annoying problem of how to conceal the pipe. The plumber will want to take the most direct route ... which often means exposed piping.

IN THIS SITUATION, it will pay you to know about the pipe chases and other "secret passages" in the walls of your house. Telling the plumber where you want the vent pipe to run may cause him to mumble and grumble ... but if you've thought it through carefully, he'll do it.

LEAD PIPING

IF YOU HAVE ANY LEAD supply or waste pipes, this stuff is probably 75–100 years old ... and near the end of its service life. Although you should plan on replacing it as soon as is practical, circumstances may require you to live with the lead pipes for a little while longer. Which means that you should know how to patch the pinhole leaks that inevitably occur.

SIMPLEST METHOD OF REPAIR is based on lead's softness. The procedure was demonstrated by a plumber that a fellow brownstoner called in one day when a lead supply pipe sprouted a pinhole leak. When the plumber arrived, he smiled at the dismay my friend exhibited while looking at the gentle rain of water. The plumber reached into his tool box and took out a ball peen hammer. He gave the pipe a sidewise rap in the area of the leak. The little spout of water stopped immediately. The lead was soft enough so that the lead closed over the pinhole after it was struck with the hammer.

IF YOU FIND YOU DON'T HAVE THE MAGIC TOUCH with a hammer, leaking lead piping can also be mended in the following manner: (1) Turn off water supply so that pipe empties of water; (2) Dry the area around the leak thoroughly with heat from a hair dryer, heat lamp or high-wattage light bulb. (If you use a propane torch as a heat source, be gentle—the flame is hot enough to melt lead!); (3) Thoroughly clean the pipe with steel wool or a wire brush on an electric drill so the lead is shiny at least 3 in. around the leak; (4) Apply plastic lead, plastic steel or equivalent patching compound to the leak. Build to at least 1/8-in. thickness and spread 2 in. all around the leak. Allow to dry thoroughly in accordance with manufacturer's directions.

LEAKS IN THE DWV SYSTEM

MOST LIKELY, the Drain-Waste-Vent system in your house is a combination of galvanized and cast iron. Horizontal drain lines are usually 1 ½-in. or 2-in. galvanized; the vertical soil stacks are normally 4-in. cast iron, as is the main horizontal waste line in the cellar that leads to sewer or septic tank.

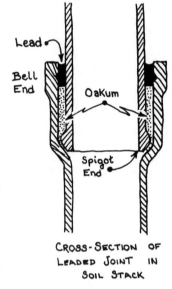

CROSS-SECTION OF LEADED JOINT IN SOIL STACK

THE 4-IN. CAST iron pipe is subject to two kinds of problems: (1) Loosened joints and (2) Leaks caused by rusting and/or cracking. Joints in the 4-in. cast iron pipe are rather complex affairs. First, the spigot end of one section is fitted into the bell end of the adjacent section. The joint is then packed with oakum (a specially treated fibrous material) and is driven tight with hammer and calking iron. Molten lead is then poured into the joint, on top of the oakum. On horizontal runs, an asbestos joint runner has to be clamped in place to hold the molten lead in place. After the lead cools, it is packed tight using a hammer and calking iron.

MOVEMENTS SUCH AS SETTLEMENT of the house can disturb the lead seal in these joints. The symptoms: Slow leaks ("weeping") from a horizontal line; the smell of sewer gas from either vertical or horizontal lines.

REPACKING THESE JOINTS is beyond the ability of most homeowners; handling molten lead is not something you un-

dertake casually. However, there is one thing you can try if you are absolutely determined to avoid another encounter with the plumber. Take a hammer and calking iron (or blunt cold chisel if you can't locate a calking iron at a plumbing supply store) and with sharp blows re-work the entire face of the lead. The object is to move the lead enough so that it once again seals tight against the iron.

CAST IRON PIPE can also fail due to cracking or rusting through. Cracks in vertical stacks are especially insidious. They can dump water into the walls intermittently for months before surface discoloration gives them away.

A PIPE THAT has cracked or that has a rust hole can be repaired so that it is serviceable for many months. But realize that the section (and maybe most of the waste pipe) is seriously flawed and probably will have to be replaced within 24 months.

1. Thoroughly Clean Area Around Leak

2. Brush On Epoxy Or Polyester Resin

3. Wrap With Fiberglass Cloth. Re-Coat With Resin.

TO REPAIR a small crack or pinhole leak in a cast iron pipe, you can use plastic lead or plastic steel, following the procedure outlined earlier for patching lead pipe. For larger holes and cracks, you can use the procedures shown at the right: Shut off flow of water and dry the pipe with heat. Clean the pipe with wire-brushing. (Use strip of coarse emery paper if pipe is close to wall and hard to get behind.) Coat cleaned pipe with polyester or epoxy resin—at least 6 in. on either side of the hole. Wrap with fiberglass strip; coat with resin then put on a second wrap of fiberglass. Finally, coat the whole patch with a topcoat of resin. Allow to cure overnight. This patch will last a long time; it's the rest of the pipe that you have to worry about.

Calking Iron

QUIETING A STEAM HEATING SYSTEM

MANY OLD HOUSES have steam heating systems that were installed 50 or more years ago. Although steam heat is considered old-fashioned, these systems can be efficient, economical, reliable—and silent—when they're working properly.

WHEN A STEAM system isn't adequately maintained, however, they can produce a veritable symphony of thumps, gurgles and hisses when the steam starts to circulate.

EVEN IF YOU HAVE a brand-new boiler, you're likely to have the thump-gurgle-hiss problem. That's because these noises usually originate in the steam distribution system (the pipes and the radiators). The heating plant (burner plus boiler) merely burns the oil or gas to generate steam. The job of the distribution system is to take the steam from the boiler to the rooms where you need the heat.

WHEN THE HEATING plant is replaced, it's usually hooked up to the old distribution system because of the heavy cost of replacing the pipes and radiators. And the old distribution system is the likely source of any noises that you hear.

ANATOMY OF A STEAM SYSTEM

TO DIAGNOSE the cause of your particular noise, you need to understand the anatomy of a steam heating system.

THE DISTRIBUTION system operates in what engineers call two-phase flow. That means there is a gas (steam) and a liquid (water condensed from the steam) both flowing in the same pipe—and they're going in opposite directions. The steam is rising by convection from the boiler up to the radiators where it condenses—liberating the heat that warms the room. The condensed water flows by gravity from the radiator down through the steam pipe back to the boiler.

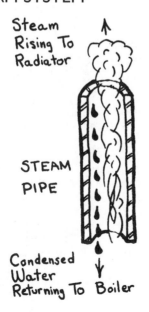

UNDERSTANDING THIS flow scheme is essential to tracking down the various noises you hear.

NOW LET'S SEE how you actually go about finding and silencing the sources of your steam symphony.

CURING THUMPS AND GURGLES

THUMPS AND gurgles are caused by bubbles of steam slugging through pockets of water. The cure is merely finding where water is collecting and eliminating these pockets.

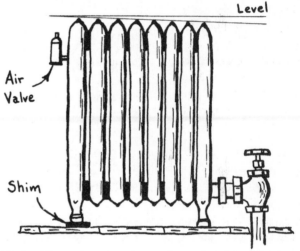

Placing shims under radiator assures that condensed water drains out properly.

FIRST THING to check is water level in your boiler. If it's too high, water can be entrained in the steam and carried up into the distribution pipes amid much sloshing. There's a sight glass on your boiler, and water level should be no higher than the indicated line—when the boiler isn't firing. If you fill to this line while the boiler's firing, you'll end up with too much water when all of the condensed steam returns.

IF THE GURGLES aren't caused by boiler water level, chances are the trouble is in one or more of the radiators. Probably the radiators are tipping the wrong way; i.e., sloping away from the steam valve. This will cause condensed steam to collect at the far end of the radiator, with resulting gurgling as steam bubbles through this little puddle.

Cure: Put wooden shims under the two feet farthest away from the steam valve. This makes the radiator tip slightly toward the valve (check with a level). Result: All condensed steam will drain back to the boiler.

SILENCING THOSE HISSES

THE ONLY TIME a radiator should hiss is from the air vent valve—just as the steam is starting to rise. But after 2–3 minutes the air valve should close with a noticeable pop.

ANY CONTINUOUS hissing means trouble somewhere. If the continual hissing comes from the air valve, it's a signal that the valve is shot and should be replaced.

AN AIR VALVE is an inexpensive hardware store item, and replacement is as simple as twisting the old one out and threading the new one in. Usually a wrench isn't needed. Caution: The new air valve should be installed in a vertical position for proper operation.

An air valve can be stuck open or stuck closed.

IF YOUR AIR valve *never* hisses, that's also a sign it should be replaced. An air valve that doesn't hiss isn't venting air. Result: Steam can't enter and radiator won't heat properly.

IF THE AIR VALVE isn't the source of your particular hiss, it's probably coming from the steam valve. This valve can leak at three places: At the packing nut, union nut or bonnet gasket (see diagram above).

A LEAK AT THE packing nut is most common—and easiest to fix. First, try tightening the nut with a wrench. (Be gentle! Those are brass threads.) By tightening, you compress the stem packing a little more and this usually seals off the leak. But there comes a time when the stem packing is so old that no amount of tightening is going to stop the leak. Then it's time to repack the stem.

FIRST, be sure the boiler is turned off. Do this by either throwing the Off/On switch or by turning the thermostat to its lowest setting.

STEM PACKING is a special graphite-impregnated cord available at hardware stores. To replace the packing, back the packing nut off completely and remove all of the old packing. Wrap two or three turns of the new packing around the stem *clockwise*. Tighten packing nut snugly—but not too tight.

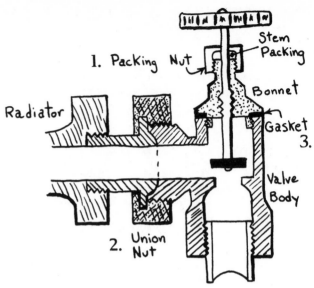

A steam valve can leak at Packing Nut (1); Union Nut (2); or at the Bonnet Gasket (3).

After you've turned the boiler back on, wait to see if the new stem packing leaks. If it does, tighten down on the packing nut until the hissing stops.

YOU MAY ALSO find steam leaking at the union between steam valve and radiator. (And water will probably be dripping on the floor.) First try tightening the union nut with a monkey wrench. Don't tighten too hard, though, because the threads are brass and it's fairly easy to strip them.

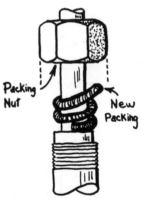

Leak at valve stem can be fixed with two turns of stem packing. Retighten Packing Nut after installing packing.

IF THE HISS doesn't stop, it means somebody else has *already* stripped the threads. At this point, you really should replace both the steam valve and union. For a do-it-yourselfer this is quite a production. But if you don't want to spend the money for a plumber to do it, you might get by with the following stop-gap:

BACK THE UNION nut off completely with a monkey wrench. Then wrap threads on the union with plumber's twine (available at hardware stores). Use only one strand from the multi-stranded twine, running it in the groove of the thread. Apply generous amounts of pipe dope to the threads, then tighten union nut snugly.

ALTHOUGH THIS is a stop-gap, a repair like this can last many years.

OTHER GURGLE-CAUSERS

Improper operation of the steam valve can also lead to gurgles and bangs.

Frequently people try to regulate the heat in a steam radiator by partially closing the valve. This practice will only lead to grief. A steam valve is meant to be *completely on or completely off*.

A partially closed valve may impede the return of condensed steam back to the boiler. As a result, you get hammering when the upcoming steam bubbles through the accumulated water adjacent to the partially closed valve.

You may inadvertently have the same thing happen with an old steam valve that has a worn-out seat. Result is that the valve won't shut off steam-tight. So when the valve is closed, rising steam can seep in, but the condensed water can't flow out. Water accumulates inside the radiator, and the steam leaking by the worn-out seat through the condensate can create quite a racket.

The only cure—short of replacing the valve entirely—is to leave the valve fully open all the time.

A MOST RARE MALADY

Most rare type of problem with a steam valve is a leak between the bonnet and valve body. Cause: The gasket between these two parts has deteriorated.

You can make a satisfactory replacement gasket out of stem packing. Here's how:

1. Back bonnet off, using a large adjustable wrench, so there is a 1/8" gap between the valve body and bonnet.

2. Remove what's left of the old gasket.

3. Wrap one turn of stem packing—liberally daubed with pipe dope—around the bonnet threads, overlapping the ends of the packing about 1 in. Be sure to wrap the packing *clockwise*.

4. Tighten bonnet down snugly.

THE ART OF GETTING PLASTERED

MINOR REPAIRS

RARE IS THE OLD HOUSE that doesn't have some problem plaster. If it's not a section of old plaster bulging from loose lath, then it's a bunch of holes made by zealous electricians or plumbers.

COPING WITH THESE PLASTER PROBLEMS ranges from simple to difficult. But hard or easy, problem plaster should be viewed as a challenge to restoration craftsmanship. Ripping plaster out wholesale should be a last resort. Since one of the reasons for living in an old house is the charm and sense of history it provides, it doesn't make sense to alter the architectural design of the house by covering old plas-

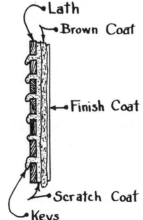

ter with Masonite panels, or tearing plaster off to expose the bricks below.

THIS JOURNAL SERIES on plastering will range from simple patching jobs to replastering entire walls and ceilings. Depending on your own level of craftsmanship, you can decide how many of these tasks you wish to undertake yourself and when you want to call in the plasterers.

BEFORE PLUNGING INTO PLASTER REPAIR, make sure you understand the design concept behind the particular wall you are working on. Construction of plaster walls has changed considerably as building methods evolved in the United States.

NORMALLY, PLASTER is held to the wall by a mechanical bond between the base coat (scratch coat) and the lath. Lath can be any of a number of materials that provide a lot of holes in the surface. The plasterer, in applying the scratch coat, forces plaster into the holes with his trowel. Plaster squishes through the holes, then starts drooping down the back of the lath. When this drooping plaster hardens, it forms "keys" behind the lath.

MODERN ROCK LATH doesn't have holes in it, but rather forms a bond between the plaster and the specially treated paper fibers on the surface. Plaster will also adhere to the paper surface of ordinary sheetrock. Adhesion of plaster to non-porous surfaces such as painted plaster can be increased with a bonding agent, such as Aqua-Weld, which is brushed on the surface before plaster is applied.

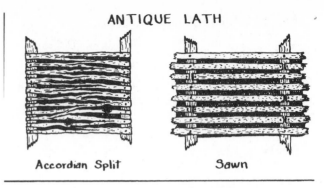

ANTIQUE LATH

Accordian Split   Sawn

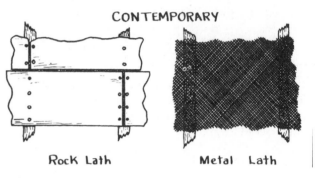

CONTEMPORARY

Rock Lath   Metal Lath

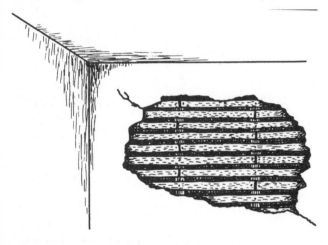

IN EARLY AMERICAN HOUSES, lathing was hand-split from thin hemlock or oak boards. Splits were made alternately on opposite sides of the board, and then the board was stretched like an accordian. Cracks thus formed provided space for the plaster keys. Hand-split lathing was uneven, which imparted a wavy appearance to the plaster that is characteristic of early American houses. In these buildings, plaster walls frequently were coated with whitewash—partially as a sanitary measure—and as the lime layers built up, the wall took on a scaly look of age that was added to its wavy look.

SAWN PINE LATH began to replace hand-split lath early in the 19th century, and as a result plaster walls became much flatter—and lost some of their "character."

SO IF YOU'RE ATTEMPTING to restore an old plaster wall, check to see if it has hand-split lath behind it. If you use new lath in a wall that has hand-split lath in other sections, your patch will likely be quite noticeable because it will be flatter. Obviously you can't buy hand-split lathing, but it's possible to fashion it from ¼-in. hemlock, split along the grain. If hemlock can't be obtained, next best thing is to install sawn lath, bowing it outward slightly as you nail it in place. As the water from the wet plaster expands the lath differentially, it will simulate the wavy effect of hand-split lath.

SOME VERY OLD AMERICAN HOUSES have plank walls, with siding applied to one side of the planks and plaster directly to the other side. Since the lath was applied directly to the planks, there's little room for the plaster to form good keys. If you are restoring a wall of this type, lath should be held out from the planks with furring strips.

PLASTER was usually applied to lathing in three stages. First was the scratch coat, rich in lime and containing animal hair

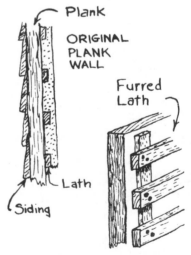

Plank

ORIGINAL PLANK WALL

Furred Lath

Lath

Siding

for additional strength, which was forced into the lath to form keys. The surface was "scratched" with the trowel or other tool to roughen the surface so next coat would adhere firmly. Second coat, the "brown coat," contained a high percentage of sand and additional animal hair. The third coat, "finish coat," had a high lime content, but no animal hair, and was troweled on thinly to avoid cracking on setting.

CRACKS IN PLASTER are endemic to old houses. Most common are cracks in walls and ceilings caused by settling and shrinkage of the structural timbers. These cracks extend through the plaster right down to the lath.

SOME OF THESE CRACKS you will come to regard as old friends since they will show up again and again no matter

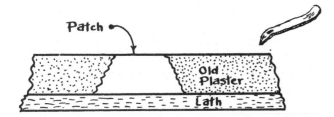

how often you patch them. These you will have to consider part of the charm of the house. Other cracks, once you patch them, will docilely disappear forever.

LARGER CRACKS should be undercut with a beer-can opener or putty knife to make the bottom wider than the top. This provides a solid anchor for the patch. With smaller cracks, undercutting is more trouble than it's worth.

SPACKLE IS EASIER TO WORK WITH than plaster of paris for patching cracks since it does not set up as rapidly. However, there is no single "best" plaster patching material. As you proceed, you'll find there's a wide variety of materials available to you, each of which has advantages for certain kinds of jobs.

CANNED SPACKLE IS EXTREMELY HANDY to make a quick patch of a small crack or dent. This pre-mixed material saves the trouble and mess of mixing a batch of spackle powder and water. It can also be used successfully instead of wood filler to patch nail- and screw-holes in woodwork. Canned spackle shrinks on drying, however, so it can't be used for big patches. It's also expensive to use in large quantities.

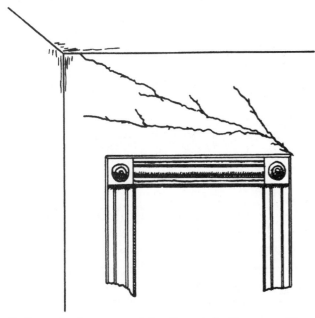

Settling cracks show up around door frames and ceiling corners. If house is still settling, cracks will recur.

TRICKS AN OLD FARMHOUSE PLAYS

I've made a couple of interesting discoveries since moving into this civil-war vintage farmhouse.

The ceiling of one room was severely damaged by moisture, causing the paint to hang in festoons from the plaster. A plasterer I had called in to do other work informed me that my plan to scrape the ceiling and repaint was doomed. The plaster had been moisture-damaged to the point that new paint wouldn't adhere and would quickly peel.

Solution was to nail sheetrock to the ceiling, tape the joints and paint. This removed only ½ inch from the room height.

One interesting sidelight: The beams under the old plaster ceiling were not the expected 16 in. on centers. Spacing varied randomly from 12½ in.–20 in. Each had to be located individually by driving exploratory nails.

R. Christian, Katonah, N.Y.

SPACKLE POWDER is more economical than canned spackle, and can be mixed in various consistencies to match the job at hand. It's the workhorse for most crack filling jobs. For hairline cracks, a thinner mixture—the consistency of heavy cream—will work best. For bigger cracks and holes you'll want a stiffer mixture—the consistency of bread dough. When there's a lot of patching to be done, some renovators mix up a thin and thick batch at the same time and have both on hand as they work their way around a room.

NOTE: Cutting the tops off plastic Chlorox bottles and using the bottoms for mixing containers is a convenient—and ecologically sound—way to get a big supply of spackle pots. Then it's not big catastrophe when a batch goes hard on you in the bowl.

SPACKLE POWDER doesn't shrink on drying as much as canned spackle. But it sets rock-hard and is difficult to sand, so you should smooth the surface as cleanly as you can with your putty knife while the spackle is soft and workable.

SHEETROCK JOINT CEMENT is handy if you have a lot of hairline cracks to fill, or shallow depressions where paint has chipped out. Joint cement is sold pre-mixed in cans for taping sheetrock seams. (One brand name is "Perf-Tape" compound.) Joint cement is applied with a wide tape joint knife. It adheres well to painted surfaces, feathers beautifully to a thin edge and sands easily after it has dried. However, joint cement shrinks a lot on drying, so it can't be used for filling large cracks.

IN ADDITION to these standard materials, there are many "secret formulas" for patching compounds. Some painters use plaster of paris powder mixed with paint to fill cracks before painting. Others swear by a mixture of plaster of paris powder mixed into joint cement.

YOU'LL WANT TO EXPERIMENT with varying materials and tools until you find the ones that fit your workstyle best. Making a modest investment in a big selection of putty knives, scraping knives and joint knives with blades of various stiffness will allow you to select the one that's right for a particular job. (Also, it's impossible to lose all these knives simultaneously, so you'll always be able to find one to work with.)

FOR PATCHING MOST CRACKS, you'll probably find that a wide-bladed knife (about 3 in.) with a flexible blade will give the neatest results. Once you have the crack stuffed with spackle, finish the patch off with long, smooth strokes, dragging the blade across at a flat angle to the patch. For hard-to-reach corners, you may find that your fingers are the best tool yet invented.

BEFORE PAINTING OVER PATCHWORK, the patch

should be lightly sanded, then primed either with shellac or a primer paint. This will prevent the final coats of paint from drying unevenly.

AFTER FILLING CRACKS, next most common plaster repair is patching holes made by electricians and plumbers. One particularly vexing type of repair is the "bottomless hole"—made when a workman pokes a hole through both plaster and lath, and there's nothing at the bottom of the hole for the plaster to adhere to. One way to cope with this situation is to rip out enough additional plaster so that the two adjacent studs or beams are exposed. New lath or sheetrock can then be nailed to the studs and plaster applied in the conventional manner. (More on this later.)

A SIMPLER AND less messy solution is to stuff wadded newspaper into the hole until it catches firmly on the sides and back of the interior partition space. Then after wetting edges of the old plaster thoroughly, apply thin coating of plaster of paris to the newspaper and the edge of the hole. Let plaster set for 20 min., then rewet and apply another thin coating of plaster. After repeating a couple times, you'll build up a firm plaster base and can then proceed to patch in the conventional manner. Build plaster up to within 1/8 inch of the wall surface. (Leave base

Wadded Newspaper Fills "Bottomless" Hole

coats rough to give adhesion for the top coat.) Use trowel to get smooth finish on the final layer.

MAJOR REPAIRS IN PLASTER SURFACES

FINISH PLASTERING is quite an art—although not as difficult as some believe. In this article we'll review some of the major types of plaster repairs the old-house owner may encounter. At some point—depending on your own level of craftsmanship—it doesn't pay to do these repairs yourself. After surveying these techniques, you can decide which jobs you want to tackle yourself—and when it will pay to send out a call for help.

A COMMON PROBLEM in old houses is loose or bulging plaster. This is caused by one of two things: (1) Lath has pulled loose from the studs; (2) Plaster has pulled loose from the lath. The former condition is less serious than the latter. To determine which type of condition you have, you may have to poke an exploratory hole or two.

IF LATH HAS PULLED LOOSE FROM STUDS, the plaster can be pushed back into place and held with countersunk screws and washers. (See description of ceiling anchors following.)

IF PLASTER HAS COME OFF THE LATH, in most cases you'll have to rip the loose plaster off and patch as described elsewhere in this article.

THERE IS A SPECIAL CASE of plaster pulled loose from the lath in a ceiling in which it may be possible to salvage the old plaster if you are really in love with it. Salvage depends on being able to work on the ceiling from above, either from an attic or by lifting floorboards. The procedure involves:

1. Pushing the old plaster back into place and holding it firmly in position with wooden braces that extend up from the floor;

2. Removing the old plaster keys from behind the old lath;

3. Pouring a fluid mixture of plaster of paris over the lath and the old ceiling plaster. Linen cloth can be laid in for additional strength. The plaster of paris layer will adhere to the old ceiling plaster and re-anchor it to the lath. This technique is rather involved, however, and if you're not sure of your own skills you had better consult a professional plasterer.

PATCHING HOLES IN PLASTER is a relatively simple matter. You have several techniques to choose from, depending on your work preferences and materials at hand. Whichever method is selected, first step is to undercut the old plaster with a putty knife or beer can opener so the new plaster will be firmly locked to it.

ONE PATCHING PROCEDURE involves replacing all of the missing plaster with new plaster. This means there must be lath at the bottom of the hole for the plaster to grab onto. If any lath is missing, you can tack some salvaged lath in place, or nail in some new wire lath, rock lath or plain sheetrock. NOTE: This occasional need for replacement lath means you should save a bundle of random lengths from any wall demolition you undertake.

BEFORE APPLYING PLASTER, thoroughly wet the old plaster and lath. This will prevent the old material from sucking water from the new plaster and impeding a proper set. One convenient way to accomplish this wetting is to use an old plastic detergent squirt bottle filled with water.

IF THE HOLE TO FILL is more than 1/8 in. deep, it should be filled with two or more layers of plaster to prevent cracking of the final coat. Since plaster of paris will harden in about 20 min., this won't take an inordinate amount of time. Depending on depth of the hole, the undercoat should be built up to within 1/8 in. of the surrounding wall in one or two applications. (You can check clearance with a board laid across the hole.)

IF YOU ENCOUNTER DIFFICULTY with plaster of paris setting up too fast, you can retard set-up by adding vinegar 50–50 to the mixing water. Or you can throw in a handful of powdered spackle into the plaster powder and mix well before adding water.

THE UNDERCOAT, or "scratch coat," could be made from perlited plaster if you have a large hole to fill. Perlited plaster is lighter and less expensive than plaster of paris (because of its lightweight filler) but you should let it dry for at least 48 hours before applying the final coat of plaster.

TO INSURE GOOD ADHESION of the finish coat, the intermediate layers of plaster should be left rough. You can use an old comb, the point of a trowel or a small piece of metal lath to make cross-hatch scorings in the undercoat.

TO APPLY FINAL COAT of plaster, surface of the previous coat should be thoroughly wet down. Then fresh plaster is troweled on to bring the level up to the rest of the wall. A board that's long enough to span the patch can be worked back and forth across the hole to knock down any high spots and fill in valleys.

A RECTANGULAR PLASTERER'S trowel should be used

to obtain a smooth finish. It takes some practice to use this tool properly. So give yourself every advantage by purchasing a top-quality trowel.

FOR PATCHES UNDER 6 inches in diameter, plaster of paris is a satisfactory material for the final coat. Its disadvantages are its fast set-up and the fact that it doesn't work as smoothly as lime-plaster. For patches larger than 6 inches across, lime-plaster is better because of its superior workability.

TO APPLY FINAL COAT OF PLASTER, work trowel from left to right, starting at the base and using the upward stroke to force in the new plaster, then seal with a downward stroke. Trowel should be held against the plaster with its leading edge raised only slightly, bearing down firmly on the trailing edge. To get a glassy surface on the plaster, it should be allowed to set for a few minutes, then re-worked continually with the trowel. A clean brush is used to wet the plaster just ahead of the trowel as it is stroked across the surface from top to bottom. Rough spots will be discovered and removed in this process. The more the plaster is worked, the smoother the final coat will be.

KEEP TROWEL CLEAN by frequent dunkings in a bucket of water.

PLASTERING IS GREATLY SIMPLIFIED if plasterboard or rock lath is used as a base instead of a plaster scratch coat in large patches. If old lath is still in place, plasterboard can be nailed right on top. Just be sure that it's nailed to the studs. If needed, thin wooden shims can be tacked to the studs to bring the plasterboard to within 3/16-in. of the wall surface. (Old pieces of lath make handy shims.)

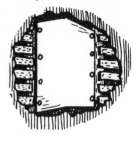

WITH PLASTERBOARD NAILED IN PLACE, you can apply finish coat of plaster directly, follow-steps outlined above. Be sure to pack plaster tightly in crack between plasterboard and old plaster.

SHEETROCK CAN BE USED in place of plasterboard if you have some handy. However, sheetrock lacks the specially treated surface that makes plaster stick hard to plasterboard. You can increase the adhesion of plaster to sheetrock by using a latex bonding agent such as Aqua-Weld.

THIS TRICK CAN BE MODIFIED in making ceiling repairs where the overhead plastering required is beyond most renovators' skills. Old ceilings that seem in bad shape may really have only one section that needs replacement. By repairing this one section, the rest of the ceiling can be saved.

TIPS ON MIXING PLASTER

By Francis Valentine

WHILE I DON'T CLAIM to know everything about plastering, I've learned some things while renovating my brownstone that may be of value to other renovators.

ONE TRICK is the proper way to mix plaster, whether you're applying pure plaster to a small patch, or are making lime-plaster for covering larger areas. The trick is: DON'T STIR THE PLASTER WHILE MIXING IT WITH WATER! Mechanical action of stirring hastens set-up. Stirred plaster of paris will start to harden within 5 min.; when properly prepared it will remain workable for 15–20 min.

THE PROPER TECHNIQUE is to sift plaster powder slowly into water until the water is completely absorbed. DO NOT stir during this operation. If you're making pure plaster for small holes, simplest way is to prepare it in a clean plastic pan. Start with COLD water, and use same volume of water as volume of plaster you want to end up with. The plaster powder combines with the water and will not increase volume significantly.

FROM THE PLASTERER'S LEXICON

QUICKLIME—Calcium and magnesium oxides formed by firing limestone over 1700° F. Slaking quicklime with water sets off a violent reaction that brings the whole mass to a boil. Principal use of slaked quicklime is in masonry mortars because of the high degree of workability it imparts to the mixture.

HYDRATED LIME—Prepared at the factory by adding controlled amount of water to quicklime. Two basic grades are available: Mason's hydrated lime and finishing lime. Finishing lime is used in final plaster coats to impart plasticity to the plaster. Although partially hydrated, finishing lime should be allowed to soak in water for 24 hrs. to improve its workability.

PLASTER—When gypsum rock is heated to 266 F., three fourths of the water is driven off. The resulting fine white powder is known by many names—the most common being plaster of paris. Other common names are gypsum plaster and gaging plaster. Gaging plaster comes in quick-set and slow-set varieties.

HARDWALL PLASTER—Gaging plaster mixed with perlite aggregate to form a lightweight base-coat plaster. Sold under trade names such as "Structolite."

BROWN COAT—Coat of plaster directly beneath the finish coat. In two-coat work, brown coat is the base-coat applied over the lath. In three-coat work, brown coat is applied over the scratch coat.

SCRATCH COAT—First coat of plaster in three-coat work.

FINISH COAT—Last coat of plaster. Usually consists of lime putty and gaging plaster mixed ratios ranging from 5:1 to 2:1.

PUTTY—Product resulting from mixing lime and water together.

THE BAD SECTION is cut back to sound plaster, ending on the mid-point of a beam. For additional strength, you might want to secure the edges of the old plaster with ceiling an-

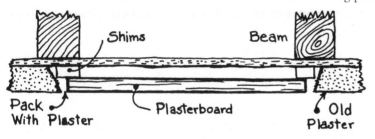

chors (see next column). A piece of sheetrock is then cut to fit the hole you have just made. Use 3/8-in. thick stock, since it's easiest to work overhead with this light-gage material. Determine thickness of shimstock that must be nailed to the beams to bring sheetrock out to surface of the old ceiling.

USING SHEETROCK NAILS, fasten sheetrock patch to ceiling beams. Then fill crack between sheetrock and old ceiling with plaster, feathering the plaster out to make a smooth joint. If necessary, you can go over the plaster seam with joint cement to get a perfectly smooth, sandable joint.

SIFT PLASTER THROUGH YOUR FINGERS into the pan until all water has been absorbed. Rapping the pan will jog any remaining water to the top of the mixture. Sift more plaster onto the surface to absorb these last traces of free water.

GOBS OF PLASTER PUTTY can then be lifted out of the pan onto your trowel. (Be careful not to disturb the remaining plaster when removing the small amount to work with.)

If the plaster on the trowel is too moist, sift on some additional plaster powder and mix in with a smaller second trowel. Even though this mechanical mixing will start the plaster setting up, it doesn't matter because this material will be used up immediately.

MIXING IN A PLASTIC PAN simplifies cleanup because you simply allow any excess plaster to harden completely in the vessel. Hardened plaster can then be removed by twisting the pan. If you've got a lot of patching to do, you may want to have two or three mixing pans on hand so you can work out of one while the excess from the previous batch is hardening in the other pan.

PURE PLASTER HAS SEVERAL ADVANTAGES for patching holes: (1) It sets quickly so that successive layers can be applied at 30-min. intervals; (2) It can be painted as soon as it is completely dry—usually overnight. (In contrast, lime-plaster should cure for at least several weeks before painting.) (3) Plaster takes a smoother finish than spackle; (4) It's simpler to mix than lime-plaster.

HOLES THAT ARE 6-in. dia. and under can be successfully patched with pure plaster, with the apertures larger than 1 in. across being best handled with two or three coats. All loose plaster is first cleaned from area to be patched. After thoroughly wetting lath and old plaster, new plaster is pressed firmly into place with trowel. Purpose of this first coat is to establish a bond to lath and old plaster and provide firm foundation for subsequent coats. Surface of this coat should be left rough. Second coat, if needed, is applied 30 min. later, bringing surface of plaster to within 1/8–3/16 in. of the wall surface. Final coat is applied with wide taping knife or or rectangular plasterer's trowel. After the final plaster coat has set for a few minutes, it should be re-wet with a water brush and smoothed in one direction with the trowel to produce a glassy surface.

FOR HOLES LARGER THAN 6 in. dia., base coats should be made of perlited plaster or plasterboard as discussed elsewhere in this article. For these larger patches, you'll want to consider finishing with limeplaster because of the greater workability of this material. To make lime-plaster, start by soaking hydrated lime at least 24 hrs. according to directions on the bag. (A plastic garbage pail makes a good soaking vat.) Mixing the soaked lime with the plaster is accomplished on a large (4 ft. × 4 ft.) plywood mixing board.

PLACE ON THE BOARD as much lime putty as you can use in a half hour. For inexperienced plasterers, this will mean about a half-gallon of lime. A ratio of 5 parts lime to 1 part plaster is about right for beginners (professional plasterers will use about 3 parts lime to 1 part plaster). So if you've put 2 quarts of lime on the board, this means you'll need approximately 1/2 pint of plaster.

TO MAKE THIS MIXTURE, form the lime putty into a ring on the mixing board. Place a pint of water into the center of the ring. Sift plaster powder into the center until all of the water is absorbed. Don't touch the plaster with the trowel at this stage.

TO MIX LIME AND PLASTER, take a wedge of lime and plaster or as many wedges as needed and mix on the edge of the board. (Don't disturb the rest of the plaster when removing the wedge with your trowel.) This will allow 20 min. of workability for the material in the center ring. If mixture is too thin, you can sift a little more plaster powder onto the

Brace made from 2×4's holds sagging ceiling plaster and lath in place while ceiling anchors are attached to beams.

batch you've pulled aside for mixing. Transfer the lime-plaster mix onto your hawk and trowel into place. Follow the leveling and smoothing techniques discussed in this and the previous article.

HOW TO USE CEILING ANCHORS

WHEN BULGING PLASTER is caused by lath pulling loose from the beams, the condition can be remedied with simple anchors—as long as the plaster is still firmly keyed to the lath. This condition is frequently found in old ceilings, where the lime in the plaster corrodes the lath nails—allowing the ceiling to sag.

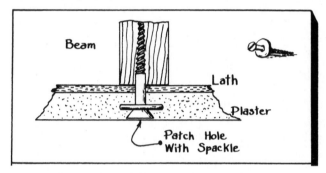

Ceiling anchors can be made from a wood screw and washer. Conceal with spackle.

WHETHER USED ON CEILING OR WALLS, principle of the anchor is the same: (1) Bulging plaster is pressed back into proper position; (2) Hole is drilled through plaster and pilot hole for screw is made in the beam; (3) Hole in plaster is countersunk; (4) Anchor is screwed in place and concealed with spackle.

HOLE IN PLASTER should be drilled with a carbide-tipped masonry bit. Countersink is made with a big masonry bit or an old countersink that you don't mind dulling on the plaster. After drilling pilot hole in beam, screw in anchor until it holds plaster firmly in place. For most applications, a 3-in. screw is about right.

IF A LONG CRACK in a ceiling is to be reinforced, use ceiling brace to hold plaster in place while anchor is inserted. Space anchors about every 24 in. NOTE: In old ceilings, beams may not be spaced evenly every 16 in. You may have to drill exploratory holes to find each one.

DUPLICATING PLASTER CORNICES

ORNAMENTAL PLASTERWORK is very beautiful but it is, alas, also very fragile. All too often the old house that is otherwise in good shape will be missing all or some of its original decorative plaster. Decorative cornices contain plasterwork of two types: (1) Running moldings; (2) Cast moldings.

A RUNNING MOLDING is characterized by its smooth continuous lines—resulting from its having been "run" in place with a template. Cast moldings (also called enriched or ornamented moldings) usually have indentations that require their being cast in a stationary mold and then affixed to the wall with a "glue" consisting of plaster of paris.

THIS ARTICLE WILL DEAL with duplication of running moldings.

A MAJOR PROBLEM WITH DECORATIVE PLASTER is the shortage of craftsmen who can (or will) do the work. Most of the plasterwork in 19th-century houses was installed by plasterers who had been trained in Europe (especially Italy). Very few workmen today carry on that craft.

AS A RESULT, one method of duplicating running moldings calls upon the skills of the carpenter rather than the plasterer. Just about any running molding can be closely approximated by building up with standard wood moldings. While not totally satisfying from a purist's standpoint, when carefully done a built-up wooden replica will be indistinguishable from the plaster original.

FOUR BASIC SHAPES can handle many of the duplicating jobs:

| 1 x 1 | Cove | Half Round | Quarter Round |

A WIDE RANGE OF OTHER WOODEN MOLDINGS are available to handle more complex replications. If your lumber dealer doesn't have a convenient display that you can examine, you can obtain an excellent samples on numerous web sites. The best way to illustrate fabrication of moldings from wood is with an example:

IN THIS CASE, the old house was missing a 6-foot section of running molding on the ceiling. Since the missing piece was short, duplicating in wood seemed the simplest solution. A 6-foot wooden molding was assembled in the following fashion:

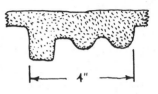

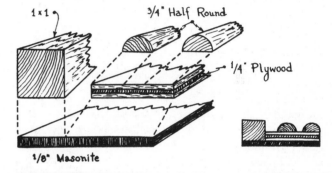

THE MOLDING WAS PUT TOGETHER with brads (with holes countersunk and filled) and glue. The edge of the plywood was filled with wood putty to make a smooth surface and the entire assembly was lightly sanded.

WOODEN MOLDING was secured to the ceiling with wood screws that went into the ceiling joists. (Toggle bolts can be used to hang the assembly from the ceiling if the molding runs parallel to the joists and there's no beam overhead to screw into.)

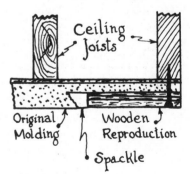

IT'S POSSIBLE at this point you'll find that the ceiling has a bow in it that will impart a noticeable curve to the molding if you drive the screws tight. In this case, use wooden shims to level the molding. Fill all gaps and screwhead holes with spackle or plaster. Apply shellac or primer to the wooden section and paint to match the rest of the ceiling.

IF YOU WANT TO RE-CREATE THE cornice molding with plaster, you've got two choices: (1) Cast or run the cornice in sections on a table and then fasten it in place; (2) Run a new cornice in plaster right on the wall. Running in place was the way plaster cornices were originally applied. You can still find plasterers who will do this work—if you look hard enough.

IF YOU CAN'T FIND SOMEONE IN your area to do this work, it is possible to do it yourself. But running a cornice is NOT a project to be undertaken lightly. It will doubtless involve several false starts and a lot of chipping out of mistakes before you get the hang of it. Even under the best of circumstances, it can take a professional over a week to run the cornices for a single room—especially if there are a lot of corners and angles.

THE THEORY OF RUNNING A MOLDING is very simple: (1) Make a template that is an exact reverse of the cross-section of the molding you want to make; (2) Throw wet plaster up on the wall; (3) Run the template over the wet plaster to shape it.

AS WITH MOST THINGS, the actual practice is a lot more complex than the theory.

MAKING THE TEMPLATE OR MOLD is not too difficult. It can be cut from sheet metal and backed with wood to give it stiffness. You should try to avoid undercuts in the pattern because it makes it harder to separate the template from the plaster. The wood backing should be recessed slightly behind the template and beveled so that the pattern will cut cleanly through the wet plaster.

Bad: Under-Cut

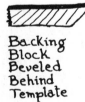

Backing Block Beveled Behind Template

THE TEMPLATE is then mounted in a wooden frame so that it can be held at a right angle to the wall and guided along the temporary wooden track (or "screed") that is tacked in place on the wall to ensure the straightness of the molding.

MOLDINGS ARE NORMALLY RUN over the brown coat. However, one could be run over a finish coat if it's not too heavy. A bonding agent could be applied to the finish plaster to assure good adhesion.

AS FOR THE PLASTER MIXTURE to be used, each professional seems to have his own secret formula. A concensus mixture would seem to be two parts of finishing lime to one part of plaster of paris.

IF THE MOLDING IS NOT TOO THICK (not much more than 1 in.) it can be made of solid plaster. Plaster shrinks on

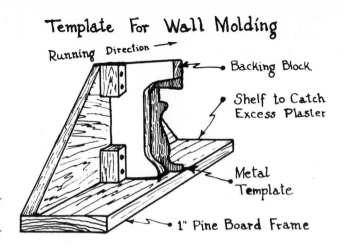

Template For Wall Molding

Running Direction

Backing Block

Shelf to Catch Excess Plaster

Metal Template

1" Pine Board Frame

drying and if laid too thickly, the cornice will crack. A thick ornate cornice would be made by attaching wooden brackets to the wall in the approximate form of the cornice and about three-quarters of an inch below the level of the finished cornice. Brackets are attached every 12 inches and then lathing is nailed to the brackets.

Template For Wall/Ceiling Cornice

Guide For Ceiling Track

Metal Template Backed With Wood

Guide For Wall Track

TO FORM THE CORNICE, the template is run continuously across the surface of the plaster—always in the same direction. Excess plaster is pushed off the face of the mold, and can fall either onto a hawk you hold in your hand or onto a shelf built into the mold. Additional plaster is thrown back into those voids that still need building up and the mold is run back over it. A water brush can be used to to keep the surface of the plaster from drying out and setting too rapidly.

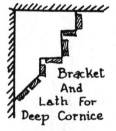

Bracket And Lath For Deep Cornice

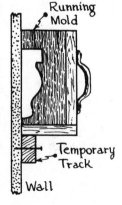

Running Mold

Temporary Track

Wall

YOU CAN see that speed is of the essence You have got to get the cornice perfectly formed before the plaster takes its final set. Also, the consistency of the plaster is critical; it can't be so fluid that it sags, yet it must be plastic enough to be shaped by the mold. Only practice will help here.

THE CORNICE MOLD works tolerably well on straight runs, but it doesn't do you any good at all at the corners. Because of its guides, the running mold has to be stopped about 6 in. short of every corner. Then you've got two choices. You can run sections of molding flat on a table and make mitered corners while the plaster is still plastic. When dry, these cast sections can be fitted to the run molding and then glued to the wall or ceiling with plaster of paris. Seams between pieces can be filled with plaster. Or, if you have artistic hands, you can shape the corners by hand with a trowel, putty knife or any other implement that gives the desired result. It's the finishing of the corners that can be the really time-consuming part of cornice installation.

BECAUSE OF THE COMPLEXITIES of running cornices in place, often restorers will run them in sections on a table. When dry, the sections are affixed to wall or ceiling and the joints filled with plaster.

HOW TO DUPLICATE PLASTER CASTINGS

ORNAMENTAL PLASTERWORK divides into two main categories: Run-in-place moldings characterized by their straight lines (detailed in the February issue) and "enriched" moldings that contain designs in three-dimensional relief. Enriched moldings are always cast. It's not uncommon for complex cornices to contain plasterwork of both types.

IN THIS ARTICLE, we'll review various methods for reproducing enriched moldings from fragments you may have on hand. And if you don't have anything left to take impressions from, we'll tell you where you can get new ornamentation, either made from plaster or new lightweight materials.

COMMONLY, THE ORNAMENTAL plaaster-work in an old house is partially damaged or totally missing. The case of Samuel E. Gallo, the noted sculptor, is not uncommon: Gallo's Brooklyn town-house had been "modernized" 30 years ago, complete with dropped ceilings and acoustical tile. As part of these "improvements," workmen had carefully removed all of the decorative plaster—both from the ceiling and from the wall friezes. However, above the dropped ceiling he found a portion of the original ceiling molding that had survived. And in the back of a closet that had been added during the alterations Gallo found a 3-foot section of the wall frieze. Starting with just these two fragments, Gallo was able to totally restore the plasterwork to the same state it was in when Victorian ladies and gentlemen graced his front parlor.

ASSUMING YOU HAVE A FRAGMENT to work from, your first problem is to make a mold from which you can make future castings. The method that will be described here is the most commonly followed procedure—making a mold from rubber latex. This is suitable for making large molds. Special techniques for making small molds will be described later in this article.

MOLDS CAN BE MADE of fragments that are still attached to walls or ceilings, but it's a lot easier if the piece can be detached so that you can work on a table or on the floor. Some ornate plasterwork like ceiling medallions were usually glued in place (often with a thin layer of plaster of paris) and gentle prying often will free the piece. In other cases, you might want to cut out a chunk of wall or ceiling that contains the fragment and bring it down to ground level for further operations.

A LITTLE SCULPTURE MIGHT BE in order to patch the fragment or fill in any portions of the pattern that have been damaged. Spackle or your favorite patching compound can be used here. Next, prepare the fragment for mold-making by carefully cleaning it. It can be coated with shellac or Krylon spray to give easier separation from the rubber latex. Most restorers report that they get good separation from clean plaster without using any coating. If the plaster is painted with bronze or any copper-containing pigment, however, the Krylon or shellac coating is essential.

MAKING THE MOLD

NEXT STEP IS TO BRUSH THE master piece with the rubber latex. Be sure all crevices are coated. Latex should be allowed to cure or vulcanize according to manufacturer's instructions. The Cementex product cited below, for exam-

ple, gives optimum results when cured at about 110° F. You can obtain this temperature with infrared heating lamps, an electric hair dryer, sticking it in a slightly warm oven, or using some other heating system of your own design. After the rubber has cured for the correct period of time (usually at least 1 hr. when heat is used) it's ready for the next latex coating. The number of coats that will be required is dictated by the size of the original and depth of the relief. The bigger and deeper the piece, the thicker the mold you'll need. It's imperative that each layer be cured according to instructions or else the layers may not bond properly to each other.

YOU CAN CUT DOWN on the number of latex coats needed if you incorporate cheese-cloth into the mold layers. The cheesecloth acts much like the steel bars in reinforced concrete. With this type of reinforcement, you'll probably need only four to six layers of latex, even for large molds.

IF YOU HAVE TO MAKE A MOLD on wall or ceiling because you can't detach the original, you'll probably have to let time do the vulcanizing rather than heat. This will usually mean several days between latex coats and then leaving the whole mold in place several weeks while the final curing takes place.

BUILDING A MOTHER

BEFORE STRIPPING THE LATEX MOLD from the original, the next task is to make a "mother." Function of the mother is to support the mold when it's filled with wet plaster so that it doesn't distort. The mother is made of plaster, reinforced with coarse burlap.

BEFORE POURING PLASTER FOR THE MOTHER, check latex mold for undercuts. These should be filled with wet paper towels. Otherwise, the mother will lock in there and you'll never separate it from the original. A thin layer of wet paper towels should also be laid over the entire surface of the rubber mold. This will prevent the plaster in the mother from sticking to the rubber.

Latex Mold

Undercut

Wet Paper Towels

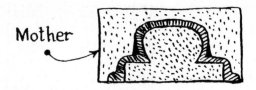

Mother

A FRAME around the mold will let you pour a mother that has square sides and a level bottom. The mother should be at least ½-in. thick at the highest point of the mold. As plaster is poured for the mother, incorporate generous amounts of coarse burlap. This will not only greatly increase the strength but will also considerably reduce the weight.

THE MOTHER CAN BE PULLED from the mold as soon as the plaster has set . . . in less than an hour.

IF YOU HAVE BEEN FORCED TO make a mold of a fragment that is still attached to the wall or ceiling, you'll have to peel the mold from the original before making the mother. The problem is making a mother for the mold without crushing and distorting it with the weight of wet plaster. Here's one way: Make the mold with a 4-in. flange while on the wall so it will lay flat face down on the floor. After filling undercuts with wet paper towels, saturate cheesecloth with wet plaster and lay it carefully on the rubber mold so it isn't distorted. After plaster has set, you'll have a stiff surface and you can brush on another coat of plaster. Once this is dry, you can pour the final application of plaster and the coarse burlap.

AFTER SEPARATING THE MOTHER from the rubber mold, you can pull mold from the original. Care must be exercised because the mold will tend to pull away the plaster where there are undercuts. Also, sometimes the inside of the mold will stick to itself if you happen to squash it while handling.

INTERIOR OF THE MOLD should be washed with soap and water to remove any residual byproducts from the vulcanizing process.

SPECIAL SMALL MOLDS

IF YOU JUST HAVE TO MAKE A SINGLE CAST of a small fragment, there are simpler mold-making procedures you can use—especially if the original doesn't have any undercuts on it.

ONE WAY is to take paraffin and soften it by gentle heating in warm water. Simply press the soft paraffin over the original to make the mold. Or you can use modeling clay, exercising care not to distort the shape in handling. Both wax and clay molds can only be used once because you destroy the mold when removing the plaster cast.

Restoration of elaborate cornice and ceiling moldings in New York townhouse. Photo courtesy of Felber Studios.

FOR EXTREMELY SMALL AND FINELY DETAILED reproductions, you can borrow the technology of the dentist. You can use dental alginate to make a mold. This gives a soft, flexible mold that faithfully reproduces all undercuts and detail From this, you can make a plaster cast. Or if you want an especially hard and durable reproduction, you can use Lucite molding compound. Both the alginate and Lucite can be purchased at dental supply houses.

SILICONE RUBBER also works well for molds up to about 6 inches across. See box on opposite page.

CASTING TECHNIQUES

ONCE YOU HAVE THE MOLD, making a casting is a fairly simple process, although there will be some tricks you pick up as you go along. Plaster of paris is the most common casting material, although you might want to use some of the special molding plasters that have a very fine particle size, which gives a smooth dense surface to the casting.

A GOOD CASTING MIXTURE will be 7 parts by volume of plaster to 4 parts water. To retard set-up time, always use cold water and put the water into the mixing container first. Then sprinkle plaster powder in slowly, stirring as little as possible. Stirring hastens set-up and may also entrain air bubbles in the plaster. If you need to retard set-up even more, add a teaspoon of vinegar to the water before sifting in the plaster.

FOR A MIXING VESSEL, you're best off using a flexible plastic container such as a cut-off Chlorox bottle. To clean out excess plaster, just let it harden in the vessel, then squeeze. The excess plaster will crack and fall right out of the vessel.

IF YOU DON'T HAVE ENOUGH PLASTERWORK left to restore, you can order new plaster ornaments—or you can have your own custom moldings prepared.

BEFORE POURING PLASTER INTO MOLD, fill it first with water and then pour water out. This will moisten the walls and ensure penetration of the plaster into all crevices. Make sure the mold is nestled snugly into its mother, then use a small brush to work plaster into all nooks and crannies so you won't have any trapped air bubbles. Then add plaster and cheesecloth or burlap strips for strength. Even very delicate frieze tracery will turn out amazingly strong when cheesecloth is incorporated into the cast.

ONCE THE MOLD IS FILLED WITH plaster, jog it gently to nudge plaster into all the indentations. Then level the plaster by working a straightedge across the top of the mold.

PLASTER SHOULD BE HARD ENOUGH to remove from the mold in 30 min. But castings should be allowed to air-dry for 24 hr. before attempting to install them.

LARGE THICK CASTINGS can be made hollow. Use a thick plaster mixture and plenty of burlap to build up the sides. In this way, the casting will be strong and not terribly heavy.

A SPECIAL TRICK that's used in making beaded molding is to insert a loop from a long piece of string into each bead. The string also runs in the channel between beads. The plaster between the beads inevitably cracks, but the string holds the whole line together.

INSTALLING PLASTERWORK

TO AFFIX PLASTER CASTINGS TO WALLS or ceilings, the old-timers often used a thin coating of plaster of paris as an adhesive. They'd just hold the piece in place for a few minutes until the plaster set. The advantage of using plaster as an adhesive is that it won't deteriorate with age as organic glues will.

LIGHT PLASTER MOLDINGS can be put in place using a mastic adhesive or epoxy. Gypsum board joint cement also makes an excellent adhesive for light pieces.

ROOM-TEMPERATURE VULCANIZING

There is room-temperature vulcanizing silicone rubber that will make molds a lot faster than regular latex. A silicone rubber mold can be made in one pouring and will cure at room temperature in 24 hours. It makes a soft, flexible mold that will accurately reproduce undercuts. The material is quite expensive, and will work best for small castings.

FOR HEAVY CASTINGS, you may want to drill holes in them with a carbide-tipped bit and secure them to the ceiling beams with screws. Once the casting is in place, you can fill any seams, holes and crevices with spackle.

FOR VERY LARGE PIECES, you might want to make the casting out of fiberglass and plastic resin rather than plaster to cut down on the weight. You can use the rubber molds constructed in the manner described above, but the casting procedure is considerably more complicated.

ORNATE PLASTERWORK is one of those finishing touches that make old houses so distinctive. Although restoring plaster can get pretty involved, the end result of your craftsmanship will be a pleasing display that you'll enjoy for all the years you're in the house.

Staircases and Floors

SURGERY ON A STAIRCASE

QUESTION

One staircase in my 1890 Victorian frame house has developed a noticeable sag. Is this likely to be serious—and if it is what can be done about it?

R. Bradley Andover, Mass.

WHILE EVERY CASE IS DIFFERENT, your problem reminds me of a situation I encountered in a brownstone row house. I had lived there for about a year and had been busy coping with electrical and plumbing problems when I began to notice little things about the top-floor staircase . . .

. . . LITTLE THINGS like a noticeable increase in the amount of rhythmic bouncing as one ascended the stairs. Little things like a hole in the plaster under the staircase . . . a hole that wouldn't stay patched no matter how many times I plugged it with plaster.

I DECIDED THAT OPEN-STAIR SURGERY would be necessary. Now do-it-yourself stair surgery is not for everyone; you need a strong back and must be able to withstand the sight of spilled plaster. However, the following description may help you diagnose a similar condition—or help you direct the ministrations of a specialist you might call in.

TO DETERMINE why the plaster was always falling out of the patch, I performed an exploratory operation. The plaster on the underside of the staircase was ripped out in the area of the hole-that-wouldn't-stay-patched. Enough plaster and lath was removed so that both a flashlight and the surgeon's head could be inserted into the opening.

WHAT I SAW REVEALED that part of the staircase framing had come loose and was bearing down on the plaster below every time someone went up the stairs. Radical surgery was needed.

FIRST STEP IN THE OPERATION was far and away the messiest and most unpleasant—removing all of the plaster and lath from the underside of the staircase. Opening the underside in this fashion revealed the full extent of the problem—and the remedies that would be necessary. The first diagram shows a simplified view of the framing that the original builders put together—before the treads and risers were nailed on.

MIDDLE OF TREADS were supported by 1×6's fastened with nails to center stringer.

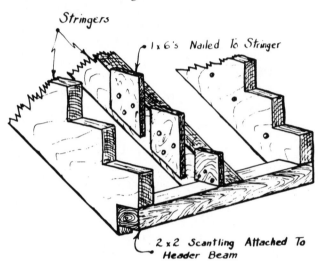

AFTER THE SHIFTS and shrinkages that occur in 100 years, however, this is the condition that confronted me:

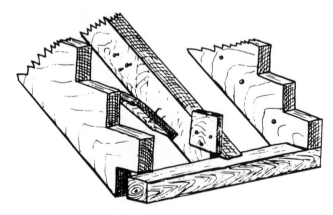

THE 1×6 BLOCKS had come loose and two stringers were perilously close to slipping off the scantling block.

The outer stringer had come almost totally off the supporting scantling and was held up only by a faint hope. Also, most of the 1 × 6 blocks used to support the middle of the treads had come off. I decided to totally disassemble the staircase and rebuild it.

IN DISASSEMBLING A STAIRCASE, first thing to remove is the balusters. On this staircase, they were keyed into the treads and held in place by the end trim. End trim is held with nails and should be worked loose gently. Slip a stiff putty knife into the joint between tread and end trim. Open the joint wide enough so you can slide in a pry bar. (Don't use a screwdriver to open the joint; it will damage the wood.)

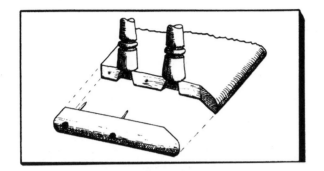

WHEN END TRIM is removed, the balusters can be slipped out of the keyway. Tops of the balusters are usually glued into the hand railing. If these joints haven't already worked loose, you can twist them by hand and the glue will give way.

ONCE THE BALUSTERS are removed,★ next comes the treads and risers. Note: Since the balusters are hand-fitted to each tread, reassembly is greatly simplified if you number each baluster and tread so you can put all parts back in the same order in which they were removed.

★ With all of the balusters removed, it's an ideal time to consider stripping them. You can make a vat and dip them easily. Also, it's easier to refinish them when you can pick each one up and turn and twist them as you apply the finish.

JUDICIOUS USE of the stiff putty knife followed up with the pry bar will allow you to work treads and risers loose without damage. (I found it easiest to start with the bottom riser.)

Treads and risers are mortised into each other and held together by nails.

ONCE TREADS AND RISERS were removed, next task was to secure the two stringers that had worked loose. (The third stringer had been fastened to the brick wall with cut nails and was still solid as a rock.)

THE STRINGERS were shoved back into position—but there had been enough shrinkage so that simple toe-nailing to the scantling would not provide a secure joint. The answer was two heavy 6" corner braces.

CORNER BRACES were fastened to the stringers and header with heavy 4" lag screws. It's hard to drive screws in

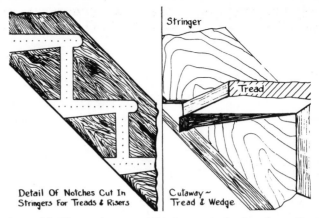

Detail Of Notches Cut In Stringers For Treads & Risers   *Cutaway ~ Tread & Wedge*

Original builders used auger and chisel to cut notches in stringers for treads and risers; wooden wedges held treads in place.

the old dried beams. Pilot holes are a must, as well as lubricating the threads with soap before driving. Lag screws were used so a hefty wrench could be used to drive them.

NEXT, NEW TREAD SUPPORTING BLOCKS for the middle stringer were cut from 2 × 6 and nailed and glued in place. In order to fit the blocks exactly against both tread and riser, treads and risers were put back one by one, and the support blocks fitted snugly against them and secured with nails. The original wedges were re-inserted between the underside of treads and the two outside stringers.

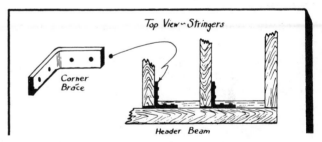

Loose stringers were secured by attaching them to header beam by means of heavy corner braces held with 4" lag screws.

WEDGES THAT were missing were replaced with new ones cut from 1-inch pine board stock.

NOTE ON NAILING: On a staircase, which is subject to continual working and stress, it is important that nails be driven at opposing angles to resist being pulled out.

RE-INSERTION OF THE BALUSTERS was quite easy, and sheetrock was nailed to the underside of the stringers to replace the plaster that had been pulled down.

THE OPERATION was a success.

SAGGING FLOORS

IT'S HARD TO IGNORE a sagging floor. A cracked ceiling can be avoided by never looking up. You can hang pictures over holes in the wall. But a defective floor nags its way into your consciousness continually . . . the ominous bounce . . . spongy boards . . . having to adjust your posture to accommodate the tilt in the floor . . . these things have an annoying way of calling themselves to your attention.

SO BEFORE YOU START refinishing those lovely old wide plank floors, or restoring that magnificent parquet, make sure that the floor itself is structurally sound. Some of the tilt and wobble may just be part of the house's character; in other cases it may be the signal of real trouble ahead.

IN THIS ARTICLE, we'll review some of the major structural ailments that can afflict old-house floors and what can be done to correct them. In subsequent issues we'll deal with patching and refinishing wooden floors.

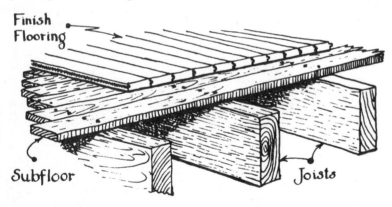

THE DIAGNOSTIC TECHNIQUES for identifying floor problems are simple enough; fixing them may be another matter. Rolling a marble or rubber ball across a floor will identify the direction and severity of any sag. Jumping up and down on a floor will tell you if it is adequately supported (if the floor vibrates and the windows rattle, you've got a problem). Walking around a floor will locate any loose and springy boards.

MOST FLOORS HAVE THREE major components: Supporting joists; subflooring laid at right angles to the joists; and finish flooring at right angles to the subfloor.

A SAGGING FLOOR is the result of a problem with the supporting joists. Only careful inspection can tell you which

problem you have. You're lucky if the sag is on the ground floor because it is easy to inspect the underside of the floor from the cellar or from the crawl space under the house.

THE PROBLEM COULD BE AS SIMPLE as the joists having shrunk or sagged a bit. This commonly results in a gap between the top of the joists and the subfloor. If the gap is small, thin wooden shims can be inserted between joist and subfloor. This will also eliminate any springiness in the floor above. If the gap is large and the joist is otherwise sound, a 2 × 4 can be nailed to the joist, snug up against the floor boards. So doing should also help silence squeaks.

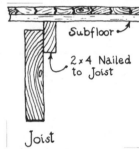

MORE SERIOUS is the case where the joists themselves are not adequately supported. Where the joists span 15–20 ft. or more, there's likely to be (or should be) a girder supporting the joists near the center of the house. If it's merely a problem of girder shrinkage, solution could be as simple as driving wooden shims in gaps between girder and joists and/or between girder and post.

IF THE GIRDER has sagged because of inadequate support, the remedy will be more of a project. The problem may simply be an insufficient number of supporting columns. Or it can be a more insidious problem like the one illustrated at the top of the next column. Upon superficial examination, it seemed that the girder was firmly supported by a stout 10-in. tree trunk resting on a concrete footing. Closer inspection, however, revealed that the post had lost much of its carrying capacity because it was riddled with termites.

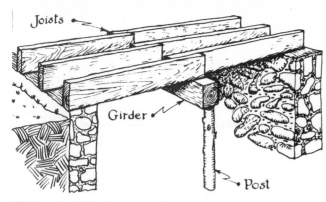

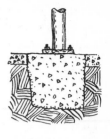

Girder carries the load in center of paired joists used to span long distance.

AFTER A TEMPORARY JACKING POST had been installed and the old post removed, the cause of the trouble was located: The original post had been set on a large flat rock for a footing when the house was built in 1825. The rock was just resting on dirt. When a later owner decided he wanted a concrete floor in the cellar, he had just poured concrete around the post. The termites, ranging far afield in search of food, had managed to burrow under the foundation and find their way into the bottom of the post that was protruding below the concrete.

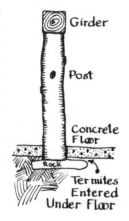

REPLACING THE WOODEN POST with a steel column made the chewing a little tougher for the termites.

SUPPORT FOR A GIRDER can be added fairly simply by using metal jacking posts. If you have a thick cellar floor (4 in. or more) you may be able to get by with setting the posts directly on the floor. Base plate of the post should be secured to the floor by drilling 1-in. deep holes in the concrete and fastening the plate down with bolts and lead expansion anchors set in the drilled holes. Top plate should be fastened to the girder with lag bolts.

IF THE CELLAR FLOOR is dirt, or the concrete isn't thick enough, new footings will have to be poured for the jacking posts. This could be a 24" × 24" concrete pad 6-in thick poured on top of an existing concrete floor. Better still, break through the old floor and dig a hole 18 in. square and 18 in. deep. Anchoring bolts can be set in the concrete while it is still wet.

AFTER SECURING BASE PLATE to the footing, movable top of the jacking post can be raised to the girder. If the girder has to be raised more than a small fraction of an inch, adjustment should be made slowly over several weeks' time.

The jacking post should be raised only a quarter turn at each adjustment. This will allow the new stresses to be equalized throughout the frame of the house and will prevent cracks in the plaster.

IT'S ALSO POSSIBLE that the floor is sagging because the foundation has crumbled where ends of joists or girders rest. In this case, beams can be propped up temporarily with timbers or metal jacking posts while the damaged foundation is repaired. All loose masonry is removed with hammer and cold chisel. Wall is then rebuilt with fresh mortar. Bricks are probably the best material to use for patches because they are easy to cut to odd shapes. After mortar has cured (wait at least a week) temporary posts can be removed and beams set down gently on the new masonry.

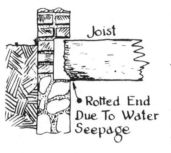

ANOTHER VERSION of this problem has been found in some old houses where joists were set in foundation masonry below grade level. Not surprisingly, water seeps into the foundation and after the passage of the years the ends of the joists completely rot away. With a condition like this, one morning you could find the floor had dropped into the cellar!

THERE ARE two repair options in this case: (1) Rebuild the entire floor, replacing the rotted joists with new timbers heavily treated with preservatives. Wall should also be treated to minimize water penetration. (2) Arrange a new supporting system by adding girders made from 2 × 10's bolted together and supported by jacking posts. In this case, the joists no longer rest on the foundation at all. This system, while simpler than rebuilding the floor, does subtract room from your cellar because of the space taken up by the girders and posts.

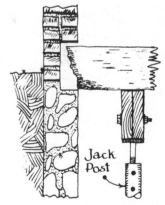

IN SOME OLD HOUSES, a sagging floor may be caused by lack of a girder altogether. Although addition of a girder is a fairly major undertaking and usually requires a contractor, it is possible for the competent do-it-yourselfer to handle some jobs. You can make a girder by bolting two or three 2 × 10's together. Girder is temporarily held in place with propping timbers, then metal jacking posts are installed every 8 ft. Be sure footings for posts are adequate as discussed above. Use jacking posts to raise the sagging joists slowly—a quarter turn at a time—spread out over a period of several weeks.

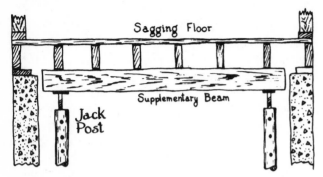

Girder and jacking posts can be installed to push up inadequately supported joists.

IF THE FLOOR ISN'T SAGGING but bounces and vibrates excessively, the joists may be undersized or inadequately bridged. Bridging stiffens a floor by transmitting loads to adjacent joists. It's very tricky to install crossed X wooden bridging once the floor is on, but you can toe-nail 2 × 6's between the joists and get much the same stiffening effect. Compression type metal bridging is also available that can be installed from underneath with a few hammer blows.

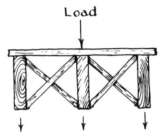

Bridging Transmits Load To Adjacent Joists; Helps Stiffen Floor.

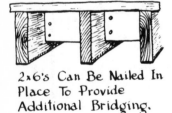

2x6's Can Be Nailed In Place To Provide Additional Bridging.

IF JOISTS ARE undersized and you don't want to install a girder because it will subtract headroom, you can nail a 2 × 4 to each side of the joist. Doing this increases the effective width of the bottom of the joist and adds to its ability to carry tension.

IN OTHER CASES OF BOUNCING FLOORS, you may find the joists have been damaged by cutting. The diagram below shows that it's bad to notch a beam on the edge—and especially bad to notch a beam in the middle where the compression and tensile stresses are greatest. Some plumbers seem to regard joists merely as obstacles to be cut through so they can run their pipes. But if a

2 × 4 Stiffeners Nailed to Joist

3-in. deep notch has been cut in a 2 × 8, its effective carrying capacity has been reduced to that of a 2 × 5.

IF A JOIST IS SAGGING because of such notching, it can be jacked into place and the notch bridged over with 2 × 4s. Or it can be supported with permanent posts.

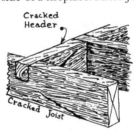

AN ESPECIALLY vulnerable point is at the joists on either side of a fireplace. These joists have to be notched to let in the header beam—and they have to carry extra weight. If not properly sized by the builder, these joists can sag and crack. Repair of such a condition can get pretty complicated. A new joist might have to be added and tied in with the header using an iron stirrup or joist hanger.

Cracked Header

Cracked Joist

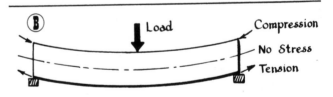

New Joist

Iron Stirrup Used To Tie Cracked Header To New Joist.

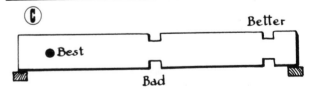

CHARACTERISTICS OF A BEAM: (A) Bending stress from a point load is greatest at center of the beam. (B) Under load, top of beam is in compression, bottom is in tension. There is no stress in middle of beam. (C) Because of the above, worst possible place to notch a beam is in the middle. Best way to pierce a beam is to make hole in center where stress is zero.

REPAIRING OLD FLOORS

A SAGGING FLOOR on the ground level of a house is less of a problem than on the upper storeyss–because on the ground floor you can make repairs from the cellar. And your handiwork will be visible only to those you invite down to the workshop.

A SAG IN AN UPPER FLOOR is more vexing because with the joists covered by flooring above and plaster below you can't tell whether there is structural damage or merely harmless shrinking and settling.

ONE SPECIAL CASE is when structural beams have been left exposed as part of the basic design of the house. In this event, it is easy to see if any cracks have developed. But repairs have to be made carefully because the mends will be visible. Two methods for making such repairs are shown at the right.

IN SKETCH A, a T-shaped angle iron is used to bridge a crack. The beam is slotted with a circular saw to accept the web of the angle. Bottom of the beam is mortised to let in the flange of the T so that it is flush with the rest of the beam. Holes are drilled in both ends of the flange so it can be fixed to the beam with long screws.

IF YOU'D RATHER have exposed metal on the sides of the beam because of a particular sight line, sketch B shows a beam mortised on both sides to accept iron plates, which are fastened with heavy screws.

IN EITHER CASE, you may have to use a couple of jack posts to move the beam back into correct alignment before fitting the mending plates.

REPAIRS GET MORE COMPLICATED when the joists are hidden by floorboards and ceiling plaster. The situation is greatly simplified if you are planning to replace the ceiling anyway. The plaster can be torn down so you can see what the real trouble is. If you do not have to replace the ceiling—and you suspect structural damage—there is no alternative to lifting some floorboards to take a look.

IT MAY WELL BE that joists have been weakened by plumbers hacking away to make room for pipes. This is especially likely around bathrooms where there are lots of pipes and the joists in all likelihood weren't designed to take tile floors and heavy fixtures (especially bathtubs filled with water).

IF THE CONDITION is severe enough to require exposing the joists, 2 × 4 stiffeners can be spiked to the joists. Additional bridging can also be nailed in place to help spread the load. Where notching has weakened beams, cuts can be bridged over with 2 × 4's. If after these repairs there is still a bothersome sag that has set into the joists, you can level the floor by nailing long wedge-shaped pieces (cut from 2-in. stock) to the tops of the joists.

AN ALTERNATIVE SOLUTION would be to install a a girder to support the upper joists. This pre-supposes that you've got some headroom to spare on the lower floor. Since the girder would be a load-bearing element, your best bet is to get an architect or engineer to develop the design. The girder can be boxed in and made a design element. Inside the girder enclosure you can also run wiring, ductwork and piping that has to be concealed.

ANOTHER WAY TO HANDLE a need for additional support is to install columns and then camouflage them with bookshelves, storage units or a partition. Such a post, however, shouldn't just rest on the floor below—in all probability you'll just make that floor sag, too. The load has to be transferred to a load-bearing surface—usually the foundation or footings in the cellar or the central girder beneath the ground floor. It is acceptable practice to line up columns vertically with intervening joists. The joists will transmit the load from one column to the next.

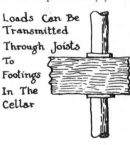

Loads Can Be Transmitted Through Joists To Footings In The Cellar

Two Methods For Mending Cracked Beams

(A)

(B) Iron Plates Set Into Each Side Of Beam

REPAIRING FLOORBOARDS

IN MANY OLD HOUSES the floorboards impart much of the antique character to a room. So floor restoration should be approached gingerly, recognizing that variations in color and texture are what gives it an old appearance.

DEPENDING UPON ITS AGE, a house will have a floor consisting of heavy boards laid directly on the joists, or it will have a finish floor laid on top of a rough sub-floor. We'll look first at houses with no subfloors, a type of construction common in the 1700s and early 1800s.

IN HOUSES WITH PLANK FLOORING, there are at least four possible ways that the boards could be joined:

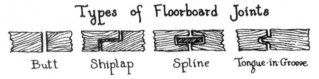

Types of Floorboard Joints

Butt · Shiplap · Spline · Tongue-in-Groove

BUTT JOINTS make it easy to take up floorboards for repairs without disturbing neighboring boards. But shrinkage can create wide gaps between the planks. To prevent drafts blowing up through cracks in butt-joint floors, some housewrights laid thin strips of wood, 4–6 in. wide, on the joists beneath each joint. If there are no strips beneath the joints and the cracks are bothersome, there are several possible remedies.

On a floor over a cellar, you usually can nail a strip of thin wood over the crack on the underside of the floorboards. Where you can't operate from the underside, there are several ways to fill cracks from above. A long wedge of wood, stained to match the rest of the floor, can be inserted in the crack and fastened with small finishing nails to the edge of one of the floorboards. (Fastening to only one of the boards allows for expansion and contraction.) Small cracks can be filled with a variety of proprietary fillers. Or you can make your own filler from sawdust and white glue, or sawdust and varnish. If the floor is to be painted, an even better filler is a synthetic-type caulk (such as butyl). These remain flexible for many years and expand and contract with the floor.

FLOORING TECHNIQUES changed little between pre-Revolutionary times and the Civil War. The wide floorboards used are thicker (1–1/8 in.) than today's because the joists were more widely spaced. White pine was the favored material, planed smooth on the top and left rough underneath. Attics were floored with the rejects, so that although you may be able to find replacement boards in your attic, it's unlikely they will be top-quality pieces.

PLANK FLOORS will need attention if the boards are loose, badly warped or very deeply worn. Loose boards must be re-fastened to the joists. Occasionally you can re-tighten the boards just by pounding the old nails in further. But in most cases this has been tried so often by previous owners that the nails will no longer bite.

HAND-MADE NAILS were used on many old floors, and their exposed heads form part of the pattern of the floor. If you need more of these old-style nails for a patch, contemporary sources are available. If you have to re-nail a board that already has exposed nailheads, you'll want to make the new nails invisible so that you don't disrupt the nail pattern. If the board can be pushed back into the proper position merely by standing on it, you should be able to re-secure it with a couple of flooring nails. Drilling small pilot holes (about three-fourths the diameter of the nail) will help avoid bent nails as you nail into the old dry joists. Driving the nails at an angle will help prevent their working loose under foot traffic.

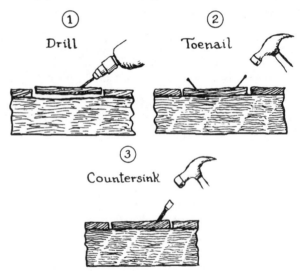

① Drill ② Toenail ③ Countersink

Nailheads should be countersunk and the holes filled with wood filler or a color-matched putty.

SCREWS CAN BE USED for boards that need extra holding power to keep them in place. Too, screws are less likely than nails to work loose over the years. Pilot holes in the joists are a must. Screw holes should be counter-bored and plugged with wooden dowels stained to match the rest of the floor. For this kind of work, a power screwdriver is a real asset. If you encounter difficulty driving screws into the joists because

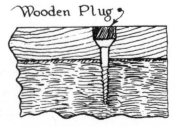

Wooden Plug

they're so dry, try lubricating them with soap.

IF BOARDS ARE badly warped, they can be straightened by saturating the wood with water ... keep damp rags on the boards for several days. Then screw and plug as described above.

SOMETIMES A BOARD OR section of board has to be re-placed. If the boards are butt-jointed, it's not hard to lift one without damaging neighboring pieces. If the boards are interlocked, however, the procedure gets more involved.

Soak With Water

IF THE BOARD is cracked, you can probably work it loose with a hammer and chisel. If there's no crack, it will probably have to be cut out. You don't want to take out more than the damaged portion, which may not be a whole board. In this case, drill a hole next to a joist big enough to admit the blade of a keyhole or sabre saw. A lengthwise cut will allow you to free the damaged portion. Since the board is cut off flush with the edge of a joist, you'll need to attach a 2 × 4 nailer to support the end of the replacement board.

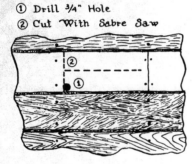

① Drill ¾" Hole
② Cut With Sabre Saw

FOR REPLACEMENT boards, you may be able to salvage an old piece from an inconspicuous part of the house or barn. But such "borrowed" lumber is likely to be thicker or thinner than what you require ... and probably won't match very closely in color. So it's no great tragedy if you have to go to the lumber yard to get a new board.

2 × 4
Nailed To Joist
Provides Nailing Sur-
face For End Of
Patched-In-Board

NEW LUMBER, HOWEVER, will doubtless require cutting and fitting. For one thing, new lumber will be thinner than its old counterpart, due to changes in lumber standards. This dictates use of thin wooden shims on the joists to bring the new board up to the level of the rest of the floor.

IF THE NEW BOARD IS considerably different in color, experiment on a scrap with various stains until you come up with the right combination that blends the new in with the old.

IN CASES WHERE DAMAGE is confined to the surface, you may be able to get a quick replacement by turning the board over. In pre-1850 houses, the undersides of the boards will probably be quite rough ... and planing will be required. The board shouldn't be sanded glass-smooth, however, because the overly level board will present too much of a contrast with the rest of the floor. Planing will reduce the thickness of the board so you'll have to use shims to bring it up to the proper level.

AN EXTRA-LARGE SQUARE

A VERY LARGE SQUARE can come in handy for jobs like laying out partitions. One can be made very simply based on the classic 3–4–5 right triangle. Fasten long straight 2 × 4's in an approximate right angle using a lapped joint. Measure 30 inches along one leg and 40 inches along the other. Then nail a 50-inch piece of 1 × 2 connecting these two points. The result will be a perfect right angle—and you can make it as big as you need.

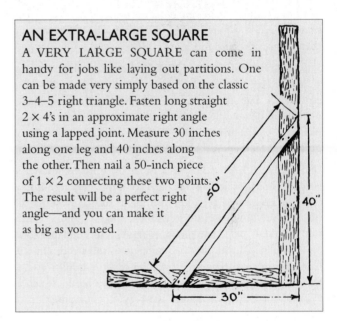

50"
40"
30"

REFINISHING OLD WOOD FLOORS

A NICELY FINISHED FLOOR is one of the crowning touches that pull a room together. But the old-house owner confronts an amazing number of techniques and finishes that can be used.

IN THIS ARTICLE, we'll deal strictly with clear natural finishing that let the grain of the wood show through. Although naturally finished floors are immensely popular today, this was not always so. In the 1700s and early 1800s painted floors were in favor. If you have a house of this vintage—and the wood in the floors is in bad shape—painting may be the answer. A painted floor is quite authentic for Early American houses—and it is much easier to prepare a floor for painting than for natural finishing.

REGARDLESS OF THE FINISH to be used, obviously you shouldn't start work on the floors until all plastering has been completed. This usually means that wall and ceiling painting should be completed, too, since repainting often requires patching of the plaster. And nothing damages a new floor quite like feet grinding plaster dust into the finish.

IF YOU ALREADY HAVE a naturally finished floor, the first decision is whether you need to completely refinish, or whether renewal of the old finish might suffice. Washing the old finish with mineral spirits or turpentine—rubbing gently with fine steel wool, and mopping up with lots of paper towels—will lift old dirt and wax. Sometimes this treatment will bring about an amazing rejuvenation of an old dull finish. If there are worn spots that require touch-up, a product such as Fabulon's Epoxy Gym Finish will provide good adhesion to both the bare spot and the edges of the old finish.

IF THE OLD FINISH IS SO SCARRED and chipped that complete refinishing is required, then the old finish has to be removed. There are two ways to do this: Paint removers or sanding. Neither is a particularly pleasant task.

OF THE TWO TECHNIQUES, sanding is the fastest and probably the most satisfactory for the majority of hardwood floors. There is one case, however, where one should hesitate before setting a power sander to the floor. And that is the house with old softwood plank floors that have acquired a pleasing texture of uneven wear from generations of foot traf-

fic. A power sander will remove the variations and produce a flat, even surface that will have none of the pleasing character that the unevenly worn floor possessed.

THE ALTERNATIVE TO POWER SANDING, alas, is hand scraping. A shellac finish can be taken up with alcohol, steel wool and lots of paper towels. Shellac is the easiest finish to remove. Paint or varnish require a chemical remover—and a lot of elbow grease. Beware of liquid removers that contain wax; traces of the wax may remain in the wood and create problems when the finish is applied. You're best off sticking with the paste-type water-rinseable removers. If you do use a wax-containing remover, you should thoroughly rinse the floor afterwards with mineral spirits and paper towels, or use a water-soluble wax-removing powder such as Wax-Off.

POWER SANDING IS QUITE APPROPRIATE for most hardwood floors such as those found in Victorian houses and other city rowhouses.

A COMMON PROBLEM is to find linoleum glued to a  nice old wood floor. After the linoleum is pulled up, there frequently is a mastic and felt residue left on the floor. This can be softened with turpentine or mineral spirits so that it can be taken up with a hand scraper. Or it can be taken off with a power sander; just be prepared to use lots of open-coat coarse paper. The mastic fills the paper very rapidly, dulling its cutting power, and requires frequent changes of paper.

ASSUMING YOU'VE DECIDED TO SAND off the old finish, the next decision is whether to do it yourself or hire a professional to do it for you. Sanding a floor is hard, dusty work. The only reason to do it yourself—besides saving money—is that you are more likely to take more time with the medium and fine papers that are required to get a really smooth surface. The fine sanding is a time-consuming step and is the area where a hired workman is likely to skimp. If you decide to do it yourself, some guidelines are set out below to help you achieve top-quality results.

TIPS ON SANDING

FLOOR SANDING CHURNS UP a lot of very fine wood dust. So the first step in getting ready to sand is to remove all furniture, pictures, shades, drapes, etc. that can act as dust-catchers. This dust can return to haunt you as you are applying the finish to the floor. All loose boards should be fastened and damaged boards replaced.

ALL PROTRUDING NAILHEADS should be counter-sunk. Taking special pains at this step will save you a lot of grief later on. Protruding nails will tear the sandpaper—requiring frequent changes of paper—and can even damage the rubber on the drum of the sander itself. You may also want to remove the shoe molding at the bottom of the baseboards. This step will allow you to sand

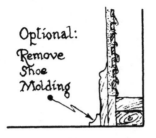

Optional: Remove Shoe Molding

more neatly at the edges. But the moldings should only be taken up if they will come off easily under the gentle prying of a putty knife; if they show a tendency to splinter then better leave them in place—or else be prepared to totally replace them with new moldings.

DOORS TO ADJACENT ROOMS and halls should be closed to contain the dust. Opening the windows top and bottom will provide ventilation and also an escape route for some of the dust.

SETTING UP THE SANDER

SANDERS CAN BE RENTED at many large hardware, paint and tool stores. (Consult your Yellow Pages under "Floor Machines—Rent-ing.") You'll need two sanders: A large drum sander for the major areas and a small disk sander for the edges. Be sure to get thorough instructions from the rental person about how to operate the machine and change paper. Many people in rental shops assume that everyone was born

Drum Sander

knowing how to operate power sanding equipment. Also be sure to get a good look at the condition of the rubber on the sanding drum. If someone else chewed it up, you don't want to get blamed for it.

ONE CAUTION: Drum sanders draw a lot of current and may blow the fuses on 15-amp. circuits. If you have 220-v. circuits in your house, you should see if the rental shop has 220-v. machines, since these draw only half as many amps as a comparably-powered 110-v. sander. Also, be sure to rent extension cords sufficient to reach from the selected power source to all work areas; the large amperage drawn by these machines dictates special heavy-duty cords.

PROFESSIONAL FLOOR SANDERS who only have 15-amp. 110-v. circuits to work with frequently will by-pass the circuit breaker with a jumper in the fuse box. (But this procedure should never be attempted by anyone who is not totally familiar with the hazards involved.) To re-move an old finish and prepare the floor for refinishing requires three sanding steps:

Edger

• FIRST CUT—Sanding with coarse open-coat paper breaks up and lifts the old finish;

• SECOND CUT—Medium paper removes all of the scratch marks left by the coarse paper;

• THIRD CUT—Fine paper removes scratches left by the medium paper and leaves floor perfectly smooth.

NORMALLY, all cuts are made parallel to the length of the boards—to avoid roughing the grain with cross-cutting. One major exception to this rule is when you have a very thick, gunky finish to take up. In this instance, many old-timers will make one cross-grain pass with the coarse paper to help break up the finish, then make a pass parallel to the grain with the coarse paper to lift the remainder of the old finish.

COARSE PAPER'S function is not only to lift off the old coating, but also to smooth out any discrepancies in the sur-face that are bothersome. The amount of material taken up is regulated by the speed at which the machine advances across the floor. It will try to pull you along at a brisk clip; by hold-ing back and slowing it down, more material is removed.

SOME POINTERS ON USING THE DRUM SANDER: Never allow the sanding drum to contact the floor while the sander is stationary—the drum will grind a hole for itself faster than you can say "there's a hole in my floor!" Use the clutch lever on the handle to lift the drum every time the sander stops. Begin your cut at one wall and walk the sander to the opposite wall. Then pull the sander back along the same path. The return pass picks up some of the dust thrown out by the first cut. Lift the drum, then re-align the sander to make the next pass, overlapping the first cut by 2–3 in.

AS THE COARSE PAPER becomes loaded with the old finish, it loses cutting efficiency and you should install new paper. The gummier the old finish is, the more frequently

DIFFERENT SANDING PAPERS FOR DIFFERENT JOBS

SELECTING THE CORRECT ABRASIVE for a job involves: (1) Type of grit; (2) Size of grit; (3) Backing. Among the grits used are:

• Flint—A quartz material resembling white sand, flint is the least expensive—and softest—of the grits. Flint paper is especially useful for hand-sanding heavily painted or pitchy surfaces, throwing it away as it clogs. When clean, wood can then be sanded with garnet paper.

• Garnet—Garnet is sharper than flint and does not crumble as easily; best for hand-sanding clean wood. Though more expensive initially than flint paper, garnet is more economical in the long run.

• Silicon Carbide—Hardest of all abrasives, silicon carbide grit is used for most floor sanding papers.

• Aluminum Oxide—For power sanders of the hand-held variety, aluminum oxide is most satisfactory. More expensive than garnet, aluminum oxide will prove less expensive on the job.

GRIT SIZE—To make things nice and confusing, there are two systems for classifying grit size. The old system uses a numerical code; the newer system uses numbers that represent the number of openings per inch in a screen through which the abrasive particles can pass. Here is a rough table of equivalents:

Grade	Grit Size (Old System)	Grit Size (New System)
Very Fine	6/0–10/0	220–400
Fine	2/0–5/0	100–180
Medium	1–0	50–80
Coarse	2½–1½	30–40
Very Coarse	4½–3	12–24

BACKING—Abrasives are glued either to a cloth backing (stronger and more flexible) or to paper. Abrasive particles may be glued close together so that no backing shows ("Closed Coat") or spaced widely so that 30–50% of the backing is visible ("Open Coat"). Open coat paper is used for gummy material that tends to clog or "blind" the paper.

you'll have to change paper. You'll also find yourself changing paper often (a dreary task!) if you didn't do a thorough job of countersinking protruding nailheads.

ONCE ALL THE OLD FINISH HAS BEEN LIFTED with the coarse paper, load the medium paper into the sander. Repeat the sanding sequence until all the marks from the coarse paper have been removed. Follow the same sanding sequence with the fine paper, polishing off all the scratches left from the medium paper. Even though the floor seems quite smooth after the medium paper, it still needs a thorough going over with the fine paper to give first-class results. The finish you apply to the floor, rather than hiding sanding imperfections, will magnify them. A thorough fine sanding is the difference between the "quick and dirty" job and a superior one.

ONE EXCEPTION to the sanding sequence outlined above is encountered with a parquet floor. Because of the crisscross way parquet pieces are laid, there is no single direction to the grain. Therefore, "sanding with the grain" has no meaning. Also, parquet strips generally are much thinner than other types of flooring, so you have to be careful not to remove too much material. The answer is to remove the old finish by starting with a finer paper—a #2½ closed coat—in order to avoid deep scratches across the grain. This procedure takes longer because you'll have to change papers more frequently—but it will conserve the floor.

EDGER IS A DISK-TYPE SANDER and thus tends to make circular scratch marks on the floor. You have to develop a gentle touch when using the edger—especially when using the coarse paper—so that you don't make deep swirl marks that are difficult to remove with the medium paper. Avoid pressing down; let the weight of the machine do the work. One hallmark of a slap-dash sanding job are the circular marks near the baseboard caused by careless use of the edger.

BECAUSE THE EDGER MAKES A circular cut you can't work it into the corners. Here you have to resort to hand scraping. This is a tedious, time-consuming chore. When hiring someone to sand floors for you, checking the work they do in the corners is a clue to how many pains they are taking with the whole job.

SINCE TWO SANDERS ARE USED in floor refinishing,

it is an ideal job for two people. One becomes the specialist with the drum sander and the other with the edger. Two people should be able to sand an average-size room in 4–5 hours of steady work. Two rooms can be sanded in one long day by two people—but be prepared to collapse from total exhaustion after if you are not accustomed to heavy physical labor.

WHEN DOING THE FINE SANDING, either work in your stocking feet or else in crepe-soled shoes so you won't leave marks on the bare wood. After the final pass with the fine paper, vacuum thoroughly—not only the floor but also baseboards, moldings and any other place where wood dust may have accumulated. Otherwise, this dust may come floating down onto your newly applied finish.

IF THE FLOOR HAS BEEN STAINED BLACK in patches by leaking water, probably the best time to deal with these is after all the machine sanding is done. You can probably remove the spots by bleaching with oxalic acid. You should be

---

FIRE DANGER

The super-fine dust created by floor sanding is highly combustible. When finished sanding, all collector bags on the machines should be emptied into boxes and the boxes placed outside where they can do no damage—even if they should burst into flame. Fires have been started many hours after work stopped by sparks that had been sucked up into the dust bag and which smoldered for hours before breaking out in flame.

---

able to get oxalic acid crystals at a large paint store or a drugstore. Make a solution of ½ cup crystals in warm water. Brush the solution on the stain and let it soak into the wood. When the solution has dried, vacuum up the dried crystals and re-sand the surface by hand or with an orbital sander.

SELECTING THE BEST FLOOR FINISH

MANY OF THE CURRENT do-it-yourself manuals would lead you to believe that the choice of a floor finish today is very simple: "Polyurethane." But after extensive contacts with users, the technical staff of *The Journal* has concluded that the advantages of polyurethane have been vastly over-sold to the consuming public.

THERE IS A RANGE of highly satisfactory finishes available to the old-house owner . . . and polyurethane is only one of them. The choice of the best finish for your application depends upon: (1) Amount of traffic the floor will have; (2) Final appearance you want; (3) Amount of time you are willing to spend applying and maintaining the finish.

BEFORE STARTING ANY FINISHING OPERATION, be sure to vacuum the room thoroughly to remove all traces of dust. This includes dust on baseboards, windowsills, etc. that could be blown onto a wet finish by a stray breeze.

WHETHER OR NOT TO STAIN is the first decision after the floor has been sanded. Bear in mind that once the finish is applied the floor will appear darker than the raw sanded wood. You can get a good idea of what the floor will look like with a clear finish by sloshing mineral spirits (benzine)

or turpentine over several square feet. This "wet look" gives a good approximation of the finished floor.

IF YOU DECIDE YOU WANT a darker color, you can use any of the commercial oil stains. Be sure, however, that the stain is compatible with the final finish you have picked. Polyurethanes, especially, are not compatible with certain stains. Lighter shades are obtained by letting the stain soak in only a few minutes, then wiping off excess with soft, absorbent cloths. Or you can lighten a stain by thinning with turpentine. Darker shades are achieved by letting the stain soak in for 15–20 min. before wiping.

OIL STAIN SHOULD BE ALLOWED to dry at least overnight—and preferably 48 hr.—before applying the finish. It is advisable to wipe the stained surface down with soft cloths one more time. If a conventional varnish is to be used over stain, it's best to seal the stain with a shellac wash—one part 4# white shellac thinned with 6 parts denatured alcohol—allowing the shellac to dry at least 24 hr.

UNDER NO CIRCUMSTANCES should a paint store person ever talk you into using a varnish stain! This is a varnish into which coloring matter has been pre-mixed. Whereas an oil stain can enhance grain, a varnish stain will vastly diminish the grain. Using a varnish stain is like applying a sheet of Formica.

TO PATCH OR NOT TO PATCH

IN OLD HOUSES, floors often have "discrepancies" that are so deep that they can't be sanded out. Real philosophical questions arise as to how far one should go to remove these blemishes.

BADLY DAMAGED BOARDS, of course, should be completely replaced (see *The Journal,* May 1974 p. 10). But there is another kind of damage where there can be real differences of opinion as to whether repairs are called for. Some people want to restore surfaces so they look exactly like new. Others prefer to leave the imperfections—because they are part of the history and character of the entire house.

FOR EXAMPLE, a woman recently contacted *The Journal* about the best way to plug bullet holes in a floor. It seems that she had just purchased an old rooming house and evidently one of the previous occupants had a rather spectacular way to request more heat.

SHE WAS TOLD that the holes could be drilled and plugged with dowels; or filled with white lead tinted with the proper colors-in-oil; or filled with a mixture of sawdust and white glue, then stained.

BUT, WE SUGGESTED, shouldn't the bullet holes be considered part of the history of the floor and just left alone? After all, people with an 18th-century house would point with pride to scuff marks made by horses stabled there during the Revolution. So 100 years from now, won't people be pointing with equal pride to early-20th-century bullet holes?

DIFFERENT COATS
FOR DIFFERENT FOLKS

CHART ON THE NEXT PAGE summarizes the pros and cons of the various floor finishes. The longest-lasting finishes are those that put a film on the surface. Foot traffic then wears away the film of finish rather than the fibers of the floor. One drawback of these film-forming finishes is that the film that protects the floor also acts as a light reflector. So that any varnished floor—even the "satin finish"—will have some sheen.

THE SOFT, RICH LUSTRE that one associates with old wood comes from the penetrating type finishes—the ones that soak into the pores of the wood. These finishes, such as penetrating sealers and linseed oil, act by filling in between the wood fibers at the surface, rather than by forming a protective coating on top of the wood. Thus the penetrating finishes

have less abrasion resistance than the film-forming types. So the homeowner who opts for the penetrating finish is faced with the prospect of either waxing (for added wear life) or frequent touch-ups in high traffic areas. Penetrating finishes, however, are easier to touch up than most varnishes. Just brush on more of the penetrating finish, allow to soak in and wipe off any excess.

THERE ARE TWO BASIC TYPES of varnish: Oil varnish and spirit varnish. Oil varnish polymerizes on exposure to air and forms a coating that is chemically bonded to itself and to the wood. Polyurethane and commercial varnishes (of the long-drying type) fall into this category. Once dried, only a chemical varnish remover will dissolve the film. This presents the problem of getting good adhesion between touch-up coats and the old film of varnish. To obtain adhesion, the old finish should be sanded with #0 sandpaper to eliminate all gloss. This provides a "tooth" for the new varnish coat to adhere to. (After sanding, carefully wipe up all dust with a soft cloth moistened with turpentine.)

SPIRIT VARNISHES form a coating by evaporation of the solvent. These varnishes can be re-dissolved by applying more solvent. Shellac and the quick-dry varnishes (such as Fabulon) fall into the category of spirit varnishes. It is easy to touch up a spirit varnish by blend-patching. The solvent in the fresh coat

---

FORMULA FOR OLD-FASHIONED
OIL FINISH

The following recipe has been used with good results on old pine plank floors:

>   1 qt. Boiled Linseed Oil
>
>   1 pt. White Vinegar
>
>   1 qt. Turpentine
>
>   Burnt Umber Pigment In Oil

Mixture is to be applied to floor from which all traces of old finish, wax, grease, etc. have been removed. Mix vinegar, linseed oil and turpentine in large container. If darker color is desired for floor, mix small amount of burnt umber into mixture and test on some little-seen section of floor. Let dry overnight, buff, and add more umber if necessary. NOTE: floor will darken with age, so there's no need to hurry to get immediate dark effect. Apply finish sparingly and wipe up excess with soft cloths. Buff. Allow to dry at least 5 days. Repeat process. Finish can be cleaned by damp mopping with mild soap. In high-traffic areas, additional coats can be applied as necessary. Be sure to clean floor with mild soap and allow to dry overnight before applying and buffing the touch-up coats.

FLOOR FINISH SELECTOR

FINISH TYPE	ADVANTAGES	DISADVANTAGES
SURFACE FILM TYPES		
Shellac	Inexpensive. Easy to apply and touch up by blend-patching.	Not long wearing. Should be waxed. Vulnerable to water. Becomes brittle with age.
Conventional Varnish	Moderate cost. Longer wearing and more stain resistant than shellac.	Long drying time. May require filler on oak floors. Surface has gloss. Waxing recommended.
Quick-Dry Varnish	Fast drying allows room to be put back in service sooner. Easy to touch up by blend-patching. No waxing needed.	Medium wear life. Surface has a gloss.
Poly-Urethane	Hardest surface of all varnishes. Long-wearing and highly resistant to staining and scarring when properly applied. No waxing.	Can be mis-applied. Not compatible with certain stains; plastic film can separate from wood. Can't blend-patch. Surface has a gloss.
PENETRATING TYPES		
Penetrating Sealer	Easy to apply and touch up. Doesn't leave glossy reflective film on the surface.	Not long wearing. Waxing is recommended.
Oil Finish	Final finish has rich lustre and patina; easy to touch up.	Not long wearing. Long drying time. Will darken with age.

partially dissolves the old surface so that the two coats fuse tightly together. (If there is any wax or dirt on the old finish, this would be washed off, of course, before blend-patching.)

FOR OLD PINE AND SOFTWOOD FLOORS, there's no doubt that an oil finish will give the richest appearance. The only question is whether the homeowner can afford the slightly longer drying time these finishes require and is willing to do the touch-up maintenance that will be needed. Touch-up is quite easy, however: Just wipe on more oil.

SOME VERY PERSONAL PREJUDICES

IN THE CHART on the opposite page, we have attempted an even-handed evaluation of all the finishes—giving them all "equal time." But based on personal experience, the author has acquired a set of preferences and prejudices that I'll pass along for what they're worth.

FIRST, I can't see the sense of anyone using shellac or conventional varnish on floors. Shellac has little abrasion resistance and so requires continual waxing. Who needs that? As

for conventional varnish, if you are willing to put up with the long drying time you might as well go for the longer-lasting polyurethane.

MANY DO-IT-YOURSELF MANUALS knock the quick-dry varnishes because they are not long-lasting. Nonsense! I have used quick-dry varnishes on hardwood floors with excellent results: 6 years of wear (and still going), no waxing needed, with only minor touch-ups required in a couple of high-wear spots. Quick-dry varnish dries tack-free in 15 min. and can be re-coated in 1 hour. This means you can sand and finish a floor in one (albeit a long one) day.

I USED A LAMBSWOOL APPLICATOR and wiped on three thin coats of the varnish (four in high traffic areas). Three thin coats are more effective than two thick coats. Floor thus coated should dry 24 hr. before being subjected to much foot traffic. I obtained excellent results with "Quick-15" made by Mantrose-Haeuser, New York. Another excellent product is "Fabulon" made by Pierce & Stevens.

A QUICK-DRY VARNISH is the best compromise when you need a tough, no-wax finish and you need to get the floor back in service as soon as possible. Polyurethanes have a much longer drying time—and I have never been particularly happy with the results. Others I know swear by polyurethane. So if you use a polyurethane and aren't pleased . . . don't blame me!

WHEN YOU WANT TO LAVISH A LOT OF LOVE on a floor . . . and get a soft lustrous result . . . oil is definitely the thing to use. But to do the job right you should use at least two coats . . . allowing a week's drying time for each coat. You can get by without waxing if you wipe on more oil as needed.

– R. A. Labine

AN ARCHITECT'S SPECIFICATION
FOR RESTORING A 1795 PINE FLOOR

Sanding can do harm to pre-1800 flooring, especially to the type of pine flooring used in Tidewater, Virginia and similar areas.

I have recently written a specification covering repair and refinishing of some 1795 flooring. I am indebted to Mr. P. Buchanan of , Williamsburg, Va., for some of the technical data included.

In some areas, badly damaged boards had to be replaced with new pieces of 5/4" (nominal) boards of quarter-sawn air-dried heart pine. So the specification covers the finishing of both the new and old boards.

Finishing New Flooring

a. Go over floor with steel wool pads on buffing machine and hand scraper . . . DO NOT USE SANDER . . . to obtain proper smooth surfaces.

b. Seal boards with liberal coat of boiled linseed oil and let dry completely (3 to 10 days, depending on weather).

c. Apply second coat of boiled linseed oil to which a small amount of coloring has been added as required to obtain a uniform appearance of the floor. (Do not put coloring into first coat.) Allow to dry completely.

d. Apply light coat of floor wax.

Finishing Existing Flooring

a. Remove any paint, etc., with a water-soluble paint remover.

b. Clean boards with a caustic cleaner, with bristle brushes. Do not use wire brushes.

c. Buff floors with steel wool pads and hand scrape as necessary to obtain smooth clean surfaces. Do not use sanders.

d. Apply light coat of floor wax.

– Frederick Herman, A. I. A.

FLOOR REFINISHING
A RADICAL ALTERNATIVE

By Daniel J. Mehn

I AM GOING TO MAKE a statement that many readers will challenge: I believe that using paint & varnish remover on old floors is easier, less messy and usually less expensive than machine sanding or hand scraping methods. Further, when one adds up all the time involved, I'm certain that the paint remover method takes less time—and as a bonus puts less strain on the family unit than the sanding/scraping way. And the end result looks better.

NOW, YOU SAY, how can this character make such sweeping claims for a method that isn't given any serious consideration by any of the standard "how-to" manuals? The answer is easy: I've tried both ways. I'll never sand again.

I INCLUDE IN MY SWEEPING statement all types of floors: Hardwood, softwood, wide and narrow, toe-nailed and face-nailed, painted and varnished/waxed floors. It can also assist those facing the "gunk" of old linoleum and tile paste.

WHEN I BOUGHT my first old house, I faced all the typical problems: Too many coats of paint on what had been beautiful woodwork; too many layers of wallpaper in every room (except where there were too many coats of paint on *top* of too much wallpaper) . . . and floors that had been waxed weekly for too long, with (maybe) an occasional cleaning and re-varnishing.

	SANDING	CHEMICAL STRIPPING
PRO	No wet mess "New floor" look Major unevenness fixed Gets it all done at once	Containable wet mess "Old floor" look, including both patina and natural bumps No loss of thickness
CON	Potential fire hazard from sanding dust Inhalation of dust Dust everywhere for long time Loss of patina and character Nailheads need resetting Loss of thickness (a major problem with old parquet floors) Unevenness at sides and corners	Potential fire hazard (if flammable remover is used) Wet mess Inhalation of vapors More cleanup stuff required (steel wool, scraper, rags, etc.) Possible disposal problem

FINANCIAL & OTHER FACTORS

	SANDING	CHEMICAL STRIPPING
PRO	Can contract out; larger the job, the lower the price per unit If do-it-yourself, sanding machines can be rented. Only belts need be purchased	Most amenable to do-it-yourself a piece at a time
CON	Should be done all at once, both for best price and to contain the sanding dust to a single occurrence	Lots of expendable "use-it-up" items Not likely to be contractable Requires bent-over diligence & perseverance; uncomfortable

AFTER COPING WITH the ceilings, walls and wood-work, it came time to face the floors. Having some previous experience (helping my father lay floors) plus the usual assortment of "how-to" books, I set out to do the conventional sanding job. I obtained the usual assortment of sanders: A walking belt sander for the large open areas; a small belt hand sander for the edges and (because I was wary of disk sanders) *both* orbital and disk sanders for the corners—plus the usual collection of large and small hand scrapers for small corners, door saddles, etc.

NUMEROUS COATS OF WAX and varnish gummed up many sanding belts, but the job got done. Ultimately, I obtained a job that I could take pleasure (but not pride) in. Friends thought I had a new floor. (They didn't see the pits and gouges along the edges and in the corners.) Besides, does one *want* a new floor in an old house? And, they didn't live with the weeks and months of sanding dust slowly settling down, again . . . and again . . .

THE HAPPY ACCIDENT

MARRIAGE AND A FAMILY brought me to another (and, I hope, final) old house, with precisely the same set of problems I had encountered before. And it was on this set of floors that I learned . . . a better way!

THE HOUSE HAD strip pine flooring. Underneath the wax and discolored varnish was what appeared to be a fine patina from years of sunlight streaming in through the windows. The floor fairly shouted at us that it needed to be refinished, and I vowed to do it . . . as soon as the other projects were completed.

AND THEN . . . the great accident occurred. While working with paint remover on the wainscotting, some paint remover fell on the floor. In scooping up the gunk, I found that it picked up all the wax and varnish from the floor. One thing led to another, and after some experimentation I concluded that stripping a floor with paint remover was superior to sanding. The pros and cons of each method are summed up in the chart above and on the preceding page.

LOSS OF THICKNESS can be especially troublesome on thin parquet floors. I know of at least one case where a parquet floor was totally destroyed by sanding; it simply curled up at every corner and exposed edge. The moisture content was severely disturbed by the loss of the surface coating and the outer compressed and surface-coating-impregnated wood cells.

HINTS ON STRIPPING

HERE ARE SOME SPECIFIC tips for stripping floors with paint remover (subtitled: "Don't be stupid like I was!"). Some of these hints are also applicable if you are sanding floors in the conventional way.

1. SCHEDULE the project carefully. Allow more time than you think necessary. I can now do a 15 ft. × 15 ft. floor in 6–8 hr., but it took more than twice as long the first time.

2. MOVE ALL THE FURNITURE out of the room and then live that way until the floor is completed. Though the speed of the job will be affected by such things as the weather and your physical endurance, allow about a week for the complete stripping and refinishing job.

3. DECIDE IN ADVANCE what you want to do about connecting surfaces, such as baseboards, shoe mouldings, door saddles, floor registers and the floor area leading to the next room, etc. Here are my suggestions for these areas:

a. REMOVE THE FLOOR REGISTERS. Put a plastic wastebasket into the void so that people don't step into the hole.

b. STRIP THE FLOOR about one foot into the adjoining room (unless it has already been done). Later, finish that part maybe six inches into the room, leaving a not-done area for catching up with when the next room is done.

c. IF THE BASEBOARDS are going to be stripped, now is the best time to do them. The mess from each helps the other. This also means that you won't have to remove the shoe mouldings . . . avoiding all the problems of possible splitting, replacement, etc.

d. If THE BASEBOARDS aren't to be stripped, then you'd best remove the shoe mouldings. If the baseboard is painted, run a sharp knife between the shoe and the baseboard to cut the paint film so it doesn't chip or flake.

e. AREAS AROUND PAINTED DOOR FRAMES that you don't want to have to repaint require careful stripping. Strip an area about 2 in. wide, using a ½-in. brush and very clean wiped spatulas first. Then, clean a wider area to about a 6 in. distance with a wider brush—before progressing to the floor itself. This way, you've cleaned the critical areas first—before fatigue and the temptation to rush sets in.

NON-FLAMMABLE REMOVER

BE SURE TO USE a non-flammable remover to eliminate any danger from an accidental spark or flame. And be sure to ensure adequate ventilation. (See The Journal May 1976, p. 9, for a discussion of potential hazards of paint remover fumes and safety procedures to follow.)

PLAN YOUR MOVEMENT through the room, not only in terms of avoiding painting (or, rather, stripping) yourself into a corner, but also in terms of supply or materials, removal of gunk, rest area, etc.

HAVE MORE CLEANUP MATERIAL than you think you'll need. This includes newspapers, plastic or cardboard buckets or cans (to wipe tools with and to contain the scraped-off gunk), lots of #3 (coarse) steel wool, extra rubber gloves, and lots of rags (old towels or wash cloths are ideal).

DO CORNERS FIRST, and then the edges. If there are any other unique or problem areas, get them done first—cleaning around them to a width of 6–12 in.

IN DOING THE CENTRAL FLOOR area, I'd suggest a space about 18 in. wide (a width you can easily reach across) by 4–5 ft. long—running with the flooring—as a basic working unit. Coat the first unit with remover, then go on to coat a second unit. By then, the first unit should be ready for scraping with a wide-bladed spatula. If necessary, wait a little longer until the remover has soaked all the way through. Let the remover do the work.

USE THE SPATULA to get the wax and floor coatings off, sweeping the gunk to the second unit. Then, coat the first unit a second time, coat a third unit, and scrape the second unit. I find I can work three units at a time this way—but never more than three!

BACK AND FORTH

WHEN YOU COME BACK TO THE first unit (having scraped the second, coated a third and recoated the second), get a good fistful of steel wool in your gloved hand, and, with a circular motion, stir the residue in the area. The object at this point is not to pick up the gunk, but rather to use the cutting edge of the wool to cut through the more stubborn spots. Now, go on to the second unit and do the same circular swirling stirring up.

COME BACK TO THE FIRST UNIT, and with a "picking up" motion of the wool, try to wipe up much of the gunk. (If the finish is very thick, you may need some more stirring. But I've done most floors with just two coats, using this technique.) Once you've used the steel wool to wipe up—always in the direction of the next unit—as much sludge as you can, use a piece of absorbent rag to wipe up the residue, working with the grain of the wood.

YOU SHOULD SEE FLOOR, cleaned, at this point. Use a clean rag to wipe *hard* again to really clean the area. Then go on to the next unit for the steel wool and rag pickup. The floor that is cleaned, but still slightly damp from the remover, will look the way the floor will ultimately appear after the final finish is applied.

AS YOU CONTINUE, you may see a spot or two that still has finish remaining. Unlike sanding, this is easily remedied by going back with a bit more remover, steel wool and rags.

REMEMBER, as you progress, to overlap units slightly to ensure that no lap marks show up. When you start to work across the floor, the new units should overlap the completed ones by the width of one floorboard.

FINISHING TOUCHES

ONCE YOU'VE finished the entire room, the temptation is to relax. Don't! Go over the entire floor again with a careful eye. With a sharp scraper in one hand, and a terry cloth rag wet with remover in the other, hit any of the minor spots that need further work. The reason for not waiting is that any finish remaining will still be internally soft from the big job. They are much easier to remove while in that softened condition than when they've had a chance to dry. A thin-bladed, rounded-edge screwdriver often is an asset at this point in clearing grooves and cracks between boards. A nutpick is also helpful.

IF THE FLOOR HAD BEEN STAINED, you should find that much of the color came off with the original coat of remover. But if you still want more of the stain up, use another medium coat of remover. Leave it on until it has almost dried out, then attack the surface again with medium or fine steel wool and the terry cloth rags for pickup. It's fairly easy—since the remover is doing all the work—but it does take more time.

IF THE FLOOR HAS SLIVERS or board edges that must be reattached, wait a couple of days for the remover to evaporate fully. Then, in stockinged feet, go over and lift the sliver edges. With whatever tool works best, get the dirt, sludge and wax off both surfaces. Then glue the splinter back down. I've had good luck with epoxy; but if you don't get the surfaces thoroughly clean, the epoxy won't hold. Keep whatever glue you use off the surface of the floor. The glue will seal the pores of the wood and will keep any stain or finish from sinking in.

FINALLY, reset any nailheads that showed up during the stripping operation. Now you are ready to apply the final finish.

THE BEST FLOOR FINISH

EVERYONE HAS his or her favorite floor finish. Several articles on this have appeared in other chapters of this book. I'll pass along my experiences which may be of benefit to some.

I AM TOTALLY DISENCHANTED with polyurethane varnishes. Scratches and nicks seem to be magnified by the slight crazing of the plastic coating around the scratch or nick. As these nicks and scratches accumulate, the floor looks worn beyond its years.

NOR AM I PLEASED with the "gym" floor finishes. Not only is the coating too evident for my tastes, but the drying times touted on the can can only be considered an optimistic estimate for a very dry day. Never have I had the drying time less than three days. Once I waited five days to recoat. You can imagine the problems of dust control while waiting for the tackiness to go away.

I PREFER a satin finish for a floor rather than a high-gloss appearance. I find I get best results with a penetrating oil finish.

BESIDES THE SOFT SATIN appearance the penetrating oil gives, it has several other advantages that I like:

• It's easy to touch up a heavily worn area by simply applying more of the penetrating oil (after surface cleaning). No need for sanding or stripping.

• You can refinish one floor and then go on to strip and re-finish an adjacent room. When the two refinished floors are joined, there are never any overlap marks where the new and old work meet.

THE ONE DRAWBACK of the penetrating oil is that it is not the easiest finish in the world to apply. You flood the sur-face with penetrating liquid, reflood after 30 min., and then rub the excess off after another 30–60 min. If you don't rub the excess off in time, the surface residue gets tacky, and has to be "dissolved" with more liquid. No big deal, but it is easy to let your belief in your own rubbing ability get the best of you and cause you to coat a bigger area than you can rub in the alloted time.

FLOOR MAINTENANCE

LIKE MANY PEOPLE, I'm lazy, and frequently my inten-tions are better than my follow-through. Floors with a pene-trating oil finish should be waxed. And I have used a paste wax (Trewax) on some of my floors—hand applied and buffed. But there are other rooms where I just haven't gotten around to waxing. With the single exception of the entry area (where the traffic is the greatest) the unwaxed floors have held up fine.

ON THE WORN AREAS of *both* the waxed and unwaxed floors, I've successfully come back a year or two later and touched up the bare spots with more Watco. I just let it soak in, then buff off the excess. The surface looked as good as new, with no "patched look."

WAXING TWICE A YEAR is a good idea for rooms that get heavy use. In lighter wear areas it's not really necessary—as long as you touch up the bare spots once a year or so.

REFINISHING WOOD FLOORS

By Frank Broadnax

WHEN YOU DECIDE to refinish your floors, the preparatory work is difficult and somewhat special. *The Old-House Journal* did an excellent job on this in its December 1974 issue. You may wish to refer to that article in preparing your floor for its new finish.

ONCE YOUR FLOOR IS nice and clean, free of any old finish, dust, dirt, wax, etc., you are ready to apply the new finish. Here I'm assuming that you'll want a clear finish that will allow the beautiful wood grain to show through.

BEFORE THE FINISH GOES ON

FIRST OF ALL, the weather plays a major part in applying a successful finish. NEVER apply a sealer or finish in damp, humid weather. I prefer the humidity to be 50% or less . . . and the temperature to be somewhere between 50–95° F. Make sure the floor is dry and that you have good ventilation.

IF YOU USED a mineral spirits or turpentine-soaked cloth to remove dirt or dust, you saw what the floor will look like when it has its new finish. If you did not use such a cloth, at this point I suggest that you moisten a small section of the floor with turpentine or mineral spirits. This will tell you whether or not the floor will be too light with its natural finish . . . and whether you'll want to stain. Obviously, you have to stain before sealer is applied.

WHEN AND IF you stain the floor, allow the stain to dry at least 12 hr.—and preferably 24 hr. You should buff lightly with fine steel wool . . . using a machine if you have access to one. Otherwise, it's hands-and-knees time. Anytime you buff with fine steel wool, you should vacuum to remove the fine dust and bits of steel.

SEALERS & VARNISHES

TO SEAL THE FLOOR, I prefer to use refined tung oil. It is quite easy to apply: Use a good soft bristle brush and apply a thin coat, brushing with the grain of the wood. By putting on a light coat, you avoid the need to wipe out excess with a soft cloth as one would when refinishing furniture. Allow the tung oil to dry 24 hr.

NEXT I APPLY A good floor varnish. I prefer one that has a tung oil base. Two such brands that we have available locally are Var Tung and Tung-Roc. Among the nationally distributed brands, McCloskey's is the one that I use most often.

IF I WANT A HIGH GLOSS, I go with gym-coat. This is the type of varnish used on gym floors. Always apply at least two coats, allowing 24 hr. drying time between each coat. Remember that applying several thin coats is always far superior to one thick coat.

SHOULD YOU NOT WANT a high gloss, use a satin finish varnish. Again, apply at least two thin coats.

I THINK THE MOST BEAUTIFUL floor I've ever done used a combination of high-gloss and satin finish varnish. Here is the procedure I followed:

1. Apply a thin coat of tung oil to seal the floor;

2. Apply one coat of gym-coat high-gloss varnish;

3. Apply a final coat of satin-finish floor varnish.

The top finish had a soft, satiny look. But by using the high gloss as an in-between coat, the finish had a deep, rich appearance—even though thin coats had been used.

HOW DOES THIS TYPE OF FINISH hold up? Great! It will last for years. And if you use a good quality varnish that doesn't darken with age, you can apply a touch-up coat as the finish wears off in high-traffic areas.

FLOOR CARE

TO CARE FOR the finished floor:

1. I never recommend waxing. This only leads to trouble . . . especially if you ever want to add a touch-up coat of varnish. Should you use wax, use a paste wax. Carnauba wax is the hardest available and does not turn yellow. Carnauba will last 8–12 months longer than other waxes.

2. To care for the floor, vacuum regularly and dust with a treated dust mop. You can treat your own string mop with a product such as Endust.

A WORD ABOUT POLYURETHANE. I personally feel the virtues of polyurethane have been oversold. I no longer use it, nor do many of the experienced floor finishers that I know. It is quite possible to get unpleasant surprises with polyurethane, many of which stem from its rather long drying time. If you are using polyurethane, be doubly sure not to apply it in humid weather and to allow plenty of time between coats.

PLUGGING CRACKS BETWEEN FLOORBOARDS

To The Editor:

SOLID MATERIALS can't be used to plug cracks between floorboards because of the constant shrinking and swelling of the boards due to varying moisture content. I thought your readers might be interested in my inexpensive and reversible solution to cold air drafts between old floor boards:

FORCING INEXPENSIVE felt weather stripping into the cracks with a broad bladed knife neatly solves the problem of drafts. Wider cracks require two or three thicknesses of felt. Width of the felt is less than the thickness of the boards so that the filling lies below the plane of the floor. Friction holds the material in place so that not even a vacuum cleaner will dislodge it. Being resilient, the felt compresses and expands in concert with dimensional changes in the boards.

I SUPPOSE THAT PAINT could be flowed into the felt to match it to the boards. But I find that when it is pushed down, the neutral graybrown color is scarcely evident. Best of all, like any good conservation procedure, the process is readily reversible and can be easily undone by using an awl or other pointed instrument to pry out the felt.

John O. Curtis

CRACKS BETWEEN FLOORBOARDS: THERE'S NO MAGIC SOLUTION

EDITOR'S NOTE: In another article, Phil Walton asked a question about what to do with floorboards over a crawl space that had shrunk alarmingly. We received a number of comments on this problem, and all seem agreed on one major point: Any attempt to fill the cracks with a rigid filler such as wood putty or sawdust and glue is doomed to failure. Even the use of wooden splines—a frequently mentioned remedy—has its drawbacks, as the following letter points out:

To The Editor:

Generally, cracks in wood floors are caused by compression shrinkage. A board that cannot swell in width because of its neighbors when its moisture content rises is put into compression. Upon drying out again, the board shrinks to less than its original width because of this compressive stress. After 30 or 40 heating seasons, the board has become sufficiently narrow that it no longer is put into compression when the moisture content rises—and thus the shrinking stops.

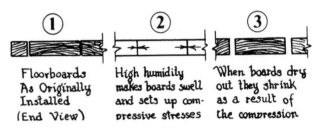

(1) Floorboards As Originally Installed (End View)
(2) High humidity makes boards swell and sets up compressive stresses
(3) When boards dry out they shrink as a result of the compression

If the cracks are repaired with cements or splines, the compression process starts all over again. The solution we recommend is to first reduce the high moisture content (which generally occurs in the summer) by applying an adequate vapor barrier over the crawl space. This could be a polyethylene sheeting taped and lapped. After the moisture condition has been corrected, then relay the floor, realizing that several boards may have to be added.

This problem is quite common in areas of the country where humidity numbers exceed the temperature, and where wood floors have been installed over earth basements and crawl spaces.

J. Henry Chambers, Restoration Consultant

To The Editor:

Phil Walton's proposal to put tarpaper on the underside of the floor sounds plausible. Better yet would be to put 3 ½ inches of insulation—with vapor barrier toward the heated part of the house—between the joists. This will stop the breezes, as well as adding insulation. The insulation can be stapled in place fairly easily. If the fiber glass shows any tendency to pull away from the vapor barrier, you can staple chicken wire under the insulation. What about the cracks? One method is to slip in narrow strips of wood. The strips can be angle-nailed with long thin finish nails to one of the floorboards. (If you nail them to both floorboards, the expansion and contraction will pull the nails loose.) Another ingenious solution I have seen is to put a piece of hemp rope in the crack. It can be varnished, and the final result is quite attractive—as well as keeping high heels from getting caught in the cracks.

In my own house I have taken up several floors and re-laid them. I picked up the boards, numbered them, and then took them outside to scrape and sand all of the crud that had gotten into the cracks over the years. Before resetting the boards, I put down roofing felt or sheathing paper on the subfloor. I do this during the winter, when the boards are at their narrowest due to drying out.

Peter C. Hotton, House & Garden Editor

THE STICKY PROBLEM OF LINOLEUM PASTE

EDITOR'S NOTE: In a recent issue, Elizabeth Tully asked for help from the readers with a floor problem. She wanted to know how to remove linoleum paste from an old floor without sanding. She was afraid that sanding would remove a lot of the character from the old pine boards. Below is a composite of the answers that we received:

THE READERS ALL AGREE that removing old linoleum adhesive without using big power equipment is a messy, time-consuming chore. With that advance warning, here are some of the suggestions passed along:

1. *TRY WATER FIRST*. Most of the old-time linoleum pastes were water soluble. So they can be softened with water and then removed by mopping or scraping.

START WITH HOT WATER. Some people add a dash of detergent or trisodium phosphate to increase the water's soaking ability. Slosh water on with a mop and cover with a layer or two of newspapers. The damp newspapers will retard evaporation and keep the paste in contact with the water. Allow to soak for 20–60 minutes, then test for softness with a putty knife. If the paste needs more soaking, you may have to dampen the newspapers again with more hot water.

AFTER SUFFICIENT SOAKING, many of these old adhesives can then be removed with mops or sponges and more hot water—followed by a thorough rinse. If there's a lot of felt stuck to the adhesive—or if the stuff is proving difficult—you may have to remove the softened material with a putty knife or wall scraper. The most favored implement seems to be a wallpaper scraper—the kind with replaceable blades. Any residue left on the floor can then be cleaned up by scrubbing with hot water with a bit of detergent added.

MANY OLD WIDE BOARD FLOORS may also be covered with paint underneath the linoleum. The paint can be removed with a floor sander, but of course this will also grind off all of the patina, the tops of the hand-forged nails, and will level all the hills and valleys that give an old floor its character. Chemical paint removers, a lot of elbow grease, and a small belt sander will clean up most of these floors. But if you run into milk paint, reports G.S. Schmidt of Darien, Conn., the only method of attack is a scraper and a bottle of ammonia. Knee pads (like basketball players wear) and rubber gloves are also worthwhile investments for this grueling task.

2. *TRY HEAT NEXT*. Most of the modern adhesives are not water soluble. When you are confronted with this type, the procedure outlined in (1) will not work. So the next step is to try softening with heat, then removing with scrapers. Best source of heat is a hot-air gun (see *OHJ*, April 1976 p. 3). You could also use one of the heat lamps that is sold for paint stripping purposes. One reader had good results with a wallpaper steamer. A propane torch with a spreader tip will also work, but there is the added hazard of fire and the possible scorching of the wood floor.

3. *THE CHEMICAL METHOD*. Linoleum adhesives that resist water can be attacked chemically. But chemicals are recommended only if the heat method in (2) proves impractical. The reason: Potential health hazards from the chemicals used.

MODERN LINOLEUM AND TILE ADHESIVES can be softened with paint removers—the water-rinseable type. These removers contain methylene chloride, and all the ventilation precautions (see *OHJ*, May 1976 p. 9) should be observed. Professionals doing the job will often dilute the paint remover 50–50 with lacquer thinner to get greater coverage. This procedure introduces the added danger of fire, however.

AS THE ADHESIVE SOFTENS, it can be scraped up with a metal scraper or rubber squeegee. Be careful in disposal of the sludge as it is toxic—and flammable if lacquer thinner has been used. Rinse surface with mop and water or mild detergent solution. If stubborn spots remain, treat them again with the paint remover.

Painting

DANGER: RESTORATION MAY BE HAZARDOUS TO YOUR HEALTH

By The Old-House Journal Technical Staff

THIS IS A SCARE CHAPTER. We don't want to scare you into abandoning restoration. Rather, we want to scare you into observing sensible precautions for your own well-being. After reviewing a lot of literature in the field, we sure have succeeded in scaring ourselves. None of us on *The Journal* staff were aware of all of these health hazards. The new information is not going to stop our restoration activities. But it sure is going to change *how* we do some things.

A EUROPEAN CONSERVATOR on a recent trip to the U.S. remarked that American restorers are "chemical crazy." He was astonished at the number of organic chemicals that are used in such a casual way by old-house owners.

WHAT FOLLOWS is by no means an exhaustive survey of all physical and chemical hazards encountered in restoration work. But it does summarize some of the most common dangers that all of us face.

THE WORST: PAINT REMOVING

REMOVAL OF SURFACE COATINGS is probably the single most dangerous restoration activity. There are toxicity hazards both from the removers themselves and from the paints being removed. For extra excitement, there is the added danger of fire.

THE FUMES from many, if not all, commercial paint removers are toxic to one degree or other. Severe damage to lung tissue has resulted from prolonged exposure to such fumes. Even more serious is the recent discovery that methylene chloride—the active ingredient in many removers—can have *fatal* short-term effects. When inhaled, methylene chloride is broken down in the body to form carbon monoxide—a toxic substance. Exposure for 2–3 hours can result in levels of carbon monoxide combined with hemoglobin in the blood that adds stress to the cardiovascular system. This can be quite serious for people with a weakened or diseased cardiovascular system. Cases of fatal heart attacks following exposure to paint removing substances have been reported in the medical literature.

METHYLENE CHLORIDE is not the only bad actor. The solvent benzene is especially dangerous. Benzene can be absorbed through the skin—and the presence of as little as 25 parts per million in the air is considered dangerous. Benzene has been linked to some forms of liver cancer and to failure of the bone marrow.

AN EXAMPLE of the type of hazardous chemicals that some stripping formulations contain:

> Methylene Chloride
> Toluene
> Acetone
> Methanol or Denatured Alcohol
> Benzene

VAPORS FROM ALL THESE CHEMICALS (except toluene and denatured alcohol) are considered hazardous to a greater or lesser degree. Also, as noted previously, benzene can be absorbed through the skin as well as inhaled.

THE PRECAUTIONS to be observed in handling chemical paint and finish removers are:

1. Use adequate ventilation. Preferably, work outdoors. Never use paint removers in an enclosed basement workshop. If you are stripping wood inside the house, be sure to have windows open—and use a fan to disperse concentrations of chemical vapor. It is especially difficult to ventilate properly in cold weather. But it is better to turn off the heating plant, open the windows wide and work shivering in layers of sweatshirts than it is to risk the health hazards of breathing chemical fumes in a warm enclosed room.

2. Use rubber gloves to avoid absorption of solvents through the skin. Be wary of pin-hole leaks in rubber gloves; they immediately render the gloves useless. Whenever a fingertip or other part of the hand feels cool, it is a sign that there is probably a leak.

FIRE HAZARDS

FLAMMABLE PAINT REMOVERS (the benzol-containing types) and organic solvents (such as alcohol, mineral spirits, etc.) present special fire hazards. The danger is not just from throwing a lighted cigarette into the can. Vapors from the organic solvents are heavier than air and tend to accumulate at floor level. If you are working in a cellar, these vapors can be ignited by a furnace or water heater.

THERE IS ALSO a potentially lethal combination in flammable remover, steel wool and electrical outlets. If you are removing paint from panelling and your steel wool contacts an electrical outlet, the resulting sparks can ignite any flammable remover that may be spread on the adjacent woodwork. The Journal staff knows of several serious fires that have been started in this way.

TO AVOID FIRE HAZARDS:

1. When working inside, use only nonflammable removers whenever possible;

2. If a particular procedure dictates the use of a flammable remover or solvent, be sure to work with windows open and a fan blowing to avoid buildup of combustible vapors at floor level. NEVER use flammable removers in the cellar;

3. If you must work with steel wool and flammable materials near electrical outlets, cut off the power by pulling fuses or throwing the circuit breakers.

IN HANDLING paint removers, keep the material off the skin—and especially out of the eyes. Make sure there is a source of running water at hand to immediately flush away any accidental spills on the body. If there isn't any running water, be sure to have a large bucket of clean fresh water in the area. An eye cup (available at any drugstore) is valuable for rinsing out the eyes and should be a standard piece of safety equipment.

LEAD POISONING

LEAD POISONING is another hazard associated with paint removal. Lead poisoning is one of mankind's oldest environmental problems. Physicians of ancient Greece and Rome recognized the toxic nature of lead. Lead has long been acknowledged as an occupational hazard for painters. Yet many old-house owners who enthusiastically start out sanding and torching off old paint do not recognize that they are exposing themselves to possible lead poisoning.

SOME SYMPTOMS of lead poisoning are dizziness, nausea and a general malaise. Renovators who have gotten lead poisoning may mistakenly ascribe their symptoms to fatigue or a cold. Prolonged exposure to lead paint particles can do permanent damage to vital organs and the central nervous system. Children and pregnant women are especially vulnerable.

ANY HOUSE BUILT PRIOR TO 1940 probably contains some lead paint. So EVERY old-house owner should be aware of the potential hazards. Lead can be absorbed both from the dust created by sanding and scraping lead paint, or from the vapors created by burning paint off with a blowtorch or propane torch. Using torches inside is especially dangerous because the vapors become more concentrated.

SAFEST WAY TO REMOVE lead paint is with an electric hot air blower. The heat gun—which has a low fire risk—is quite efficient and easy to operate. The stream of hot air softens and lifts the paint. There are no toxic lead fumes created because the operating temperature of the gun is lower than the volatilization temperature of lead.

CHEMICAL REMOVERS can also be used to strip paint without danger of lead poisoning. Chemical removers, however, have their own hazards as described previously. Dip tanks, where appropriate, can also be used to remove lead paint safely.

THE RESIDUE of removed lead paint still presents a hazard and should be packaged and disposed of in a way that won't attract small children.

IT SHOULD BE EMPHASIZED that lead paint that remains tight to the wall presents no hazard to the occupants of the house. It is only when the paint comes off the wall—either through peeling or active removal procedures—that any danger is created.

IF IT IS EVER NECESSARY to sand lead-based paint, do it outdoors if possible and be sure to wear a good-quality tight-fitting dust mask.

TESTING FOR LEAD PAINT

IF YOUR HOUSE WAS BUILT before 1940, there probably is some lead paint present . . . and you should observe the precautions outlined above. If there is any doubt and you want to test, there is a simple procedure you can follow to determine the presence of lead-based paint. It is called the "sodium sulfide test" or "spot test." It is based on the principle that a a drop of sodium sulfide solution will turn black in contact with lead paint.

ROGER A. RENSBERGER of the Lead Paint Poisoning Project at The National Bureau of Standards has provided The Journal with this description of the spot test:

• Wash any dirt, grease or oil off the area you wish to test. Dry it thoroughly.

• Scratch a corner of the painted surface to expose any hidden layers of paint. Test may also be performed at the edges of cracked or chipped paint, providing that *all* layers of paint are exposed.

• Apply a drop of the nearly colorless sodium sulfide solution on the fractured paint surface with a medicine dropper.

• After 90 seconds, check the solution drop for color. It will turn grey to black if lead paint is present. If it remains colorless, there is probably no lead compound in the paint.

NOTE: The sodium sulfide solution will not change color if the old lead paint has been covered over with a non-lead paint. That's why it is necessary to scratch through all layers to expose a sample of every paint that is present.

ONE CAUTION IN INTERPRETING results: There are a few uncommon forms of lead in paint that will not give a color change in the spot test. Also, if the paint is dark in color, it may be difficult to observe the color change in the sodium sulfide drop.

LOCAL PHARMACISTS can prepare the spot test solution by dissolving sodium sulfide in distilled water to form a 5%–8% concentration. An ounce of the solution will be enough for several dozen tests. Some pharmacists may require a doctor's prescription in order to fill a request for the chemical solution.

IT IS ALSO POSSIBLE to make the test solution from a photographic chemical: Kodak Sepia Toner #1691757. Although other manufacturers make sepia toner, only the Kodak product contains enough sodium sulfide to react with lead paint.

TO MIX THE SOLUTION, use only Part B of the two-part package. Fill a clean glass container with one pint of distilled water. Pour Part B toner into the water while stirring with a clean glass or plastic stirring device. (Do not use metal.) Mix solution thoroughly and transfer 2–4 oz. of it to a dark glass bottle fitted with an eyedropper cap for protection from sunlight. (Do not let the solution come in contact with metal bottle caps or container lids.)

CAUTION: Sodium sulfide is poisonous. Keep solution out of reach of children. Do not allow it to come into contact with eyes. In case of accidental ingestion, notify a physician immediately. Dispose of any excess solution by pouring it down a sink and flush with plenty of water.

OTHER HEALTH HAZARDS

• Puncture wounds are an occupational hazard of restoration work—and so is the lockjaw that could result. Be sure your tetanus shots are up to date. Richard Byrne, a leading restoration consultant, notes that he will not allow a workman on one of his jobs unless the worker can show evidence of having received a tetanus shot within the last 2 years.

• Some joint taping compounds contain asbestos. Sanding these materials puts asbestos fibers into the air, which is then inhaled into your lungs. Asbestos has been linked to some forms of cancer. The safest course is to use only taping compounds that specifically say "No Asbestos." If it doesn't say, then assume the material contains asbestos and level it only by "wet sanding"—smoothing with a damp sponge.

• Inhaling plaster dust is not desirable. The lungs have no way to eliminate the plaster dust that may accumulate there. In extreme cases, silicosis could result. If you are going to be generating large amounts of plaster dust during demolition work, be sure to wear a good-quality, snug-fitting dust mask.

NOT EVERY POSSIBLE restoration hazard has been set forth in this article. But from what we have discussed, we think most people will realize that we all should be a little more wary of some of the materials we deal with all the time. The objective is to keep from doing bad things to ourselves while we do good things for our houses.

Painting Tip: Latex Caulk For Wood Cracks

WHEN PREPARING FOR PAINTING, patching cracks in woodwork and the joints between woodwork and plaster is essential for a good-looking finished job. Materials often used for this job—spackle and wood putty—are rigid and sometimes fall out after a year or so as the wood expands and contracts.

HOWARD ZUCKER, professional grainer, offers this tip to *Journal* readers: Use latex caulk, the same material used for exterior caulking. The caulking gun makes it convenient to run the material into long cracks. A damp sponge will wipe away any excess. Most important, the latex is flexible and will expand and contract along with the wood. And after being allowed to dry a day, it takes paint well.

DEALING WITH CALCIMINE PAINT

By Clem Labine

CALCIMINE is a dirty word to many old-house people. We became acquainted with calcimine the same way that many old-house owners do—the hard way. We had just purchased our brownstone and one of the first things Claire wanted to do was to paint the closets so she would have a place where her clothes would be at least partially safe from the plaster dust.

SHE SPENT ABOUT FIVE HOURS on a sweltering summer afternoon stuffed inside three different closets, coating each with a fresh coat of white paint. Finally finished—tired but with a sense of satisfaction at a job well done—Claire went back to admire the first closet she had completed. Whereupon she burst into tears! The fresh paint was hanging from the walls in foot-long ribbons.

THE PROBLEM, as we subsequently discovered, was that the walls were coated with old calcimine paint. The fresh paint we were putting on was a water-based latex. Since calcimine is water-soluble, it was partially dissolved by the water-based paint. Result: The new paint wouldn't stick to the walls. Disaster!

THE NATURE OF CALCIMINE

CALCIMINE PAINT was used in America from the 18th century up to the early part of the 20th century. Calcimine was a water-based wash, usually white—but sometimes tinted blue or other pastel shades. It was mixed right on the job from whiting (chalk), glue size and water ... plus tinting pigment if desired.

CALCIMINE WAS POPULAR in Early America because it could be made inexpensively by the householder from materials at hand. Calcimine retained its popularity—especially for ceilings—even after premixed paints became available. The attraction was the soft, lustrous flat finish that calcimine gives ... quite unlike the effect given by oil-based or latex paints. The noted restoration architect, Joseph J. Roberto, plans to use calcimine on the ceilings of The Old Merchant's House restoration that he is supervising in New York City. He made this choice not only because calcimine is an authentic finish for the Greek Revival period, but also because he likes the soft, silky effect it creates.

Montgomery Ward & Co.'s Kalsomine Colors.

1st. It is the only strictly Sanitary Kalsomine in the world and contains the best Hygienic disinfectant known to science.

2nd. It is prepared dry, and made ready for use by simply adding hot water. Full directions on every package, and can be applied by an inexperienced person.

3rd. It can be applied to old, hard finished walls and make them as good as new. It can be used on iron, wood, brick, stone or plaster walls, wooden partitions, &c.

4th. Our White, of which no sample is shown, is a purer white than ordinary kalsomine, and will remain so much longer.

Will always make a perfect finish, one package covering about 400 square feet.

16 Kalsomine Tints and White.

G2729--

White, per pkg.	$0.30
Tints, per pkg.	.35
25 packages in case, white	7.00
25 packages in case, tints	7.50
100 lb. drum, white	6.00
100 lb. drum, tints	6.50

4 Fresco Colors, for Bordering, Striping, Etc.

No. 22, per ½ lb.	$0.20
No. 21, per ½ lb.	.40
No. 25, per ½ lb.	.35
No. 23, per ½ lb.	.30

Write us for Kalsomine Color Card.

From the 1895 Montgomery Ward & Co. catalog.

From the 1895 Montgomery Ward & Co. catalog.

ONE DRAWBACK OF CALCIMINE was that it had to be washed off before another coat was laid on. If layer was added on top of layer, the whole mass tended to crack and peel. Some old-time painters would take the short-cut, however, and not wash off the old calcimine before recoating. The buildup caused peeling problems that many old-house owners are living with today.

WHAT TO DO ABOUT CALCIMINE

AN OLD-HOUSE OWNER may confront the calcimine problem in two guises: (1) The wall or ceiling may have a calcimine finish still exposed; or (2) the calcimine may be covered over with subsequent layers of oil-based paint.

IF YOU AREN'T SURE whether you are facing a calcimine-finished surface, you can test by scrubbing with hot water. If it is calcimine, it will wash right off.

WHEN CONFRONTED WITH a calcimine finish, you have two choices: (1) Paint over it; or (2) strip the calcimine off before repainting. If the calcimine coat is tight to the surface and shows no signs of peeling, you are probably safe in just over-painting. Be sure to use an OIL-BASED paint.

IF THE CALCIMINE FINISH shows much inclination to peel, you are best off stripping it before repainting. The following procedure is recommended: Fill a pail about half full with hot water. With a large bristle brush, soak a section about 3-ft. square with water. With a sponge, scrub off the old calcimine, and then move on to the next section. Change water frequently—to avoid leaving a fine calcimine dust on the surface. Adding a little trisodium phosphate (TSP) to the wash water will hasten the process.

MORE DIFFICULT is the situation where the calcimine has been coated with an oil-based paint . . . and the calcimine is starting to peel. In this case, the calcimine can't be washed off because the water can't penetrate the oil paint film. The two options in this case are: (1) Chip out the loose places and patch with spackle or joint compound; or (2) undertake the tedious process of stripping all the paint off.

THE DRAWBACK of just patching a peeling calcimine surface is that nothing is done to correct the cause of the peeling. In fact, the addition of yet another layer of paint is likely to accelerate the peeling process. It is probable that your beautiful new paint will start flaking off in 6–18 months as more of the calcimine base coat comes loose from the plaster.

STEAM STRIPPING

THE ALTERNATIVE—stripping the layers of oil paint and calcimine—is equally unappealing. However, in the long run it is the soundest procedure. The easiest method (relatively speaking) is stripping by steam soaking. Steam will pass through the oil paint layer and loosen the calcimine. The only problem is getting an adequate source of steam.

HOMEOWNERS WHO HAVE steam heat have a ready-made source of steam. You can disconnect a radiator, unscrew the steam valve from the steam pipe, and attach a standard

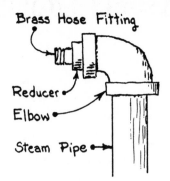

1. Remove steam valve from steam pipe.

2. Attach elbow and fittings.

set of plumbing fittings that will allow you to hook up a heavy-duty garden hose to the steam pipe. Surprisingly, a heavy duty garden hose has proved quite satisfactory for handling the low-pressure steam that comes from home heating plants. When the thermostat is turned up, the heating plant becomes a continuous steam generator that propels steam through the hose and out the nozzle. By holding the nozzle directly at the painted surface, the calcimine will start to loosen in a few seconds. A wall scraping knife will scoop the old paint off in long continuous ribbons once the steam has done its work for a few minutes. An entire ceiling can be scraped clean in about 4 hours. It is, however, hot, messy work—definitely not the type of activity you'd want to schedule for a hot summer day. Lots of condensed steam will end up as water on the floor, so plenty of newspapers are in order.

OBVIOUSLY, handling live steam requires care. Steam can inflict painful burns if the nozzle is directed against the skin. Taping the nozzle to a long broom handle with friction tape allows you to control the nozzle while keeping your hands at a safe distance. The procedure works best with two people; one handling the steam hose and one scraping.

HOMEOWNERS WHO DON'T HAVE steam heat can use a wallpaper steamer. This device puts out a lot less steam, however, so the procedure will take quite a bit longer.

AFTER STEAM STRIPPING, there will still be some calcimine residue left on the surface. This can be washed off using the procedure outlined earlier. When the calcimine is removed, all cracks should be patched, the patches primed, and then the entire surface coated with a good quality primer (tinted a shade darker than the ultimate finish coat).

19TH-CENTURY HOUSE COLORS

By Carolyn Flaherty

NEARLY AS MUCH judgment and taste is required to paint the 19th-century house appropriately as is needed to design one. Also required is a bit of time and hard work and an understanding of how old houses were painted originally. The 19th-century house has all those decorative features because the builder and owner thought them to be beautiful. Therefore, they were painted to call attention to the construction and decoration of the house.

PERHAPS THE MOST IMPORTANT aspect of painting the 19th-century house is the selection of a basic color for the body of the house and at least two or three colors for the porch, eaves, window mouldings, etc. Picking out the details is the most neglected area of house painting today. The biggest mistake made in painting the post-Greek Revival house (the Italianate, Gothic Revival, Carpenter Gothic, Queen Anne, bracketed style, etc.) is to paint the house white. White was never used after 1850. There were no "white elephants" in the Victorian Era. Disregarding the various styles of architecture and its carefully planned decoration by making it a big white mass is a 20th-century abuse of our architectural heritage.

JUST AS THERE WERE philosophical and cultural reasons a house was designed in a style resembling an Italian villa or a small castle, there were reasons they were painted in the various shades and colors fashionable from decade to decade.

COLONIAL HOUSES were generally left unpainted until mid-18th century. Barn red (inexpensive because it used iron oxide as pigment) and pumpkin yellow were 18th-century favorites, along with white and cream. Window and door mouldings were trimmed in white and doors were generally painted black, red, green or blue. The heavy bars and muntins in the windows were often painted dark to make them appear more slender. Most paint manufacturers have attractive lines of Early American colors from which to choose.

THE GREEK REVIVAL HOUSE (1820–1850) was invariably painted white with green shutters. White was thought to resemble the white marble of the ancient ruins–the inspiration for the Greek Revival style. The Greek-style house continued to be popular in the South and West even after mid-century and it was always white even though other colors for other styles were fashionable.

BUT IN THE REST OF THE COUNTRY white went completely out of fashion after the middle of the 19th century. The influential romantic architects Davis and Downing changed the landscape with their designs for Gothic Revival, Italian and Bracketed houses. Their designs were quite different from the box-like Greek Revival and it was important for the effect that they not be painted white.

SO AFTER THREE DECADES of white houses, white was now completely out of fashion. Instead, the colors were light but not bright–gray, cream, fawn–colors that resembled stones found in nature. Shutters and blinds, if any, were painted the darkest green or stained in a wood color.

AS DOMESTIC ARCHITECTURE BECAME larger and more complicated in design in the last quarter of the 19th-century exterior paint colors changed again. The late Victorian house (Queen Anne, Eastlake, Mansard, Stick, and Shingle, etc.) was painted in darker and more somber hues. Main body colors ranged in the deep earth tones of brick red, dark terra cotta, brown, deep sage or olive green.

THE FASHIONABLE architectural embellishments–wood ornament, gable trim, finials, elaborate porch trim, carefully planned stick and shingle decoration–required that the house be painted in two, three or more colors to articulate these decorations.

THERE WERE ALWAYS REGIONAL variations. Sunny southern and western areas painted in lighter and brighter shades but with same use of two or more colors for decorative details. The South used more white for all styles of houses perhaps because the Greek Revival style remained popular for so long.

THE FOLLOWING COLOR SCHEMES are given as examples for some of the more common 19th-century house styles. They all have their basis in historical fact. Some are taken from specifications in old architectural pattern and paint books, some worked out from general theories of architects like Downing.

BECAUSE IT IS QUITE DIFFICULT for two people to discuss color without an actual sample of the color to refer to–and because of the difficulty of doing an article on color in a black & white publication–actual colors are referred to by number from the Pittsburgh Paint line. Pittsburgh Paint was chosen because it is a good quality paint, has a wide variety of colors, and is distributed to a large number of paint stores around the country.

THESE COLOR SCHEMES are meant merely as a guide for the old-house owner who would like to paint a 19th century house in the manner to which it was accustomed in the last century. Substitutions can be freely made. Some of the late Victorian colors, for instance, are difficult for the modern eye and sensibility to like. For example, even though white was rarely used, a white porch is certainly pretty to the contemporary eye.

Gothic Revival

Body: A warm gray. Eaves, porch, window trim: Dark grayish-blue. Blinds: Dark Blue

-or-

Body: Drab. Eaves, porch, window trim: Light brown. Blinds: Dark brown.

This section of a Gothic Revival cottage designed by Andrew Jackson Downing is a good example of the Victorian manner of painting houses. Architectural decoration is emphasized by the use of light and dark paint. (Photo courtesy of the Dutchess County Planning Commission)

Note: The color combinations for the Gothic Revival and Bracketed farmhouse are appropriate for many styles—Carpenter Gothic, the Bracketed and the wood Italianate—built throughout the Victorian era. A plain house may have no more than a steep gable, a pointed (lancet) window or sawn wood ornament to show its Gothic influence. According to the directions given by the architects these color schemes can be reversed. That is, light trim on a dark body or dark trim on a light body. But shutters and blinds were always very dark and usually the darkest brown or green.

Bracketed Farmhouse

Body: Warm Sage Green.
Porch, Brackets, Window Trim: Straw.
Shutters and Blinds: Dark Brown.

-or-

Body: Fawn, cream.
Porch, brackets, window trim: Medium Brown.
Shutters, Blinds: Dark Green.

LATE 19TH CENTURY STYLES

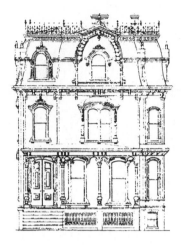

Mansard

Body: Maroon Porch, Trim, Cornice: Green.
Blinds: Gray.
Sash: Brown.

-or-

For Sunny Climes-

Body: Yellowish Beige.
Porch, Trim, Cornice: Tan.
Blinds: Dark Brown.
Sash: Same color as body.

Stick Style

Body: Light Sage Cornerboards, Bands, Porch, etc.: Orange-yellow.
Cut-work and chamfered edges: Black

Italianate

Body: Light grayish-green.
Porch, cornice, doors and window mouldings: Dark Olive Green.
Blinds, moulding strip on cornice, door trim, etc.: Reddish-brown.
Sash: Same as Porch.

Note: The above color scheme is from the Late Victorian period. But the Italianate house had been popular since mid-century. At that time it was painted in light shades resembling stone (particularly Italian stone) and in sunny areas like San Francisco where it was especially popular, it was always painted in light colors. Here is a lighter version of the Italianate:

Body: Peachy Tan Porch, Cornice, doors and window mouldings: Cream.
Blinds (if any), moulding strip on cornice, porch grilles: Medium Brown.

Stick and Shingle

First Story Body: Maroon.
Shingle Work of Second Story: Terra Cotta Red.
Panels in Gables: Peachy Tan
Trimmings: Dark Green Window Sash: White
Carved Work: Chrome Yellow
Blinds, if any: Green

Queen Anne

Shingles: Dark red—stained or painted
Woodwork: Dark Green.
Panels, Base of Blue Oriole Window: Old Gold

Sash: White

THE COLOR COMBINATIONS given here show the variety of shades and hues used on a single house. The scheme for the Queen Anne house is the most unusual, but not for its own time–about 1885. Today's homeowner may not like these specific combinations at all. An alternate color combination can be worked out by staying in the range of colors suggested for the period. The important factor is the use of two or more colors for picking out the details.

IT IS NOT EASY TO GENERALIZE about the delineation of details because the Victorian period encompasses so many different types of decoration. But here is a suggestion: Before you select colors, stand in front of your house and look at it with an eye to what makes your house (or row) look different. That decoration and trim, or anything that might be labeled "unnecessary" today, is what should be painted to call attention to itself. It could be said that an authentic period house painting is comprised of paint, knowledge of precedent, time and a little love.

AVOIDING MISTAKES
IN EXTERIOR PAINTING

By Edward F. Gola

FOR MANY YEARS, the biggest selling house paint was a product based on linseed oil with high levels of zinc oxide—a product with both plus and minus features. It provided good performance with proper application, but it had a built-in affinity for moisture—with a strong tendency to blister.

THOUGH A NEW ERA of chemical-based coatings and resins has emerged to give the homeowner a wider range of paints to choose from, the old-house owner faces a special problem: You also have to think about what has already been applied to the structure. An old house has probably been patched, repaired and repainted five or more times. It not only has acquired a brittle build-up of old paint film that may be reaching (or at) its saturation level, but it is also a build-up of different paint formulations that may not be compatible with each other.

QUESTIONS TO BE ANSWERED first are: (1) Will the surface take still another coat of paint? (2) If yet another coat of paint is to be added, what kind of surface preparation is necessary? (3) What kind of top coat will be flexible enough to counteract the brittle character of the surface to be covered? (4) If the old paint is to be removed, what is the best primer and finish coat combination? (5) Is there evidence of a moisture condition that should be corrected before any new paint is applied?

PREVIOUS PAINT –
SALVAGE OR REMOVE?

ABOVE 16 mils thickness (0.016 in.), an old paint film can be considered at the dangerous saturation level. What this means is that above this thickness the paint film presents a greater and greater barrier to the escape of moisture—moisture that is often generated within the home itself. Since moisture tends to collect at the interface between the wood surface and the original first coat of paint primer, pressure mounts at this point as the moisture tries to push its way through the paint film. At high film thicknesses, this pressure can cause cracking and peeling down to the wood surface.

THERE IS NO WAY—short of extensive laboratory testing—to predict with 100% certainty whether or not a new coat of paint will cause peeling. New paint, regardless of qual-

ity, will peel if applied over an old film that is not anchored firmly to the wood, since expansion and contraction of the new paint film will pull off the old loose material. The only guide for the old-house owner is to make a careful appraisal of the condition of the siding, soffits, trim, etc.

WHEN THERE IS general deterioration of exterior surfaces—with continuous patterns of deep, down-to-the-bare-wood cracks—the old finish should be removed. This is a difficult, time-consuming job that can be accomplished best by burning off the old paint or by sanding.

GREAT CARE should be taken in burning off paint since this process can char the outermost layers of wood cells and contribute to defiberization. When charring occurs, it is difficult to get the proper paint adhesion. Surface charring should be removed by sanding whenever possible. When all charring can't be removed, reasonably good performance can be achieved by using a primer that does not contain zinc oxide or other reactive pigments, since these pigments are hydrophillic (water-loving) and contribute to prime coat blistering. Also, finish coats containing zinc oxide will blister if applied over bare wood without a proper prime coat.

BLISTERS may also appear within a very short time after a coat of paint has been applied in hot weather or in direct sunlight. This causes skin-drying and traps the thinners before they have had a chance to evaporate. This is known as solvent blistering—and is more apt to happen with darker colors that absorb more heat from the sun.

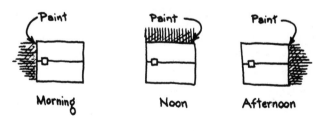

Avoid direct sunlight by painting in the shadows during the day.

IF PAINT HAS BEEN REMOVED by burning or sanding, prime the wood with two coats of solvent-base primer. Allow sufficient drying time (as indicated by the label) between coats. Thin the first coat four-to-one with a solvent such as mineral spirits (1 qt. of mineral spirits for every gallon of paint). This reduced prime coat helps to lower viscosity and allows the paint to penetrate and glue the loose wood fibers together so they won't break away. Second primer coat should be full strength; this provides assurance that you have "cemented" the wood fibers.

FOR THE TOP/FINISH COAT, one coat of an oil-type quality house paint should be sufficient with proper priming. If you choose a latex house paint, one coat is recommended for Northern areas, and two coats where mildew is a problem. The second coat creates a more effective barrier to external moisture (rain, dew, etc.) and moisture is a prime agent for mildew growth.

IN SOME CASES, cracking and peeling may be confined to single boards or small sections of siding, or in the so-called "protected" areas, such as the soffits. Careful cleaning, scraping, sanding and priming of these problem areas can avoid the last resort of complete paint removal.

MOISTURE – INSIDE OR OUTSIDE?

PRIME CAUSE OF PAINT FAILURE on exterior surfaces is moisture migrating to the surface from inside the structure—or moisture getting behind the paint film from the outside. Most of the complaints aimed at "bad paint" are in fact misdirected; they result from failure to take proper precautions against moisture.

MOISTURE CAN ENTER from the outside through faulty flashing, inadequate caulking, leaking gutters, etc. Moisture can also originate from the inside from high-humidity areas such as bathrooms and laundry rooms.

YOU CAN THWART EXTERIOR MOISTURE by sealing all cracks. On the roof, defective shingles should be patched or replaced. Faulty flashing should be repaired with flashing cement. Leaking gutters can be repaired with fiberglass and epoxy resin. Any cracks or holes in siding should be plugged with putty or caulk. And all joints between siding and woodwork trim, and joints between wood and masonry, should be sealed with a good quality latex caulk. Latex caulk costs quite a bit more than the old oil-based caulks, but they will give much longer service.

DEALING WITH MOISTURE from the interior is more complex. Better ventilation is usually the key. In bathrooms, for example, inexpensive tile that may have been used for walls will have to be replaced—and an exhaust fan installed to give the moisture a way out. Attic spaces may require instal-

lation of louvers—or bigger ones if you already have them. There should be at least two attic vents, with 1 sq. ft. of vent area for every 350 sq. ft. of attic space.

CAULKING CHECKLIST

• Between siding and drip caps on windows and doors;

• Between siding and window sills;

• Between siding and frames of doors and windows;

• Between siding and corner boards;

• At joints between masonry and woodwork;

• Between siding and decorative moulding;

• Around columns, capitals and gingerbread;

• Between porches, masonry steps and house foundation.

WASHERS AND DRYERS generate a tremendous amount of water vapor inside the house. You should be sure that dryers, especially, are properly vented to the outside.

ADDITIONALLY, siding that has been installed close to the ground will usually be saturated with moisture drawn by capillary action. The moisture vapor is drawn upward into other parts of the wood structure and may condense on the back of the siding—only to migrate through and push off paint wherever it goes. Wooden wedges under clapboards—or metal vents in more extreme cases—can provide moisture with a way to escape to the atmosphere without pushing through the paint.

ANY ROTTING BOARDS should be replaced—after treating the new board with wood preservative and priming edges and both sides before installing.

'PROTECTED AREAS' – A SPECIAL DANGER

GREATEST IMPACT of exterior moisture is on the so-called "protected areas"—soffit areas such as under eaves and roof overhang, or areas protected by trees. These areas are protected from direct sunlight and from driving rain . . . which means normal cleaning and weathering does not occur. Dirt and grime accumulation can become excessive. And any moisture that does collect (such as dew) does not dry quickly and water remains longer on the paint film. This promotes expansion and contraction of the top paint film, which may weaken the bond of one coat to the other.

KEY TO GETTING good paint adhesion in these protected areas is proper surface preparation. If surface is hard and glossy,

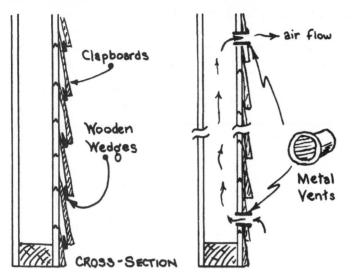

Clapboards

Wooden Wedges

CROSS-SECTION

air flow

Metal Vents

Two Ways To Vent Excess Moisture From Exterior Walls

it should be sanded. If peeling, it must be thoroughly scraped. If dirty or grimy, it must be cleaned. And if the soffit area has been painted many times, be sure the new top coat has sufficient flexibility to handle the dimensional fluctuations of the previous coats.

TIPS ON SURFACE PREPARATION

SURFACE PREPARATION is vital for good paint performance, since it provides the basis for adhesion—and adhesion is what good paint performance is all about. Anyone restoring the finish on a piece of fine old furniture knows the importance of careful surface preparation. Unfortunately, old house exteriors rarely get the same loving attention—even though a lot more is at stake.

TO CLEAN A SURFACE FOR exterior painting, first remove all loose material such as flaking paint, dust, etc., with wire brush, scraper, sandpaper and/or steel wool. Tight stubborn material may have to be removed with a motorized wire brush. Old paint that is smooth and shiny should be roughened by sanding to provide a good "tooth" for the new paint.

WHEN THE OLD PAINT has been chalking (surface is powdery) it is especially important to wash off the chalky powder. Same is true if there is much suface dust and dirt. Make up a mild detergent solution by mixing ¼ cup household detergent (such as Tide) in a gallon of water. Scrub the exterior using this solution and a bristle scrub brush. Rinse off thoroughly with a garden hose and allow the house to dry completely before proceding to paint.

EXCESSIVE CHALKING may be due to the use of or quality paint, or abnormally long exposure to weather, or inadequate surface preparation. Some paints do not have enough binder for long life and are too highly pigmented. Premature chalking will also occur if badly weathered surfaces are not properly prepared and primed. An improper primer, for example, may result in the wood absorbing the binder from the finish coat. Also, cracking, peeling or chalking may result if a latex house paint is applied during freezing weather or below temperature specified on the label.

NAILHEADS should be countersunk, patched with filler and pre-primed. Where old paint has flaked out in big pieces, edges of the holes should be sanded to feather edges, and pre-primed if you are down to bare wood.

IF THERE ARE a few small rotted areas that don't warrant complete replacement of the wood, you can use some of the epoxy wood consolidating systems.

EXTERIOR PAINTS are made in many different formula-

Find and correct any moisture problem. Then remove peeling and chalking paint.

Use bristle brush to remove all dirt and dust. Wash surface if dirt and grime are excessive.

Apply primer and finish coat that are compatible with each other—and with the old paint film.

EXTERIOR PAINTS are made in many different formulations—each designed to give best performance under different conditions. For example, mildew is one of the most common causes of paint failure. There are specific treatments—and paints—designed to deal with mildew conditions.

MILDEW is the visible result of fungus growth on the surface of organic matter. It is fairly common on exterior painted surfaces, especially in warm, humid or shady locations. It appears as tiny spots of brown, black or purple discoloration. The unattractive appearance becomes progressively worse due to growth of the fungus and entrapment of dirt in the mold web.

LIKE ANY LIVING ORGANISM, mildew fungus requires food. It flourishes on the nutrients found in house paint, on the surface under the paint film, or both. Often, mildew on the surface will grow completely through the paint film to the wood below, much like the roots of a tree. Result: Deterioration of the entire paint film.

PAINT MANUFACTURERS have tried to solve the mildew problem by developing paints with the most mildew-resistant materials, supplemented with specific mildew fighters. Unfortunately, a mildew resistant paint film is only as good as the surface preparation prior to painting. If mildew is definitely present, it is necessary to thoroughly clean and sterilize before any painting is started. Since mildew sometimes looks just like dirt, it is wise to test a surface for its presence.

A SIMPLE MILDEW TEST consists of placing a few drops of common household bleach on the suspicious patch. If the bleach causes the spot to lose its blackish or brownish appearance, then there is reason to believe mildew is growing on the surface.

TREATMENT FOR MILDEW

ONCE MILDEW has been diagnosed, the following procedure is recommended:

1. Prepare a cleaning and sterilizing solution of 3 qt. warm water into which you add 1 qt. of liquid bleach containing 5% sodium hypochlorite; ⅔-cup trisodium phosphate or borax; ½-cup detergent.

2. Remove mildew by scrubbing with this solution. A medium soft brush will give good results. When applying solution, avoid getting it on skin or in your eyes.

3. After scrubbing, thoroughly rinse with fresh water from a garden hose. Allow surface to dry completely.

4. Apply mildew-resistant paint as soon as possible after the house dries. This prevents possible contamination by fresh fungus spores.

WHEN SELECTING a paint from the many types available to today's homeowner, remember that the primer and topcoat should be considered together as a single system. If these two don't react well together, you are merely painting on more problems for yourself in the future. When in doubt, the safest course is to buy a primer and finishing coat made by the same manufacturer.

SELECTING THE BEST EXTERIOR PAINT

By Clem Labine

NOW, WE'LL LOOK AT the many types of exterior coatings available and the characteristics of each.

FIRST RULE IN REPAINTING is: Don't rush it! Repaint only when the old paint has worn thin and no longer protects the wood. Faded or dirty paint can often be freshened by washing. Too-frequent repainting produces an excessively thick film that is more sensitive to the weather and also is more likely to crack across the grain of the paint. (The grain of the paint is the direction of the last brush strokes.) Complete paint removal is the only cure for cross-grain cracking.

IF THERE ARE PATCHES of bare wood that have been exposed to the weather for several years, it is best to recondition these places before applying *any* paint. These places are so dried out and porous that they will drink in paint like a thirsty sailor. To treat these areas, use two parts of *boiled* linseed oil thinned with one part of turpentine. Apply the oil liberally with a brush. If the wood still seems porous, wait a day and then repeat the process. When the wood has been thoroughly saturated with linseed oil, the surface will have a slight sheen when dry. Then spot-prime the patch with a zinc-free linseed oil primer before applying the finish coat.

FACTORS IN PAINT SELECTION

PAINT CONSISTS OF THREE basic elements: (1) A binder such as linseed oil or a latex resin; (2) a thinner such as mineral spirits, turpentine or water; (3) a pigment. The binder is the key to good paint performance. A poor binder—or too little of a good binder—will give disappointing results.

THERE ARE TWO GENERAL TYPES of binders: Those thinned with organic solvents and those thinned with water. The latter are characteristic of the so-called "water-based" paints. (This is actually a misnomer, because the paints aren't based on water, but rather on the latex binder emulsified in water.)

THE MOST COMMON solvent-thinned binders are the alkyd resins and linseed oil. Binders are usually the most expensive component in paint, so cheap paints are likely to be lean on binder—which will result in a short service life for the paint film.

PRICE OF THE PAINT usually only amounts to 10–20% of the total job cost when you are having a job done professionally. So it doesn't pay to use anything but the highest quality paint—even when you are doing the job yourself. Cheap paint is just going to require the added expense of repainting several years sooner than would have been needed if high-quality paint had been used. Too, the paint build-up from these more-frequent repaintings is just going to hasten the day when the entire paint film fails and all the old paint has to be removed from the house.

PRICE ALONE DOESN'T tell you which is the best quality paint—although it is an indicator. Careful reading of the labels on the paint cans should tell you which is the best buy. You are looking for the maximum of binder resin and hiding pigment. High binder resin gives a long service life; high content of hiding pigment gives you more coverage per gallon.

LABEL ARITHMETIC

INFORMATION ON PAINT CAN LABELS isn't laid out quite so neatly, however. You have to do a couple of quick calculations to find out what you need to know. The first set of numbers given to you are for "Total Pigment" (hiding pigment plus fillers) and "Vehicle" (binder resin plus thinner). For instance, a label might read:

Pigment	33.4%
Vehicle	66.6%
	100.0%

BY ITSELF, this doesn't tell you much because you don't know how much of the Pigment is filler, and how much of the Vehicle is thinner. So read on. The analysis of the Vehicle given is:

Alkyd Varnish	85.1%
Driers	0.5%
Mineral Spirits	14.4%

THE 85.1% OF BINDER (the alkyd varnish) looks very good, until you read the footnote indicated by the asterisk. The footnote tells you that the alkyd varnish has the following composition:

EXTERIOR PAINTS – PROPERTIES & USES

TYPES	PROPERTIES & USES
Primer/Sealers	Used for unpainted wood, or old surfaces that have lost most of the original paint. Has high percentage of pigment that prevents paint from soaking into the wood; provides uniform painting surface for the topcoat.
Primers	Designed to promote adhesion between paint films rather than to seal wood. Used on old work when old paint is in poor shape—especially when there is a chalking condition. Unsuitable as topcoat. Should be covered with finish coat within a week of application.
Topcoats (Oil or Alkyd)	Excellent brushing and penetrating properties. Provides good adhesion, elasticity and durability. Apply with brush to obtain strong bond, especially on old work. Many oil-based paints offer "controlled chalking," which makes them self-cleaning—rain washes off the chalk, and with it the dirt. Oil paints give a glossier surface than latex. Usually get a heavier film and greater hiding power with oil paints.
Topcoats (Latex)	Have durability comparable to oil-based paints. Quick drying; can be applied in damp weather. Easy to apply with roller. Provides better color permanence than oil paints. Provides matte finish, making touch-up easier. (A glossy oil-based finish that has dulled with age may look blotchy when touched up with fresh glossy paint.)
Trim Enamel	Usually made with oil-modified alkyds. Slow drying (overnight). Made in high sheen, bright colors. Have good retention of gloss and color. More expensive silicone-alkyd enamels are substantially more durable than oil-alkyd enamels.
Anti-Rust Primers	Priming of iron and steel surfaces when good corrosion resistance is required. Slow-drying types provide good penetration into cracks and crevices. Fast-drying types should be used only on smooth, flat surfaces. Use water-resistant types for metal subject to severe humidity or to fresh water immersion.
Galvanizing Primers	Priming of new or old galvanized metal and steel surfaces. Satisfactory as finish coat if metallic gray color not objectionable. High percentage of zinc dust provides good anti-rust protection and adhesion. Galvanizing/zinc dust primers give excellent coverage, one coat usually being sufficient on new surfaces. Use two coats for surfaces exposed to high humidity.

Non-Volatile (Soya Alkyd Resin)	51.3%
Volatile (Mineral Spirits)	48.7%

BY READING THIS FOOTNOTE, you find out that nearly half of the alkyd varnish is thinner (mineral spirits). By calculating these percentages back, you find out that the total binder content is about 29% of the total paint. This is actually a pretty good percentage; cheap paints may have only half as much binder.

ANALYSIS GIVEN for the pigment in this particular paint:

Titanium Dioxide	13.2%
Calcium Carbonate	85.5%
Silicates	1.3%

THE PIGMENT IS COMPOSED substantially of hiding pigment (as opposed to fillers). So the total "active" ingredients in the paint are: Binder (29%) plus Hiding Pigment (32%) for a total of 61%. This is a good quality paint.

ABOVE A CERTAIN POINT, the ratio between binder and hiding pigment becomes a trade-off. Adding more binder means you get a more durable paint film . . . but you get less pigment so you don't get as much hiding power.

STEER CLEAR OF PAINTS that don't list their contents by percentage on the label!

Guidelines For Paint Selection

IT IS IMPOSSIBLE TO PICK a single "best" paint for every conceivable exterior paint job. Having outlined the characteristics of the most common paint types above, these additional guidelines can be given:

• If the paint currently on the house has performed satisfactorily, use the same brand and type (if known) when it is time to apply a new coat of paint.

• If the old topcoat isn't chalky or peeling and is in generally good shape, you can add a new topcoat without worrying about a primer. If dirty, however, surface should be washed before laying on the topcoat, and any patches that have been scraped down to bare wood should be spot-primed with a zinc-free oil-based primer.

• A primer is indicated where there is excessive chalking.★ To test for chalking: Rub an old T-shirt across 10 inches of the surface. If pores in the cloth plug up with old pigment, chalking is excessive. Before applying primer, chalk should be washed off.

★ Some causes of excessive chalking: Last coat of paint may have been spread too thin; paint may be excessively weathered; paint may have been applied over a porous substrate that absorbed much of the binder; inferior paint was used.

AN OIL-BASED PRIMER is best for overpainting old chalking surfaces because oil gives better adhesion than latex primers.

• In selecting a topcoat to go over a primer, remember that the two should be considered together as a system. Big problems can be created by choosing a topcoat that wasn't designed to be used with the primer. If you are using an oil-based primer, you are safest using an oil-based topcoat made by the same manufacturer.

• On new wood, a primer/sealer should be used as the first coat.

OIL-BASED VS. LATEX PAINT

THE OLD ARGUMENTS about oil-based vs. latex exterior paints largely come down to a matter of personal preference in most cases. Good quality oil-based and latex paints will give about the same service life in the majority of applications.

WHEN IT COMES DOWN TO A COIN-TOSS between the two, most old-house owners opt for oil-based paint . . . mainly for reasons of tradition. Oil-based paints have a longer history of proven service. And most houses were originally coated with oil paints. So using oil-based paints seems appropriate to many.

LATEX PAINTS offer more convenience in use. Rollers and brushes clean up with water. And you can apply latex in damp weather. (Surfaces must be *completely dry* for oil paints.)

LATEX probably has an edge in painting new wood where you are worried about passage of moisture from inside the structure. On old work, however, the main barrier to moisture is the many coats of old paint beneath the new layer. So the slightly greater porosity of latex doesn't give any significant advantage.

AS NOTED ABOVE, oil-based paint has the edge on old chalky paint where it is desirable to apply a coat of oil-based primer first. In this case, you are best off using an oil-based topcoat over the oil-based primer.

MOST TRIM PAINTS are oil-based, too. So in spot-priming trim work, you should also use an oil-based primer.

FOR COATING SHAKES AND SHINGLES, many people prefer stains rather than paint because stains let the natural beauty of the wood show through. Stains are basically varnish binders colored with transparent iron oxide or dyes. Stains are easier to apply to rough textured surfaces because they have a lower viscosity than paints, and so penetrate better and provide more adhesion.

HOWEVER, no clear finish will have the durability of a binder protected by an opaque pigment (such as a paint). Stains are more subject to degradation by the sun and so you have to renew the finish more often.

PREPARING TO PAINT

By Clem Labine

FEW PEOPLE REALIZE that, in painting, the actual application of paint is the easiest—and in many ways the least important—part of a paint job. Proper surface preparation is EVERYTHING. In old houses, you can easily spend 4–8 hours or more in preparation for every hour that will be spent actually painting.

BEFORE PLUNGING into preparation for painting, however, ask yourself the basic question: Is repainting really needed? Or will just a thorough cleaning (and maybe some touch-up) suffice? Too often, people lay on a new coat of paint rather than cleaning. But repainting year after year has two serious drawbacks: (1) Thick paint layers blur detail in woodwork and ornamental plaster; (2) Heavy paint layers create lumpy surfaces and increase the likelihood of alligatoring and other paint problems.

A CLEANING SOLUTION of Soilax (or similar nonrinse soap powder) can provide an amazing rejuvenation of old paint. And since old painted work should be washed free of dirt and grime before repainting anyway, you can delay a final decision until the cleaning step is completed.

IF THERE IS WALLPAPER on the wall—painted or un-painted—you're best advised to strip it off. Wallpaper that is tightly bonded to the wall can be painted—but it doesn't look as good as paint on flat plaster. Also, the paper can always come loose at a later date—ruining the whole paint job.

THE CALCIMINE FACTOR

BEFORE 1940, calcimine paint was widely used on ceilings (and sometimes walls) to avoid problems of paint build-up. Calcimine—essentially a tinted chalk in a weak glue—was meant to be washed off before a new coating was applied. That way, you always had only a single layer of paint on top of your plasterwork, and all outlines were crisp and sharp.

WHEN OIL-BASED PAINTS began to replace calcimine, often these new paints were applied right on top of the old calcimine. This was a mistake. Over the years, the glue that holds the calcimine to the plaster weakens . . . and as it peels it takes all the other paint layers with it.

THERE ARE ONLY TWO WAYS to deal with chronic peeling caused by old calcimine:

1. Allow the surface to continue peeling and touch it up periodically;

2. Remove the calcimine and covering paint layers. Calcimine dissolves in water—but you'll have to use heat or chemicals to remove the water-impervious paint on top of the calcimine.

IF YOU HAVE A SURFACE that is still covered with its original calcimine (you can tell by its solubility in hot water), be sure to wash it ALL off before painting. (The May 1976 article has tips on washing calcimine.)

BEWARE OF ALLIGATORS

THE MOST FRUSTRATING of paint problems is alligatoring—an over-all series of cracks in the old paint film. The cracks originate not in the plaster or woodwork below, but rather somewhere in the layers of paint on top. One common cause is applying a flat paint over varnish or glossy enamel.

ONCE ALLIGATORING is occurring, you can do only one of two things:

1. Treat the problem symptomatically by filling the cracks with spackle or joint compound. Recognize, however, that the alligatoring will probably show up again within a year;

2. Remove all the paint layers with a heat gun or chemicals and start all over again.

IF YOU ARE EVER painting over varnish or glossy enamel, prevent future alligatoring by sanding thoroughly, or use a liquid deglosser.

ELBOW GREASE NEEDED

AFTER WASHING (and having determined to repaint), the next step is to thoroughly scrape all loose and flaking paint. This is a boring—but essential—part of the job. Proper scraping not only removes blemishes and loose material; it also calls your attention to cracks and loose plaster that will need more work.

IT'S AMAZING what a difference the proper scraper makes. Although there are many types on the market, most professional painters find that the best scraper is a homemade "short scraper." They take a good quality flexible scraper (such as a

Russell or Warner) and have it cut down as per the sketches at the right. Best way to cut them is at a metal shop that has a sheet metal cutter. In a pinch, you could cut one with a hacksaw and straighten the edge with a grinding wheel or file. A file is used during scraping to sharpen the scraper should it become dull. Professional painters usually have a number of short scrapers—cut to different lengths from different width blades. For the homeowner, a good all-purpose scraper can be made from a 4" flexible scraper cut so that about 2" of blade remains.

PROPER LIGHT is a great asset in the scraping and subsequent patching operations. Best way to get this is with an extension light fitted with a reflector. Hold the lamp in one hand and the scraper in the other. You'll be astounded at the imperfections that show up in the glare of your hand-held lamp that aren't noticeable in ordinary lighting conditions.

LOOSE PLASTER

OFTEN THE SCRAPING will turn up areas of loose plaster in walls or ceilings. In severe cases, the only solution is to remove all the old loose material and replaster or replace with sheetrock. But if the problem is localized, there are a couple of short-cut repairs.

PLASTER OF PARIS can be used to make a "key" to anchor the old plaster. Cut away the heart of the loose material, exposing the lath. Make sure that the lath is firmly attached to the studs. After thoroughly wetting the lath and surrounding plaster, trowel in a stiff mixture of plaster of paris—making sure that some of it oozes behind the lath strips. Trowel the plaster of paris firmly against the old plaster to obtain a good bond.

RUN A BOARD across the patch to make sure that none of the new wet plaster is higher than the surrounding surface. Much better too low than too high. Low spots can be filled in later with spackle or joint compound. If any plaster of paris gets on adjoining painted surfaces, sponge it off while wet—or else remove it after it is dry with your short scraper and coarse steel wool. Plaster does not adhere well to painted surfaces, so if you don't remove this slopover before painting, you run the risk of chipping at a later date.

BEWARE ESPECIALLY of ceilings that seem spongy to the touch. Lath nails can work loose from old dried joists. Or the plaster keys may have broken loose from the lath. In either case, loose plaster in a ceiling is just an accident (possibly fatal) waiting to happen.

IF INSPECTION SHOWS the lath are still secure to the joists, small loose areas can be repaired with plaster of paris keys as described above. If the lath is loose—or the area involved is several square feet—you can drill through the plaster with carbide bits, and secure the plaster with 2" washers held by 3" wood screws driven into the joists. The washers can be camouflaged by feathering out with several applications of joint compound. These anchors should be placed at about 18" intervals throughout the loose area.

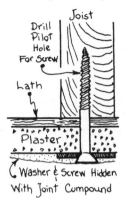

JOINT COMPOUND: THE MAGIC MATERIAL

TO BRING OLD PLASTER SURFACES up to snuff for painting, many professionals rely heavily on joint compound (also called "wallboard compound," "taping cement," etc.). They use this in preference to commercial spackle. The advantages of joint compound: It has good adhesive properties (it will stick to paint), works smoothly and can be easily sanded when dry. The premixed joint compound, although more expensive than the powdered form, has better working properties and is worth the added cost.

JOINT COMPOUND is excellent for leveling imperfections in walls or ceilings . . . such as places where old paint has chipped out, cracks caused by alligatoring, etc. Used in conjunction with joint tape, it's also useful in covering structural cracks. When professional painters are preparing an old room that's in bad shape, very often every square inch will be gone over with a thin layer (or layers) of joint compound to even out all irregularities.

ONE DISADVANTAGE of joint compound is that it shrinks on drying. Thus if any build-up more than 1/32" is required, you should put the material on in several applications. Each coat should dry thoroughly before the next one is applied. Try to get the bulk of the material put on in the first application—and smooth it out as much as possible without fussing excessively. The subsequent coats . . . applied thinly . . . will complete the smoothing of the patch.

THE WIDER THE AREA being worked, the wider the taping knife you should use. Some professionals have taping knives as wide as 12". For the homeowner, however, a 3", 5" and 6" knife should handle 99% of the situations you'll encounter.

AFTER THE JOINT COMPOUND dries, it can be smoothed by sandpaper or "wet sanding" with a damp sponge. If you've worked carefully with the taping knife, however, the need for sanding should be minimal.

JOINT COMPOUND is highly absorptive of paint. Therefore, before the finish coat of paint is applied, all patches—both raw plaster and joint compound areas—should receive a coat of primer. The primer should be tinted the same color—or slightly darker—than the finish paint that will be used.

PATCHING CRACKS IN PLASTER

By Clem Labine

BAD STRUCTURAL CRACKS–the kind that tend to reopen year after year–require a different treatment than the surface repair described in the last chapter. Structural cracks are the result of movement. Few people realize that a house is constantly in motion due to changes in temperature, humidity, winds, foundation movement, etc. Expansion and contraction of structural elements at differing rates sets up stresses in plaster walls and ceilings. Although the amount of movement is normally quite small, it can be great enough to cause cracks to develop along lines of greatest stress. Cracks are the building's way of relieving tension.

THE FACT OF CONSTANT MOVEMENT dictates the best approach to mending structural cracks. If you use a rigid material like plaster of paris or powdered spackle to patch a stress crack, it's likely that the structural movements that created the crack in the first place will cause it to reopen in a year or so—sometimes almost immediately.

THE SECRET lies in using a mending system that has some "give" to it. An excellent mending system can be created by using the materials used for covering sheetrock joints: Premixed joint compound (such as U.S. Gypsum's "Durabond Wallboard Compound") plus a cloth or paper reinforcing tape.

PREMIXED JOINT COMPOUND is more expensive than the powdered mix-it-yourself variety, but it more than makes up for the added cost in better workability. If you have a lot of patching to do, you can save quite a bit of money by buying the joint compound in 62-lb. pails.

THE CLOTH REINFORCING TAPE is better for flat surfaces than the paper tape. The open weave of the cloth tape allows the joint compound to ooze through easily and thus beds the tape securely to the compound. This characteristic

is especially important when you have to overlap tape when following jagged cracks (see diagram on next page).

THE CLOTH TAPE is difficult to find in certain parts of the U.S., however, and so you may have to make do with the paper tape. This shouldn't cause any great problem except when overlapping tape on jagged cracks: You'll have to make sure there is an adequate bed of compound between the two layers of paper. In any event, the paper tape works best on corner cracks, as explained later.

APPLYING THE TAPE

TO PATCH CRACKS, apply joint compound with a wide (5–6 in.) joint knife. Butter the compound into the crack, spreading it about 3 in. on either side of the crack. Center the reinforcing tape over the crack, and force the tape down into the bed of joint compound with the knife. It should be pushed hard enough so that some of the compound oozes up through the fibers of the cloth tape—but not so hard as to disturb the fibers of the tape. If you are using paper tape, push hard enough to bed every portion firmly against the bed of compound—but not so hard as to squeeze all the compound out from under the tape. There should be a thin layer of compound left under every square inch of tape to form a bond between the tape and the plaster surface. Remove any excess compound by wiping with the joint knife.

AS SOON AS the tape is bedded, cover with a thin layer of compound and smooth as much as possible by working with the joint knife. When first coat has dried (at least 24 hr.), smooth out any ridges by "wet-sanding" with a damp sponge or a heavy-nap cloth folded flat or wrapped around a suitable block. (You can also sand with sandpaper, but it creates a lot

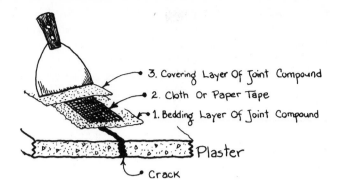

3. Covering Layer Of Joint Compound
2. Cloth Or Paper Tape
1. Bedding Layer Of Joint Compound
Plaster
Crack

of dust.) Apply a second thin coat of joint compound and feather the edge at least 1 in. beyond the first coat. After second coat has dried, wet-sand lightly and apply a thin finishing coat. The finishing coat can be worked quite smooth with the joint knife. A professional can work it so that no further sanding will be required. But most of us will find that our work will need a final light wet-sanding.

WHEN WORKING WITH joint compound, be sure to keep any crusted material that forms on the taping knife out of the fresh material. The old stuff will just cause lumps that make it impossible to feather out the joint compound smoothly. Throw away any material that shows signs of losing its workability. Better to waste a little than risk fouling all the material remaining in the can.

TO KEEP JOINT COMPOUND in the can from getting fouled—and for ease of working—a second tool is used to hold a working amount of compound. (Plasterers would call this tool a "hawk.") A large joint knife or finishing trowel will serve for this purpose. Just be sure the holding tool is bigger than your  working knife; you need a long edge to wipe the edge of your working knife against.

INSIDE CORNERS

PAPER TAPE works best on cracks in inside corners because it can be folded easily to conform to the shape of the corner. Apply compound to both sides of the corner, then fold tape along center crease and press into position. Firmly press both sides of tape into compound with the joint knife. As noted before, it's very important that every square inch of tape have an adequate bed of cement underneath it. Otherwise, it will pull away from the plaster surface sooner or later.

WIPE EXCESS off both sides of the angle. Immediately apply a coat of compound over one side of the angle only and allow to dry (at least 24 hr.). After compound has dried, apply coat to other side of angle and allow to dry. (It is possible to cover both sides of the angle with a single application, but the twostep process ensures that you don't disturb your work on one side while you are smoothing out the other side.)

APPLY A FINISH COAT, and feather it out beyond the edge of previous coats of compound. Wetsand as needed.

CRACKS IN COVES

A SLIGHT VARIATION in technique works best when dealing with cracks in curved surfaces, such as a cove between ceiling and wall. The bedding layer of joint compound can be brushed on with a 2½-in. nylon paint brush. The cloth tape is then pressed into position by hand, and then a covering layer of joint compound is brushed on. Brush back and forth until it looks smooth. If the compound is too stiff to brush smoothly, you can loosen it by adding a small amount of water.

AFTER DRYING, the first coat can be wet-sanded with a damp sponge, and then a finish coat is brushed on. The brush adapts itself to these curved areas much better than a joint knife.

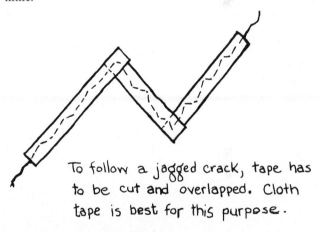

To follow a jagged crack, tape has to be cut and overlapped. Cloth tape is best for this purpose.

PROBLEM CRACKS

IF YOU HAVE a structural crack that you know from experience is subject to an unusual amount of stress and strain, it may break through the sheetrock tape and compound. For these special problem areas, the best thing to use is a commercial patching system called Krack-Kote. It uses a pliable adhesive and a glass-fiber reinforcing tape, and thus has more flexibility and strength than ordinary joint compound.

KRACK-KOTE, manufactured by Tuff-Kote Co., Woodstock, Ill., should be available through large paint supply stores. The main drawbacks of this system: It is more expensive than the joint compound, and also takes much longer to apply.

GAPS BETWEEN PLASTER surfaces and surrounding woodwork are also subject to a lot of movement because of the shrinking and expanding of the wood with changing temperature and humidity. Thus you need a filler that has some flex to it. Acrylic latex caulk, applied with a caulking gun, works very nicely for this purpose. Any excess can be cleaned off with water and a sponge before it sets up.

A FINAL WORD on the taping system: Don't go "tape crazy." Minor cracks can be handled with the surface spackling techniques described the last chapter. Only experience, unfortunately, can sometimes distinguish between major and minor cracks. Also: If a wall has so many cracks that it would take an undue amount of time to tape them all, consider either totally replastering or else canvasing the surface.

Chimneys, Fireplaces, Stoves

REPAIRING OLD CHIMNEYS

By Matt Huff, The Clean Sweep

Restoring old chimneys to working order is usually a job for a professional. But competent pros are hard to find. In this article, an expert lays out the ABC's . . . so you'll know what you can do yourself—and when it's time to call for help.—Ed.

IN FIREPLACE WORK—as in washing windows—the sensible approach is to start at the top. There's not much sense in worrying about renovating the firebox if the flue is plugged and the chimney toppling. First step in checking out a chimney is to see if the flue is clear. One simple way to do this is to light a fire: Open the damper (if it has one) and light a crumpled sheet of newspaper in the firebox. Add other sheets of newspaper slowly so that you won't have too much smoke in the room should the flue be plugged.

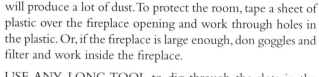

IF THE FIRE BURNS satisfactorily, smother the fire with a folded newspaper to see if the flue can accommodate all the smoke produced.

IN SOME FIREPLACES, you can hold a hand mirror above the damper and see the sky reflected in it. This only works in flues that are straight or nearly straight—but it does offer convincing proof that the flue is clear.

OR, IF YOU CAN REACH the top of your chimney, you can lower a weighted rope down to the fireplace, and then pull a burlap bag stuffed with papers up through the flue to check for obstructions.

ALL THREE OF THESE METHODS presume that you can open the damper. But in many old houses, especially those in which the fireplace has seen little use, the damper will be stuck shut. Many years' accumulation of debris may be piled atop the damper to a depth of several feet. Flues in old houses were lined with mortar, not tile, and the weathered mortar deposits a lot of sand and lime on top of the damper.

IF YOUR DAMPER has a sliding plate on it (as is common with many 19th century fireplaces), tap the sliding plate back and forth to loosen the debris behind it. It will probably move very little at first because of the weight of the debris, but continued tapping will eventually loosen it. The falling dirt

will produce a lot of dust. To protect the room, tape a sheet of plastic over the fireplace opening and work through holes in the plastic. Or, if the fireplace is large enough, don goggles and filter and work inside the fireplace.

USE ANY LONG TOOL to dig through the slots in the damper. As you dig the dirt out, more and more debris will cascade down. When you finally dig out enough debris to open the damper, the digging goes a lot faster. As soon as you poke through the deposits and establish a draft, the dust will begin to go up the flue instead of out into the room—making your task easier. When all the debris has been dug out, apply one of the tests described earlier to see if the rest of the flue is clear.

IF THE FLUE is still plugged, you must locate the blockage. Look at the top first, because a previous owner may have capped the flue to keep cold drafts out. If the flue isn't capped, pinpoint the obstruction by lowering a weight on a rope. When you feel the weight go slack, you have reached the plug and can measure the length of rope you've played out. Try breaking the plug free by hauling the weight (a window weight is ideal) up a few feet and dropping it on the plug. This may free an obstruction that is only composed of a few bricks.

MOST OBSTRUCTIONS are formed when the brick divider that separates flues tumble down. The resulting plug can be several feet thick and quite resistant to pounding with the weight. If your plug is of this stubborn variety, it can only be removed by surgery. Knock the plaster off the inside wall where the plug is located, then break into the flue by removing several wall bricks with a hammer. (A rented electric hammer may save time.) And beware—the operation is very dusty!

DIG OUT THE RUBBLE plugging the flue and test again for a draft. When it is working, brick up the hole and replaster.

INSPECT THE CHIMNEY TOP next. If it leans, it should be torn down and rebuilt. You may want to raze the chimney to roof level because it is nearly impossible to match new bricks to existing bricks. If sections of the chimney are covered with white powdery efflorescence (often in attics, just below the roof), it means the bricks have been saturated with water for a long time. If the water leak can be stopped and the bricks given a chance to dry out, the bricks may be saved. But if water has deteriorated the bricks too badly, the chimney should be rebuilt.

IF A LOT OF MORTAR has weathered out of the joints, tuckpoint with fresh mortar. If your chimney needs extensive tuckpointing, it may be worth your while to tuckpoint every joint because it is so difficult to match the color of the new mortar to the old.

LINING THE FLUES

YOUR OLD CHIMNEY probably has more than one flue. The flues are separated by brick dividing walls—usually only one brick thick. These dividers are typically in worse shape than any other part of the chimney. The top few feet of these dividers may be missing altogether. You can line the flue with metal pipe to prevent the dividers from tumbling down the flue as they continue to erode.

METAL PIPE for lining flues is available in sizes from 6 in.–12 in. diameters. Local heating suppliers may have only small sizes, but large sheet metal shops should have a complete range.

STAINLESS STEEL PIPE must be used in furnace flues because furnace exhaust gases corrode ordinary metals very quickly. In a fireplace flue, you may use the much cheaper (but shorter-lived) galvanized steel pipe. Choose the largest diameter that will fit down your flue without binding. 3-foot sections are the most convenient to install.

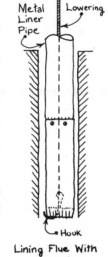

Lining Flue With Metal Pipe

INSERT THE PIPE, crimped end first, from the top of the chimney—one section at a time.

TIE A ROPE to a hook and hook the first section of pipe so that you can keep the liner from getting away from you as you lower it. Just before each section enters the flue, secure it to the previous section with metal screws.

IF THE BRICK DIVIDERS between flues are decrepit, put one section of pipe part way down the other flues so that you won't knock any loose bricks down into the other flues while you work.

LOWER THE LINER down the flue until the bottom end reaches the top of the fireplace throat. Seal the bottom end by forcing screen around the liner and dumping mortar down from the top. Seal around the liner at the top, too, to keep water out.

INSTALLING A METAL LINER is simple in a smooth straight flue. But in a flue that bends too much, or whose inside surface is rough with mortar and broken brick, you may be unable to slide one down. In this case, you will probably have to break into the chimney to install flue tiles. Also, if your fireplace has a weak draft, do not install a metal pipe liner because it will reduce the cross-section of the flue and thus reduce draft.

INSTALLING TILE FLUE LINERS requires breaking into the chimney as described earlier for the removal of major obstructions. But in this case, you have to open up ALL of the chimney. When the chimney brickwork is exposed on the outside of the house, the work can be done from the exterior—but it requires scaffolding. If the chimney is inside the house, the work has to be done from the interior. The process is quite messy—and also expensive. It could run $700–800 or more to have a professional tile-line a flue that runs from a ground floor fireplace to the top of a three-storey house. This is definitely not the normal do-it-yourself kind of job.

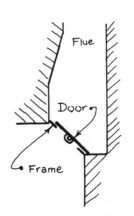

Plan For A Simple Damper

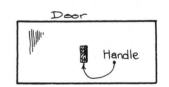

Steel plate is cut to fit opening and to rest on frame. Bottom edge rests on smoke shelf.

An Alternative Simple Damper Without Hinge

FIREPLACE REPAIRS

IF YOUR HOUSE is over 120 years old, its fireplaces were probably designed to burn wood. If newer than that, the fireplaces may be designed for coal grates or gas logs. Most coal fire dampers were made of two slotted plates—one behind the other. To open these dampers, slide the back plate left or right until the slots line up. Total area opened by these slots is small—probably too small to handle the smoke from a wood fire.

IF YOU PLAN to burn wood and need a larger damper opening, sometimes the slotted coal dampers can be pushed back together to provide the larger area. If the plates are fixed, you will have to remove the old one and replace it with a fabricated flat damper.

THE OLD DAMPER is probably made of cast iron and can be broken and removed with a hammer. Flat dampers must be custom-made because you will not be able to buy any damper to fit the small opening of a late 19th-century fireplace. A welder should be able to make one for about $50.

WHEN INSTALLING THE DAMPER of your choice, wrap the edges with fiberglass insulation. This fiberglass buffer will allow the steel damper to expand and contract without breaking the adjacent mortar. If you have to re-mortar areas around the damper, mix some fireclay with the mortar to increase its resistance to heat.

IF YOUR FIREBOX is still in good condition, you will probably need to do little more than tuckpoint the joints. Again, use fireclay.

IF YOUR FIREBOX has crumbled or is completely gone, begin the rebuilding by laying a level hearth. You can remove the existing hearth and lay a brick hearth, or pour a fresh slab of cement with a high sand and fireclay content over the existing rubble. A level hearth is the most important factor in building a neat, even firebox.

USE FIREBRICK throughout the firebox. The joints should be as thin as you can make them—about 1/8 to 1/4 in. Allow the mortar to set at least three days before lighting any fires.

INSTALLING A MANTEL

SHOULD THE MANTEL and the facing on the front of your fireplace be missing, you'll have to locate an appropriate mantel from an architectural antiques shop. After any refinishing, the mantel can be hung above the fireplace by securing two or three flat hooks to the wall and to the back of the mantel (see sketch below). You will need accurate measurements—and perhaps several tries—to position the hooks so that the mantel just touches the floor. Mantels can also be wired to the wall using heavy picture-hanging wire.

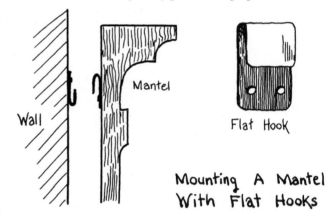

Mounting A Mantel With Flat Hooks

THE FIREPLACE FACING that covers the area between the fireplace opening and the mantel can be made of tile, marble or brick. Your taste, the size and shape of the mantel, your purse, and the original facing (if known) will all help

DANGER: WOOD FIRES & UNLINED FLUES

BUILDING A WOOD FIRE in a fireplace that has an old unlined flue is an invitation to a house fire. Often, the mortar in the old flues has eroded, providing many side exits for the combustion products. To make matters worse, sometimes old house builders rested wooden beams right in the chimney wall. These beams can be ignited by a stray spark.

WOOD FIRES are particularly hazardous because, in addition to sparks, the fire gives off soot and tar that can build up as deposits inside the flue—and which can suddenly ignite as a spectacular chimney fire. In a well-lined flue, a chimney fire can be harmless. But in an unlined flue, a chimney fire can easily spread to the rest of the house.

THE CHIMNEYS in many late 19th century houses were not lined—because they were meant only for gas logs or coal fires. These burn more cleanly than wood—and don't create the extensive deposits that a wood fire does. You could still use a gas log safely in an unlined flue. And a coal fire burning anthracite (hard coal) produces a clean flame. Cannel coal, however, tends to produce a lot of sparks.

THE PROPER LINING for old flues may be governed by your building code. Some localities insist upon tile linings for flues used with wood fires. Cost of a tile lining can run around $20–30 per ft. installed.

you determine which facing to use. Bricks can be laid up with regular mortar. Most other facings can be applied using plaster of paris as a "glue."

THE FACING SHOULD fit behind the mantel and behind the metal frame that surrounds the firebox opening. This is much easier than trying to butt the facing up against the frame and mantel.

IF YOUR FIREBOX was lined with metal firebacks and sides, they can be reinstalled in your renovated fireplace. Prop them in the desired position and wire them to masonry nails pounded into the surrounding walls. Fill behind them with rubble and pour a new concrete hearth around their base.

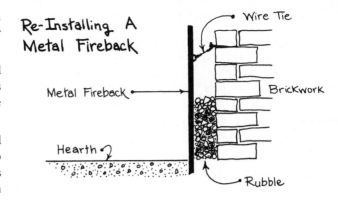

REPAIRING & RESTORING MARBLE MANTELS

By Richard Mazan

DO-IT-YOURSELF RESTORATIONISTS should have no fears about removing, repairing and installing marble mantels. Once you understand the anatomy of their construction, assembly and repair procedures are relatively simple.

SOME OLD-HOUSE OWNERS who are missing mantels are able to locate replacements in buildings that are scheduled for demolition. The hardest part of the removal and installation process is removing the mantel from the wall without damage. It can be done . . . it just takes time and patience.

MARBLE MANTELS installed in the late 1800s were almost always joined together with plaster of paris. The entire assembly is joined to the chimney breast with the same plaster "glue"—plus a few wire ties. So the dismantling procedure is basically one of breaking these plaster of paris bonds. And make sure you have a helper on hand to hang onto the marble pieces as they are worked loose.

HERE ARE THE STEPS you'd follow to disassemble a marble mantel:

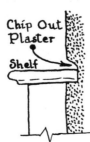

FIRST, REMOVE THE SHELF. The shelf may be set into the wall, requiring that you chip out the plaster just above the inset along the entire length of the shelf. The shelf can then be worked loose by hitting upward with the palms of your

hands along its length. DO NOT attempt to use heavy tools to hurry the operation or you'll just end up with marble chips for your garden.

NEXT, REMOVE THE KEYSTONE. It is held in place on a centering dowel with plaster. Try twisting first. If that doesn't work it loose, use a few gentle taps with a cold chisel at the seam to loosen it, then twist keystone off.

THE SPANDRELS—the arched face pieces—can be released by first unfastening the hook-and-eye arrangement of the iron liner in the arch. Pull in several directions on the spandrels and they will give way. The trim pieces left on the wall will need some gentle persuasion with a pry bar. If the hearth is not visible, it may be under the floor as a result of remodeling. Probe for it if the floor is expendable.

INSTALLING THE MANTEL

CENTER THE HEARTH STONE square to the wall and test for level in two directions. If you do not wish to cut out the floor to fit the new hearth, it will work satisfactorily to set it right on the present flooring—if the fireplace will be for decoration only. Edges of such a raised hearth can be trimmed with a suitable wood molding.

CEMENT MORTAR or plaster of paris and wooden shims

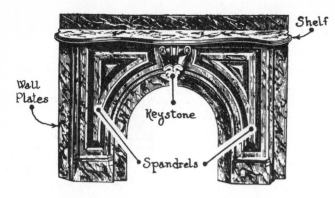

Shelf

Wall Plates

Keystone

Spandrels

can be used under the hearth in the leveling process. The rest of the assembly process should be preceded by a "dry run"—test-fitting all the remaining pieces without plaster.

EXCESS HEIGHT can be cut from trim pieces with an ordinary hack saw. (You'll probably be surprised to find how easily marble cuts!) To keep trim, spandrels and other pieces plumb and square, it will be necessary to brace them with 1×3 scrap lumber while the plaster is setting. Nail small cleats to the floor to anchor one end of the braces; cut braces a mite longer than you measure so that they will bow and exert pressure when they are in place.

WITH ALL ADJUSTMENTS made for fit, scribe pencil marks where necessary to permit parts to line up correctly after the plaster adhesive is applied. Mix enough plaster to glue the trim pieces to the wall. You'll want a slow set-up plaster for this operation. Use a commercial retarder in the mixing water, or add a teaspoon of vinegar or animal glue to the mixing water. To get more working time out of the plaster, always use cold water and put the water into the mixing container first. Sprinkle plaster powder in slowly and stir as little as possible.

APPLY ¼-inch of plaster to the mating surfaces and fit marble to the pencil marks. Be sure that structural walls (especially bricks!) have been thoroughly wet down before applying plaster. Check for plumb on all sides. Because of the retarder, you have time to slide pieces around as need be. When trim pieces are properly positioned, lock in place with braces.

IF NEED BE, at any point you can always scrape the plaster off and begin anew. At any time the plaster shows signs of setting, throw it out and mix a new batch (be sure container has been thoroughly cleaned out before starting new batch).

NEXT, APPLY PLASTER TO the spandrelsand fit to pencil marks on the trim pieces. Plumb, then brace with 1×3's cut previously. After the plaster has set, apply plaster and fit the two arched trim pieces to the back of the spandrels. These can

be held to the spandrels with C-clamps or bracing.

THE KEYSTONE was originally positioned with a wooden dowel. If the dowel is missing, insert another dowel or bolt and set in plaster, checking for squareness. Apply ¼-inch of plaster and fit keystone to original position at the apex of the arch. Brace keystone until plaster is set.

CENTER THE SHELF and draw a pencil line on the wall along the upper back edge. Remove shelf and rout out plaster deeply enough to allow shelf to set into wall the proper depth. There will usually be stain and plaster marks to show exactly how the shelf was positioned previously. Apply plaster at every point where the shelf is to rest and set in shelf. Wipe off all excess plaster that oozes out. Plaster remaining in small recesses can be picked out easily after it dries.

FIT IRON LINER to the opening in the spandrels and tie hooks into the side firewalls. This can be done by drilling holes in the masonry with a carbide-tipped bit and anchoring the hooks in the holes with a fast-setting patching cement, such as Rockite.

REPAIRING DAMAGED MARBLE

BROKEN MARBLE can be repaired reasonably well with epoxy glue and large bar clamps. Or you can fashion your own large clamp by nailing two cleats to a board that is a little longer than the piece to be repaired. After the pieces have been glued, force them together with wooden wedges driven between the cleats and the marble. CAUTION: Marble will bend, so it may bow if you apply too much pressure.

CHIPS AND GOUGES can be filled with epoxy resin and marble dust (which is an ingredient in the manufacture of cultured marble). Fill hole with the mixture and leave slightly higher than the surrounding area. Use fine-grit wet-type automobile paper to sand down after drying. If you need to apply graining, try dry colors and a fine-tipped brush while the epoxy adhesive is still tacky.

ABRASIVE PAPER—the type used in auto body shops for wet rubbing—is great for refinishing marble. Start with 200 grade and work up to 600. The paper will cut for a long time as long as it is kept wet. For final polish, use tin oxide powder (sometimes referred to as putty powder) and water with a rubbing pad. Or you could use the white kind of auto rubbing compound as a final finish. Marble can be given a final touch with a good grade of furniture wax, or a marble polish such as Goddard's.

CARE AND CLEANING OF MARBLE

FOODS AND BEVERAGES that will mar wood may very well damage marble surfaces. Fruit juices, for example, are acidic and can eat away marble. Moisture rings may result from sweating glasses. Coasters should always be used under glasses and any spills wiped up promptly.

THE MARBLE INSTITUTE OF AMERICA offers these pointers for removing stains that may work their way into the marble surface:

• POULTICE—Most stains require a poultice for removal. A poultice is a device for keeping the stain moist and in continual contact with the treating liquid. A poultice can be made of white paper napkins, white cleaning tissue or white blotting paper.

THE POULTICE SHOULD BE SOAKED with solution appropriate to the stain being treated (see below) and kept moist while the treatment is going on. Poultice can be prevented from drying out by covering with Saran Wrap or a piece of glass. It may require two to three days to draw the stain out of the marble.

• ORGANIC STAINS—These are caused by natural substances such as fruits, coffee and tea, and organic dyes from papers and fabrics. To remove, wash the marble with water and then apply a poultice soaked with household ammonia (full strength) or 20% hydrogen peroxide solution.

• RUST STAINS—Rust rings often result from tin cans, flower pots, nails and other metallic objects. Remove by applying a poultice soaked in commercial rust remover.

• OIL STAINS—These result from spills of such materials as butter, salad oil or peanut butter. Remove with a poultice saturated with acetone or amyl acetate.

REBUILDING FIREPLACES

By R. C. Hunter

QUITE OFTEN IN OLD HOUSES the original fireplaces have been removed because they had become unfashionable, unused or decrepit. Now, with escalating fuel costs, a working fireplace is again a highly desirable asset. Even more important, the growing interest in the sensitive restoration of old homes is bringing more and more people up against the problem of replacing a missing fireplace. Perhaps my experiences in restoring fireplaces in my 1890 Victorian house can help others to begin this task.

ASSUMING THERE IS NOTHING LEFT of the original fireplace, the first challenge is to figure out where the original fireplaces may have been. This can be quite difficult if the earlier owners did a careful job of removing them. The first step is to identify all the chimneys from the outside and the walls of which rooms they pass through. This may be harder than it seems. Not infrequently, the tops of chimneys were pulled off when fireplaces were no longer being used. The only remainder may be the chimney breast alongside an outside wall or in an attic.

USEFUL CLUES may also be found in the cellar where you can look for the base of chimney stacks. A cleanout door for the ash pit is a sure sign of a fireplace having existed somewhere overhead.

HAVING IDENTIFIED WALLS with chimney breasts that may conceal plastered-over fireplaces, there are a couple of other clues to look for before you start swinging the sledge hammer:

1. Check for patched flooring where the hearth would have been;

2. Remove the baseboard along the face of the chimney breast. The wall is usually not as carefully finished behind it and may show signs of the original opening (When I pulled away my baseboard, 40 years of debris poured into the room!);

3. Try punching a small hole through the middle of a suspected opening. My fireplaces were just covered over with metal lath fastened to the opening and then plastered over.

IF THESE PRELIMINARY TESTS convince you that there is a fireplace opening behind the wall, now is the time for the sledge hammer! It's best just to knock the plaster off first. If there's brickwork behind the plaster, look to see if the shape

of the original opening is apparent. If it isn't, stop! You don't have a fireplace. But if there is the outline of an opening, knock the brickwork patch out, starting in the middle, and try not to break up the old masonry any more than necessary.

ONCE THE OPENING IS CLEARED, you can then fully assess the extent of the project. You already know whether you'll have to rebuild the top of the chimney ($350–$1,000). You may also have to re-line the flues, depending upon the condition of the masonry and local building codes. Sure danger signals: Badly crumbling masonry lining or missing or cracked, loose brickwork. Many house fires have been started by sparks that escaped through deteriorated flues. So it pays to take a safe and conservative course in evaluating the condition of the flues.

NOW COMES THE FIREPLACE ITSELF. It will almost certainly need a damper, a partial or complete firebox, a new hearth and the chimney breast extended out around the firebox.

THE DAMPER POSED THE GREATEST PROBLEM in rebuilding the fireplace in our bedroom. The only commercial dampers I could find were in very limited sizes and none of them fit the existing brickwork or scale I needed (our bedroom fireplace is rather small). I finally fabricated one myself, which has turned out to be far superior to anything else I have seen. It consists of a rectangle formed of angle iron, set into the masonry in the throat in front of the smoke ledge. A heavy piece of plate steel cut to size fits into the frame. The weight of the iron keeps the damper closed; a chain pulled through the front of the fireplace facing opens it.

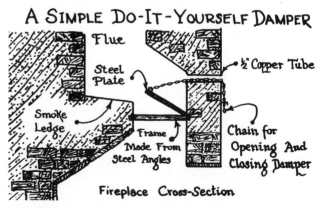

A SIMPLE DO-IT-YOURSELF DAMPER

Flue

Steel Plate

½″ Copper Tube

Smoke Ledge

Frame Made From Steel Angles

Chain for Opening And Closing Damper

Fireplace Cross-Section

THIS TYPE OF DAMPER has some distinct advantages: You can always tell whether the damper is open or closed (by looking at the chain); if it is closed you don't have to fumble around in the flames for the pull chain; and it is cheap—the materials only cost about $6.

THE FIREBOX is built out of firebrick or any hard brick, and mortared—ideally—with fireclay (although you can probably get by with well-tooled joints of portland cement mortar). The firebox is built out beyond the chimney breast to give depth to the fireplace and should be extended as far out as your mantel is deep.

Removing the baseboard reveals evidence of old firebox hidden behind the plaster. Debris from the old masonry that had accumulated in the firebox spills into room through slits in the patchwork.

IN SOME TYPES OF FIREPLACES (such as mine) a cast iron frame is mounted into this brickwork. I drove four masonry nails into the breast and fastened the frame to them with lengths of wire. The iron frame was held out the correct distance with blocks of wood, then the void was filled in with bricks. The firebox should be extended with additional brickwork (common brick) to the width and height of the opening formed by the arch.

THE FIREBOX is usually not as large as the mantel opening . . . the difference generally being an area covered in decorative tiles or marble. Build the masonry out to within ½ in. or so of the mantel, leaving enough room for the finish material (tile, etc.). Too, if you are using an iron frame, also leave a ½-in. groove behind it so you can slip the facing material in behind. This is a lot easier than trying to cut and fit the facing flush against the iron.

THE FACING MATERIALS are affixed directly to the masonry. For the tiles I used, I found plaster of paris an ideal adhesive. It sets up very quickly and dries hard and tight.

THE MANTEL IS NOW SET IN PLACE over the tiles and masonry. It should be fastened to the wall at the top and bottom with appropriate anchors. The hearth, if it must be rebuilt, should only involve tearing out the new floorboards to the original opening. I found the easiest approach was to pour and finish a cement slab in the usual manner, and then apply the decorative surface to it once the slab was dry. I used ceramic tile set in mastic, which I then grouted.

Knocking lath and plaster away reveals the old firebox (left). It clearly needs a new firebrick lining. Additional brick-work (right) extends chimney breast out to the iron framing arch.

Temporary wood piece (in lieu of tiles) is slipped behind the iron frame.

Finishing touch: Mantel attached to wall.

THAT'S IT. I think the average old-house handy person can do everything (I have) except the chimney work—and my biggest handicap there is my total fear of heights! So go look for those plastered-over fireplaces now . . . before you really need them.

RESHAPING AN OLD FIREPLACE

By John L. Lloyd

I HAVE INSTALLED DAMPERS in three existing fireplaces in two houses in which I've resided and renovated and have been quite successful each time.

WITH ANY EXISTING FIREPLACE there's one unalterable given—the flue size. Measure yours, then consult a table of fireplace dimensions (most any fireplace book—or a lumber yard or hardware store if you can look at the directions included with the dampers they have for sale). Working the table backwards, see if your fireplace opening (W × H) approximates one of the acceptable sizes for the size flue that you have. If it doesn't, change the opening so that it does. I poured 6 in. of concrete to raise the floor of one fireplace and lowered the top of another about 3 in. by dropping my wire lath and plaster stop when I refinished the face of the fireplace.

NEXT, REMOVE ANY BRICKS not part of the actual chimney structure to make the firebox as large as possible. This is the time to examine your fireplace and chimney carefully. Repoint wherever necessary and within reach. Clean out as much soot and dirt as possible.

IF YOUR CHIMNEY HAS a flue liner consider yourself fortunate. It can be repointed by lowering a canvas bag stuffed with rags and newspapers and weighted down with bricks. Stuff the bag so that it will just fit down the chimney. Prepare mortar to pancake batter consistency and ladle a generous amount on top of the bag toward the edges. Lower the bag to the first joint in the flue and swab up and down a few times. Then lower to the next joint, etc.

IF YOU HAVE NO flue liner, check to see if any wooden floor, ceiling, or roof members tie into the chimney. If they do, extensive carpentry is required to cut them free structurally and box in around the chimney. I was fortunate in only having to do this on one side of one fireplace. When the chimney is free of wood members, I would suggest, as added insurance, wire lath and plaster all the way up to the roof line. A brown coat of plaster is all that is necessary in places out of view.

THE NEXT STEP is to purchase the largest cast-iron damper that will fit into the fireplace *above* the lintel. Don't buy a steel damper if you can avoid it–they warp. Make sure your damper has a removable door and handle that can be installed after the damper body has been installed. Next, measure the

size of the firebrick available at your local lumber yard and purchase enough to line the three sides of your fireplace. Ask if you can return the unused ones–they're expensive.

NOW COMES THE HARD PART. Refer to drawings A through D and to your table of fireplace dimensions. You're going to line the fireplace with firebrick in a manner to create angled sides and a sloping rear wall. Try to stay as close to the applicable dimensions as possible. The front of the damper body must touch the back of the front wall of the fireplace on or above the lintel. It doesn't have to rest on the lintel—side walls of firebrick will support it. The back of the damper body then, is the top of the sloped rear wall (call it point M).

START LAYING YOUR FIREBRICK, one course at a time in a fairly dry mortar mix around all three sides of the fireplace. Lay the brick straight up to whatever full course brings you to the approximate height to begin the slope. Get this height from the table and temper it with the reality of having to slope outward from the rear wall to point M. It will usually be 3 or 4 courses. Begin the slope by using a mortar joint on the back wall that's thin in front and thick in the rear. From here on in, lay one course on the back wall clear across. Don't worry about tying-in or interlocking the side walls.

THEN LAY ONE COURSE on the two side walls. The brick that meets the back wall on each side will have to be cut at an angle—more on cutting later. The horizontal mortar joints will no longer be continuous since the side walls, rising straight up, will be higher than the sloping rear walls.

CONTINUE LAYING one course at a time, back wall first, then side walls until you are one course below point M. This should put your side walls above, even with, or no more than 1 in.–2 in. below the bottom of the lintel. Carefully lift the damper body into approximate position and prop, wedge, or hold it there.

LAY THE LAST COURSE of brick—the course on the back wall may have to be cut to come out level with the side walls. Place a generous amount of mortar on top of the last course and lower the damper into place.

USING A WET MORTAR MIX, reach up through the damper and pack mortar down to seal the line of contact between the front of the damper body and the lintel. Pack mortar around all 4 sides of the damper to seal. Using sand or ashes, pack cavities behind angled side walls and sloping rear wall. (It's easiest to do this after each course is laid.)

THE WAY YOU PLAN to treat the sides of your fireplace opening determines how you treat the frontmost brick on each course of the side wall. If the fireplace opening is to be narrowed (determined by table dimensions and esthetics) you may not have to do anything. However, in all three of my cases the fireplace width remained the same. Thus, I had to make an angle cut on each frontal brick.

BEFORE STARTING this job, make sure you have access to a masonry saw—preferably water-cooled with a diamond blade. Firebrick is softer than most common brick and cuts fairly easily, especially if you use the above mentioned saw. If you don't have to make the angle cut on the frontal bricks,

and if you're good with masonry hammer, you may not need a saw at all. However, I've always used one.

IF YOU MEASURE carefully before starting and are able to determine the various angle cuts necessary, you may be able to gather up all the bricks that need cutting and go to a local construction site. A few dollars to the masonry foreman may work miracles. Plan on going back at least once, though, for a few unforeseen cuts. Don't forget that these angle cuts are not simple since the side walls don't meet the back wall at a right angle.

INSTALL THE DAMPER DOOR and handle and that's about it. It's a lot of work—about 1 to 2 days for the firebrick and damper part—but it's worth it on a cold winter's evening.

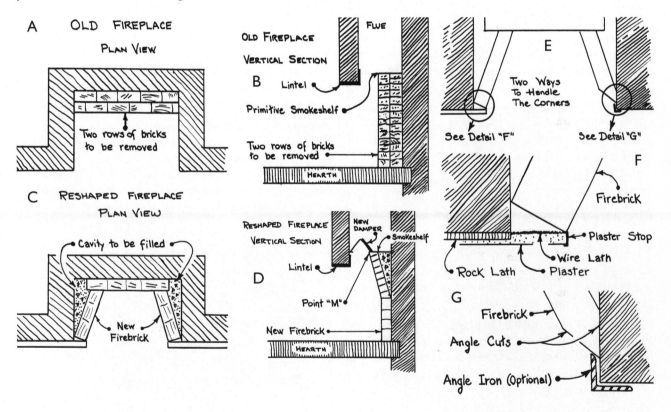

TEACHING A FIREPLACE NOT TO SMOKE

By James R. McGrath

A WORKING FIREPLACE can be a comfort and a joy on a cold winter evening. But a fireplace that doesn't work properly can literally bring tears to your eyes.

I RECENTLY MOVED into a renovated 1888 house in which one of the selling points was the working fireplaces. Flues were newly relined, new firebrick in the fireplaces . . . everything looked really great.

THE FIREPLACES LOOKED GREAT until we tried to light a fire in them. Then . . . SMOKE. Lots of smoke in the room as well as a minimal amount going up those beautifully lined flues.

I TRIED USING different types of fuels. Still lots of smoke. Opening the windows did improve the draft and reduce smoke, but the wind blowing through the house rather defeated the whole idea of having a fireplace.

I THEN WENT DOWN THE standard checklist for a smoky fireplace:

• The damper was checked to make sure it was functioning properly. It stayed open after the fire was started and didn't flop closed. Next . . .

• I shoved a piece of newspaper up into the damper opening and lit it. Flames and smoke all went up the chimney. This indicated that the flue was clear.

RELUCTANTLY, I CONCLUDED that the fault lay in the structure of the fireplace itself. The masons who had relined the flues and rebuilt the fireboxes may have been wizards with bricks and mortar. But they didn't know beans about the theory of fireplace design.

A LITTLE RESEARCH revealed there are several critical elements in fireplace construction that can cause it to smoke:

• No smoke chamber or smoke shelf in the chimney;

• Chimney improperly located on the roof or lacking a chimney cap leading to insufficient draft;

• Damper improperly located;

• Incorrect dimensions in the firebox.

I DECIDED TO INVESTIGATE the possibility of improper firebox dimensions since this is the easiest problem to correct.

THERE ARE SEVERAL CRITICAL dimensions in a fireplace, all of which are interdependent:

> Size of flue
> Throat dimensions
> Height of firebox opening
> Width of firebox opening
> Depth of firebox

VERY OFTEN, THE VOLUME of the firebox is too great for the capacity of the flue (especially if the flue has been narrowed by the later addition of a flue lining). When this occurs, the flue simply can't carry off all of the hot gases generated in the firebox.

THERE ARE TABLES that indicate proper dimensions for fireplaces of various proportions. The tables indicated the proper volume for a fireplace with my particular throat and flue dimension was 12,544 cu. in. (You measure throat dimensions inside the fireplace; to get flue dimensions you have to go up to the roof and measure at the chimney top.)

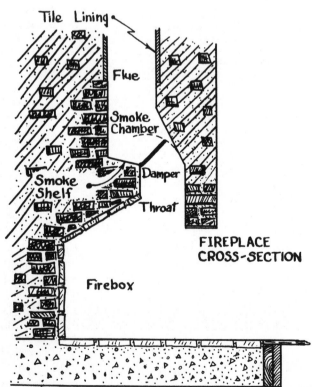

FIREPLACE CROSS-SECTION

THE ACTUAL VOLUME of my fireplace was about 15,660 cu. in. To arrive at this, I did a simplified calculation merely using the width and height of the opening times the depth; I didn't attempt to take into account the slope of the back wall. This exercise confirmed my suspicion, however, that the opening was too big. The fireplace as I inherited it had an opening that was 30 in. high, 29 in. wide and 18 in. deep. To reduce the volume to the indicated 12,544 cu. in. would require a reduction of 6 in. in one of the dimensions.

SINCE THE PROPORTION of height to width to depth is also important, I decided at this point that a little experimenting was in order.

WARNING ABOUT UNLINED FLUES

OLD CHIMNEY FLUES were originally built from bricks and mortar, without benefit of any terra cotta tile lining. With the passage of time, the mortar used in these flues will deteriorate, allowing cracks to develop and bricks to fall out. Sparks from a wood fire can penetrate these crevices and start fires in the internal wooden timbers of the house.

YOU CAN TELL whether your chimney flue is lined by inspecting it from the roof. If it isn't lined, have it checked out by an expert before using it for wood fires.

TO REDUCE VOLUME, I placed two layers of brick in the bottom of the firebox. This decreased the height of the opening by 4½ in. A fire was lit and—Voila!—no smoke.

Three ways to reduce fireplace opening, depending on the surrounding decoration.

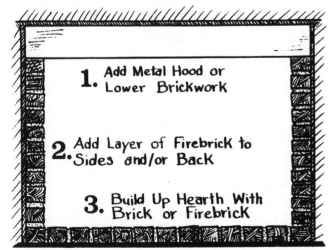

1. Add Metal Hood or Lower Brickwork

2. Add Layer of Firebrick to Sides and/or Back

3. Build Up Hearth With Brick or Firebrick

THE QUESTION NOW was how to make a permanent modification. Since I had a nice firebrick base in the firebox, I didn't want to mortar the common brick on top of them. So

1. Remove Bricks Using Masonry Drill Bit & Cold Chisel

2. Lay Steel Angle In Thin Bed Of Mortar

I decided to see if lowering the opening from the top would have the same effect. I cut a piece of sheetrock about 12" wide and long enough to cover the width of the fireplace opening. I lit a fire in the fireplace and then experimented holding the sheetrock hood at various levels across the top of the opening. I found that decreasing the opening by about 5 in. from the top had the same effect of stopping the smoke.

BECAUSE I HAD A PLAIN BRICK FRONT on my fireplace, I decided to lower the brickwork by two courses. I had brick on hand that would closely match the bricks around the fireplace.

IF YOU HAVE A FANCY MANTEL with tile or other facing around the front of the fireplace, however, my solution wouldn't work for you. You would have to reduce the firebox opening by adding brick to the bottom or sides of the firebox, or by adding a metal hood to the top of the opening. To build up hearth, you can use common brick set in standard mortar. To add a layer of brick to the sides, you should use firebrick—and point the mortar joints with fireclay since they are exposed to the hot gases generated by combustion.

To install additional courses of brick, a new steel brace must be inserted.

TO BRING THE BRICKWORK DOWN, I used a carbide-tipped masonry bit to drill out the mortar holding the two bricks at the level where new brickwork would come. After the mortar was drilled out, a cold chisel loosened the bricks so they could be pulled out. Half bricks at the corners were also removed to provide keys for the new brickwork.

A STEEL ANGLE was inserted into the holes left by the removal of the bricks. The angle was about 8 in. longer than the width of the opening. (Steel angle can be purchased at many large hardware stores, or at building supply dealers.)

TO INSTALL THE ANGLE, you must make sure that all loose mortar has been cleaned out of the brickwork. Thoroughly soak bricks with water so they won't suck all the water out of the new mortar. (This applies to the new bricks as well as the old.)

WHEN CORRECT POSITION of the steel angle has been determined, lay a thin bed of mortar on both end bricks, put angle in place, and true up with a mason's level by adding or removing mortar from one end. Don't make too thick a mortar bed, however, or you won't be able to fit all the bricks on top.

LAY A THIN MORTAR BED on the angle and proceed to lay in the new brick. The only trick is in laying the top course of brick; you have to force the mortar into the crack between the old and new bricks. At this point I abandoned my trowel and did the stuffing with my fingers.

WHEN COMPLETED, the new brickwork was almost totally indistinguishable from the original work. And a perfectly working fireplace awaited Santa on Christmas Eve.

MATCHING BRICKS & MORTAR

THERE ARE THREE THINGS TO watch out for if you want to create new brickwork that is indistinguishable from the original:

• New bricks must be selected to match the originals with regard to size, color and texture;

• New mortar must match the old, both in color and texture;

• New mortar joints must be shaped the same as the old.

MANY OLD HOUSES were built with sandlime mortars. This can be closely matched with a mortar consisting of one part Portland cement, two parts lime and nine parts sand.

IF YOU'RE DOUBTFUL about matching the mortar color, safest thing to do is to mix up a small test batch, apply it to a brick and see what it looks like after it dries. In general, increasing the amount of Portland cement will make the mortar darker; adding lime makes it whiter. For added color flexibility, you can also get white Portland cement; silica or flint sands can be obtained in shades ranging from off-white to a light brown.

SHAPES OF MORTAR JOINTS

Flush   V-Joint   Concave

Raked   Weathered   Stroked

THE SHAPE OF MORTAR JOINTS have a surprising effect on the appearance of a wall because they determine depth of the shadow line between bricks. You may have to experiment with your pointing trowel, tuck pointer or joint tool to find the right combination of tool and technique to achieve the same shape joint that the old-time masons created.

ADDING A DAMPER TO AN OLD FIREPLACE

A DAMPER IS MERELY a device placed in the throat of a fireplace flue to prevent drafts from coming down the chimney (and heat escaping from the room) when the fireplace is not in use. In a properly designed fireplace, the damper has no regulating function. It is either totally open (when there is a fire going) or totally closed (when the fire is out).

MANY EARLY FIREPLACES were built without dampers . . . probably because they were going all the time during cold weather, and during hot weather a draft down the chimney was welcome ventilation. Other fireplaces have had dampers removed during previous "remuddlings" when fireplaces were bricked up. In either case, a lack of a damper is a serious drawback for contemporary lifestyles. Since few of us are going to have a fire going all the time during cold weather, we want a damper in every working fireplace.

AND WHAT IF THE DAMPER is missing? There are a number of ways to retro-fit a damper to an old fireplace. The readers of *The Old-House Journal* have passed along a number of methods they have used. But damper problems should not be considered alone; they should be analyzed in conjunction with fireplace geometry. To get a fireplace that will give—maximum heat, minimum fuel consumption, without smoking and requires a combustion chamber and flue that conform to some pretty rigorous geometrical standards. Often in making the modifications in brick-work required to make a badly designed fireplace more efficient, it is a relatively simple job to insert a damper in the new masonry. We'll discuss fireplace geometry later in this article.

A CHIMNEY STUFFER

BUT WHAT ARE THE alternatives if you don't need new masonry? By far the simplest solution was sent in by Robert W. Frasch, Chairman of the Rochester, N.Y., Preservation Board. Here's his answer:

FOR AN EFFECTIVE and no-cost seal to eliminate heat loss, cut an old foam rubber seat cushion and insert it in the throat. If you cut it about 1" wider than the opening on all sides, the foam rubber plug will hold itself in place.

CAUTION: Foam rubber is flammable and will burn if a fire is accidentally lighted before removing it. I forgot to take it out once, but was able to poke the plug up the chimney with the fire tongs before it began to burn.

SUGGESTION: Clean the flue throat well before inserting the foam plug. This greatly reduces the amount of dust created when the plug is removed. For safety's sake, attach a tag on a string to the foam damper with a safety pin. This will remind you that it is there.

Robert W. Frasch

A BUTTERFLY-VALVE DAMPER

HERE'S A SOLUTION worked out by reader Bob Davis of Alburtis, Pa. He had a rather *large* problem, as you'll see:

I NEEDED a large damper—4 ft. × 6 ft.—for our walk-in fireplace. No commercial dampers are made that large.

I DESIGNED and installed a unit that works just fine. The frame is made from 3" × 3" angle iron, 1/4" thick. A piece of 1/4" steel plate was then fitted to the frame as shown in the diagrams.

THE ¼" STEEL PLATE should overlap the angle iron 1/2" front and back as shown in the diagram below. A piece of pipe was welded to the steel plate lengthwise to act as a pivot. The pipe should be welded a little bit off center so that the weight of the plate will keep the damper closed.

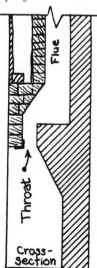

I USE A CHAIN to position the damper. One end is fastened to the far side of the steel plate; the other end is looped over a hook on the underside of the lintel.

MOUNTING SUCH A large, heavy damper is quite a chore. It takes several people to hold it in place during the mounting process. My fireplace has irregular stonework, so we had to drill the mounting holes in the steel angle to correspond with the mortar joints between the stones. To determine the position for the holes, we raised the damper inside the chimney several inches above where it was going to be mounted. We then marked points on the

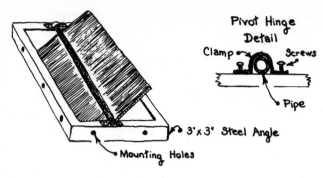

Pivot Hinge Detail

Clamp   Screws

Pipe

3" x 3" Steel Angle

Mounting Holes

points on the angle that corresponded with mortar joints (see diagram).

HOLES WERE THEN DRILLED in the angle. Since we were using 1/4" lag bolts for mounting, we drilled 1/2" holes to allow for slight misalignments. After drilling holes in the angle iron, we positioned the damper and marked the mortar through the holes. At these points we drilled holes big enough to accept splitlead sheaths for 1/4" lag bolts.

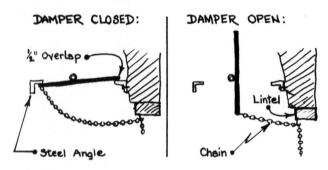

DAMPER CLOSED:

1/4" Overlap

Steel Angle

DAMPER OPEN:

Lintel

Chain

THE LEAD SHEATHS were pounded into the holes, and when the damper was raised into position, the lag bolts were inserted through the mounting holes and screwed into the lead sheaths. The damper was quite rigid and sturdy.

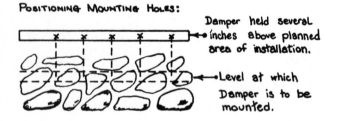

POSITIONING MOUNTING HOLES:

Damper held several inches above planned area of installation.

Level at which Damper is to be mounted.

BECAUSE OF IRREGULARITIES in the stone, there were numerous gaps between the damper and the masonry. I didn't want to fill these with fireclay or mortar because constant expansion and contraction of the damper would cause any rigid filler to work loose. So I stuffed all the cracks with fiberglass insulation. The fiberglass works beautifully: It is nonflammable, doesn't work loose, and completely seals off drafts that would otherwise leak around the damper.

THE ENTIRE DAMPER was assembled for me by a welder. The cost was under $75, including materials. This is cheaper than most commercial dampers.

Bob Davis

LEVER-OPERATED DAMPER

BOB KERR of Keokuk, Iowa, sends along these comments: While renovating our brick house built in the 1830s, we have found the dampers shown on the following sketches to be very effective. They can be fabricated with the basic tools found in most welding shops. Basically, the design consists of a frame made of angle irons. A piece of 1/8" or 3/16" steel plate sits on top of the frame, hinged on one side.

THE DAMPER IS OPENED and closed by a lever that is welded to the door. Position of the lever is fixed by stops on the flat metal quadrant welded to one side of the frame. Between the flex in the lever rod and the play in the hinges, there's enough give in the lever to manoeuvre it past the stops.

THE FRAMING CAN BE ADAPTED to fireplaces with either straight or sloping walls. If the throat is deep and the weight of the door makes it difficult to open, the door can be cut in two pieces. One lever and quadrant can control the front section; another lever and quadrant can be used for the rear section.

FOR FIREPLACES WITH VERY WIDE throats, we have used multiple units, placing the damper doors side by side.

Robert T. Kerr

THE RIGHT SHAPE FOR A FIREPLACE

BEFORE PLUNGING AHEAD to fit a damper to an old fireplace, you had best make sure that the shape of the firebox and throat are of the correct proportions. To get a clean-burning fire that throws maximum heat without smoking requires a combustion chamber built to fairly rigid specifications.

MANY 18TH CENTURY FIREPLACES (and 20th century fireplaces, for that matter) were built with incorrect proportions. One symptom is the chronically smoking fireplace. Too, many late 19th century fireplaces were designed only for gas logs, and don't have the right shape for burning wood.

SO YOU MAY FIND that you'll have to put in some new brickwork to get maximum efficiency from the fireplace. Thus, there's no sense to start out by fitting a new damper to the throat—only to discover that the new brickwork is going to alter the throat dimensions.

LEVER-OPERATED DAMPER

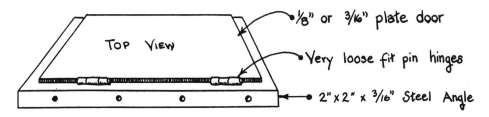

TOP VIEW
- ⅛" or 3/16" plate door
- Very loose fit pin hinges
- 2" x 2" x 3/16" Steel Angle

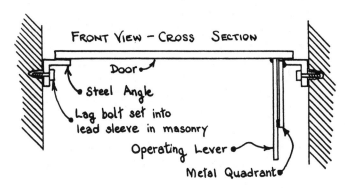

FRONT VIEW—CROSS SECTION
- Door
- Steel Angle
- Lag bolt set into lead sleeve in masonry
- Operating Lever
- Metal Quadrant

INTERIOR VIEW OF LEVER MECHANISM
- Full Open
- Shut
- ¼" x 1" Flat Quadrant
- ½ Open
- ⅜" Thick Stops
- ¼" x 1" Flat Lever

STRANGE AS IT MAY SEEM, the definitive research on fireplace design was done by Count Rumford at the end of the 18th century. His essay, "Of Chimney Fire-places," published in 1796, set out principles for efficient fireplace construction and modification. His principles have not been significantly improved upon in the two centuries since.

18th century and which you still see today—are all wrong for maximum heat efficiency.

PLAN VIEW

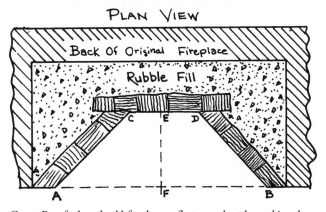

Back Of Original Fireplace

Rubble Fill

Count Rumford made old fireplaces reflect more heat by making them shallower and sloping the side walls. In his system:

$$CD = EF \quad AB = 3\ CD$$

In actual practice, opening AB can vary from 2 CD up to 3 CD.

RUMFORD DISCOVERED that the primary heat from a fireplace is radiant heat. Therefore, it is critical that the back wall (fireback) and side walls (also called coves or jambs) be placed in such a way as to reflect the maximum amount of heat into the room. The kind of deep fireplace with coves perpendicular to the back wall—which were common in the

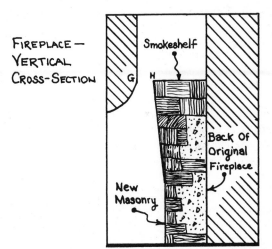

FIREPLACE— VERTICAL CROSS-SECTION
- Smokeshelf
- G   H
- Back Of Original Fireplace
- New Masonry

In addition to making the back shallower, Count Rumford's modifications included adding a smoke shelf and narrowing the throat. Rumford's dictum: Depth of throat (GH) should never be less than 3 inches nor more than 4 inches.

RUMFORD BUILT QUITE A REPUTATION in London as a fireplace doctor. It became quite the fashion to boast of a fireplace that had been "doctored" by the master himself. Commonly, he made four basic changes to improve fuel efficiency and reduce smoking:

• Reduced fireplace opening by lowering the lintel (or raising the hearth);

- Moved the fireback closer to the front of the hearth;

- Added slanted coves;

- Reduced depth of the throat and added a smoke shelf.

RUMFORD'S IDEAL FIREPLACE is tall and shallow, with sides and back angled for maximum heat reflection. Ironically, masons are still building fireplaces at variance with Rumford's principles—and homeowners are suffering the same consequences as our 17th-century ancestors.

ESPECIALLY IMPORTANT when considering dampers is the depth of the chimney throat (GH in diagram at right). Rumford's experiments determined that for best drawing power, the throat should be no more than 4" deep—with a flat smoke shelf behind it. Many old fireplaces have throats much larger than this. The smoke shelf's job is to deflect cold air coming down the chimney and mix it with the column of rising hot gases and smoke.

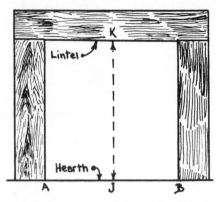

Best shape for fireplace opening is square; i.e., AB = JK. In old fireplaces, factor controlling actual dimensions is the cross-section of the flue. Area of fireplace opening should be 8–10 times the cross-section of flue. This relationship fixes all the other dimensions.

USING WOOD STOVES SAFELY

By Lynn Diller

WE LIVE IN NORTHERN MICHIGAN where wood is readily available. As a result, we know more and more people who are turning to wood as a source of heat—either as a total home heating system, or as a supplement to other types of heat. Unfortunately, we also know of a rising frequency of house fires in our area caused by wood stoves. Wood heat can be very satisfying—but it can also be dangerous if you have no prior experience.

THERE IS A BROAD SPECTRUM of stoves available, but I will confine myself in this article to two main types: Box stoves (illustrated below) and Franklin fireplaces. I will also make no secret of my dislike of Franklin fireplaces. Although they were a great improvement over conventional fireplaces 200 years ago, they cannot compare in efficiency with box stoves. The reason: Air flow.

THE WAY TO CONTROL how a wood stove burns is by regulating the air flow. The more you can control the flow of air through the stove, the more heat you can get out of a given amount of wood. We learned a long time ago that there is a great deal of difference between *burning* wood and *heating* with wood.

OUR NEIGHBORS heat with a Franklin and we with a 40-year-old Ivy box stove. We can go over to their house and in an evening they will feed their fire 3 or 4 times. When we come home, our box stove is just ready for more wood.

FRANKLIN STOVES also require special safety precautions. I know of serious house fires started when logs rolled out of the doors of the stove. The doors have catches—but I guess people are reluctant to fiddle with them when they get hot. There's also a very real danger from sparks; I've seen many a rug with little black dots all over it from flying sparks. Never go away with the door to a Franklin stove left open!

BESIDES CONTROL of air flow, another important factor is the amount of cast iron. A general rule of thumb is: The more cast iron, the greater the heating capacity of the stove. An efficient stove will have cast iron chambers and baffles to absorb every bit of heat possible from a fire.

SOME NEW STOVES also have thermostatically controlled drafts. The cooler the room gets, the more the thermostat will open the draft to get a more vigorous fire. The only drawback to this system is that on a long cool night all the wood will be burned up while you sleep and you'll wake up to a cold stove in the morning.

CHIMNEY HAZARDS

MOST OF THE HOUSE FIRES caused by stoves result from faulty chimneys. All old chimneys (and some new ones) should be lined. You can buy metal chimney liners that go together in sections and which can then be slipped down into your chimney. (This procedure obviously won't work with chimneys that have bends and doglegs in them. These call for tile liners.)

WE FOUND IN LINING our old chimney that even "straight" flues aren't always that straight. We were finally able to wiggle the liner into position—but with much difficulty. We then wired it to the top of the chimney.

THERE IS A SLEEVE or "thimble" where the stove pipe enters the chimney wall. Make sure that the sleeve is tight and doesn't wiggle; all openings should be cemented tight.

MAKE SURE ALSO that the stove pipe has adequate ventilation around it wherever it passes through floors or walls. An old house will probably already have a "donut" or some kind of grate that holds the pipe safely as it passes through a partition. A hot stove pipe that contacts a partition directly can easily start a fire. The gases in our stove pipe travel 17 ft. before they enter the chimney—and the pipe is very hot to the touch at the chimney sleeve.

AS A GENERAL RULE, it is advisable to have the stove pipe travel as far as possible vertically before entering the chimney. This allows the gases to cool down somewhat—and gives you better control of the draft. A pipe that goes directly from the stove to the chimney through a wall (as it has to in a one-storey house) is a potential hazard.

STOVE PIPE

STOVE PIPES come in different gauges of metal. Get the heaviest gauge possible. Light gauge pipe will be eaten away by the accumulation of crud inside. (Sheet metal stoves will also burn away in a couple of years!)

THE METAL-ASBESTOS PIPE is a great improvement over the old plain sheet metal pipe. This is a pipe with a layer of asbestos over it—with a cladding of metal on the outside. With metal-asbestos pipe, you can run a complete chimney almost anywhere you want it.

OUR NEIGHBORS had a chimney fire last winter, and it burned the paint off the outside of their metal-asbestos pipe all the way up to the upstairs ceiling. Had this been ordinary stove pipe, they probably would have lost their house. Metal-

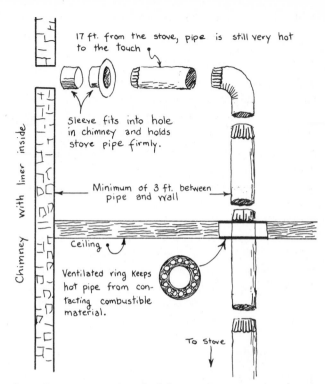

Stove pipe arrangement in author's house.

asbestos pipe is fairly expensive (about $35 per yard), but isn't your house worth it?

METAL-ASBESTOS PIPE can be run right up through the roof if you don't have a chimney to connect to. But one caution: Some of these chimney kits have metal rain caps for the top that are supposed to be safe for use with wood stoves. But our firechief told us that some of them have screens that can trap soot and cause chimney fires. ALL WOOD-BURNING STOVE SYSTEMS SHOULD BE CHECKED OUT BY A HOME HEATING EXPERT, FIRE MARSHAL, OR OTHER QUALIFIED PERSON!

CLEANING STOVE PIPE

AS A PRECAUTIONARY MEASURE, you should clean out the stove pipe periodically. Ash will collect in an elbow and should be scraped out every few weeks to maintain a good draft. Tap your pipe every few days, and if you hear pieces of soot falling it means that the pipe is ripe for cleanout.

FOR CLEANING, you have to let your fire die completely out. Even a warm stove pipe will smoke . . . so be prepared for a period without heat while the apparatus gets cool enough to work with.

STOVE PIPE is fitted together with just friction; the crimped end being shoved into the open end. So it's fairly easy to jiggle them apart for cleaning. Any accumulations in elbows can be scraped out. For longer sections, take an old burlap bag and stuff it with rags or newspaper to give it bulk and shape. Tie the bag to a rope and pull it through the pipe to scrape the soot off the inside. You can also buy contraptions that will do this job. When the heating season is over, you can take all the pipes down and have them cleaned at the carwash.

THIS MESSY PROCEDURE is quite necessary to prevent combustibles from building up inside the pipe. If the buildup goes on unabated, it is quite likely that you'll get a roaring fire inside the stove pipe . . . which is very dangerous!

AFTER YOU HAVE GONE THROUGH the awful job of cleaning a stove pipe once, you'll ask: "Isn't there any way to avoid this?" There is . . . or at least ways to increase the intervals between cleanings. Burning only dry, seasoned wood will cut down on the need for cleanings. You can also buy soot destroyers. You throw the soot destroyer into the fire every few days. After using it for several days, the soot will detach itself from the pipe and fall back into the firebox. You will still have flyash settling in elbows and flat spots, but the creosote and soot problems are greatly diminished. If you can't find soot destroyer locally, you can buy it by mail from Cumberland General Store.

ANOTHER SAFETY NOTE: Always be very careful if you use a vacuum cleaner to clean ashes and soot from the inside of your stove. The air rushing into the bag will fan even a very small spark and set the inside of your cleaner on fire.

KEEP YOUR DISTANCE

STOVES AND PIPES should always be placed a good distance from walls and furniture. The dry radiant heat from the stove will crack furniture and loosen veneer. A good rule of thumb: Keep stoves and stove pipes at least 3 ft. from walls; keep furniture at least 10 ft. from stoves.

IF IT IS NECESSARY to place stoves closer than 3 ft. from a wall, you can buy asbestos sheets or special reflective panels to protect the wall.

IT IS ALSO NECESSARY to have something under the stove to protect the floor. Some people use bricks or slate under the stove. I prefer the metal-covered asbestos pads made especially for this purpose. You should select one that sticks out at least a foot on all sides of the stove. They are good for catching falling ashes and coals—and a good place to lay hot stove pokers and shovels.

IT'S A GOOD IDEA to keep two inches or so of sand in the bottom of your stove. This will protect the bottom from warping and cracking—and keep a lot of heat from being radiated towards the floor.

BURNING WOOD

ONE MAJOR FACTOR determining how well your stove will work is the fuel you use. Soft woods such as pine, spruce and poplar burn more quickly and give less heat than hard woods such as maple, oak or beech. Pine and spruce also have a lot of sap which means a lot of creosote up your chimney. This goo coats the inside of your chimney and a stray spark can easily set it afire. If you are lucky, the fire will be contained in the chimney—but some people are not so lucky. Hence the need for the chimney cleaning mentioned earlier.

THE GREENER THE WOOD, the greater the creosote problem. We know of a fellow who was boasting that he had gotten a really good deal on some "freshly cut, slow-burning pine." It would have been funny if it hadn't been so serious. If he could get the wood to burn at all, his chimney would have enough soot inside to catch fire in a couple of weeks. It wasn't such a good bargain for him!

SOME PEOPLE consider dry oak the next best fuel to coal. But green oak, unlike the well-seasoned material, will gum up a chimney after a while . . . just as soft woods will. All firewood should be allowed to dry a year before burning. (If you leave it to dry too much longer than that, it will start to rot and be full of ants and other creepy-crawlies when you bring it into the house.)

A LITTLE BIT of rotten wood is good for starting fires and quick heat in the morning. Small pieces of wood give you a quick, hot fire. Larger pieces will burn longer and are good for nighttime when you can't feed the fire so often.

YOUR BOX STOVE can also be used as an auxiliary kitchen range. We leave a water kettle on the stove at all times. It helps to combat winter dryness—and it provides us with a steady source of hot water for coffee or hot chocolate. We rinse the kettle out every day and put fresh water in. Otherwise, deposits will build up and the water tastes funny. Too, don't let a pot on the stove boil dry; the bottom will burn out.

TWENTY CAUSES OF CHIMNEY TROUBLES AND THEIR CURES.

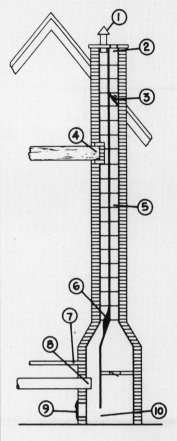

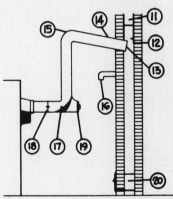

NO. FAULT	EXAMINATION	CORRECTION
1. Pipe extension not of same area as chimney opening, and extension below opening of cap.	This is ascertained by measurement.	Pipe to be extended and opening to be same as chimney opening.
Chimney below gable of roof.	Determined by actual observation.	Extend chimney above gable of roof.
2. Chimney opening smaller than inside dimension.	Ascertained by measurement.	Widen opening to same dimension as chimney area.
3. Obstructions in chimney.	Found by lowering weight on a line.	Use weight to break and dislodge.
4. Projection into the chimney.	Lower a weight or light on extension cord.	Must be handled by brick contractor.
5. Break in Chimney linings.	Build smudge fire blocking off other chimney opening, watching for smoke escape.	Must be handled by competent brick contractor.
6. Collection of soot at narrow space in the opening.	Lower light on long extension cord.	Clean out with weighted brush or bag of loose gravel on end of line.
7. Two or more openings into same chimney.	This is found by inspection from basement.	The least important opening must be closed, using some other chimney flue.
8. Smoke pipe projects into flue but beyond surface of the wall.	Measurement of the pipe from within or observation of pipe by means of lowered light.	Length of pipe must be reduced to allow end of pipe to be flush with wall.
9. Air leak at base of clean-out door. through the cracks.	Build small fire, watching for smoke or flame	Cement up all cracks around the base.
10. Failure to extend the length of flue partition down to floor level.	This is found by inspection.	Extend partition to floor level.
11. Broken clay tiles. mirror reflecting condition of walls.	Can be found by light and patched with cement.	All breaks should be
12. Clay lining fails to come below opening of smoke pipe.	Found by observation through flue opening into chimney.	Clay tiling should be extended below flue opening.
13. Partial projection of smoke pipe into flue area.	Found by measurement after pipe is withdrawn or by sight from chimney opening, using light on a cord.	Projection must be eliminated.
14. Loose seated pipe in flue opening.	Air leaks can be determined by smoke test or examination of chimney while fire burns below location.	Leaks should be eliminated by cementing all pipe openings.
15. Smoke pipe enters chimney in declining position.	This is observed by measurement.	Correct the pipe to permit smoke to enter in an ascending pipe.
16. Second flue opening below that for smoke pipe.	This is found by observation from within basement.	Change to allow only one opening in each chimney.
17. Accumulation of soot narrows cross sectional area of pipe.	Examine pipe from cleanout out opening.	Remove soot.
18. Hand damper in a full closed position.	If handle does not give true position of plate remove section of pipe to ascertain position.	Allow sufficient opening of plate for needed escape of gases,
19. Clean-out opening on pipe leaks air.	Flames visible when furnace is under fire.	Tighten or cement to eliminate inate leak.
20. Clean-out pan not tightly seated in base of chimney.	This air leak can be determined by watching action of small fire built in bottom of chimney shaft.	Cement to eliminate all leaks.

Reprinted from Washington Stove Works' "Parlor Stove Installation Manual."

Mouldings, Woodwork, Shutters

MAKING WOOD MOULDINGS THE OLD WAY

By Burton L. Brown

JUST AS THE SLOW, MEASURED TICK of a grandfather clock evokes a warm feeling, so also does the classic beauty of an old home. When each was constructed, the builder was not in the habit of being rushed. A sense of beauty, balance and symmetry was worked into each—which still brings forth appreciation today, even though most people can't say why.

AMONG THE THINGS that add to the beauty of an old home are the mouldings in all their variety. In most houses built before 1850, these mouldings were made by hand—many times right there in the house. The method of making these mouldings has been all but lost. If you should suggest that your carpenter of today make mouldings for your house, he'd think only of a custom woodworking shop that produces mouldings by machine. He'd then mumble something about costs being too high, and nothing more would be said.

HANDMADE MOULDINGS come from wooden planes called—appropriately—moulding planes. They were widely used up through the middle of the 19th century. A carpenter might have anywhere from 40 to 60 of them. The shapes of the cutting blades and the soles (bottoms) of the planes were all different. Each produced a part of the beautiful woodwork

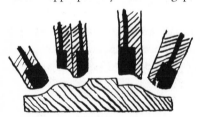

Several different planes were needed for complex mouldings.

that formed the trim in a house. In looking at the sole, it sometimes takes imagination to see what shape comes from it. By and large, these beautiful old tools are now being sold as curios to be hung on a kitchen wall—never to be used again.

MY FIRST INTEREST in moulding planes came from an unsuccessful attempt to buy an old house that I had always loved. A carpenter friend of mine knew that I was going to look at the house and he told me to take special note of the woodwork—he had always admired the workmanship. This led to an interest in mouldings—and eventually to the method of using the planes.

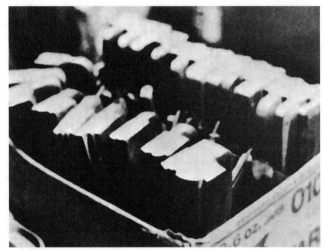

Moulding planes are stored on end so blades won't get nicked. Note profiles on soles of the planes.

VERY LITTLE SEEMS TO HAVE been written or the subject. Although I still have a great deal to learn, I have been successful in mastering the basics of these old planes and in reproducing many old mouldings.

IF YOU WANT to give it a try, the first thing is to obtain the planes. Antique shops, attics and auctions are the best place to look. About 15 years ago, an antique dealer offered me a whole box of them for $3. I didn't know a thing about them at the time—and couldn't have raised the $3 besides. The planes I eventually accumulated over the years cost much more.

BEFORE STARTING, you should have some idea of what you are trying to achieve. A trip to your local library might be a good idea. The Fine Arts section usually has books of measured drawings of architectural details. You'll find that mouldings vary with the section of the country. Any mouldings you produce should be in keeping with what was done in your area at the time your house was built. If your house is Victorian, don't try to make it into a Colonial. It will never look right.

BESIDES PLANES, you'll need a tablesaw, a 12-ft. bench, hammer and nails, a strong back and a steady hand. You'll also need some odd-shaped sharpening stones to sharpen the blades of the planes. You'll also need a patient spouse—you'll have shavings everywhere!

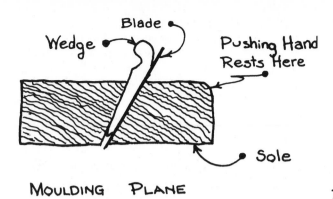

Wedge — Blade — Pushing Hand Rests Here

Sole

MOULDING PLANE
Cross Section

VIEW FROM REAR

Depth Gauge Or Stop — Blade Offset

Guide Or Fence

YES   No

Blade Should Align With Shape Of Sole.

NOW TO WORK. Suppose you want to reproduce a baseboard with a simple bead at the top edge. Take a piece of either clear or choice pine and cut it to approximate size. Then fasten it to the bench. This can be done with a stop nailed to the bench for the work to rest against. Or you can nail the work itself to the surface of the bench. Holes made by the small finishing nails can be filled later when the piece is put in place and painted.

THE ROUGH-CUT BOARD is first "dressed" with a flat plane to get rid of saw marks. Now you are ready to start cutting the moulding. Take your plane and adjust the blade so it will cut a thin shaving. The blade should be carefully aligned with the sole of the plane. The wedge should be tight. You can tighten it by tapping with a wooden mallet or by tapping it against the bench. To loosen the wedge (to move the blade) tap the wedge in its notch so it slides upwards. To lower the blade, tap the top end of it against the bench gently until it is low enough. Place your index finger on the sole to judge the blade's position. The blade can be raised by striking the front end of the plane against the bench. You can also remove the wedge and start over again.

Clamp plus stop nailed to bench keeps work steady and vertical.

IN MAKING A CUT, you need a fence to keep the plane from wandering. Many times the fence is part of the plane. You rest the fence against the outside of the work and move the plane along the length of the board—taking off a shaving of wood. As you push the plane, let your fingertips of the left hand slide along the work. (You'll get slivers at times; it's an occupational hazard.) This is done to guard against the plane tipping off to one side or the other. Each time you push the plane down the length of the board you'll take off a shaving, gradually bringing out the shape of the moulding.

IN PUSHING THE PLANE, there are three directions of push: (1) along the length of the board; (2) downward thrust to take off the shaving; (3) a thrust to the right—across the board. This last thrust is important—especially on the first few cuts—to keep the fence of the plane in line so as to produce a full moulding. All this is done, of course, while keeping the plane from tipping from side to side.

WHEN MAKING A PASS, you try to keep the depth of the cut uniform the full length of the board. This is almost impossible because of variations in the grain. Often, the plane cuts less at the beginning of the board and more at the end. Any high spots have to be touched up by short passes in order to make it all uniform.

THERE IS A PECULIAR MOTION used in setting the plane down in the middle of the moulding and in raising it up that keeps you from getting chips and nicks. In setting the plane down, you put the front of it onto the moulding and as you move the plane forward, you gradually lower the rest of it onto the work. This gives a gradual start to the pass. In taking the plane off the work at the end of the high spot, you lift the back of the moving plane first—and the front edge comes up only after the rest has lifted clear. In cutting a moulding, you soon develop a "feel" so that you know when you've hit a soft spot, or when the grain is wrong. This sense of touch is essential to good workmanship—so a protective glove on the guiding hand would detract from your ability to feel the progress of the plane.

ONCE YOU'VE CUT A FEW MOULDINGS, you will find yourself getting fussy about wood. You will want to go to a quality lumber yard where you can go and pick out your own pieces from the pile. You'll want the grain as straight as it comes—and NO KNOTS! A plane can be forced through a knot, but it isn't good for you or the plane.

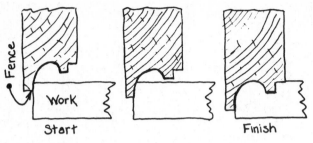

Cutting A Simple Beaded-Edge Moulding

MANY EARLY AMERICAN HOUSES had a bead at the corner of the window trim or door jambs. To reproduce these, starting with a board of the proper thickness, make the first cut as described above. Then stand the board on edge and make a second cut as shown in the diagram below.

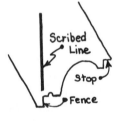

THIS TYPE OF CORNER BEAD can be used in many places. I am planning to use it to help hide some hot air heating pipes. In many Early American houses of post-and-beam construction, beaded-edge boards were used to box in the large framing timbers. By locating the heating pipe in a corner—and boxing it in with some of these beaded-edge boards—the heating run will be disguised to look like an authentic boxed-in beam. Plumbing pipes may be hidden in the same way.

ALL MOULDING planes work on the same principle. Some, however, have to be held at an angle in your hands. You can tell the angle by two methods. The first clue is to note the angle of the stops and fences on the plane. Second, on the front of the plane should be a vertical line scribed into the wood. This line is to be held vertical. In order for the scribed line to be vertical in the plane shown in the sketch at the right for example, the plane has to be held at an angle of almost 60°. (The plane in the diagram is a post-Colonial plane.)

Make Corner Bead With Two Cuts

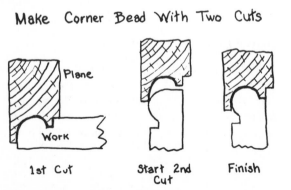

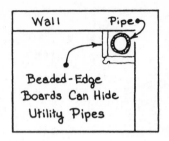

THIS TYPE OF plane comes together with the work as shown in the diagram below. Most planes of this type have fences that guide you in this angle work. With a fluting plane, however, there is no fence and you'll have to nail one to your work. There are even some planes in my collection that I don't understand yet. But I'll get to them one day!

ONCE YOU CAN CUT MOULDINGS, you can put them together with unlimited effects. For example, a single plane of the type shown above was used to make mouldings for a cap and base for pilasters used in a doorway. A section was sliced out of one moulding and added to the top of a second moulding to make the cap. The large plane was then used in the reverse position to make a base for the pilaster as shown below. Incidentally, the wider the plane, the harder it is to push. A 1-in. plane is hard; and you should try a 2-in. plane!

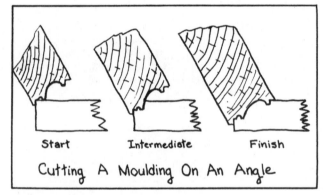

Cutting A Moulding On An Angle

SHOWN ON THE NEXT PAGE is a cross-section of a cornice cap I made for a replacement window using old moulding planes. As you can see in the photo above, the 1974 work is indistinguishable from the 1823 original.

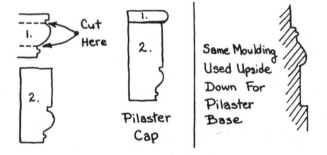

I ALSO HAVE A "SASH PLANE" that will make muntins for windows. With this plane I rebuilt six windows in our old Greek Revival. The old muntins had been removed for some reason and a single pane of glass installed in its place.

Window at left had been taken out during the late 19th century and a door put in its place. Author Brown restored the window and created the cap on the window cornice to match the original woodwork (shown on the window at the right).

moving the wooden pins at the corners. The new muntins were put in place and the sash reassembled using new wooden pins that I fashioned. The reassembly was done without nails or glue. Small wood wedges were driven between the muntin and sash at the point where the muntin was mortised through.

Sash Plane

Muntin Cross-Section

AS FOR TENDER LOVING CARE of planes, linseed oil is always a good dressing for wood parts; a thin film of sewing machine oil will prevent rust on the knife. Sharpening the blade requires very hard stones (such as "Arkansas white") in various shapes. I have four stones: A flat one for sharpening flat knives; a diamond shaped one; an elliptical one; and a tapered cylindrical stone. With these I can sharpen almost any blade. An edge is worked up to the point where it will take a small shaving from your fingernail. If the blade is sharp, you won't have to sand the finished moulding. If it isn't, there won't be any end to the sanding!

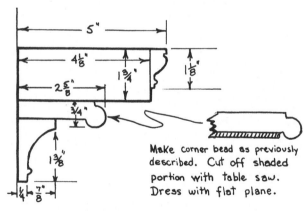

Make corner bead as previously described. Cut off shaded portion with table saw. Dress with flat plane.

Replacement Window Cap Is Built Up From Several Mouldings

REMEDIES FOR 'DARK, UGLY' WOODWORK

By Clem Labine

A COMMON OLD-HOUSE COMPLAINT: "I can't stand that dark woodwork. What should I do?" Most people turn automatically to paint remover. But this can be a needlessly messy—and expensive—solution. Chances are that there is a serviceable finish obscured beneath many layers of wax, grime and shellac. Often, this finish can be *revived* with a lot less effort than completely stripping and refinishing.

IN PARTICULAR, late 19th-century and turn-of-the-century houses often have paneling and woodwork of walnut, mahogany and oak that looks practically black—but which can be revived with minimum effort.

ABOVE ALL, don't plunge in and strip everything off, automatically assuming that the wood will look better "natural." In many cases, a dark finish was applied originally . . . sometimes because dark woodwork was integral to the design of the house . . . and sometimes to disguise the fact that cheap, uninteresting woods had been used for the woodwork. More than one person has stripped off dark ugly finish . . . only to find that they are left with light ugly wood.

THE FIRST RULE is *test*. There are a variety of revivers you can use. So find the least conspicuous area of woodwork and run a series of test procedures . . . starting with the easiest and working up to the more drastic and time-consuming.

IF YOU ARE WORKING with the original finish, in all probability it is shellac rather than varnish. Unlike varnish, shellac is readily dissolved by several mild solvents, which means that there are several fairly easy tricks short of total stripping that will rescue the original finish.

FREQUENTLY, the dark color is a combination of the shellac (which darkens with age) plus pigment that was sometimes added to give the finish a darker color. By selectively removing a portion of the finish, you may be able to arrive at a color you like.

• TRY CLEANING first. Mineral spirits (benzine) or turpentine will remove any of the heavy wax build-up. Use plenty of rags or paper towels to wipe the surface. If the rags come off dirty, you are removing considerable surface accumulation. This will leave the surface dull looking. If the color is promising, let the surface dry, and then apply a thin coat of lemon oil or Butcher's wax.

• TRY STRONGER cleaners next—cleaners that will dissolve a portion of the finish. These include proprietary cleaners like Fantastik or full-strength Top Job. Or you can make your own strong cleaner by dissolving 1 1b. of washing soda (sal soda) in a gallon of hot water. Use rubber gloves, and rub down the woodwork with this solution and 2/0 steel wool. Ammonia will also dissolve shellac.

RUB WITH THE CLEANERS until the wood is a shade you like. Then finish as above.

• NEXT COME THE CHEMICAL SOLVENTS. There are several different formulas you can try:

▸ 15% (by volume) lacquer thinner in mineral spirits;

▸ 50–50 mixture of lacquer thinner and denatured alcohol;

▸ Pure denatured alcohol.

START WITH the first mixture because it will take off the least amount of finish. Apply with fine 3/0 steel wool, wetting surface and changing pads as necessary. The appearance of the surface while wet with the solvent is the look it will have when the final coat of wax or lemon oil is applied. When you have taken off enough of the old finish and have the look you want, wash the surface with rags saturated with benzine or mineral spirits.

IF YOU WANT A HARDER FINISH on the woodwork than that provided by lemon oil or wax, you can apply a satin finish varnish, or a hard oil finish such as that provided by Minwax Antique Oil or tung oil.

CAUTION: Never apply wax over a surface that has been treated with lemon oil. Unlike tung oil or linseed oil, lemon oil doesn't dry. So the wax will dissolve in the lemon oil and make a gummy mess. Likewise, don't apply lemon oil to a surface that has been waxed. If this disaster does occur, the resulting glop can be removed with mineral spirits or turpentine.

ONLY AFTER all of the above cleaning and reviving procedures have been tried should you move on to the ultimate step of removing all the old finish with paint & varnish remover. Sometimes woodwork that has been stripped entirely of its dark old finish looks very dull and lifeless, leaving the homeowner disappointed—and tired and poorer to boot.

UNSTICKING A BALKY SLIDING DOOR

By Clem Labine

THERE IS SOMETHING VERY SATISFYING about a pair of sliding doors that roll smoothly out of the wall . . . appearing as if by magic. And when the host parts the doors silently to announce to the guests in the front parlor that dinner is served . . . well, that is the height of elegance.

BY THE SAME TOKEN, nothing is quite so frustrating as a sliding door that won't slide. It is quite difficult to maintain that air of elegance while tugging and hauling on a 100-lb. hunk of wood that steadfastly resists your efforts to withdraw it from its hiding place inside the wall.

WHEN A SLIDING DOOR WON'T SLIDE, the first instinct is to think that it needs new rollers. In fact, new rollers are usually that LAST things that are needed. In most cases, the problems are more complex. A sliding door is a more delicately balanced mechanism than most people realize; there are at least 6 major things that can go wrong. And many door problems involve two or more of these hazards.

THE ONLY WAY to trouble-shoot a balky sliding door is to check out all the possibilities . . . starting with the easiest ones first.

HOW IT SHOULD WORK

IN ORDER TO REPAIR a malfunctioning sliding door, you should understand how one works under ideal conditions. This analysis is based on the repair of half a dozen sets of sliding doors in houses built from 1840–1890. Some houses may have different door mechanisms than the one to be described, but all doors examined in this 50-year construction span were built about the same.

IN THEORY, a sliding door mechanism is quite simple. There are two wheels mortised into the bottom of the door that roll on a metal track fastened to the floor. Normally, there are also wooden pegs that extend about ½ in. from the top of the door. These pegs travel in a slotted groove in a top wooden track and keep the door aligned at the top. In some doors examined, however, these pegs are missing and apparently never were installed even when the doors were new. In these cases, the door is held in alignment at the top only by the stop mouldings.

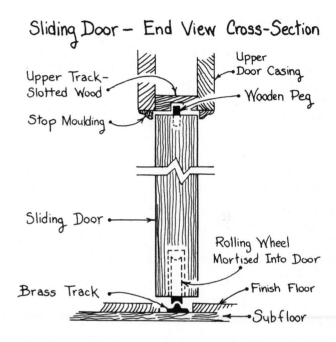

Sliding Door – End View Cross-Section

- Upper Track – Slotted Wood
- Stop Moulding
- Upper Door Casing
- Wooden Peg
- Sliding Door
- Rolling Wheel Mortised Into Door
- Finish Floor
- Brass Track
- Subfloor

THE SECRET: CORRECT ALIGNMENTS

ALIGNMENT IS THE KEY WORD in analyzing sliding door problems: Alignment between the door, the top track, bottom track, and sides of the wall pocket. The alignment problem is complicated when the door is warped—which is not uncommon.

MANY OF THE CLEARANCES involved in a smoothly operating door are only ¼ in. or so. But in 100 years of existence, the shifting and shrinkage of a house's timbers can easily amount to an inch or more. So it should be no surprise that a door that glided silently when the house was new now grinds and grumbles like a freight train. The remedy, in most cases, is merely to correct the alignments so that the geometry of the door, upper and lower tracks, and side walls is the same as when the doors were installed. This process isn't simple; it often requires a lot of trial-and-error.

WHEN A DOOR ROLLS HARD . . . or jumps the track . . . the first thing to check out is the track itself. Sometimes the solution is as simple as clearing debris from the channel around the track, especially the portion inside the wall. In other cases, the brass track will be battered and bent from

Top View of Sliding Door Pocket in Wall

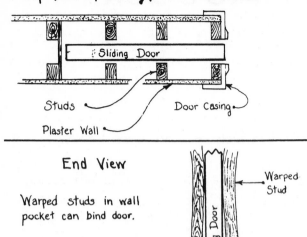

Studs

Plaster Wall

Door Casing

Warp In Upper Track Can Cause Binding

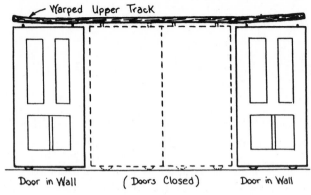

Warped Upper Track

Door in Wall   (Doors Closed)   Door in Wall

When upper track is warped, doors can get out of alignment when sliding into wall.

End View

Warped studs in wall pocket can bind door.

Warped Stud

Sliding Door

floor traffic. Careful work with a hammer and pliers often can set things aright. Other times, the finish floor boards will have shifted so close to the track that the wood binds the rolling wheels. Remedy: Cut back the old board, or else lay in a new, smaller piece. In yet other cases, the treatment may require lifting the entire track, straightening it out, and relaying it in the exact center of the groove in the floor. If the floor has settled, some shims under the track may be required.

SURPRISINGLY, the brass track often is not tacked to the floor inside the wall. If the track has drifted out of position inside the partition, the door may bump into some of the wall studs. Often, this can be corrected by working through the opening in the door frame. Here's how:

REMOVE THE METAL STOP from the top of the door frame. This allows you to roll the door being worked on all the way across the opening—to occupy the space normally taken up by its mate. (The mate door is tucked into the wall.) The vacancy created allows you to get a good look inside the wall pocket. Usually you can get a hammer far enough inside so that the track can be straightened and tacked in place.

IF YOU CAN'T get a hammer far enough inside to totally reposition the drifting track, the only option is to break open the plaster wall opposite the end of the track. Then nail the track firmly in place in the precise middle of the wall pocket.

FLOATING TOP TRACK

IF THE DOOR IS BINDING inside the wall—and you have determined the bottom track isn't the culprit—the next thing to investigate is the top wooden track. Frequently, the top

track is not fastened in any way inside the wall; it just sort of floats. Thus it can—and often does—warp in any of four directions. If it warps to the right or left, it may run the door into the studs at the side of the pocket. If the track has warped upwards, it may no longer hold the pegs and may allow the door to flop.

IT MAY BE POSSIBLE—working from outside the door frame as described earlier—to correct a left-right warp by inserting shims between the track and the first set of studs. If this doesn't work, the only alternative is to open the wall and nail some braces to the studs to hold the wooden track in the correct position.

IF THE TOP AND BOTTOM TRACKS are perfectly positioned in the middle of the wall pocket, and the door still binds inside the partition, the problem is probably caused by studs that have bowed inward. Often you can spot the offender visually with a flashlight. If not, you can make a gauge by cutting a block of wood the exact width of the opening in the door casing. Tack the gauge block to the end of a broomstick and push it into the wall pocket, checking clearances between all the studs.

IF THE AMOUNT OF BULGE is small—less than ⅛-in.—and located in the first set of studs, you may be able to remove a sufficient amount of material with a drum rasp attachment on a power drill. But if you can't reach the trouble spot, more drastic remedies may be required. In special cases where the problem is in the last set of studs, it may be possible to pry them apart with wedges inserted through the door frame . . .

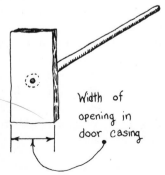

Width of opening in door casing

and to keep them at the proper spacing via an inserted block. (Be ready for some cracked plaster.) Otherwise, the only answer may be to open the wall and to turn or replace the studs.

WHEN ROLLERS NEED REPLACING

SOMETIMES the roller wheels do need replacing—or perhaps they are missing altogether. The large rolling wheels that the doors originally had are no longer made. You may be fortunate enough to find a set of the correct size as a salvage item. But if you can't, there are modern substitutes that will suffice.

IF THE TRACK IS STILL IN PLACE, for example, and all you need are the wheels, there are large window pulleys made that may fill the bill. The Grant #1415 Sheave has been used with success; this is just a large window pulley with a nylon roller and pot metal housing. Certain types of patio door rollers can also be used.

BECAUSE THE OLD ROLLER WHEELS were larger than the ones you can buy today, the old mortise will have to be adapted. The best idea is to get as many rollers as possible into the old mortise (see diagram below). Just be sure that the rollers are carefully aligned with each other and with the centerline of the door.

REPLACING SLIDING DOOR ROLLERS calls for dismounting the door. Here's how: Remove the stop mouldings at the top of the door frame. With many doors, this gives you enough clearance to lift the door off the bottom track and to tilt the door free of the top track. If the top pegs are still caught in the groove, you can usually raise the upper track sufficiently by pushing up on it with a 2×4.

IF THE DOOR IS MISSING a peg and you wish to add one to improve the alignment of the door at the top, use

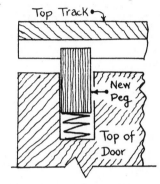

a piece of wooden dowel of sufficient diameter to fill the existing hole. Put about ½ in. of coil spring into the bottom of the hole. Then cut off the dowel so that it will extend half way into the groove in the upper track when there is no compression of the spring. (The function of the spring is to allow you to depress the peg sufficiently so that you can slip the pegs into the upper track when remounting the door.) The pegs should not bear against the top of the groove when the door is mounted on the tracks.

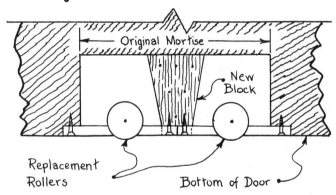

Fitting New Roller To Bottom Of Door

Original Mortise

New Block

Replacement Rollers

Bottom of Door

REFINISHING PAINT-STRIPPED WOODWORK

By Clem Labine

THIS CHAPTER ABOUT REFINISHING paint-stripped woodwork is based on some very recent personal experience. But before getting into tips for dealing with stripped wood, I want to make some comments about "The Cult Of The Stripper."

OBSERVATIONS OVER THE PAST MONTHS have convinced me that entirely too much wood stripping is going on. In many cases, stripping woodwork is not only historically inappropriate, but the process can involve a lot of needless work and expense. And often the results are downright disappointing.

SOME PEOPLE SEEM TO FEEL that "restoring" means stripping every piece of wood in sight. In Early American houses, especially, this can lead to absurd results. Most wood in pre-1840 homes is soft . . . lacking the pretty grain of hardwood . . . and was originally painted. Stripping wood of this type is inappropriate . . . and it is almost impossible to produce a really good-looking result.

THE JOURNAL EDITORS were recently given a tour of an 1830 Greek Revival townhouse in which the owner proudly pointed to the woodwork in the main hall that he had just "refinished." The wood was pine, and surely had been painted when originally installed because the wood was not especially attractive and painted wood was the custom in Greek Revival decoration. Yet the new owner had stripped off the paint and applied a clear sealer. The woodwork looked awful! Not only was the grain itself quite drab, but there were flecks of white paint everywhere—clinging to every crevice and pore in the wood. But the owner was quite pleased with his handiwork because he had "stripped the wood."

OTHER TYPES OF COMPLEX WOODWORK, such as panelled wainscotting, may be made of hardwood that was originally finished naturally but is now languishing under layers of paint. This is often found in "remuddled" Victorian homes. Unless one is willing to spend a lot of time digging paint out of cracks and crevices, the end result of paint stripping on such large, complex surfaces is likely to be quite disappointing. The bits of leftover paint peeking out from countless holes and cracks loudly proclaim: "This was a quick-and-dirty stripping job!"

RATHER THAN DO A SLAM-BANG stripping job, two alternatives should be explored first. By careful scratch-testing you can probably determine what the original finish was. If it was paint, you are much better off repainting in the original color—or in a color that is appropriate to the period and style of the house. Painting is a lot faster, easier—and less expensive than the stripping process.

AND EVEN IF THE WOOD had originally been finished with a clear shellac or varnish, you would be better off applying a grained finish than doing a half-hearted stripping job. A grained finish will give a better-looking result for less work than badly done paint removal.

ANOTHER POINT TO WATCH FOR—especially in Victorian houses—is a mixture of woods. The late 19th-century builders tended to use fine hardwoods for the woodwork in the more formal rooms, but were apt to use lesser grades of wood in the family rooms. From the outset, the true character of the lesser woods was disguised with graining, paint or colored varnishes. Only removing paint from small patches in each room will tell you whether you have this kind of mixture of woods in your house. Only the hardwoods are worthwhile candidates for full-fledged paint stripping.

WHEN THE WOOD IS WORTH STRIPPING

OUR PARTICULAR PROJECT was the panelled wainscotting that runs through the front parlor and hallways in The Journal's 1883 Victorian brownstone. Test stripping had shown that the wood—underneath about six layers of gloppy white paint—was beautiful American black walnut. Even though the amount of wood to be stripped was staggering, we decided the beauty of the wood warranted the enormous amount of time it would take.

THE WOOD WAS STRIPPED using a paste-type stripper ("Rock Miracle"). The bulk of the paint came off with one application of the paste-type remover, followed by scraping with putty knives and a rinse with a liquid-type paint remover. Just this much had taken about 20 person-days of work. The wood looked OK . . . but not great. A haze of white paint clung tenaciously to it.

EXPERIMENTING ON A SMALL SECTION, we found that enough rinsing with liquid paint remover followed by washing with denatured alcohol would clean up the flat surfaces to a visually acceptable level. Additional hours spent with screwdriver and nutpick finally got the white residue out of the flutes, grooves and corners. After figuring out the time and cost of cleaning up that one section . . . and multiplying by the number of sections remaining . . . Claire and I fainted!

CLEARLY, A DIFFERENT APPROACH was called for. We knew that we would have to settle for something less than total paint removal and work out some of the imperfections during the finishing steps. The process we evolved worked quite well. It's based on the principle of covering up everything you can't remove.

WE RINSED ALL THE WOODWORK one more time with liquid paint remover until our patience was totally exhausted. After these additional hours, there was still a faint white haze on the wood, as well as bits and flecks of white in deep grooves and crevices of the mouldings. It was obvious that digging out every last bit of the deep-down white residue could become a lifetime project.

FOR THE BASIC FINISH ON THE WOODWORK, we had selected Minwax Antique Oil Finish. This is a clear, penetrating-type oil finish (with a linseed oil base) that is quite easy to apply and which gives a soft, lustrous finish. Tests on a small patch of woodwork, however, revealed that the residue of the white paint showed through the finish as well as the grain of the walnut.

CAMOUFLAGING THE WHITE RESIDUE

THE ANSWER TO THE WHITE HAZE PROBLEM was found by making what amounts to an antiquing liquid. To the Oil Finish itself we added pigments ground in oil (the tinting colors you can buy at large paint stores used mainly in coloring paints). We obtained a walnut-colored liquid by using two pigments—burnt umber and burnt sienna—in these approximate proportions:

> 1 quart Antique Oil Finish
>
> 2 Tablespoons burnt umber pigment
>
> 1 Tablespoon burnt sienna pigment

PROPORTIONS, obviously, would be altered to fit the color of the wood being finished. Test the liquid on a small inconspicuous area following the procedures outlined below. Once you've got the right mixture, be sure you've made up a big enough batch so that you don't have to go through the whole mix-and-match process again halfway through the job.

THE PIGMENTED OIL was applied liberally with a brush. Special attention was paid to working the oil thoroughly into all corners and grooves. All excess was wiped off with cheesecloth within 15 minutes.

WHEN THE SURFACES ARE WIPED DOWN, most of the oil on the flat panels comes right off on the rag. Just a small amout of pigment is left on the surface of the wood . . . just enough to mask the suggestion of white left from the stripping.

IN CORNERS AND GROOVES, however, where the cheesecloth doesn't reach, the pigmented oil accumulates more thickly. But that's OK, because that is also where the steel wool wouldn't reach when the paint was being removed. And these are the areas that have the greatest concentration of paint pigment. The end result of this process is that all the white blobs are covered by a semi-opaque walnut colored layer that dries hard like a varnish. So the corners and grooves, instead of having white ghosts, have a darker cast that gives a pleasantly antique look.

IF YOU TRY A PIGMENTED OIL wiping liquid like this and find that it doesn't give adequate hiding power, you can either add more pigment or else wait until the first application dries (at least 24 hr.) and then put on a second coating.

WE HAD INITIALLY TRIED a walnut oil stain for this purpose. But stain colors by penetrating the wood and dyeing the fibers. And where you need the color the most is on top of the residual paint—which doesn't take the stain. The pigment-in-oil, on the other hand, deposits a layer of walnut color right on top of the white residue.

THE FINISHING TOUCHES

IN CASES WHERE there is no white haze left on flat surfaces—but there is paint pigment left in gooves and cracks—the procedure should be altered slightly. The wood should be given a coat of the clear, unpigmented oil first, which would then be wiped down and allowed to dry thoroughly for 2–3 days. Then the pigmented oil liquid can be brushed into corners and gooves where there is still paint residue showing. All excess is wiped off with cheesecloth. The first coat of oil finish will keep the pigmented oil from sinking into the flat surfaces where the color isn't needed; it will wipe off completely. Pigment will accumulate in corners and grooves where it is desired to hide the paint residue.

THERE WILL DOUBTLESS be small spots where residual paint still shows through. Easiest way I found to cope with these small blemishes was to make up a small amount of walnut "paint": A thick mixture of pigment and the finishing oil. With a small artist's brush, I put a small dot of walnut color over each of the white blips. It took time—but less time than trying to dig out each bit . . . and the cover-up is gentler on the wood, too.

AFTER ALL ADJUSTMENTS had been made to get rid of the white ghosts, two more coats of the clear, unpigmented Antique Oil Finish were applied, wiping each one down thoroughly with cheesecloth. After the final coat had dried for three days, it was buffed lightly with very fine (0000) steel wool to give it a softer luster.

THIS PROCEDURE CAN BE ADAPTED to refinish any type of stripped wood. Any wood color can be reproduced using combinations of one or more of the following pigments: Burnt umber, burnt sienna, raw umber, raw sienna.

WE ARE EXTREMELY PLEASED with the results we obtained using this technique. Although the grain isn't as brilliant as it would have been had we been refinishing virgin walnut, it is the best stripped woodwork I have seen.

TIPS ON STRIPPING SHUTTERS

SHUTTERS COME IN TWO DEGREES of difficulty as far as stripping goes: Hard and Very Hard. Because of the many irregular surfaces, under the best of conditions stripping shutters is a time-consuming and frustrating process. We've collected the techniques and suggestions from a number of old-house people who have been through it so that if you're undertaking a similar project you can get through it with a minimum of ulcers and deleted expletives.

IN THIS ARTICLE we're using the term "shutter" to cover both both blinds and shutters. True shutters have solid panels and are usually used on the exterior—to literally shut up a house. Blinds have movable louvers that are used to regulate light. Stripping techniques are the same for both—although blinds are harder because they have more ins and outs.

BECAUSE SHUTTER STRIPPING is such a major project, it shouldn't be undertaken casually. There are three situations in which you should consider stripping:

1. You have hardwood shutters that have been painted and you wish to go back to a clear natural finish;

2. You have hardwood shutters with old darkened shellac or varnish on them that you wish to remove before refinishing;

3. You have softwood shutters that have been painted so often that they are thickly covered with old cracking paint. It may be desirable to strip off the old material before repainting. It usually is not worthwhile to strip paint from softwood shutters in order to apply a clear finish.

SOFTWOOD HAS AN OPEN PORE STRUCTURE and paint tends to cling tenaciously—making it very difficult to get the wood really clean. And once it is clean, softwood grain isn't particularly interesting. So you put in a lot of work for a result that isn't terribly exciting.

IF YOU HAVE A LOT OF SHUTTERS TO STRIP, you may want to farm the whole thing out to a commercial stripping service. Cost usually is in the range of $5–10 per shutter—and the charge might well be worth all the time and mess saved.

CAUTION: Commercial services usually use a variation of the lye bath process—although each will claim he has his own magic formula. These dips can be rough on fine hardwood (see discussion later in this article). So before consigning your precious mahogany shutters to a caustic soaking, you're best off if you can see examples of the stripper's previous work on hardwood. It can save futile weeping over ruined wood later on.

HOWEVER, if personal desire or economics impels you to do-it-yourself stripping, here's what you need to know to make the process as painless as possible. First, because shutters have so many irregularities, dipping in a bath simplifies the stripping process because all surfaces are contacted simultaneously by the treating liquid.

WHEN REMOVING SHUTTERS FOR DIPPING, be sure to mark the original location of each shutter. Although they look identical, the odds are that the sizes will differ slightly—as will the mounting holes. Pencil marks on the ends usually aren't sufficient because the dipping process will likely obliterate them. If you're equipped with metal numeral dies, use them to stamp numbers into the end-grain in an inconspicuous place. Otherwise, cut numbers into the end with a pen knife.

THEN THE QUESTION ARISES: What to dip in? The best answer is a tub made from galvanized metal In some restoration neighborhoods, several families have chipped in and split up the cost of having a suitably sized tub made up at a local tinsmith shop. A tub 60"dp × 24" × 10" is adequate for work with shutters. If the dip tub will also be used for larger pieces like doors, then obviously a larger tub should be ordered.

OTHER MAKESHIFT EXPEDIENTS can be pressed into service for dipping tubs. An old bathtub . . . a 55-gal. drum . . . a big plastic garbage pail. As long as the container is at least half the depth of the shutter, you can use it for dipping by dunking one-half of the shutter at a time. You can also make a dipping box from clear pine boards (knots will cause leaks) The joints can be sealed with silicone bathtub caulk. This type of wood box will serve pretty well for everything but lye (the lye would eat through the boards in fairly short order). For lye service, a wood dipping box could be lined with fiberglass and epoxy—the type used for marine repairs.

Dipping Box
Cross-Section

Silicone Caulk
1×10
1×12 Clear Pine

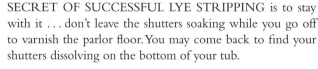

Dip One End At A Time

LYE IS THE QUICKEST and least expensive stripping agent to use. Cans of lye are available at many supermarkets and hardware stores (it's sold for cleaning drains). Strength of the lye solution you'll need depends on the amount of paint to be removed. In general, the stronger the better. Some use a solution of one pound of lye per gallon of solution. If there's only one coat of paint to cope with, you could get away with one pound for every five gallons. The idea is to use a strong solution that will attack the paint quickly—before the lye has a chance to soak into the glued joints. Shutters should never be left in a lye bath one minute longer than required to soften the paint.

LYE WORKS BEST WHEN IT'S HOT, so you're best off working on a warm sunny day. Bricks can be used to hold down the shutters to totally submerge them in the solution.

SECRET OF SUCCESSFUL LYE STRIPPING is to stay with it . . . don't leave the shutters soaking while you go off to varnish the parlor floor. You may come back to find your shutters dissolving on the bottom of your tub.

WHEN THE PAINT HAS SOFTENED SUFFICIENTLY, you will be able to remove it by scrubbing with a stiff-bristle scrub brush . . . the kind you'd use to scrub floors. This scrubbing can be done while the shutters are floating in the vat (and while you are wearing rubber gloves to keep the lye from dissolving your hands).

AS SOON AS THE PAINT HAS BEEN SCRUBBED OFF, remove the shutters from the bath and flush them thoroughly with a garden hose to remove all traces of lye. Some people recommend neutralizing the lye by dousing the shutters with vinegar, but this really isn't necessary if you flush thoroughly. Besides, who wants shutters that smell like salad dressing?

FINAL TRACES OF PAINT in corners and crevices should be picked out while the shutter is still wet. Use an old screwdriver, nutpick or your favorite crevice tool. While lye is an inexpensive and effective stripping agent, it is not a universal cure-all, and there are several cautions to be observed.

FIRST, while lye will do an effective job on softwood and oak, it is not recommended for hardwood—such as mahogany and walnut—to which a clear finish will be applied. Lye will turn wood dark, and although it can be bleached back with Clorox, all this back and forth definitely does not enhance the grain.

SECOND, lye will dissolve skin—so use rubber gloves and protect your eyes. Flush thoroughly with water if you get any lye solution on you.

FINALLY, the spent lye solution presents a disposal problem. Don't dump it on the ground if you ever expect grass to grow there again. If you are connected to a central sewer system the solution can be flushed down a drain—diluted with copious amounts of cold water to minimize wear and tear on the pipes.

PAINTED HARDWOOD SHUTTERS are the biggest bother because in order to preserve the hardwood under-

SHUTTER STRIPPER SELECTOR

Type of Shutter	SOFTWOOD or OAK			HARDWOOD		
Stripper	Paint	Shellac	Varnish	Paint	Shellac	Varnish
Lye Bath	✓					
Chemical Strippers		✓	✓	✓	✓	✓
Alcohol		✓			✓	

neath, the paint should be removed with chemical strippers rather than lye. There's no pleasant way to use a chemical remover. But there are a few tricks that will make it a little less gruesome.

THE FIRST TRICK IS: Don't be stingy with the material. Although stripper is expensive—it runs around $8/gal. these days—you might as well get the maximum amount of work out of it by using it properly . . . and that means generously.

THE BEST REMOVERS are the water-rinseable paste types. Sold under a variety of trade names such as Strypeze, TM-4, Old Reliable, etc. Selection of remover is pretty much a matter of personal preference.

ONCE THE REMOVER IS APPLIED, resist the urge to start scraping away immediately. Wait until the remover has soaked through to the bottom layer of paint. You may have to lay on a second—or even third—coat of remover in order to soak through. Don't let the remover dry out . . . keep it wet with successive applications of remover. It's easiest to conduct this operation in a tub or dipping box . . . with the shutter supported on blocks or bricks. This allows you to recycle some of the remover that drips off.

Cross-Section of Shutter Being Stripped in Box.

TEST WITH A PUTTY KNIFE to see if paint will come off in a continuous ribbon, leaving the wood clean. If not, wait longer. If it will, the remover has done its job and now it's your turn. Remove as much paint as possible by scraping with the putty knife. Then wipe up the remainder with fine steel wool.

AFTER MOPPING UP WITH steel wool, there will still be some paint remaining. Rinse with a liquid paint remover, followed by a wipe with more steel wool.

EVEN WITH GENEROUS USE OF remover, it usually takes at least 4 hours to strip a painted shutter.

AN OLD DARKENED FINISH on shutters is probably shellac. If so, you're lucky—because shellac is the easiest finish to remove. It dissolves readily in denatured alcohol . . . and liquid paint remover will cut right through it.

THE MOST PLEASANT METHOD is to set up a two-vat dipping system with denatured alcohol. Very effective . . . but also expensive. Shutter is dipped in first alcohol bath and allowed to soak for 15 min., then is scrubbed with very fine steel wool. The shellac dissolves into the dipping solution. After a few shutters are done, the alcohol bath absorbs quite a bit of finish—becoming essentially a dilute shellac solution. Rinsing shutters in a second, clean alcohol bath removes the traces of shellac solution.

LESS ALCOHOL—but more elbow grease—is used if you just flood the shutter surface with alcohol and scrub with fine steel wool and paper towels. With this process, you're lifting the surface off mechanically rather than floating it off as you do with the alcohol bath.

IN SOME CASES, the shellac contains additives that cause it to ball up in alcohol rather than dissolve. In this event, add one part of lacquer thinner to 3 parts of the alcohol. If neither alcohol nor lacquer thinner will touch the finish, then you're dealing with real varnish and you'll have to use chemical strippers as described below.

LIQUID PAINT REMOVERS can be used with shellac or varnish—although the action is a lot faster on shellac. Working in a horizontal tub, flood on the liquid remover. Remover that drips off can be picked up from the bottom of the vat with a paintbrush and recycled to the top of the shutter. When the remover has soaked through the finish, mop it up with fine steel wool. Add more remover to keep the finish wet and to rinse off the last traces of the old surface.

RESTORING SHUTTERS TO WORKING ORDER

WITH ALL of the attention being focused on the energy crisis, it's time to look at that great energy-conserving invention: the window shutter.

FOR THE ORIGINAL OLD-HOUSE OWNER, shutters weren't just pretty decorations. They can also be a practical tool in running the house. In winter you can cut consumption of heating fuel by closing the shutters at night. This cuts radiation losses through window apertures. During winter days, you capitalize on the sun's warmth by opening the shutters on the sunny side of the house.

IN SUMMER, the process is reversed, and can cut—or eliminate—the need for air conditioning. During the day, close the shutters on the sunny side of the house to keep out the sun's rays. At night, open the windows and shutters to let the house fill with cool night air.

THE TRICK to this energy-conserving scheme, however, is having shutters that work freely. In many old houses they have been pretty well battered after 100 or so years of use. Here's a review of various mechanical ailments that afflict shutters and some remedies that have been used successfully.

SHUTTER SAG

FREQUENTLY, LOOSE HINGES CAUSE SAGGING that prevents proper closure. These loose hinges in many cases can't be fixed by merely tightening screws because after numberless retightenings the screws have stripped all of the wood from their holes. One obvious remedy is the Old Matchstick Trick—stuffing a matchstick into the hole to give the screw more wood to bite into.

A MORE PERMANENT SOLUTION is to fill the hole with plastic wood. (A very satisfactory filler is Elmer's glue mixed with fine sawdust.) Re-insert screw while the filler's soft—but tighten all the way. When the filler has set in a couple of hours, tighten down the screw.

SECURING LOOSE JOINTS

SHUTTER JOINTS may have come unglued to the extent that the shutter won't close properly. Method of repair depends on how badly it's unglued.

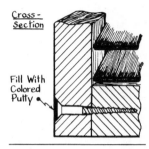

Screw reinforcement.

IF JOINTS ARE PARTIALLY LOOSE, you may be able to open them far enough to force more glue in and clamp while glue sets: To get new glue into a crack, run a line of it on top of the crevice and blow it in through a drinking straw. An alternate method is to use a 3" wood screw to reinforce the joint. Drill a shank hole (large enough to pass the body of the screw) through the outer frame section, and drill a pilot hole in the second frame piece. Countersink hole so that screw head is hidden. Cover screw head with linseed oil putty colored with pigment (burnt umber, raw umber, raw sienna—available at paint stores) that match the wood.

IF JOINTS ARE COMPLETELY LOOSE, the simplest thing is to totally disassemble the shutter, reglue joints, and reassemble. Getting all louvers back into their sockets is something of a Chinese puzzle, but with patience it can be done. Two or three bar clamps will hold the shutter together while glue is setting.

PINWHEELING LOUVERS

LOUVERS MAY BE MISSING THE YOKE PIN that connects them to the vertical post—so that some louvers don't move in unison with the others. This can be fixed with a common pin, file, and needle-nose pliers.

CUT OFF HEAD and bend pin into a U-shape. Sharpen blunt end with a file. With needlenose pliers, slip new yoke pin through loop on vertical post and force it into old pin-holes in louver.

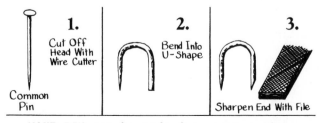

YOKE PIN can be made from common pin.

REPLACING MISSING BEARING PINS

IF THE WOODEN BEARING PIN at the end of a louver breaks off so that the louver hangs down like a broken bird-wing, replace the missing bearing pin with a wire pin.

MAKE A U-SHAPE from a common pin, as shown in the diagram. Sharpen the blunt end. With needle-nose pliers, force the two legs of the U into the louver where the old pin had been. When new pin is inserted deeply enough so that louver can be pushed back into frame, use needle-nose pliers to withdraw pin so that it telescopes into the bearing socket.

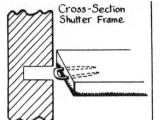
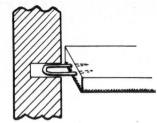

New bearing forced deeply into louvre.　　*Bearing pin extended into socket hole.*

IF THE SHUTTER FRAME WAS totally disassembled reglueing, the new louver should be cut with wooden bearing-pins at both ends and inserted when reassembling the shutter. Then fashion a new yoke-pin as described above.

IF THE SHUTTER IS STILL IN ONE PIECE, the new louver should be cut with only one wooden bearing-pin. After slipping the wooden bearing into its socket, anchor the other end using the telescoping bearing-pin technique described above. Then attach a new yoke-pin.

YOUR SHUTTERS—now in perfect working order—are not only aesthetically pleasing, but also ecologically sound.

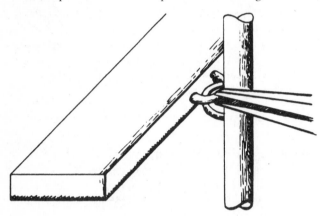

Yoke pin inserted with needle-nose pliers.

FAKING A LOUVER

NEW LOUVERS CAN BE CUT from thin wood, patterned after the ones still in place. Orange crate slats are about the right thickness, and are easily cut and stained.

FIXING SAGGING SHUTTERS

To The Editor:

IN WORKING WITH OLD BLINDS, I have found that a number of mine had a noticeable sag. Joints in these blinds are all mortise-and-tenon, with wooden pegs holding the assembly together. I have found that you can straighten up these blinds by driving in small wooden wedges at the middle mortise.

A WOODEN MALLET is used to drive the wedges so as not to break the small wedge. You use the middle mortise rather than the top or bottom mortises because the wood is usually in better condition in the middle of the blind.

Burton L. Brown

To The Editor:

I HAD A SET OF BLINDS with a couple of pegs broken off the ends of the louvers so that those few slats flopped around like a bird with a broken wing. I didn't want to take the blinds completely apart to insert new louvers. So I cut a "V"-shaped notch in the slats where the peg was missing, then carved a new peg with a wedge-shaped end that matched the "V."

A GLUE SUCH AS quick-set epoxy is applied to the wedge. The new peg can then be slipped into the hole in the side rail and the wedge fitted into the "V" notch in the louver. The peg can be held in place with the fingers while the glue sets. (Since there isn't a lot of stress on the joint, it doesn't have to be super-strong.) Stain to match.

Robert Costello

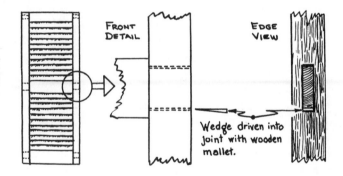

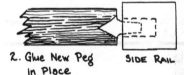

ADDING STORAGE TO THE OLD HOUSE

By Stephen MacDonald

STORAGE IS ONE OF THE MORE vexatious problems besetting the owner of an old house. We have so many possessions these days—many of which hadn't even been invented when the house was built. Even articles that had been invented—like books—weren't owned in the abundance that they are today. This means that today's old-house owner will either have to throw away some of his or her possessions (which might not be a bad idea at that) or add some storage space to the house.

LET'S BEGIN WITH THE UNDERSTANDING that in adding storage facilities to your house you are adding an anachronism—however necessary it may be. If you don't want it to LOOK like an anachronism, the unit will have to be custom-made to suit your particular house. Fortunately, many kinds of storage units are reasonably easy do-it-yourself projects.

SHELVES FOR BOOKS, records and the like are a good place to begin, because they are easy enough to build so that a novice carpenter can have a confidence-building success. And the experience introduces skills that can be expanded into more ambitious cabinet-making projects later on.

DESIGN FACTORS

SHELF-BUILDING PROJECTS involve two basic steps: (1) Construction of the basic unit, which is pretty much the same for everyone; (2) adding the finishing touches (mouldings, etc.), which have to be tailored to you specific house. The following instructions will guide you through the carpentry of the basic construction and then give you some ideas on tailoring the result so that it looks as though it were built with the house.

THE FIRST STEP IN DESIGNING the bookcase (we'll call it that, even though the unit could be used to accommodate other things) is to plan out such functional matters as how much capacity you require and where the unit will stand. Then you have to add aesthetic factors such as what dimensions will give you the desired capacity in a shape that makes sense in the room you have selected. You might want to build tall cases that reach to the ceiling . . . or door height . . . or wainscot height. In these considerations you'll do well to consult books that have photos of houses of similar vintage to yours, and visit neighbors who own old houses.

HOW FAR APART should shelves be? It's possible to make them adjustable, of course, and some people think this is the safest course. On the other hand, most people don't adjust their adjustable shelves very often (if ever) after they are in place. And fixed shelves are both stronger and better looking than the adjustable kind. Usually, good advance planning can eliminate the need for adjustable shelves.

FINAL PROCEDURE in this first part of the design is to draw up a detailed plan of the basic structure and include all dimensions.

SPECIAL TRIM

NEXT STEP IS TO CONSIDER what special touches will make the basic shelf unit look as if it had been in your house forever. Many old bookcases tended to be ornate, with such features as elaborate carvings and beveled-glass doors. If you have the woodworking skill to bring off this kind of thing, by all means go right ahead. But it isn't necessary. A simpler but quite satisfactory effect can be achieved by selecting an architectural detail that's part of the room where the bookcase will be and incorporating it in the design. For example, copy the room baseboard and extend it around the bottom of your unit. Select a crown moulding for the top that is similar to your cornice moulding or framing woodwork in the room. Perhaps you'll also want to add strips of decorative moulding to the fronts of the uprights.

ANY WELL-STOCKED LUMBERYARD carries a variety of ready-made mouldings in softwood that can be stained or grained to match hardwood. It's almost always possible to combine two or three stock mouldings in a way that comes close to matching old mouldings.

SELECTING WOOD

WHAT MATERIALS should you use? If the unit is to be painted or grained, possibly even stained, softwood lumber will be the logical choice because it's the cheapest—although lumber prices have gone so high in recent years that nothing can be considered cheap. For the genuine hardwood look you'll have to use either solid hardwood or else a plywood veneer. Solid hardwood is available in some lumberyards in some cities—but it's always expensive. Veneered hardwood plywood is an excellent substitute—and it's somewhat cheaper and easier to find. You can find plywood faced in almost every kind of wood.

EDGES OF PLYWOOD VENEER can be covered with a strip of veneer (sold in hardware stores and lumber yards) attached with contact cement. Even better is to face the edges with moulding strips of the appropriate hardwood—if you are fortunate enough to locate some.

PERHAPS A WORD IS IN ORDER on lumber grades, which can confuse even an experienced handy-person. Softwood boards are sold in two broad grades—Select and Common—but there are several sub-grades in each category. Few yards stock the full range of grades, so mostly you'll be choosing between the Select and Common that your yard carries. Select costs roughly twice as much as Common, so it's worth considering whether you can make Common do the job. Sometimes you can cut several good pieces out of a Common board; other times you can fill and seal knots. But when you need a long piece of clear wood, you'll have to pay for Select.

IT IS VITALLY IMPORTANT that your lumber be dry. Wet wood is hard to cut, it dulls blades, and shrinks and warps as it dries to the humidity level of your house. The best wood is kiln-dried.

HARDWOOD IS GRADED DIFFERENTLY. The top quality is known as FAS—meaning Firsts and Seconds—followed by Select and Number 1 Common. FAS has few defects, Select has a few more (especially on the back face), and Common is usually unsuitable for large pieces such as bookshelf units.

Simple storage unit (which can be used with or without doors) from Downing's 1850 edition of "The Architecture of Country Houses."

AS FOR PLYWOOD, the softwood variety is frankly not recommended for quality work—even if the plan calls for painting. Its interior plys are soft and loose. Hardwood plywood is available in several grades. The highest, Premium, is probably not worth the extra expense unless you need matched graining. The grades known as 1 or 2 are adequate. Many yards term their plywood "G2S" (meaning Good on 2 Sides), or "G1S," (Good on 1 Side).

PLYWOOD IS SOLD IN PANELS, usually 4 ft. × 8 ft., in 1/8, 1/4, 3/8, 1/2, 5/8, 3/4 and 1 in. thicknesses. Boards are sold in "nominal" dimensions—which means the size before finishing and drying. Thus a board nominally 1 in. thick actually measures about 3/4 in. A nominal 5/4 (called "five quarter") measures a little over an inch thick. These are the two most likely thicknesses for shelves. Board widths are nominally 4 in., 6 in., 8 in. and up, increasing by twos. Board lengths are actual dimensions, beginning at 8 ft. and increasing by 2-ft. increments.

BACKING FOR SHELVES can be made of Masonite (if it is to be painted or grained), or else 1/4-in. hardwood plywood.

MYSTIQUE OF THE LUMBERYARD

WHAT ALL THIS MEANS is that you must get to know your way around the lumberyard if if you expect to do much woodworking. First step is to know exactly what you want. Using your plan of the bookcase, make a rough sketch of each component with its dimensions (you won't be able to do this until you have read the following sections on joinery).

USE YOUR COMPONENT DRAWINGS to work out a cutting plan. Try to figure out on paper the minimum amount of lumber you need to buy and how to cut it. Use your cutting plan to derive the lumber list—which is the shopping list you take to the yard. Take along your component sketches and cutting plan, too. You may be planning to buy four pieces of 8 ft. 1×10, but if the yard is out of 8 ft. lengths you'll need to recalculate in a hurry!

LUMBERYARDS HAVE A MYSTIQUE for many people, but they're really quite straightforward when you get to know them. The typical operation has an office and a yard. You place your order in the office, and then take your receipt to the yard to get the order filled.

THE MOST IMPORTANT PERSON in the place, as far as you're concerned, is the yard man (or the yard foreman in a large yard). He is the one who is going to select your wood—or better yet, allow you to select it. Yards vary in their attitude about do-it-yourself lumber selection.

Some insist that if you are buying three boards in a size then you must take the top three on the pile. Others let you pick through till you find the three you want.

STILL OTHER YARDS fall somewhere in the middle; they'll allow you to reject an occasional board but not grope through an entire pile. Whatever the yard policy, it's important that you be on hand, if for no other reason than to let the yard people know you are concerned about the quality of the lumber. This is especially true if you are trying to build with Common lumber, where there may be great variations in boards that cost the same.

DO NOT—unless your brother is the yard man—phone in an order for delivery. You are likely to get the dregs that everyone else has rejected. If the yard man is helpful, it's not a bad idea to tip him a dollar or two. That way he'll remember you the next time you come in.

CUTTING AND FITTING

BACK HOME at your shop, you begin by squaring an end of each board, crosscutting it in the appropriate lengths, following your cutting plan. If you're using plywood, you'll begin by ripping the sheets into boards, then crosscutting to length. In this and in all cabinet work and other ambitious carpentry, it is essential that all cuts be square and accurate to 1/16 in. or better. The way to assure this is by measuring carefully ("Measure twice, cut once," as the saying goes), keeping your blades sharp and being sure that your saw—especially if it is a radial-arm saw—is in perfect alignment. A radial-arm saw is one of the most versatile and useful of home shop tools, but it gets out of alignment notoriously easily. A dull blade that drags through the wood will pull it out of adjustment in just a few passes.

NEXT, cut the dadoes and rabbets. These are basic wood joinery cuts, used in almost all cabinet work. A dado is simply a channel in a piece of wood where another piece joins it (in this case where a shelf fits into the sides). A rabbet is like

The addition of an appropriate crown moulding and baseboard bring a simple box shelf unit into harmony with the rest of the room.

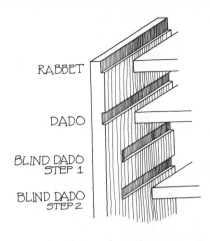

RABBET

DADO

BLIND DADO
STEP 1

BLIND DADO
STEP 2

a dado, but along an edge. Bookcase sides are often rabbeted along the inside back edge to accept the back, and across the inside top to accept the top shelf.

THESE CUTS are easy to make with special blade sets. Dado sets for radial-arm and table saws include two cutters that look much like regular blades, several chippers and some small shims. You make up a sandwich of the cutters, putting as many chippers and shims between them as are needed to make a dado the width you want. Dadoes and rabbets can also be cut with a router or, if you prefer the old-time hand skills, with special planes. In any case, the position, width and depth of the cuts are critical, and great care must be taken.

SPECIAL CUTS

DADOES MUST BE just wide enough for the shelves to fit snugly. Too narrow and the shelf won't fit without an unholy struggle; too wide and it will be sloppy—leaving a gap. It's a good idea to sand the shelves before measuring them for the dadoes, because sanding makes them slightly thinner. Dado depth should be about 1/4 in. for bookcases made of nominal 1-in. stock or 3/4-in. plywood. At the outset, you should make a few trial dadoes in scrap wood before cutting "for real."

SOMETIMES YOU'LL WANT to use a "blind dado," as for instance when the shelves don't extend to the front of the sides. To do this, cut with the dado blade to the point where the shelves will stop, then use a very sharp chisel to square out the channel.

AFTER CUTTING AND DADOING, put veneer or moulding strips on any plywood edges that will show, then sand and dust all pieces. If the finished unit will be too large to conveniently carry through a doorway, move the components to the room where the bookcase will stand. If there is a baseboard on the wall, cut out the rear bottoms of the uprights with a sabre saw. If the bottom shelf is at baseboard height, you'll have to make it less deep than the others. And the back must also stop above the baseboard.

LAY OUT AND ASSEMBLE the bookcase according to your design. Use good quality yellow (not white!) cabinetmakers' glue and finishing nails in all joints. (Franklin's "Titebond" glue is a good high-strength, long-lasting adhesive.) Shelves can be face-nailed from the outside of the uprights, but the nail-holes will be less obvious if you toenail them from the inside—a more difficult job. The nails should be sunk with a nailset and the holes filled with wood putty. If the wood will be finished naturally, the best filler is linseed-oil glazing putty colored with pigments to match the finished wood. This filler should be added after the natural oil finish has been applied to the wood.

Hanging Shelves.

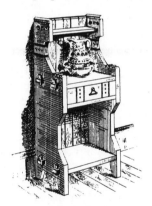

ONCE THE SHELVES, sides and tops are in place, attach the back and hoist the unit into position. Then you can install the mouldings and other trim that will give your basic bookcase its special character. You may want to tack small strips of moulding over the front edges to cover the dadoes.

IF THE BOOKCASE is tall, it may be necessary to anchor it to keep it from toppling. The simplest way to do this is from the top—if there is room to work between the top shelf and the ceiling. First, find a stud in the wall, then screw an angle bracket to the wall and the top of the bookcase. If there's no room on top, use the top of a high shelf.

ADDING STORAGE TO THE OLD HOUSE

By Stephen MacDonald

MY PREVIOUS ARTICLE described in general terms how to add stock mouldings to a home-built bookcase or storage unit to give it a "period" feeling. In this chapter, I'll give some specific illustrations of how standard mouldings can be combined in built-up assemblies to closely approximate the dimensional richness of some of the old-time moulding trim.

THE EXAMPLES that will be shown here, of course, represent only a tiny fraction of possible combinations, and are not offered as a uniquely suitable solution for any particular house. Rather, these illustrations are intended as idea-starters to stimulate your own creativity. The best approach in designing decoration on your bookcase is to choose an existing moulding or decorative motif in the house and adapt it as closely as you can using available materials and skills.

ALL OF THE MOULDINGS shown in the illustrations on the following pages come from a pattern catalog published by the Wood Moulding And Millwork Producers, an industry association. The numbers on the drawings correspond to the moulding numbers specified in the catalog, which shows many dozens of mouldings by style and size. The booklet is an invaluable reference because few lumberyards carry a complete selection of mouldings, and they would rather that you select only from what they have in stock. With the book in hand you can see the full range of profiles that is produced—and what a yard can order for you if it wants to be helpful.

WORKING WITH MOULDINGS

FOR BOOKSHELF-STYLE storage units, a crown or cornice moulding along the top is usually the most prominent feature. It is possible, of course, to use a single piece of stock crown moulding. But a single moulding might not have the depth and profile that you need. Two or more mouldings can be combined to produce the added dimensions. Assembly of mouldings such as shown on following page 228 is quite simple: All you need is glue and some small brads. Any nailing holes can be easily filled.

WORKING WITH MOULDINGS is fairly simple. The basic tools needed are a coping saw, mitre box and backsaw (a

Robert Potts constructed this handsome and practical storage unit for his Brooklyn brownstone. Speakers for a hi-fi system are at either end of the bottom section, with storage in the middle. Unit was made from clear pine and then stained. A crown moulding and carved shell ornament (which Potts carved himself) pick up the theme of classical detailing that's found elsewhere in the home's interior.

rectangular saw designed for use in a mitre box, named for its stiffly reinforced top or "back"). The mitre box holds the saw in position for precise 45° or 90° cuts.

WHERE A MOULDING travels around the outside of a corner, mitre two pieces of moulding at opposite 45° angles

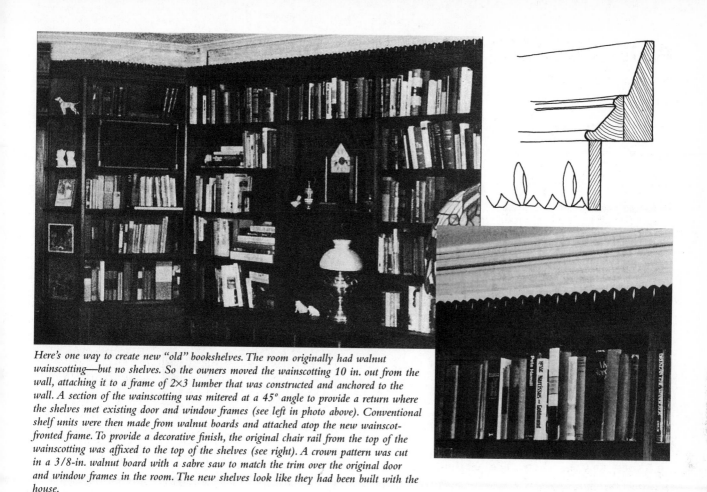

Here's one way to create new "old" bookshelves. The room originally had walnut wainscotting—but no shelves. So the owners moved the wainscotting 10 in. out from the wall, attaching it to a frame of 2×3 lumber that was constructed and anchored to the wall. A section of the wainscotting was mitered at a 45° angle to provide a return where the shelves met existing door and window frames (see left in photo above). Conventional shelf units were then made from walnut boards and attached atop the new wainscot-fronted frame. To provide a decorative finish, the original chair rail from the top of the wainscotting was affixed to the top of the shelves (see right). A crown pattern was cut in a 3/8-in. walnut board with a sabre saw to match the trim over the original door and window frames in the room. The new shelves look like they had been built with the house.

and fit them together to form a tight right angle. When running around an inside corner, a better fit will result from a coped joint.

FOR A COPED JOINT, first cut a 90° end on one piece of moulding and butt it into the corner, fastening it in place with finishing nails. Cut a 45° mitre in the other piece to the correct length, then use a coping saw to follow the cut line made by the back saw on the first cut. Keep the blade on the waste side of the line, and cut at 90° to the direction in which the moulding runs (see diagram above). Test the coped moulding against the piece already in place, and trim or file the coped piece as necessary for a tight joint.

WHEN NAILING MOULDINGS in place, it's a good idea to leave the heads protruding about 1/4 inch until you're sure everything fits correctly. That makes them easier to remove in case adjustment is needed. When all is in alignment, set the nails about 1/16 in. below the surface and fill the holes.

THE ONLY PITFALLS in this kind of work are that you'll cut the mitre in the wrong direction, get the moulding in the mitre box upside down, etc. Taking correct measurements at corners can also be a little tricky at first. It's always wise to experiment a little before you begin assembling things for real.

Coping An Inside Joint

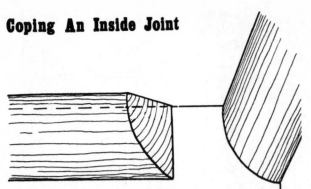

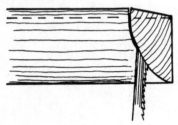

1. Butt one piece of moulding square into corner. Mitre 2nd piece at 45°.

2. With coping saw, cut along mitre line at 90° to back of moulding. Keep saw on waste side of line.

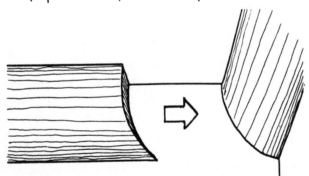

3. File or sand joint as needed for tight fit.

Typical Assemblies For Cornices

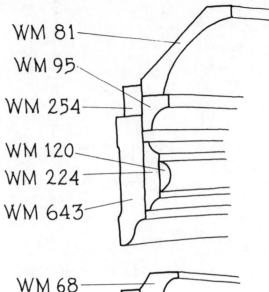

WM 81
WM 95
WM 254
WM 120
WM 224
WM 643

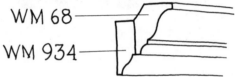

WM 68
WM 934

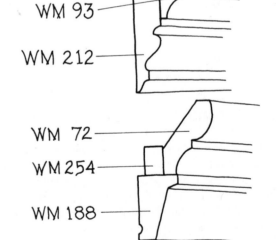

WM 93
WM 212

WM 72
WM 254
WM 188

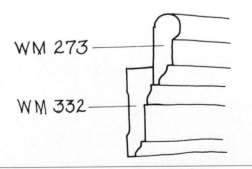

WM 273

WM 332

SAWN WOOD ORNAMENT

by Carolyn Flaherty

THE GREAT VICTORIAN ENERGY and enthusiasm for imitating, adapting and creating new forms in building have left us with a wealth of detail to appreciate and, hopefully, preserve.

ONE OF THE MOST INTERESTING FACETS of the vitality of the era is the sawn wood ornament. Created by carpenter/builders with many levels of knowledge and sophistication, it is apparent that the reason for sawn wood ornament was simply a desire to create design for its own sake. For this reason, the sawn wood ornament is a folk art that should take its place with other respected early American artistic expressions such as primitive painting and quilting.

THE MORE SOPHISTICATED AND PROSPEROUS Victorians had homes built for them by trained architects who used every previous style and form to erect Grecian, Roman, Italian and Gothic Revival buildings. Contemporary fashions such as the mansard roof in France were quickly incorporated into Victorian building. But lack of wealth did not prevent the burgeoning middle class from striving to erect a home of "quality."

LOCAL CARPENTER/BUILDERS did their utmost to satisfy both their own and their client's desire for the rich detail and proliferation of decoration that marked the era. Sawn wood was often a cheap substitute for the carved and turned wood that ornamented more lavish buildings.

HOME BUILDING WAS SOMEWHAT standardized by popular "house-pattern" books. One of the most popular was Andrew Jackson Downing's *Cottage Residences.* Downing published plans and pictures for country houses in Gothic, Italian villa and Elizabethan styles among others. He also used the Alpine chalet with its deeply overhanging eaves and sawn wood ornamentation as inspiration for a typical Downing cottage. Architects like Calvert Vaux and Samuel Sloan were also putting out books with designs and suggestions.

THESE STYLES WERE USED BY LOCAL builders as models and inspirations in a wonderous combination of styles and imitations. Using indigenous wood and a jigsaw, bandsaw or scroll saw driven by steam or foot treadle, they made ornaments for eaves, brackets, porches and gates by sawing out shapes, drilling or cutting holes, and by adding wooden appliqués. Just as Downing himself felt that the immensely popular

Greek Revival style with its horizontal, masculine line was not sufficiently decorative, so did many local carpenters. They may have simply rebelled against the plain box-house within their limits of architectural capabilities or their client's financial means.

THE LOCAL CARPENTER/ builder often let imagination guide him, recreating classical motifs as they remembered them, and usually mixing periods. If classical knowledge was limited, they created flowers, sunrises, unique shapes of their own liking, and sometimes even religious or sexual symbols of a naive sort.

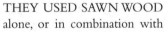

THEY USED SAWN WOOD alone, or in combination with turned or chiseled ornaments if the budget permitted. Often the wood they used was left over from the actual house they had built.

A FAMILIARITY WITH the Victorian heritage we have left to us today gives some knowledge of the wealth of ideas that found their way onto many houses from grand to simple. In many of these, sawn wood ornamentation is the distinguishing feature of certain styles, many of which are found exclusively in just one part of the country.

THE HUDSON RIVER AREA OF New York in particular, and much of upstate New York featured many of the aforementioned Downing and Calvert Vaux inspired houses. Downing popularized the verandah, and great detail is concentrated on the verandah, gables and eaves of these houses.

THE RATHER AUSTERE ITALIAN villa style took on a different look in this area. Wood ornamentation was added and became more and more fanciful. The use of large, decora-

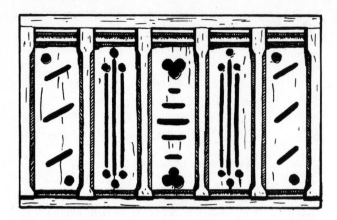

tive brackets under the cornice gave this Americanized Italian style the name "Hudson River Bracketed."

THE ALPINE CHALET style recommended by Downing as being "quaint in ornaments and details" depended on carved wood cut-outs or graceful shapes on the bargeboards on steeply sloped roofs for its style. The fact that most carpenter/builders had never seen an Alpine chalet probably accounted for the fact that they could add these Swiss-style details freely to houses in completely different proportions and shapes from a chalet.

WHILE ANOTHER TASTE-MAKER of the Victorian era, Charles Locke Eastlake, was influencing both interior and exterior design with his Gothic Revival in England, Victorian Gothic became a popular American style. Popular periodicals spread news of impressive buildings being built in this style. Once again the carpenter/builder took what appealed to him and incorporated it into his ornamentation. Simple houses around the country often featured a trefoil or quatrefoil in vergeboard, gable or porch trim. Wood trim adorned pointed gothic windows, or as in the illustration at the left, cut-out leaf forms topped diamond-shaped window panes. These decorative hoods make the windows of the Vermont cottage on which they are found appear taller and pointed.

OUT OF THESE ADAPTATIONS came a style known as Carpenter Gothic. Usually a box-like house with high peaked roofs, it was distinguished by very fanciful wood trim, somewhat resembling Gothic forms. Differing from other wood trims in that it usually painted dark colors against a lighter house, the trim was curved, swagged, scrolled or lacy. Meriting the term "gingerbread" more than any other type of wood ornament, it gave a doll-house appearance no matter how large the house.

VICTORIANS avoided monotony not only with a great variety of architectural styles but also by using a wide variety of paint colors. Houses were seldom painted a monotone color and were rarely white. Downing and Vaux recommended earth tones with a slightly darker trim for country houses. The use of colors found in the surrounding landscape was one school of thought, but just as often fanciful combinations such as pink with red trim

were used. Paint colors were used to point up the rich details of the house. Sawn wood ornaments were often painted two shades of gray in city houses.

SOME OF THE MOST imaginative uses of wood ornament can be found on the decorative board covering the projected portion of a gabled roof, called a vergeboard or a bargeboard. Decorative wood pieces were also added in the triangle at the top. Starting with plain wood boards, usually 1 or 2 inches thick (Downing specified 2" stock) the carpenter, with saw and drill, set out to add the finishing touches to his handiwork. With a bandsaw he would cut patterns on the edges of the boards. Having shaped the outer edges, he could go on to create more complex patterns by cutting away some of the middle of the board.

WITH BRACE AND BIT, he bored holes—in many fanciful combinations. For example, 4 holes grouped together became a quatrefoil—or with a slot-stem added the 4 holes could become the head of a flower.

MORE ELABORATE HOLE patterns were created by using a drill and keyhole saw to cut slots, squares, diamonds, and curves. Sometimes more than half the wood was cut away—the remainder forming delicate wood tracery.

FOR GREATER DIMENSIONAL EFFECT, the carpenter used the applique technique—cutting a pattern from a board and then nailing the cut-out to another board. Very elaborate effects were created using this build-up process.

TOWARD THE END OF THE 1800's, the stick-style ornament became very popular. Economics undoubtedly played a part, because less drilling and sawing was required on the carpenter's part. This style also appealed to the thrifty carpenter, for he could use all of the leftover scraps of wood to put the final ornamental touches on the house.

MOST PATTERN BOOKS OF THE ERA did not illustrate many bracket designs therefore the local carpenter-builder had to create his own patterns. The endless variety of brackets that resulted show every technique of scrollwork, holes, slots and applique used on other areas of the house.

THE LATE VICTORIAN QUEEN ANNE STYLE, most eclectic of all, combining so many styles (except the architecture of the period of Queen Anne which it had virtually nothing to do with) was tall and graceful. Some of the lovliest ornamental wood porch decoration can be found on these houses.

QUEEN ANNE and elements of the Swiss chalet combined to form a mode known as "Stick Style."

THE MAIN CHARACTERISTIC OF THE Stick Style was the arrangement of horizontal and vertical timbers, semi-exposed. Geometric stick arrangements often adorned gables and porches. Wood ornaments, scrolled and pierced, ran along the bottom of horizontal timbers and beneath windows and cornices. Unfortunately, this style has too often been re-painted white in modern times, obliterating the details which had distinguished it. Two-tone painting, particularly in soft tones, picks out the details and retains the visual interest.

AS VICTORIANS WENT WEST, further away from the sources of these particular styles, carpenter-builders depended more on their imaginations. Exotic Far Eastern touches on gables and eaves, and Chinese porch railings are not uncommon features of far western Victorian houses.

THE SAN FRANCISCO AREA still retains a wealth of Victorian houses. Built mostly with "gold" money, even the average "workman's" house has an enormous amount of decorative detail. Using native California redwood, carpenters freely copied motifs from the most elegant homes onto ordinary city houses.

ONE OF THE MOST POPULAR STYLES IN THE BAY AREA is an Italian villa type constructed of wood. Queen Anne and Stick Styles are numerous often with an Eastlake-type motif. Possibly inspired by the beauty of the sun over the San Francisco Bay, carpenters of the area used sunbursts and sunrise motifs in profusion.

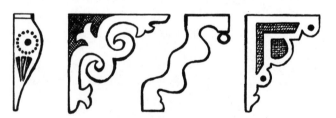

RESTORING & RE-CREATING SAWN WOOD ORNAMENT

ONE NICE THING about sawn wood ornamentation is that it is easy to restore. Its original popularity derived from the fact that the carpenter could cut and install it at the building site—which made this type of ornament inexpensive.

IF THE TRIM HAS SMALL PATCHES OF ROT, you may be able to salvage the original by using specialized marine repair products.

PIECES THAT ARE LOOSE can be re-secured with stra-

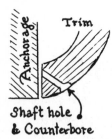

tegically located nails or screws. Some 4" (or longer) screws give maximum holding power. To install, drill a hole in the trim just big enough to pass the shank of the screw and counterbore so that screwhead is below surface of the wood. If wood in the anchorage is tough, you may also want to drill a pi-lot hole for the screw threads. A power screwdriver makes screwing into tough wood easier, as will lubricating the threads with soap. Cover screwhead with putty before painting.

TO DUPLICATE MISSING TRIM, most patterns can be closely matched using only a sabre saw and a portable drill, shaping replacement pieces from standard 1" or 2" pine lum-ber. If you can't match the original exactly, the important thing with exterior trim is to duplicate the *mass* and *rhythm* of the original. As long as you can fill in vacant spaces with rea-sonable facsimilies, very few people will ever detect the new

work. Seemingly complex detail can be built up from simple pieces. For example, this ornately sculpted gingerbread can be duplicated from three pieces of 1" pine stock that are shaped with sabre saw and drill:

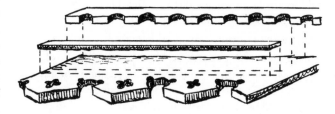

WHERE PAINT IS PEELING BADLY, thoroughly remove loose flakes with putty knife and wire brush. If wood has been unpainted for a long time, it would be a good idea to saturate it with a pentachlorophenol wood preservative. The preserva-tive will retard rot, provide water repellency and act as primer for the paint. Special attention should be paid to flat surfaces and areas that trap water.

Painting trim is such a laborious task that you want to do the best possible job the first time so you don't have to re-do the job in 18 months. Be sure to use a high-quality paint and ap-ply carefully in accordance with manufacturer's directions.

Architectural and Decorative Styles

THE CLASSICAL ORDERS

CLASSICAL ARCHITECTURE—the designs of ancient Greece and Rome—has influenced the appearance of countless old houses in the U. S. Such diverse architectural styles as Georgian, Federal, Greek Revival and Renaissance Revival are heavily influenced by classical designs. And other styles such as Second Empire will show classical touches here and there.

THE OLD-HOUSE WATCHER will find classical influences such as columns, capitals and entablatures on house exteriors around doorways and porches, window trim and cornices. Inside, you'll find classical touches in plaster ceiling moldings and decorative woodwork.

THE TERM "ORDER" refers to a complete design for a column plus base, capital and entablature. The proportion for each and every element in the order was meticulously spelled out—based upon the diameter of the column as the fundamental unit of measure. In later centuries, however, house builders and architects would feel free to alter the proportions (and even the arrangement of elements) to suit their own needs.

ILLUSTRATED ON THIS PAGE are the capital and entablature sets of the five basic classical Orders. The Greeks had three Orders: Doric, Corinthian and Ionic. The Romans adapted these three Orders (slightly altering the proportions and some details) and added two more: Tuscan and Composite.

THE TUSCAN, a simplified Doric, is the plainest and most massive of the five. The Doric is distinguished by the triglyphs in the frieze and the upward-turned "D" shape at the top of the column. The Greek Doric has a fluted column while the Roman Doric has a plain

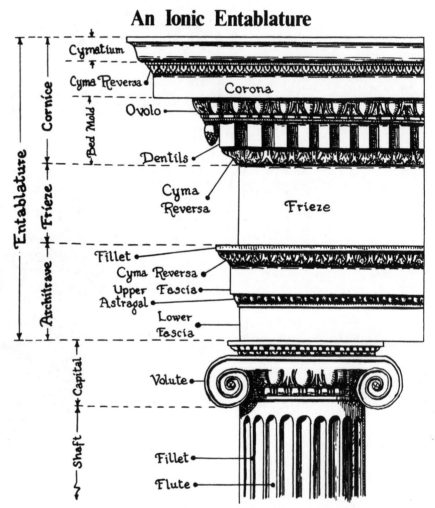

An Ionic Entablature

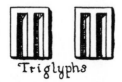

Triglyphs

shaft. The Ionic Order is distinguished primarily by the volutes in the capital.

THE CORINTHIAN ORDER is most readily identified from its bell-shaped capital ornamented with acanthus, olive or laurel leaves with 8 small volutes at the top.

THE COMPOSITE ORDER is the most elaborate of the five—and the one with the most variations. Its capital is a combination of the Ionic volutes plus the acanthus leaves of the Corinthian capital.

Acanthus

Doric

Tuscan

Corinthian

Composite

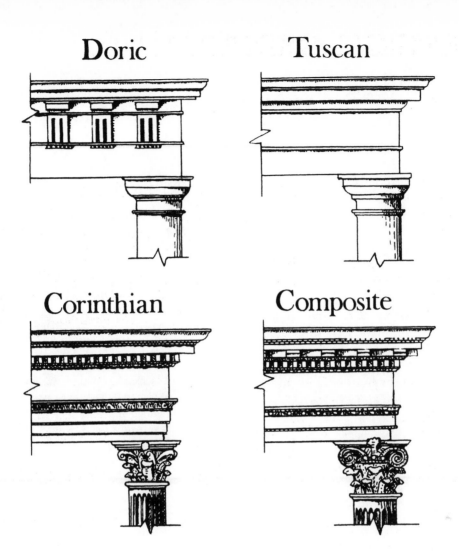

THE DOMESTIC ARCHITECTURE OF DOWNING

by Carolyn Flaherty

A CAREFUL LOOK AT ANY HOUSE built between 1850 and 1870, or a city park of the same period, will most likely show to some degree the influence of Andrew Jackson Downing.

IN THE EARLY PART OF THE 19TH CENTURY, architects were rarely employed for building a private residence. The usual practice was for a man to look around, decide what he liked best, and then hire a carpenter-builder to make one like it. In fact, builders, carpenters and bricklayers commonly called themselves architects and the distinction between them and a professional architect was of little importance to the general public.

THE GREEK REVIVAL STYLE was in its heyday in the decades of the twenties and thirties. A severe style, it left the cheaper versions looking rather like plain wooden boxes. Downing detested the practice of building private homes to look like smaller versions of public buildings. He referred to the Greek Revival houses as "tasteless temples."

THE GOTHIC REVIVAL had just begun to make its way across the ocean but had not yet made a dent in the great popularity of the classic architecture.

DOWNING WAS BORN IN NEWBURGH, New York in 1815, where his father owned a nursery. After his father's death, Andrew Jackson ran the nursery with his brother, Charles, ending his formal education at 16. Although he was self-taught in botany, he soon became an expert landscape gardener.

When he married in 1838, he designed a house for himself and his bride to be built in Newburgh, high above the Hudson. The Gothic style (then known as Elizabethan when it applied to houses) fit in with his theory of "expression of purpose" or "truthfulness" in architecture. It offended him that the Greek style was used for church and bank alike. The Gothic also suited his idea of himself as a serious and poetic man. And it suited his informal, asymmetrical, woody landscaping.

Downing's Own House

THE GREAT SUCCESS OF HIS DESIGN and the admiration it received led him to be interested in the design of houses as well as landscaping. In 1841, at 26, he published "A Treatise on the Theory and Practice of Landscape Gardening, Adapted to North America." It was a popular and influential book and he followed in 1842 with "Cottage Residences," which incorporated designs for houses, along with floor plans, complete instructions for building them, cost of each design and a complete landscaping design for each style.

THE FAVORED STYLE for cottages was the "Pointed" or "English Rural Gothic." This style, more than any other, suited his ideas of the picturesque. He favored irregular roof shapes, and asymetrical design. Although he recognized that the cheapest way to build a house was in a square or rectangle, he recommended the addition of bay windows, verandahs, and decorative trim to give a more irregular and richer appearance.

THE MOST OBVIOUS DECORATIVE FEATURE was the vergeboard. He achieved a sculptured effect by using thick wood, cutting out Gothic motifs and enriching with wooden moldings.

DOWNING'S GOTHIC COTTAGES are sometimes called "Carpenter's Gothic." This is misleading. When a carpenter-builder took a plain, thin piece of wood and cut out a Gothic design or any other fanciful motif on a vergeboard it was a Carpenter Gothic. There were even a few of these types around when Downing was writing, and he scorned their "card-board" appearance. Although these naive versions were often meant to imitate Downing, and are quite charming, they are not really what Downing had in mind. Downing's designs had a richness and sophistication that few carpenter-builders could match.

THANKS TO DOWNING, bay windows became a mid-Victorian fad. They were often added to the simplest farm-house, and even today, you can spot a house built many decades before the mid-19th century and tell by its bay window that the owner had probably read "Cottage Residences."

THAT AMERICAN-AS-APPLE-PIE FIXTURE, the porch, also grew out of Downing's ideas. The Colonial, Georgian, Federal, Greek and other popular earlier styles had at most a small portico. But Downing loved the verandah. Along with the practical function of keeping the entrance dry, he felt they were "a neccessary and delightful appendage" in a country with hot summers. "Hence a broad shady verandah suggests ideas of comfort, and is highly expressive of purpose."

DOWNING DEVOTED A LARGE PART of "Cottage Residences" to his first interest—landscaping. He had been influenced by many rural landscape architects in England, particularly J. C. Loudon, who had also written books describing how a cottage could be treated with different facades. Like Loudon, he preferred informal landscaping in a more "romantic" manner than the formal Georgian gardens or the geometric Dutch gardens. He did, however, favor the Georgian method of using a running ditch, instead of fence, hidden by shrubbery to separate portions of the landscape, particularly from cattle. This was called a "ha-ha." He used vines and creepers to integrate house and garden, and also to hide the ugliness of badly designed houses.

FOR VERY SMALL COTTAGES, with a limited space for planting, he designed various forms of the parterre, with perhaps a vase on a pedestal or a sun-dial for the center. He was continually searching to find indigenous trees and plants that would bloom successively and provide the best color and odor.

Parterre

WITH A TRUE VICTORIAN SENSE OF "APPROPRIATENESS," Downing preferred tall, pointed trees surrounding the vertical lines of the Gothic style, and round-shaped trees for the flatter Italian style.

ONE OF DOWNING'S MOST popular designs was a type called the "Cottage Ornee." To a rural English cottage he added a verandah and perhaps a small balcony made of slender logs, with vines and creepers abounding. This would give a picturesque appearance to even the simplest house. The French flavor of "ornee" added to the humble English word "cottage" caused this style to become instantly dear to the mid-Victorian heart.

ALTHOUGH THE GOTHIC WAS DOWNING'S FIRST LOVE, and "Cottage Residences" featured many versions of the pointed style, some other romantic styles were included. It was from his major work, however, that the full impact of his taste and influence was felt.

THIS BOOK, "THE ARCHITECTURE OF COUNTRY HOUSES," fully developed his ideas about architecture, and was so complete in its attention to detail that builders used it for decades to imitate the cottages, country houses and villas he described. These designs were for farm houses, stables, gate houses as well as Elizabethan cottages, Italian and Tuscan villas, and the bracketed style he made famous. It was published in 1850, just two years before his tragic death in 1852. Over sixteen thousand copies were sold by the end of the Civil War.

Villa in the Norman Style

DOWNING ON COLOR

DOWNING HAD VERY DEFINITE THEORIES regarding the use of color on both the exterior and interior of houses. The one color he really disliked was white. Most of the Greek Revival and other wood frame houses were painted white in the early part of the 19th century.

ACCORDING TO DOWNING, "The glaring nature of this color, when seen in contrast with the soft green of foliage, renders it extremely unpleasant." It was so unpleasant to him that he presented three pages of arguments against this "great breach of good taste" in "Country Houses."

THE OBJECTION TO WHITE was based mostly on the glare and harsh effect caused by the sun on the white house and its conspicuousness in the landscape. To compound this solecism, shutters painted in bright green rendered the effect even more appalling. He recommended a cool, dark green as a less offensive shade than the bright green. He preferred, however, to have oak shutters. If real oak was not within the means of the home owner, he advised staining a cheaper wood in imitation of oak.

COLOR WAS GIVEN A LOT OF ATTENTION by Downing because it is the first impression of a house to be perceived the eye. After doing in, in no uncertain terms, the universal white house, he rightly felt bound to make recommendations for the colors appropriate for his designs.

THE DOWNING THEORY IN COLORING HOUSES was to "avoid any colors that nature avoids. In buildings, we should copy those colors that she offers chiefly to the eye—earth, stone, bricks and wood are the materials of which houses are built." Since houses are not built of foliage, there was no reason to paint a house green.

THE ORIGINAL "COTTAGE RESIDENCES" contained six color samples, three shades of gray and three of drab or fawn. Barns or stables, because they were meant to be unobtrusive, should be dark browns or grays. But a cottage, small country house or villa should be of a mellow, cheerful shade that harmonized with the countryside. A mansion could have a graver color than a cottage to express its greater dignity and size.

HOUSES SURROUNDED BY TREES should be lighter in shade than those more exposed. A general recommendation was, "The safest color, for general use, is something between a cream and a dust color." This tint was the color of English freestone, and usually called fawn. He recommended that cheap stucco and cement cottages be washed in this shade.

DOWNING LIKENED THE FEATURES OF A HOUSE such as window facings, cornices, eaves, etc. to the features on a human face. To have them all the same shade would give the same insipid effect that colorless features do to the face.

THE RULE WAS SIMPLE. If a light shade was used for the house, a darker shade of the same color would be used for the features of the house, and a still darker shade or the darkest green or brown for the shutters, if they were to be painted. The variety would produce a cheerful effect and avoid the dull, heavy look of a house painted in monotone.

IF THE TINT CHOSEN FOR THE HOUSE was a dark one, then a much lighter shade of the same tint would be used for the features. Or, perhaps several tints in a light shade that would harmonize with the dark tint.

IN *COUNTRY HOUSES* Downing gives a list of approved colors and tells how to make them for those who "have to depend on their own wits." It may be of interest to those trying to find a Downing-type color in the labyrinth of color charts in our modern paint stores. The method he describes would also produce a durable paint by today's standards.

"THE COLORS ARE SUPPOSED to be first finely ground in oil, and then mixed in small quantities with white-lead and boiled linseed oil. A few trials will enable the novice to mix agreeable neutral shades—especially if he will be content to add a very *little* of the darker shades at a time, and try the effect with the brush. After the proper shade is obtained, enough should be mixed at once to go over the whole surface."

- Fawn color: White, yellow ochre, and Spanish brown.
- Drab: White, Venetian red, burnt umber, with a little black.
- Gray stone: White, lampblack, and a little Venetian red.
- Brown stone: Spanish brown, chrome yellow, a little white and lampblack.
- French gray: White, ivory black, with a little Indian red and Chinese blue.
- Slate color: White, lampblack, and a little Indian red.
- Sage color: White, raw umber, Prussian blue and Venetian red.
- Straw color: White, yellow ochre, and orange chrome.
- Chocolate: Spanish brown and black—or, for a light shade, Venetian red and black.

DOWNING SINCERELY HOPED that "at no very distant time, one may have the pleasure of travelling over our whole country, without meeting with a single habitation of glaring and offensive color, but see everywhere something of harmony and beauty."

THE ROMANTIC STYLES OF A. J. DOWNING

ALTHOUGH DOWNING PREFERRED THE GOTHIC, it was by no means the only style he proposed in his efforts to create for all "the beautiful, rural, unostentatious, moderate home of a country gentleman."

DOWNING BELIEVED there were "no buildings, however simple, to which either good forms or something of an agreeable expression may not be given." To do this, he made even the simplest house "picturesque"—a quality he felt was created by "power exposed." This could be done by projections and emphasis on architectural features of the house, such as brackets and hoods. Downing's artistic nature even saw drama in the deep shadows these features created.

A SMALL STRUCTURE SUCH as this was intended for a family that "that takes care of itself." In other words, servantless. It was most important to Downing that every working-man have the civilizing effect of "smiling lawns and tasteful

cottages"—a necessity in a true republic prosperous enough to have so many of its people able to build a home of their liking.

FOR A HOME WHERE SERVANTS would also live, Downing designed "country houses," larger and able to incorporate more beauty and picturesqueness in their design than the cottage. A "villa" was simply a slightly larger country house, but as picturesque and romantic as possible.

HIS DESIGNS WERE sometimes his own, or executed by A. J. Davis (Downing lacked formal training and couldn't draw well) or Davis' own designs, or those of Wheeler or Loudon. He specified where they had come from—the object being to show people as many good designs as his imagination and wit could find. These designs drew on architecture from many countries and past eras that fit his idea of the romantic.

DOWNING BELIEVED that the two most beautiful styles for country residences were the pointed Gothic and the horizontal Italian modes. Their outlines were irregular and picturesque, and harmonious with nature. All modes referred back to two original styles, and everything else was a modification or variety. They were the Gothic, with vertical lines prevailing, and the Grecian, with horizontal lines prevailing, and both had been adapted to domestic styles.

THE PURE GRECIAN STYLE, with its rigid form that did not bend to domestic needs, Downing thought most appropriate for a temple with its "elegant simplicity."

THE MODERN ITALIAN STYLE—a modified form of the Grecian—featured an "elegant variety" of forms harmonious with the needs of domestic life.

The Italian Style

DOWNING THOUGHT THE ITALIAN STYLE somewhat inferior to the pointed and high-roofed Gothic in expressing rural life—its spirit being somewhere between town and country—but its mingling of both was expressive of modern life.

THE ELEGANCE OF AN ITALIAN VILLA was produced by the simple lines of its exterior, but enhanced by the introduction of such "beautiful and refined" features like terraces, balconies, verandahs. The picturesque quality was attained from these irregular features and the variety of shapes. Windows were simple but massively framed rectangles with round or round-headed windows combined in the same building. Arched doorways were often incorporated.

"POWER" was expressed by projecting roofs, often with brackets, and over all the dignity of the Italian square tower, the campanile, bringing elevation and unity to the composition.

SINCE THE IRREGULARITY OF ITS COMPOSITION was one of the elements that contributed to its beauty, future additions, made as a family grew in wealth or number, only added greater picturesqueness to the Italian villa.

THE GREEK STYLE, on the other hand, was marred by any addition to its original pure and simple form.

DOWNING preferred the Italian style built in stone as it was in Italy. He acknowledged, however, that since Italy was a tree-poor country and America was not, it would often be more feasible to build with wood.

HE ALSO FELT THE ITALIAN STYLE, with its broad verandahs and projecting roofs, and balconies with stone balusters, to be more suitable to the southern and western portions of America. However, since even the North had such hot summers, these features were not inappropriate in any part of the country.

ANOTHER PRACTICAL recommendation for building in the Italian, or closely related Roman and Tuscan styles, was the fact that builders were experienced with building the Greek style and would have less difficulty with it than the pointed style.

The Bracketed Style

DOWNING'S MAIN WEAPON against the plain, regular, box-shaped house, lacking in "Beauty" was the decorative bracket. To even the plainest style, built out of economy, a verandah and a projecting roof could be added. He called these simple cottages an "American Bracketed Farmhouse." He prophesized the immense popularity of this mode in his description of
the design. "If we call this style American, it is only because we foresee that our climate and the cheapness of wood as a building material, in most parts of the country, will, for a long time yet, lead us to adopt this as the most pleasing manner of building rural edifices of economic character."

DOWNING PROTESTED AGAINST THE simple, unadorned roof lines of the Greek style. "Expression of purpose" demanded that the roofs of buildings should be shown and be ornamental. Since the "secret source of the Picturesque is the manifestation of Beauty through Power," then the support of the roof should be boldly and powerfully exposed.

FOR PRACTICAL PURPOSES, the projecting roof kept the house dryer and more thoroughly protected from the weather, and made the upper storey rooms cooler in summer.

WOOD WAS PLENTIFUL, and the local carpenter/builders could freely imitate Downing's designs or create original brackets. So the bracketed, projected roof began to appear on not only the Italian style and the simple cottage style, but became a decorative feature for decades on houses of every kind.

DOWNING'S INFLUENCE was felt most in his native region, the Hudson River area. Bracketed roofs became so popular and indigenous to the region that Edith Wharton wrote a novel titled *Hudson River Bracketed,* featuring a typical, bracketed mansion. The name "Hudson River Bracketed" is still applied to the many homes of that type in the area.

A Tragic End

BEFORE A. J. DOWNING, books on architecture had been "builder's guides" addressed to the carpenter. But Downing spoke to the owner, convincing a large portion of the country that beauty and harmony were possible for all.

ALTHOUGH HE LOVED the kinds of architecture that lent themselves to grand buildings—and many thought his own home resembled a castle—he argued against very large and ostentatious houses as inappropriate to a young republic. "...The true home still remains to us. Not, indeed, the feudal castle, not the baronial hall, but the home of the individual man—the home of that family of equal rights, which continually separates and reforms itself in the new world—the republican home, built by no robbery of the property of another class, maintained by no infringement of a brother's rights; ... large enough to minister to all the wants, necessities, and luxuries of a republican, and not too large or too luxurious to warp the life or manners of his children."

IN THE SUMMER OF 1850, while abroad, he met and formed a partnership with Calvert Vaux. It was a very brief association. On July 28, 1852, Downing was killed in a steamboat accident on the Hudson River. Downing had been one of the first advocates for public parks in large cities, and Vaux (with Olmstead), carried out Downing's ideas in his designs for Central and Prospect Parks in New York City.

AT THE TIME OF DOWNING'S DEATH, at the age of 36, he was supervising a landscape gardening design, at the request of President Fillmore, for the grounds of the Smithsonian and the entire area from the Capitol to the White House. Never completed, nothing remains of his design today. Only the memorial urn erected on the Mall is left to remind us of the great romantic influence of Andrew Jackson Downing.

DOWNING ON INTERIOR DECORATION

DOWNING WAS NOT REALLY promulgating anything new in interior decoration. The decor of the early 19th century was still classical and much lighter in tone than the later, more opulent decades of the Victorian period. Downing was trying, however, to encourage "taste" in even the plainest home, and a sense of "fitness."

THIS FITNESS WAS EXPRESSED by the use of color and simple furnishings that were appropriate and "essentially country-like" to rural homes. His guidelines can be useful today in re-creating interiors in the many houses built in the decades following 1850, in the styles Downing popularized.

DOWNING ARGUED THAT THE INTERIOR of a house should reflect its exterior architectural style. While a large villa could use brackets, beams and cornices in large rooms to do this, even a small, plain house could introduce some appropriate architectural detail in the wainscotting and woodwork.

HE RECOMMENDED THAT THE ROOMS OF A HOUSE be finished in colors that fit the use of the rooms. ". . . Nothing is so insipid as to find all the principal apartments (rooms) of a house of one color . . . without any regard to their use."

HALL, STAIRCASES AND PASSAGES: Cool and sober tone—gray, stone or drab. Simple in decoration, enhancing the effect of the richer hues of the other rooms. Floors of tile—more fitting and durable than carpet.

DRAWING ROOM OR PARLOR: Should exhibit more beauty and elegance than any room in the house. Color should be lighter, more cheerful and gay than other rooms. Walls should be light so that the brilliancy of effect is not lost in the evening. White relieved by gilding, while popular for town houses, should not be used in the country where gilding should be used sparingly. Instead, use delicate tints such as "ashes of rose," pearl-gray, pale apple-green, with darker shades for contrast.

DINING ROOM: Rich and warm in coloring, more contrast and stronger colors than parlor.

LIBRARY: Quiet and comparatively grave in color. Fawn or neutral for walls, bookcases and furniture preferably dark oak, and a carpet to accord with the severe and quiet tone of the walls. Leather best covering for furniture.

BEDROOMS: "May vary from the greatest simplicity and chasteness of color to any light and cheerful style of decoration." (Apparently "chaste" and "cheerful" did not go together.) Paperhangings also recommended.

WAINSCOTTING FOR THE INTERIOR should be made of native wood of the district where the house is built—maple, birch, ash, black walnut, oak. If, for economical reasons, a hardwood was not used, it should be stained and varnished for the same effect.

WOODWORK: Paint to harmonize with the prevailing tone of the room. It may be lighter or darker than the walls, and generally a quiet, neutral tint, but never the same color, and never white.

WALLPAPER: With papered walls, the ceiling is left white or a neutral tint harmonizing with the prevailing colors of the paper. Popular patterns of the period featured Gothic, Italian or Grecian architectural motifs. Downing disliked the representations of church windows and carved church work, etc. as being too grand for houses, but approved of the "plain" types featuring panels and cornices. He also recommended papers giving the appearance of oak wainscotting—"well-suited to the entry or living-room of a cottage"—because they would give architectural detail to the plainest room. Other types he favored were flocked papers that imitated woven stuffs, and fresco papers that formed the walls into compartments or panels.

Another inexpensive method of creating architectural details was to use "decorative" paper in one solid color on the walls, with strips of paper in harmonious or contrasting colors, cut in strips, and pasted on to form lines, panels and compartments.

CURTAINS: Chintz for the plainest cottages—inexpensive but giving a "pretty effect" is selected to harmonize with walls and carpets. For a heightened effect, there were printed cottons with separate borders to be sewn on. For better curtains—"moreens" (a popular woolen fabric) of a single color; brown, drab, crimson, or blue—more expensive but more durable than cotton.

THE MOST "ARCHITECTURAL" mode of arranging curtains is from a projecting cornice of wood. The molding should be Gothic for a Gothic house, and Grecian for any other classical style. (The May issue of *The Old-House Journal* gives instructions for making this kind of cornice and a source for period molding.)

TO GUIDE THE PEOPLE who would furnish the houses they built after his designs, Downing also gave extensive recommendations on furniture in "Country Houses." He recommended some manufacturers in principal cities and used their illustrations, because they were making "cheap, light furniture for cottages." The pieces were either "Grecian modern"—a slightly classical look to plain furniture, often painted gray, drab, or light blue—or else French and Gothic pieces for larger houses and villas.

DOWNING ABHORRED THE PRACTICE of using ornate furniture in country homes even if the owner could afford it. Extravagant decoration was "in bad taste and out of keeping with the comparative simplicity and ease of manner which ought to characterize rural life."

EASTLAKE

by Carolyn Flaherty

MANY AMERICAN HOUSES built in the late 1800's feature "Eastlake touches" or are known as "Eastlake inspired." This is a curious fact since Charles Locke Eastlake was not American but English and—although an architect—was best known for his designs for furniture and other domestic items. How then did all that "Eastlake" get onto all those houses?

FOR THOSE OF US WHO ARE NOT AT HOME in the field of art history, but want to know more about the old houses we love, we can only detect the Eastlake influence by tracing it back to the period that produced this amazingly popular style.

BY THE MIDDLE of the 1800's, High Victorian decor had too often become a hodge-podge of excessive upholstery topping badly designed imitations of French furniture. This furniture, curved in every possible manner, floral carpets and florid colors fought for attention with the doilies and knick-knacks that rested on every surface and nestled in every niche.

Chair from the Crystal Palace Exhibition, 1851.

An Eastlake design for a chair in medieval style.

THE CRAFTS HAD BECOME HIGHLY commercialized by the middle of the 19th century. Instead of the precision given to every piece by lengthy hand labor, workshops were now equipped with steam-driven machines. The rapidly growing middle class demanded more and more articles and were willing to replace them—and often—with the latest fashion. The glued-on curlicues and excessive padding in imitation of French Rococo and the use of veneers and varnish dictated by speed of manufacture offended the discerning eye and caused a desire to return to good, honest English workmanship and style.

IN REACTION TO WHAT THEY considered the degeneration of taste, an "Art Movement" in the decorative arts began to take shape. Men like John Ruskin, architect, and William Morris, poet, painter, and philosopher, were in the forefront of the attempt to raise the standard of contemporary domestic arts. They associated art with morals and saw in the return to handcraftsmanship a vision of a new society. Eventually they went from the reformation of design directly to the reformation of people—turning to philosophy and politics.

ALTHOUGH GOTHIC ARCHITECTURE really needed no reviving—it had always been nicely surviving—by now it had attained a more important place in contemporary British architecture. In 1836 the decision had been made to replace the burned Houses of Parliament with Gothic buildings. The Romantic Gothic literature of Sir Walter Scott had also created a feeling for the medieval. One of the most popular figures of the time, he himself lived in a neo-gothic house.

CHARLES LOCKE EASTLAKE published his *A History Of The Gothic Revival* in 1872. Beautifully timed! It came out at the height of the Gothic Revival movement. In it he supplied details of 343 neo-Gothic buildings from 1820–1870 and it firmly connected him in the public mind with Gothic architecture.

THE ARTS AND CRAFTS PHASE or "art movement" part of the Revival had remained a rather esoteric part of Victorian culture. The stylized wallpapers and handcrafted furniture of William Morris was far too expensive for all but a few believers. A good deal of its fame had come from the pokes that magazines like "Punch" were fond of taking. It was facetiously suggested in one issue that dust should be allowed to accumulate on the walls so that colors would be properly subdued. Cartoons portrayed the inhabitants of these "aesthetic" rooms as languid figures in unfashionable "arty" dress, bearing a strong resemblance to the "hippie" of our past decade.

EASTLAKE SIMPLIFIED many of their ideas for a general market and made the "art" movement a popular movement. His common-sense, practical and helpful book, "Hints On Household Taste" was first published in 1868. And it made Charles Locke Eastlake perhaps the first "household name" in architecture.

HE TOOK A LOOK AT every aspect of the Victorian home and found every inch of it to be badly designed, vulgar, and non-functional. He blamed it all on shopkeepers and women, even condemning the "dangerous and ungraceful crinoline." What the book lacked in originality it made up in forcefulness. Drawing on many ideas, including the chunky, simplified furniture of Pugin, he laid down guidelines for a reformation.

REJECTING THE ROSES AND ribbons of popular Victoriana for Morris-type stylized designs, he declared "decorative art is degraded when it passes into a direct imitation of natural objects. Nature may be typified or symbolized, but not actually imitated."

HE CHOSE FOR HIS OWN textile designs for drapes, etc. strong classical patterns like the Greek key, diagonal stripes, or horse girth bands. His common-sense approach is typified by his recommendation of washable fabrics like cretonne and the striped cottons from the Orient. He favored curtain poles over dust-gathering cornices and valances. He liked these poles adorned with medieval ornament.

DETESTING THE common practice of attempting to make a thing look like something it was not, such as painting walls to look like marble, he called for the honest use of materials and rejected veneering. Today, when it seems wood paneling (the latest shade being rasberry) covers everything from ornamental plaster to old wainscotting and threatens all but the TV screen, perhaps this principle ought to be recirculated.

DECORATION SHOULD be limited to surface ornament—inlaid wood, embossed leather and embroidery. The encaustic tile (tiles in dull, earth tones with geometric designs) met with Eastlake's approval and he promoted them for floors, the lower part of the vestibule wall, and for fireplace decoration.

HIS LOVE FOR STURDY, simple (relatively speaking in the late Victorian era) and functional furniture, unvarnished instead

of French polished and made with basic structural pegging instead of glue, sprang from a desire to revive good, honest craftsmanship. Although the illustrations in his book were Gothic, he said in the preface to the second edition: "It is the spirit and principles of early manufacture which I desire to see revived, and not the absolute forms in which they found their embodiment." However, his strong medieval predilection was evident in the design motifs he chose for his own illustrations:

 Gothic crosses   trefoils

 quatrefoils   A series of holes in a circle

He also liked an individualized crocket and finial. The crocket refers to the carved decorations on the edges of a gable or arch. The finial is an ornament crowning a spire, gable or arch. Classical fluting, stylized flowers incised in wood, and carved borders in geometric shapes were used in his illustrations for furniture.

HE NOT ONLY BELIEVED IN form-following function, he thought it should be stressed. He adapted medieval and Renaissance ironwork in hinges, knobs and studs that declared their purpose dramatically on a piece of furniture. The drapery rods and poles atop metal beds had imposing finials reminiscent of medieval spears. It was one of the most easily imitated aspects of his designs, and a chunky piece of hardware or ironwork with spear-type motifs became a popular "Eastlake touch."

LEAVING NO INCH COVERED, he deplored the excessive carpeting covering Victorian floors. The scrolls and ribbons horrified him even more. He once referred to "horticultural rugs and zoological hearthrugs" in utter disdain. Replace with quiet colors and small, geometric patterns or oriental "Turkey" rugs of a square shape and leave a parquet border around them.

HIS ZEAL FOR TOTAL REFORMATION led him to recommend or design metal beds, lighting fixtures, and even jewelry and cutlery.

Impact in America

THE BOOK HAD A STRONG IMPACT in England, but its effect in America was startling. A media marvel, it had four English editions and six American. He stopped short of being the Jacqueline Susann of his day in that technology precluded a movie version.

HIS DIRECT TONE AND COMMON-SENSE attitude appealed to the American personality and Eastlake's good, solid English name, easy to pronounce, was a blessing after all those years of imitating those fancy "Louis" styles.

THE BOOK WAS GIVEN TO PROSPECTIVE BRIDES as a solution to all their forseeable problems. It became for many a simple "bible" with which they could tell right from wrong. The words "artistic" and "inartistic" replaced "fashionable" and "unfashionable." Harper's Bazaar reported, "Suddenly the voice of the prophet Eastlake was heard crying in the wilderness, 'Repent ye, for the Kingdom of the Tasteful is at hand!'"

AND SO AMERICANS WANTED EASTLAKE FURNITURE. Of course, there wasn't any. There were just a few illustrations in a book everybody was buying. But the demand was now there and the supply soon followed.

MANUFACTURERS QUICKLY HAD A LINE to offer of furniture "after Eastlake." Unfortunately, the term blanketed every article manufactured that looked different from former products. Some good quality furniture was produced, adapting many of the real Eastlake principles. But anything slightly chunky, slightly Gothic, or with a geometric detail or two was accepted as Eastlake or even "East Lake" as was often featured in advertisements. In fact anything that purported to be in improved taste became known as "Eastlaked."

Eastlake's Disavowal

IN THE 1878 EDITION he found it necessary to defend himself: "I find American tradesmen continually advertising what they are pleased to call "Eastlake" furniture, with the production of which I have had nothing whatever to do, and for the taste of which I should be very sorry to be considered responsible."

THE GREAT POPULARITY OF THE Eastlake style was not without criticism, nor was it unanimously accepted by other members of the design and decoration establishment. Upholsterers in particular were in a snit over the prospect of an unpadded fad.

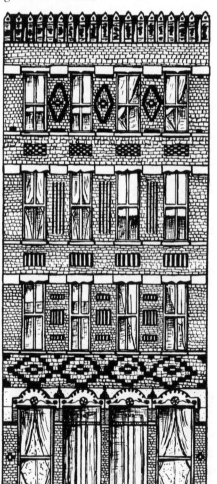

A MODERN VERSION OF THE TYPE OF criticism "Hints On Household Taste" received, in typical words, is found in "The English Interior." Referring to Eastlake's Turkey rugs, "golden oak horrors" and geometrical tiles, the author called them "pieces of calculated hideousness."

IN A LIVELY BOOK ABOUT THE Victorian period, "Victoria Royal" the author, Wellman, labels her chapter on Eastlake "Friar Eastlake's Grocery Gothic." While being rather harsh on poor Mr. Eastlake, she makes an interesting comment, perhaps expressing the reason why he is often considered by experts to be merely a popularizer and not an original force. "He made the mistake of believing that the only possible future design could have lay in the past." After the Eastlake fad went out of fashion, the very name "Eastlake" became an epithet of reproach. This was unfair to a man of sincere principles whose reputation suffered mostly from bad imitation.

Our Square And Circle

EASTLAKE WROTE ONLY one other book after "Hints On Household Taste." Not a best-seller, it was called "Our Square And Circle." First published under the pseudonym Jack Easel, it was a charming autobiographical sketch. In it he recounted his disappointment over his lackluster career in the National Gallery of London. His uncle, Sir Charles Lock (to the eternal confusion of historians—there is no "e" on the end) was a famous painter, art historian, and first director of the National Gallery.

CHILDLESS, he had taken a deep interest in his nephew's education. The younger Eastlake had begun as an architect and had then turned to painting. For a short time he was a roving correspondent for "Punch." He ended up as an administrator, like his uncle, and served in his later years as head of the National Gallery. All of these fields proved disappointing except for interior design and the fame that "Hints" had brought him.

IN "OUR SQUARE AND CIRCLE," written in 1895, he refers to the mid-century period as "that terrible time when our homes were at the mercy of the upholsterer." And, reflecting on his missionary work among the tasteless, "Heaven save us from a return to that phase of ugly conventionalism, of life-less ornament, of dull propriety and inartistic gloom!"

Eastlake On Houses

THOUGH HE SHARED THE BELIEF of Ruskin and others that a house should be similar in style in both interior and exterior and, if possible, be designed by the same person, he designed few houses and none after *Hints*.

ONE OF HIS BASIC principles was that function should be visible and even stressed. This was also an element of the Queen Anne style—having the structural members visible and even ornamented. Since Eastlake espoused this principle for his furniture designs along with his preferences for lines rather than curves—the early Queen Anne style that featured linear arrangement of timbers is also known as "Eastlake."

THE DECORATIVE PANELS illustrated below were created by house builders who thought they were following

Eastlake's admonition (regarding furniture) to reduce non-essential carving and restrict it to inlaid panels. These panels (often found between windows, under eaves or between ornamented timbers) were further meant to reflect the Eastlake influence by using stylized flowers and sun motifs or geometric designs.

THE USE OF POLYCHROMATIC color is often associated with Eastlake. He popularized the use of soft, earthtone shades for his interiors. So a house painted in a quiet shade with its borders, features in decorative panels and structural ornaments picked out in compatible shades is often thought of as "Eastlake influenced."

TERRA COTTA was one of Eastlake's favorite materials. He liked it for decorative elements of all sort, and his own house was nicknamed "Terra Cottage." Like the Queen Anne style in England, a red brick house with geometric designs picked out in terra cotta is another "Eastlake" house.

ONE OF HIS MOST POPULAR INNOVATIONS was the overmantel. It was designed by Eastlake in an effort to reform the homemaker's habit of placing gewgaws all around the parlor. Instead, Eastlake recommend a "little museum" of shelves over the fireplace to hold only objects of quality such as the blue and white oriental china of which he was so fond. Many houses with exterior Eastlake influences also have an overmantel built in over the fireplace.

San Francisco

IN SAN FRANCISCO, Eastlake and the gold rush building boom coincided. Since most of the city's housing was built in the same period as the Eastlake popularity, it is a goldmine of Eastlake influence. The style is considered one of the main types in the city. It is often referred to as Stick/Eastlake because of the visible timbers. Very like the eclectic Queen Anne style in the rest of the country, San Francisco's houses have more geometrically arranged boards and paneling and less of the graceful curved shapes associated with Queen Anne around the rest of the country. In the great surge of building so many highly individual houses, almost anything that isn't specifically Greek or Italian does seem to have found a convenient label in "Eastlake."

MANY SECTIONS OF THE COUNTRY have houses built in 1870–1890 period that conform to Eastlake's "basic principles" or which have geometric detailing that is commonly referred to as "Eastlake touches." Some of the following are clues to architectural details that are often attributed to Eastlake's influence:

• Ornamental iron with medieval motifs, especially iron cresting on roofs and balconies.

• Decorative incised stylized flowers or geometric patterns on lintels or the front of a building.

• A gallery effect of spindles on the outside of a house—in front of a window or under the eaves, using baluster-type spindles. This echoed the gallery (a railing around the edge of a table, cabinet or shelf) that was a popular element of Eastlake-influenced furniture.

Many of these elements are also found in the interiors of an Eastlake-influenced house. For instance, the incised flowers on a brownstone front will be found inside on the woodwork over doors and windows.

• The arrangement of sticks in a geometric pattern on a porch or as a gable decoration is often thought to be Eastlake in inspiration.

In the gabled dormer illustrated below, the Eastlake influence shows in the geometric pattern on the eaves, the iron cresting on the roof, and the use of a finial ornament topping the gable. Also, colored glass was used in the window, reflecting the popularity of stained glass in an Eastlake house. Daylight was still considered vulgar in the late 19th century.

ONCE YOU START PICKING OUT "EASTLAKE" on old houses it's hard to stop. And you can't help but wonder how they got there. Did the owner, architect or carpenter-builder read Eastlake and try to duplicate a principle? Or did they see a popular decoration somewhere and copy it? Or a grand house they liked and wanted one as much like it as they could have? No one can really know the answer and so it is truly an old-house mystery story.

THE LATE VICTORIAN ART MOVEMENT

By Carolyn Flaherty

A TREMENDOUS EFFECT on the way English and American homes looked—both inside and outside—in the latter decades of the 19th century was due to the Arts and Crafts Movement. It began in England with a few architects and designers who wanted to reform the taste of the English public. By the 1880s the Art Movement had become an important influence on architecture, furniture, wallpaper, decorative objects, textiles, color schemes, and even women and children's clothing.

IT WAS A PERIOD in which people wrote, talked, and thought about taste and decoration to an amazing degree. It preceded, and contained the origins of, the Art Noveau or Modern period generally thought of as the end of the Victorian era.

IT IS ESPECIALLY IMPORTANT TODAY to the owner of a Victorian home built in the second half of the 19th century. Too often, because Victorian decoration has been so misunderstood, the stereotyped version of the overstuffed parlor with unwieldy furniture is all that is commonly portrayed as Victorian decoration. But the Art Movement popularized an elegant, simple mode of decoration that is appropriate to any late Victorian home and at the same time is pleasing to the modern eye.

BY MID-19TH CENTURY, those in the field of design were unanimously lamenting the state of English decoration. Household goods and ornaments were being mass-produced for the first time and were often poor in quality and design. Standards of taste in design had gotten lost in the advance of technology, and the home of the average middle-class Englishman was crammed full of furniture and objects, stuffed and trimmed or covered with glass. Lavish and complicated design motifs were cribbed from every period in historey, with the exception of the preceding century, which was scorned for its simplicity. Color and pattern ran rampant through the house.

WILLIAM MORRIS

ONE OF THE FIRST AND MOST influential of the missionaries of good taste was William Morris. He thought English interiors either "costly and hideous, or cheap and hideous" and the main road to salvation to be a return to the honest work of the medieval craftsman. An excellent craftsman himself, he said, "Handicraftsmen are the only group who are really happy because in their daily work they experience their greatest pleasure." He designed what later became known as "Art Furniture"—furniture with simple lines and with decoration limited to inset panels or repeated, incised carvings. The wood was often stained black, dark green or blue and the designs in gilt. He rejected the elaborate moldings, carving and glued-on ornament that was fashionable in the mid-1800s.

MORRIS AND CO. manufactured a chair with wooden arms with padded tops, supported by spindles, with an adjustable back that worked on a simple peg system. Enormously popular, almost every home had a "morris chair" of a similar kind by the turn of the century. Today the term "morris chair" is still applied to any adjustable easy chair with loose seat and back cushions.

From the 1902 Sears, Roebuck Catalog.

IN 1861 WILLIAM MORRIS and a group of fellow artists and craftsmen began the firm that was to become Morris and Co. They engaged in interior decorating commissions, murals, architectural carving, the manufacture of furniture, wallpaper, stained glass, metal work and jewelry, and "every article necessary for domestic use." Although the return to handcrafted work was not economically possible, many of his innovations were eventually absorbed into the mainstream of commercial manufacture. Their acceptance had a great deal to do with his exceptional personality which attracted other brilliant people to join with him in his crusade.

MORRIS WAS AN EXCELLENT painter, poet, architect, manufacturer, printer, book designer, publisher, maker of furniture, wallpapers and textiles, dyer, gardener, protector of ancient buildings, commentator on public affairs and self-designated conscience of his age. He was also one of the most famous cuckolds. A much-loved man by others, his wife, a beautiful former model of his, was in love with his good friend and mentor, Dante Gabriel Rossetti, the pre-Raphaelite painter and poet. It was common knowledge that Rossetti returned her affections. Many of Morris' psychology-oriented

A typical William Morris design.

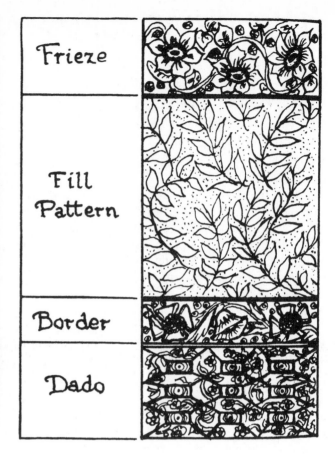

biographers claim that his incredibly complex, intertwining flowering vines which are the hallmark of his wallpaper, textiles and book illustrations, were a compensation for his failure to interwine with Mrs. Morris.

NOT ALL OF THE Art Movement wallpapers were as complicated in design as were the original Morris papers. Many of the designs of Day, Talbert, Crane and others are of a sophisticated but simpler design. But they all have the flat, unshaded representations of non-realistic flowers, vines, or Japanese motifs. After checking with many of the American firms that formerly carried English-made Morris papers, it was found that they have been discontinued mostly because they were so expensive and delivery was lengthy and erratic. There is a firm in London, Sanderson, which manufactures the original papers. However, it costs about $75 just to have the sample book shipped to American customers. There are, however, many Morris-type papers available from American wallpaper companies, although they do not bear the Morris label. An economical alternative to Aesthetic-type wallpaper is stencilling. Stencilling gives the flat, two-dimensional look so essential to Art Design.

MORRIS WAS ALSO RESPONSIBLE FOR PAINTED mouldings and woodwork trim. One of the first decorating commissions undertaken by Morris and Co. was the Green

Dining Room at the Victoria and Albert Museum. A range of dull greens predominated in the color scheme and the woodwork was painted dark green. This was a room used by architects, designers and art students, and had a great effect.

WOODWORK WAS PAINTED TO HARMONIZE with the colors used in wallpapers. It became fashionable the latter part of the 19th century to divide walls horizontally into: Dado (about 3 ft. up from the floor) topped by a wooden moulding or paper border; Fill paper for the main upper wall; Frieze. Between filler and frieze there was usually a picture rail or a narrow shelf for the display of porcelain or blue and white china.

SOMETIMES DIFFERENT PATTERNS would be used on the parts of the wall—or the same pattern would be used on the dado and the fill portion but in different colorways.

A GREAT DEAL OF ATTENTION WAS paid to the dado; it was no longer just an architectural term but a household word. A very popular covering for the dado was also Indian matting (widely used, too, for a floor covering). Its pale golden color was a good foil for the black and gold Art Furniture and an attractive companion to the subdued shades of the Art Wallpapers. Japanese imitation leather was also imported for use on the dado. It was slightly embossed with some gilt, and was also used for inset panels on furniture as an alternative to more expensive hand-painted decoration.

THE AESTHETIC COLORS

THE FOUNDATION OF THE Aesthetic Movement was the new use of color. A whole range of subdued colors was developed for interior decoration. Morris could not bring himself to use the bright aniline dyes which were then being produced. They were "hideous in their extreme purity," and, in fact, were often garishly bright. Writers on decoration often advised extreme care in the over-use of these scarlets, and vivid blues, greens and purples. They particularly warned against painting ceilings or walls white in combination with these bright hues. Morris experimented with vegetable dyes to produce more neutral shades. Some of his first attempts were dull yellow-greens and khakis—which he later rejected—but which were forever associated with him.

THE COLORS USED by Morris were secondary or tertiary shades—a range of dull greens, particularly sage green, rust, ochre, citron, gold, and peacock blue. So complete was the eventual alteration of color schemes that even the bright cheerful favorite house plants like the fuchsia, geranium and begonia were discarded for the decorous dullness of the aspidistra and the olive-green palm.

ART DECORATION

IN GENERAL, THE AESTHETIC INTERIOR contained less furniture and of lighter appearance than the High Victorian room with its heavy, carved pieces. Colors were subdued and ornament was confined to porcelain, china and paintings instead of bric-a-brac and glass domes. The new decorative motifs were the sunflower, lily, peacocks, cranes, and fans. Because these motifs became so popular, they were often used out of context in many Victorian rooms that made no other concession to the Art Movement.

SUNFLOWERS

THE POPULARITY OF the ubiquitous sunflower began with Talbert, who was designing textiles and wallpaper even before Morris. His designs had great freshness and originality and were widely imitated after his early death. His "Sunflower" series of wallpapers, embossed leathers and flocks won the Gold Medal for England in the Paris Universal Exhibition of 1878. His characteristic style involved the use of sharply-delineated flowers, fruit and leaves—all without shading—on a ground that often used Japanese design as its source.

It was probably Talbert's sunflowers that were most imitated on woven and printed fabrics of all kinds, particularly stamped velvet and plush, that appeared in the 70's and 80's.

Sunflowers carved on a Victorian newel post.

ALONG WITH the sunflower many other tall flowers had their day—the lily, iris, cattail—plants that were bold and unsentimental. They were always represented in a non-realistic manner and in flat colors; the opposite of the realistic roses and forget-me-nots so lushly portrayed in French fashions.

An illustration by Walter Crane, the English Art Movement designer, drawn for The House Beautiful—*a book that helped popularize Art furnishings in America. The fireplace is tiled, the furniture "modern" and the fans Crane liked so much decorate the mantel.*

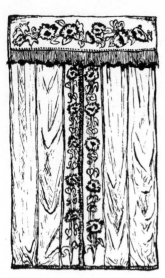

"The Queen's Curtain," a simply hung pair of rich brown velvet drapes with a flat, straight-edged valance. Queen Victoria herself suggested the bucolic sunflower as a motif, assuring its future popularity. They were designed for use at Windsor Castle and displayed at the Great Exhibition in London in 1851. These simpler lines for drapery became fashionable in later decades.

LEWIS F. DAY also liked the sunflower for his textile and wallpaper designs, but he added a series of mantelpiece clocks with the sunflower as the clock face. They contained in miniature all the features of Art Furniture and were very popular.

THE SUNFLOWER BECAME the symbol of Art design and soon appeared on every decorative surface—moulded in terra cotta on buildings, cast in iron for trim on railings and fences, painted on tiles, incised in furniture and woodwork, and in "Art Embroidery" used for quilts, drapes and clothing.

PEACOCKS, CRANES AND FANS

JAPANESE GOODS (just beginning to be imported into England and in high favor with the Art Movement) were directly responsible for the popularity of the cranes, peacocks and fans that newly decorated Victorian homes.

THE PEACOCK, either the whole bird or just a few of its feathers, had as many possiblities for stylization as the sunflower. It, too, was incorporated into all kinds of Aesthetic decoration. Particularly in America, a vase filled with peacock feathers was thought to be the latest fashion.

THE CRANE WAS A FAVORITE of the English designer Walter Crane. He used it often on his wallpaper and tile designs. He also introduced a classicism into Art Design. He favored lanquid ladies draped in costumes of early centuries, and favored narrative themes. One of his most famous wallpaper designs depicted scenes from Sleeping Beauty.

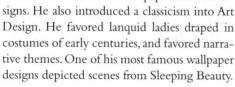

TILES WERE AN IMPORTANT PART of the new decoration. They were particularly popular for fireplace surrounds. Victorian houses built in the latter decades of the 19th century will often have fireplace or hallway tiles with one of the favorite Art motifs or a classical subject like King Arthur and the Round Table.

THE JAPANESE FAN was another popular exotic fashion. Crane admired it for its design elements as did Whistler, the transplanted American painter. Whistler advanced its popularity by using a few purple fans to decorate the walls and ceilings of a blue room in his own home. It became a fad till the end of the century to have a Japanese fan tucked, with artful carelessness, behind a picture, criss-crossed over doorways, and bedecking mantels. If one fan was "artistic"—then a lot of fans were thought to be very artistic. They were imported into England and America in such great numbers and were sold so cheaply that they eventually lost their "exotic" flavor.

WILDE IN AMERICA

OSCAR WILDE was the most conspicuous advocate of the Aesthetic Movement. His genius for attracting publicity made him the butt of most of the satire directed at the "Aesthetes."

WILDE POPULARIZED the Art Movement in America with as much impact as Eastlake's *Hints On Household Taste.* He began his 18-month tour of the U. S. in 1882, appearing in his velvet knickerbocker suit with a sunflower or lily in his buttonhole and never failed to create a stir.

HE HAD COME TO "instruct and elevate our rich, clever but not particularly cultured transatlantic cousins." He soon developed a fondess for the country, however, enhanced by its natural beauty and by its enthusiastic receptions. He scorned the French decorative arts in fashion, attributing their vulgarity to the monarchy—winning him great favor with American audiences. They allowed him to tell them how badly their homes were designed and furnished, and even the critics who laughed at him in print adopted the "Art" principles he espoused to some degree.

AN INTERESTING FIGURE in the Art Movement was the young English designer, Kate Greenaway. She designed tiles and book illustrations featuring children in high-waisted

frocks and sun-bonnets, colored in soft yellow and greens. The simple lines of the garments were closer to the styles of preceding centuries than the "little adult" manner children were dressed in during Victorian times. She managed to liberate children's clothing and inspired many imitators who sentimentalized her drawings on greeting cards and figurines for decades.

THE AESTHETIC MOVEMENT was a well-intentioned effort on the part of many creative people to bring art into everyday life. Eventually, the missionary aspect died out as new fashions caught the public's attention. But the influence on color, furnishings and architecture remained. In almost every part of England and the U. S. where 19th-century buildings remain, the sunflower can still be seen—if you look carefully—reminding us of a time when so many cared, talked and wrote about how houses should look both inside and outside.

GREEK REVIVAL DECORATION

by Carolyn Flaherty

MORE OLD HOUSES WERE BUILT, and converted to, the Greek Revival style than any other type in America. For decades it was our national style and had its own particular form of decoration. And yet this style of interior decoration, so appropriate to the classical features of the Greek Revival interior, has been curiously neglected. Old-house owners have often wondered why the popular Early American and Victorian colors and furnishings do not quite "fit" in their Grecian-style houses. A room of this period may be wanting a touch of the Greek to bring out its original character.

HOUSES AND PUBLIC BUILDINGS imitating classic Greek architecture were built in every part of the country, from 1820 to 1840. Towns that were just beginning during the period were built entirely in the Greek style, often having Greek names as well—Troy, Euclid, Ithaca, Athens. The style lingered until the Civil War, particularly in the middle and western parts of the country.

THE MOOD OF THE American people played an important part in the Greek mania. There was a revolt against British imitation, formerly so popular, after the unpleasantness of the War of 1812. Nor did they care too much for the imperious Napoleon. On the other hand, Americans were in sympathy with the Greek people's struggle for freedom. The columns, porticos and colonnades that appeared in such profusion were thought to symbolize the democratic

principles of the ancient culture. Men like Jefferson believed the temple style to be the perfect expression of the ideals of the American republic.

THERE WERE ALSO MORE PRACTICAL REASONS the Greek Revival house became as popular as today's ranch house. House builders built for clients who wanted a maximum of impressiveness with a minimum of cost. The white columns—round and square, plain and fluted—that held up the classic triangular pediment were certainly impressive. And they could be executed with great economy for the sugar planter, banker or farmer alike, all of whom deemed them appropriate.

AS TRAINED ARCHITECTS WERE RARE, the builders required a style that was easily translated into their own vernacular. The temple style, particularly in its simplest form of a few columns or pilasters added to a new or existing box-type house, fit the bill. It could also be built in wood—an important factor in a tree-rich country. Books by Asher Benjamin and Minard Lafever were published as "Builder's Guides." They included instructions on basic geometry and gave drawings of classic and their own versions of "classic" columns, mantels, pediments, etc., to be used by local carpenter/builders around the country.

ONE OF THE MOST COMMON features of the style was the portico—a

covered or roofed space at the entrance. It was held up by 2, 4 or more columns. In its simplest version, it was often grafted onto a plain colonial style house to give it the "modern" Greek look.

IF A HOUSE DID not feature a portico, it at least had corner pilasters and a suggestion of the classical pediment by emphasis on the gable end of the house. Heavy cornices were used on the gable, with the amount of classical detailing depending on the cost of the house.

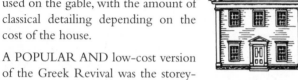

A POPULAR AND low-cost version of the Greek Revival was the storey-and-a-half house. It managed to have all the worst features of the style as far as comfort was concerned, while adding a few of its own. In this type there was only one one main storey recessed behind white columns of the same height. The half storey, usually the children's and servants' rooms, crouched in the triangular half storey, pierced by small, often round, windows. The low pitched roof, covered with tin, made these rooms oven-temperature in summer, and tended to sag and leak under the snow in winter. But since it was the comfort of the children and servants that was sacrificed to fashion, the storey-and-a-half house remained popular. The parlors and "master chambers" were on the main floor.

THE COLUMNED FRONT OF the house admitted little sunlight to the interior—a fact that was not acknowledged until the Greek style began to decline. There were also certain oddities connected with the attempt at classical symmetry. Both town and country houses had floor plans with two of everything—two parlors or two matching bedrooms. Additional rooms like the kitchen and pantry had to be fitted in jigsaw fashion to the back of the house. Often non-functioning doors were built to keep a symmetrical appearance.

THE CITY ROW house was also adapted to the Greek style. Higher ceilings caused them to be taller, and they were usually deeper than they were wide. They had a long, narrow hall to make room for the two symmetrical parlors. The high stoop—a Dutch leftover—remained fashionable in New York, but Philadelphia and Boston built their Greek row houses with white marble steps. Expensive houses sported a Grecian front door with fluted Ionic columns on each side,

supporting a flat entablature. The flat cornices had decorative dentils (small toothlike blocks). Grecian motifs in iron-work decorated fences.

DESPITE THE PREOCCUPATION WITH SYMMETRY, the front door—usually square-headed with vertical side-lights—was moved from the center towards the side of the house. This was actually an experiment in "modernizing"—an attempt to reduce the draft in the rooms caused by the old-fashioned central hallway.

TO CREATE THE IMPRESSION of stone, weatherboards were often butt-jointed rather than overlapped, and brick-work was painted white or gray.

THE INTERIOR

THE GREEK REVIVAL INTERIOR had a restrained elegance. Color and furnishings gave a look of cool simplicity. Elegance was achieved by symmetry in architectural details and placing of furniture, and the use of similar colors for walls and woodwork and a contrasting color for both upholstery and window hangings, usually in the same design and fabric.

THE PRECEDING FEDERAL PERIOD had been noted for delicacy in design and neo-classical motifs. Many of the first Greek Revival houses were decorated in the Federal style, but as the Greek style became more popular, there was more emphasis placed on purely Grecian lines and motifs. The influence of the Empire style in France and the Regency in England combined to produce the American Empire. With this style, the furniture that was designed for the Greek Revival houses became heavier and more massive, and eventually became what is now thought of as "Victorian" by mid-century. Because the Greek Revival style in architecture lasted so many years, most houses in the Greek style built in the 50s and 60s were decorated in the Victorian style. But here we will explore that decorative period from 1820 to 1840, when furnishings were still related to the exterior Greek Revival style.

COLORS

THE CLASSICAL LOOK REQUIRED a backdrop of pale walls that would simulate the ancient marble or stucco of classical Greece. Painted plaster walls were more in favor than wallpaper. They were tinted in delicate shades of gray, lavender, pink, blue and yellow, with woodwork in the same shade or in white. Pale buff walls with white woodwork were used occasionally.

THERE WERE MANY CHANGES in the interior from colonial fashions: Wood panelling was ommitted or painted white; the dado disappeared, and high ceilings were decorated with delicate plasterwork, a chandelier hanging from a center rosette. A symmetrical look was achieved by the balanced arrangement of doors, windows, etc. Mantels were smaller and decorated with molded composition in wreaths, swags, honeysuckle and gouged fans and cameo-like discs. Mythological figures and draped Muses graced some mantels.

GRANDER HOMES imitated the cool grandeur of Grecian interiors by marbleizing the columns that often separated parlors and by gilding the tops of columns and mouldings. Hallways often had niches large enough to contain classical sculptures.

WALLPAPER

WHEN WALLPAPER WAS USED, it was often the expensive and fashionable Chinese landscape type, very popular for large entranceways. Pale-colored papers with vertical lines or classical swags and urns were sometimes used. J. C. Loudon, in his widely-read encyclopedia of home furnishings, specifically recommended types of wallpaper for the room decorated in the Grecian style. He thought "architectural" wallpapers with "sculptured honeysuckle which decorates the many friezes of ancient temples" to be most desirable. For the hall, he recommended a plain paper in imitation of stone, and graining the woodwork in imitation of oak.

ARCHITECTURAL AND CLASSICAL motif wallpapers are hard to find today. However, pale colors and papers with textured surfaces are easily found. There are also many patterns that have vertical lines and medallion and snowflake-like designs, although they are usually grouped in a "colonial" collection. Any formal paper—like the floral stripes that are still popular—give the cool appearance desired for a Grecian room.

WINDOW TREATMENTS

WINDOWS WERE LARGE AND SLENDER in the Greek Revival house, contributing to the lighter look in in-

This is a typical Greek Revival parlor with American Empire furniture and a bulls-eye girandole over the mantel. The fabric is a woven cotton and silk in a dark mossy green. It is used for the chair and window curtains in its plain ground version and with an Empire snowflake design to cover the Grecian sofa. "Davout Snowflake Damask" was recreated by Brunschwig & Fils, Inc., for the Bayou Bend Chillman Empire Parlor in Houston, Texas.

teriors. Rich fabrics and strong colors were used to provide accent to their austere settings, although the lines of the drapery were kept simple.

THE OPULENT COLORS of the French Empire were used in rooms of grand proportions—royal purple, emerald green, wine red, and brilliant yellows and blues. Most window hangings, however, used fabric in less rich colors—grays, golds, peaches, and quieter blues and greens. But the fabrics were elegant and formal. Silk, satin, damask, brocade, taffeta and velvet were the most fashionable and furniture was upholstered in the same fabric and color.

VERY POPULAR WERE SATINS AND TAFFETAS striped or dotted with medallions. Toiles printed with patriotic French and American scenes were used, and are reproduced today by many fabric firms. These scenes were printed on cottons and linens.

THE FRENCH ROD was commonly used in window treatments. Elaborate finials in Empire motifs gave a strong decorative accent. The formal English boxed valance was another elegant treatment, and less expensive windows had plain wood cornices. Wooden cornices were gilded for added elegance.

THE BEAUTIFUL FABRICS USED ON Greek Revival windows were expensive even then, because they were imported and woven with a great deal of real silk. But today,

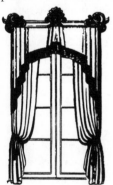

the cost of a heavy damask is mindboggling. The toiles are more readily available and will probably be found in most stores in a "colonial" grouping. But the key factor—elegance—can be found in ready-made fabrics by using solids with a formal texture, striped patterns, medallion or snowflake designs or chintz in cool colors. Chintz is a popular fabric with decorators who refurnish period rooms with today's fabrics, often with a floral design in a symmetrically arranged manner such as the "English garden" prints.

FLOORS

HOOKED AND BRAIDED RUGS on painted floors were commonly used in houses until mid-19th century when factory-made carpets were available. Those who could afford them often had "Brussels" carpets or other expensive, imported types.

THERE WAS A FASHION FOR PAINTED FLOORS in large black & white squares in imitation of the marble squares used in grand European parlors. Sometimes the squares were marbleized to make them more like the original, and other color combinations like peach and black or gray and black were used.

FURNISHINGS

IN THE 1820s, when the Greek Revival began to make its appearance, the light and delicate look of the Federal period

Klismos

was still fashionable. Hepplewhite, Sheraton and Phyfe, who had been using Grecian motifs, were the foremost cabinetmakers. They had replaced the heavier Chippen-

dale style. With the Greek mania, furniture took on the lines of the ancient Greek furniture. The splayed legs of the "klismos" were used in chairs and sofas.

THE TYPICAL PLAIN SOFA of the period was a solidly proportioned piece of furniture with two identical headrests in the forms of scrolls that curved gracefully into the seat rail. The girandole, a round mirror with the Federal eagle on

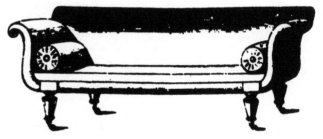

top, was a particularly popular decorative item. But mirrors in general were widely used to enhance the spaciousness and elegance desired. Diamond and fan motifs were popular for glass and silver, and earthenware from England displayed figures from the ancient culture or patriotic scenes from American historey.

MIRRORS, CHAIRS, SOFAS AND TABLES were used in pairs to create the classical balance and dignity that typified the Greek Revival home.

THE QUEEN ANNE STYLE

By Renee Kahn

AMERICA GOT ITS FIRST LOOK at the Queen Anne style at the Philadelphia Exposition of 1876, the great "Centennial." It was love at first sight for this "tossed salad" (as Russell Lynes calls it) of Elizabethan, Jacobean, and Classical elements. For the next 20 years it was every man's dream house, his castle, his retreat from the growing pressures of American life.

QUEEN ANNE was largely the creation of an English architect, Richard Norman Shaw. Nostalgic by nature, it was supposed to be a return to the simple, solid construction methods of the days of good Queen Anne (150 years earlier), when workmanship was emphasized over superficial architectural detail. In that sense, it was the architectural counterpart of William Morris and the Arts and Crafts movement of the time.

THE GREAT PUBLIC ENTHUSIASM for Queen Anne swept away both the Gothic and French Mansard styles. Its only competitor was the Romanesque, which had the weight, both figurative and literal, of Henry Hobson Richardson behind it. Romanesque, however, was a stone construction style, and therefore out of reach of most American pocketbooks. On the other hand, a wooden Queen Anne house could be put together quickly and cheaply by any competent carpenter and his helper.

QUEEN ANNE'S NICKNAME, the "bric-a-brac" style suited it very well. Earlier examples looked more Elizabethan, as though they had come out of Shakespeare's England, later came Jacobean towers and turrets, and still later, the more classical elements like Palladian windows and Grecian columns. The entire style was finally snuffed out by the Colonial wave which swept America at the turn of the century.

ALTHOUGH IT WAS POPULAR for only two decades, its impact on the American scene was enormous. The rapid growth of our cities and towns, along with innumerable technological advances, resulted in the construction of hundreds of thousands of Queen Anne houses. Although it is probably the most common "old house" we have around today, next to nothing has been written about it.

THE BASIC SHAPE

THE SIMPLE RECTANGLE of earlier days was gone: Asymmetry ruled the day. Wings and gables protruded in all directions, and modest porches expanded into full scale verandahs or piazzas. Balconies, overhanging gables, and bay and oriel windows dotted the facade. The house grew organically, from the inside out. Its inner structure determined its outer shape. Adding to the style's picturesque effect were the towers and turrets. "Here," according to one Builder's Plan Book, "the fastidious housekeeper could banish the smelly smoker." Towers were round, octagonal, or square, but the most fascinating were onion domed, like Arabian Nights fantasies. Rooflines varied: A street of the period often displayed many different styles. Whether gabled or hipped, roofs were high, in keeping with the medieval effect. Dormers were commonplace and not placed symmetrically. One rather charming roof variation was called "jerkin head," and the end tipped downward.

THE SKIN

THE DOMINANT DECORATIVE element was texture. A typical "skin" consisted of a clapboard or stone first storey, a shingled second storey, and a half-timbered attic floor. Sometimes, instead of half timber, still another variety of shingle was used. It was not uncommon for a house of the period to have three or four different kinds of shingles on it.

THE BANDSAW, which was perfected after the Civil War, made it possible to turn out shingles in great quantity and variety. Common forms re-resembled fish scales or feathers, while the more unusual versions looked like playing cards, or even

This block in Stamford, Conn., shows a typical conglomeration of Queen Anne rooflines–hipped, onion dome, turrets.

GABLES provided space for considerable decoration. Finials rose and pendants descended. The gable peak was frequently filled in with sunbursts and sunflower designs, or an arrangement of spindles. Bargeboards, unlike previous Gothic styles, were relatively plain and unadorned.

QUEEN ANNE architecture was frequently called the "Free Classic" style because of its use of Greek and Roman decorative motifs. Dentils (rectangular toothlike projections) appeared under the cornice, along with swags, garlands, urns, and columns. These elements, plus the reappearance of the Palladian winow, forecast a full return to "Colonial" architecture in the 1900s.

fruits. An imaginative home builder could combine these ready-made forms with abandon, even placing them in wavy patterns so that the whole surface seemed to undulate.

THE TRIM

WHILE WOOD TEXTURES and window patterns created most of the visual interest, there was no shortage of other kinds of trim. The typical Victorian carpenter looked upon ornament with great enthusiasm. Factories all over the country produced ready-made gingerbread, and one could browse through their catalogs with abandon. The dominant motifs of the period were the stylized sun-burst and sunflowers as-

sociated with the English Arts and Crafts Movement. Innumerable variations of the two turned up on gables, brackets, over windows and doors.

MOST ORNAMENT however, was "turned" (because of improvements in turning equipment). Spindles shaped like interior balusters and posts were used on porch railings, and other trim. Brackets were generally smaller, and less ornate than in preceding periods, and were often incised in an "Eastlake" manner.

WINDOWS

TO ENHANCE the picturesque, medieval quality, window panes were often small and squarish. These units were combined with larger "plate" glass areas in a number of different ways. The most common arrangement was a small-paned top sash over a solid glass lower half. Another version consisted of a border of small panes (frequently colored) set around a larger one. Sometimes only a transom on top was small-paned, and even less frequently, the entire window was made up of small squares. Stained glass was used mainly for hall or staircase windows

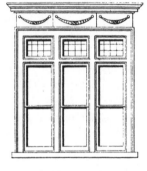

where the filtered light added to the "times gone by" atmosphere. Both windows and doors often had glass panels with a decoration etched in the glass.

PAINT

DURING THE FIRST HALF of the 19th century houses were generally painted white with dark green trim. Under Downing's influence in the middle of the century, this changed to fawns, greys, and drab green. During the last quarter, however, colors became deep and intense. Lewis Mumford refers to this period as the "Brown Decades," and ties the color choices to the depressed mood of the times (brought on by the Civil War, Lincoln's death, and the severe recession of the 1870s). At any rate, a warm red-brown seems to have been the most popular color, with deep greens, umbers, and

The top sash of the window seen through the arch has small panes as a border. Other details frequently found in the Queen Anne style: Decorative panel, dentils, columns, varied texture of brick, board and shingles.

golden ochres not far behind. Other color schemes called for maroons, burnt orange, and stone gray–all colors made possible by technological growth in the paint industry.

THE QUEEN ANNE HOUSE was rarely painted in only one or two colors. The body, trim, shutters, and sash were all treated differently. It was not uncommon for as many as five contrasting, but harmonious, shades to be used on one house. Only in an era of cheap labor could such elaborate color schemes be considered on an everyday basis. To invest in such a paint job today is a true act of love.

INTERIORS

THE DOMINANT FEATURE of a Queen Anne house was the large, squarish entry hall. Lined with dark oak wainscotting and woodwork, it was designed to impress and envelop the visitor. If finances permitted, it contained a baronial fireplace and a built-in bench beneath the stairs. A vestibule led to the outside door and protected against drafts.

ABOVE THE PANELLING there was either wallpaper (Lincrusta-Walton, a glazed, textured variety was popular, or fabric–preferably damask or velour.) Patterns were exotic: Japanese or Moorish in influence, with numerous friezes, borders, and dados. Three dimensional looking designs were branded "dishonest" and flat patterns were considered the only appropriate designs for flat wall surfaces. Plain plaster walls, when used, had stencilled borders beneath the cornice. If one could afford it, the ceiling had boxed-in beams or coffering. Other-

wise, pale tints of plaster sufficed. The ornate plaster rosettes of previous periods were no longer used, and light fixtures hung from unadorned ceiling plates. Light came from stained glass, or stained glass bordered windows, which lent an appropriately medieval air to the room.

A drawing room corner furnished in the "artistic" manner fashionable during the period when Queen Anne houses were built.

THE MAIN ROOMS came off the central hall, in an asymmetrical manner. As central heating came into popular use, it was no longer necessary to close off spaces with heavy doors–portieres were sufficient. Doors were still recommended for places where quiet and privacy were needed, such as the library. Despite heating systems, fireplaces remained important features and builder handbooks of the period recommended that they be made as elaborate as one could afford.

AS LATE AS THE 1880s the indoor toilet was considered a luxury and was found only in "better" homes. Except for mansions, there was rarely more than one bathroom, and that was next to the master bedroom.

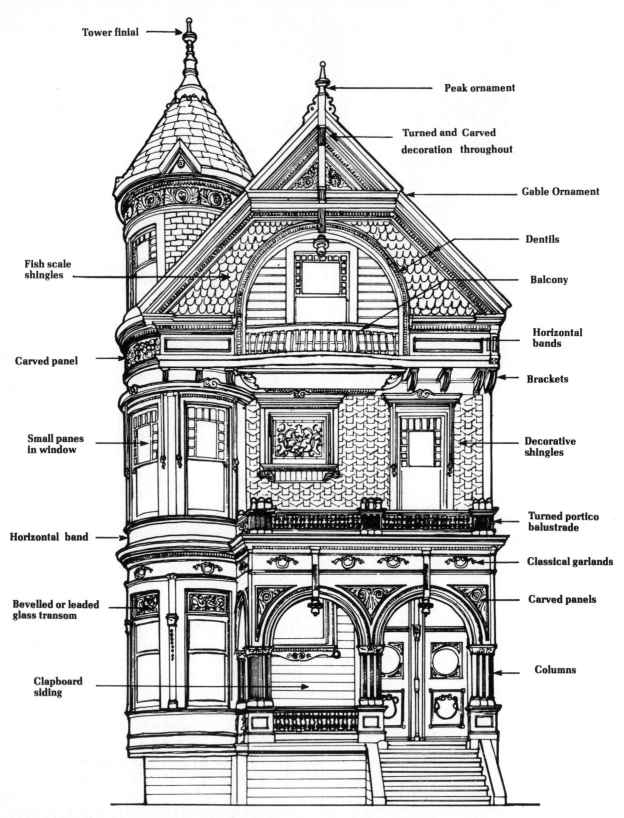

Tower finial

Peak ornament

Turned and Carved
decoration throughout

Gable Ornament

Dentils

Fish scale
shingles

Balcony

Horizontal
bands

Carved panel

Brackets

Small panes
in window

Decorative
shingles

Turned portico
balustrade

Horizontal band

Classical garlands

Bevelled or leaded
glass transom

Carved panels

Clapboard
siding

Columns

This Queen Anne house contains many features found in this picturesque style – a variety of textures with 3 different types of shingles plus clapboarding; many different kinds of windows; and different kinds of wood decoration. The drawing is adapted from an excellent book about Victorian architecture in San Francisco, A Gift To The Street.

This restored Queen Anne is a good example of how elegant the style can be. . . .

FURNISHINGS

GONE WAS THE red plush and white marble of the Civil War Era. In its place stood a hodge podge of "artistic" furniture, which claimed its roots in "medieval simplicity." Like the wallpaper, it was more than medieval. Any household with a pretense to good taste had its "Turkish Corner" and Japanese screens.

THE MAJOR influence, however, was Charles Eastlake, whose *Hints On Household Taste* was a runaway best seller when published in 1868. "Art furniture," or "Eastlake," as it was called, dominated public taste for the next twenty years. Although it gave lip service to "simple, honest craftmanship," it ended up as ornate, and as poorly made as the furniture that preceded it. Despite Eastlake's disapproval, the cabinetmaker disappeared under the weight of the upholsterer. Fringes and tassels were everywhere.

EVEN THOUGH machine made, furniture had a handcrafted, rectilinear look. Decoration was incised and gilded, or carved in a flat, stylized manner. Spindles provided an acceptable alternative to the squared-off lines, mainly because Eastlake saw them as a revival of the medieval "turners" art. He also deplored varnished furniture, and wood finishes were either ebonized or left natural.

THE CENTENNIAL EXPOSITION of 1876 brought in yet another fashion, one which outlasted all the others. It was the collection of American antiques. One small exhibit, a colonial kitchen, set off a wave of patriotic collecting that still exists today. Since the supply could not possibly meet the demand, increasing quantities of reproductions were made.

QUEEN ANNE TODAY

THE IMPACT OF the Queen Anne style on the American scene was enormous. Today, we tend to make light of these romantic, overly embellished fantasies. We call them "white elephants," and complain about how much they cost to heat. Many of them are in run-down neighborhoods, unloved and exploited. However, they were solidly built, and respond well to a loving hand. Be brave! Tear off those asphalt shingles, let the original skin shine through. Strip off that louvered glass porch! Find another stained glass window for the hall, and just watch it come back to life! Top off your efforts with a real Queen Anne coat of paint (not white). How about rust color with maroon and orange trim?

. . . but, typical of the plight of so many Queen Anne houses today are these two empty buildings in Stamford.

TUDOR HOUSES

By Carolyn Flaherty

ONE OF THE MOST POPULAR styles of house building in America is the Tudor. The style began with the first English settlers and continues today. Although the original English Tudor is well documented in the architectural books, hardly a word has been written about the American Tudors. The Tudor homeowners have been asking The Journal for more information about the style and its history, as well as help in decorating it to enhance its architectural charm.

THE TERM "Tudor" in American houses refers to the house that has some half-timbering in the picturesque style of the old English house. Other readily identifiable features are the small, diamond-shaped panes in bay and oriel windows, and large medieval chimneys. An American Tudor might be a small suburban cottage built in the 1880's or a huge country mansion of the '20s and '30s.

THE ORIGINAL TUDOR PERIOD in England was the 16th and first half of the 17th centuries. The great social and religious changes began with Henry VIII in 1509 and continued till the death of Mary Tudor in in 1558. It was during the reign of Henry's daughter, Elizabeth Tudor, from 1558 to 1603 that life in England was peaceful and prosperous enough to begin the great adventure in domestic building. In 1603 the Stuart dynasty began with James I. Since Jacobus is the Latin

for James, the period is known as Jacobean. The Early Jacobean period is included in the label "Tudor" as house building and decoration did not change dramatically. The Late Jacobean period ending with the Commonwealth, saw enough decorative changes to make another article.

THE TUDOR IS REALLY THE FIRST house as we know them today. Previously, real houses had been built only for the wealthy and the rest of the population lived in temporary, roughly built dwellings. But under Elizabeth's reign houses began to appear in great numbers built of oak beams and plaster. Interestingly, as the peaceful times did away with the need for real castles, the Englishman began to look upon his his castle. It was a time of great pride in the domestic house and of good, cheerful living.

SHAKESPEARE'S PLAYS and the many Elizabethan fairy tales we grew up with have kept this "Merrie Old England" alive in our memories and perhaps explains the emotional attachment America has had to the old English house.

IN HALF-TIMBER CONSTRUCTION the actual timber framework of the building was left exposed to view and the spaces between the timbers filled or "nogged" with brick work often covered with stucco. English workmen have al-

A typically American Tudor built c. 1914 in Pennsylvania adds Colonial features (shed dormer, shutters) as well as regional characteristics (fieldstone front, pent roof over the oriel window) to the old English form and half timbering.

Not as commonly found in the American versions, this 1929 Pennsylvania Tudor has varying brick patterns in the "nogging" between the beams. These decorative brick patterns were often used in old English half-timbered houses.

always loved oak, and in the 16th century it was plentiful. The timbers were heavy and broad and gave the house a decorative look. Beams were often shaped into circles, herring-bone patterns, or cut out in trefoil and quatrefoil shapes. These "black & white" houses often had elaborately carved verge boards.

LEFT OUT IN this discussion are the many buildings of the Tudor period built in stone. These large masonry structures were generally manor houses and were ornamented with crenellations, sculptured finials, Tudor arched doorways and combined both Gothic and Italian Renaissance ornament. This style has been copied in America mostly for public buildings and is often labelled "Collegiate Gothic." A typical masonry Tudor is illustrated above

TUDOR IN AMERICA

THE PURITANS BROUGHT the half-timbered style with them to America as well as the more austere aspects of Jacobean decoration. Houses in New England, however, quickly took on a different appearance than their English counterparts due to the harsh climate.

From Palliser's "New Cottage Homes"—1887

THE TUDOR STYLE was revived dramatically in the late Victorian period when "picturesque" styles were the fashion. The Elizabethan style (as it was called then) was adapted for large country houses as well as smaller town and suburban houses. The use of cement stucco, which was weather resistant, made half-timber construction feasible.

AS THE QUEEN ANNE STYLE reached its height and began to decline around the turn of the century, the Tudor style again became very popular. From 1900 to the First World War, Tudors were the rage. Some historians have, rather coyly, labelled this period "Jacobethan" Revival.

The main staircase from Sheldon Hall, in Leicestershire, England. It was characteristic of the first wooden staircases to build them around a square well and break them up into short flights with a low pitch.

UNLIKE MANY OTHER BUILDING styles, the Tudor did not go out of fashion. Another enormous surge of popularity took place in the 20s and 30s. Author Russell Lynes remembers a contractor in the 20s, who had a good business converting Queen Anne houses into half-timbered ones by removing the porches, nailing irregular timbers to the outside, and filling in the interstices with stucco.

ORIGINAL TUDOR INTERIORS

DURING THE ELIZABETHAN and early Jacobean eras everything was made from oak, giving the Tudor age the name "The Oak Period." This sturdy wood was used for walls, to make furniture, hewn beams and floors. Walnut was not used until the Late Jacobean period.

A FAVORITE FORM of Elizabethan decoration was the vine with leaves, tendrils and grapes carved on exterior and interior beams. It is the lavish carving and exuberant decoration in wood that is the main characteristic of the Tudor interior.

BEFORE THE TUDOR PERIOD houses were on the order of castles—with comfort and decoration taking a place far behind defense. Small windows protected against seige and interiors were fairly grim. Now, with peace and progress afoot, and the need to defend gone, the house builder could let in light and air and begin to give thought to decorating walls, ceilings, fireplaces and furniture.

"LINEN-FOLD"   HERALDIC   CARVED
OAK PANELLING

WALL PANELLING transformed crude interiors into rooms of architectural beauty never surpassed. Intricate panelling appeared even in smaller homes. The linenfold motif—taken from the chalice napkin covering the host—was most popular and used for wall panelling, chests and furniture.

EARLY TUDOR FURNITURE was still structurally dependent on walls. Beds extended from the wall panelling and were decorated with the same carving. Beds were actually like little cabins with heavy drapes of leather or fabric to keep out the chill. Most seats and cupboards were also attached to walls.

LATER INTO THE Tudor period wood turning began to take the place of carving and more furniture appeared. With the introduction of coffee in 1645, chocolate in 1657, and tea in 1658, a need for tables for serving arose.

CUSHIONS were all there was in the way of upholstery and, often as not, there would be no more concession to comfort than a piece of Turkey carpet on a bench or chair.

An Early Jacobean oak room from Herefordshire, England. The brass chandelier is of the kind Colonists made or imported to America in later centuries, and is still reproduced today.

WINDOWS

TUDOR HOUSE BUILDERS brought as much light as possible into the house. Tall bay windows rose from the ground often to the roof line. The frieze window, a horizontal band of windows above the wood panelling, was a common way to admit light, particularly in the half-timbered cottage. The small, diamond-shaped panes were often brightened with insets of stained glass with heraldic patterns.

TUDOR WINDOWS, one of the most recognizable features, have been copied in all the later revivals. Palliser and Palliser, an architectural firm prominent in the 1880s, gave specific instruction for windows with "heraldic effect in art glass."

cotton.

LIGHT CAME FROM elaborate iron or brass chandeliers and tall iron standards. Helmets, armour and hunting implements were also hung on walls.

This is the entranceway of a Tudor style house, built in 1914, in Waterford, Conn. Typical of Tudor revivals, the walls are oak panelled and the floor is polished oak.

DECORATING THE TUDOR HOUSE TODAY

THE TUDOR HOUSE OWNER will most likely have many features in the interior that are reminiscent of original style and probably have a great deal of oak. A widely imitated feature of the old English style is the massive fireplace. In chilly England it was a vital part of the house and was often a colossal floor-to-ceiling structure. Revival styles often feature a large carved wood chimney piece. Heavy wrought iron fire-place accessories should be used, minus the Colonial decorative motifs.

DECORATION AND FABRIC

IF THE DESCRIPTION OF abundant oak and massive furniture in the Tudor house gives the impression of drabness, this is wrong. Tudor interiors, although dignified, were actually bright and cheerful. The windows, of course, did much to create brightness with daylight and colored light from the small bits of stained glass filtering in. Another element was the use of stucco ornament.

CEILINGS WERE a vital part of decoration. Ornamented with rich plaster Renaissance motifs or strapwork, we still marvel at their elegance in pictures of great English houses. Smaller homes usually had some ribbing, relief work or oak beams to produce a decorative effect.

RUSHES WERE OFTEN used to cover floors of public rooms and, in grand houses, Oriental carpets were used for private rooms.

IN THIS PERIOD of flourishing trade, rich velvets, damasks and tapestries were imported to England. The richest fabrics were used for bed hangings. Tapestries (many made at the Mortlake factory in England) were used as wall hangings and for cushions and drapes. Embroidery, an art at which the English have always excelled, appeared on crewel work—wool patterns on linen or

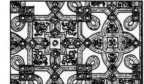

PLASTER CEILING

STRAPWORK ORNAMENT

FURNITURE

TO GET THE EFFECT OF dignity from heavy pieces of furniture and the warmth of wood, it is necessary to keep small articles and trimmings to a bare minimum. Furniture is very important in the Tudor house because the large proportions of the panelling, staircases, windows, etc. make delicate or fragile furniture look quite out of place. If you are lucky enough to have Jacobean style furniture, you don't need much more in the room. But if you have to add furniture here are some suggestions for achieving the right proportions.

Antiques—The Puritans brought the Jacobean style (in its most austere form) with them. Any of the very early New England chests, large refectory tables, etc. would be appropriate. The 1850's saw a great revival in "Elizabethan" furniture recognized by the many turnings and leather or tapestry covered seats, bulbous carved legs, stout stools. There is quite a lot (it was made up to the turn of the century) of this kind of furniture still around. The Mission Style, just coming into vogue now, also looks well because of its large proportions.

Contemporary—If you are furnishing in contemporary or a mixture, stick to the large, solid types: campaign furniture, classics like the Chesterfield leather sofa. Some of the large reproduction oak pieces are suitable.

WHILE A BENCH with a piece of carpet may not be our idea of comfort, beware of too much in the way of stuffed pieces in the room and use a bench with cushions where possible.

FABRIC

CREWEL WORK was done in "long and short" stitch on natural cotton or homespun with brightly colored wool and used to relieve the monotone of the wood in the room. The "Tree of Life" pattern from India was widely copied as it was later on in New England. Crewel (sources in *The Old-House Journal* Catalog) is excellent for drapes, bed-spreads and cushions. For the same reasons, printed India cottons are excellent.

THE MOST widely used textile in Tudor times was tapestry. Tapestry, however, is almost impossible to buy today. While some is advertised in the back pages of decorating magazines it is of poor quality and, even worse, French, of the pastoral scene with the "Empress as Milkmaid" type. There are some new fabrics that have a rough burlap-type finish. If they are patterned with a medieval type, naive floral design or a plain, dark color they can be effective. Plain wools are also good.

RICH TUDOR HOMES used elegant fabrics—velvet and damask mostly. Colors here are very important—crimson (which looks beautiful with oak) was very popular as were all the dark and rich colors—deep reds, greens, blues, browns and perhaps dark yellow.

PERHAPS THE MOST IMPORTANT thing with fabric is what not to use. Any material in a pastel—pink, violet, etc., will throw a Tudor room off, as will any fussy patterns: Little flowers, large roses, etc. Thin materials—light silks, sheers, etc. are also inappropriate.

CURTAINS WERE USED to keep out the draft and they were hung in a utilitarian manner—on rings from a heavy iron bar and pulled across the window by hand. Heavy gold gimp and braid were sometimes used for trim and as a rope to pull the curtains. Since it is virtually impossible to find any good old-fashioned heavy trimmings, macrame could serve for cords and trimmings.

FURNISHINGS, FLOORS AND WALLS

MIRRORS WERE IMPORTED during Elizabeth's reign and were rare and expensive. When used they had rich frames. Use mirrors sparingly and frame them elegantly. Holbein portraits were fashionable and a portrait or two will give a nice flavor.

ALTHOUGH ARMOUR was an important decorative accessory, as was heraldry, modern replicas do tend to look quite tacky and evoke the image of a brand new "Ye Olde Tavern" on the state highway.

FLOORS SHOULD BE polished to a rich, dark lustre and any floor coverings used should be small enough to leave plenty of wood showing. Straw mats are appropriate as are small Oriental or "Turkey work" carpets. Small strips of carpet were used in old English houses on chests, cupboards and tables as well as floors.

WALLS ARE preferably white or creamy beige. White is especially effective with beamed ceilings. Since wallpaper was rare, hand-blocked and very expensive in Tudor times, it is best to say away from paper. Most patterned papers will be anachronistic and give an undesirable look of fragility to the Tudor room.

LATE 19TH CENTURY DECORATION

By Carolyn Flaherty

AS MORE AND MORE old-house owners become involved in restoring Victorian houses to their original architectural charm, the question of how to decorate them becomes more urgent. Many people never had any intention of getting into period decoration, but after a few years of very hard work they have on their hands a house with lovely plasterwork, beautiful parquet floors, and period lighting fixtures.

THEY HAVE GOTTEN THIS FAR, and they want to continue the Victorian look and feel of the house they have so lovingly restored. But they also may not be overly fond of the stereo-typed image of antimaccasars, beribboned lamps, and frou-frou all atop a carpet of bright red cabbage roses.

THE VICTORIAN ERA produced many theories of decoration usually voiced by cranky gentlemen who decried the poor taste of the day. One such man was Charles Eastlake whose influence was felt throughout the late Victorian era. Another was Henry Hudson Holly. Holly is mainly remembered for his very popular books concerning architecture. His volume, "Holly's Country Seats," published in 1863, presented designs and plans for rural and suburban houses which were widely copied around the country to build for a growing nation.

BUT HOLLY did not confine himself to the design of the house itself. A large section of his later book, "Modern Dwellings," published in 1878, is addressed to the decoration and furnishing of the house. Written in high Victorian dudgeon, he attacks the craftmanship, taste, manufactured goods, and attitudes of the day. But Holly is more than a negative voice of his time.

WITH A DEFINITE SET of guidelines for painting and decorating, use of color, fabric and furniture, he presents a sophisticated and elegant mode of decoration for the late 19th century house. He formed his theory of interior decoration by drawing on the more original work of A. J. Downing, Eastlake, and the creative genius of Dr. Christopher Dresser in England. But by putting it all together in an easy-to-read, popular book, it was easily digested by the public and had a wide influence on the American reader.

SOME OF MR. HOLLY'S suggestions, culled from his writings in his own words, are presented here as a practical set of guidelines for decorating in an authentic late 19th century manner:

COLOR AND WALL TREATMENTS

COLOR CAN GIVE prominence or subordination. Blue produces the effect of distance, and if placed upon the ceiling, causes it to appear higher, or, if in a recess, will deepen it. Yellow, on the contrary, appears to advance toward the eye; and, if used upon the ceiling, will seem to lower it, or if upon a projecting moulding, will exaggerate its prominence. Red is the only color that remains stationary.

IT IS GENERALLY ADMITTED that furniture and costume show to a better advantage when the walls of an apartment are dark, while pictures look well upon a light background. In order to accommodate these requirements, the dado, or lower three feet of the walls, may be dark in color; the surface, where the pictures are to be hung, of a neutral tint; while in the cornice and ceiling any number of brilliant hues may appear. By this means a harmonious gradation of colors is achieved. Indeed, it would be well if this arrangement of colors were to be made the rule in decorating apartments. The heaviest and richest colors should be upon the floor or near it, and the lightest and most brilliant either upon or in the neighborhood of the ceiling.

A DARK COLOR, also, when applied to a skirting or dado, gives the effect of strength, which is always desirable to suggest in parts bearing a super-incumbent weight. Brown, rich maroon, dull bronze-green, or even black, may be used here to advantage.

Brown, rich maroon, dull bronze-green, or even black, may be used here to advantage.

THE ASSOCIATION OF COLOR with strength claims a larger part in decoration than is generally supposed. Thus, the trimmings of the exterior of a dwelling, if painted a color darker than the body, seem to produce a constructive effect, and convey the idea of ribs and stanchions supporting the house. So, too, the frame of a panel, if painted darker, gives the idea of strength, while the panel itself, being light, appears to be supported.

A SKIRTING OR MARGIN ALSO, having in any way the effect of a frame, should be emphasized by a stronger color. This includes cornices and trimmings of doors and windows. These trimmings, or architraves, as they are called, should be of a color more pronounced than the wall, but not so dark as the surbase, unless black be introduced, in which case one or two narrow lines of bright color or gold may be added. When black is used, it would be well to have a portion of it polished, thus producing a contrast between a bright and dead surface.

DOORS SHOULD BE DARKER than the walls—something in tone between them and the trimmings. Thus if a wall be citrine, the door may be low-toned Antwerp blue or dark bronze-green; but in either case a line of red, being complementary to both, should be run around the trimmings.

CEILINGS AND MOULDINGS

HOLLY ALSO has some definite opinions about the treatment of ceilings and mouldings:

CEILINGS ARE ESPECIALLY susceptible to ornamentation, for the reason that their entire surface may be seen at once. If we wish to limit the decoration of our rooms, let us expend our efforts here, as the walls and floors canbe relieved by pictures and furniture.

I WOULD RECOMMEND the avoidance of structural members, and especially of that chef d'oeuvre of plaster art, the centre-piece, with its impossible flowers and feeble ornaments. It would be better to use some flat design in color, making it the principal feature of the ceiling, reaching, if you choose, to within a few inches of the border. I say border, as the cornice, unless broad, is much improved by being extended with a margin of color. Now, these borders on the ceiling are like the dado on the wall, and have the effect of breaking up its broad surface. The same rule applies to floors. By surrounding them with a margin of darker color, a similar advantage is attained.

IT MAY NOT BE INAPPROPRIATE to introduce around the ceiling a margin of some tasteful design in wallpaper—one, for instance, in which brilliant colors appear on a gold ground. In a large room, the effect would be good if this margin were the entire width of the roll. It might also be appropriately edged with a wooden moulding.

A LARGE MOULDING on top of the dado may frequently be employed with advantage. It not only improves the appearance, but, if placed at the proper height above the floor, it will also serve to protect the wall from the chafing of chairs and other furniture.

LOWER MEMBERS ought never to be light and so gilt mouldings should not be placed below the level of the eye. Therefore, black walnut or ebony are more appropriate here.

AS A GENERAL RULE, if light, transparent tints are used, the moulding should be black. If a dark or maroon inlay is employed, gilt mouldings would make a pleasing contrast. The remainder of the ceiling, if low, should be of some tint calculated to give an appearance of elevation, such as, for instance, one of the many delicate shades of blue or violet.

DECORATION IN GENERAL

HOLLY WENT TO ENGLAND in 1856 and was very impressed with the new "Queen Anne" movement. Many architects, designers and craftsmen in England were rejecting the Gothic style as too church-like for domestic living. The "free classic" or Queen Anne style was emerging. Holly was the first to bring these ideas back to America. Here are some of his miscellaneous remarks about decoration in general:

WALLPAPER

LIKE OTHER INDUSTRIES that have come under the influence of the general advance in decorative art, the manufacture of wallpaper has greatly improved. (Holly, did, however complain that there was not enough interest in good wallpaper to warrant the import of the famous William Morris papers.–Ed.)

THE BREAKING UP OF WALL SURFACES with frieze and dado is one of the peculiar characteristics of the English designs, and in this way some of the best combinations of color and pattern are produced. The dados are sometimes of a checkered chocolate pattern, relieved with gold and black, while the intermediate space above contains a neutral design, as introducing moss or delicate ivy.

THE FRIEZE is of an utterly different treatment, sometimes Japapnese in character, positive in color, and either conventional or natural in design. In some, storks, or other fowl, in various attitudes seem gliding through the air. In others, vines and trellis-work, laden with vivid green and golden fruit, relieve the frieze as if the intermediate space represented a wall or screen, over which the various scenes of the vegetable and animal kingdom are made to show in bold outline.

FOR A ROOM in which convivial conversation, wines, and viands are to be enjoyed, the color should never be light, but of neutral or complementary tint. In reception rooms or parlors, the eye should be gratified, the senses of the palate not being brought into competition; and hence floral designs and gay colors–something of an enlivening nature–would be appropriate.

THE FLATNESS OF A WALL should be left undisturbed, and the decoration as little obtrusive as possible. For instance, use a diaper pattern (a diagonal pattern made up of regular repeats of small geometric or floral motifs, often surrounded by connecting lines) that imitates a flat stencil design. No attempt should be made to show figures in relief with shades and shadows which are in bad taste and produce a disagreeable effect. Such vulgarisms are, however, happily passing away; yet the public taste is far from being cultivated in these matters; and paper, instead of forming a background to pictures, is apt to assert itself far beyond its due importance.

GENERAL

DINING ROOMS–Dining rooms, as a general thing, should be treated in dark colors, so that their walls may form an agreeable background for the tablecloth and fixtures. A white tablecloth is generally too glaring in its effect and out of keeping with the surroundings. For general purposes, one of a cream tint is preferable.

PLANTS–An inexpensive method of decoration is the introduction of flowers, according to a system quite common in England, but only recently introduced here. It consists of an arrangement of plants in the fireplaces in summer. Of course, in a position like this, where the sun cannot reach them, there are only certain plants which could thrive, as for instance, the English ivy, or some varieties of fern. If cut flowers, which can be changed as they fade, are added, the effect will be as bright and cheerful as that of a wood or sea-coal fire in winter.

THE BUNGALOW STYLE

By Renee Kahn

THE PEOPLE NEXT DOOR live in a bungalow. They were quite surprised to hear this, having assumed that their modest cabin just grew, without any aesthetic rhyme or reason.

THEY WERE EVEN MORE SURPRISED when I explained that their humble bungalow was far more than a winterized cottage, and that its heritage was a combination of Japanese, Spanish, Bengali, and Swiss architecture, to say nothing of our native barns, log cabin, stick, and shingle style. As if this wasn't impressive enough, I threw in Frank Lloyd Wright and the Prairie style. "A variation of Bungalow," I explained.

THE TERM ITSELF comes from the Hindustani word "Bangla" (literally "from Bengal") and signifies a low house surrounded by porches. These houses were not typical native dwellings, but were the "rest houses" built by the English government in India for the use of foreign travellers. Rambling one storey structures, they were designed to withstand the heat of the Indian climate, and had wide overhanging eaves, stone floors, and long, breeze-filled corridors. Deep verandahs (another Indian word) provided additional shade. The word "bungalow" was brought back to England by retiring civil servants, and eventually came to describe any modest, low-slung residence of picturesque lines.

IN THE UNITED STATES, the term "bungalow" supplanted the word "cottage" and was popular because of its euphonious sound and exotic connotations. During its heyday, prior to World War I, thousands of bungalows were built.

SOME WERE EXTRAORDINARY examples of fine craftsmanship, such as those built by Greene & Greene in California, while most were hastily slapped together from $5.00 mail order plans.

DESPITE WIDE VARIATIONS in style, cost and location, the bungalow had certain, almost universal characteristics. Its lines were low and simple, with wide, projecting roofs. It had no second storey (or at most a modest one), large porches (verandahs), and was made of informal materials. It was primarily for use as a summer, or resort house, except in the warm California climate, where it was easily adapted to all year round use.

CONSTRUCTION MATERIALS emphasized the humble and the unostentatious. One wit defined the bungalow as "a house that looks as if it had been built for less money than it actually cost." Another famous remark was "the least house for the most money." Although low cost materials such as rough boards and fieldstone were emphasized, the bungalow was not an inexpensive house to build. With all, or most, of the rooms on one floor, there was a need for more of the costly wall and roof area than in a two-storey house of comparable size. In addition, more land was needed to accomodate this spread-out plan. Despite these cost factors, the one-storey house, without stairs for the housewife to climb, was enormously popular, and was eventually transformed into the ranch house of today.

And advertisement for bungalows that appeared in House Beautiful *in May 1908.*

Greene and Greene designed this bungalow in Pasadena, California, in 1905. Although the large overhanging eaves are designed for a sunny clime, this feature was copied in the north and east in many bungalows inspired by this design. Photo from the Greene & Greene Library appears in the book, **Greene & Greene.**

PORCHES WERE an essential part of the Bungalow style, but unfortunately, they were designed for sunnier climates, and darkened the interior of the house. This was often overcome by constructing the porch with an open roof, like a trellis, which could be covered by vines or an awning. Porch roofs frequently echoed the gable of the house, but were placed off to one side. Posts were made of boulders, or covered with shingles, contributing to the desired "natural" look. This natural look also extended to the outside wood finish, which was either left plain or stained, sometimes with a lump of asphalt dissolved in hot turpentine.

WHILE THE NAME and original concept of the Bungalow style came from India, it was native Japanese, Spanish, and Swiss architecture that influenced it the most. There were other influences as well: Creole plantation architecture, and American Stick and Shingle styles. Even barn and log cabin construction played a part. In other words, the entire repertoire of international timber building styles.

IT MAY SEEM DIFFICULT to comprehend, but the Chicago World's Fair, the great Columbian Exposition of 1893, which plunged America further into a Classical revival, also encouraged the development of the Bungalow style.

THE ECONOMIC SETBACKS of the 1890s provided a need for simpler residences, and the Fair showed the public how these might be made to look. Much attention was focused on the Japanese buildings, as well as the Louisiana exhibit, styled after a Creole plantation house. In the decades following the exposition, Chicago's wealthy North Shore became dotted with bungalows, largely influenced by Louis Sullivan, who had experimented with the form a few years earlier.

IT WAS CALIFORNIA, however, that became the hotbed of the bungalow. Here, the one-storey cottage, planned more for comfort than elegance, became a symbol of the state. A number of factors were responsible. First of all, California was traditionally receptive to experiments and new ideas. The mild climate and spacious terrain lent themselves to informal construction and casual living. There was also no conservative colonial tradition to return to, as there was in the East. Whatever tradition there was was the Spanish hacienda style, which was readily compatible with the bungalow.

THE PROXIMITY to the Orient also encouraged an interest in the Japanese house, and contemporary magazines referred to "Bungalows in the Japanese style" or "the Japanese Bungalow." These buildings were rambling and irregular in plan with much open timber work, lightweight siding, and

deep eaves. Other Oriental touches were posts resting on sunken round stones and turned-up eaves, pagoda style.

THE CALIFORNIA BUNGALOW reached its zenith in the turn of the century work of the brothers, Charles and Henry Greene. They were architects in the Craftsman style, not as famous as Frank Lloyd Wright, but arising out of the same tradition. They succeeded in creating a rambling, informal house that used natural materials, and was superbly integrated with the landscape. While Japanese, Swiss, and Spanish influences are evident, they managed to transform them into a uniquely Californian expression.

AT THE OTHER END of the quality spectrum were the innumerable plan books which spread the California Bungalow style. "Direct from Bungalow land," they advertised. Henry L. Wilson, the "Bungalow Man," one of its most successful promoters, produced a book in 1910, partially entitled: *The Bungalow Book, A Short Sketch Of The Evolution Of The Bungalow From Its Primitive Crudeness To Its Present State Of Artistic Beauty And Cozy Convenience* . . . It cost a dollar, and in two and a half years time went into five editions. While Wilson claimed Oriental and Spanish Colonial influences, his most obvious source of ideas was the Swiss chalet.

IT WOULD BE ALMOST IMPOSSIBLE to list all the variations of the bungalow style. There were almost as many as there were bungalows. However, certain broad classifications do exist.

ONE OF THE MOST POPULAR would have to be Southern California type and its offshoot, the Patio bungalow. Next, was the Swiss chalet, which was easily adapted to the bungalow form, most because of its wide, overhanging eaves. These were frequently built on a hill, or mountainsides, and had quaint balconies with sawn board railings.

ANOTHER PROMINENT VARIETY was the Adirondack Lodge, or Catskill summer home, which was usually a glorified log cabin. They soon became a fad with wealthy city families, and provided an elaborate mountain retreat for entertainment purposes. Built out of horizontally laid logs, they came the closest to a, Early American style of construction.

ALSO COMMON IN THE EAST was the New England seacoast bungalow, which had a strong Colonial flavor. Long and narrow, it stretched out along along the dunes, capturing the view and the ocean breezes. In keeping with bungalow philosophy, the seacoast bungalow harmonized well with its surroundings. Low, horizontal lines repeated the rhythm of the dunes, and silvery shingles captured the reflections of the water.

THE IDEA OF HARMONIZING a house with its natural surroundings also lay behind much of the work of Frank Lloyd Wright. His versions of the Bungalow style were known as Prairie houses, and contributed significantly to the Bungalow vogue. Like the prairie, they emphasized gentle, horizontal lines. Their dormerless, wide-eaved roofs enhanced the feeling of closeness to the ground. While Wright was reluctant to acknowledge it, he was greatly influenced by Japanese architecture, especially in the strong relationship of his indoor and outdoor areas. Unlike the typical resort bungalow, Wright's houses were meant for year-round use, and were often two or more storeys high.

INTERIORS

THE FLOOD OF LITERATURE after the turn of the century brought much advice on how to furnish the bungalow. Simplicity and lack of pretension were the main goals. Gustav Stickley, the furniture maker, was also editor of the magazine *The Craftsman,* and was one of the major promoters of the Bungalow style, which he referred to as "Craftsman Homes." In 1909 he wrote: "When luxury enters in, and a thousand artificial requirements come to be regarded as real needs, the nation is on the brink of degeneration."

STICKLEY, a disciple of William Morris, was also responsible for the sturdy oak furniture commonly known as "Mission." These comfortable, handcrafted pieces were considered appropriate for the bungalow, as were the plainer versions of wicker and rattan. Easy-to-care-for leather or canvas cov-

Rancho de Santa Fe, in California, circa 1924, combines the Spanish hacienda style with the popular bungalow.

ered the seats. No pretty bric-a-brac lay about, only sturdy Art pottery and brass or copper bowls. Matting and shag rugs were suggested for the floors; however, Orientals were "never out of place." Surfaces were simple, and covered with natural looking stains.

Described in the 1908 Sears, Roebuck catalog as a "strictly Mission rocker," this style of furniture was proclaimed by Sears to be "no longer an experiment but one of the most popular styles for all those who appreciate beauty and simplicity of design."

$5.65

PLASTER WALLS WERE TO BE avoided unless the house was for year-round use. One possible wall treatment left the studding bare, another created a panelled effect with boards and battens placed at right angles to each other.

STILL OTHER acceptable interior finishes were burlap, matting, or panelling made out of stock lumberyard doors nailed together. Ceilings were often beamed, especially in the living room.

FIREPLACES were a dominant feature of the bungalow, and one publication flatly stated that "a bungalow without a fireplace would be as strange as a garden without flowers." In keeping with the informality of the house, these were usually made of large, untrimmed rocks, and were without fancy mantels.

A FIREPLACE in the living room was an absolute necessity, but smaller ones could also be placed in other rooms. Generally speaking, "inconspicuous informality" was the goal.

THE STYLE

IT SEEMS IRONIC that the bungalow originally had its greatest impact upon the intellectual upper-middle class who valued it for its "honesty" and "practicality." Despite its lofty aspirations and exotic sources, the style ended up sloppily imitated in thousands of tacky boxes. It has come to represent both the best and the worst in American architecture from the turn of the century until the 1920s.

IT DID, HOWEVER, make positive contributions to the American home with its lack of pretentiousness, its use of natural materials, and its effort to integrate the

house with its surroundings. Its direct descendant, the ranch house, a somewhat characterless version of the bungalow, remains today one of the most popular forms of domestic architecture.

STICKLEY SAW THEM as ". . . the kind of houses that children will rejoice all their lives to remember as 'home,' and that give a sense of peace and comfort to the tired men who go back to them when the day's work is done."

NO SMALL TASK.

Special $8.49 Complete

These wood and glass lighting devices were popular for the bungalow along with pierced metal lanterns.

1OK6040 Beautiful Large Mission Style Hexagonal Electric Chandelier that hangs on

AMBER ART GLASS SHADE
WOOD MISSION
WEATHERED OAK FINISH

Electric and Gas—Ht. 19 in., fumed oak finish, 1½ in. amber art glass shade, 2 in. skirt, square base and column. 1 in shipping carton, 10 lbs.
C3182—Electric..) Each
C3183—Gas........) $3.25

One Corner of a Man's Room in the McHugh-Mission Style

An Arts and Crafts interior–bungalows were meant to be furnished in a similar style. The predominately wood rooms were highlighted with touches of brass, copper, and lighting fixtures with colored glass or candles. Illustration from **The Forgotten Rebel,** *a monograph on Gustav Stickley by John Crosby Freeman, published by Century House.*

Kitchens and Bathrooms

EARLY AMERICAN KITCHENS

By Carolyn Flaherty

IN MOST EARLY AMERICAN houses the room that was originally the kitchen has long ago become the dining room or living room. The large room featuring a brick or stone fireplace, and often surrounded by moulded wood panelling–an anachronism for preparing food–is often the lovliest room in the house. There is little reason to place a stove and sink in such a room and so the actual kitchen is relegated to another room. It is the intent of this article to deal with the problem of that room, often lacking in any built-in charm of its own but which should harmonize with the rest of the house.

IF YOU DO HAVE A ROOM WITH A fireplace that you wish to use as a kitchen, the problem is to work-in the modern appliances while maintaining the atmosphere of the warm colonial kitchen. The cooking and keeping apparatus should not be the first thing to strike the eye.

THE ESSENTIAL FIREPLACE, around which the early kitchen functioned, dominated the room with its large size and ample hearth. The fireplace provided heat, a cooking place, and lighting, and most of the the living in a small house was done around it. Kept continuously burning with whatever wood was locally available, some were so huge that they had seats built in the sides for old people and children to warm themselves. Large iron firebacks with raised designs were placed at the back to reflect the heat and prevent crumbling of the brick or stone from the intense heat of the constant fires.

WHILE THESE HUGE early fireplaces are attractive they were not very efficient as they were so cavernous that they did not throw enough heat into the room. They were used mostly in the 17th century and the early part of the 18th and so are not really "authentic" to many homes.

MANY EARLY KITCHENS in the South were relegated to a separate building. This lessened the danger of fire and kept the family's living quarters cooler in summer and free of cooking odors.

EARLY AMERICAN KITCHENS were starkly simple, with decoration and color found only in the ornamental gourds, ears of corn or string of peppers hung over the fireplace.

IN THE LATTER PART OF THE 18th century and the early part of the 19th, fireplaces became smaller and the kitchen became more cheerful and colorful with the addition

This typical 17th century kitchen is quite medieval in character–low-ceilinged, dark and showing the solid frame of the house with its exposed ceiling beams and posts. The vertical boards were left unpainted as were all interiors in that century.

THIS IS THE KITCHEN in the Hurley Patentee Manor in Kingston, New York, a large stone house built in 1745 and attached to a 1696 Dutch cottage. The house is owned by Stephen and Carolyn Waligurski.

WHEN THE WALIGURSKIS bought the manor in 1963, the kitchen was only half the size it is now because the original back wall of the kitchen had fallen off in 1924 and it had been partioned. To restore the room to its original plan, Stephen followed the lines of the original foundation and built up with stones from the property. The only change he made (from a description given him by a descendant of the original family) was to add another window from old wood and glass that exactly duplicates the exisiting ones. The ceiling beams were set into place with the help of the family car and block and tackle (also brains and brawn).

A WARM AND CHARMING EARLY AMERICAN kitchen was then created by the Waligurskis using their knowledge of Early American settings, their ingenuity and some plain hard work.

THIS HALF OF THE large 20' × 16' room shows an Early American kitchen much as it would have been, but less austere. The wallpaper is a documentary reproduction, from the local wallpaper store, of a colonial fruit and vegetable pattern. Carolyn made the simple curtain arrangement from a deep red homespun fabric.

STEPHEN MADE THE large trestle table from 200-year-old wood found on the property, and the ladderback chairs are old reproductions. The fireplace was completely reconstructed out of salvaged bricks.

BOTH THE CONE CHANDELIER and the fireplace screen are Hurley Patentee reproductions made by Stephen. The large iron pot in front of the fireplace is an old hog-scalding kettle that was found on the property.

IN THE MANNER of early colonial housewives, Carolyn has hung sage from the beams for drying. The large bench at the right of the picture is an old settle. It provides seating in front of the fire, but then swings into a hutch table to provide extra work surface in the other part of the kitchen.

CAROLYN WALIGURSKI loves Early American houses, history and antiques. But she is also a very busy lady with four children, a full-time teacher, a creative homemaker who does all her own sewing and decorating, and an active participant in church and community activities.

SO ALONG WITH THE CHARM of a restored period kitchen, she also requires one that is totally up-to-date with all the modern conveniences. And they are all there in the working part of the kitchen but cleverly arranged so that they are inconspicuous. The room is harmonious because the textures and colors found in the room are carried into the work area.

APPLIANCES and fixtures are tucked into a floor area of approximately 8' × 5'. The efficient storage space is carefully worked out to utilize all available space. Stephen and Carolyn built all the cabinets and panelling themselves with birch. The refrigerator is boxed in, leaving a 6 in. space above for ventilation. The end closet, next to the refrigerator, is a full-length grocery cabinet with door shelves. The dishwasher, a KitchenAid, was bought with an empty-frame front, in which a panel could be slipped. They added a birch panel to match the cabinets. A platter rack is closeted above the stove and beside the stove is a hanging pot rack and lid drawer. The corner cabinet contains revolving shelves.

REFRIGERATOR AND STOVE are copper brown. A bakery board covers the top of the stove when it is not in use. Not visible is a set-in light housed at the bottom of the cabinet beside the sink. The pierced lantern with four candle arms is another Hurley Patentee reproduction.

THE ENTIRE FLOOR area of the kitchen is covered with practical Armstrong 12-inch vinyl tiles in a pattern called Cinnamon.

of painted walls and painted decoration on floors and furniture. This is the traditional Early American kitchen that is so admired and imitated today. There are many houses built in a later period like the plain Greek Revival style or the rural farmhouse that do not have any particular architectural features in the big old room that is the kitchen and can benefit from decorating in the earlier colonial manner.

WALLS AND CEILINGS

THE FIRST AREAS to consider when decorating the Early American kitchen are the walls and ceiling. They certainly do not have to be all wood. Only the very early kitchens were all wood and if you are lucky enough to have a room that has original moulded panelling it is probably the dining room now. By the second quarter of the 18th century the colonists began to use paint—more as a preservative than for decorative purposes. It must be remembered that paint was expensive and wood was cheap. But as soon as they could afford it—or had the time to make it—the colonists used paint to relieve the monotony of the all-wood kitchen.

IT WAS THEN that they began to use cheaper woods—like knotty pine—because they were to be painted or stained a color anyway. So, contrary to the urging of the plastic-panelling manufacturers, covering a room with knotty pine (real or ersatz) is not the way to decorate a colonial kitchen. If you wish to have a lot of wood in the kitchen, use only real wood such as clear pine and coat with a varnish that will give a slightly antiqued effect. Other fads for the rustic look, like using weathered barnboards for wallcoverings, are also a matter of personal taste but are not appropriate to the Early American kitchen.

RATHER THAN BUYING NEW WOOD, use paint and wallpaper to decorate for economy and authenticity. There are very many documentary wallpapers available at moderate prices that have been reproduced with washable surfaces that do not detract from their appearance and are very suitable for a kitchen.

EVEN BEFORE paint was commonly used, the colonists relieved the monotony and darkness of the small-windowed, dark room by building plaster walls. The plaster was made of crushed oyster shells, sand and sea water. They lightened its brownish shade with a coat of whitewash, made by slaking quicklime in water, and often added vegetable dyes for color. They later learned to make milk paint and then oil paint. Color-starved colonial housewives loved the cheerfulness this brought to their kitchen.

THESE EARLY COLORS WERE STRONG and vivid. Never use a pastel shade when painting the Early American kitchen. Some of the colors used in decorating were yellow ochre, Prussian blue, Indian red, and strong greens. A coat of varnish tinted with raw umber will give a mellow, aged look to painted surfaces. A neutral shade like beige for walls is effective with a deeper color like Indian red for woodwork or cabinets.

AS PAINT BECAME more available, the fancy-painting techniques of stencilling, marbleizing and graining also became popular; these techniques will add atmosphere and interest to walls and cabinets and are the most economical way to decorate. The kitchen is a terrific place to try out some of these crafts. Covering the fancypainting with a coat of washable varnish will provide a durable surface that is easily cleaned.

AMERICAN FOLK DECORATION

THE DECORATIVE PAINTING done in the 17th, 18th, and 19th centuries is a very important part of Early American decoration. Not confined to walls or floors, it was used to decorate chairs, chests, tinware, clocks, glass, etc. This kind of decoration can be used in the Early American kitchen for cabinets, walls, furniture or even a refrigerator door. But to use it effectively it is necessary to know its history, the types found in different regions and periods as well as precise instructions for each kind. This would mean writing a book. Fortunately, somebody has written an excellent one. *American Folk Decoration* by Jean Lipman with practical instruction by Eve Meulendyke gives an excellent background as well as complete instructions for the decoration of all the above-mentioned areas as well as for fabrics, houses, and even barns.

FLOORS

COLONIAL KITCHEN FLOORS were made of random wide board planks, stone or brick. Wood floors were washed every day with soap and sand as an abrasive. New dry sand was spread in the morning and housewives swept it into scroll or herringbone patterns.

UNATTRACTIVE WOOD FLOORS with no particular distinction will give added color and character to the kitchen if they are painted in a rich color or in one of the fancypainting techniques.

THE EARLY AMERICAN HOUSEWIFE made wool and cotton striped carpets. There is a record, in 1830, of a minister's wife who painted her floor "carpet-like" with stripes of red, green, blue, yellow and purple. Covered with a clear protective finish, this old way of painting a floor would be an authentic, practical and lively kitchen floor treatment.

THE HOUSEWIFE was Mrs. Bascomb and an excerpt

from her journal is recorded in an excellent paperback, *Floor Coverings In New England Before 1850,* by Nina Fletcher Little. She gives an illustrated history of the rag rugs and wool carpets made by New England housewives. Also discussed are the manufacturered carpets, floor cloths, and the painted and stencilled floors done by fancypainters.

THE POPULARITY of the colonial decorating style has caused manufacturers to offer a wide range of floor coverings that are appropriate for Early American decoration. Armstrong, in particular, has quite a few patterns resembling brick or stone in tiles and linoleum that come in attractive clay and brick tones.

STORAGE SPACE

WHEN PLANNING STORAGE SPACE in the Early American kitchen utilize any antique chests, dressers or cupboards you can. These were storage spaces for linens, etc. in the Colonial kitchen. Wood cabinets will look good but if you don't have good wood you can refinish old painted cabinets with a rich Early American paint color and perhaps add some painted decoration–either freehand or stencilled.

THERE IS NO RULE that says cabinets can only be above a counter top and, in fact, in colonial times they never were. When planning cabinets try to include one or two of the old-fashioned full length kind.

REPRODUCTIONS OF EARLY AMERICAN hardware on cabinets, doors, and windows give a dramatic period effect. *The Old-House Journal* Buyers' Guide lists quite a few blacksmiths that make these reproductions.

ONE THING THAT will ruin a period atmosphere in the Early American kitchen is the kind of overly-bright lighting so often used in kitchens today. There is a large number of companies making reproductions of early lighting fixtures–chandeliers, sconces, lanterns (listed in The Buyers' Guide). If additional light is needed it is usually better to use a recessed light enclosed at the bottom of a cabinet so that it is not visible.

IF CURTAINS ARE USED they should be simple and hung from a rod placed inside the window frame. Fabric should be cotton or a homespun type, or a synthetic that looks similar.

KITCHENS IN THE VICTORIAN HOME

By Carolyn Flaherty

THE VICTORIAN KITCHEN is the one room in the house that the old-house owner may not want to re-create as it was. Most kitchens in the Victorian period were inconvenient, uncomfortable and unattractive. The kitchen in the well-to-do Victorian home was given about as much consideration as the topic of sex at a Victorian dinner party.

IT IS UNUSUAL to find a picture of the kitchen in the many books that feature period rooms. That is because most of the kitchens of the Victorian period were for the use of the servants. Generally painted all-over in an institutional green or cream colored enamel, they contained none of the decorative elements found in the rest of the house. With the burgeoning prosperity of the Industrial Revolution, even comparatively simple homes had at least one kitchen servant.

SIMPLER HOMES without servants had utilatarian kitchens that were equipped for the hard work it was to prepare food one hundred year ago, but usually without thought to decoration.

THE FARMHOUSE KITCHEN was inconvenient and poorly equipped by today's standards—freezing cold in winter until the fire was lit, and hot in the summer. But because the family meals were generally eaten in the kitchen, the room was large and cheerful. But one thing all types of kitchens had in common was the plainness of their decoration. It was only after the practice of hiding the cooking utensils and food from view became popular in the 20th century that wall-papers and fabrics designed especially for the kitchen became popular.

TODAY'S OLD-HOUSE owner wants a more attractive and convenient kitchen than the one that was originally there. Because of the different way food is packaged, we will also want to hide many of the cereal and cookie boxes that fill the grocery shelves. So we need to add eye-appeal with decoration.

ONE OF THE MOST ATTRACTIVE features in an old house is the large size of the kitchen rather than the tiny-box room that houses of recent vintage have allotted to the kitchen. These large rooms make cheerful and comfortable eat-in kitchens whether or not there is an additional dining room.

MANY OF THESE OLD KITCHENS will have some Victorian architectural features in them—wains-cotting, plate rails, glass-door cabinets. Whatever their condition, they are worth reviving. Some details like wainscotting and plate rails can be re-created in a plain room with stock mouldings.

WHEN PURCHASING STOVES and refrigerators, the ones with the simplest lines and least amount of shiny control panels will not only look better in the Victorian kitchen but will most likely work better and last longer than their overly-designed and under-engineered counterparts.

PROBABLY THE MOST IMPORTANT element in decorating the old kitchen is a negative—what to avoid. Under this heading comes any of the splashy vinyls. They will say "modern" and ruin the nostalgic effect. Fortunately there are many vinyl floorings available in uncomplicated patterns and a wide variety of neutrals and colors. Choosing materials for kitchen surfaces depends a great deal on the budget. Real ceramic tile for floor, backsplash or wall decoration or butcher block for worktables or counters are quite expensive. They are, however, well worth the investment for the durability and beauty they provide.

LETTING COOKING UTENSILS show—on shelves or hanging—will give a "real kitchen" look that is appropriate even if the objects are not antiques. Out of place aesthetically are the many gadgety appliances that are unnecessary and demand a great deal of time to take them in and out of storage, clean and (if possible) fix them—the electric hot dog broiler, grilled cheese sandwich maker, etc. The appliances that are real aids to food preparation and make kitchen work easier are really few in number—blenders, toasters, mixers.

ALSO ADDING TO THE WRONG KIND OF kitchen clutter are the many cutsie "reproductions" that are not reproductions of anything that ever was—colonial paper towel holders, toaster covers with gold eagles—they are not only the wrong period but downright ridiculous.

LIGHTING IS A VERY IMPORTANT FACTOR in achieving a period look in the kitchen. Along with the all-white, gleaming chrome kitchen resembling an operating room that became fashionable around the 1930's, kitchens also became very over-lighted. Usually one overhead light is suffcient and this should be an old or reproduction fixture if possible as it sets the mood for the room. If additional lighting is required

ADD A PLATE RAIL FOR AUTHENTIC TOUCH

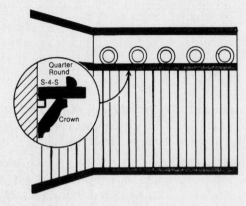

THE PLATE RAIL can also be made wider than shown in the diagrams to become a shelf. It can then hold crockery and pots instead of plates. The WP specifications for mouldings in the diagram below are from the Western Wood Moulding Producers.

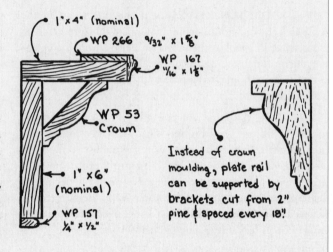

A PLATE RAIL CAN ADD decoration and storage space to a kitchen. A plate rail is like a chair rail in that it divides a wall for architectural interest. Used in old Pennsylvania Dutch kitchens, the plate rail was also a popular feature in Victorian homes—particularly in the dining room, above narrow-board wainscotting. Wainscotting can still be purchased at lumberyards (may require a special order) and a plate rail installed at the top. Or the plate rail alone can be used around the whole room—or just one wall.

TO GIVE THE VICTORIAN KITCHEN the character of the rest of the house, feature floor and wall treatments that are traditional and play down the modern appliances. Wood, wood-graining, and architectural detail mixed with some old or reproduction items will contribute to an old-fashioned kitchen atmosphere.

THE KITCHEN in the Harriet Beecher Stowe house in Hartford, Conn. exemplifies the best kind of kitchen of the Victorian period. It is light, cheerful and efficient. There was no evidence of the actual kitchen that belonged to Harriet in the restored house. This re-creation embodies the ideas of Mrs. Stowe and her sister Catherine Beecher, authors of a revolutionary book, *The American Woman's Home,* published in 1869. The book was an invaluable guide in the re-creation of this model kitchen.

THEIR BOOK was a treatise on the formation and maintenance of an economical, healthful and Christian home and covered child care, decoration and a good bit of theology. But the part that is interesting to us today is the section on home decoration and particularly the kitchen. These ideas are still modern a century later. They introduced the thought that the kitchen should be the core of the household. Some of their ideas, effected in the kitchen shown are:

• Bring the outside in. There are no curtains in the window. They were against the heavy draperies of the period as being unsanitary and felt curtains in the kitchen to be superfluous. If a curtain must be used, a thin, white fabric was recommended.

• Use plants wherever possible. Although there are no plants in the particular window shown, plants do abound in the windows of the Stowe House.

• The use of paint as a practical, easily cleaned and inexpensive decorative surface. The floor is painted–a common practice in both kitchen and bathroom. The painted, chestnut-grained cabinets are rich looking and yet are as easily cleaned as any other painted surface.

• The open shelves are attractive and quite convenient. They are patterned after an illustration in the book which is shown at the bottom of the page.

CATHERINE AND HARRIET thought the kitchen should be like a cook's galley in a steamship, with every article and utensil used in cooking arranged so that with one or two steps the cook can reach all that is needed. This was quite a departure from most kitchens of the period. While servants suffered the most from the lack of organization in large kitchens, even the smaller, servantless kitchens were generally laid out with little regard for the amount of steps taken by the woman who was doing the work.

A MODEL VICTORIAN KITCHEN

HARRIET BEECHER *Stowe's kitchen was a model of efficiency for its time. The bins, window casings, cabinets and shelves are bass wood and have been grained to resemble chestnut. Shelves are shallow so that one would not have more than one row of objects on a shelf. Walls are painted sunny yellow and the floor is painted gray. The coal range, patented in 1873, was rather sophisticated for its time as it was built into the chimney. Coal ranges were generally free-standing with a pipe going into the chimney.*

AN OLD-HOUSE KITCHEN THAT COMBINES CHARM AND CONVENIENCE

WHEN JOAN AND JOE FUDJINSKI moved into their 1909 limestone house in Brooklyn a decade ago, the first room they had to restore was the kitchen.

THE ENTIRE ROOM was covered with about five layers of paint–the outside coat a horrid shade of apple green. The floor was covered with a badly-worn, dark green linoleum. There was an old stove on legs that was falling apart and a 5-foot long sink. In Joan's words, "a dismal looking mess."

THE KITCHEN, a medium-sized "L" shaped room, is in the back of the house in the extension and when they moved in it was unheated and very cold. The first thing Joe did was to drop the ceiling and put in insulation.

NEXT THEY STRIPPED the paint from the cabinets, doors, window frames and corner beads. Under the layers of paint was a fine, solid oak.

FORTUNATELY, the Fudjinskis did not have a lot of money available for the kitchen when they began. For one thing, they could not afford the "kitchen contractor" so popular in city house restorations to put in the ubiquitous plain cabinets and formica counter tops.

THEY HAD TO GO SLOWLY–it was almost three years before the kitchen was finished. This provided the time to get used to the room, find out what would be convenient and discover what they really liked.

THE ONLY EXPENSIVE ITEMS in the room are the stove and the floor. Joan is a fine gourmet cook who does her own baking, etc., and she requires a kitchen that is functional, easy to clean and has adequate storage.

JOE WAS ABLE TO DO the work in the kitchen himself. He built all the shelves, cabinets and counter tops in the room, except the original oak cabinets.

AN UNUSUAL AND practical idea is the built-in wine rack shown on the next page. It occupies a space in a wall that would otherwise be dead space–opposite the stove and next to the entrance to the basement.

THE WALLPAPER, actually a contemporary pattern, is vinyl-coated and has a Victorian flavor. It is a rich red and blue and covers two walls; the other walls are painted white.

THE REFRIGERATOR had to be cater-cornered because of the lack of wall space in the room. When Joe suggested building shelves around it, Joan thought it would be corny. But after they were built, she found them to be a good place for storing large pieces, and wants to add a few more shelves for seldom used large pots. Most important for the old kitchen, however, they effectively play down and draw the eye away from the necessary modern refrigerator. The shelves are painted a rich flat red as are all the cabinets and radiator enclosure.

The counter tops are left in their natural color.

THE RADIATOR ENCLOSURE under the window adds another working surface and the shelf below doubles as a plate warmer. A dishwasher is inconspicuously tucked under the sink enclosure.

RANDOM-WIDTH oak floorboards made by Bruce Hardwood Floors were installed by Joe. They came very light in color and he stained them a walnut color. The boards have wooden pegs that add character. It is amazing that a wood floor has withstood ten years of abuse from a busy cook and four children. But it looks wonderful. Joan washes it with Spic and Span (never actually sloshing water–just a damp mop) and waxes it with Preen or a similar wood wax about three times a year.

JOAN NEEDED a no-nonsense, reliable stove. She also wanted a black one. The one she selected is a Crown semi-professional model. It has six burners, two ovens and two broilers, and has proved to be a dependable appliance. Joe plans to make a hood with an exhaust that will hang from chains.

NEATLY SOLVING THE PROBLEM of unattractive groceries, Joan put dotted swiss shirred curtain panels on the inside of the glass-door oak cabinets.

AN IMPORTANT CONTRIBUTION to the old-fashioned mood of the kitchen is the soft lighting. The only source of light is the reproduction lighting fixture. It is gray (unpainted) wrought iron and although it is of a quite earlier period, it looks very much in character with the wood and brick textures of the room. Dried thyme, basil and sage are hanging from it for ready use in cooking.

THE SOLID OAK ROUND TABLE was found in a second-hand store–a few years before these kind of pieces moved into the "almost antique" category. Because there is still such a large quantity of oak around, they make good buys and fit in nicely with the nostalgic kitchen.

THE WARM AND PLEASANT, yet very functional kitchen, that the Fudjinskis have created is largely a result of hard work and good taste. It also owes its success to the care given to what was already there, the lack of flashy non-essentials, the plain and reliable equipment, and the attention to detail that creates its individuality.

BATHROOMS IN THE OLD HOUSE

by Carolyn Flaherty

THE BATHROOM can be a real problem for the old-house restorer. Since many old houses didn't even have bathrooms in their previous life, it is sometimes a room that cannot be restored. The problem is more of relating it in general appearance to the rest of the house.

WHILE IT IS often easier and preferable to the old-house owner to have a completely modern bathroom, there are those who do not like the impact of a modern room in an old house. There is a great deal of available information for the planning and decoration of the modern bathroom and, therefore, there is no need to repeat any of it in this article. Rather, this is an effort at assisting the old-house owner who wants to retain or re-create a functional room with an ambiance related to the rest of the house.

THERE WAS, of course, no such thing as an Early American bathroom. Therefore there are no reproduction toilet articles that are not gimmicky. The sight of the valiant U.S. eagle adorning a cutesy plastic-pine "Colonial" toilet seat cover is accompanied by the apparition of early statesmen whirling in their respective graves. The little gold eagle on every practical and decorative object has become as much of a nuisance as the city pigeon.

A BATHROOM in an Early American house is either a much later addition or a converted bedroom with plain 20th-century fixtures. Decoration is therefore the only way to relate the bathroom to the main body of the house. A converted bedroom-to-bathroom usually means a rather large bathroom by modern standards.

COLOR, TEXTURE and pattern are the necessary ingredients. With a good choice of paint, paper and lighting fixtures, the room can be an extension of the style and period of the rest of the house.

WALLS can be papered with one of the many good reproduction wall-papers. Many of these papers come with a vinyl coating that makes them more durable but does not affect their old-fashioned appearance. Stencilling will give an Early American look to plaster walls. The patterns can be protected by apply-

ing a polyurethane or conventional varnish. The bathroom is a wonderful place to experiment with the stencilling technique because of the smaller size of the room. A small all-over design in a wallpaper or stencilled application will camouflage the irregularieties of an oddly shaped room.

SOME OF THE NEW colored bathtubs and other fixtures look good in the "new" Early American bathroom. Major manufacturers have bayberry greens, rich blues, and soft golds in their lines–hues that go well with the colors found in many of the reproduction wall-papers and fabrics. These deep shades are enhanced by the look of wood. You can buy ready-made or custom-made tubs enclosed in wood and sinks set into a wooden cabinet. If the present bathroom includes some worn, painted cabinets that are not very attractive, they can be grained to simulate the appearance of wood.

OBVIOUSLY, REPRODUCTIONS of Colonial lighting fixtures and hardware will help create a traditional look. A bathroom window offers another opportunity to restate the decorating theme. A simple arrangement of white or documentary print fabric in a tie-back or plain Shaker-style (similar to café curtains) would be appropriate.

VICTORIAN BATHROOMS

HOUSES BUILT AROUND 1850 and later demand an entirely different point of view. It is possible to re-create a late 19th-century bathroom. Even if the period you restore to is later than the house itself, it will most likely marry well in character. An understanding of the 19th-century bathroom is useful in this effort.

IT WAS NOT UNTIL THE 20TH CENTURY that bathrooms were in general use. As late as the 70s, even in affluent households the zinc tub was still placed in front of the bedroom fire for adults and the kitchen fire for children. Fortunately for the servants who had to fill and empty the large tubs, frequent bathing was thought to bring on lung disease and so the job was generally a weekly procedure.

THE VICTORIANS were also wont to go to great lengths to disguise sanitary fittings with wash-basins hidden in dressers, huge hooded baths in wardrobes, and toilets inset into all manner of cabinets. Actually, this latter custom was not new. Fine cabinetmakers like Sheraton and Hepplewhite did some of their finest work when turning out commodes for the wealthy.

EARLY BATHROOMS, with tub, sink and toilet all in one room, were large. Pipes were concealed by boxing-in tubs and toilets, usually with varnished mahogany. Wash-basins were set in bureau-like cabinets with marble tops. Other articles of furniture were placed in the bathroom for storage or relaxation—chairs, sofas, bureaus with heavily framed mirrors. Stained glass windows provided both privacy and elegance.

JUST BEFORE THE TURN OF THE CENTURY, a more open look, in the interests of cleanliness, became fashionable. Pipes were exposed so that they could be cleaned more easily and germs could not gather in enclosed spaces. Floors and walls were tiled, and tubs had ball and claw feet. A new innovation was the shower bath.

BY 1900 cast iron bathtubs with a porcelain coating had replaced the wooden box lined with sheet lead and sunken tubs with ornamental tiles were coming into use. Bathrooms tiled in pastel colors were not common until the 1920s.

BATHS WERE OFTEN placed in the center of the room during the Victorian era—a "new" idea being used by many decorators today for large bathrooms. In the 19th century, it sometimes didn't occur to the houseowner to have the bath installed any place other than were the old zinc hip-bath had been

– in front of the fire. Plumbing was generally installed in a former bedroom as the house-builder had not thought to make provision for a separate room to hold bathing and toilet facilities.

THE MOST ELEGANT and comfortable bathrooms were designed in the prosperous Edwardian era. King Edward VII, a man much concerned with pleasant surroundings, commissioned the gentleman dapper, one Mr. Crapper, to devise some of the most innovative sanitary fittings and fixtures ever made, then or now. The bathroom Mr. Crapper designed at Sandringham House in England is still in perfect working order. In fact, the few that could afford them were offered a wider choice of tubs, toilets, lavatories and hardware than the many are offered today.

THE TECHNOLOGY of bathroom plumbing has really advanced very little since the beginning of the century, and if some of the elegant, old fixtures were available today as reproductions they would no doubt find a large market. Today's fixtures tend to be less well designed for the body. Tubs are too small, wash-basins are too low with the faucets placed so close to the back that you can't get your hands wet, and the hardware is awkward to handle.

THE ESSENTIALS of a good bathroom are simplicity, style and cleanliness. Early bathrooms had as much attention paid to floor, wall and lighting treatments as to the fixtures themselves. It is the care given to all these elements as well as to the decorative acessories that gives an old bathroom its charm.

AS IN ANY OTHER ROOM, a bathroom can be given character and visual interest by emphasizing architectural details and wall divisions. Wood mouldings can be added for finishing at the top of wallpaper, or to divide the walls into panels. Keep wainscoting if you are lucky enough to have it. Probably made of softwood, it will most likely not be worth stripping but can be painted, grained or antiqued. Wallpaper borders can lend an old fashioned effect. Old walls that tend to crack and peel can be covered with a texture paint and accented with ceramic tile borders.

TEXTURES play an important part—real marble, ceramic tile, wood. Granite was a favorite English surface for lavatory tops and slate was often used. Painted imitations of these materials were also quite common. But the modern plastic versions of these materials—plastic marbelized tiles, plastic wood panelling, etc.—will destroy the nostalgic atmosphere.

STAINED AND LEADED GLASS WINDOWS were used for elegance and privacy in Victorian and Edwardian bathrooms. If you don't have one, and installing a new one is too expensive, a panel over the existing window can be used for the same effect. It is much less expensive than installing a window.

A Real Victorian Bathroom

The bathroom in the Harriet Beecher Stowe House in Hartford, Connecticut. Built in 1871, Mrs. Stowe lived in it from 1873 until her death in 1896.

The side walls are papered over tongue-and-groove wainscoting. The floor is spatter-painted in five colors, commonly done in the 19th century. The small cherry mirror belonged to Mrs. Stowe and the spool-turned towel rack is a typical Victorian accessory. The very ingenious contraption on the end wall combines a tin-lined bathtub and sink with a kerosene heater. At the very top is a tank, which feeds the heating tank. The marble sink is on two tracks with a brass pull. Folded doors can be closed to completely hide it from view. The tank toilet (the top is hidden in the picture) is a "front flush" type with the bowl in the shape of an elephant trunk.

WOOD SHUTTERS are an attractive, sensible way to treat windows as is the Roman shade—a shade that folds accordion-style and pulls up and down like a Venetian blind.

A CERAMIC TILE FLOOR IS the most practical kind for the bathroom. It has the greatest moisture-resistance and is very attractive. It can also be quite expensive. However, a good deal of the cost is for the installation and the competent do-it-yourselfer can save a large portion of the cost by installing it himself. If you have a practical, old-fashioned little-white-tiled floor, you can add a bit of comfort and color with an area rug. But the wall-to-wall carpeting shown today for bathrooms is out of character in the period room. If there is an old wood floor in poor condition, spatter-painting or stencilling can give it a lift. They would have to be coated with a water-resistant polyurethane or conventional varnish.

IF THE BATHROOM does not have a period lighting fixture and adding one is not practical, there are many plain globe types of modern fixtures that look very well with Victorian decoration. Attractive hardware also adds a great deal of charm to the room. The Old-House Journal Buyers' Guide lists many firms who make good reproduction hardware. A wood or brass drapery pole makes an elegant towel rack. An oval Victorian mirror instead of an antiseptic medicine chest mirror makes a world of difference, but then it is necessary to find another old wall-cabinet for the medicine.

WHEN ADDING A NEW BATHROOM to the old-house the fixtures can be installed on one wall to save money; that is, on the "wet wall"—the one that contains the piping. Although this is not always the best arrangement for decoration, it does save a great deal in plumber's fees. When installing a shower, remember that a shower curtain and rod is not only less expensive than glass doors but also more in keeping with the old house.

IF YOU PLAN TO DECORATE in period style then white fixtures are the best choice, as colored ones are a recent innovation. When buying fixtures from a plumber remember that they usually purchase only one brand and if you want another type you will have to study the catalogs of various firms yourself.

CAST IRON tubs with a porcelain finish are the highest priced but the most durable. They hold heat well insuring a comfortable bath and holds a finish well and resists chipping. Steel tubs are almost as good and slightly lower in price. But the new fiberglass-reinforced polyesters are overly sleek in appearance and will scratch easily.

SOME SUGGESTIONS FOR THE OLD BATHROOM

WHEREVER POSSIBLE, keep the old fixtures and replace or repair parts. The old porcelain fixtures frequently are chipped and stained. Often these can be salvaged by resurfacing with epoxy, such as the Marshalls' did with their old bathtub (see pg. 11). The two-part epoxy systems are the best. The porcelain first has to be thoroughly cleaned to remove all traces of soap and grime.

THOROUGH WASHING with trisodium phosphate or washing soda, followed by rinsing with mineral spirits will remove both water-soluble and oil-soluble contaminants. Chips in the porcelain have to be filled in with epoxy metal fillers. Then the entire fixture is sanded with wet-and-dry sandpaper to create a "tooth" for the epoxy surface coating. After mixing according to manufacturers' directions, the epoxy material is applied with a brush. A second coat is normally applied about 24 hr. later after scuff-sanding the first coat. One brand of epoxy that has been used with good results is "Klenk's Epoxy Tub & Tile Finish," manufactured by Zynolyte Products, Compton, Calif. An epoxy finish can be expected to last several years; then it will have to be sanded and new coating applied.

IT MAY BE THAT the old fixtures are awkwardly arranged. A plumber can re-arrange them and and perhaps storage space can be added at the same time. An attractive old cabinet or bureau will lend period atmosphere. While looking over the old fixtures, it can also be decided whether the pipes and plumbing are to be exposed or boxed in with wood. Both

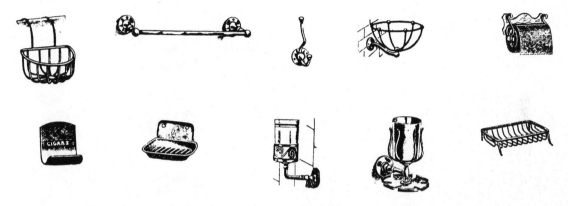

Some of the bathroom accessories offered in the Sears, Roebuck and Co. Catalog of 1902.

AN EDWARDIAN BATHROOM IN BROOKLYN

WHEN NORMA AND JIM MARSHALL moved into their brownstone in Brooklyn they had an old bathroom with everything in it painted parrot green. They suspected that there might be some nice wood and brass under all that paint. The first step was to win the argument with the local plumber who wanted to take it all out and put in new. The second was to strip off the old paint. The faucets are brass and the roll-rim on the tub and the toilet tank and seat are wood with marble sink and slabs under the sink and tub. The tub had to be resurfaced.

THE SOPHISTICATED, APPEALING bathroom they have today is the result of paint, paper and attention to details. Norma wanted a large-patterned wallpaper reminiscent of the Art Noveau period. A semi-custom-made paper, she was able to pick the colors that filled in the flowers. She picked two of

her favorite earth-tone shades—a dark burnt orange and an olive-drab similar to bronze. The wainscotting is painted in the olive-drab. They bought a mixed-in-the-store paint but had to add a little of this and that to match. The outside of the tub, rug, shower curtain and chair are in various shades of the burnt orange-rust color.

THE LARGE WINDOW presented a large decorating problem. After rejecting curtains, shades, etc. they selected a very modern Levolor Venetian blind with narrow slats. This type of blind does not have the tapes and assorted hardware of the usual kind, and they come in unusual colors. The Marshalls' is a bronze tone and blends beautifully with the similar shades in the room.

SINCE THERE WAS ONLY a wood-framed mirror over the sink, Norma added a small oak wall-cabinet on the opposite wall as well as a standing one underneath for additional storage. The old fixtures that the Marshalls were so adamant about keeping have not only lent themselves well to the charming period bathroom they have created, but they also work as well as any modern counterparts they could have installed.

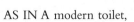

KEEPING HIGH-TANK TOILETS IN WORKING ORDER

By Don Yule

BELIEVE IT OR NOT, the inventor of the reservoir tank flush toilet was named Thomas Crapper. He and his family operated a large factory in 19th-century England that was devoted to the manufacture of plumbing fixtures. Mr. Crapper was a respected member of the English industrial establishment.

AN EARLY VERSION of one of Mr. Crapper's inventions is placed in a closet-sized room on the top floor of our house, in between the two bedrooms. Open the frosted-glass-panelled door and—voila—the ceramic "throne" mounted on its slate base. The seat and lid are golden oak, as is the flush box which sits on iron brackets seven feet above the floor. A brass pipe leads from the flush box down to the bowl, and a chain with a wooden handle on the end hangs down from the left side of the box.

ALTHOUGH THE FUNCTIONING of this type of toilet is similar to the modern variety, there is a fundamental difference in the operating principle. Whereas in a modern toilet the water descends from the box into the bowl by gravity flow, in the earlier high-tank toilets the water is siphoned down.

FIGURE 1 SHOWS THE FLUSH BOX in the full position. The float valve (A) is held closed by the high position of the float ball (B), buoyed up by the water level. In operation, the chain (F) is pulled down, raising the valve sleeve (D) and the outer cannister (S). Water starts rushing through the perforated tube (G). The water rushing down through the pipe to the bowl creates a partial vacuum inside the valve sleeve. When

the chain is released, a water-tight seal is again formed at (J) when the valve sleeve (D) drops. However, the vacuum inside the valve causes the water to rise between the cannister (S) and the outside of the valve sleeve (D) until it reaches the overflow hole (0) at the top of the valve sleeve. A siphoning action is thus started, and the rest of the water in the flush box is drawn out through the overflow until the water level reaches a hole in the bottom of the cannister (S) and the siphon is broken.

AS IN A modern toilet, the float falls with the descending water level, opening inlet valve (A) and admitting water to refill the tank. This type of flush box is inherently more durable and trouble-free than the modern type, but after a century of use, naturally some repairs were required. If you have a similar toilet, you may

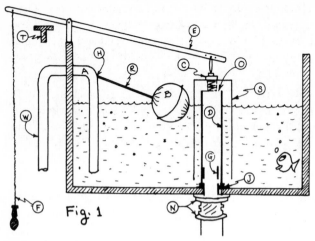

Critical elements are the valve sleeve (D), the valve gasket (J) and the outer valve cannister (S).

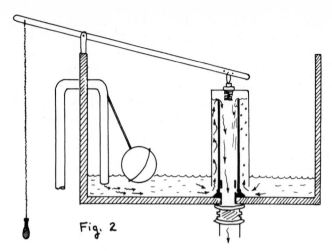

When valve (D) is lifted, water rushes into pipe (G), setting up a siphon that draws rest of water through (0).

have encountered some of the following problems, for which I offer my solutions.

A PERPETUAL DRIP

IF YOU HAVE THE FAMILIAR situation of a perpetual drip from the flush box into the toilet bowl, the flush valve gasket (J) may need replacing. This is a collar of rubber or leather that fits under the flush valve unit. To reach it, unfasten the flush valve cylinder (S-D) from the lifting arm and remove it from the tank. (I am assuming that you have first turned off the water supply to the flush box!)

THE GASKET WILL BE FOUND fitting snugly around a perforated pipe (G) that sticks up a short distance into the tank. If this gasket is old, it may be very hard and you may have to cut it with a blade to get it off. Try to keep it in one piece, however, as it will be very handy when trying to find a new one. The rubber "dripless" kind can be found at most large plumbing supply stores (in Brooklyn, at least). But they come in many shapes and sizes—which is why it is handy to have the old one with you. To install the new one easily, oil it first, then slip it down over the perforated pipe and press it down evenly all over.

IF YOUR GASKET is the flat leather variety, you can make a new one yourself from single-ply leather . . . most easily obtained from the tongue of an old shoe. Just trace the outline of the old gasket with a pencil and cut it out with scissors.

FAULTY GASKETS

TWO OTHER GASKETS that may cause problems are located where the flush tube exits from the tank. If either leaks, first try tightening the collar nuts (N). If this doesn't work,

you can remove either gasket and make a new one from leather or rubber. For double leak insurance, coat the new gaskets with Permatex gasket cement before installing.

TIGHTEN THE COLLAR nuts only snugly, as the gasket might bunch up or be squeezed out to the side if the nut is turned too tight.

ANOTHER CAUSE OF DRIP is if the float valve is incorrectly adjusted, allowing water to run out the overflow (0). This is remedied by bending the rod (R) downward so that the float is lower—achieving a correspondingly lower water level in the flush box.

SOMETIMES THERE IS A GASKET under a collar nut that connects the float valve to the water supply line (W). I find that a 1/2-in. faucet washer works perfectly here. Another cause of valve malfunction can be a worn screw (H) that acts as the hinge for the float rod and ball. Be sure to replace with a brass screw, as steel would rust quickly.

ALSO, THERE IS A RUBBER SEAT inside this valve that might need replacing if the water cannot be completely stopped by lifting up the float ball. The float valve may be unscrewed in half to reach this rubber seat. Clean off all corrosion with brass polish while the valve is apart.

MENDING COPPER

THE FLUSH BOX normally has a lining made of copper. Mine had several pinhole leaks caused by corrosion and by the float ball rubbing against the inside of the tank as it rose and fell. The seams of this liner can be re-soldered—as can any holes—but I found plastic steel also works well for this repair.

ONE PROBLEM PECULIAR to siphon-type flush boxes is a leak in the copper shell (S) that surrounds the flush valve is a leak in the copper shell (S) that surrounds the flush valve (D). If there is a major air leak here, the siphon action will not work and you will be obliged to hold the chain down to get all the water in the box to drain down into the bowl.

THESE COPPER SHELLS are held in place by a nut (C) on the center rod of the flush valve unit. This nut may be loose, or the gasket under it may need replacing. An open seam or other hole in the shell may be soldered or repaired with plastic steel. If the shell is too far gone, you may be able to obtain a new one at the plumbing supply store. Or you can fashion your own from an appropriately sized plastic bottle. Just cut the top off so that you have the same length as the original shell, punch the correctly sized hole in the bottom, and you'll have a unit that will work as well as the original item.

I HAD ONE FINAL PROBLEM with out flush box. When the chain was pulled too vigorously, the flush valve would pop up farther than its normal distance of travel and get hung up on the valve guide. To operate properly, the flush valve needs be raised only about 1/4 in.

TO GUARD AGAINST this malfunction, I fashioned a stop out of a metal ell brace (T) and screwed it to the wall in back of the tank so that the lifting rod would bump against it when it had travelled far enough to open the valve. I glued a piece of rubber to the brace where the rod strikes it for silent operation.

NOW THE VALVE WILL only open the correct distance, no matter how vigorously my five-year-old son yanks the chain!

RESTORING MARBLE SINKS

By David S. Gillespie,

AT ONE TIME or another most of us have come across those fine marble sinks so common to Victorian buildings of the 1870's and 80's. They usually stand against the walls of junk shops gaping forlornly. The marble is stained, the bowls cracked or missing, and the faucets are corroded beyond recognition. We scratch our heads and think, "If only I could use that," and then go out and buy an imitation marble thing.

WHEN MY WIFE AND I set out to restore an 1883 home in Michigan we discovered one such sink in the original bathroom. Local garage sales yielded three others in various states of disrepair so that we now had sufficient sink tops for the house.

THESE TOPS can usually be had in this area for between five and fifteen dollars and are thus a good cheap sink as well as being authentic. Moreover, they are not difficult to use and any old house owner can do it with easily available tools and small expense.

THE FIRST STEP IS CLEANING the top. One of ours had been painted black (modern?) but paint, we found, comes off quite easily with common paint remover. Stains, particularly rust and water stains, are very difficult to remove since marble is a porous, soft stone. Cleanser will clean off most grime and surface stains but for deeper stains a weak solution of muriatic acid worked fairly well.

SCRATCHES AND SMALL PITS are more difficult but they can usually be worked out with a very fine grade of wet/dry sandpaper. In some areas there are shops which will polish the marble to give it a harder surface which will resist stains in the future. For the very deep stains there is just no solution and you should either avoid buying tops that are badly stained or be prepared to live with the stains.

REPLACEMENT BOWLS are really no problem. (See box below.) Since marble is very soft it is easy to work with common shop tools. Re-aligning the mounting screws (necessary when using some replacement bowls) is not hard but must be done with care. Place the sink top upside down on a work table and place the bowl where you want it, marking the location of the four mounting points. Then set the bowl aside and shim up the top between the work table and the top. This step is crucial because the sink top is made with a lip which contacts your work table but the flat part of the top itself does not. Attempting to work on the sink top without properly supporting the face can result in a cracked or broken top.

NEXT, DRILL NEW MOUNTING HOLES using a half inch masonry bit. Be careful not to drill through the top and lubricate the bit with water as you are working. Drilling

cool both the bit and the stone to minimize the possibility of cracking. The holes will need to be about three quarters of an inch deep. Once this is accomplished set the new mounting screws. The old way of doing this was to drip hot lead into the hole around the screw head.

IF YOUR TOP HAS MOUNTING SCREWS that need to be removed simply heat the lead with a small propane torch and the screws will come out easily. An easier method for the amateur is to buy four star anchors at the hardware store.

THESE ARE SIMPLY a machine screw nut surrounded by a lead sleeve. Place one in each of the half inch holes, and, using the tool provided with the anchors, tap them until the lead expands and the anchors feel solid. Be sure that the face of the marble beneath each hole is firmly resting on a block of wood or other shim. Otherwise you will break right through the face. If the original mounting brackets are on the sink top, new ones can be fabricated quite easily out of flat steel or bars.

USING A PIECE of ⅛-inch metal about ½ in. wide and 2 in. long, bend one end at right angles so that you have an "L" with the short side about ½ in. long and the long side 1½ inches.

DRILL A HOLE large enough to take your machine screw in the long side and you are ready to go. The short end of the "L" braces against the marble and the long end goes over the bowl edge to hole it firmly in place.

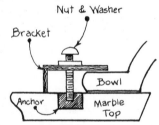

FAUCETS ARE ALSO no problem. If you have the original faucets you may want to use them. They will need to be thoroughly cleaned (I recommend having them boiled out at a local radiator shop) and possibly will need to be replated. Replacement of the rubber washers will then yield a perfectly functional and original faucet.

IF, LIKE US, you have gone soft and prefer mixers, almost any wide-spread faucet set will do. Most sink tops had two holes for the faucets and a small hole in the middle to which the chain on the rubber stopper was connected. The faucet holes are usually too far apart for modern wide-spread faucet sets so you will have to go to the plumbing supply house to get a short length of 3/8 in. copper tubing to replace the pieces which come with the set (18 in. should be more than enough).

YOU WILL ALSO FIND that the faucet holes in the sink top are just a bit too small. A 1 in. grinding wheel in an electric drill will enlarge the hole sufficiently to use modern faucets. These are available at most hardware stores or through the Sears catalogue. The central hole will have to be made much larger and for this I recommend a large masonry drill bit if one can be had. If not, it can also be made with a series of grinding wheels though it is a tedious job.

SOME SINKS WERE MADE with only one hole for a faucet and a large hole in the center for the drain plunger. I discovered that Delta makes a faucet which requires only one hole for mounting. The center hole in the sink top, which had once held the drain plunger, was much too large, however. To solve this problem I had two stainless steel washers made and, by placing one above and one below the surface of the marble, was able to reduce the size of the hole to fit the new faucet set. The hole for the old faucet was used up by the new drain plunger.

WITH THE NEW FAUCET SET and the bowl firmly installed on the sink top, the next step is to hang the sink on the wall. On my sinks they mounted from 22 in.–26 in. apart which isn't very handy for hitting pre-existing studding. If your wall is torn up for plumbing anyway, don't forget to install new studs or braces in the proper location before sealing up the wall. If you are hanging the brackets on a finished wall, try to hit a stud on at least one side and then use toggle bolts on the other.

IN MANY CASES THE BRACKETS will have been lost. If there are no brackets with your sink you have several alternatives. Any metal shop (including the local high school) can fabricate new brackets cheaply. Another alternative is the chrome posts used to support more modern wall-hung sinks though I don't think they look very good in an old house.

A CHEAP ALTERNATIVE I used is to support the sink with old stair balusters salvaged from a demolition site. Brackets are probably preferable as they are easier to clean around.

INSTALLATION is the last and easiest step requiring only that the sink be level from side to side and that you allow a very slight drop from back to front to prevent water running back toward the wall. Another thing to consider is height. Both my wife and I are tall and so we installed the sinks 36 in. above the floor. Normal height of 32 in. will be too low for most people over 5 feet tall.

NOW HOOK UP the water supply and turn on the faucet. You will have an authentic addition to your bathroom. It is both inexpensive and easy to maintain. No Victorian home should be without one.

Period Design
and Decoration

DECORATING THE VICTORIAN HOUSE

A PRIMER FOR BEAUTIFYING HOUSES BUILT FROM 1837 TO 1914

THE OWNER of the Victorian house is often beset by some very special decorating problems. The problems are generally not the fault of the house itself but result from efforts to make it into what it is not.

WHAT IT IS NOT is a series of plain-box rooms. And most of what is written today about the decoration of houses is an effort to get the home owner to buy more new things or constantly alter what they have. But the old Victorian house was built to last for many years and not to look like something different every year or so. The same yards and yards of splashy fabric or plastic wall panelling that are recommended for rooms without architectural interest will look out of place in the 19th-century home or alter its features for the worse.

FEW PEOPLE CARE TO have a "museum-type" recreation of the style in which their house was originally furnished. There is no need for the clutter that gave the Victorian period its bad reputation. Many of the reasons for the objects that made their way into the Victorian house have disappeared with our ancestors. We no longer require a table in the hallway, laden with decorative objects, for the sole purpose of containing calling cards left by visitors. Nor would we use the ubiquitous table placed in the center of the parlor in the same way. It was meant to display the "fancywork" laboriously produced by the ladies of the house. Nor do many of us have the army of servants required to dust and clean a variety of unnecessary objects.

OF COURSE, some of the old pieces are fun to have and can add a nostalgic charm to a room. If one is a collector, many Victorian pieces can be found at reasonable prices, especially those that do not pass the "100 years old" antique test.

BUT WHETHER FURNISHINGS are antiques, or a mixture of contemporary, reproductions, and some hand-me-downs, they are details. And details should come last. The important factor in an old house is its interior architecture and proportions. This is where the old-house owner has the advantage. Because the woodwork, mouldings, ceiling medallions, mantels, etc., are not decorating "problems" but rich backgrounds that cannot be duplicated today.

BECAUSE THE MOST IMPORTANT features in a house are the proportions—height of the ceiling, windows, etc.—and the architectural style and ornamental detail found on the interior features—this is the place to begin interior decoration. The colors and textures you add create the old-fashioned harmony the Victorian house deserves.

THIS LITTLE PRIMER will take a new look at the old house by going back to some of the principles used in the 19th and early 20th centuries in the decoration of houses. They are as appropriate now as they were then for the many styles of interior and exterior architecture built in the Victorian era.

An 1833 illustration of a Grecian room, this was the model for many interiors built in the Greek Revival style. This most popular Early and Mid-Victorian house was built from 1820 to about 1870 in the West. Although most rooms patterned after this type were simpler, the low dado, rectangular wall panelling outlined with composition moulding, and Greek ornament were typical components. Usually painted in pale shades of blue, yellow, lavender, and green, the composition trim and mouldings were often painted in buff or cream. Gilding articulated the decorative features and added elegance to these formal rooms.

THE FIRST STEP TO TAKE when decorating the Victorian house is to take stock of the architectural details. Ceiling height, window heights and placement are important and so are the division of the walls. 19th-century walls were divided horizontally and these divisions are the decorative key to a room. Equally important are the mouldings, wainscotting, panelling, etc. that may have been removed over the years, or covered up by modern wall coverings.

OFTEN THE POOR "white elephant" room that nothing seems to look good in is a well-proportioned room with its architectural features removed or ignored. A single color paint or one-patterned paper cannot be expected to cover such a broad expanse of wall and look attractive.

A HOMEOWNER faced with this kind of large, plain room can often discover what type of interior architecture it once had. Usually, there will be houses of similar style and age in the area and one is bound to still have its original features. Local historical societies and libraries can be of assistance.

WOOD PANELLING and wainscotting are reproduced today in old styles. A few excellent firms also make plaster and composition mouldings, ceiling medallions and decorative trim that will restore the character of a room.

THE DADO is the lower portion of the wall—right above the baseboard—generally topped by a moulding called the chair rail. Originally meant as a background for furniture, it rose higher up the wall as the 19th century wore on and furniture became more massive. By the turn of the century it was often 3/4 of the way up the wall and eventually became obsolete.

WHEN THE DADO was made of softwood (common in wainscotting) it was often grained. Graining is a technique that used paint, pigment and varnish to create a durable economical imitation of wood. It is a wonderful trick, actually, and does wonders for wainscotting that is in poor condition or painted over many times. The dents and bumps on the surface actually contribute to the real look of wood.

IF A COLOR is preferred, the wainscotting can be painted and then given an antique glaze with varnish containing some brown pigment—similar to the "antique kit" effect. The glaze makes the finish more durable but also hides imperfections and gives a richer appearance.

A DADO EFFECT can also be created with other materials. It was fashionable around the 1880s to use straw matting below the chair rail. In the early 20th century, decorators often recommended burlap, felt or denim for the lower portion of the wall, particularly for hallways. A dado can be re-created in this way today, using stock mouldings for the chair rail.

WALLPAPER WAS USED in quite a different way in the 19th century. It was put up in sections: Dado (unless the dado was wood), border paper, fill portion and freize. Papers were made in related patterns and solids with coordinated border and freize designs. When walls were divided with mouldings in long rec-

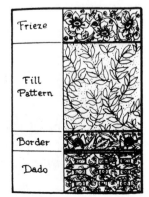

This old illustration begat many an "Olde English" room in America. This kind of wood-panelled dado is found in many parlors, dining rooms, libraries and some master bedrooms. The top of the wall (or bottom of the ceiling) is the cove. They were usually stencilled or papered—even when the ceilings were simpler. If wallpaper covered the walls above the dado, then the paper in the cove was a different pattern, although related. Mixtures of Gothic, Elizabethan and Jacobean designs in furniture, woodwork and mantels were a typical form of Victorian decoration and lasted well into the 20th century.

tangular panels (the mouldings were made of wood, plaster, composition and even papier mache and can be bought today in many materials) the panels were often papered and mouldings painted a different color than the rest of the wall. The owner of the Victorian home often has a difficult time finding wallpaper with patterns large enough for the scale of the main rooms. But many of the Early American reproductions of French and English florals and stripes will look right if related textured and solid papers are used in dividing the wall.

AN ALMOST LOST decorating technique that was widely used in the 19th century is stencilling. Very different from the simple patterns used in Early American houses, Victorian stencilling was a sophisticated application of elaborate designs. Unfortunately, most of this work has been painted over.

THE MOST IMPORTANT THING TO LEARN about the stencilling of the Victorian period was *where* they stencilled. A typical Victorian parlor, library, or dining room often had a wood-panelled dado, wallpaper in the fill portion of the wall, and a stencilled frieze or cove. A pattern for the frieze or cove can be adapted from the design in the wallpaper used below.

STENCIL PATTERNS can be taken from books, rugs, or drapery fabric. A design from the room itself—ornament on the mantel, over windows or doors, etched in glass in a door panel, or floor or fireplace tiles—will provide a pattern inspiration that will harmonize with the room.

AN UNUSUAL DECORATIVE note is added by the old method of stencilling a "wipe-line" above the chair rail.

A SMALL PATTERN—a Greek key, a row of stylized flowers, or Gothic crosses—was stencilled above the wooden chair rail and the surface where the pattern was applied was then varnished. This provided a durable finish for the constant dusting done by the housekeeper.

STENCILLING was also a very popular way to decorate hallways. Often the walls and ceilings in vestibules had very decorative treatments done in this manner. In the last few decades of the 19th century, many homes were built without the fancy embossed plasterwork found earlier.

THIS WAS BECAUSE the "Eastlake" or Art Movement

A classic vertical wall division that never went entirely out of fashion in the Victorian era.

influence had dictated a new form of decoration. Subdued, grayed shades of green, rust, ochre and gold replaced the rich reds, browns and purples then in vogue. And flat, stylized ornament in geometric shapes replaced the roses and ribbons that

generally covered floors and furniture. This made stencilling even more popular because the flat appearance of stencilled designs was an effective way to display the new designs. If your room has all the Victorian divisions of frieze, cove, etc., but does not have any raised plaster ornament in them, it may very well have been stencilled.

WHITE IN THE inside of houses was fashionable in the Adam period (1783–1815) and did not return to fashion until the 1930s. The feeling for light colors continued after the Federal period into the Greek Revival style. Light shades of green, lavender, blue and yellow were used on walls, but drapes and upholstery were in deep shades of red, green and blue.

BY MID-19TH CENTURY, a variety of colors were used, and they were selected in accordance with the Victorian feeling for what was consider "fitness" in decoration—the function of the room.

PARLORS AND DRAWING ROOMS were the most elegant rooms in the house. Delicate tones with darker shades for trim and gilding were combined. Later in the century much darker shades became fashionable—crimson, purple and liver brown. It was these dark tones that gave Victorian decor its "gloomy" epitaph. These colors are very difficult to use. For

instance, the dark reds absorb light. But if you have a High Victorian parlor with elaborate plasterwork and wood carving it was probably decorated in these darker tones.

HOWEVER, MODERN paints come in many subtle tones that were not available then. It is possible today to use more attractive shades of these darker colors. For instance, a deep rose would give a Victorian feeling without having the oppresive effects of a dark red. The most important factor in painting the Victorian room is to decide on more than one shade of a color or to use a contrasting color for the architectural features—the composition or plaster mouldings, frieze, cove and ceiling. Picking out these interior architectural details is the way to restore its original beauty.

THE PARLOR is the room that accommodated the fads and fashions of the period. Because it was mainly a room for visitors, it was often redecorated in the latest style. The parlor also contained the fancywork—shell pictures, woolwork

flowers, wax fruit—done by the ladies of the house. Also displayed prominently were many objects that were considered to be symbols of culture—usually items that showed an acquaintance with the arts and European visits. Postcards, shells from far-off places, reproduction prints and sculpture, souvenirs from various archaelogical digs, all had their place. To add to the number of things found in this room, many glass domes covered the ob-

jects. It is no wonder that Victorian decoration was remembered as "cluttered." But so many of these articles, belonging to a bygone way of life, really had nothing to do with the real interior decoration of the home—the pleasing and sophisticated manner in which walls, ceilings and woodwork were treated. Meanwhile, in contrast to the busy furnishings of the parlor, the rest of the rooms tended to be more restrained and avoided the whims of fashion.

THE LIBRARY never varied. Painted in neutral shades it presented a sober, quiet appearance. Shades of gray and brown for walls and floor, and leather upholstery were always in fashion.

BEDROOMS were decorated in cheerful and light tones. Wallpaper in floral and striped patterns in the French and English styles were used throughout the century.

HALLWAYS were treated with neutral tones and the dado and woodwork was often grained. Tiles were popular for floor covering. They are attractive and durable.

CEILINGS were always painted in a lighter shade than the walls—never darker. A darker ceiling causes it to look lower. This is often done today to produce the lower ceiling effect. But the Victorians built rooms with high ceilings because they liked them that way.

ANOTHER EFFECT never found in Victorian homes was the bare brick wall. Many fine craftsmen were at work in that period and a beautifully finished plaster wall was something both craftsmen and owner took pride in. In fact, excepting an intricate kind of garden furniture called "rustic"—anything really rustic was frowned upon. Because the brick behind plaster walls was not meant to be exposed, the the results of stripping off the plaster will most likely be very disappointing.

AN IMPORTANT FINISHING TOUCH for an elegant Victorian background is the addition of the kind of hardware used then for draperies, doors and shutters. There are some firms reproducing these elegant fixtures. Often, the old Victorian house has a good deal of its original hardware in place, but not noticed because it has been painted over many times.

Victorian Stencil Patterns

A GUIDE TO LIGHTING THE OLD HOUSE

by Carolyn Flaherty

PERHAPS THE MOST DIFFICULT area to cope with in re-creating an appropriate interior style for the old house is lighting. It is the subject our readers ask most about.

THERE ARE A NUMBER OF REASONS lighting is such a problem. Few of us would care to read by candlelight or spend hours cleaning and filling oil lamps. Of course, fixtures can be electrified. But then the amount of light has to be worked out. Candle-power bulbs can be used but more lamps and fixtures will be needed. There is no question, however, that modern lighting fixtures do not look good in the period room. But reproductions are expensive (and Victorian reproductions almost non-existent) and antiques can be costly and require a great deal of shopping time to locate.

SO THE ANSWER FOR most old-house restorers is a compromise–a subtle use of unobtrusive modern lighting combined with as many period fixtures as you have the good fortune to come across.

HOWEVER, the period fixtures must be the right style and vintage. A massive black wrought iron antique or reproduction chandelier made for an Early American farmhouse would be ludicrous in an elegant Queen Anne. Old is not enough!

THIS GUIDE is meant to aid the old-house person in selecting those fixtures that will enhance the architectural style and age of your house–whether you are shopping in catalogs, yard sales, antique shops or Aunt Hattie's cast-offs.

COLONIAL: UP TO 1790

IN COLONIAL AMERICA there were four ways to provide lighting in the home:

1. The huge, cavernous fireplaces provided some light for nighttime activities.

2. Tallow candles. Early chandeliers were suspended candlesticks. Candles were very costly, however, and used only by very prosperous families. Many ingenious devices were constructed to hold candles on the backs of chairs or hang from beams.

3. Crude substitutes for the tallow candle like the rushlight. Rushes were cut green from the marshes, soaked in grease and mounted in holders for burning.

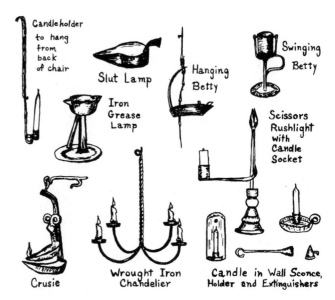

Candleholder to hang from back of chair

Slut Lamp

Iron Grease Lamp

Hanging Betty

Swinging Betty

Scissors Rushlight with Candle Socket

Crusie

Wrought Iron Chandelier

Candle in Wall Sconce, Holder and Extinguishers

4. Primitive lamps. By arranging a wick in a container of grease, oil, lard or any inflammable material, a bit of light could be provided at the cost of a good deal of smell and smoke.

LITTLE CHANGED in the development of lighting before the 19th century–most primitive lamps in Colonial America bear a remarkable resemblance to the kinds used by the Romans in the first century. These lamps were made of tin, iron and pottery in Pennsylvania. Some of the most popular were the "crusie" (the English name; sometimes called a "Phoebe" in New England); the "slut" ("slut" referred to a rag dipped in grease); and the "betty." The betty was made in many forms–on a stand, on a chain, or a small pot-like vessel sometimes having a cover.

EARLY AMERICAN: 1790–1850 (FEDERAL AND GREEK REVIVAL)

ELEGANT CANDELABRA and chandeliers had been used in the Georgian houses of America before the Revolution. Towards the end of the 18th century, publications from England popularized the Adam style, which had long been fashionable in Britain. The graceful decoration of the Adam period required beautifully made fixtures with a good deal of crystal to enhance the light of the many candles used. These were used only by the wealthy merchants and ship owners who could afford both the English and French imported fixtures and the many candles they used.

AFTER INDEPENDENCE, popular taste ran to an emulation of the classical Ancient Greece and taste was no longer solely influenced by Europe. American interpretation of the classic style called for simple and delicate ornament. However, cooking was still done at the huge fireplaces and for most of the population whale oil lamps were the chief source of light.

THE GREEK REVIVAL in architecture and decoration began during the Federal period and continued on to the Victorian. One of the most popular decorative features in the well-furnished parlor of the Federal or Greek Revival home was the girandole—a large, convex mirror with an eagle surmounting it, usually with candle brackets at either side. A typical parlor or dining room would

have, in addition to the girandole, an elegant chandelier suspended from a richly decorated ceiling rosette, candelabra and additional candle brackets on the walls.

THE SIMPLE WHALE oil lamps used throughout this period were commonly made of tin and

pewter, with pewterers turning out very lovely styles. Glass whale oil lamps also became widely used in a great variety of shapes and styles—both blown and pressed glass.

THE FIRST REALLY NEW IDEA in lighting devices was the Argand lamp. In 1783 a Swiss chemist, Aime Argand, invented a lamp that increased the draft and made the flame brighter—equal to ten candles. The Argand lamp burned vegetable or whale oil. It had a cylindrical wick that admitted air on both the inside and the outside of the burner, which made the light brighter, as well as the glass chimney that held the flame steady. The Argand became very popular although never inexpensive.

TWO IMPROVEMENTS on the Argand lamp were the Astral and the Solar type. The Astral worked on the Argand principle but had a flat, circular tube with radiating arms attached to the lamp. It was meant to eliminate the annoying shadow cast by the Argand burner. Many Astrals

were very well proportioned, with lovely shades of ground or cut glass, and often had crystal prisms hanging from the circular reservoir.

THE SOLAR LAMP was patented in Philadelphia in 1843. Similar to the Argand and the Astral, with the wick closely fitted into a round tube that extended through the bottom of the oil font—an inverted bell-shaped reservoir. The Solar had a bulb-shaped chimney. Like the Astral, they were usually graceful with brass or bronze columns rising from a pedestal base.

ONE OF THE FEATURES OF interior decoration in the Greek Revival period was the use of classic symmetry. The Argand, Astral and Solar lamps were often made in pairs, especially for the mantel. Because they were made of fine metals and glass, they were too costly for general use.

THERE WERE MANY simple glass lamps in popular use from 1800 to mid-century. One of the most interesting is the "sparking" lamp. A cork was fitted tightly into the opening in the lamp, and running through it were one or two parallel, short metal wick tubes. The little lamp gave about 15 mins. of light, since it held only a small amount of oil. They were often used to light the way to bed.

ONE OF THE MOST widely used lighting devices in the first half of the 19th century was the peg lamp. This was a thrifty device to use oil (as well as camphene and commercial fluids developed from 1830 on) and yet retain the

many candlesticks most families had accumulated. Bowls to hold the fluid were made of tin, silver or glass with a peg at the bottom. The bowl was then inserted with the peg in the candle-stick where the candle used to go. Like the sparking lamp, the peg lamp did not hold very much fluid and gave a poor light.

IN ELEGANT FEDERAL AND GREEK revival houses many of these lighting devices could be found in the same room. Argands and Astrals were also made as chandeliers for hallways. But no one lamp or fixture gave much light compared to today's electric bulb. So when using period fixtures electrified, use bulbs in low wattage—and preferably candlelight bulbs—except for reading lamps. Simpler farmhouses used only whale oil and peg lamps, and one or two antiques or reproductions of this type will add an authentic flavor to the house.

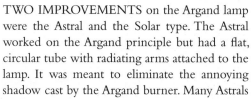

THE VICTORIAN ERA (1851–1901)

DURING THE LAST HALF of the 19th century a wide variety of lighting devices were used in the home. While the gadget-conscious Victorians readily accepted the new types of fixtures developed for the new fuels and the wealthy Victorians used elaborate chandeliers and decorative fixtures, many homes continued to be lit with the older oil lamps.

THE FIRST IMPORTANT CHANGE in lighting after mid-century was the development of kerosene as a fuel. Kerosene was far safer than camphene and less expensive than all other fuels. It also gave a stronger light. With the use of the flat wick burner, arranged so that a clear glass lamp chimney could be attached, the turnip-shaped oil reservoir replaced the elongated type. The burner could be easily unscrewed from the font for filling and cleansing.

THE FIRST POPULAR TYPE of kerosene lamp was the peg lamp formerly used with oil. At first made for candlesticks, the pressed glass industry now produced them in enormous quantities for insertion into lamp mounts. They were very similar to the earlier types in form.

ONE OF THE MOST ELEGANT glass lamps of the 1850s and 1860s was the Overlay lamp. Made by manufacturers like Sandwich in New England, the cased glass was cut away in spots to show the color of the base layer. They often had marble and brass bases. All of the table lamps of this period were similar in form to the oil lamps of previous decades, though usually converted to use with kerosene.

AS LAMPS DEVELOPED specifically for use with kerosene, the variety of burners, lamp chimneys and globes were enormous. Kerosene lamps are hard to date because the most popular types were made throughout the 19th century and are still produced for use in rural areas. A kerosene lamp will be appropriate in any setting after 1860.

THE STUDENT LAMP was the most popular of the patent and novelty lamps. The distinguishable feature is a detach-

able oil or kerosene font that fed the fuel through a tube to a burner part arranged on an arm so that shadows were not cast on the table. It was similar to the Astral mantel lamp, but of a much more functional design. It had a heavily weighted base to prevent it from being knocked over. Student lamps were made in double or single lights, and in bracket, hanging and stand versions as well as the table lamp type. Although their widest popularity was from 1875 to 1900, they are still reproduced today in colonial types, Victorian styles, and modern adaptations, and almost always electrified.

BEFORE KEROSENE, hanging oil lamps could be used only by the well-to-do because the hanging lamp required such a large amount of oil. But the kerosene hanging lamp became quite popular. Working on a chain and counterpoise principle, the lamp could be pulled down for filling and cleaning. Hanging lamps were most commonly used for hallways and the glass globes were cranberry, blues and pinks or etched glass. Also used frequently in the library, prisms were used dangling from a decorated glass shade to add to the brilliance.

CHANDELIERS were made to use all the various fuels; oil, kerosene, and later on, gas. They were made in an endless variety from plain to fancy, of brass, bronze and ormulu with decorative white and colored globes. Some of the most elaborate chandeliers of the late 19th century imitated 18th century candle chandeliers.

BRACKET LAMPS became widely used. They were made of metal or glass and set in a swinging iron frame attached to the to the wall. Bracket lamps were favored for kitchens and bedrooms. Bracket lamps sometimes had a reflector of mercury glass or tin, and those used in hallways often had an additional decorative glass shade.

GAS LIGHTING was known in England as early as 1792. It gradually came into use in America at first for street lighting and was piped into many houses during the latter part of the 19th century.

The most commonly used gas fixture was the gasolier–or gas chandelier. Clear glass globes were seldom used for gas fixtures. Kerosene lamps had often used clear glass chimneys so as not to diffuse its relatively feeble light, but the higher candle power of gas light caused glare. So domes, shades and globes were colored, frosted, milk and egg white and later were made in a wide range of brilliant hues.

GAS BRACKET LIGHTS were used throughout the house and the brackets were often quite elaborate. A popular form of gas fixture was the newel light. Set atop a newel post in the hall, the base was often a metal statue holding aloft the globe. Clusters of imitation candles were also common.

THE MAJOR INCONVENIENCE with gas as a fuel was that fixtures had to be stationary. (The quickest way to spot a gas chandelier is the pipe leading to the ceiling in which the gas line is contained.) To use gas for a table fixture an unsightly hose was attached to the ceiling or wall fixture.

GAS WAS NOT available outside the larger cities. Individual acetylene plants were sometimes used used out in the country, but they were dangerous and could explode.

BY 1890 gas was being widely used for lighting and electricity was making inroads. But it was during the 1890s that the parlor oil or or kerosene lamp had its golden age. The most popular was the ball-shaded glass lamp usually decorated with painted flowers. The bottom glass portion held a concealed oil font. These parlor lamps are often known today as Gone With The Wind lamps because of their use in the famous motion picture. But they were used incorrectly in a background for the Civil War era as they were not introduced in the U.S. until the 1880s.

WHILE THE Gone With The Wind lamp was the most popular, many other kinds of lamps were in use and usually many different kinds in one home. The plainer oil lamps like the Rochester were used in bedrooms. And the banquet lamp, shaded lamp with a fanciful metal base generally in form of a cherub, had its place in the parlor.

LATE VICTORIAN LAMPSHADES were frilly affairs trimmed with silk, lace and ribbons. They were used on the banquet lamp, piano lamps and standing lamps. The Victorian matron also spent many hours making shades of fabric, of heavy paper with cutout designs, and even hand-painted glass shades.

THE EDWARDIAN ERA (1902–1914)

IT WAS AFTER THE TURN OF THE CENTURY that the public showed a real interest in using electricity for domestic lighting. The first electric fixtures were nothing more than a naked bulb hanging by wires from the ceiling.

SOME PEOPLE BEGAN TO ADAPT the parlor lamp to electricity by placing an incandescent bulb inside the flowered globes or even in the glass bowl surrounding the old brass oil font. Converters were sold specially for converting the parlor oil lamp to electricity. Wires were generally hidden under table covers.

COMBINATION ELECTRIC AND GAS fixtures in both chandelier and bracket form were used in the latter part of the 19th century and continued to be be used after the turn of the century to provide an alternate means of light during the not uncommon power failures.

THE FIRST WIDELY MANUFACTURED type of electric fixtures were simulated candles. Candle sockets in which a bulb was screwed and then covered with a shade appeared in the early 1900s. Until the 1920s electric chandeliers, wall sconces, newel fixtures and some lamps aped the 18th century candle-holding type of lighting device. Glass prisms were used for added brilliance. True to their earlier counterparts, these electric candle chandeliers were hung from the ceiling by a chain—with the electric wire winding unattractively through it up into the ceiling.

THE DOMED LEADED lamp was popularized by Louis comfort Tiffany at the turn of the century. It was actually the first type of lighting designed for the electric bulb. The Tiffany style exemplied the sinuous lines of Art Noveau and were made in tulip-shaped chandeliers, or wisteria and lily-of-the-valley designs for library lamps. Tiffany lamps, as well as their imitations, are quite sought after today.

ALSO DESIGNED ESPECIALLY for electricity during the same period were the boxy-shaped lamps of the Arts and Crafts style. These fixtures were often wood-framed and resembled the Mission furniture of the period. Like the Tiffany styles, these fanciful creations often did not provide sufficient illumination (by today's over-lit standards).

DRAPES AND CURTAINS

by Carolyn Flaherty

OLD-HOUSE OWNERS who want to use curtains or drapes the way it was done when the old house was new will find themselves delving into a rich and complicated part of decorative history.

PART OF THIS HISTORY CONCERNS the development of textiles in the 18th and 19th centuries and their importation into this country. The varied climates from North to South and the ways in which homes were heated changed the functions of bed and window hangings and required adaptations of the way they were used in Europe. How much the French or English style influenced home decoration depended on the social and economic status of the American home owner and their desire to imitate Old World culture. The simpler, servantless colonial home created an indigenous, thriftier style of decorating with fabric.

FASHIONS IN EUROPEAN window dressings derived from the bedhangings that were used in France and England for centuries—a practical way of keeping drafts away from a bed or couch. Harmonizing fabrics were used on bed and window in the 18th century, and changing attitudes about the vices and virtues of fresh air made the bedhanging merely an ornamental device by the early 19th century.

FRENCH DESIGN INFLUENCED all other countries for many years. The lambrequin (a French term meaning scallop) was a stiffened, flat piece that adorned the tops of bed and window curtains and was originally designed as a background on which to embroider elaborate patterns. Lambrequins, valances (a skirt-like hanging of fabric across the tops of drapes or curtains) and cornices (wooden projections from the wall which hid the tops of curtains and hardware) gave draperies their main distinctions in period and style.

IN THE FASHION OF LOUIS XIV, the formal lambrequin was used either plain or cut in dentils or tabs which were trimmed. The Louis XV style was less formal but very rich. The lambrequin was decorated with, or replaced by, loops and drapings ornamented by fringe and lace. The XVI style became more classic and  restrained, lessening the amounts of materials used and with lighter fabrics such as taffeta.

Mid-19th century English print used for lambrequins and curtains of the bed and window hangings in the Borning Room of the Stenton Mansion in Philadelphia. The fabric, Partridge Print, was reproduced from an original document by Brunschwig & Fils, Inc.

ENGLAND, as did other countries, adapted from the French, adding and subtracting their own style. Since English fashion dominated American life in the 18th century and their fabrics and trimmings were available in all the larger cities in America, our 18th-century homes largely imitated the popular English window treatments of the time.

THE SIMPLEST KIND of drape was two strips of cloth tacked to a lath at the top of the window, sometimes held back by cords or tie-backs. A valance or lambrequin, secured by brackets, concealed the the tacks.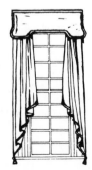

THE SWAG EFFECT eliminated the need for a cornice or lambrequin with a simple

valance-like draping of material across the top of the window. The sides fell 1/2- or 3/4-length down, ending in a jabot. The material was draped over a lath across the top of the window. The draping was sometimes sewn up in the center and often trimmed with a tassel. Usually done in richly-colored fabric, it allowed a full view of an attractive window. It would seem easily duplicated today, using small brackets, decorative loops or wooden rings to hold the material at the top of the window.

THE VENETIAN CURTAIN, which extended the width of the window and had no center opening, was simply raised

to the top of the window by cords which were run through rings stitched in vertical rows to the back of the curtain. Lighter materials that gathered attractively were used for elegant effect, but heavier materials were also used in less formal rooms.

PELMET IS AN ENGLISH TERM for a lambrequin and was used interchangeably. Confusion with the terms "valance" and "lambrequin" probably stems from the omission of a stiffener in some lambrequins. Very heavy materials such as

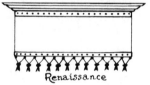
Renaissance

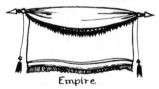
Empire

linen, wool (often combined) or brocades did not need any extra weight to lie flat. These fabrics were made with more threads and in heavier weights than commonly available today. Brunschwig & Fils, who reproduce material for museums and restorations, use complicated, time-consuming processes to duplicate these fabrics.

EVIDENCE OF THE HAND-LABOR that was involved with fabric can be seen in the bedroom of the Sewall House in the Brooklyn Museum. The hangings are made of a heavy linen fabric entirely hand-embroidered with wool. This crewel work imitates designs found in the tree-of-life motifs of the Indian painted cottons which were widely imported into the colonies.

THE CUT OF a lambrequin is a key to its period. Simple, delicate scrolls were popular in the mid-18th century. A more elaborately scalloped profile was used in the decades after the Revolution. A fabric much in fashion in the 18th century was

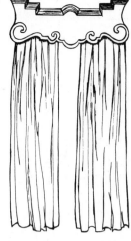

the toile. Imported from France or England, the toile had copperplated scenes printed on it depicting historical events or pastoral scenes. The lambrequin illustrated on the right is a typical Queen Anne style very popular in the late 18th century, often in sheer wools trimmed with gold.

FRENCH FESTOON drapery is one of the oldest and most popular forms used in many variations over the centuries. The vertical strips are held back to form a jabot under the tie-back. Cords running through rings were sewn to the back of each curtain in a diagonal line extending from the bottom center to the upper outer corner. The cords were secured on knobs at the sides of

the windows. A valance was draped across the top. The festoon drape was adapted in the 18th and 19th century to suit all kinds of houses by the use of plain or rich fabrics and ranged from a simple tie-back to elaborate versions with voluminous pleats and cascades. The illustration on the left is of a festoon drape used in a Victorian home. Popular in rich fabrics—velvets, heavy silks and damasks—and opulent trimmings of gold braid, fringe, loops, and tassels adorned valances, lambrequins and tie-backs.

As the Victorian desire for decoration grew more elaborate, so did the manner in which they dressed their windows. The monumental proportions of Victorian rooms and windows encouraged monumental cornices. They were often elaborately carved with birds, wreaths and flowers and gilded.

THE LUSH DRAPES WITH their folds, cross-folds and flutings had under-curtains of Irish lace, tambour or loom-lace. It became fashionable to have a "glass curtain" under the drapes and lace. Made of sheer materials like point d'esprit, nets, marquisette, it was the layer that actually went against the glass window.

GODEY'S LADY'S BOOK, the style dictator of the period and forerunner of today's fashion and decorating magazines, states in the 1852 edition: "No heavy curtains are now in use without one of lace or muslin to soften the effect." Crimson, maroon, deep blues, purples and greens were favored colors for the heavy drapes.

The curtains fell to sill length or to the floor, or were sometimes drawn up with a tie-back. Originally they were hand-drawn and sometimes two rods were hung so that the drapes could be overlapped. By the end of the 18th century French rods came into use that operated in a manner similar to today's traverse rod, with cords, rings and pulleys. The illustration at bottom left shows a simple, early 19th century version in which the drapes remained stationary.

THE CORNICE, VALANCE AND CURTAINS illustrated below represents a suggested window treatment described as Grecian

A sumptuous Victorian parlor in the Wickham-Valentine House in the Valentine Museum, Richmond, Virginia. The life-size portrait is of the young Queen Victoria. The elaborate gilt cornices top deep rose wool damask draperies over lace curtains. The Victorian Damask pattern is reproduced from an 1840 document by Brunschwig & Fils, Inc.

THE TIME AND LABOR necessary for the cleaning of these voluminous drapes, lace curtains and glass curtains, taking the heavy drapes down for the summer, etc. boggles the mind in today's servantless society.

GODEY'S LADY BOOK CONTAINED ILLUSTRATIONS, often as part of an advertisement, that were used by the Victorian homemaker as models for their homes. The Lady Book spanned the decades of the Victorian era and is probably available in the reference section of many libraries around the country. Today's owner of a Victorian house who would like to duplicate period window hangings can go right to the source with Godey's Lady Book.

ALTHOUGH HANGING DRAPES OR CURTAINS from a rod had been a basic method in Europe and the colonies from very early times, the French Rod method became very fashionable at the end of the 18th century. Up to that time, they had been used in rooms of all kinds,

in an 1833 *Encyclopedia For The Home.* The author recommends the style for "a cottage finished in a Grecian or Italian manner." These early 19th century styles are in keeping with homes of simpler architecture, such as the Italianate, and were popular before Victorian elaboration became the fashion.

OCCASIONALLY, THE PURCHASER of an old home will move in and discover that poles, usually of heavy wood matching the woodwork, are installed in the doorways. These poles originally held portieres. Portieres were drapes hung with wooden or brass rings on the poles in front of the doors and sometimes in place of doors. Usually, they were only hung between the larger, formal rooms of the house—parlor, library and dining room. They were drawn to keep the heat from the fireplace in one room—and sometimes for privacy. In the Victorian home tapestries, brocades and velvets were popular. During warmer seasons, the portieres were taken down along with the heavy drapes and replaced with light silks or cottons in pale shades.

WHILE THE FASHIONABLE HOMES IN THE CITY were imitating and adapting European styles, the early colonists in rural areas were using simple fabrics like muslin, calico (at that time an unprinted cotton) and linsey-woolsey (a combination of linen and wool) for simple, functional, and economical window hangings.

The illustration below left is of a style seen often in Early American homes in which the curtain is tied-back on only one side. Sometimes used in large formal rooms in an elegant, sheer fabric on a series of windows. This particular one is a representation of a linen curtain found in the bedroom of the Schenck House in the Brooklyn Museum. The curtain is on a rod of small diameter, held by loops of the same material—a common method. Rods of wood or iron were used, but it is a common museum practice to substitute the widely available brass rod of today.

RE-CREATING PERIOD WINDOW HANGINGS

by Carolyn Flaherty

OLD-HOUSE OWNERS WILL FIND very little relevant information in print that deals with window treatments. Oddly, even the manufacturers who reproduce documentary fabrics and re-create 18th- and 19th-century patterns do not tie in their fabrics with good suggestions on how to use them.

ONE LARGE MANUFACTURER'S current advertisement in the "house and garden" magazines shows some nice documentary patterns—and then suggests that you send $2.50 for a booklet and a cocktail apron made out of this historic fabric.

OBVIOUSLY, THIS WILL NOT HELP you treat your windows to an 18th-century lambrequin or a Victorian valance in keeping with the period of your home.

A LITTLE do-it-yourself research of period windows will result in more authentic and often simpler ideas for decorating than the abundance of glossy photos depicting acres of pinch-pleated curtains and wall-to-wall fabric usually offered by decorating magazines.

ALTHOUGH PERIOD DECORATING is rarely done outside of museums and historical societies, it can be simple and rewarding. Since your house is not a museum, you can be free to experiment: You can substitute less expensive and easier-to-care-for fabrics and modify styles, while still restoring much of the original look and feel to a room.

TO GIVE YOU A HEAD START with your own research we have put together some ideas for the handyperson and suggestions about fabrics.

FOR PERIOD WINDOW TREATMENTS requiring lambrequins, certain valance styles and decorative cornices (illustrated and explained in the April 1974 issue) you will need a basic cornice board.

FIRST CUT a 1 × 6 in. pine board to a length that will extend to the outer edge of the window casing. Attach to the top of the window using

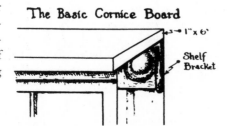

The Basic Cornice Board

a small shelf bracket, held in place with 3/4 in. screws.

ABOUT THE ONLY CAUTION is to make sure that the cornice board is level before tightening the screws down.

TO MAKE A LAMBREQUIN YOU must first make a pattern. You can do this by simply looking at pictures of period rooms or by visiting museums or historical restorations and copying the scalloped or scroll shape you like best. When using cotton or other lightweight fabrics, it will probably be necessary to stiffen the material. Buckram can be cut in the same shape and glue-stiffened to make it easier to pin or baste the material over it. When covering the buckram with the fabric, be sure the pattern design is centered properly.

WHEN USING A VERY HEAVY fabric such as crewel, wool, or brocades, it will not be necessary to use more than a lining. Many colonial lambrequins were made in such heavy wools that they were used without a lining. This kind of lambrequin doesn't have a tight-stretched look to the fabric but is soft and heavy in appearance. Welting, gold braid and other trims outlining the bottom edge also give the lambrequin additional weighting.

TO ATTACH the lambrequin, sew hooks on the back of it, and place screw eyes in corresponding positions on the cornice board. The fabric can then be removed when necessary while leaving the board in place. Curtains or drapes are then hung on a rod behind the cornice board.

Attaching A Lambrequin

IF YOU WISH TO MAKE A FLAT, STIFF lambrequin, glue the fabric onto a Masonite pattern that has been tacked to the cornice board. Wallpaper paste works well for gluing fabric.

HOW TO MAKE A CORNICE

FOR A MORE FORMAL APPEARANCE, some period wondow treatments used a wooden cornice that projected from the window casing and covered the top of the valance, drapes and curtains.

WHILE OLD-TIME CARPENTERS USED many different jointing techniques in cornice construction, it's possible for the old-house handyperson to fabricate a basic cornice that will will be in keeping with the period of your particular house. Many basic design ideas can be copied from cornices seen in period rooms.

WE'LL SHOW HERE HOW TO MAKE a simple cornice that would be appropriate in not-too-formal rooms, especially early 19th century. The basic idea is to make a cornice that will slip over the basic cornice board.

THE CORNICE can be built up from standard lumber as shown in the cross-section. The 1" × 6" pine board is cut so that it surrounds the front and sides of the cornice board. These three pieces are glued and nailed. A 4" wide plywood strip (or similar stock) is glued and nailed to the 1" × 6" frame. Strips of 1" × 1" square molding is nailed to the inside of the frame at a point that will allow the cornice to rest at an appropriate height on the cornice board.

Cornice Cross-Section

WP 47 Crown Molding
½ x 4" Plywood
1" x 6" Board
1' x 1"
Cornice Board

FINALLY, 3 pieces of crown molding are cut and attached to the outside of the frame. Careful planning is required here because the corners

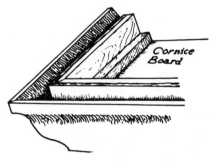

Cornice Board

require a compound miter—cutting two angles simultaneously. It's hard to explain in words, but you'll quickly discern the problem once you get into it. If the cornice is going to be painted or gilded, you can use wood filler to compensate for a near-miss at the corner.

THIS SIMPLE COR-NICE will slide right onto the cornice board, resting on the 1" × 1" molding strips. It can be held in place with hooks and eyes fastened to the top of the cornice board.

THE HANDYPERSON WHO'S A WHIZ with a sabre saw and router can fabricate more elaborate cornices with scrollwork, scallops, etc. There is also more elaborate period molding that you can use instead of the lumber-yard standards.

SWAG VALANCES

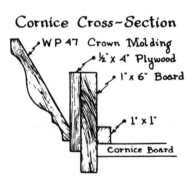

IT IS EASIER TO HANG A SWAG valance if you alter the position of the basic cornice board by turning it 90 degrees. (See diagram below.) A swag valance can be simply tacked to this lath board, letting the sides fall into a jabot effect. For a simple window treatment, this valance—with the sides falling to mid-length or sill-length—was used commonly in the 18th century without under curtains. The skirt-like valance across the top was sometimes drawn up in the center with stitching. Modern gathering tape simplifies the task. A tassel hanging from the middle was a popular trimming.

Two Ways To Install A Lath Board

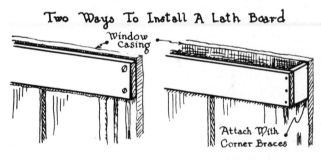

Window Casing

Attach With Corner Braces

IN FORMAL ROOMS with large windows, the swag valance is often seen made in rich silks and velvets with drapes of the same fabric. Large decorative rings or ornate metal tiebacks can be screwed into the lath board at each side. The material is then pulled through the rings, falling into a jabot on each side. To hold a heavy fabric in place, it will probably be best to staple the back of the valance to the back of the lath board.

FORMAL VALANCES

SOME FORMAL VALANCES REQUIRE A tight, square corner with the sides of the valance hanging down in a precise manner. To facilitate hanging this kind of valance, you can construct a window board.

ADD TWO SHORT boards at right angles to the underside of the basic cornice board.

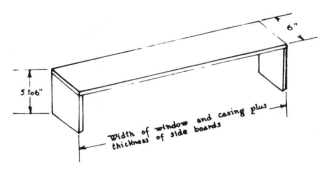

AN ELEGANT BUT SIMPLE VALANCE can be made by stapling a long, rectangular piece of material (brocade, brocatelle, velvet, wool, moire, satin, etc.) across the top of the window board. Drape the center portion to fall into a graceful curve and staple to each side. The side pieces are brought from the top to drape over stapled

portion on each side and carefully placed in folds that fall into a jabot effect down the sides of the window. They are stapled to the back of the window board to hold them in place.

ANOTHER FORMAL, MORE COMPLICATED TREATMENT is the Austrian valance. It requires an elegant but lightweight fabric, such as silk taffeta, that will gather attractively. The fabric is fitted and stapled to the window board and drawn up in two or three places with gathering tape or stitching. Trims and tassels can dress an Austrian valance to the desired degree of 18th century elegance or 19th century Victorian opulence.

THE VENETIAN CURTAIN

VENETIAN CURTAINS ARE A SIMPLE WAY to combine shade and drapery in one piece of fabric. It was a forerunner of the Venetian blind and the Austrian shade. Early Venetian curtains were made simply to draw up in one pice, forming a bunchy gathering when raised to the top. The simplest kind, illustrated below, were mounted on a board at the top, with a stiffening strip of wood at the bottom. A series of rings were sewn in a row along both sides of the curtain.

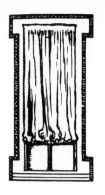

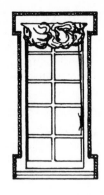

Cords, attached to the stiffening strip, ran up through pulleys or eyes. The cords, used to raise or lower the curtain, were secured to a hook or a knob on the window casing.

VENETIAN CURTAINS of this type, made in heavy, rough fabrics (linen, cotton, wool or combinations) were popular in England and introduced widely into the colonies in the 1700s.

LIGHTER FABRICS such as silks or cotton dimity, which formed graceful festoons, were used for Venetian curtains in more formal rooms.

ONE OR MORE additional rows of rings would then be sewn up the back with corresponding cords. With softer fabric, the wood stiffener at the bottom was often omitted. A cornice or lambrequin was frequently used to cover the apparatus at the top.

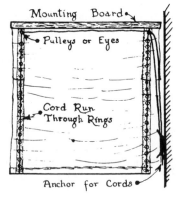

THE AUSTRIAN SHADE of today is really a Venetian curtain made of a thin, opaque material, often with many sections for wide windows.

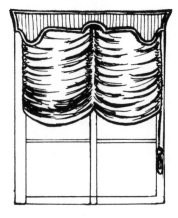

WHILE IT IS FAIRLY easy to purchase a standard Austrian shade, suitable for a formally furnished room, the Venetian curtain usually has to be made to order. Even then, it is usually a narrower version of an Austrian shade in a slightly heavier fabric.

IF YOU WISH TO MAKE THE EARLY type of Venetian curtain, heavy cotton, wool, or one of the rough-textured synthetic fabrics, perhaps with cotton or wool fringe, would be appropriate. You will then have a simple and authentic window treatment particularly attractive in an early 18th century room.

THE FRENCH ROD

THE FRENCH ROD offers the simplest way to duplicate period window hangings. It has been used for centuries in wood, iron and brass in Europe and America in every period. Popular all through the 18th century, the decorative French rod became very fashionable around the beginning of the 1800s. Drapery hardware firms manufacture a large selection of plain and ornamental rods that are widely available.

CLASSIC WINDOW TREATMENTS
FOR THE EARLY AMERICAN HOUSE

THE SWAG VALANCE is the most adaptable window treatment for the period house. Used throughout the 18th century, the swag was then called a festoon and the cascading sides known as jabots. Most early hangings were simply the swag and short cascades (they were rarely long enough to reach the sill) used alone without additional drapes or curtains.

IN THE PICTURE ABOVE, the 3 large windows are draped after the fashion shown in Chippendale's "Director." The fabric is a rare silk brocade with red, blue and green floral sprays (symmetrically placed) against a salmon ground. These hangings are typical of the early swags in that they are simply one long rectangle of fabric, gathered at the corners with a heavy cord. The back edge of the swag is tacked to a cornice board.

THE MOST INTERESTING FEATURE of this window treatment is the varying length of the cascades.

IN THE CENTER PHOTO, a swag is tacked to the cornice board and a French rod (under the swag) holds a single drape. In the first half of the 19th century many variations were used: swag-and-cascades; swag-and-cascades over one or a pair of drapes; or swag-and-drapes.

IN THE GREEK REVIVAL HOUSE swags, cascades and drapes were quite popular. The length of the cascades or drapes were longer—to the sill or floor, and a glass curtain was often used in addition. The keynote of Greek Revival decoration was simple elegance and drapery fabric was silk–brocades, taffetas, damasks. Colors were either light and cool, (light blue, silvery gray, apricot) or (if the furnishings were French) rather royal: purple, emerald green, royal blue, and often trimmed in gold. Window treatments were graceful in line—reminiscent of a Greek toga.

HOW TO MAKE A SWAG AND CASCADES

Materials Needed

Muslin for pattern, drapery fabric for swags and cascades, lining fabric for cascades (Lining will show–select to match or contrast), twill tape, staple gun and staples.

Swag

THE HEIGHT of the window determines the depth of the swag–generally about 16–18 in. deep. The width of the top of the swag is the same as the width of the cornice, but the bottom width of the fabric for the swag should 8–12 in. wider, depending upon the desired finished depth.

Diagram A

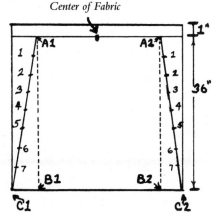

PLACE A PIECE of fabric 37 in. deep and as wide as needed right side up on a flat surface, and mark center of width at top edge. Draw a line 1 in. below top edge of fabric; on it indicate width of top of swag by marking points A1 and A2, centered on width of fabric. Mark corresponding points B1 and B2 on bottom edge of fabric. Decide how deep the finished swag will be. If finished depth of swag is to be 16 in. allow 5 in. from B1 to C1 and from B2 to C2; if finished depth is 17 in. allow 6 in.; if finished depth is 18 in. allow 7 in. Draw diagonal line from A1 to C1 and from A2 to C2. If you want 5 folds, divide the diagonal line into 6 equal parts; if you 6 folds, divide it into 7 equal parts, etc.

TACK SWAG TO cornice board along one inch allowance at top edge of fabric. Fold at points 1 and pin to A on both sides. Fold at points 2 and pin to A and continue folding and pinning on both sides until all folds are pinned in place, smoothing folds from center out to sides as you work.

CUT OFF EXCESS fabric on both sides in a straight line perpendicular to the floor. Place twill tape along top raw edge

and staple it and the top edge of swag to top of cornice; staple through folds at either side into cornice, making certain staples will be hidden by cascades.

LEAVING ABOUT 3½ IN. beyond last fold, trim away excess fabric along curved bottom edge. Turn under a ½ in. hem.

Cascades

CASCADES CAN BE MADE to any length. For classic proportions, the inside edge should be the same depth as the deepest point of the finished swag. The average cascade is made with three pleats.

Diagram B

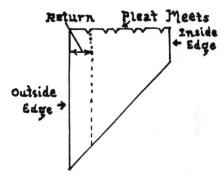

Diagram C

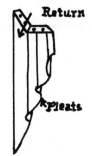

FIRST, MAKE A MUSLIN pattern. Cut it to shape as shown in Diagram B, with a diagonal line from bottom of inside edge to bottom of outside edge. Allow enough fabric (usually about 4 in.) from outside edge for covering cornice return before starting pleats. Also allow about 1 in. along top edge for folding over cornice, and ½ in. on other three sides for seams. Starting at long side where corner of cornice will fall, fold in three pleats; notch fabric to indicate folds and depths of pleats (Diagram B).

USE MUSLIN PATTERN to cut cascades and lining pieces. With right sides together, seam fabric and lining together along sides and diagonal edge. Turn to right side and press. Pin top edges together and stitch ½ in. from edge and press. Fold and pin pleats in place; then stitch across top. Bind top edge with matching fabric or finish with tape to hold pleats in place. Make second cascade, reversing long side and direction of diagonal edge. Staple cascades to top of cornice (Diagram C), overlapping ends of swags and covering staples.

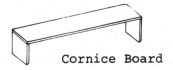

Cornice Board

PORTIERES

A PORTIERE is a curtain or drape used over an arch or doorway. They were both decorative and functional and can serve the old-house owner for these two purposes today.

THE USE OF PORTIERES began in castles to keep the heat from the fireplace in a room and the drafts out. Colonial homes seldom required portieres as our first American houses were small and generally had doors between the rooms.

THE VICTORIAN HOUSE, with its high ceilings and generously proportioned rooms, brought back the portiere. Hanging an elegant drape in a doorway also fit in well with the Victorian's love of luxurious fabric and desire to leave no space undecorated. Often a portiere would be hung just for appearance and fastened to the doorframe so that it could not be drawn.

BUT IT IS THE FUNCTIONAL use of the portiere that is of interest in our present economy. By drawing a heavy velvet drape across a door of the room in use, and leaving the room not being used unheated, the big old house will require far less fuel. They can also keep heat in rooms and out of halls.

IN THE 19TH CENTURY portieres were almost always made with a cut or uncut velvet fabric. They were often made with a different color fabric on each side so that each room could have, in effect, a different drape on the same rod. Occasionally, in a richly furnished set of rooms, portieres would be hung on both sides of a door—usually the huge sliding doors between parlor and dining room.

FROM THE 1880's up to the turn of the century, maroon was the favored color. And maroon was most often combined with buff—maroon on one side, buff on the other. Also popular was maroon with crimson or olive. Deep browns and greens were the next most favored colors. Applique, embroidery and gimp were added for decorative interest.

THE HEAVY PORTIERES were generally taken down for the warm weather and lighter silk drapes were hung for strictly decorative effect. Because late Victorian houses had so much wood—walnut or oak—in the main rooms, the color, pattern and texture of the portiere was a desirable break in the austerity of the woodwork.

AS HOUSES BUILT after the turn of the century came under the influence of the Classical Revival and walls and wood became lighter, the portiere was made in lighter fabrics and in lighter colors—such as striped silk. But these were not much more functional than the beaded curtain that had a brief popularity in the 1890's. What we are concerned with here is the functional portiere.

MAKING PORTIERES

TO MAKE A PORTIERE it is necessary to have a good, heavy fabric. Velvets are available in mohair, cotton and silk. Brunschwig & Fils and Clarence House (see OHJ Buyers' Guide for addresses) can do embossing with 19th century rollers in many patterns. They also have the tassels and trim that were used for the most fashionable types of portieres. These firms deal only with the professional, however, and fabric and trim are quite expensive.

WASHABLE SYNTHETIC VELVETS are widely available and their appearance is very much the same. They are durable and far less expensive. The trimmings are not available but a little creativity can substitute. For instance, with a maroon velvet drape, stop about a foot from the floor and finish with a buff velvet. This would give the same proportion to the panel as it would have with trim. Horizontal bands of fabric in contrasting colors will also add to the period look and substitute for expensive gold trimmings.

Two portiere designs from the popular decorating book, "Hints On Household Taste" by Charles L. Eastlake, 1878.

FOR FULL INSULATION BENEFIT (also for sound-

proofing) the drapes should be lined. In England, where portieres are commonplace, cotton flannel is used for a lining.
Good results can also be obtained with a dacron filler normally used for making comforters.

INGRAIN CARPETS were often used for portieres. An ingrain carpet has double or triple woven cloth and is reversible.
They were quite popular and relatively inexpensive. Usually
woven in 36 in. widths, they required no more than adding
rings on one end and to be hung on a rod. The Oriental rug
was also used to make portieres, in particular, the type known
as a "Turkey carpet."

THE MOST COMMON WAY to hang portieres was on a
wooden pole with wooden rings attached to the drapes. Poles
were either set inside the door frame or hung on brackets attached to the face of the door casing. When attached to the
casing, a deep valance was often used over the drapes.

A MORE UNUSUAL WAY OF HANGING the portiere
was to drape the curtain over a rod and let a portion hang
down to form a valance. Called a "Queen's Curtain," they were
embroidered and appliqued and could be ordered through the
mail from drapery firms. Since the part hanging down from
the rod could be any length, and because they were meant to
bunch up at the hem, it was truly a "one size fits all" item.

Portiere made from a patterned fabric and edged with tassels are hung from brass rings on a pole painted white.

MOST PORTIERES were simply pulled to one side of the
door when not in use, but some were fastened to the doorframe with a looped metal chain. Hardware stores sell a similar
chain that is used for hanging lamps or plants.

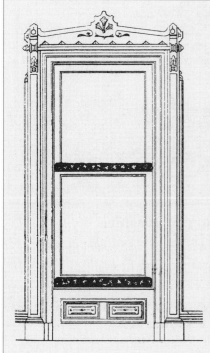

The Draft Excluder

THE ENGLISH VICTORIAN homeowners
had a clever but simple trick they used to keep
drafts out of the house. A long, sausage-shaped
object made of fabric and stuffed with sawdust,
was placed along the joint between the upper
and lower window sash or along the sill and on
the floor in front of the doors.

TRADITIONALLY made of fabric that was
red in color, the draft-excluder can be sewn
from any remnant of material. When making a
portiere, a yard or two of the same fabric could
be used for a draft-excluder, giving this homely
little object a touch of class.

IN LIEU OF not-so-readily available sawdust,
any heaver filler–like beans–can be used. If
there is a chance the draft-excluder might get
wet–as one on the floor on a wet day might–it
would be better to use a filler that would resist
water. Aquarium gravel would be ideal.

WALLPAPER IN OLD HOUSES

By Carolyn Flaherty

The old-house owner can do a lot to restore the original look and feel of a house with wallpaper. And there are many ways to approach it.

You may be fortunate enough to have an original paper on your walls. If so, experts advise that you do no more to it than dust with a clean paint brush, as chemicals and coatings can ruin an antique paper. Antique papers were often hand painted in tempera or water colors. There are companies that will reproduce an antique design if the piece of original paper is large enough to contain at least one repeat of the pattern.

If you find a piece of an original paper and do not wish to go to the expense of having it reproduced, or if you find only a fragment, there are many historical societies and museums around the country that would appreciate receiving these samples.

There are also firms that carry original antique papers. These designs are often the scenic murals or historical depictions that were so popular in the 19th century, or antique English imported reproductions of Oriental patterns and papers directly from China. Some firms also reproduce antique papers using the old method of hand-blocking, a very time consuming (and expensive) method.

More likely, the old-house owner will just want to re-create some of the original spatial effect and period of the room with a more moderately priced paper, manufactured in the modern way. These wallcoverings, however, because of the attention given to the authenticity of reproduction, will maintain the feeling and period of the house.

The available designs in reproduction papers seem to be preponderantly 18th century. The reasons for this, so far as I can determine, are many. By mid-19th century, when America began mass-producing its own, the enormous popularity of wallpaper led to some rather overdone styles and badly printed paper. As one decorator said, "You really wouldn't *want* to copy anything done after 1820." This, to me, seems an arbitrary judgement. The wild

Panel, Plaster, and Border

This type of decoration, which divided walls vertically, reached the height of its popularity in the mid-19th century.

and wonderful whimsies of the Victorian period express the mood and character of that particular era so forcefully that even its excesses hold a charm and fascination to many of us. Also, it is an attitude that neglects much of the truly fine design done here and abroad in the 19th century.

ANOTHER, MORE practical difficulty with 19th century papers, is that, aside from murals, even the all-over patterns were much larger than in the 18th century. Many 19th-century houses, particularly the brownstone, had rather grandiose proportions in the formal areas of the house (parlor, dining room), which made these large-scale designs necessary.

AND THE fashionable mode of dividing walls for decorative effect into horizontal or vertical portions also led to some quite complicated coordinated designs used in combination with one another in the same room. Paper was often used to represent moldings, panels and even used extensively on the ceilings, often representing ornate medallions.

These intricate styles and the methods of combining them have limited the amount of 19th-century paper that today's manufacturers can profitably reproduce. Few home owners care to use paper for the same purposes or in the same overwhelming quantities as the Victorians often did.

ALONG WITH THE popular murals and historical depictions, often quite large, with borders and frieze carrying related designs, the Victorians made use of some rather sentimental themes. One, which won a design prize in the 1880s, had a growth of clover and swarms of bees over a band of clover heads in the dado. The fill pattern was a field of clover with bees, while the frieze above carried out the theme in a hexagonal pattern suggesting the honeycomb cells in a beehive.

WALLPAPER was so popular in the 19th century that it was used to cover bandboxes, so called because they were originally used to store men's collar bands. They soon became the 19th century answer to overflow packing problems. The earlier ones

This bedroom in a Merrimack, Massachusetts landmark home is papered with a reproduction of an early 18th century pattern by Thomas Strahan Company, originally found on a chintz fabric. Early American rooms (this one is c. 1757) were usually papered ceiling to baseboard.

were usually covered with common French and English border papers, but later in the 19th century special commemorative and topical scenes were printed especially for large bandboxes.

THE 18TH CENTURY home owner has a wide and excellent selection of reproductions to choose from. Many lines are "documentary" (designation by historical societies or museums of the authenticity and origin of the paper).

MANY FIRMS INFORM the buyer as to the origin and period of their designs. Thomas Strahan Company, for example, prints the history of the paper on the back of the page in their sample book. Collections are often grouped by period or places of origin.

OTHER REPRODUCTION wallpapers reflect many areas of 18th and 19th century decorative art. Design is adapted from old plates, fabrics, tapestries and crewel-work and are often reproduced with a matching fabric.

KATZENBACH AND WARREN'S *Waterhouse Wallhangings* contains reproductions collected by Dorothy Waterhouse in New England homes. These wall paintings represent brocades, tapestries and other exotic decorations seen by sea captains in foreign ports.

A standard comercial pattern, c. 1848, showing a a striped design with scrollwork and flowers.

A typical horizontal wall division popular in the 19th century. The frieze was commonly 14" to 16" wide. The dado (also an architectural term) was often papered. Dadoes in the 18th century were usually wainscotting or panelling. The proportions of division changed from from decade to decade in the 19th century with the dado portion rising.

MANY COLLECTIONS, like the Williamsburg, reproduce designs up to 1820. And because the patterns are often French and English in origin (in turn sometimes reproduced from Indian and Chinese design) they blend in well with the eclectic temperament of the 19th century home.

Frieze

Border

Fill Pattern

Border

Dado

Base-Board

FINDING A LATE 19th century Victorian paper requires a little more hunting. However, most of the wallpaper firms are giving the 19th century more attention these days, perhaps prodded by the increasing numbers of people who are buying, renovating and living in 19th-century houses around the country.

The same French Directoire wallpaper now covering the walls of the Cabell Bedroom (named for Henry C. Cabell, Governor of Virginia from 1805 to 1807) in the Wickham-Valentine House at the Valentine Museum in Richmond, Virginia. Photographs courtesy of Brunschwig & Fils, Inc., specialists in documentary fabrics and wallpapers for museums and restoration houses.

Photo of a "document" (as the original piece of wallpaper is called) of a block printed French wallpaper, c. 1815.

The document as reproduced by Brunschwig & Fils, of this striped design with nesting birds, squirrels and flowers.

VICTORIAN FANCYWORK

by Carolyn Flaherty

VICTORIAN DECORATION EARNED its often bad reputation in large part because of fancywork. This was the name given to the endless variety of ornament produced by the Victorian woman in an effort to "beautify" her home.

OTHER THAN NEEDLEWORK—making clothing for herself and her family—which was a necessary skill for all females before the sewing machine—fancywork was the only outlet for the "genteel" middle- or upper-middle class woman.

THE ROLE OF SUCH A WOMAN was to show the world how well her prosperous husband was doing. This necessitated servants and often a governess. With even "novel reading" considered somewhat of a vice, making fancywork objects was the only proper way to spend a long afternoon.

UNFORTUNATELY for the appearance of many a parlor, too many women did not find this pursuit rewarding, nor were they very good at the crafts at which they so earnestly and diligently worked.

POPULAR PUBLICATIONS URGED them on, however, with high-minded advice. "The wife is the presiding genius of the home. Let her learn to create those adornments that make her home pleasant and attractive." And so they did ... often with such a vengeance that one wonders, looking at some of the worst examples, if there was not some subconscious retaliation directed at the Victorian male who kept her in her ribbon-bedecked, stuffed parlor.

BUT THEN, as today, there were some who truly enjoyed these creative efforts and, far more often than we should expect, some lovely things were made. Even most of the more naive efforts show an industry and charm that would be readily admired if they had been produced in colonial rather than Victorian times.

SOME OF THE MOST POPULAR TYPES of fancywork, most of which can be duplicated today, are described in this article. Left out, as being of only historic interest, are the many items associated with the bygone pastimes and customs of the era. Because needlework played such an important part in their lives, ladies spent a great deal of time ornamenting pincushions, needlecases (needles were an expensive item) and thimblecases. These were popular gift items and they usually rested in an elaborately decorated workbasket.

THE CUSTOM OF PRESENTING a calling card when paying a visit provided many more opportunities for decoration. The cards themselves were usually quite elaborate, and a table was placed in the hall for the sole purpose of holding a fancy card box in which to place them. Another table, covered with a fancywork cloth, was placed in the parlor to exhibit the current projects the young ladies of the house were engaged in, for the admiration of the visitor. These objects, no longer useful in contemporary life, may have caused much of the Victorian clutter, but they were very dear to the heart of a 19th-century lady.

BERLIN-WORK

KNOWN TODAY AS "petit-point" or "needle-point," it was then called "wool-work," "canvas-work," but most commonly it was known as "Berlin-work." Originally, a pattern was printed, requiring many skilled colorists, on which each tiny square represented a stitch. These patterns originated in Berlin. The needleworker would look at this paper pattern and then duplicate the square with a stitch on a canvas. It was an extraordinarily painstaking but popular pastime. Woolwork was used for ottomans, chairs, and footstools and fireplace screens.

BY MID-19th CENTURY the method of printing the design right on the canvas (as it is still done today) had been perfected. This spurred Berlin-work on to even greater popularity. From the traditional birds and flowers, patterns went on to historical figures and scenes and copies of great paintings, much of  them earning Berlin-work its bad name.

THE CRAFT LATER degenerated to cardboard cards with perforated holes, and to patterns sold with the difficult parts already filled in.

MANY PEOPLE STILL ENJOY doing needlepoint and it is recognized as an historically authentic textile to use with colonial or Victorian antiques.

BEAD WORK

GLASS BEADS were produced in abundance in Venice in the early part of the 19th century and they were used in needlework to decorate purses, work boxes and pincushions.

THE BEADS WERE ALSO worked on a loom to make lamp or table mats, vase covers, hanging baskets and lambrequins. Or, in other words, a covering for just about anything it could be made to fit. Crystal and metal beadwork was also used lavishly for fringes and tassels on upholstery and drapes.

FRETWORK

INTRODUCED in the 1860s, fretwork—also known as scrollwork, jigsaw work, and Sorrento carving—soon became one of the most popular crafts in the next few decades with both sexes. A delicate handsaw or "jigsaw" was used to cut out patterns on a small wooden article.

PUBLISHERS OF needlework and other fancywork patterns soon put out portfolios of designs for fretwork. These patterns were traced on wood—an inexpensive material at the time—and then carved out with the jigsaw.

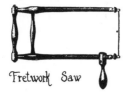

Fretwork Saw

BRACKETS FOR THE ubiquitous knickknack shelf were the most popular items. Fretwork also was widely used to make wallpockets or "catch-alls"—a favorite Victorian item. They were carved in wood with a pocket of beadwork or embroidered cloth. They often held no more than the weekly newspaper or (an obviously necessary item) a dustcloth! Fretwork was also used to make picture frames, towel racks and other numerous small items.

SPATTERWORK

TO PRODUCE A spatterwork or "spraywork" pattern, an arrangement of leaves, ferns and/or flowers was pinned to a light board or piece of fabric. A wire sieve was placed over this and india ink was "spattered" through, usually with an old toothbrush. A modern spraygun would quickly give the same effect.

A WELL-DEFINED, delicate silhouette remained after removing the foliage. "Graceful, waving grasses" and even seaweed were popular, and it was recommended that the "spattering" gradually thin out towards the edges to give a graduation of tints. The patterns were then used for lampshades, curtains,

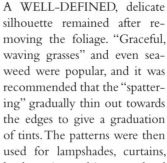

lambrequins, and insets on book covers, boxes, and workbaskets. The most common use—a framed picture—still adds a nice, nostalgic touch to a Victorian parlor.

LAMPSHADES

LAMPSHADES WERE MADE from ornamented cardboard for many years before the Victorian period. One of the most popular methods was known as "embossing on cardboard." To do this, a series of slanting incisions was made on paper or thin cardboard with a sharp knife held obliquely. The cuts raised the face of the paper slightly to make a shadowy decoration.

THE DESIGN ILLUSTRATED ON the left is an actual pattern for another version of embossing on cardboard known as "diaphne." Diaphne was a form of window decoration that vaguely imitated the effect of stained glass, but with colored paper. This method, used for lampshades, called for colored tissue paper behind the slits. According to *Godey's Lady's Book,* this method would "give a soft shading to the old-fashioned biscuit lamp shade."

SOME OF THE MORE elaborate versions added fretwork or beadwork. Later, actual slits were made through the cardboard and the light of the electric bulb filtered through. Along with floral decorations, birds, swans and landscapes were popular motifs.

SHELLWORK

MORE THAN ANY OTHER SINGLE OBJECT, the seashell filled the Victorian desire for intricacy of detail, delicacy, and variety of curved lines. Collecting shells was a popular pastime at English resorts. The tiny "rice" shell from the West Indies was also enormously popular. Great numbers and varieties of shells were glued together to form floral arrangements for mantel decorations, figures, vases, jewelry and hair ornaments.

SHELLWORK PICTURE FRAMES were well-suited to the Victorian theory of "appropriateness" in decor. If a landscape scene was framed in a rustic manner with twigs and acorns, what could be more appropriate than a seascape framed in seashells?

SOME CHARMING EXAMPLES of the complicated floral arrangements that were used for mantel decorations still retain their delicacy a century later due to the practice of placing them—like many other types of handwork—under a glass dome for protection.

UNFORTUNATELY, the over-abundance of fancywork produced in so many endless hours was often jumbled together along with many other fussy decorations and knick-knacks. Taken out of its muddle and placed in a more serene atmosphere, many of these fancywork objects can be as delightful to us as they were to the Victorians. And a few of them, whether antique or newly-made, can give a charming nostalgic touch to an old Victorian house.

GOTHIC DECORATION
IN THE AMERICAN HOUSE

CONTEMPORARY FASHIONS in home decoration are influenced by pictures–movies, television, magazines. But the great fad for Gothic decoration in the 19th century was inspired by words–mostly the words by and about Sir Walter Scott. It was not just the popularity of his "Gothic" novels but the romantic figure he himself presented to the public. He built himself a new Scottish castle, Abbotsford, imitating in its construction and decoration the medieval associations of his novels. Publications such as *Godey's Lady's Book* kept avid American readers informed of its progress.

THE DECORATION OF ABBOTSFORD was completely different from the early 19th-century style of decoration. The cool, light shades and white woodwork of the Adam period were then common. But Scott liked black oak and rich colors and the art of simulating rare surfaces like hardwood, stone and marble with painted decoration. English oak wainscotting was used in his mansion, but the oak was simulated on ceilings and cornices. Crimson wallpaper complemented the real and grained wood.

IN AMERICA, this combination (using native black walnut or oak) and deep red continued in popularity until the turn of the century–particularly in dining rooms. Tapestry-like wallpapers as well as reproductions of colored or embossed leather (made of papier mache or stencilled and glazed) were popular for their association with the romantic.

THE ROOM IN ABBOTSFORD that had the most lasting effect on American Victorian decoration was Scott's library. Somber, with dark panelling and walls painted to resemble stone, it presented the "ideal" atmosphere for scholarly pursuit. This version of a library was so established in the Victorian mind that although Abbotsford was completed in 1824, the Victorian homeowner would have a grave and Gothic library until the end of the century–no matter what style the rest of the house was decorated in.

ANOTHER OF SCOTT'S interesting contributions to interior decoration was his popularization of collecting antiques and salvaged house parts. He took many items from the ruins of Melrose Abbey for his new home. In a lumberyard, he came across an ancient porch dismantled from an Edinburgh prison. He rescued it for its carved panels, which he used for wainscotting.

A BOOST FOR THE Gothic style in decorating was provided by Queen Victoria herself. She had the private dining room at Windsor Castle decorated in Gothic motifs. Its pointed arch panelling, carved tracery ceiling and carpet with a Gothic cross pattern was much admired and imitated.

IT IS DIFFICULT TO imagine the way the Victorians used the trefoil, quatrefoil, and other Gothic motifs to decorate furniture, wallpaper, cast-iron stoves, jewelry and other common household items. That is because we think of Gothic as ecclesiastic and see it mostly in cathedrals.

BUT THAT WAS NOT the way the Victorians thought of it. To them it was romantic and there was nothing incongruous about furniture that resembled architecture on a very small scale. This kind of popular decoration often had little to do with the style of the house in the early 19th century.

AS THE Industrial Revolution produced more wealth in America, real wood tracery and vaulting was found in interiors. And as Downing and Davis popularized the Gothic styles for houses, even simpler rural houses began to sport an arch or two or the type of square-headed drip mouldings as shown in the drawing on the previous page (a design for a bedroom by A. J. Davis) for interiors.

IN HIS WIDELY-READ BOOK, *The Architecture Of Country Houses* Andrew Jackson Downing gave advice for decorating the interiors of houses in the Gothic mode. In general, he recommended lighter shades such as rose or gray for parlors and dining rooms as being more appropriate for rural homes than the deep crimsons and purples.

HE DID, however, recommend a painted imitation of stone for hallways and graining for wood in all parts of the house to create a rich, dark hardwood effect when less expensive woods were used. He supplied drawings for oriel and bay windows with heavy drip moulds and diamond-shaped panes, and many illustrations of simple furniture with a Gothic motif.

FOR LIBRARIES, of course, he gave only one decorating theme: "Comparatively grave."

FOUNTAINS FOR THE CONSERVATORY

By Tom H. Gerhardt

IN *THE GREAT HOUSES OF SAN FRANCISCO*, Thomas Aidala describes the use of plants in the Victorian house.: "If money allowed, you could almost always find a conservatory, a wonderful glass room, just off the drawing room on the first floor, filled with plants growing around an artificial pond fed by trickling water, which often contained goldfish and occasionally frogs." The conservatory fountain is really one of the more delightfully whimsical, exciting, and unusual decorative pieces that is allowable in the Victorian scheme.

THERE ARE THE SMALLER VERSIONS of the larger outdoor fountains, usually consisting of a figure on an iron basin around 2½ ft. in diameter that is set up on iron legs. Also, usually on pedestals following the same motifs as the ones under spills on exterior fountains, are often found iron octagon-shaped aquariums piped with a spray in the middle and having a drain and overflow. The plumbing is very similar to an exterior fountain. One could then watch the fish through the glass sides while enjoying the sound of the splashing spray.

HIGHLY ORNAMENTAL rectangular aquariums were also produced, a very early model being on a cast iron stand that looks like rustic pieces of tree limbs nailed together. The corners of the conservatory fountain-aquarium often have iron brackets for flowerpots and/or iron eagles gazing down into the pool of water.

GOLDFISH along with standard aquarium plants are excellent for ornamenting these aquariums. There are even miniature water lilies available that will do well in the proper light. A long algae scraper equipped with a razor blade takes care of the "green stuff" that forms on the glass and is not consumed by those helpful scavengers, pond snails. Coarse gravel and rocks make the bottom very interesting. The addition of fresh water by the use of the spray and avoiding the introduction of too many fish or overfeeding will eliminate the need for frequent cleanings.

DRY SPELLS FOR THESE AQUARIUMS should be avoided as the lack of water causes the seal to give out, necessitating the use of aquarium cement to form a watertight bond once more.

RESTORING CAST IRON

EXCELLENT SUGGESTIONS for restoring cast iron are given in another chapter of this book. To these suggestions might be added an emphasis that cast iron should not be sand-blasted, as this removes the smooth, rust-resisting (to some extent) finish that was placed on the item at the foundry. Stripping through the use of chemicals and then wire-brushing the pieces is much safer (to the cast iron) methods of removing the paint and rust.

MISSING PIECES, especially urn handles, can often be recast by a local foundry if they are willing to make a mold. Although it is tricky, broken pieces may be welded through the use of nickel rod on an evenly heated surface (often, the cast iron will break elsewhere while the welded place is cooling if the whole surface has not been heated).

AN INTERESTING VICTORIAN color scheme for iron urns and fountains consists of dual (compatible) colors that bring out the features in sort of a "Wedgwood" design. White with pale blue, pale green, pale gray, or cream were often used on these garden ornaments during Victorian times. Less "Wedgwood"-looking but also used were black with silver or dark red and green with dark red.

IT MUST BE REMEMBERED in painting fountains that regardless of the colors used the water will always stain the paint according to the chemicals that are in it. Fountains supplied by artesian wells often will have an iron coating all over the wet surfaces within days. This staining might to some extent dictate the color scheme; otherwise its evidence must be regarded as an artistic patina and a necessary evil.

THE BLUE SWIMMING POOL LOOK for a fountain basin must be avoided. If a coat of paint must be applied to the cement basin, it should be black waterproofing tar. Most people think at first that this might be gloomy-looking. However, the black surface gives an illusion of depth, causes the surface of the water to reflect beautifully, and hides the dirt between cleaning.

FOR THOSE WHO WISH TO acquire iron urns and fountains for use in restoring Victorian houses, the search for the old is not easy. There are only a few antique and restoration shops that specialize in these iron ornaments. Sometimes nurserymen, florists, and caretaking services that do cemetary work have several of the relic urns that are surplus. Pieces and parts should not be overlooked and left behind, as they will most likely interchange with others that may be found.

Graining and Stencilling

HOW TO GRAIN LIKE A PROFESSIONAL

by Howard Zucker

GRAINING IS A PAINTED IMITATION OF the grain of wood. It is an authentic, economical and interesting technique that can produce amazing results with a little practice.

BECAUSE IT IS SUCH AN inexpensive and durable finish, it is very practical for hallways, old kitchen cabinets, exterior doors, old doors, furniture, woodwork and floors.

GRAINING IS MUCH LESS EXPENSIVE than stripping, hanging paper or new carpentry. For instance, if a room contains old wainscotting that is not worth stripping but is unattractively painted, by graining the wainscotting you get the effect of wood and keep the architectural detail. This is much less expensive than new wood panelling that alters the look of a room and usually "modernizes" it.

IN OTHER INSTANCES, you may want to "match" a wood surface. If a new shutter is installed next to older ones, the new wood will most likely be more inexpensive than the type used in the past and not have the grain of the older wood. It is possible to grain the shutter in imitation of its neighbors.

GRAINED SURFACES do not show dirt and scuff marks as do painted surfaces and they retain their attractiveness far longer. It is also a useful finish for non-wood surfaces like: cabinets, radiator covers, convectors, grilles and switchplates.

YOUR FIRST ATTEMPTS AT GRAINING may not result in works of art, but the effect will be similar enough to wood. For areas like baseboards, this is sufficient and will give you the necessary practice for tackling more decorative jobs.

THERE ARE TIMES WHEN IT IS BETTER to hire a professional decorator. If you apply the background coat and do your own final varnishing, you can save a great deal of money by having the professional do just the actual graining. And you can learn a lot by watching him.

THERE ARE THREE PARTS to the graining procedure: Applying the background coat, making the wood grain with the graining stain, and varnishing. There is no magic in graining—it is a craft that anyone can learn. It is helpful to have a sample board and some pictures of wood you can copy if you don't have the real thing.

I USE MASONITE BOARDS 12" × 16" for testing colors. A practice or sample board lets you see how closely you are matching a natural wood and make necessary adjustments. The novice should limit the graining at first to the straight grains rather than the more complicated swirls of heart growth.

YOU ARE NOT TRYING FOR photographic representation of wood but rather the lines and patterns that resemble the real thing. Organic wood has imperfections and many accidental things you do may simulate real wood. Actually, color is the most important factor.

BACKGROUND COAT

THE SURFACE TO BE GRAINED should be painted with an oil-base semi-gloss paint. The color you use for the ground coat is very important to the finished result. Pick out the lightest shade in the wood you are going to imitate and select a paint that is just a little lighter.

YOU CAN TINT THE OIL PAINT yourself by using colors in oil—raw umber, raw sienna, burnt umber, burnt sienna (Benjamin Moore oils preferred). Mixtures of some or all of these shades should duplicate any natural wood you are imitating. Or bring a piece of wood to the paint store and match the color you want to achieve from the color gallery. Let the store mix it for you.

I PERSONALLY PREFER to use a mixture of ½ semi-gloss and ½ enamel undercoater. It dries hard quicker and seems to be receptive to my stains.

BUT, BEFORE YOU EVEN PUT the ground coat on— clean the wood! On previously painted surfaces use deglosser (or liquid sandpaper). On really dirty surfaces like kitchen cabinets, wash down with a strong solution of Soilax to remove grease. Rinse clean.

FURNITURE SHOULD BE CLEANED even more thoroughly. Any wax residue will cause the finish to chip easily. I use a washing soda solution so strong that it must be applied with a brush. Coat the area and then scrub with fine steel wool to soften the wax. Then wash *all* of it off with clean water. Let a washed surface dry for a day.

ONE APPLICATION OF GROUND COAT is usually enough on previously painted surfaces. However, if it is an unsealed surface such as raw wood, unpainted plaster or sheet rock, you must use one or two coats of primer-sealer or enamel undercoater before the coat of semi-gloss.

WHEN LAYING ON THE PAINT, it should be brushed in the direction the wood goes. Sanding done before the ground coat should also be in direction of the simulated grain.

WHEN PAINTING A BACKGROUND for exterior work, avoid exterior finish house paints. They take too long to dry  and are too shiny. Play safe and use exterior oil primer only. I recommend Ox-Line Trouble Shooter Exterior Primer. It also is fine for interior work. Since it comes in white only, tint it yourself, or let the paint store do it for you.

ALLOW the background coat to dry one day. It may take longer outside. Test by scratching sharply with fingernail to make sure it is hard.

TOOLS

THERE ARE MANY TOOLS AVAILABLE that can be used for graining:

• Cotton waste, rags, cheesecloth or natural burlap.

• Rubber combs. These are available in some paint stores. I buy compounding rubbers in an auto store and cut out the teeth with a razor. Rubber combs create a vivid effect such as you often see on exterior doors in a yellowish oak-type graining. Putting the rubber inside a rag gives a more subtle and softer effect.

• Steel graining combs. Used for the same purpose as rubber combs.

• Check or pore rollers, overgrainers, stipplers, mottlers. (Available in some paint stores.)

• Badger blender.

• Liner: Striping or pencil brush.

• Steel wool.

THE TOOLS YOU USE TO GRAIN will come from personal preference. Most grainers only use some of the above.

GRAINING STAINS

TRADITIONALLY, graining has been done with oil stains or water stains—or a combination of both. Some grainers have found that a water stain achieves better appearance for certain types of wood. One advantage of water stains is that they dry immediately and the varnish can be applied right away. Some grainers use a water stain to simulate the pores of the wood and then apply an oil stain for the figured grains.

WATER STAINS CAN be mixed using ⅓ stale beer to ⅔ water or vinegar and water in equal parts, using dry colors. Or poster colors can be used alone with water.

THE OLD-TIME STAINS were usually made up of 1 part raw linseed oil, 2 parts turpentine, a fractional amount of dryers, and a "megilp." The megilp is what prevented the grain lines of the stain from running together. Whiting may be used as a megilp. But in general, the formulas used by old-time grainers are so complicated that describing them in detail will discourage most amateurs and send them back to their antiquing kits.

THERE ARE TWO STOREBOUGHT PRODUCTS that can be used successfully in lieu of the traditional mixtures. Either of them can be used as a staining mixture by adding oil colors. (I prefer Benjamin Moore.) They are glazing liquid or flatting oil. Either will achieve similar results.

HOWEVER, LIKE MOST DECORATORS, I use my own stains to achieve the effects I am aiming for. One I commonly use, for 1 qt. of stain, is:

> 3 parts mineral spirits
> 1 part pure benzine
> ½ shot glass of boiled linseed oil
> A fractional amount of flat white paint
> Oil colors to achieve desired shade.

THE STAIN IS APPLIED VERY THIN. Brush it out sparingly as you spread it on. In general, the equivalent of one brushful of stain will cover ten times the area as one brushful of paint.

THE BIGGEST ADVANTAGE of this stain is that you don't have to grain it while wet as you do with other stains. When you have to work stains wet, you can only apply the stain to a small area at a time. My stain is used when it sets up and has dried "tack-free." It can set for 15 min. to a half hour. This gives more flexibility and allows you to apply it over a large area all at once.

GRAINING

THE FIRST STEP is to cover the surface with the stain and let it set up. Constantly stir the mixture to keep the oil from settling to the bottom. When it has set up, dip cotton waste or cheesecloth into stain, squeeze out, and make the graining patterns. Go in the direction that wood would go. When it has set up again, you can use fine steel wool or blender brush to make pores or soften effects.

IT IS DIFFICULT TO PUT THE ACTUAL process of graining into words. However, by just drawing a rag or brush back and forth, you can get some effect of wood. And the various

Howard Zucker is spreading the stain very thinly over the dry ground coat.

After stain has set up, graining figures are made with cotton and stain.

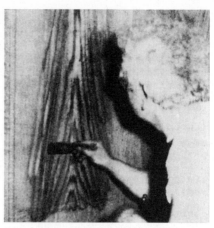
The vivid lines are blended and softened with a dry brush or fine steel wool.

tools you select—rubber combs, brushes, etc., will add more variety. The stain itself is an almost magical thing.

IF YOU WISH TO IMITATE PANELLING, as in a hallway, use a hard carpenter's pencil to mark out the wall into stiles and panels. (Soft pencil lead will dissolve in the stain.) The vertical and horizontal stiles can be straight grain and the panels more complex swirls of heart growth. Make sure there is a clearly delineated change of grain direction where joints would butt.

NOTE: Don't try to use store bought wood stains for graining. They are intended for staining natural wood only.

OVERSTAINING

FURTHER ENRICHMENT WILL be achieved by overstaining—letting the first graining coat dry a day, and then repeating the graining process. Each time you go over it, you will add more depth and richness.

FOR AN ANTIQUE FINISH, a good overstain can be made with white flat paint made very thin with mineral spirits. Try an overglaze out on the sample board to make sure it does not dissolve the stain. If it does move it, shellac or varnish before overglazing.

OVERSTAINING OR OVERGLAZING can be used to darken your grain, alter the color or antique it. It is done at least a day later, when the original job is dry. The original stains as an overgrainer will darken it considerably.

PICKLING

PICKLING IS A DECORATIVE FINISH that gives a frosty effect to wood. It is achieved by reversing the graining process of putting dark over lighter. You grain with a thin white stain (white paint thinned as for the antique overglaze) on a darker background. This effect is often used on natural wood and on colored backgrounds such as red or blue paint.

Making "medullary rays" with a brush—regular, horizontal patterns that occur in wood.

A straightedge is used to create the sharp outlines of vertical stiles.

A sample board is handy to test color and the reaction of the stain to finishes.

VARNISHING

THE PURPOSE OF VARNISHING is to protect the graining so that it can be washed. Other finishes are possible as an alternate to varnish, but I think varnish is the best bet. It is durable and long-lasting and the easiest to do. The polyurethane varnishes are fine.

I USUALLY ALLOW THE STAIN to dry for two days before I varnish. The exception to this is a water stain, which may be ready to coat almost immediately after staining.

DIFFERENT LUSTRES ARE POSSIBLE, ranging from a high shine to a dead flat finish with a satin finish and a semi-gloss in between. Some paint-makers have all four, such as McCloskey. Others have only three, such as Valspar, while still others may only manufacture a semi-gloss and a high-gloss varnish.

AND THE FINISH IS NOT necessarily what you may expect from the label. One concern's semi-gloss may have the same lustre as the satin finish from another concern. Only experience will tell you if you are getting the finish that you were looking for.

VARNISH ALSO brings back the color to what it was when wet. Graining stains dry differently and usually lighter. Water stains sometimes dry out to a fantastic degree. It is important to remember that varnish darkens when you are matching to a previously grained piece of wood or natural wood.

MAKE SURE THAT you use an exterior varnish for outside work. If the grained area is exposed to the sun it will require varnishing about once a year because sun attacks the varnish. Follow the instructions on the label for the proper thinning agent. Some varnishes ask for turpentine, others may permit any mineral spirits. Be methodical in applying the varnish. Criss-cross your brush strokes and then finish off as the wood goes, just as you did with your grounding and staining. If you skip, you'll find out when you wash it, because you will be washing off the graining.

TOUCH-UPS

SOMETIMES THERE IS DAMAGE right after the graining, before I've had a chance to varnish. But I still varnish before touching-up to avoid disturbing the stain. It is possible to do extensive touch-ups on work that has been done years before.

DON'T TRY TO TOUCH-UP with your same graining stain. It can't be done. The basic idea is to take white, some thinners, and your basic colors on a palette along with an artist's pencil brush of some kind, and to adjust the color for each touch-up.

IF I WANT TO SAVE THE JOB of re-varnishing, I use durable materials—either enamel that has the same luster as the varnish on the area being touched-up, or I use an appropriate varnish in the touch-up mixture.

GRAINING IS A TRADITIONAL TECHNIQUE

GRAINING has ongoing a rich history in America. In Colonial times, "fancypainters" advertized their skill at graining as well as stencilling, marbleizing, gilding and lacquering. Natural wood was often grained. This was usually plain pine that was grained to imitate cedar, mahogany, oak or maple, for the express purpose of giving elegance to the wood. Wood panelling and doors were the most common areas that were grained.

CEDAR AND MAHOGANY were the most popular grained finishes. Much of the early graining looked very different from the 19th-century type. Cedar, the richest in color, usually had a pink painted background and the over-color, usually olive or drab, was blended into it while wet. This gave a colorful and vibrant effect.

THE TECHNIQUE of graining was brought over by English craftsmen. Regency England used graining in very elaborate decorating schemes. Good graining was thought to be a "conversation piece," and was done in many wealthy homes in conjunction with gilding and marbleizing. But along with the kind of graining that looked just like wood, there were types

there were types that were meant to give an exaggerated appearance of wood. Leather combs and feathers were often employed.

IN THE 19TH CENTURY, "faux bois" (literally false wood) was used extensively. A. J. Downing, in *Architecture of Country Houses* recommended grained woodwork as the most easy surface to care for "made smooth by varnishing." He recommended imitation of ash, maple, birch and oak. He deplored that "peculiarly yellow oak" as a better imitation of molasses than wood.

MANY GERMAN DECORATORS immigrated to the U.S. in the 19th century and brought the graining technique with them. It has always been very popular in large cities like New York and Baltimore for that reason. Hallways and exterior doors are frequently grained even today, and the city house often had grained floors and woodwork on the ground floor where the kitchen and servant's pantry were built with cheaper wood than the upper storeys. Graining in the Victorian period imitated wood as closely as possible. Decorators often used mechanical rollers and steel combs to do the job quickly and economically.   —C.F.

EARLY AMERICAN WALL STENCILLING

by Carolyn Flaherty

A GREAT DEAL OF THE WARMTH and charm of colonial rooms was contributed by stencilled walls. Popular through the last quarter of the 18th century and up to about 1840, walls with bold, simple patterns and clear, strong colors were part of the environment for many an Early American homeowner desiring to add color and ornament to his home.

JOURNEYMEN ARTISTS WERE no doubt responsible for a great many decorative walls. There are lengends in many New England towns surrounding stencilled walls in a tavern, painted in return for prolific feats of wining and dining on the part of the wandering painter. A picture emerges of the routes of some of these itinerants from the similarity of patterns, probably made from the same stencils, in a tavern and nearby homes in a town, then another town, following a path back and forth across the northeast.

ONE OF THESE JOURNEYMEN was Moses Eaton, who later turned to farming. His kit of stencils and brushes was found in the attic of his house in Dublin, New Hampshire, and is now in the possession of The Society For The Preservation Of New England Antiquities. Eaton's designs were cut on heavy paper, usually coated with shellac, paint, or oil to make them more durable, and one set has been found made out of leather. Stencils for the journeyman artist had to be durable not only to be used over and over, but to withstand the rolling and packing as they went from place to place.

EATON'S STENCILS do not have any register marks for accurate placing of one stencil next to another, indicating that he probably depended solely on his eye and the upper straight edge of the stencil. It is likely that a chalked cord was used by many artists, especially for vertical bands.

LOCAL ARTISANS, often with other trades and occupations, probably did stencilling when it was requested. Once a pattern is chosen and a stencil made, no great skill is required to apply it to a wall. Unlike wallpapering, there is no need for a smooth wall, or cutting and measuring.

FRIEZES (the border running around the top of a wall) and borders over the chair rail (the molding about 30 in. up from the floor) and large, all-over patterns are fairly simple.

PAINT IS APPLIED SPARINGLY to the open portions, taking care not to get paint on the underside of the stencil. From the old walls that remain, there is no evidence that any colors were shaded.

OF COURSE, WHEN A ROOM is stencilled in some of the more complicated versions, with freizes, borders, and large patterns separated by uprights, either a very good natural eye or a careful room plan is needed. However, the stenciller has the advantage of being able to leave out certain parts of a pattern when approaching a door, etc., and being able to cheat slightly with the open spaces.

SOME OF THE MOST original and charmingly naive patterns found were probably done by a person who had seen a stencilled wall in a tavern or on a visit to a neighboring town, and tried their hand at decorating their own walls.

UNLIKE MORE DURABLE decorative features of Early American life such as furniture, pottery, and paintings, the walls surrounding the colonist's everday life have been most vulnerable to time. Repainting, washing and papering have left little to record this art.

BUT WHAT REMAINS shows that stencilling was very popular in New England, particularly away from the commercial centers where wallpapers could be bought. Wallpaper was imported from France and England and although much in favor, it was still fairly expensive. The popular papers of the time no doubt influenced both the artist's designs and the homeowner's desires. All-over patterns most obviously simulate wallpaper, and many of the papers featured representations of architectural features like freize, chair rail border, etc. Stripes were very fashionable, and were reflected in the vertical uprights used by the stenciller.

ONCE MACHINE-MADE AMERICAN wallpaper became readily available and inexpensive, stencilling as a means to decorate walls all but disappeared by the second half of the 19th century. But the unique quality of stencilling, with its ability to adapt to the individual proportions of a room and its irregularities, has never been duplicated.

ALTHOUGH MOST OF the stencilled wallsthat remain or have been uncovered

are in New England, some have been found as far west as Ohio, often with the same patterns found in New England. Stencilled walls have not found in significant numbers further south than New York.

Stencilled frieze in a bedroom in New Canaan, Connecticut. The design is a Handcrafted Walls adaptation of a pattern found in New Hampshire. Colors are medium blue and pastel pink on a white ground.

ALTHOUGH PENNSYLVANIA is rich in the stylized floral and geometric stencilling on furniture and barn walls done by the early German settlers, they apparently did not use this means of decoration on the inside walls.

COLORS AND PATTERNS

A VARIETY OF geometric and foliage patterns were popular. Some seemed to have special meanings. Moses Eaton was fond of the pineapple which was a symbol of hospitality in colonial times. Bells are found very often, particularly in friezes. They were  probably wedding bells, and there is evidence that a homeowner often had wedding bells stencilled to welcome a new bride into the house.

 MANY FRIEZE BORDERS have swags, festoons and tassels reminiscent of French drapery. Weeping willows, the Federal eagle, sunbursts, woven baskets and vases filled with flowers were also popular for the larger decorations, particularly over the mantelpieces.

BORDERS FAVORED FLOWERING VINES, roses, laurel leaves and stylized leaves. They were often edged with dot and dash patterns, or combined with small hearts or flowers.

THE FLAT COLORS USED FOR STENCILLING were either milk or oil paints. Pigments ground in oil, and ready for mixing, were sold as early as 1724 in Boston. Paint was frequently mixed with oil as a vehicle. In many rural dwellings, however, the thriftiest medium was one that every household had a large supply of—skimmed milk.

UNFORTUNATELY, MILK PAINT was not very durable and even the tavern owner and housewife's warnings not to wash the painted walls did not prevent the loss of many of these walls.

BLACK, GREENS, YELLOWS, PINKS and reds with some red-browns and blues are the colors that have predominated in the walls remaining. For background color, either the original plaster or yellow and red ochres were most common, and some deep pinks and blues.

WHILE MOST STENCILLERS probably used the dry pigments mixed with oil or milk, restorationists occasionally have only been able to duplicate some of the odd shades by using berry or beet juice, or some other vegetable substance. Whether some artists made their own natural dyes as a rule, or only when they ran out of pigment, is guesswork.

THE COLORS ARE NOT EASY to duplicate today unless a good, well-pigmented oil or milk paint is used, but more difficult is to conceive of the use of color as boldly as did these artists. There is a huge difference in the "bold and clear" colors of yesterday and the "bright" colors shown in slick magazines today.

IT TAKES SOME LOOKING at pictures of old walls in museums or source books and paint chips from manufacturers of reproduction colors to get the feel of the richness and warmth they created.

FOR EXAMPLE, Moses Eaton's daughter remembered a room in their house with soft raspberry walls and deep green and red decorations! That Moses Eaton liked strong red and green is evident from the traces of paint on his stencils.

VERY DIFFERENT is another house in New Hampshire with a room with pale pink walls, divided with a black line from the light gray background of the frieze with festoons, tassels, and medallions in two shades of light blue with blue-black markings.

THESE DARING COLOR SCHEMES and sharply defined patterns were the background for the simple lines of Early American furniture. Such rooms had a minimum of colored fabric. A room today would have to be as simple as the original to contain so much color and pattern on the walls. But

Dining room walls in a Ridgefield, Conn., home. Stencilled by Handrafted Walls, the larger designs are separated by vertical uprights, and bordered by a frieze and chair rail design. All patterns are close adaptations of originals from Ohio and New England, except for the birds, taken from an old quilt. In five colors: umbered green, ochre, red, blue and black on a white ground.

Stencilled sunburst design in a bedroom in New Canaan, Conn. An original Handcrafted Walls design—colors are ochre, Venetian red, and Prussian blue. The pattern is carried around the window, emphasizing an important architectural feature of the room. An important advantage of stencilling—as compared with wallpaper—is its flexibility to adapt to specific features in a room.

even if the room has more color, fabric and "things" than its original state, a border or frieze pattern can give an authentic and colorful effect.

THE PALE, WASHED-OUT LOOK often associated with Early American decoration and painted walls is not the way these walls look when they have been found under paper, in closets, or other protection, but rather the way an unrestored stencilled wall looks after 150 years of the ravages of time have washed it out.

MANY OF THE REDS, GREENS, and blues used were "umbered" or had ochre added. This gave a deep but not dull look—the dark colors like mulberry, Prussian blue or chrome were always quite intense in appearance.

STENCILLING IS A FAIRLY SIMPLE technique and requires few tools. Paint, stencils, cutting tools and paint brushes are about all that is necessary.

PAINT—Any good oil or milk paint with a lot of pigment is suitable.

STENCILS—Can be made from a variety of paper types. There is no need for the heavily coated paper or leather used by the original stencillers since they will not be used as often

or carried around for a great length of time. Handcrafted Walls uses different kinds of material: simple brown paper coated with shellac to sheets of Mylar (plastic sheets available at art supply stores), which are very durable and easy to cut. Any weight of paper can be used, with judgment as to how much you care to spend, how often they are to be used, and how long they are meant to last. (They can be stored for touch-up or restoration work later on.)

CUTTING TOOLS—An X-acto knife (available in art supply stores or hobby and craft shops) makes the best cutting tool. A single-edge razor will also work well on most papers.

BRUSHES—A variety of brushes is needed. Round brushes work best and you will need small ones for small cut-outs and a couple of larger ones.

STENCIL PATTERNS can be made from original designs, a design adapted from a plate, carpet, quilt, books featuring traditional motifs, or any simple, pleasing pattern.

A WHOLE DESIGN CAN be traced onto one stencil, or you may want to make more than one. Two stencils help in separating the colors. For instance, a bouquet of red flowers and green leaves could have one stencil for the green leaves. The one for the red flowers could have one leaf (an extra) to

help match up the pattern. Stencillers mostly match by eye, but it also helps to make a chalk mark on the wall where the next stencil goes. It is sometimes a good idea to try them out on the basement or attic walls, or inside the closet, to get the hang of it.

THE MOST IMPORTANT THING TO REMEMBER is to apply the paint very sparingly. Otherwise it can run. With very little paint on the brush, start in the middle of a large space and work it out to the edges. For a small space, you can start on the apron of the stenil and work back and forth over the cut-out.

FOR FRIEZES AND BORDERS, the top or bottom edge of the stencil acts as a guide in keeping the patterns running in a straight line. All-over patterns will require careful layout, using a plumb bob and chalk line.

STENCILLING WILL look good in any room in an Early American house. But its flexibility to adapt to the proportions of a room make it a useful decorating technique for rooms of any period that have irregular features or a lack of architectural features. Stencilled walls and floors can brighten and enrich otherwise dull areas of house—dark hallways, walls along the stairway or old, bumpy walls.

VICTORIAN STENCILLING

by Carolyn Flaherty

STENCILLING IS AN EFFECTIVE, inexpensive and imaginative way to decorate a 19th-century house. It adds color, elegance, enhances architectural detail and is a form of decoration that was in wide use during the period.

STENCILLED DECORATION CAN SOLVE a decorating dilemma encountered by many homeowners who want to add to the life of a room, but find that Victorian wallpapers are either difficult to find or quite expensive. The large proportions of Victorian rooms also raise the cost of hanging wallpaper. But more important, the divisions of wall space (friezes, borders, moldings) and various arches and irregularities often do not lend themselves to a neat arrangement of an all-over patterned wallpaper.

STENCILLING WAS USED to enhance these very same architectural features that often are so confusing to the modern eye. And with Victorian stencilling the most important thing is *where* to use stencilling, not what pattern to use. The great eclecticism of the period makes it easy to be authentic, since the Victorians used decorative motifs from the Roman, Egyptian, Gothic, Moorish, and Pompeian periods with a merry disregard for what was "proper" but rather what was "fashionable" that year. So the pattern chosen to make a stencil can depend on personal taste but with an eye to what motif will adapt well to the space chosen.

WALLPAPER AND STENCILLING were very often used together, typically with a large-patterned paper on the walls and a stencilled frieze and/or ceiling. This was usually too much of a good thing, and the stencilling alone can re-create the original feeling with a less cluttered effect.

DURING THE LATTER two-thirds of the 19th century, wallpaper was quite popular and inexpensive. Most Victorian walls were covered with paper or richly colored paint. There was little need to use stencilling to cover walls with an all-over pattern.

LARGE, FORMAL ROOMS sometimes had stencilled walls, but in very complicated designs. One type called for a "pounce," a stencil with punched holes. It was held against the wall and a charcoal bag applied to leave a pattern on the wall. A craftsman could then apply the paint, in designated colors, to this form, enabling many men to carry out portions of an artist's design. The final effect resembled a mural more than a stencilled wall.

ANOTHER USE OF STENCILS was to apply a "diaper" pattern. This is an elaborate floral or geometric repeating pattern, which interlaces. Often done in gold leaf, these small patterns require great precision in matching.

THESE ELABORATE WALLS cannot be reproduced by a person not trained in the craft, and so it is more profitable to focus on the areas where the homeowner might wish to use stencilling in conjunction with painted walls.

• FRIEZE: The decorative band at the top of a wall. There is usually a cornice molding at the top of the frieze. If there is no architectural frieze defined by moldings, a decorative border can be stencilled to give richness to the room. A frieze is generally 1 ft. to 2 ft. deep, so a large pattern should be used for the stencil.

• COVE: A large concave moulding between the ceiling and the cornice of a room. The cove was often stencilled in Victorian homes, alone or in combination with a frieze. A flexible stencil paper—such as simple brown paper—is needed to bend to the shape of the cove. This is a portion of the room that is often a problem when painting. Do you paint it the same color as the ceiling, or the same color as the wall? Ornamented with stencilling, it becomes an attractive transitional feature instead of a problem wall space.

• CEILINGS: Borders, lines and designs stencilled on a plain ceiling can give it a richness that is lacking if it does not have ornamental plasterwork. Stencilling also distracts the eye from the lumps and oft-covered cracks common to many ceilings. Small ceilings, as in vestibules or hallways, were often stencilled in all-over patterns.

• WIPE-LINE: The beginning of the wall, right over the wainscotting or dado, was called the wipe-line because the housekeeper would eventually get a dirty smear from dust-

ing the top of the panelling. To camouflage this smear, a small pattern was often stencilled above the projecting wood. For further practicality, the pattern was usually glazed over with a varnish, dulled with an ochre or umber tint. Stencilling above the wipe-line can be a striking decorative note either as the only pattern on the wall or in conjunction with other stencilled parts of the room. A small pattern, with a bold outline, is needed here, A single flower, a Gothic cross or trefoil, or a French fleur-de-lis are good designs for this space.

TO SEE IF YOUR HOUSE ORIGINALLY had stencilling, you can do a little detective work by using the technique described for the Glenview restoration to see if some old stencilled patterns might show up. They can be traced and made into stencils.

ALTHOUGH THERE ARE FEW RECORDS left of the stencilling done in the Victorian era, designs can be found in many places that fit in character and period—and have the sharp outlines required for a good stencil pattern.

HOUSES BUILT IN THE FIRST HALF of the 19th century, particularly the Greek Revival type so popular, were decorated with classic motifs, particularly Grecian. Any strong, simple outline of classical origin makes an effective stencil. The later Victorian houses, more eclectic and ornate, leave even more room for personal taste and imagination. Gothic ornament, stylized or conventional foliage, and various geometric designs are authentic and appropriate.

A RICH SOURCE FOR PATTERN INSPIRATION is fabric. Old fabrics in quilts, drapes, etc., or reproduction fabrics provide many adaptable designs. China, antiques, books and magazines will provide many ideas.

AN IMPORTANT FACTOR in making a stencil is the ties. The ties are what hold the pattern together on the stencil—the portion in the design not cut out. Some stencils, like the one shown in the grid, have a simple enough design not to need ties to keep the stencil from falling apart. Others boldly show their ties, as on page 1, declaring that the pattern is a stencil. The ties can also be part of the pattern itself, as with the veins of leaves. Or, the ties can be painted in free-hand if desired.

TECHNIQUES FOR VICTORIAN STENCILLING are the same as for Early American stencilling. Two additional suggestions: (1) For larger spaces, a small roller with a very sparse amount of paint, will give a good, even effect, and (2) For very small spaces, paint can be applied with a small piece of velvet cloth wound around a finger.

SIZING PATTERNS

Enlarging A Gothic Cross Pattern

To enlarge or reduce a pattern, trace the pattern and then make the grid over it. The squares of the grid can be any size, ½ in., 1 in., etc. Make a second grid with squares bigger or smaller by the desired size change. Then transfer the pattern free-hand, square by square. Finally, you can cut out the pattern, shellac or otherwise make the paper paint-repellent, and you have your stencil.

GLENVIEW: VICTORIAN STENCILLING RESTORED

THE GLENVIEW MANSION is part of the Hudson River Museum in Yonkers, New York. It was built in 1876 for John Bond Trevor and his young second wife.

IT IS KNOWN as a "Centennial House" because many of its furnishings were bought at the Centennial Exhibition in 1876. While in Philadelphia, the Trevors met the famous cabinet-maker, Daniel Pabst, and commissioned him to make the woodwork and decorative features at Glenview.

THE ENORMOUS popularity of Eastlake's ideas on home decoration greatly influenced the style of Glenview. The Ebony Library's massive fireplace and overmantel has Eastlake-inspired incised decoration. These stylized motifs are reflected in the stencilled patterns of floral and geometric designs. The colors—grayed greens, greenish blues, ochred yellows, Venetian red—are the colors favored by the Aesthetic Movement in England which Eastlake popularized in America. These colors were often further subdued by the application of an umbered glaze.

STENCILLING WAS A PERFECT MEDIUM for the flat, sharply delineated patterns espoused by Eastlake. The appeal of these subdued decorations was in their vast difference from the conventional representations of flowers and foliage and the bright, harsh colors so fashionable in the previous decades. The very flatness of the stencilwork increased the stylized effect of the patterns and replaced embossed plasterwork on ceilings, borders and friezes.

WHEN THE RAMBUSCH DECORATING COMPANY, of New York City, undertook the restoration of Glenview, they had only old photographs of the Library and the Drawing Room to give evidence of the original stencilling. The walls and ceilings had been painted over many times.

THE EBONY LIBRARY, now completed, was the first room to be restored. Workmen uncovered a portion of each part of the complicated stencilled patterns, traced the designs and made the stencils for use in the restoration. Because of the intricacy of the designs, most of these stencils are "multi-stencils"—meaning there are quite a few stencils made for each design. One for each color is generally used, and they are matched by a key portion on each stencil.

Section of frieze (lowest band in above picture) as it looked when workmen uncovered it. It has been restored in its original colors—black lines and gilt petals on a deep, brick-red background.

Another view of the stencilling in the above picture. Starting from the bottom, it shows the frieze (detail at left), gold leaf stars on the cornice molding, and geometric designs and stylized flowers on the cove and ceiling panel, all on gray-green backgrounds. The main ceiling is white with striped borders and flowers.

THE VESTIBULE, not at first thought to have any stencil work, was found to have an all-over geometric design of circles inside squares, with geometric borders and frieze, incorporating a great deal of gold leaf in the patterns.

A DETERMINED WORKMAN uncovered the designs by taking a floodlight and holding it up to the ceiling. He was then able to see small ripples in the paint that repeated across the ceiling, thus giving him a clue as to where to look for the pattern underneath the many layers of paint.

THE HUGE, WAINSCOTTED HALLWAY has a large frieze pattern in subtle, almost-pastel colors above sage green painted walls. Above the wainscotting, a stencilled flower in a darker shade of green runs in a horizontal line.

THE DRAWING ROOM, shown on this page in progress, will be completed soon and the dining room will be restored next. Already, in a square on the ceiling, a spectacular polychromatic bird on a gold leaf background has been uncovered.

The restoration work in progress in the drawing room of Glenview is being greatly aided by this photo taken in the 1890s. The walls were covered with wallpaper, but from the frieze to the ceiling, all other decorations were stencilled. The Rambusch workmen are uncovering patterns, making stencils, and reproducing the original paint colors. The room will soon be restored to its High Victorian elegance. Picture is from the Hudson River Museum.

Howard Zucker, of Rambusch, has uncovered enough of the lotus flower design in the frieze to make a stencil. After removing 5 or 6 layers of paint with paint remover, until a trace of pattern appears, he then sands with very fine wet/and dry sandpaper.

Jim Geraghty is priming the ceiling. The stencils have already been made and are ready to be applied. The tan paint is a few shades darker than the final coat will be—the way to prime when painting with colored paint.

CREATING A VICTORIAN HALLWAY

By Carolyn Flaherty

WHAT CAN YOU DO WITH a nondescript hallway? How can you transform it into an attractive space? Not only attractive, but give it a Victorian period effect? These questions–faced by many old-house owners–had special significance for us.

THE OLD-HOUSE JOURNAL editorial office is on the ground floor of an 1883 brownstone. The hallway was painted white–the brownstoner's all-purpose solution for decorating problems. It had been painted frequently over the years and was covered with layers of old enamel. There was nothing of distinctive character to be found in the long entrance way, and a good deal of work was needed to get it into even an ordinary painted condition.

The hallway, in its former "boardinghouse transitional" style, as we began patching in preparation for painting.

BUT THE JOURNAL STAFF did not want a monotonous white-walled area. We felt we should practice what we preach and do some period decoration. It required a lot of thinking, planning and time for the execution. It did not, however, cost very much money for materials. The old-house owner who is willing to spend the time required can create the same effect by using the techniques described, adapting colors and patterns to fit their own house. So here is a step-by-step recreation of our thinking and and the methods we used in the decoration.

STRIP OR PAINT?

THE FIRST DECISION had to be whether or not to strip the old paint off the woodwork. By chipping off the paint in a few strategic places we were able to determine that the wood underneath was an inexpensive softwood that was originally grained. It was common practice to use cheaper woods, often grained, on the ground floor of brownstones even though the parlor floor above might have real walnut or mahogany.

WE COULD NOW AVOID the messy and difficult task of paint stripping but were left with woodwork with a very unappealing surface. A coat of paint, mo matter what color, would not improve its appearance. So we decided to grain it as described in another chapter.

BECAUSE THE WOOD upstairs is walnut, we easily made the decision as to what wood to imitate. But we decided to grain the vestibule portion of the hallway in golden oak for variety and to lighten the darkest part of the hallway.

TO CREATE A VICTORIAN look it it often necessary to divide the wall spaces either horizontally or vertically. Therein lies one of the biggest drawbacks to using wallpaper. Manufacturers are just not making Victorian papers. When they do manufacture an occasional Victorian pattern, they neglect to make the accompanying borders and friezes that were used in the 19th century. So we rejected wallpaper and turned to paint.

WALL DIVISIONS

NOTHING SAYS "Victorian" quite so dramatically as a wall with a dado and a frieze. The dado could be created with graining (in imitation of wainscotting) and would tie-in with the grained doors and mouldings. We could create a frieze with stencilling.

THIS IS THE MOST DIFFICULT part–the selection of a pattern and colors for the stencilled frieze. First, you need a focus to zero in on a particular kind of ornament from the myriad of design sources available–books, fabrics, furniture, etc. Take your clue from the house itself.

THE JOURNAL BROWNSTONE was built in the period when flat, stylized decoration popularized by Charles Eastlake was popular. There is a sunrise pattern incised on the mouldings of the parlor floor that is reminiscent of some of the Eastlake-inspired American furniture. But we didn't like it enough to duplicate it in a stencil pattern, nor were we creative enough to adapt it as a more handsome design. But we took from it the knowledge that our decoration should be of a flat, stylized and geometric type–in other words, no flowers or leaves that look like the real thing.

THE EXTERIOR OF THE HOUSE is neo-Grec–composed of flat planes broken by horizontal moulding bands. Although there is no Greek ornament inside or on the outside of the house, we knew we could incorporate a classic Greek design into our frieze and be on the right track.

SO WE COULD NOW LOOK to a source used by designers for centuries–ancient Greek ornament. We found what we wanted in a book of historic ornament–a very flat, stylized anthemion (Greek for "flower"–often called honeysuckle.)

NOW THAT WE HAD the pattern we next had to decide on colors. We knew what we wanted. There are many choices–bright and cheerful, vibrant and dramatic, pale and elegant. We opted for soft and sophisticated, the kind of palette used by Art Movement designers in late 1870's and 80's.

THE WALL PORTION HAD TO BE LIGHT for two reasons–the hall itself is a dark area and could not take a deeply colored wall, and the walnut-grained dado needed contrast. The wall color is an antique parchment, created by applying a glaze over a light yellowish-beige paint.

THE FRIEZE IS A COMPLICATED arrangement of tertiary colors–colors arrived at by mixing two secondary colors. A soft yellow, an off-white, and a touch of gold leaf were added for accent. Sample boards were used over and over again before making a final decision.

A HALL ALLOWS more leeway for the use of many colors in the wall treatment because there is not the problem of the wall colors clashing with upholstery or drapery fabric.

ALTHOUGH WE LOVE OUR FRIEZE, we would like to point out that it is not necessary to have such a complicated arrangement for a Victorian effect. In fact, we recommend beginning the stencilling experience with a pattern that requires only two or three colors.

WIPE LINE

WE KNEW THAT a wipe line was often stencilled above a wainscotted dado and we cided to carry trompe l'oeil (French

---

PRIOR TO PAINTING . . .

PROPER SURFACE PREPARATION is the key to any successful paint job. Here's what we did on the hallway project:

CALCIMINE PAINT (covered with several layers of oil paint) had to be removed from the ceiling to prevent future peeling. We used the steam process (see OHJ May 1976, p. 2).

ALL LOOSE PLASTER was broken out and the voids filled with sheetrock nailed to the studs. Before any further patching was done, all wall surfaces were primed with an oil-based primer/undercoater (tinted to the approximate color of the finish coat). The primer not only helps increase the adhesion of the patching materials, but it also helps highlight small areas that need minor patching.

HOLES REMAINING around sheet-rock patches were filled with plaster of paris. Sheetrock joint compound—applied with wide-bladed joint knives—was used as a final finish on patched areas. Two or more coatings were used where significant buildup was required. Cloth tape was used on all joints between the sheetrock patches and the wall plaster.

JOINT COMPOUND was also used to fill minor surface blemishes. Major cracks were covered with cloth tape set into joint compound. All joint compound patches were spot-primed before finish coat was applied.

CRACKS IN PAINTED WOODWORK were filled with acrylic latex caulk—as were cracks between plaster and woodwork. Excess acrylic caulk cleans up easily with damp sponge. Caulk also has the flexibility to yield when wood swells and contracts. All woodwork to be painted was cleaned with liquid sandpaper to remove accumulated grease and grime.

The honeysuckle wipe-line is stencilled above the chair rail of the real walnut and burled walnut wainscotting.

Here the honeysuckle wipe-line is above our grained imitation of the walnut wainscotting.

for "fool the eye") to its fullest with a stencilled border above our grained wainscotting. The pattern is a simpler version of the honey-suckle taken from the frieze and painted in the color of the background of the frieze.

DADO

WE ACTUALLY created two dadoes in the hall. On the wall leading up the stairs, walnut wainscotting was made to match the wainscotting on the floor above. The wall along the stairs is a very high traffic area and real wood is better for long-term durability. It is also aesthetically pleasing. The carpenters

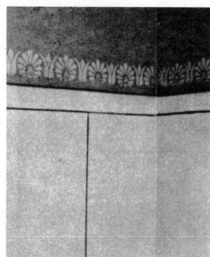

This is the vestibule dado after it has been painted yellowish-tan and striped, before the grained patterns are applied.

who actually made the wainscotting are writing an article about it and it will be featured in an upcoming issue of the Journal.

WHILE THE REAL wainscotting was fairly expensive, it was worth it for the stairway wall but would have been too expensive to use as a dado in the entire hall and vestibule area. But it gave us the idea to imitate it for the remaining dado portion of the wall. It was actually an experiment and is a rather complicated and difficult work of graining.

A MORE PRACTICAL and easy-to-do kind of graining is the type we used in the vestibule. It is golden oak and the key to making it look like wainscotting is to block out lines where the boards would end and to stripe the lines in a dark brown. Each section is then grained in a wood pattern ending at the striped lines as if each section were actually a separate board.

THERE ARE OTHER WAYS to create an authentic-looking dado. Marbleizing, for example, was a popular 19th century treatment for halls. (See OHJ March 1975.) Even simpler is a painted simulation of a leather wallcovering. This can be done with a light reddish-brown painted undercoat topped with a mottled darker red-brown glaze.

AN IMPORTANT DESIGN consideration when planning a dado is the border that separates the dado from the upper wall. This can be a simple line, a painted border or a wood moulding chair rail painted in harmonious or contrasting colors.

GLAZING

THE MELLOW, AGED PATINA of the walls is an important element in the antique Victorian look we wanted. We created this effect by glazing the walls. A glaze is a liquid finish applied over a painted wall that produces a translucent top coat under which the ground coat glows through.

THE LIQUID USED for the glaze coat can be made with Glazing Liquid to which you add oil pigments. We recommend Benjamin Moore pigments, and with a selection of raw and burnt sienna and raw and burnt umber you can create a large variety of glaze colors.

A LITTLE MORE COMPLICATED is this recipe: Flatting oil, a few drops of white alkyd flat paint, and oil pigments.

This view of the hall shows the duplicated walnut wainscotting on the left. The rest of the woodwork, including the radiator enclosure, is grained.

THERE IS REALLY NO WAY to give instructions for how much pigment to add. Start with a small amount and apply the glaze over the sample board, adding more pigment until you arrive at the right effect. Make sure you apply each new version of your glaze over a board with the wall paint on it so you will see the finished effect.

AFTER YOU APPLY the glaze to the wall, immediately take cotton waste and dab the finish to produce a textured effect. You control the mottled effect by dabbing lightly or dabbing and stroking to produce more contrast. Other effects can be created by using stiff brushes, crumpled tissue paper, etc., but we wanted a soft effect produced by light dabbing.

IF YOU FIND THAT THE FINISH sets up too quickly—before you can use the cotton waste to move the glaze—a small amount of kerosene or linseed oil can be added to slow the set.

AFTER THE GLAZE HAS DRIED—two or three days—the surface can be varnished with a flat or satin finish. The varnish will protect the glaze and provide a washable surface that will last for many years. The best varnish is Benjamin Moore's eggshell finish.

CEILING AND MOULDING

THE CEILING WAS PAINTED in the same shade as the walls but left unglazed, creating a different, but related, appearance. Without the glaze, the ceiling is lighter making it appear higher. To have glazed it, too, might have been overdoing the effect. Or, as Chesterton said, art, like morality, is dependent on drawing the line somewhere.

THERE IS A LARGE MOULDING at the top of the walls that we had also left unglazed. However, the flat, light paint seemed to magnify its imperfections as well as making it disappear as an achitectural feature. As it was quite battered with many indentations and chipped paint, it would have consumed many hours filling in the nicks and dents. So we mixed a glaze deeper than the wall shade (adding raw umber) and applied it to the moulding. We then wiped it off using the same method as in antiquing furniture.

WITH THE DARKER GLAZE the moulding again became an architectural feature as well as a subtle transitional element from the dark background of the frieze to the light ceiling. Equally important is the way the deep glaze hides the many imperfections from the eye.

AFTER THE PAINTED decoration was completed and the Victorian mood created, we found that objects that were not compatible with the period effect tended to stick out like sore thumbs.

THE DOOR KNOBS WERE the plain hardware store kind probably put on in the 1930s.

The varied tones on the glazed moulding were produced by leaving a heavier residue of glaze on the receding portions.

WE WANTED HARDWARE in the Late Victorian style with a geometric type design rather than the rococo types usually reproduced.

FORTUNATELY, THERE IS A COMPANY making solid bronze door knobs, escutcheons and hinges in the Eastlake style. The firm is San Francisco Victoriana and we found them in our Buyers' Guide.

THE OTHER JARRING NOTE was our old lighting fixtures. They hadn't been noticeable in the old setting but they now looked awful. We found two old, matching fixtures in the right period. They are brass with holophane shades. There are many salvaged and reproduction fixtures available. The Buyers' Guide can help in the search.

WE HAD NO IDEA before we started how much the planning and doing would add to the enjoyment of the final result. However, we consider it an "interpretive restoration." In the purest sense of the word, "restoration" means the process of accurately reproducing what was originally there.

ALTHOUGH WE KNEW WHAT WAS there before—a calcimine ceiling and tan walls—we felt under no obligation to recreate a plain, dull hallway. We knew that it had been grained and that stencilling was widely used for hallway decoration in the Victorian era. And we are sure that the colors and style of ornament are in keeping with the architectural style of the house.

WE HAVE, IN FACT, CREATED a nicer hallway than the house ever had before. But we are happy with it and we think the house is too.

Solid Bronze Door Knob.

THE 'HOW TO' OF STENCILLING

By Clem Labine

FOLLOWING is a description of the process used in creating the multi-colored frieze stencil illustrated in the preceding article. Although the patterns used in this example are Victorian, the procedure would be the same for Early American stencilling.

ONCE A PATTERN has been selected, it has to be drawn to the proper scale. Patterns can be scaled up or down using the "proportional squares" method on page 398. Next you need to know how many colors you are going to use and how the colors will divide—because you need a separate stencil for each color.

STENCILS CAN BE CUT on special pre-treated stencil paper available at many art supply stores. Some people prefer clear acetate (.0075 gage) or frosted Mylar (.005 gage) because it lasts longer. But just about any heavy-bodied stiff paper can be used. For example, on our job when we ran out of stencil paper, one stencil was cut from a manila file folder. When untreated paper is used, it should be thoroughly soaked with boiled linseed oil and allowed to dry 24 hr. This adds durability and stiffness to the stencil.

WHEN MULTIPLE STENCILS are used, you need "keys" on each stencil to properly position it in relation to the work that has already been laid down. These keys are cut-outs that allow you to see an element that has already been painted. But paint is never applied through the keys.

ROUND, STIFF-BRISTLED BRUSHES are used for stencilling. Paint is applied with the ends of the bristles . . . working with the brush perpendicular to the surface being sten-

cilled. Some art supply houses carry special stencil brushes. You can also use a cabinetmaker's gluing brush or a rubbing brush. (Round gluing brushes are available from many sources in the current *Old-House Journal* Catalog.)

WE USED FLAT, OIL-BASED PAINTS for our stencil. You can also use acrylic colors or Japan paint. Japan paint dries very quickly and is preferred especially for small multi-color jobs where you have to overlay several successive stencils. (If not available locally, you can get Japan colors from Behlen Bros.)

THE TRICK in using oil-based paints is keeping them as thick as possible so that they don't run under the stencil. The consistency of ketchup is ideal. We hand-tinted all of our paints with colors-in-oil and added a bit of enamel to the paints to build up the body.

BESIDES USING THICK PAINT, the other secret of stencilling lies in using the brush as dry as possible while still getting adequate coverage. Keep a palette of folded newspaper by your side. After the tip of the brush is dipped into the paint, work the bristles first on the newspaper to remove excess paint. Otherwise, paint will seep under the edge of the stencil and will blur the outline.

PROPER BRUSHING TECHNIQUE involves working with the ends of the bristles with the brush held perpendicular to the surface being painted. Paint can be applied either with a staccato pouncing motion or else by a circular scrubbing.

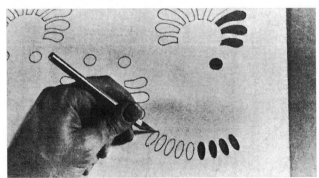

1. Pattern is drawn on stencil paper and cut out with X-Acto knife. A separate stencil is needed for each color to be used.
If not waxed, stencil paper should be treated with boiled linseed oil.

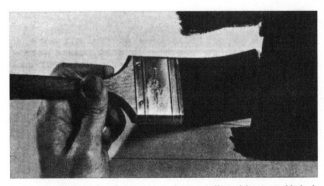

2. Limits of stencil band are measured onto wall, and lines established with a chalkline. Background color is then painted into band. We used a flat oilbased paint.

PRACTICE YOUR TECHNIQUE on a sample board. You'll soon get the hang of the proper dryness for the brush and how to work with the ends of the bristles.

BECAUSE THE BRUSH IS WORKED DRY, the colors are very thin when applied and have a certain translucence. The ground color will show through slightly . . . giving a depth, life and subtlety to the colors that is impossible to achieve with plain paint or a printed wallpaper. For example, when we went to photograph the stencilling process for this article we were amazed to find that the actual colors used in the frieze—while providing plenty of variety for the eye—didn't provide enough contrast to make clear black & white photographs. As a result, the photos you see on these two pages are a re-creation we had to make in our photo studio with special paints.

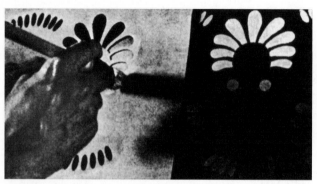

3. First stencil pattern is applied to band. Brush is held perpendicular to the work. Paint can be transferred by light pouncing action or by gently swirling the ends of the bristles.

4. Second color is applied. Note hole in stencil at right. This is a registration key—designed to line up with circle of color already applied with first stencil. No paint is applied through these keys.

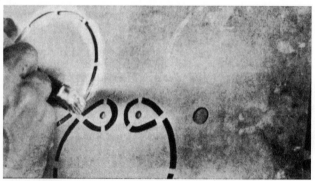

5. Third color—for the encircling ribbon—is laid down. Stencil required ties—small sections of paper running through the pattern that give strength to the stencil. Note circular key for alignment.

6. Gaps left in pattern by the ties are filled in by hand. Since paint in stencil pattern is thin and partially translucent, it takes some practice to get the painted-in areas to blend nicely.

7. Next, hearts of palmettes are added in a brownish orange. Since completed pattern contains five colors, actual shades could only be determined after much trial-and-error on the sample board.

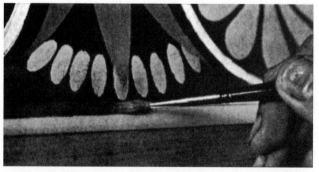

8. Striping the frieze top and bottom adds finishing touch. Straightedge is held at an angle to the surface so that paint from the striping brush can't ooze under the edge.

PAINTED FLOORS

NATURALLY FINISHED FLOOR BOARDS were not as highly regarded in the 18th and early 19th centuries as they are today. When hardwood floors were used, as in a parlor or a ballroom, they were waxed. But Early American floors were often softwood and left bare. Before the Revolution, the few carpets used in a household were generally on the tables. The early floors were often painted to add color and enrichment to a colonial room.

THERE ARE FLOORS IN OLD HOUSES today that are made of wood that is too old and stained to be finished nicely—that would have to be bleached too much, would splinter excessively, or have a flat, uninteresting softwood grain. An easy, interesting, and authentic alternative to a natural finish is a painted floor.

MOST OFTEN THE FLOOR WAS PAINTED in a solid color. Sometimes only a border was painted on a bare floor. As floor cloths, rag and hooked rugs, straw matting and carpets came into use, they were usually placed on painted floors. The most popular colors in use in the latter part of the 18th century were gray, dark green, gray-greens, pumpkin yellow, chocolate brown, and terra cotta red.

THE FIRST KIND OF ORNAMENTATION to the painted floor was freehand work. An itinerant painter, who usually grained the woodwork and perhaps decorated the walls, would often paint patterns that simulated mosaic tiles, or the English "turkey carpet" with geometric designs. A popular freehand pattern found in many old homes is a painted representation of marble, sometimes having a scroll border. A black & white checkered pattern is seen in many colonial rooms. This black & white checkered or diamond pattern, imitating expensive black & white marble floors, is found into the Victorian era.

STAIRS HAVE BEEN FOUND in old houses with a painted, figured strip running down the middle of the stairs with contrasting border edges, designed to give the appearance of a stair runner.

STENCILLED FLOORS

AFTER THE REVOLUTION, stencilled floors became quite popular and remained fashionable until about 1840. Stencilling was more complicated than freehand designs. Strong paper or cardboard, with a design cut out of it, was placed on the floor and the paint applied to the open space. When these stencil patterns were meant to imitate carpets, the stencil was a square pattern designed to match on all sides. A small star or flower was sometimes used at regular intervals of about 3 or 4 feet. The stencilled floors found in historic homes testify to the variety and colorfulness of the designs:

• An eight-petaled black flower on a deep pumpkin ground;

• Black and gray octagons (done with two stencils—the gray inside the black) on a dark green ground;

• A border pattern showing a vine in two shades of green with a red-brown fruit.

SPATTER PAINTING

SPATTER PAINTING or "spatterdash" was a widely used 19th-century method of decorating floors. It is still a very practical method of covering a floor as well as an authentic restoration technique. Originally, dark spots were spattered on a gray gound, but later examples show the reverse, with dark floors spattered in two or more light colors, giving a cheerful quality to a room. Some of the more typical early color schemes were:

• Copper brown ground with black, white, yellow and green spatters;

• Black with any variety of colored spatters;

• Blue ground with white, red and yellow;

• "Pepper and salt"—a popular New England combination for halls and stairs. Gray ground with small spatters of black and white.

To spatter paint, the ground color is applied and allowed to dry thoroughly. For the spots, flicks from a whisk broom give the best effect. It is wise to practice on a few pieces of newspaper first, to get the feel of it. Be sure to protect the baseboards and wall to at least two feet up the walls. Each set of spatters will have to dry thoroughly before the next set is applied.

FOR A SOFTER, TEXTURED EFFECT, the colors can be applied to the ground color with a pad of steel wool or a natural sponge instead of spattering them on. A thin coat of paint is applied to any flat surface (a pie plate will do) as if it were a stamp pad. Then dab the steel wool on the paint pad and apply like a rubber stamp to the floor.

IT IS NOT NECESSARY TO USE ENAMELS if a coat of light varnish or polyurethane is applied for protection. However, one of the virtues of the old-fashioned, unprotected painted floor is that worn spots can be simply touched up or painted over without eventually having to remove a coat of dirty varnish.

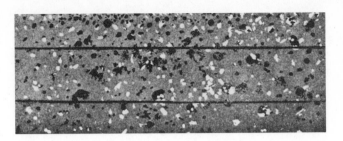

Exterior Design
Fountains, Landscaping, Fences

VICTORIAN FOUNTAINS AND URNS

By Tom H. Gerhardt

FROM MID-19th century until World War I, mass-produced cast iron supplied decorative beauty to the home and lawn. Used for fences, cresting, railings, columns, urns, statues, fountains, and lawn furniture, it was almost as common as the "molded-stone" garden ornaments that are available today . . . although far more durable and detailed. There were never as many fountains and urns as other works of art in cast iron and they seem to have had a higher mortality rate as they could be, and often were, easily removed and donated to scrap drives or sold to the dump. Therefore, the remaining ones should be considered prized possessions.

An iron octagon-shaped aquarium with plant brackets, the familiar seahorse base, and a less-familiar small umbrella boy spraying water made the long Michigan winters more pleasant in the tiled conservatory of the Edward Buckley residence, Manistee. The conservatory remains with only a cement patch in the tile floor where this beautiful aquarium-fountain once stood. Photograph courtesy of the Manistee County Historical Museum.

FOUNDRIES SUCH AS Mott, Walbridge (Buffalo, New York), and Fisk (Danbury, Conn.) cast these Victorian beauties and shipped them by train and boat throughout the country (Colorado's wealthy mining towns even had their share). Major centers of production seemed to be located for the most part in the Northeast. Often sparking the interest of owners of private residences in such finery, public parks and streets boasted large examples of this iron art–decorative horsetroughs; man, dog and horse drinking fountains; and huge decorative fountains complete with life-size figures and smaller drinking fountains around the edges.

FOR TODAY'S VICTORIAN HOMEOWNER, iron urns and fountains are important elements of decoration that are often missing from the lawn or the conservatory, or are still present but in poor condition. On the other hand, they are often added to provide greater interest and authenticity for the Victorian house where the owner can find no evidence of this decorative art ever being present.

IRON URNS

IRON URNS WERE USED in greater proliferation than the fountains as the latter works of art took plumbing and water to operate. Being available in basically just a few styles, these urns were manufactured with square bases or with more decorative, figured bases and were made in sections so that they could be taken apart and moved around very easily. For the most part, the pieces are interchangeable and usually, starting with a base (of which the larger ones are made of separate iron panels held together by tie rods), the pedestal, water reservoir, and bowl with or without bolted-on handles (handles were optional and if present at one time are often missing) are all stacked together without being bolted. The dead weight prevents them from being turned over by the wind; however, they are still vulnerable to the thrust of vandals.

THE IRON URNS are often used on balustrades near the house, along driveways, or just out in the center of the yard. In the house, the smaller versions can be used in the conservatory or plant room. When iron urns are placed on the lawn, a concrete pad should be provided so that the hollow base does not start sinking to one side; and when they are placed indoors, a heavy wooden pad with casters makes it easy to roll them around.

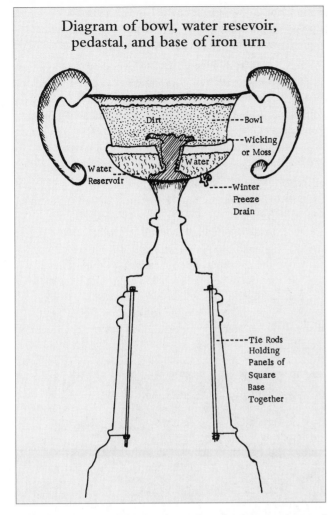

Diagram of bowl, water resevoir, pedastal, and base of iron urn

Dirt

Bowl

Wicking or Moss

Water Reservoir

Water

Winter Freeze Drain

Tie Rods Holding Panels of Square Base Together

THE WATER RESERVOIR is often the least understood part of these urns. It is the pan that receives the bowl where the flowers are planted. And in the bottom of the bowl, there is usually a funnel-shaped opening that extends downward into the water reservoir. This is where wicking or moss is placed so that the bowl is to some extent self-watering when the water reservoir is kept filled with water. If the urn is left out during the winter it is a good idea to place a drain in this reservoir to prevent it from filling with water and breaking. If a drain is not already present, a hole drilled at the lowest point and tapped eighth-inch pipe threads can be equipped with a pet cock to be opened in the winter.

WITH PLANTS AND FLOWERS selected according to geographical location, these urns are beautiful when filled with appropriate and compatible plants that seem to spray upward and overflow downward like a fountain. Plants such as the spike (Dracaenas Indivisa), that grows quite large if taken in during the winter year after year, as well as fern, caladium, geranium and coleus provide height. Variegated Vinca and Wandering Jew trail downward.

DUSTY MILLER (a plant that has now escaped to the roadsides) provides a complete variation in color with its grayish-white lacelike leaves. There are really all sorts of possibilities in planting urns that provide a very artistic and Victorian effect.

IRON FOUNTAINS

ALTHOUGH THE IRON DECORATIVE FOUNTAIN is a more complicated embellishment to the Victorian setting, nothing can duplicate a certain restful, peaceful, and yet mysterious feeling found in the sound of a fountain's falling water or can imitate the glistening spray that sparkles in the sunlight.

THE CAST IRON FOUNTAIN was the first type to be mass produced. Available with its own iron pool, it eliminated the use of dirt ponds or lead tanks and was often installed by homeowners as a most pretentious symbol of elegance in celebration of the completion of a town's waterworks.

IN ADDITION TO its presence on the lawn, it. was often used inside the house (often in the form of a large aquarium) in a bay window or a conservatory to hasten away the gloom of fall and winter by providing the sounds and delights of spring and summer through those bleak seasons of the year.

HOWEVER, because of the rising costs of water (in the beginning it was sold at cheap, flat rates based on the number of fountains, hydrants, cocks, and water closets) and the difficulty of maintenance caused by a lack of knowledge along these lines, many iron fountains were allowed to go dry, fell in poor repair, and were removed. Therefore, the few remaining ones or pieces and parts are highly prized today as ornamentation for the Victorian home. The availability of small electric pumps that consume little energy has provided a method of making them workable one more without such a great expense in water.

FOUNTAINS FOR THE LAWN

BASICALLY, the iron fountains include: (1) A central section with one, two or three spills (bowls where the water runs over the edges) that are stacked together like the urns and are often surmounted by a small iron or lead statue, (2) A large iron or lead statue on a low base. The central section is often surrounded by a round iron basin or concrete basin with a sculptured edge. The weight of course is terrific–a three-spill fountain, 8 ft., 2 in. high with a 7 ft., 6 in. iron basin costing $215 (painted) and $235 (bronzed) in 1909 from N. O. Nelson Manufacturing Company weighed 1,400 1bs. When having the iron basin on the Onekama, Michigan, Village Park fountain moved for repairs after being damaged by an automobile, the author found it necessary to find seven men to lift it onto a truck.

This fine example of a residential fountain is located in Anna, Illinois, and through repairs could run once more. It shows the typical cement basin that some of the iron fountains were constructed with.

THE ELABORATE AND WHIMSICAL DECORATIVE motifs of the different foundries for these fountains follow the same patterns with most parts being interchangeable. The iron basins have an edge with frogs or turtles nestled in rocks among waterlily and/or ivy leaves (a rare version is the one that was at the D. W. Filer home, Manistee, Michigan—it had light bulbs popping up around the edge for nighttime viewing). The pedestal under the first spill is the most ornate, commonly equipped with seahorses or cranes intertwined among cattails and arrowhead plants, or equipped with a fluted column decorated with lionheads and curling acanthus leaves.

THE PEDESTALS UNDER the other spills are usually smaller and less ornate but compatible in design, and the spills themselves often have carved edges to vary the size and location of the drip with acanthus leaves spreading outward underneath from the central column. The statue (large if alone in the pool, small if on top of one or more spills) is of iron or lead, depicting the Victorian imagination at its best in very interesting and detailed forms of time-honored favorites such as the boy and swan, the boy riding a dolphin, the umbrella boy, the boy with a serpent, the lady at the well, and the huge bird—all of which are usually perched on a base of extremely intriguing iron or lead rocks.

IF THE IRON FOUNTAIN does have a statue, the spray usually emerges from the mouth of the featured beast, the top of the umbrella, or the jug; a ring of sprays might also be used at the statue's feet. For those fountains lacking a statue, a ring of sprays or a single spray sometimes placed in the middle of two or three iron leaves and flowers in the top spill provides bubbling action.

BASICALLY, THE SPRAY IS supplied by a central pipe that in reality also holds the stacked-up parts together. Then, usually under the base of these central parts out in the basin, is the overflow pipe that carries the water off so that it does not spill out over the edge of the basin. It is typical that this overflow pipe may be unscrewed from its socket in the basin floor to drain all of the water out of the basin. A valve on the supply line is often located in the yard or under the central base to turn the water on and off.

THE ACCOMPANYING DIAGRAMS show piping for using the fountain with fresh running water and for the addition of a small electric pump to recirculate the water through the fountain. Especially in the smaller basin that contains a fountain using a pump, it is important to install a float valve on the water supply to maintain the water level as the water splashes out and evaporates.

IF NEW PIPING IS REQUIRED in restoring a fountain, copper or red brass piping are the most desirable. Adequate provision must be made for draining the supply piping so that winter frost damage will not occur. Regardless of the piping used, a copper or red brass fitting is a must for the socket in which the overflow pipe is screwed, as these threads will quickly rust out when the overflow pipe is left out to keep the pool drained in the wintertime. And the larger the drain line, the better. It is much easier to wash out a pool where the drain is large enough to carry out small bits of debris without clogging.

Color scheme of dark green with white accents this unusual ramhead fountain on the lawn of the Hamill House in Georgetown, Colorado. Iron leaves and flowers ornament the spray on the top spill while small iron flowerpots adorn the edge of the basin.

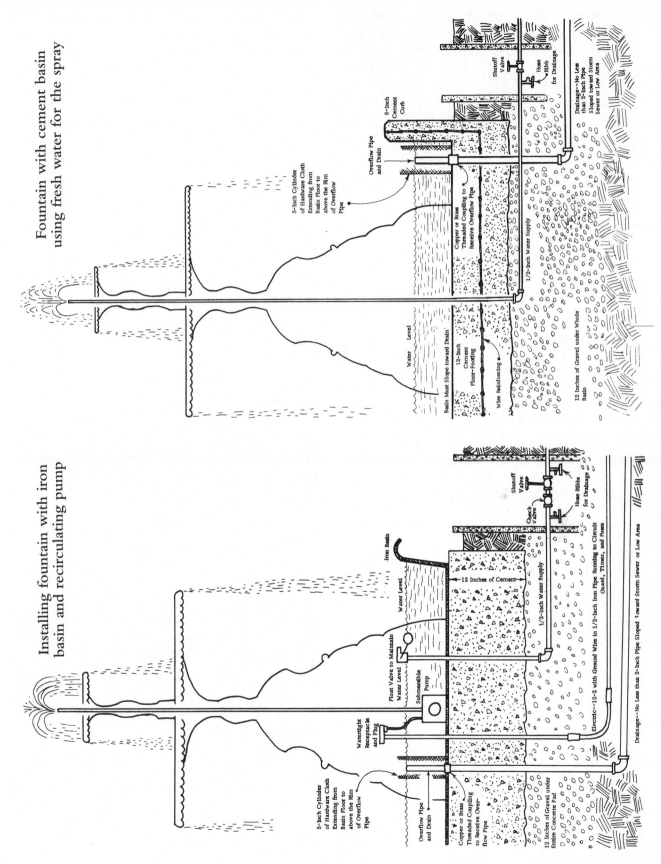

Fountain with cement basin using fresh water for the spray

5-Inch Cylinder of Hardware Cloth Extending from Basin Floor to above the Rim of Overflow Pipe

8-Inch Cement Curb

Overflow Pipe and Drain

Copper or Brass Threaded Coupling to Receive Overflow Pipe

1/2-Inch Water Supply

Shutoff Valve

Hose Bibb for Drainage

Drainage—No Less than 2-Inch Pipe Sloped toward Storm Sewer or Low Area

Water Level

Basin Must Slope toward Drain

12-Inch Cement Floor-Footing

Wire Reinforcing

12 Inches of Gravel under Whole Basin

Installing fountain with iron basin and recirculating pump

5-Inch Cylinder of Hardware Cloth Extending from Basin Floor to above the Rim of Overflow Pipe

Iron Basin

Water Level

Float Valve to Maintain Water Level

Submersible Pump

Watertight Receptacle and Plug

12 Inches of Cement

1/2-Inch Water Supply

Check Valve

Shutoff Valve

Hose Bibbs for Drainage

Electric—12-2 with Ground Wire in 1/2-Inch Iron Pipe Running to Circuit Guard, Timer, and Fuses

Overflow Pipe and Drain

Copper or Brass Threaded Coupling to Receive Overflow Pipe

12 Inches of Gravel under Entire Concrete Pad

Drainage—No Less than 2-Inch Pipe Sloped toward Storm Sewer or Low Area

IN RE-SETTING AN IRON BASIN, a level concrete pad should be built as a foundation. Then, the iron basin is placed (above ground level) on this pad using a seal of wet cement beneath the basin floor to seal around pipe openings and to adhere the basin to the pad. A level should be used in checking the basin and spills at all times to avoid the one-sided or unlevel-dish effect of a leaning fountain.

DUE TO THE UNAVAILABILITY of cement and the difficulties in forming and working it, cement basins for iron fountains were not usually used unless the desired pool size and/or depth exceeded dimensions offered in iron. Larger fountains in parks often have the hexagon- or octagon-shaped cement basin combined with an iron coping that was supplied by the manufacturer; however, the smaller residential fountans usually have a round cement basin that has a cement curb as well, when cement was substituted for the iron basin. The edges of the curb are usually simple and still can be formed by adding wooden mouldings in circular forms built with well-supported flexible sheets of wood. The author has never seen brick used originally as a coping around these basins, although several instances of sculptured sandstone coping have been evident.

IN THIS UNDERTAKING OF CEMENT WORK, it is important to follow the information given in the diagrams in order to avoid frost damage. The mixture for the cement should be no leaner than 4 parts sand, 2 parts cement, and 1 part gravel. After the forms are removed, the surfaces can be troweled and broomed. The finish should not be really slick as algae forming on the wet surfaces makes them as slick as smooth ice and very dangerous when cleaning the basin.

THE IRON BASINS are usually not more than 8 in. deep and are very safe for children. However, they may be used for a few goldfish in the summer and such water plants as water hyacinth (which produces beautiful purple bloom spikes) and parrot's feather. If one desires to grow waterlilies, water irises, or arrowheads in a fountain, the basin must be a large concrete one with a depth of not under 24 in. Generally, the water garden is kept to a minimum in a basin with an active fountain, as most of these plants do not like to be kept wet on top and do not like currents of rushing water around them. Also, a water garden must receive at least partial sunlight.

THE PLANTINGS AROUND THE FOUNTAIN should be compatible with water as the area is usually kept wet by the wind blowing the spray. Ivy is excellent around the basin.

MAINTENANCE OF THE IRON FOUNTAIN will require cleaning of the basin more often if re-circulated water is used. Algae (green water), which forms from the bottom of the basin, will always be a problem unless fresh water is added continuously. The author has found that the only real solution to this algae is to place in the basin the oxygenating plant water-milfoil or Myriophyllum, that shades the basin floor and prevents the formation of algae. The problem of mosquitos should not be evident in the fountain basin that has fresh water and fish.

WINTER AND FREEZING temperatures must bring the draining of all fountain parts and the basin (unless it is a deep one, in which logs should be placed to prevent the breaking of the cement by the freezing of the water) and the covering with canvas of the spills and statue.

DESIGNS FOR VICTORIAN FENCES AND GATES

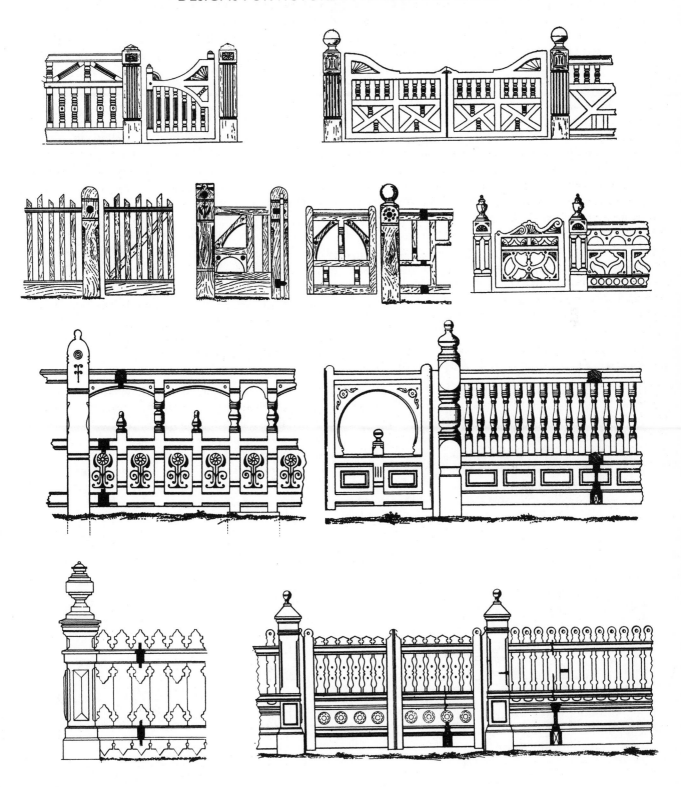

LANDSCAPING THE PRE-1840 HOUSE

By Donna Jeanloz

GARDEN DESIGN IN English-speaking America changed very little from the earliest gardens of the Pilgrims until the advent of Victorian styles and architecture around 1840. Although landscape gardening underwent a revolution in Britain during the 18th century, only the most wealthy and stylish country estates in America reflected the new naturalistic English style.

THE VAST MAJORITY OF GARDENS continued the Tudor tradition of an enclosed garden of geometrical beds of plants outlined by paths. This garden form was adapted to every architectural style from Colonial to Greek Revival, from elegant Georgian townhouses to isolated farmsteads.

SOCIAL FUNCTION OF THE GARDEN

THE EARLIEST SETTLERS in the new world planted gardens of dire necessity. They were almost totally dependent on their crops and livestock to supply their needs. Staple crops for food and fodder, such as corn, beans, and oats, were grown in fields. Everything else, including vegetables, herbs, medicinal plants, vegetable dyes, fruits, nuts, and other useful plants including some flowers, was grown on the home plot surrounding the house. Every available space was taken by these useful plants, for the health and survival of the household depended on their availability: Rue, dill, feverfew, wormwood, and other medicinal plants for various home remedies for common complaints; soapwort, teasel, madder, and woad, for processing and dyeing wool; flax, for linen and linseed oil; hops, for brewing beer; lavender and roses, to scent linen; rosemary, parsley, sage, thyme, mustard, garlic, mints, and onions, to make a constant diet of beans and root crops more palatable; plus any available sort of vegetable, herb, and fruit to vary what must have been a horrendously boring diet.

VERY LITTLE TIME and energy were expended on laying out the garden to nice effect, but rather everything was jumbled in together in patches, tall and short, according to the most suitable soil, drainage, and exposure for each plant.

LATER, AS THE COLONIES became well-established and enjoyed a degree of prosperity, necessary items became more or less available commercially so that the household was able to devote more of its garden space to non-essential plants. Especially by the early 19th century, gardens were organized and planted to please the senses as well as to supply useful herbs, medicines, and foods. The vegetable plot was usually separated from the purely ornamental plants, which might include some shrubs as well as flowers, and arbors, swings, pavillions, etc., began to appear in the garden as the garden began to be viewed as a nicety rather than as a necessity.

EVOLUTION OF AN ISOLATED FARMHOUSE TO A SMALL SUBURBAN LOT

Colonial Era

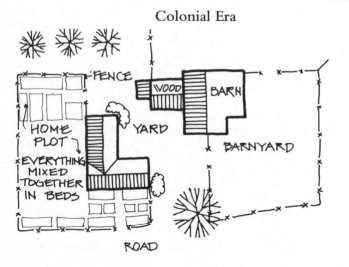

Contemporary Adaptation

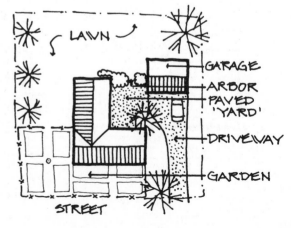

LAYOUT OF THE GROUNDS

ORIGINALLY, there was a greater distinction between the terms "yard" and "garden" than we make today. "Garden" included any area where plants were grown and tended, whereas "yard" was a smallish enclosed area where animals were kept, as in "barnyard," or where work and chores were done. A lawn of tended, mowed or clipped (scythed, in those days, or grazed) grass fell into the garden category and was a luxury of maintenance and space.

MOST HOUSEHOLDS, including urbanites, had a more varied set of outdoor activities than we do today, and therefore the organization of the space around the house itself was more complex. Areas were allocated for various gardens including orchards and fruit bushes, for yards housing at-home animals such as chickens and goats as well as for larger pasture animals, and for work such as boiling and drying laundry, making soap, chopping wood, drawing water from the well, drying fruits and herbs, and hundreds of other chores that were best done outside. There would also have been clearly defined roads and paths to the house, barns, sheds, dependencies, pastures, etc.

A CAREFUL RE-CREATION of the landscape surrounding almost any house of the pre-Industrial era would include spaces set aside for each of these uses: Gardens, yards and work areas, and access routes. An accurate restoration of the area around the house would require knowledge of how space was originally allocated, but this is usually not too hard to come by–obviously the yards for animals were adjacent to the barn and probably downwind of the house, and the work areas likely were close by the back door and sheds.

GARDEN AREAS may be harder to locate. If the house faces the street, there may well have been a garden between the house and road as dooryard gardens (enclosed by a fence which ran along the road) were popular. Usually the garden was enclosed, so old remains of walls, hedges, or fences would give a clue. Old paths and cartways often appear as sunken areas along the ground; early spring, before the grass grows up, is the best time to look for these.

YARDS CAN BE EASILY SYMBOLICALLY represented by our modern equivalent, the lawn. To be historically more accurate, this space would be enclosed by a wooden fence, but fences are expensive and if there is no good reason for enclosing the yard a fence may even look foolish. If the yard is represented by a clearly defined area it should suffice. Remember that lawnmowers were unknown in this era and relax on maintenance accordingly.

WORK AREAS, or service areas, are usually best located near the back door or in the space between a garage or shed and the house. Probably in the old days this area was simply packed dirt, but you will probably prefer some sort of informal pav-

ing. Brick is excellent in the mid-Atlantic states and in the South, where it was always popular; it should be laid in sand.

IN NORTHERN AREAS where old-style soft brick is apt to crack as a result of winter freezing the best solution is to lay random flat stones–the kind used to make dressed fieldstone walls–in sand, or river cobbles, or Belgian block ("cobblestones"). Water-struck brick can also be used but it is expensive. Less expensive solutions would include crushed stone or pea stone or crushed stone rolled into a tack coat of road tar.

PATHS AND DRIVES were probably earth or gravel, but you may prefer them paved. (Gravel gets tracked into the house and is hard on the floors.) Black top is the least expensive method and unfortunately the least appropriate.

A FAR BETTER SOLUTION is crushed stone rolled or tamped into a temporarily sticky base, usually black road tar. There are also new systems on the market which utilize an epoxy resin for a binder and crushed stone as the aggregate. Exposed aggregate concrete is also good, especially with relatively large stones (1–2 in.) as the aggregate. Crushed stone, cobblestones, and brick also look good, but when laying stones or brick in sand remember to provide a base solid enough to support the fuel oil truck if necessary. The path to the front door was often paved with brick or large rectangular dressed stones. It might be worthwhile to probe a bit in the soil where the walk is or would have been to see if the stones are still there. If grass grows vigorously in your front yard expect at least a foot of soil to have built up over any stones.

FORM OF THE GARDEN

SINCE GARDENS are primarily composed of plants–everchanging living organisms which are manipulated by humans–it is extremely unlikely that even the original form of the garden is discernible. Probably the garden has been moved, possibly several times, according to fashion, personal preference of the gardener, and worn-out soil. You will therefore almost certainly have to re-create the planted areas according to what you can learn and infer about the original gardens.

IT IS HELPFUL to first determine the social class of the house and its early owners. Is is a humble farmhouse, reflecting the needs and uses of subsistence agriculture? Or was it the home of the most important man in a small town? Or the Georgian townhouse of a professional man or merchant? Or the country estate of a gentleman? Try to imagine how dependent the household would have been on its garden, and how many hands would have been available to tend it.

THE SIMPLEST GARDENS, in terms of form and layout, would accompany isolated farmsteads and humble dwellings. These gardens would be very close to the house and composed of groups of garden beds, roughly rectangular or square, with narrow paths running between them. The beds would be small, probably only about 6 ft. wide at the widest point, and not very long.

THEY MIGHT HAVE BEEN EDGED by stones or saplings pegged along the ground, and they might have the soil mounded up somewhat higher than the level of the pathway, as good drainage was considered important. The paths might be gravel or even crushed clam shells, but probably were simply packed dirt. The entire garden would certainly have been somehow enclosed, either by a rough but tight fence or a stone wall.

VEGETABLES, HERBS, AND FLOWERS would be grown in patches in the bed according to where they would thrive best. Tall and short, coarse and fine, vegetable and flower would all be mingled together. Most of our colorful annuals were developed after this time, so consult a listing of period plants before selecting any of these. (The box on the facing apge contains only a partial list of some of the common garden plants used in the Early American period. Local libraries and garden clubs can help with research.) Almost all our common vegetables and herbs were around in the old days (except sweet corn). Probably there were few shrubs in the garden, although "laylocks" (lilacs) and roses are commonly mentioned.

ADJACENT TO THE BEDS would be fruit trees and bushes. Fruit was much appreciated and was included in every garden. Apples were a staple but almost every other kind of fruit was

AN ELEGANT PLEASURE GARDEN

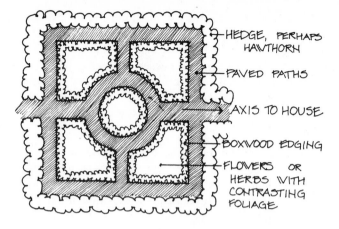

known and tried. Nuts were also carefully cultivated.

IF THE HOUSE WAS IN A VILLAGE or along a main road, it might have had a dooryard or parlor garden between the road and the front of the house. This was created by extending a fence (usually pickets) from the sides of the house out to the road and then along the road in front of the house, with a gate at the front walk. This garden was planted with flowers. Since the parlor of the house was usually at the front, these flowers provided scent and color outside the parlor windows as well as a welcoming entry to anyone approaching the front door. More utilitarian plants might be grown near the back door or in a "kitchen garden" to the side or rear of the house.

THE OWNER of a more substantial or elegant house was able to devote greater efforts to the organization of the garden. Probably servants or slaves were available to do the actual work. Flowers, herbs and vegetables might have separate areas, with each bed larger and carefully planned. Herbs were occasionally worked into knot gardens, showing off the nuances of foliage color and texture as well as the gardener's skill.

COLONIAL TOWNHOUSE GARDEN

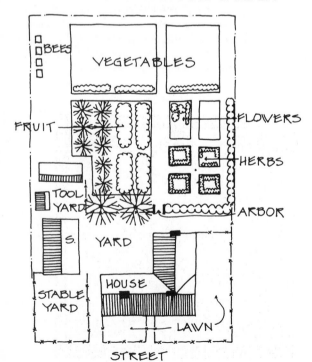

TYPICAL DOORYARD GARDENS

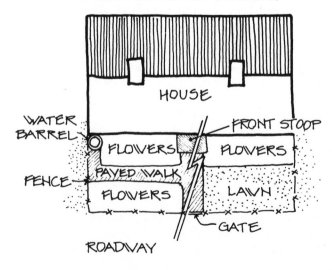

SOME PLANTS IN USE BEFORE 1840

FLOWERS

Balsam
Batchelor's Button (formerly Cornflower, Blue Bottle)
Calendula
Canterbury Bells
China Aster
Chinese Lantern Plant
Chrysanthemum
Crocus
Delphinium
Forget-Me-Not
Four O'Clocks (formerly Marvel-Of-Peru)
Geranium–Rose, Lemon, Nutmeg, Mint, Garden
Grape Hyacinth
Heliotrope
Honesty–Money Plant
Iris–Florentine, German, Sweet
Jonquil
Larkspur
Lily-Of-The-Valley
Lupine
Marigold–African, French, Sweet Scented
Mignonette
Morning Glory
Narcissus
Peony
Poppy; Opium, Rose
Salvia
Snapdragon
Sunflower
Sweet William
Sweet Violet
Tulip
Zinnia, Violet, Red, Yellow

TREES, SHRUBS AND VINES

American Holly
Bittersweet
Catalpa
English Ivy
Flowering Quince
Gingko
Hawthorn
Horse Chestnut
Mulberry
Rose-Of-Sharon
Spice Bush, Carolina All-Spice
Tree Of Heaven
Trumpet Vine
Tulip Poplar
Weeping Willow
Witchhazel

HERBS

Garlic
Garden Parsley
Chive
Anise
Dill
Rosemary
Camomile
Garden Sage
Tarragon
Summer Savory
Caraway
Winter Savory
Lavender
Tansy
Sweet Marjoram
Thyme
Catnip
Common Rue
Sweet Basil
Peppermint

IN THE SOUTHERN AND MIDDLE colonies, boxwood edging for each bed was extremely popular, as can be seen in the restored gardens of Colonial Williamsburg. Topiary work–training or trimming trees or shrubs into ornamental shapes–was especially popular with the Dutch in New Amsterdam, but might be expected to appear in any wealthy man's garden.

IN FORM THE GARDEN would be more rigidly geometric, with brick or crushed stone paths. It might be enclosed by a brick wall or a hedge of hawthorn or boxwood. Probably the central axis of the garden layout would be in line with the

A KNOT GARDEN

house or an important window. A larger area of space around the house would be devoted to a lawn of scythed grass, and for elegant country houses in the South this green could become quite large. Fruits and nuts would be included as well.

THE EFFECT THAT YOU should strive for in landscaping the old house is that of harmony between the house and its surroundings. If the house itself is elegant and refined, so should be the grounds. If, on the other hand, you are landscaping a simple cottage, you should seek a somewhat rustic effect.

PERIOD LANDSCAPING ERRORS

FOUNDATION PLANTING as we practice it today was unknown in this period. Preservationists believe that the house almost always sat on a rather low foundation with the barge board exposed. Frequently a shrub was planted at a corner of the house to soften its outline, and deciduous trees were planted to the south and west to provide summer shade. If you feel the house looks too naked without foundation planting, try planting a bed of perennials or a low ground cover along the foundation.

INDIVIDUAL SHRUBS were planted, but the shrub border was not usually an element of the garden. Shrubs were used formally as hedges and espaliers to contain and enclose rather than in naturalistic plantings to provide edges.

MUCH OF OUR MOST POPULAR PLANT material was unknown during the young days of our republic. This includes such favorites as Japanese Yew, Spirea, Weigela, White Wisteria, Hall's Honeysuckle, Pachysandra, and generally speaking, plants from the Orient, most of which were introduced in the 19th century. Furthermore, a large number of our native shrubs and plants appear to have been known but little used. Included in this group are Junipers, Mountain Laurel, Rhododendrons, etc. Favored garden plants were those brought from England which proved hardy here, such as Mulberry and Boxwood. When selecting plants for a period garden, it would be wise to consult a list of plants known to have been cultivated at that time.

PICTURE BOOKS of historical gardens are readily available in libraries to suggest ideas. If you delegate the task of landscaping to your nurseryman or landscape architect, make sure he or she understands the distinction between good landscape design and period land-scaping, and is willing to do a little research into what would be appropriate for your house.

WRONG: Colonial house anachronistically landscaped with foundation plantings popular in the 20th century.

RIGHT: Classic Colonial houses had trees, shrubs and flowers away from the house in imitation of the formal Georgian ideal.

VICTORIAN LANDSCAPING

By Donna Jeanloz

WHILE ENGLISH GARDENING STYLES underwent a profound change in the 18th century, coincidental with the Romantic Movement, American gardens continued to follow the earlier Tudor traditions of geometric gardens until well into the 19th century. It was not until the appearance in 1841 of Andrew Jackson Downing's book, "A Treatise On The History And Practice Of Landscape Gardening," that popular taste shifted toward the English naturalistic garden style.

DOWNING'S NAME is familiar to any student of the 19th century. "A Treatise" was the first of his several enormously popular books, written while he was a young nurseryman in Newburgh, N.Y. It was an overnight success, virtually revolutionizing middle-class garden styles. The neat, geometric, ordered garden was out, replaced by man-made "nature": soft, curving masses of green.

DOWNING evidently gleaned many of his ideas from the leading British landscape authority of the day, J. C. Louden, who had conveniently published a book on landscape gardening a year previously.

THERE WERE a number of reasons for the overnight success of Downing's book. For one, it was written by an American specifically for the American scene at a time when national pride and self-confidence was on the upswing. Life styles were changing with the growth of industry, and the many solid citizens benefitting from this growth felt intuitively that

their gardens no longer needed emphasis, direct or implied, on simple survival. The outdoors was increasingly regarded as a place to play rather than as a hostile environment.

ALSO, the introduction of exotic plant material including colorful annuals and a marked increase in horticultural journals and available printed information did much to interest the public in improving its surroundings. Further, the passage of fence laws starting at about this time had a strong influence on the householder's view toward improving his property. Fence laws obligated the owner of live-stock (cattle, swine, etc.) to contain the animals, whereas before the burden of fencing had been on the gardener to keep the free-roaming animals out of the garden.

IN HIS BOOK, Downing divided art into two realms, the beautiful and the picturesque, and suggested that architectural styles and landscape improvements should complement each other. He felt that the classical architectural styles–Greek Revival, Italianate, Tuscan–represent the beauty of harmony and grace and call for the beautiful landscape treatment, while the irregular architectural styles–Gothic, castellated, Norman, bracketed–require the picturesque mode of landscape improvement to balance their striking and unsymmetrical aspect. With typical American preoccupation with the new, he did not consider any of the pre-existing residential styles as candidates for either mode of the new landscape gardening.

This is an example of Downing's landscaping in the "beautiful" manner.

The imitation of wild nature is evident in Downing's "picturesque" style.

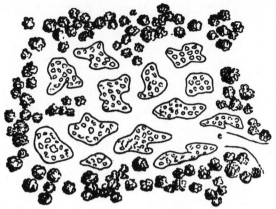

At left is Downing's "English Flower Garden," a suitable accompaniment to the beautiful mode of landscape gardening.

At right is Downing's "Irregular Flower Garden," recommended for the Gothic Revival and other romantic styles that called for the picturesque manner of landscape gardening.

HOW DID THE BEAUTIFUL in gardening differ from the picturesque? The beautiful was thought to embody grace and harmony; hence it was represented by softly flowing grassy lawns studded with stately, regularly-shaped trees and shrubs. Curving paths wound among the trees on the grounds, and in the flower garden a path might be cut through the lawn, which was punctuated with curly-shaped flower beds.

THIS "ENGLISH FLOWER GARDEN" was characterized by rather violently curved outlines. Each bed was planted with only one or two varieties of colorful blooming annuals–"the aim being a brilliant effect." Favorite plants were fuchsia,

salvia, lobelia, and red geranium. Shrubs were planted near the house, in beds along the walkways. Flowering shrubs such as mock-orange, lilacs, etc., were preferred.

DOWNING FURTHER recommended that classical-style houses should be tied to their grounds by terraces with balustrades reminiscent of the Italian gardens of the Renaissance. He recommended a terrace 5–20 ft. wide, and raised 1–8 ft. above ground level, paved with flagstones, and bounded by a balustrade with coping studded with "architectural decoration" at regular intervals. The architectural decoration might consist of vases or urns, either empty or planted in the Italian manner with formal plants (topiary work, or yuccas) or statuary. If money for the grand balustrade treatment was unavailable, vases or urns might be set on plinths or pedestals to delineate the terrace area.

THE PICTURESQUE IDEAL emulated wild nature. The total effect was much less carefully groomed and harmonious than in the beautiful mode; the goal was a kind of raw roughness appropriate to craggy stones, rushing water, and dark thickets. This effect was achieved in landscape planting by the use of irregularly-shaped or dramatic trees, especially conifers, used in tighter groups to simulate natural groves or thickets and to increase the play of light and shadows. Native shrubs might be used in naturalistic plantings. Paths through the grass and woods were even more meandering and rustic, sometimes with sharp changes in level. Rockeries, grottos, and other oddities were appropriate.

PLAN OF A "SUBURBAN VILLA" AND GROUNDS, CA. 1850.

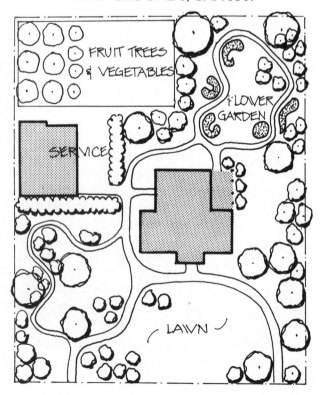

DOWNING DESCRIBES a flower garden suitable to this mode in the following terms: "The irregular flower garden is surrounded by an irregular belt of trees and ornamental shrubs of the choicest species, and the beds are varied in outline, as well as irregularly disposed, sometimes grouping together, sometimes standing singly, but exhibiting no uniformity of arrangement." This was considered a suitable accompaniment to the house and grounds of a lover of the picturesque-rural Gothic style.

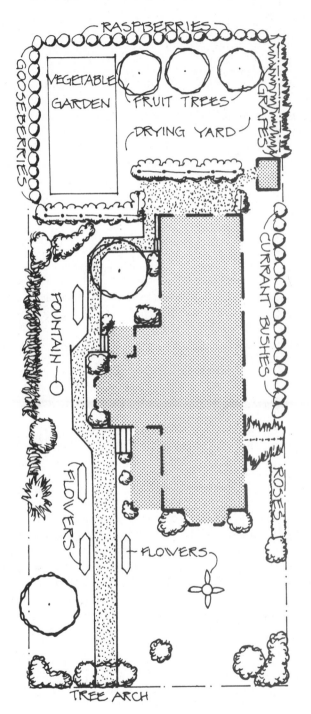

PLAN OF A HOUSE AND SMALL SUBURBAN LOT, ca. 1880

RASPBERRIES

GOOSEBERRIES

VEGETABLE GARDEN

FRUIT TREES

GRAPES

DRYING YARD

FOUNTAIN

CURRANT BUSHES

FLOWERS

FLOWERS

ROSES

TREE ARCH

DOWNING WAS ALSO a great advocate of the use of vines to soften and give character to architecture – the stylistic prelude to the use of foundation planting for the same purpose after the turn of the century. Vines growing up on wires were used to screen areas of the verandah or porch from public view, and vines were encouraged to ramble over features such as bay windows. Hall's honeysuckle, introduced from the Orient in this period, quickly became a favorite.

IT IS IMPORTANT to note that while the grounds and pleasure gardens visible from the street and house–the modern equivalent would be the front yard–followed the new stylistic trend toward "nature," every household continued to require the same service spaces as before for drying laundry, chopping wood, etc. Most homes were still outfitted with the sheds, dependencies, barns, and stables of the former era. These were carefully placed behind the house and screened in some way from the street and drive. Behind them could be found the vegetable garden and fruit trees, planted in rows.

DOWNING'S BOOK ran through 6 editions, the last of which was published more than 20 years after his untimely death in 1852. During the decades following the Civil War, the streetcar changed the shape, size, and social climate of the city as millions of well-to-do Americans moved out into newly created suburbs. The average suburban lot was far smaller than the grounds surrounding the "rural villa" of Downing's time, and its proximity to its neighbors demanded a slightly different treatment than the "beautiful" or "picturesque" advocated by Downing 30 years before.

AT ITS BEST the suburban concept was that of gracious homes set in a shared park-like environment, and the problem presented to the landscape designer was thus how to maintain the overall effect while affording privacy and individuality to each of the houses.

BY THE 1880s two features were considered essential to a businessman's home: A fine lawn and large trees. The development of the lawnmower as we know it today (almost) did a lot to popularize the fine lawn. Instead of designating certain spaces within the lot for planting grass, the entire lot was thought of as a lawn, and plantings, drives, etc., were cut out of the grass area, much as a subdivision builder does today.

TREES WERE STRATEGICALLY PLACED in the lawn to provide shade or complement architecture by providing a backdrop or accent, but they were very rarely used en masse to create a grove or a barrier. Large, stately trees such as American elm and European beech were extensively used as suitable companions to the large homes of the Queen Anne style, and fast-growing trees such as silver maple were also popular.

SHRUBS BECAME increasingly popular, both in mass plantings and as single specimens. Naturalistic plantings of shrubs in clumps and groups were used to screen undesirable views into neighboring windows and service areas, to delineate property boundaries and areas of lawn such as the croquet field, and to direct the view to and from the street.

SINGLE SHRUBS were used as accents in the lawn and as centerpieces for garden beds. Although planting to hide the house foundation had not yet appeared, flowering shrubs were often planted along the verandah's edge or under a window for their beauty and fragrance.

FLOWERBEDS REFLECTED the Victorian era's love of ornament and ostentation. Typically they were now complexly geometric: starshaped, cruciform, trefoil, and combinations. They were cut out of the lawn along walkways or in strategic and conspicuous places and planted with brilliantly colored annuals or with roses. Flowering shrubs or fountains or statuary might provide the centerpiece for a circular bed or arrangement of beds.

SUBURBAN HOUSES, like their urban predecessors, usually had two entrances from the street: a straight or elegantly curving formal walkway from the street to the front entrance, and a less elegant drive leading to the service areas hidden in the recesses of the lot. The view of the house as one approached from the street was carefully controlled. The walkway was placed to give maximum effect to the house, and plantings were introduced as necessary to enhance this view.

WHEN THE LOT WAS FENCED, as it frequently was, the fencing was of a type allowing maximum visibility, usually iron bars or rails, as the goal seems to have been a psychological sense of boundary rather than a barrier to produce privacy.

Often the ground level of the lot was raised slightly above the sidewalk by a concrete or cut stone retaining curb, which served a boundary function similar to the fence. It was considered desirable to have the land slope up to the house from the street, as this made the house appear larger and taller. If screening or privacy from the street was desired, shrubs were the usual solution.

MOST SUBURBAN HOUSES concentrated their landscaping efforts on the front yard, as the side yards were quite narrow and the backyards continued to be taken up by carriage houses, privies, wood or coal sheds, drying yards, and vegetable gardens. In Frank J. Scott's *Suburban Home Grounds,* published in 1886, almost all the suggested lot layouts show vegetable plots and fruits. Those that are simply too small to accommodate vegetables use fruit trees and bushes as the ornamental landscaping elements.

THE URBAN DWELLER of the Victorian period was generally far less concerned with landscape improvements. After all, he had less space, particularly in an attached row house with no side yards or drives to worry about. The service areas were located behind the house, with access via an alley. This rear area is now often very successfully converted into a small city garden. It need not be a period garden or a restoration since it was not originally a garden area at all.

THE FRONT YARD, usually quite small, was grassed over and often enclosed by a cast iron decorative fence. a paved walkway led to the entrance. There might be a specimen tree or shrub planted in the lawn or under a window, or a flower bed alongside the walkway, or a geometric flower bed cut into the lawn to be viewed from an upstairs window. Ivy and other vines might be encouraged to cover the masonry or twine up the downspouts.

BY THE END OF THE 19th century many of our modern annuals had been developed, and horticultural institutions were sending expeditions to the Orient to discover new plant materials suitable to our temperate climate. Japanese yew was introduced in 1855, Siebold viburnum by 1880, weigelia in 1845, kudzu vine in 1885, Boston ivy in 1862, Japanese barberry in 1875, flowering quinces before 1880, and pee gee hydrangia in 1862. In California, the eucalyptus species were introduced from Australia and New Zealand. Flower favorites, predictably, were in brilliant colors: Geraniums, coleus, cockscomb, castor beans, cannas, nasturtiums, lobelias, alyssum, zinnias. Extensive work was done in developing vegetables and fruit, especially by Luther Burbank, resulting in sweet corn and smooth red tomatoes.

WHIMSEYS OF ALL KINDS enlivened the Victorian garden. Dripping fountains and birdbaths, statues of children and animals, complex arbors, garden houses, rockeries, grottos, and fantastic and complicated topiary work were all welcomed.

An illustration from Scott's **Suburban Home Grounds** *depicts a typical iron rail fence.*

A whimsical entrance to a rural villa.

A weeping larch for the "picturesque."

DESPITE THE ever-increasing amount of exotic and Oriental plant material, there was a growing respect for native shrubs and trees. This was especially true in the prairie states, where extremes of cold, wind, and drought combined to make foreign plants less than happy. Shrubs such as box-elder and osage orange and our native willows, cottonwoods, and elms were extensively used by garden designers evolving a uniquely American landscape art which was the complement to the developing prairie school in architecture.

BY THE TURN OF THE CENTURY garden styles began a definite shift back toward naturalism from the striking stiffness of the late Victorian period. Gently curving "borders" of flowers and shrubs were used to delineate spaces, with individual species planted in clumps or drifts. Perennials became popular again, as did pastel-hued flowers. The lawn with trees remained an American institution, no longer interrupted by flowerbed cut-outs but as a continuous sweep of green carpet from border to border. And the new vogue for foundation planting decreed that every house be tied to the ground by a layer of massed shrubs.

Victorian Garden Book

Frank J. Scott's famous book on landscaping published in 1886 is now available in a soft-cover reprint. Originally titled, *Suburban Home Grounds,* it contains over 200 illustrations of plans for gardens and embellishments. The reprint version has a sewn binding and it is retitled *Victorian Gardens For Victorian Homes.*

These whimsical examples of Victorian topiary are from Frank J. Scott's book, Suburban Home Grounds.

CAST IRON FENCES

by Elaine Freed

ORNAMENTAL CAST IRON was one of the most important manufactured products of the Victorian era. It enabled the average citizen of the period to obtain, at low cost, a great show of luxury and architectural adornment.

WROUGHT IRON, hand wrought by a blacksmith, had limited decorative ironwork value to the homes of those who could afford handcrafted work and to certain uses. But cast iron could be reproduced in any form for which a mold could be prepared. The rapid evolution of fancy, cast iron work made it available to middle-class home builders. Iron work was no longer associated only with prestigious institutions and estates of the wealthy.

A FEW VOICES PROTESTED the degradation of craftsmanship but, by and large, people welcomed the proliferation of consumer goods and embellished their houses with the new cast iron products. Buildings and lawns across the land were decorated with railings, crestings, verandahs, urns, statues, garden furniture, and weather vanes all made of the newly available ironwork.

ONE OF THE MOST POPULAR uses for cast iron was for fencing. With manufacturers turning out fences with gothic motifs and romantic floral and "rustic" patterns, the owner of a new Victorian mansion no longer had to surround his lawn with anything so commonplace as a wooden picket fence.

WHILE VICTORIAN FENCING imitated traditional iron work designs, they made important concessions in size. Large estate fences maintained their monumental dimensions but the new foundry-made residential iron fences followed the more modest proportions of old-fashioned wooden picket fencing. They seldom exceeded four 4 in height. 36 inches was a popular standard; some fencing was even lower. Foundries offered both square and round vertical pickets, usually measuring ½ or ⅜ in.

19TH CENTURY iron fencing followed a common structural pattern throughout the country. Three horizontal bars—channel bars, open from the underside—supported vertical pickets, which were fastened in sections to line posts. These supporting posts were anchored in the ground with braces on stone or iron footings. Large corner posts and gate posts gave added strength.

IRON CRESTING PATTERNS FROM CATALOGS, CIRCA 1880S.

THE TOPS OF THE VERTICAL pickets were usually embellished with a cast iron ornament. Crosses and spearheads enjoyed great popularity. They were simple to make but echoed the majesty of medieval architecture. Gothic tracery could be translated easily from wood or stone carving into the molded forms of cast iron, though the limitations of the molding process blunted the effect somewhat.

AS ORIGINALLY DESIGNED, the sharp, pointed picket heads had a practical use—they were dangerous to climb over

and therefore discouraged entry. 19th-century fencing, being more akin to stair railing in scale, was benign in comparison. For a safety feature, in fact, iron rods often enclosed the picket head under a protective arch. Iron fencing was primarily decorative and offered neither privacy nor protection from intrusion.

ANOTHER VERY POPULAR motif was the "rustic." Iron morning glories and grape-studded vines twisted around iron representations of branches and trellises to form settees, verandahs and fences. Fence designs often imitated hand-made sapling fences. However curious this may seem to us, it satis-

fied the Victorian desire for "romantic" settings.

THE SCROLL, a popular motif since the Middle Ages for wrought iron work, was another common pattern for cresting and fences. Similar to many English iron gates of the 1700's, the flowing line and circular pattern of the scroll appeared on many cast iron Victorian fences.

Rustic Gate from 1887 catalog.   *Scroll Gate from 1907 catal.*

FOUNDRIES DIFFERENTIATED very little among the various motifs. Customers wanted fancy ironwork and did not bother themselves with the nomenclature or the history of design. Fence patterns were not identified in catalogs as being Gothic or Florentine or any particular style. Iron work catalog merchandise was identified by number and described with terms that bespoke its practical qualities as

much as its design: "Showy . . . handsome . . . plain, substantial . . . durable . . . elegant and strong . . . very ornamental." One popular and ornate pattern was described simply as "rich and massive in appearance and a very durable fence."

In 1890 a typical 36 in. iron fence sold for around $1.50 a linear foot, including the supportive line posts. Corner posts commanded from $2.00 to $7.00 each. Entry gates were the most expensive single item, selling for as much as $15.00.

IRONWORK FOUNDRIES frequently labeled their fences with the foundry name and address, making identification an easy task. Gates often carried name markers—cast, separate pieces attached in the center to be read by passersby as a form of advertising. Less obvious were the company name letters cast in one of the structural pieces, typically a post. Gates, unfortunately, were the most likely part of a fence to fall off or be removed, and the identifying foundry name went with it.

House in Central City, Colorado, with a simple iron fence made by the W. T. Barbee Co. of Chicago. An interesting feature is the sawn wood trim on verge board and over window.

fence to fall off or be removed, and the identifying foundry name went with it.

FENCES HAVE ENJOYED the highest survival rate of all 19th century cast iron. Over the years, the rest has been bulldozed, carted off, junked, left to rust, or recycled. During World War II, iron work was turned in by the ton to be processed as scrap for the war effort.

THE REASON so many fences remained intact, however, was not so much out of loyalty of ownership as the simple fact that they were hard to get out of the ground. You couldn't just haul the fence off to the junk dealer—you had to dig it up first. Thanks to inertia, we still have a rich heritage of Victorian fencing.

IRON, OF COURSE, IS VERY durable and, protected from rust by paint, will last for centuries.

THAT PORTION THAT DISAPPEARED WAS MORE likely the victim of changes in taste and technology than either the elements or prolonged usage.

CARE AND REPAIR OF ORNAMENTAL IRON

ORNAMENTAL IRONWORK can be one of the most attractive features of an old house—but it can be rusted by the elements. From time and neglect it can become encrusted with scale and rust—or else smothered with layer upon layer of paint that obscures the original detail.

IRON THAT IS BADLY RUSTED should be thoroughly de-scaled before painting. This can be done with putty knife, wire brush and emery paper. Somewhat faster is a wire cupbrush attached to a power drill. In really bad cases you might want to use a commercial rust remover like naval jelly.

FIRST PAINT COAT APPLIED should be a good quality metal primer like Rust-Oleum. If the final coat will be black, use gray primer rather than the red lead, as gray will be easier to cover. Finish coat can be any good quality exterior trim paint; a high-gloss enamel holds up better than flat.

IF THE IRONWORK IS IN A HIGHLY VISIBLE AREA and covered with many layers of paint, you should consider stripping before re-painting. It's amazing how much better ironwork looks when the original sharp lines are restored. Any commercial paint remover will work—or you can use a torch to burn the paint off. A torch can be very satisfactory for this operation because, unlike wood, you don't have to worry about setting the iron on fire.

WHEN APPLYING FRESH PAINT over old paint, be sure to chip out and prime any rust spots.

Rust can spread under a fresh coat of paint and cause premature failure of the new paint film.

IF YOU HAVE a particularly nice piece of iron and wish to preserve its natural beauty, you can coat the surface with wax every three months or so. But before waxing, remove all traces of rust with emery paper . . . with a few drops of turpentine if the rust is heavy. Wax thoroughly with a liquid floor wax, or beeswax dissolved in a little turpentine. After the wax has set for about 15 min., buff lightly with a soft cloth. If exposed to continual wear (such as a handrail) or harsh weather, re-waxing may be needed more frequently than every three months. Though requiring continual maintenance, this process will impart a natural beauty that no paint or plastic coating can match.

TO REPAIR IRONWORK is not too difficult. Any ironworker who is competent with a welder can handle most jobs. Most repairs consist of straightening bent pieces and strengthening those joints attacked by rust. Ends of railings and bars built into masonry can be tipped with bronze or sleeved with copper to avoid further rust damage.

IRONWORK THAT IS HOLLOW due to being cast in several pieces (such as a heavy balustrade) frequently will have pieces broken off. If the broken piece is at hand, it can be welded back in place. If lost, the hole should be plugged with portland cement mortar and painted in order to keep water out. Fencing that has been removed from its original site is often in bad shape . . . especially the footings. Since proper mounting is essential, if the original braced footings cannot be used, a similar support should be welded to the posts and then sunk in concrete to a depth of 2–3 feet.

FORTUNATELY, replacing missing iron parts is not an impossible task, as ironworking is still an active craft. Expense will vary widely. Wrought iron is relatively easy and inexpensive to fabricate. Reproducing a cast iron part is more expensive because a foundry has to make a pattern, a mold and then the casting. A number of companies offer off-the-shelf ornamental iron, but most is of the wrought scrollwork variety.

Three Ornamental Cast Iron Fences in Colorado

INDEX

V

W

Y

Z